CONSUM   SHIPS

ꓱ shown below.

The creation and management of customer relationships is fundamental to the practice of marketing. Marketers have long maintained a keen interest in relationships: what they are, why they are formed, what effects they have on consumers and the marketplace, how they can be measured and when and how they evolve and decline.

While marketing research has a long tradition in the study of business relationships between manufacturers and suppliers and buyers and sellers, attention in the past decade has expanded to the relationships that form between consumers and their brands (such as products, stores, celebrities, companies or countries). The aim of this book is to advance knowledge about consumer–brand relationships by disseminating new research that pushes beyond theory, to applications and practical implications of brand relationships that businesses can apply to their own marketing strategies.

With contributions from an impressive array of scholars from around the world, this volume will provide students and researchers with a useful launch pad for further research in this blossoming area.

Susan Fournier is Professor and Dean's Research Fellow at Boston University, USA. Her research explores the creation and capture of value through branding and brand relationships and she has received five awards for her published work. She is an Editorial Board member of the *Journal of Consumer Research* and *Journal of Marketing* amongst others.

Michael Breazeale is Assistant Professor of Marketing at Indiana University Southeast, USA. His primary areas of research include the consumption of experiences and emotional branding. Mike has published articles in publications such as *International Journal of Market Research*, *Marketing Management Journal* and *Journal of Business Research*.

Marc Fetscherin is an Associate Professor of the Crummer Graduate School of Business and the International Business Department at Rollins College, USA. His research has been published in leading academic journals such as *International Business Review*, *International Marketing Review*, *European Journal of Marketing* and *Journal of Brand Management*.

"If you want to truly understand one of the most important concepts in branding, the consumer-brand relationship, you need to read the multiple perspectives provided in this book. This is a treasure of insights that will advance your thinking and your brand."

David Aaker, Vice Chairman of Prophet, Professor Emeritus at the
Haas School of Business, University of California, Berkeley,
and author of over 100 articles and 5 books on branding

"In the midst of this global economic crisis, *Consumer–Brand Relationships* re-focuses us on the primal foundations of branding: individuals, lived experiences, relationships and humanity. This book offers a vibrant framework for re-mastering our human understanding of brands. With this as a foundation, we can fine-tune our brand measurement systems and deliver improved present and future financial performance through the discipline of branding."

Ed Lebar, CEO of BrandAsset® Consulting™,
a division of Young & Rubicam Brands

"Few subjects are more top-of-mind to marketers than the quest for resonant 'brand relationships' with customers. Yet, for all the talk in today's socially networked world, there is little real scholarship applied to the actual science of relationship-building. In *Consumer–Brand Relationships*, the authors have taken a major, comprehensive step towards understanding the real drivers of successful brand-consumer intimacy. Through scholarly assessment and pragmatic insights, the real meaning of 'brand relationships' is revealed: how they are built, nurtured and, too often, abused. Read, learn and profit!"

Hayes Roth, Chief Marketing Officer, Landor Associates

"Every marketer aspires to move his or her brand from one that is preferred to one that is loved. The consumer-brand relationship is a delicate dance that when properly choreographed can create material value for both the customer and the organization. *Consumer–Brand Relationships* provides an insightful primer in understanding the framework of what ignites, engages and sustains consumer-brand relationships over time. This book is a must-read for organizations seeking competitive advantage through deeper brand engagement."

Michael Simon, Chief Marketing Officer, Panera Bread

"A brand cannot be valuable without a true understanding of its relationship with its customers. *Consumer–Brand Relationships* provides a thought provoking and illuminating journey through one of the most complex and multifaceted components of any great brand: its bond with customers. Consumers change so fast within society. Read this if you want a more thorough understanding of their world."

Graham Hales, CEO, Interbrand London

"There are few concepts in marketing as illuminating as the consumer-brand relationship. Understanding the relationship dynamics between brands and people is a powerful tool for strategists, creatives, and CMOs. With terrific insight and vision Fournier pioneered the basis for the ideas presented in this book years ago while teaching at Harvard Business School. But in the modern marketing era, defined by connections that consumers actively choose, the framework has become more relevant and useful than ever. Relationships drive economic performance. If you understand that, and care about the relationship your brand has with customers and prospects, read this book."

Baba Shetty, Chief Strategy Officer, Hill Holliday

"Fournier, Breazeale, and Fetscherin have assembled heavy hitters to take on the big questions. I am wowed by the results. This book will transform the theory and practice of branding enormously and take us one great leap forward."

Grant McCracken, MIT Research Affiliate and author of
several leading cultural branding books including
Culturematic and *Chief Culture Officer*

"This smartly edited volume, which brings together prominent academic and practitioner branding experts, advances our understanding of questions fundamental to consumer-brand relationships: their types, their properties, drivers, and consequences to consumers and marketers alike. Critical issues regarding the consumer as co-creator of brand meanings as well as the boundaries of the human relationship metaphor to the study of brands add novel insight to our understanding of this rich topic. A brilliant concluding chapter charts a far-reaching and powerful agenda for pushing the boundaries of knowledge about consumers' relationships with their brands."

Debbie MacInnis, Professor of Marketing,
University of Southern California

"Too often relationship marketing practices have been more relationship destructive than helpful to consumers and their marketing sponsors. This book brings together leading scholars who breathe new life and understanding into the fundamental challenges of building the 'right' kinds of relationships with consumers. The insights in this book will revitalize relationship marketing in ways that will deliver value to marketers and foster ties that are valued, strong, and that can endure."

James McAlexander, Professor of Marketing, Oregon State University

"This book provides a comprehensive overview of how consumers embrace brands. With creativity and originality, the authors go beyond theory and provide great insights into the blossoming area of consumer-brand relationships."

Christian Casal, Manager McKinsey & Company, Switzerland

CONSUMER–BRAND RELATIONSHIPS

Theory and practice

Edited by
Susan Fournier,
Michael Breazeale, and
Marc Fetscherin

Routledge
Taylor & Francis Group

LONDON AND NEW YORK

First published 2012
by Routledge
2 Park Square, Milton Park, Abingdon, Oxon OX14 4RN

Simultaneously published in the USA and Canada
by Routledge
711 Third Avenue, New York, NY 10017

Routledge is an imprint of the Taylor & Francis Group, an informa business

British Library Cataloguing in Publication Data
A catalogue record for this book is available from the British Library

Library of Congress Cataloging in Publication Data
CIP data has been requested

ISBN: 978-0-415-78303-3 (hbk)
ISBN: 978-0-415-78313-2 (pbk)
ISBN: 978-0-203-12879-4 (ebk)

Typeset in Bembo
by Cenveo Publisher Services

CONTENTS

LIST OF TABLES

LIST OF FIGURES

FOREWORD

Kevin Lane Keller

E.B. OSBORN PROFESSOR OF MARKETING,
TUCK SCHOOL OF BUSINESS, DARTMOUTH COLLEGE

A topic of enduring – yet increasing – importance in recent years is the topic of consumer–brand relationships. The topic has always been at the heart of marketing strategies and a prime determinant of marketing success. In recent years, however, there has been a greater appreciation of the many different ways in which consumer–brand relationships are formed, as well as the many different benefits that can arise from those relationships.

At the most basic level, marketers value strong consumer–brand relationships because of the financial benefits that accrue from the resulting brand loyalty from customers. Loyal customers of a brand typically buy more of its products and services, buy them more often, and are more willing to pay a higher price than other customers. They can be more receptive to new product introductions and promotional and other marketing activities. And in an increasingly networked world, loyal customers can function as brand ambassadors and help to build brand loyalty with other consumers.

There is not just the potential of a commercial payoff from consumer–brand relationships as these relationships have a great deal of personal and social meaning that helps to shape consumers' lives and influence social interactions. Branding has significant cultural importance too, especially when brands are defined in their widest scope to include people, places, and things.

Clearly, the outcomes of consumer–brand relationships are many and varied. The important realization in recent years has been that of the complexity of the inputs that actually form those relationships. The fact is that many different types of consumer–brand relationships exist and the nature of those relationships has a profound effect on the social, cultural, economic, and marketing outcomes that are observed.

A deeper understanding of consumer–brand relationships – how they are formed and what form they take – is thus critical. But such relationships are an inherently multi-dimensional concept, so to understand them fully, many different points of view and perspectives must be taken. Only through such a multiplicity of viewpoints can the richness of consumer–brand relationships be captured in any way.

Fortunately, researchers in recent years have recognized this fact and are taking many different tacks and pursuing many different angles to explore the range of relevant topics. The chapters in this volume are a noteworthy example of the variety of approaches that can be productively taken to the study of consumer–brand relationships. Capturing some of the latest thinking, the chapters collectively provide a number of provocative notions and compelling insights.

To illustrate, authors delve into the intriguing concepts of brand love and brand forgiveness; they explore the fundamental defining role brands play in consumers' self-identities and how brands may function differently in the lives of children or teenagers; they build on Fournier's seminal taxonomy of consumer–brand relationships to examine new facets; and they consider the very practical managerial implications of consumer–brand relationships.

Importantly, the authors bring international backgrounds to these research pursuits, offering their inherently global perspectives to these branding topics. Researchers and practitioners alike will benefit from these contributions and emerge with a richer understanding and appreciation of the many fascinating dimensions of consumer–brand relationships. Together, the chapters offer a stimulating and challenging treatment of the topic and will be a valuable addition to the knowledge of any brand scholar or marketing practitioner.

ACKNOWLEDGMENTS

The editors of this book are particularly grateful for the institutional support provided by Rollins College, Indiana University Southeast, Boston University, and Brunel University. We would also like to thank Terry Clague, Amy Laurens, and Alex Krause at Routledge for their guidance and patience as this idea became a reality.

All the chapters in the book were double-blind reviewed, and we are grateful to the reviewers who put numerous hours of their time into improving the submissions and the overall quality of the book. Among the reviewers and assistants are:

Pankaj Aggarwal, University of Toronto, Canada
Noel Albert, Wesford Business School, France
Samil Aledin, University of Turku, Finland
Chris Allen, University of Cincinnati, USA
Claudio Alvarez, Boston University, USA
Jill Avery, Simmons College, USA
Rajeev Batra, University of Michigan, USA
Manfred Bruhn, University of Basel, Switzerland
Paul M. Connell, Stony Brook University, USA
Sara Loughran Dommer, University of Pittsburg, USA
Falko Eichen, University of Basel, Switzerland
Eileen Fischer, Schulich School of Business, York University, Canada
Tessa Gjodesen, Syddansk University, Denmark
Katharina Sabine Guese, Otto-Friedrich University, Germany
Daniel Heinrich, University of Mannheim, Germany
Hazel Huang, Durham Business School, UK
Jasmina Ilicic, Macquarie University, Australia

Velitchka Kalitcheva, Loyola Marymount University, USA
Christopher Long, Ouachita Baptist University, USA
Brett Marks, Boston University, USA
Felicia Miller, Marquette University, USA
Vivien Moinat, University of Lausanne, Switzerland
Natalie Neumann, Ludwig-Maximilians University – Munich, Germany
Leigh Anne Novak-Donovan, University of Southern California, USA
Hope Jensen Schau, University of Arizona, USA
Sharon Schembri, Griffith University, Australia
Padmini Sharma, Frito-Lay, USA
Jean Suvatjis, University of Birmingham, UK
Vanitha Swaminathan, University of Pittsburgh, USA
Scott Thompson, University of Georgia, USA
Allyn White, Mississippi State University, USA

NOTES ON CONTRIBUTORS

Pankaj Aggarwal is Associate Professor of Marketing at the University of Toronto. He received his Ph.D. from the Graduate School of Business, University of Chicago in 2002 and his doctoral dissertation on consumer–brand relationships won the Marketing Science Institute's Alden G. Clayton award for best dissertation in 2000. His primary research interest is in studying 'brands-as-people', specifically conducting research on consumer–brand relationships and brand anthropomorphism, and he also studies issues related to culture, time, and money. Pankaj's research has been published in leading marketing and psychology journals such as *Journal of Consumer Research* and *Psychological Science*, and he serves on the Editorial Boards of the *Journal of Consumer Research* and the *Journal of Consumer Psychology*. Prior to entering academia, Pankaj was Vice President at J. Walter Thompson Advertising, heading its New Delhi office.

Aaron Ahuvia is Professor of Marketing at the University of Michigan-Dearborn College of Business. Widely regarded as a leading authority on the psychology of love in non-interpersonal contexts, such as consumers' love of products and brands, he is also well known for his research on income, consumption, and happiness. Aaron is winner of the Distinguished Research Award, UM-D's highest campus-wide award for scholarship, and was also named the Faculty Member of the Year for research and teaching in 2001. He has served as Vice President of the International Society for Quality of Life Studies (ISQUOLS) and Associate Editor for the *Journal of Economic Psychology*, and his research has been quoted in *Time*, the *New York Times*, *Wall Street Journal*, major publications in Europe and Japan, and on public radio talk shows as well as popular television shows such as *Oprah*.

Christina Albee graduated magna cum laude from Ouachita Baptist University with a BA in Psychology in December 2010, having in the previous spring received the Weldon E. Vogt Outstanding Psychology Student Award. She has presented research at state and national conferences, including the Arkansas Undergraduate Research Conference and the Association for Psychological Science's 22nd Annual Convention. She was also recipient of the Best Paper Award from the First International Colloquium on Consumer–Brand Relationships. In addition to consumer–brand relationships, Christina's research interests include positive psychology and she plans to continue her education in the field of counseling psychology.

Carmen-Maria Albrecht is Assistant Professor of Marketing at the University of Mannheim. She received her Ph.D. from the University of Mannheim in 2009 and her primary areas of research encompass stress and coping, branding, and retail marketing. Carmen has published in *Psychology & Marketing* and has made numerous conference presentations relating to her research.

Samil A. Aledin is an independent scholar and a consultant. He received his D.Sc. from Turku School of Economics in Finland in 2009 and his business studies include an academic year at BSU. Samil's primary areas of research encompass teenage brand consumption, consumer–brand relationships, the evolutionary aspect of brand consumption, and the social psychological perspectives behind consumption. Prior to embarking on his academic research, Samil worked as a marketing practitioner at fast-moving consumer goods (FMCG) companies locally and internationally and he has also performed consulting duties with companies in the FMCG and media sectors. In addition, Samil has been consulted by national media as an expert on teenage consumption, and he has served as a reviewer of articles and conference papers.

Chris T. Allen is Arthur Beerman Professor of Marketing at the University of Cincinnati. He joined the UC Marketing Faculty in 1985, served as MBA Program Director from 1994 through 1996 and as scholar-in-residence with the Corporate New Ventures Group at Procter & Gamble in 1997, and is currently Interim Associate Dean for Graduate Programs. Chris has been voted "Outstanding Professor" six times by UC's MBA student association and was the recipient of the College's 2002 EXCEL Award for teaching excellence. He has published his research in all the premier marketing and consumer behavior journals, and is co-author of a leading text entitled *Advertising and Integrated Brand Promotion*, sixth edition. Previously, Chris was a faculty member in the Kellogg Graduate School of Management at Northwestern University, and in the School of Management at the University of Massachusetts. He received his Ph.D. in Marketing and Consumer Psychology from Ohio State.

Claudio Alvarez is a doctoral student in Marketing at Boston University's School of Management. His research interests include consumer–brand relationships, brand leverage, and how consumption can shape and be shaped by identity. Previously he worked for Monitor, a global management consulting firm, where he served as a project manager in the marketing strategy practice, leading projects related to branding, customer segmentation, and pricing, and also working at the marketing interface with organization and innovation. Claudio earned his bachelor's degree in Social Communication from PUC-RJ and an MBA from Coppead-UFRJ, both in Brazil.

Jill Avery is Assistant Professor at the Simmons School of Management. She received a DBA from the Harvard Business School and her interests lie in brand management and customer relationship management issues, her research on online brand communities having won the Harvard Business School Wyss award for excellence in doctoral research. Her work has been published in *Journal of Consumer Research*, *Harvard Business Review*, *MIT Sloan Management Review*, *Business Horizons*, and *Journal of Marketing Communications* and she has written a series of teaching cases on branding that are available from Harvard Business School Publishing. Prior to her academic career, Jill spent nine years managing brands for Gillette, Braun, Samuel Adams, and AT&T, and three years on the agency side of the business, as an account executive managing consumer promotions for Pepsi, General Foods, Bristol-Myers, and Citibank.

Hans H. Bauer is Professor of Marketing and holds the Chair of Business Administration and Marketing at the University of Mannheim. He received his Ph.D. from the University of Erlangen-Nürnberg and his primary areas of research and teaching encompass marketing theory, consumer behavior, strategic marketing, brand management, and communication issues. His work has been published in more than five hundred journal articles (including the *European Journal of Marketing*), book chapters, working papers and conference proceedings.

Courtney Boerstler is Assistant Professor of Marketing in the Phillips School of Business at High Point University. She is a Ph.D. candidate at the University of Oregon, with expectations to complete her doctorate in 2011, and her primary areas of research include consumer behavior, multiple methods research, decision-making, mixed emotions, and branding. Courtney has published numerous articles in publications that include the *Journal of the Academy of Marketing Science*, *MIT Sloan Management Review*, and the *Wall Street Journal*. She also received a best paper award in 2010 at the First International Colloquium on Consumer–Brand Relationships.

Michael Breazeale is Assistant Professor of Marketing at Indiana University Southeast but will be joining the faculty of University of Nebraska–Omaha in fall 2012. He received his Ph.D. from Mississippi State University in 2010 and his primary areas of research encompass retail atmospherics, consumer–brand connections, the consumption of experiences, and emotional branding. Mike has published several articles in publications that include *International Journal of Market Research*, *Marketing Management Journal*, and *Journal of Business Research*, and has made numerous conference presentations relating to his research. He has won multiple awards for both teaching and research, and serves as reviewer for several top marketing journals. Mike has performed consulting duties with clients as diverse as Millward Brown Optimor and the US military, and is a founding member and organizer of the International Colloquium on Consumer–Brand Relationships (with Marc Fetscherin, Susan Fournier, and T.C. Melewar).

Manfred Bruhn is Professor of Marketing and Business Administration at the University of Basel, Switzerland. Additionally, he has been Honorary Professor at the TUM Business School in Munich since 2005. He received his Ph.D. from the University of Münster in 1977. His primary areas of research encompass services marketing, relationship marketing, and marketing communication, and he has published in several international journals, such as *Journal of Business Research* and *Journal of Relationship Marketing*, as well as German journals, and numerous books in up to ten editions relating to his research. Manfred is president of the administrative board of the strategic marketing consultancy Prof. Bruhn & Partner AG, and has performed consulting duties for several companies.

Paul M. Connell is Assistant Professor of Marketing at State University of New York at Stony Brook. His research interests include self and identity, affective states, attitudes and persuasion, and child/adolescent consumers. His research has been published in *Journal of Consumer Psychology* and *Journal of Public Policy & Marketing*.

Mary Conway Dato-on is Associate Professor of International Business at Rollins College, Crummer Graduate School of Business. Formerly, she was Associate Professor of Marketing and Director of the International Business Center at Northern Kentucky University where she received her Ph.D. in Marketing. Mary has worked in the Philippines, Japan and the USA, her US positions including Area Marketing Manager for Ford Motor Company and Corporate Trainer for Xavier University specializing in Japanese management and cross-cultural transition issues. Mary's research interests include nonprofit branding, social marketing, cross-cultural consumer behavior, and gender and ethics in marketing. Her research has appeared in journals including *Business Journal of Hispanic Research*, *Journal of Developmental Entrepreneurship*, *Psychology & Marketing*, *Journal of Marketing Theory and Practice*, *Journal of Business-to-Business Marketing*, *Journal of East West Business*, and *Journal of Consumer Behaviour*.

Leslie de Chernatony is Professor of Brand Marketing at Università della Svizzera Italiana, Lugano, Honorary Professor at Aston Business School,

Birmingham, and Managing Partner at Brands Box Marketing & Research Consultancy. His research has been globally disseminated through books, international conference presentations and a significant stream of international journal articles, some of which have won best paper prizes. Leslie was elected a Fellow of the Chartered Institute of Marketing and also a Fellow of the Market Research Society, and his work has been reported in TV programs and radio broadcasts. He is a frequent speaker at management conferences and he has run many highly acclaimed management development workshops throughout Europe, the USA, the Middle East, Far East, Asia, and Australia. Leslie's advice on developing more effective brand strategies has been sought by numerous organizations and he has acted as an expert witness in court cases over branding issues.

Sara Loughran Dommer is a doctoral candidate in Marketing at Katz Graduate School of Business, University of Pittsburgh. Her research examines how people's self-concepts, social identities, and interpersonal relationships influence consumer behavior, primarily focusing on the use of brands as vehicles of identity expression and answering questions such as: "Who does it?", "When and why do they do it?" and "What are the larger implications of doing it?" Prior to joining the doctoral program at the University of Pittsburgh, Sara worked as an account executive at a marketing communications firm where she developed and implemented advertising plans, media relations campaigns, and special events for a variety of clients.

Leigh Anne Novak Donovan is a doctoral candidate in Marketing at the Marshall School of Business, University of Southern California. Her broad research interests include understanding the nature of evaluative processes and their influences on thoughts, feelings, and behavior, and additionally, she is investigating issues related to brand loyalty, forgiveness, transgressions, brand failures, purchasing, brand switching, and brand relationships. Prior to her Ph.D. studies, she received her BSBA and MS in Marketing from the University of Florida.

Falko Eichen is Managing Director of the strategic marketing consultancy Prof. Bruhn & Partner AG and visiting lecturer at the University of Basel. He received his Ph.D. in Marketing from the University of Basel in 2008, and he holds a Graduate Degree in Business Administration ("Diplom-Kaufmann") from the European Business School, Germany.

Marc Fetscherin is Associate Professor at the Crummer Graduate School of Business and the International Business Department at Rollins College. He received his Ph.D. from the University of Bern, Switzerland and he is a founding member and organizer of the International Colloquium on Consumer–Brand Relationships (with Mike Breazeale, Susan Fournier, and T.C. Melewar).

His research has been published in leading academic journals such as *Management International Review, International Business Review, International Marketing Review, International Journal of Market Research, European Journal of Marketing, Journal of Brand Management*, and *Journal of Place Branding and Public Diplomacy.*

Susan Fournier is Professor and Dean's Research Fellow at Boston University. Her research explores the creation and capture of value through branding and brand relationships and her current projects explore the link between brand strategy and shareholder value, brand co-creation, brand strength measurement metrics, attachment style effects on brand relationships, person–brand management, and the lived experiences of consumer–brand relationships such as flings and adversaries. Susan has received five awards for her published work and she is an Editorial Board member of *Journal of Consumer Research, Journal of Marketing, Journal of Relationship Marketing, Journal of Business-to-Business Marketing*, and *Marketing Theory*. She consults with a range of companies to inform her teaching, case development, and research. Prior to Boston University, Susan served on the faculties of Harvard Business School and Tuck School at Dartmouth. She also held a VP/Director position at Young & Rubicam and market research roles at Polaroid and Yankelovich Clancy Shulman.

Philip A. Gable is Assistant Professor of Psychology at the University of Alabama. He received his Ph.D. from Texas A&M University in 2010. Broadly, his program of research investigates the interplay of motivation, emotion, and cognition, and in order to provide a better understanding of the processes involved in these areas, his research integrates neurophysiological measures such as regional brain-activation through electroencephalography (EEG), reflex physiology, and event related brain potentials (ERP). Philip's work has been published in journals such as *Psychological Bulletin, Psychological Science, Emotion, Psychophysiology*, and *Biological Psychology*, and he has been invited to present his work at numerous international and national conferences.

Karsten Hadwich is Professor of Service Management at the University of Hohenheim, Stuttgart. He received his Ph.D. from the University of Basel in 2003, and his primary areas of research encompass service quality, relationship marketing, and customer equity management. Karsten's research has been published in *Journal of Business Research* and *Journal of Relationship Marketing* and in several international conference proceedings.

Daniel Heinrich is Research Associate and Ph.D. candidate in the Department of Marketing, University of Mannheim. His ongoing research investigates various aspects of consumer behavior within the domains of advertising, promotion, and branding, with his current projects investigating consumer–brand relationships. Daniel has made numerous conference presentations relating to his research and his work has appeared in *Journal of Advertising Research*, *Advances in Consumer Research*, and *Developments in Marketing Science*.

Hazel H. Huang is Lecturer in Marketing at the Durham Business School. Prior to joining Durham, she was a research assistant, seminar tutor, and guest lecturer at Warwick Business School, where she completed her Ph.D. degree, and before this she worked in industry for approximately ten years, mainly involved in strategic marketing and branding issues in various sectors, such as IT (Acer), retailing (Carrefour), and FMCG (J&J). Her research interests lie in symbolic consumption, particularly in interpretations of brand meanings and advertisements.

Thomas W. Leigh is Emily H. and Charles M. Tanner, Jr. Chair of Sales Management at the University of Georgia. He received his DBA from Indiana University and has served as President of the AMA Academic Council and the Sales Special Interest Group (SIG); Visiting Professor at Ogilvy & Mather (NY); Board Chairman of the ARC East Georgia Chapter; and Director of the Coca-Cola Center for Marketing Studies (1995–2001). Thomas's research has appeared in *Journal of Marketing Research*, *Journal of Marketing*, *Journal of Consumer Research*, *Journal of Applied Psychology*, *Journal of Advertising*, *Journal of Advertising Research*, and *Journal of the Academy of Marketing Science*, and he received the Lifetime Achievement Award from the AMA Sales Special Interest Group in 2006. His executive education experience includes roles for UGA, Penn State, Northwestern, Georgia State University, and Rollins College, as well as for Beatrice Foods, Marriott, Reichhold Chemicals, Siam Cement, Moore Business Forms, Inchcape/Caleb Brett, Armstrong World, CISCO, CIGNA, Digital Equipment, and SATYAM.

Maggie Wenjing Liu is Assistant Professor of Marketing at the School of Economics and Management, Tsinghua University. She obtained her Ph.D. in Marketing from Rotman School of Management, University of Toronto in 2010. Maggie's research interests are in consumer behavior and decision-making, and she has published in *Journal of Consumer Psychology*, *Journal of Economic Psychology*, *Handbook of Consumer Psychology*, among others, and presented at numerous academic conferences.

Christopher R. Long is Associate Professor of Psychology at Ouachita Baptist University. He received his Ph.D. from the University of Massachusetts in 2003 and then worked as a post-doctoral research associate at Université Catholique de Louvain, Belgium. In 2009, Chris was a visiting professor at New York advertising agency DraftFCB. His primary research areas include exploring similarities between consumers' brand relationships and interpersonal relationships, as well as understanding the effects of brand deprivation, the role of social networking (on- and offline) in consumer–brand relationships, and consumer–celebrity relationships. Chris has published in leading journals in psychology and communications and has presented his research at numerous conferences, and his work has been cited by a range of popular publications, from the *Boston Globe* to the Israeli business newspaper *Calcalist*. He recently founded the OBU Brand Lab, where he collaborates with researchers in psychology, marketing, and information science.

Deborah J. MacInnis is Vice Dean for Research and Strategy, Charles L. and Ramona I. Hilliard Professor of Business Administration, and Professor of Marketing at the Marshall School of Business, University of Southern California. She is an expert in consumer emotions, consumer information processing, and branding, and her work has been published in *Journal of Consumer Research*, *Journal of Marketing*, *Journal of Marketing Research*, and *Journal of Consumer Psychology*, among others. Deborah has served as Co-editor and Associate Editor of *Journal of Consumer Research* and Associate Editor of *Journal of Consumer Psychology*, and has won best reviewer awards at these and other journals. She is past President of the Association for Consumer Research and past Vice President of Conferences and Research at the American Marketing Association. Deborah is also the recipient of the *Journal of Marketing*'s Alpha Kappa Psi and Maynard awards for her work on branding and consumer emotions.

Felicia M. Miller is Assistant Professor of Marketing at Marquette University. She gained her Ph.D. in Marketing from the University of Cincinnati and her research focuses on brand management issues, particularly the co-creation of brand meaning and the evolution of consumer–brand relationships. Felicia has presented her research at major marketing conferences sponsored by the American Marketing Association and the Colloquium on Consumer–Brand Relationships, and she has co-authored a chapter in the most recent edition of the *Handbook of Consumer Psychology*. Her research interests and classroom insights are largely informed by her decade of work experience in the brand management organization at the Procter & Gamble Company.

C. Whan Park is Joseph A. DeBell Chair in Business Administration, Professor of Marketing, and Director of the Global Branding Center at the Marshall School of Business, University of Southern California. He is also Editor of the *Journal of Consumer Psychology* and has published many articles in a wide array of publications, including *Journal of Marketing Research*, *Journal of Consumer Research*, *Journal of Marketing*, *Journal of Consumer Psychology*, *Organizational Behavior and Human Performance*, *Harvard Business Review*, *Journal of Advertising*, *Journal of Retailing*, and *Current Issues and Research in Advertising*. C.W. co-authored *Marketing Management* (Dryden Press, 1987) with Gerald Zaltman from Harvard University and in 1987 he received the Alpha Kappa Psi award for his article published in the *Journal of Marketing*.

Nicole Ponder is Associate Professor of Marketing at Mississippi State University. She received her Ph.D. from the University of Alabama and her research has been published in *Journal of Retailing*, *Journal of Business Research*, *Journal of Marketing Theory and Practice*, *Academy of Marketing Science Review*, *Journal of Business to Business Marketing*, *Journal of Marketing Education*, and *Marketing Education Review*, among others, as well as in numerous national and international proceedings. Nicole's research interests include consumer decision-making, business-to-consumer relationships, issues in construct measurement, structural equation modeling, and issues in doctoral education.

Joseph R. Priester is Associate Professor of Marketing and Psychology at the University of Southern California. He conducts research on the psychological processes underlying consumer psychology, with a focus on the area of attitudes and evaluative processes, and his research has appeared in leading consumer behavior and social psychology journals. He co-authored *The Social Psychology of Consumer Behavior* (2002) and co-edited *The Handbook of Brand Relationships* (2009). Joe is past President of the Society for Consumer Psychology, has been Associate Editor for the *Journal of Consumer Research*, and is currently Associate Editor of the Research Dialogue section of the *Journal of Consumer Psychology*.

Hope Jensen Schau is Associate Professor of Marketing, Susan Bulkeley Butler Fellow, and Gary M. Munsinger Chair in Entrepreneurship and Innovation at Eller College of Management, University of Arizona. She earned her Ph.D. from the University of California, Irvine. Hope's research focuses on the impact of technology on marketplace relationships, branding, identity-salient consumption practices, and collaborative consumption, and she has published in *Journal of Consumer Research*, *Journal of Marketing*, *Journal of Retailing*, *Journal of Advertising*, and *Journal of Macromarketing*.

Padmini Sharma is Director in the Strategic Insights team at Frito-Lay, where she has worked on iconic US brands such as Cheetos, Lay's, SunChips, and Tostitos, as well as several portfolio initiatives. Following her MS in Advertising from the University of Illinois at Urbana-Champaign and prior to working at Frito-Lay, she was a Brand Planner at a Philadelphia ad agency, where she worked on consumer insights and creative strategies for an eclectic group of clients such as The Children's Hospital of Philadelphia, Tastykake, and The Philadelphia Foundation. Padmini's primary professional interests are consumer–brand relationships, brand stories, consumer culture, behavioral change, and cognitive creativity. Padmini won the 2009 Grand Ogilvy award for excellence in the application of research insights to address a critical business issue on Cheetos.

Stephen Springfield is Senior Director of Portfolio Brand Strategy & Shopper Insights for Frito-Lay, where he has worked for the past thirteen years. In this capacity, Stephen works as an internal strategist and consultant, leading shopper and consumer-centric brand strategy for some of the USA's largest food brands. With almost twenty years of experience, he has built unique breadth of leadership across sectors, companies, and functions, including Sales, Customer Strategy, Brand Management, Innovation, Shopper Marketing, and Consumer Strategy/Insights. In addition, Stephen has previous experience in the music and food-service industries, and is a patent-holder and published composer with an album in its fifth year of sales with iTunes.

Jean Yannis Suvatjis is a brand marketing/corporate identity consultant and currently based at Athens Graduate School of Management and Nottingham Trent University. He received his Ph.D. in Brand Marketing/Corporate Identity from the University of Birmingham and worked in the USA for twenty-five years, holding various managerial and executive positions in a range of industries including manufacturing, retailing, service, and consulting. He has taught Marketing, Management and Logistics at various academic institutions and universities, and advised several private and public companies around the world. In Greece he has advised the Greek Post Office, the Greek Telecommunication Company, the Greek Water Supply Company, the Association of Northern Greek Exporters, together with many other large companies there and in north-eastern Europe. Jean also undertook and successfully implemented a number of European Projects assigned by the European Union.

Vanitha Swaminathan is Associate Professor of Marketing and Robert W. Murphy Faculty Fellow in Marketing at the Katz Graduate School of Business, University of Pittsburgh. Her research has been published in various journals including *Journal of Marketing*, *Journal of Marketing Research*, *Journal of Consumer Research*, *Strategic Management Journal*, and *Journal of Advertising* and examines how marketing contributes to firm value creation, and how marketing strategies including co-branding, brand acquisitions and marketing alliances can strengthen a firm's value. Additionally, Vanitha's research investigates branding strategies and conditions that favor the creation of strong consumer–brand relationships, how consumer–brand relationships can be created and managed by firms, and how brand strategies can foster creation of consumer–brand relationships. She has been a participant in the Marketing Science Institute's Young Scholar Program (2003) and won the 2002 Lehmann award for the best dissertation-based article in *Journal of Marketing*, and the 2006 Best Paper Award in the *Journal of Advertising*.

Scott A. Thompson is Assistant Professor of Marketing at the University of Georgia. He received his Ph.D. from Arizona State University in 2009. His primary areas of research include new product adoption, consumer communities, consumer–brand connections, and word of mouth behavior.

Sven Tuzovic is Assistant Professor of Marketing at Pacific Lutheran University, Tacoma, WA. He was Visiting Professor in Marketing at Murray State University (2006/7) and at the University of New Orleans (2005/6), having received his Doctoral Degree in Marketing from the University of Basel in 2004. Sven has published several articles in publications that include *Journal of Services Marketing, Journal of Relationship Marketing, Managing Service Quality,* and *International Journal of Pharmaceutical and Healthcare Marketing,* and has made numerous conference presentations relating to his research. He has won two research awards, and serves as reviewer for several marketing journals.

Cynthia Webster is Professor of Marketing at Mississippi State University. She received her Ph.D. in Marketing Strategy from the University of North Texas and her research interests lie in consumer behavior and marketing research. Cynthia has published in numerous top-tier marketing journals, including *Journal of Consumer Research, Journal of the Academy of Marketing Science,* and *Journal of Advertising.* She has received several awards for her research endeavors, and also serves as a reviewer for leading marketing journals.

Allyn White is Assistant Professor of Marketing at Eastern Kentucky University. She received her Ph.D. from Mississippi State University in 2011, and her main research focus is consumer responses to negatively perceived information in the marketing environment. Allyn has published in *Journal of the Academy of Marketing Science* and *Journal of Substance Abuse,* and has received numerous awards for her research contributions. She also serves as a reviewer for leading marketing and brand management journals.

INTRODUCTION

The why, how, and so what of consumers' relationships with their brands

Susan Fournier, Michael Breazeale, and Marc Fetscherin

Over the course of the past decade, firms have come to the realization that one of the most effective tools they have to hedge against risk is the portfolio of relationships that consumers form with the company's brands. Strong relationships guarantee cash flows in the form of brand loyalties and trial of new brand extensions, create supply-side cost advantages through evangelism and word-of-mouth advocacy, and protect shareholder value in the wake of the crises that inevitably befall brands. But, as marketers have rushed to build equity though their brand relationships, they have also come to realize that the creation of value through brand relationships is a difficult and challenging task. Brand relationships are complex psychological and cultural phenomena. They must be carefully created, astutely nurtured, and judiciously leveraged if they are to thrive. They require an organization and internal culture aligned in terms of relationship principles and ideas. Today's brandscape, enabled through social media and web 2.0 technologies, has fundamentally changed the face of branding, further complicating the relationship-building task.

Consumer–Brand Relationships: Theory and Practice explores the psychological and cultural landscape of consumer–brand relationships, and identifies concepts, frameworks, and strategies directed at the hunt for resonant and strong relationships in this new brand world. Evolving from papers presented at the First International Colloquium on Consumer–Brand Relationships at Rollins College in Winter Park, Florida in 2010, this book about the art and science of brand relationships draws together current theory and state-of-the-art practices to develop usable insights into the successful creation and stewardship of consumers' relationships with their brands. The book employs a mix of theories, disciplines, methodologies, and research styles from a diverse group of international scholars and practitioners in order to cultivate:

- an appreciation of the nature and power of consumer–brand relationships, and the role they play in contemporary culture and consumers' lives;
- an understanding of brand relationships as co-creations of marketers and consumers;
- sensitivity to the diverse and varied field of consumers' brand relationships and what this means for theory and practice;
- fluency with basic brand relationship concepts and processes, including individual and communal brand relationships; relationship motives; relationship initiation; relationship decline; relationship contracts; relationship strength measurement systems; and brand love and other and emotional relationship bonds;
- a capacity to think deeply about the mechanisms and processes involved in building, leveraging, defending, and sustaining strong relationships between consumers and brands; and
- exposure to the research tools and metrics that can inform the discipline of brand relationships.

While this book has obvious relevance for researchers of consumer–brand relationships, it also provides value for a range of professionals with brand management careers in product or service markets or a simple passion for branding. These individuals might include advertising agency personnel and management consultants who are involved in formulating brand relationship strategy, or developing new or rejuvenating established relationships with brands; corporate executives who adopt major brand stewardship responsibilities; entrepreneurs with a strong interest in consumer-driven brand-building activities; and experts in the finance and venture capital worlds whose jobs involve the evaluation of brand strength and potential, and the capitalization of brand assets over time.

The chapters in *Consumer–Brand Relationships: Theory and Practice* are organized into four parts that collectively address our learning goals. Taken together, these contributions consider the consumer side of the consumer–brand relationship equation, the brand side of the equation, and the relationship as the mutually co-created unit of analysis, from both theoretical and managerial perspectives. Part I considers the essential quality and variability of consumer–brand relationships through comparisons with interpersonal relationships and depth probes of different brand relationship forms and types. Part II focuses on the explication of the emotional bonds that characterize strong brand relationships. Part III addresses the fundamental interplay between people's goals and identities and the brand relationships that they form. Part IV traverses the theoretical boundary into the managerial setting, where applied issues of relationship culture, corporate identity, customer relationship management practice, and marketer roles in community relationships are put under the lens.

Part I: The "what" of brand relationships: exploring brand relationship varieties and types

The chapters in this section focus on the relationship as unit of analysis. Authors consider general definitional issues as well as specific instantiations of different relationship forms. While an exhaustive treatment of consumer–brand relationship types is not provided, researchers collectively provide an excellent framework for further exploration. The conceptualization, definition, and measurement of consumer–brand relationships are given focus throughout these contributions.

Chapter 1, by Vanitha Swaminathan and Sara Loughran Dommer, starts at the beginning by focusing on the interpersonal relationship theories that have inspired investigations into consumer–brand relationships. The authors explore the differences between consumer–brand relationships and interpersonal relationships, and argue that while the research on consumer–brand relationships readily leverages interpersonal relationships as metaphors for brand relationships, little time has been spent distinguishing between the interpersonal relationship and the brand relationship. The authors review the use of interpersonal relationship theories in the consumer–brand relationships realm, discuss similarities and differences between interpersonal relationships and brand relationships, and provide a framework for differentiating between the two. The chapter helps researchers and practitioners to recognize when it is appropriate to use interpersonal relationship theories in consumer–brand relationship research, and when we may need to create our own theories and constructs as consumer–brand relationship researchers, and thus serves an important theory development goal.

Chapter 2, by Felicia Miller, Susan Fournier, and Chris Allen, provides an empirical look at the previous chapter's conceptual question through a lab study designed to assess the legitimacy of the relationship metaphor as applied to various relationships with brands. This research probes (1) whether direct analogues to eight different interpersonal relationships exist in the brand space (i.e. abused, adversary, committed, communal, dependency, exchange, secret affair, and master–slave) and (2) whether characteristic attributes that define and distinguish these interpersonal relationships also differentiate relationships with brands. Two surveys with a total of more than 1,500 subject participants provide data to illuminate the research questions. Results support the hypothesis that people do feel some affinity with the various brand relationships, and that people's brand relationship narratives generally conform to conceptions in the interpersonal relationships space, with some exceptions. Notably, the most commonly studied brand relationships – committed and communal relationships – demonstrate the greatest disconnects from the literature. Further, elicited brands are highly idiosyncratic, though some brands emerge as common relationship exemplars across persons and relationship types. This "relationship is in the eye of the beholder" finding violates popular conceptions of certain categories and brand characteristics as qualifiers for different (strong) relationship types.

While most research and managerial attention is dedicated to positive and strong brand relationships, negative brand relationships have received significantly less attention. This bias is corrected in Chapter 3 wherein Allyn White, Michael Breazeale, and Cynthia Webster take a look at a specific negative relationship: the avoided brand. The study employs a grounded theory approach, gathering information using in-depth interviews. The authors demonstrate that brand avoidance relationships are complex and highly involving phenomena from the avoider's perspective. Results support the idea that a brand's mere placement in a prior negative memory can result in that brand's position as a conduit for the emotions surrounding the event. Thus, in a majority of avoidant brand relationships, the brand is not an "active offender" in the relationship, but instead serves as an artifact of some negatively perceived incident. Through the resonance of the avoidant relationship construct, the authors also demonstrate that brand purchase is not always a signal of consumers' positive relationships with the purchased brand. The powerful presence of avoidant relationships can render brand choice as the incidental consequence of a negative relationship rather than a sought-after relationship event.

Chapter 4, by Claudio Alvarez and Susan Fournier, illuminates another unexplored but interesting relationship: brand flings. Leveraging data from eight phenomenological multi-hour interviews regarding brand flings and eight interviews regarding flings with other people, both using ZMET methodology and all concerning undergraduate college students, the authors support the cultural and personal resonance of the brand fling. Five themes characterizing brand fling engagements are drawn out from the data: intense emotionality, deep engagement and investment; superficial decision-making; identity signaling and experimentation; and transience. Important differences between human and brand flings are also noted. For example, while person flings are characterized by secrecy and shame deriving from cultural taboo, brand flings serve mainly as playful transitional objects. The chapter supports the notion of brand flings as a relevant mechanism for consumer–brand engagement and provides a solid conceptual foundation for future research.

Chapter 5 provides a look at yet another understudied brand relationship: the childhood friendship relationship. In this conceptual chapter, Paul Connell and Hope Jensen Schau draw upon developmental psychology theory to discuss how childhood brand friendships rooted in pre-pubescence develop and the meaningful functions that they serve. The authors argue that because young children routinely use possessions as a primary means of defining themselves, both internally and for others, childhood brand friendships are likely of critical importance to the definition and maintenance of the self. Events which heighten the relevance of childhood friendships, such as having children of one's own, are likely to make both active and latent childhood brand friendships more accessible and prone to intergenerational transfer. The authors hypothesize about processes implicated by the development and maintenance of childhood friendships, and delve into the potential "dark side" of these friendships, which have the potential to affect consumer health and well-being negatively.

We close Part I with a broader theoretical framing that considers the process mechanisms underlying different brand relationship types. In Chapter 6, Pankaj Aggarwal and Maggie Wenjing Liu explore ways in which the application of a mental accounting framework to consumer–brand relationships can yield deeper insights into the antecedents, processes, and consequences underlying consumer–brand behaviors. Mental accounting is the set of operations that people perform to organize, evaluate, and keep track of their activities, especially those related to finances and expenses (Thaler 1985). Aggarwal and Liu propose that consumers use a mental accounting framework when interacting with brands and that the principles of mental accounting are applicable in a consumer–brand relationship context. Further, they suggest that the type of relationship with a brand can lead to a variety of differences in how consumers mentally account for their brand interactions. The authors offer unique, insightful, and testable hypotheses that emanate from the mental accounting framework to encourage future empirical studies capable of advancing understanding along these lines.

Part II: Understanding consumer–brand relationship bonds: brand love and other strength indicators

This section also probes the relationship as unit of analysis and seeks a deeper understanding of one particular characterization of the relationship that is of particular interest to researchers and practitioners: the emotional attachments that qualify consumer–brand bonds. A common focus across the contributions in this section is the measurement of consumers' emotional brand bonds.

Chapter 7, by Daniel Heinrich, Carmen-Maria Albrecht, and Hans H. Bauer, provides a focal exploration of the structure and operationalization of the construct of brand love. Drawing on the concept of love as considered in inter-personal psychology as well as studies carried out in the consumer–object context, the authors develop and validate a multi-faceted brand love scale. Empirical results support a second-order love construct composed of brand intimacy, brand passion, and brand commitment. Brand love has a positive effect on consumers' willingness to pay a price premium and to forgive mistakes made by the brand. Additionally, different brand love styles are identified.

Of the few empirical studies that concern the conceptualization and measure-ment of brand love, all are based on theories of interpersonal love wherein two parties, known to each other, reciprocate and interact. In Chapter 8, Marc Fetscherin and Mary Conway Dato-on provide theoretical and empirical support for the argument that the love in the brand relationships domain is more similar to a parasocial love relationship, such as the one-sided relationships consumers have with TV stars and celebrities. The authors compare these two alternate conceptualizations, one where brand love is a reciprocating construct based on theories of interpersonal love and a model based on the one-sided view of parasocial love. Findings suggest that a love construct based on parasocial relationship theory is more suitable for explaining the concept of brand love.

In Chapter 9 by Manfred Bruhn, Falko Eichen, Karsten Hadwich, and Sven Tuzovic, we broaden our focus to a more comprehensive construct for qualifying the strength of the consumer–brand relationship: brand relationship quality (BRQ). Despite the fact that BRQ stands as the key to effective brand relationship management according to many researchers and practitioners, the authors highlight the fact that few sound validation studies exist. Bruhn and colleagues develop a comprehensive third-order measurement model that offers a more complete understanding of BRQ than exists in the literature, and test the proposed model in a robust empirical setting comprising an online survey with more than two thousand respondents across eight consumer goods markets with a total of eighty-two brands. Results support two higher second-order factors: quality of the brand as relationship partner and quality of the brand as interaction platform. Brand relationship quality drivers are shown to be industry-specific and highly context-dependent, suggesting limitations on generalized models of the strength of consumers' brand relationship bonds.

Most empirical studies that concern consumer–brand bonds focus on the positive relationship qualities that manifest in healthy brand relationships: love, trust, commitment, and attachment, for example. The unfortunate reality that confronts managers, however, is that brand relationships over the long run inevitably face crises or confront brand failures of some kind, and how consumers respond in these stressed situations fundamentally determines whether the brand relationship will survive. Forgiveness on the part of consumers is an important determinant of the effect of brand failures, and yet little brand relationship research has investigated this construct or explored why some consumers are willing to return to an offending brand while others abandon it. In Chapter 10 Leigh Anne Novak Donovan, Joseph Priester, Debbie MacInnis, and C.W. Park report on four studies designed to probe consumer–brand forgiveness. The authors find that the strength of the relationship, positive attributions, strong emotions, and brand trust support brand forgiveness. They also confirm that brand forgiveness yields repurchase, strengthens willingness to defend the brand in the future, and reduces desire to seek revenge. Just as love and commitment foster long-term relationships, so too does brand forgiveness maintain loyal customers in the face of stresses that befall consumers' relationships with their brands.

Aaron Ahuvia's Chapter 11 closes this section with thoughts on the issues and challenges researchers face when conceptualizing and operationalizing complex relationship phenomena such as brand love and relationship strength. Ahuvia directs our attention to what he calls the "brand love system," a complex, networked conceptualization of mutually reinforcing, higher-order constructs comprising interrelated lower-order constructs, many of which have sparked separate research streams in the study of consumer–brand relationships. Ahuvia discusses the pros and cons of two different options for modeling this complex system. With a latent model construct, a person's score on the higher-order construct (brand love) is determined by the shared factor variance between first-order constructs thought to comprise it. A person's score on an aggregate model construct is determined through an algebraic combination of the construct's indicators. Through Ahuvia's research with colleagues, we learn that the brand love relationship can be characterized as an aggregate model construct consisting of ten first-order constructs: a willingness to invest resources, passionate desire and a natural sense of "fit," frequent thought and use, psychological and emotional intrinsic rewards, emotional bonding and anticipated heartbreak, fusion of identities, positive affect, commitment, connections to strongly held values and existential meanings, and belief that the loved brand excels in any way a brand could excel, such as in performance, trustworthiness, and value for the money. Ahuvia provides a more comprehensive and integrated depiction of the consumer–brand love relationship than has been previously available, while preparing researchers for the challenges confronted in advancing this research.

Part III: How goals and identity drive consumers' relationships with their brands

This section shifts attention to the consumer side of the consumer–brand relationship equation. Identity is fundamental to the formation, maintenance, and very essence of this relationship, for at their core, brand relationships provide meanings that help people construct and negotiate their lives (Fournier 1998). The chapters in this section probe the fundamental question of how a person's goals and identity drive consumers' brand relationships and in so doing address various aspects of the self–brand relationship link.

Michael Breazeale and Nicole Ponder examine what they call customer chemistry and its role in identity construction in Chapter 12. The authors outline the ways in which consumers use consumption to create and express their own identities. Building on previous literature about the role of possessions in forming identity and identity construction through consumption, this chapter describes the role of favorite places, in this case, retail stores, in forming and expressing consumers' identities. In-depth interviews conducted with ten informants produce modified life histories of individuals in various life stages. These life histories provide empirical support for the phenomenon of customer chemistry – the consumption practice of forming positive, environmentally-derived attachment to a retailer – and demonstrate the role of the resultant brand relationship in identity construction and expression.

The various ways in which consumers use brand personalities and brand relationships to shape their self-identities are examined by Hazel Huang in Chapter 13. Eleven in-depth interviews with young adults, aged eighteen to twenty-two, allow close examination of consumers' use of the relationship metaphor to describe their engagements with brands. A follow-up study investigates the relationships among people's personalities, the brand's personality, and brand relationships, as explored in various high/low-involvement categories and across the FCB thinking/feeling grid. Results support the notion that people connect their self-identities to their brand relationships, sometimes including their brand partners' personalities in their self-identity statements. This purposive connection remains consistent across utilitarian and symbolic products and high-versus low-involvement categories.

Whereas the previous chapters in this section examine adults and their relationships to brands, Samil Aledin's research presented in Chapter 14 looks specifically at teenagers' brand relationships and their identity stories. Twenty-four personal interviews conducted with teenagers in the interpretivist tradition of consumer research yield both emic- and etic-focused interpretations of the identity roles played by teenagers' brands. Two categories of identity-relevant brand meanings undergird teenagers' brand relationships: self-driven meanings ("Personality traits and style," "Making an impression," "Self-esteem, mood and feelings," "Contexts") and group-driven meanings ("Immediate circle," "Subcultural and post-subcultural groups," "Specific groups," "Demographic groups"). In addition, the research provides four specific identity roles that brands fulfill for teenagers, including "Social filter," "Mature friend," "Match maker," and "A shoulder to lean on."

We close this section with a broader look at whether the same psychological processes that regulate interpersonal relationships are mirrored in consumers' relationships with products and brands. Chapter 15, by Christopher Long, Philip Gable, Courtney Boerstler, and Christina Albee, investigates ways in which consumers may draw closer to brands that facilitate specific goal pursuits in the same way that people draw closer to the acquaintances that facilitate such pursuits in the interpersonal realm. Three experimental studies conducted within the implicit goal priming paradigm indicate that consumers evaluate preferred brands more positively when brand-relevant goals are activated. Further, results support that this tendency is accentuated among consumers who have particular relational orientations, most notably, heightened needs for belongingness or, conversely, the avoidant interpersonal attachment style. Results thus support parallel processes for human and brand relationships as concerning the operation of self-relevant goal pursuits.

Part IV: Managerial applications and extensions of consumer–brand relationship ideas

The final section of the book puts consumer–brand relationship theory into practice and offers managerial suggestions for the strategic development and maintenance of strong relationships between consumers and brands. Chapters in this section provide insights into relationship work at the bench level, probing the corporate and managerial systems that facilitate and support brand relationships. The flip side of misdirected relationship management is also considered, as are brand relationships developed on the Internet, where brand control is increasingly in consumers' hands.

Customer relationship management (CRM) is the managerial discipline most formally aligned with brand relationship principles, and Chapter 16 by Jill Avery and Susan Fournier looks inside this process through consumers' eyes to understand where disconnects with core relationship tenets can be found. The focus is on firing customers, a CRM practice that has become more prevalent as firms move to maximize the customer lifetime value of their customer portfolios by jettisoning individuals with high costs-to-serve. Building from a basis of a series of interviews over time, the chapter explores the relationship trajectory of one fired customer to illuminate how a "bad customer" is often the result of an ill-informed and poorly managed customer relationship system. The authors show that, ironically, firing customers is often a case of "blaming the victim," as many managers remain unaware of their own roles in creating the bad relationships they seek to sever. The chapter offers practical advice for more sensitive relationship management, using tenets of relationality as an inspirational base.

In Chapter 17, Thomas Leigh and Scott Thompson explore and reframe the marketers' evolving role in the context of Web 2.0 and new social media. Traditionally, the marketer has served as a form of "brand curator" whose role involved designing, preserving, enhancing, and promoting brand meaning to target customers, a process for which marketers are assumed to take complete control and charge. In a world of online search, smartphones, social network platforms, blogs, Twitter accounts, peer-to-peer video sharing sites, online communities and advocacy groups, where conversations are multi-way, consumers are energized and empowered, and brand meanings are socially constructed (and not always in the brand's best interest), the marketer's role as brand curator is no longer sufficient or viable. While recent commentators suggest that the solution is one of ceding control of the brand to the social web and broader culture, Leigh and Thompson remind us that marketers have a clear stake in the branding game and that ceding control is both ill-informed and overly simplistic. The authors' contention is that the marketer's role must be defined with an acute sensitivity to the operative consumer–brand contexts in play. Leigh and Thompson leverage case study research on brands including Facebook, Skittles, BP, Apple, United, Watch Idiot Savants, and Blizzcon, as supplemented with a limited set of executive interviews to examine management perspectives on best practices for managing brand relationships in social mediated contexts. They articulate appropriate marketer roles and practices for brand relationship management for traditional authority brands, conversational brands emphasizing opinion leaders, casual social networks emphasizing multi-way exchanges, enthusiast social networks emphasizing product category loyalty, brand communities emphasizing collective social values and practices, and formal brand clubs emphasizing collective capital and institutional membership.

Chapter 18, by Jean Suvatjis and Leslie de Chernatony, takes us out of the marketing department and into corporate communications in order to assess corporate identity and its reflective relationships with brand relationships. Building from qualitative research, the authors propose a six-station corporate identity model designed to create a strong corporate identity, introduce strong brands, and guide dynamic corporate strategy, transparent communication, unique corporate personality, and strong reputation, all based on the creation and management of relational bridges required for achieving successful consumer interface. The model provides a conceptual framework for analysis of the identity development process and emphasizes the continuous and synergistic efforts involved in effective relationship management that support this goal.

Stephen Springfield and Padmini Sharma from the Frito-Lay division of PepsiCo demonstrate in Chapter 19 the real-life application and impact of many of the concepts discussed in this volume. This chapter provides an in-depth look at how one of the world's fastest growing consumer packaged goods companies puts consumer–brand relationship theory into practice. The authors explain how replacing traditional brand models with relationship-based tools has enabled a more empathic style of marketing at Frito-Lay, ultimately leading to marketing industry awards and category growth leadership. The authors discuss their experiences in challenging existing organizational narratives, processes, and metrics in order to create a relationship-centric culture – highlighting contexts in which relationship theory flourished, key points of tension in acceptance of relationship ideas, and challenges regarding how relationships can be monetized. The authors close with reflections on where there is room for improvement in consumer–brand relationships as a business application.

Conclusion

The domain of brand relationships is critically important to brand marketing, but is also quite rich and complex. Brand relationships are founded on meanings that resonate personally and culturally; they service identity, functional, and social goals. Relationships are diverse and varied, and they change in response to consumer and brand behaviors, constantly mutating and evolving. We conclude with comments on the major themes and findings presented throughout the state-of-the-art research considered in the four parts of the book, and identify areas for future research and inspirations for practice.

References

Fournier, S. (1998) "Consumers and their Brands: Developing Relationship Theory in Consumer Research", *Journal of Consumer Research*, 24: 343–73.

Thaler, R.H. and Shefrin, H.M. (1981) "An Economic Theory of Self-Control", *Journal of Political Economy*, 89 (2): 392–406.

PART I

The "What" of Brand Relationships

Exploring relationship varieties and types

1

WHEN IS OUR CONNECTION TO BRANDS LIKE OUR CONNECTION TO PEOPLE?

Differentiating between consumer–brand relationships and interpersonal relationships

Vanitha Swaminathan and Sara Loughran Dommer

Introduction

While research on consumer–brand relationships has often used interpersonal relationships (e.g., attachment styles, relationship norms, etc.) as guides and metaphors for brand relationships, little time has been spent distinguishing between the interpersonal relationship and the brand relationship. In this chapter, we will: (1) review the use of interpersonal relationship theories in the consumer–brand relationship realm; (2) discuss some of the similarities between interpersonal relationships and brand relationships, and highlight some differences; and (3) outline topics in the consumer–brand relationship domain in need of future research based on our framework.

While early research in consumer behavior viewed consumers' interactions with products and brands as a series of exchanges, this transactional view has been replaced by a relational view. However, key differences between interpersonal relationships (IRs) and consumer–brand relationships (CBRs) should be noted. Typically, CBR involves a monetary exchange (i.e., transfer of funds from consumers to brands) that is atypical in IR. Further, while most individuals enter into IR, it is not at all clear whether CBR is as ubiquitous a phenomenon. Certain individuals and certain product categories seem to lend themselves to greater levels of CBR, and there are certain "relationship averse" segments as well (Price and Arnould 1999). These differences indicate the limitations of the relationship metaphor in providing insights in the CBR context. We return to this point in the discussion, when we highlight potential areas for future research. In the next section, we provide a systematic overview of the IR and CBR research and highlight similarities and differences between the two streams. We begin with an assessment of relationship typologies across both these streams, since the development of relationship types has been a primary topic of research.

Relationship typologies in IR and CBR

Many relationship typologies have been proposed in the CBR literature, which are similar to relationship types in the IR literature. McCall (1970) sees a continuum ranging from the more formal interactions to the much more personal relationships which resemble what psychologists refer to as close relationships. Wish and colleagues (1976) conducted an analysis of dyadic relationships and found they can be summarized along the following dimensions: (1) cooperative versus competitive or hostile; (2) equal versus unequal partnerships; (3) intense versus superficial; and (4) formal versus informal.

Types of consumer brand relationships

Building on this, Fournier's (1998) seminal work on consumer–brand relationships proposed a framework and identified various types of relationships ranging across arranged marriages, casual friends/buddies, marriages of convenience, committed partnerships, best friendships, compartmentalized friendships, kinships, rebounds/avoidance-driven relationships, childhood friendships, courtships, dependencies, flings, enmities, secret affairs, and enslavements. Using a combination of case histories and survey data, Fournier made an important contribution towards developing an understanding of CBR types. Further, Fournier (1998) proposed a brand relationship quality scale comprising six facets: behavioral interdependence, personal commitment, love/passion, attachment (encompassing self-concept and nostalgic connection), intimacy, and partner quality. Building on this work, Aaker, Fournier, and Brasel (2004) undertook a longitudinal examination of consumer–brand relationships and examined whether the role of brand relationships varies based on brand personalities. They argued that relationships with sincere brands displayed characteristics that are similar to friendship templates, whereas relationships with exciting brands resembled short-lived flings. Because of these differences in CBR, their research found that sincere brand relationships suffered more following a transgression whereas exciting brand relationships were energized in a similar situation. Recently, Fournier and Alvarez (in prep.) examined brand flings as a type of consumer–brand relationship, and demonstrated the transitional identity roles that these emotive and playful relationships engage.

Relationship norms (exchange versus communal relationships)

Further research within CBR developed some of the themes that were outlined in the work by Fournier (1998). Subsequent researchers have continued to borrow frameworks that were outlined in the IR literature, albeit providing new insights in the CBR context. In the IR context, Clark and Mills (1993) distinguish between communal and exchange relationships, where communal relationships are those in which partners are expected to provide benefits (e.g., social support) to each other in response to needs as they arise. Exchange relationships are those in which members benefit each other, whereas in communal relationships the basis of benefit is concern for the other's welfare.

This research has also had an impact in the context of consumer–brand relationships. Aggarwal and Law (2005) suggested that when consumers form relationships with brands they use norms of interpersonal relationships as a guide in their brand assessments. Consistent with the interpersonal literature, Aggarwal and Law examined two types of relationships based on interdependence: exchange relationships in which benefits are given to others to get something back and communal relationships in which benefits are given to show concern for others' needs. Their conceptual model proposed that an adherence to or a violation of these relationship norms influences the appraisal of the specific marketing action and also the overall brand evaluations. Specifically, Aggarwal and Law (2005) demonstrated that priming communal versus exchange norms can moderate various information processing strategies adopted by consumers.

Brand personality and consumer–brand relationships

In consumer behavior research, the construct *brand personality*, which refers to the set of human characteristics associated with a brand, has received much attention. The personality of a brand has been shown in the consumer behavior literature to be a vehicle of self-expression (e.g., Belk 1988; Kleine, Kleine, and Kernan 1993; Malhotra 1988). Aaker (1997) developed a reliable, valid, and generalizable scale to measure the brand personality construct. Her research uncovered five brand personalities (i.e., sincerity, excitement, competence, sophistication, and ruggedness). Three of the brand personality dimensions relate to the Big Five human personality dimensions in the IR context (Norman 1963; Tupes and Christal 1958). For example, sincerity, excitement, and competence map on to agreeableness, extroversion, and conscientiousness respectively. Sophistication and ruggedness are two brand personality dimensions that are distinct to the CBR context.

More recently, there has been a shift towards understanding the emotional makeup of relationships, in both the IR and CBR literatures. For instance, Sternberg's (1986) love triangle suggests that there are three factors underlying interpersonal relationships, namely intimacy, passion, and commitment. Intimacy exists when thoughts and feelings are shared, passion is the physical desire for a person, and commitment is the value placed on the relationship. Borrowing from Sternberg's (1986) triangular theory of love, Thomson, MacInnis, and Park's (2005) three-factor model characterizes brand attachment in terms of three emotional components: (1) affection, which included emotions such as "affectionate," "loved," "friendly," and "peaceful"; (2) passion, including emotions such as "passionate," "delighted," and "captivated"; and (3) connection, characterized by the items "connected," "bonded," and "attached." There is a correspondence between the emotional attachment factors based on Sternberg's (1986) theory of love and Thomson *et al.*'s (2005) three-factor model. Passion is identical in both typologies, and intimacy can be thought of as affection (friendship without passion or commitment), and connection and commitment are similar. However, Thomson and colleagues (2005) provide a valuable tool for measuring the extent of emotional brand attachment, and much can be gained from applying the emotional brand attachment construct to the CBR context.

Attachment styles and consumer–brand relationships

An important theoretical perspective from interpersonal relationships is attachment theory. Attachment theory has its roots in the work of Bowlby (1969, 1980), who suggested that interactions with caregivers in early childhood form the foundation for systematic differences in relationships formed in later life. Attachment theory has identified two dimensions of attachment style based on the individuals' view of self and view of others, namely anxiety and avoidance, respectively, which are expected to influence the type of relationships they engage in and their potential for forming attachments in the interpersonal domain (Bartholomew and Horowitz 1991; Bartz and Lydon 2004; Collins and Read 1994; Pierce and Lydon 1998). Further, research by Hazan and Shaver (1987) suggested that the emotional bond that develops between romantic partners is based on the same motivational system that gives rise to the bond between infant and caregiver. Since Hazan and Shaver's (1987) seminal work, further research has shown that other kinds of relationships including friendships and familial bonds are also governed by attachment theoretic principles (Ainsworth 1989; Trinke and Bartholomew 1997).

Following Bartholomew and Horowitz's (1991) development of the four attachment style model, recent research on attachment theory focuses on classifying individuals based on two dimensions: anxiety and avoidance (e.g., Brennan, Clark and Shaver 1998). The anxiety dimension refers to the extent a person's view of self is positive or negative, whereas the avoidance dimension is based on the extent that one's view of others is positive or negative. The anxiety dimension (self view) assesses the degree to which the self is perceived as being worthy or unworthy of love (or one's lovability). Anxious individuals, who are perpetually preoccupied with their self-worth and self-esteem concerns, have a negative model of self (characterized by an individual's belief that they are not worthy of love), have low self-esteem (Griffin and Bartholomew 1994), and are prone to self-criticism (Murphy and Bates 1997).

Recently, attachment theory has been applied to the context of consumer–brand relationships as well. Thomson (2006) examines why consumers develop strong attachments to "human brands," a term that refers to any well-known persona who is the subject of marketing communications efforts. Thomson suggests that when a human brand enhances a person's feelings of autonomy and relatedness, the person is likely to become more strongly attached to it. Thomson and Johnson (2006) investigated the role of attachment dimensions in relationships with brands. They find that because anxious people perceive their relationships as bad, they also view their relationships as inconsistent. People who registered high levels of avoidance reported a diminished experience of reciprocity as well as lower levels of satisfaction, commitment, and involvement. Paulssen and Fournier (in prep.) have also looked at attachment in consumer–brand relationships. Specifically, they use attachment theory and longitudinal data regarding brand relationships with automotive service dealers empirically to derive *consumer* attachment. Their results regarding consumer attachment parallel those found in interpersonal relationship settings. In this way, the research by Paulssen and Fournier (in prep.), Thomson (2006), and Thomson and Johnson (2006) provides initial evidence that attachment theory can be applicable to a consumer–brand relationship context.

Attachment styles have also been shown to influence how consumers choose brands and how they react to transgressions involving brands (Dommer, Swaminathan, and Gürhan-Canli in prep.; Swaminathan, Stilley, and Ahluwalia 2009). Swaminathan and colleagues (2009) examine the manner in which brand personality and attachment style differences systematically influence brand outcomes including brand attachment, purchase likelihood, and brand choice. Results show that anxiously attached individuals are more likely to be differentially influenced by brand personalities. Across a series of studies, they show that the level of avoidance predicts the types of brand personality that are most relevant to anxious individuals. Specifically, under conditions of high avoidance and high anxiety, individuals exhibit a preference for exciting brands; however, under conditions of low avoidance and high anxiety, individuals tend to prefer sincere brands. The differential preference for sincere (versus exciting) brand personality emerged in public consumption settings, when interpersonal relationship expectations were high, suggesting that brand personality was being used by anxious individuals as a signaling mechanism, to signal to potential relationship partners. Related, Park and John (2010) examine conditions when consumers' personalities are influenced by the brand's personality. They found that for certain types of consumers (i.e., entity theorists), the personality of the brand influenced their perceptions of themselves.

Dommer, Swaminathan, and Gürhan-Canli (in prep.) linked consumers' interpersonal attachment styles to their propensities to forgive a company following a product recall, as well as to their responses to recovery efforts. Their results demonstrated that avoidant users of a brand were more likely to have lower brand evaluations following a transgression incident, and forgiveness appeared to mediate these results. Further, consumers with fearful and secure attachment were more likely to engage in punishing behaviors such as spreading negative word of mouth following a transgression, and this result appeared to be driven by blame. In terms of recovery efforts, it was found that some consumers with a fearful attachment were "lost causes," whereas consumers with a dismissing attachment were more likely to return to a company following an apology. Their results demonstrated that following a company transgression, a "one-size fits all" recovery effort does not exist and that different consumers reacted positively to different recovery efforts, based on attachment style differences. Thus, the authors were able to show that consumers' feelings about relationships in the interpersonal realm affect their responses to a company's violation of the consumer–brand relationship. Attachment styles affect consumers' propensities to blame and forgive, which in turn affect their responses to company transgressions and recovery efforts.

Park and colleagues (2010) extended our understanding of brand attachment further by describing differences between brand attachment and brand attitude. The authors identified two dimensions of brand attachment: brand prominence and self–brand connection. A key similarity between the attachment perspective proposed by Park and colleagues (2010) and attachment in the IR literature is that both appeal to the attachment literature and use known measures of attachment (e.g., separation distress). Park and colleagues (2010) proposed a two-factor model which is unique to the CBR literature. This integrates cognitive (brand prominence is a cognitive measure) with a more emotional identity-based measure.

In summary, the CBR and IR literatures share many common themes. CBR researchers have borrowed the frameworks and typologies from IR research, but have found unique and novel insights in applying them to the context of a person–brand relationship. It appears that many of the IR types are similar to those found in CBR, although with some differences.

Antecedents of relationship development

An important theme common to both IR and CBR research involves examining factors that contribute to the development of relationships. Such research has tended to focus on motivational underpinnings for IR or CBR. In the IR literature, the focus has ranged from physical attraction as a motivation, to more recent work focusing on belongingness goals (e.g., Baumeister and Leary 1995). Research on antecedents of interpersonal relationships has uncovered various constructs including self-monitoring (Snyder 1974), self-construal (Markus and Kitayama 1991), attachment styles (Bartholomew and Horowitz 1991; Mikulincer 1995; Shaver and Brennan 1992), and Big Five personality types (Norman 1963; Tupes and Christal 1958). Borrowing from the IR literature, several of these personality traits have been shown to be relevant in the CBR context as well. For example, personality traits such as self-monitoring (Snyder 1974) have been shown to moderate individuals' propensities to engage in conspicuous consumption (Ratner and Kahn 2002). Self-construal has also been shown to moderate the extent to which consumers form relationships with brands which strengthen either unique self or collective self (Escalas and Bettman 2005; Swaminathan, Page, and Gürhan-Canli 2007). Finally, as described previously, attachment style has also been shown to predict CBR (Swaminathan, Stilley, and Ahluwalia 2009).

An important goal that brands serve is self-expression and self-definition, particularly with a view to impress relationship partners and groups to which one belongs. In this way, possessions have long been shown to define one's self. Since Belk (1988) introduced the concept of possessions "extending the self," various researchers have demonstrated that consumers use products in a symbolic way to narrate their identities to others (Kleine, Kleine, and Allen 1995; Levy 1959; McCracken 1989; Reed 2004). Brand names enable consumers to express their self-identities (Escalas and Bettman 2003; Fournier 1994; Swaminathan, Page, and Gürhan-Canli 2007) and marketers often link aspects of brands with a target consumer's identity to influence consumer preferences. For instance, Escalas and Bettman (2003) link self-construal to brand preferences. They demonstrate that consumers' goals for self-differentiation from others can be attained via purchase of in-group brands and rejection of out-group brands. In summary, interpersonal relationship goals (e.g., belongingness to groups, self-differentiation) have been shown to foster consumer–brand relationships.

There are two ways by which IR goals influence CBR. First, IR can result in choices of brands that fit with consumers' current IR contexts; alternatively, IR can, under certain conditions, result in choices of brands that compensate for what is lacking in the IR context. Past research has shown that consumers react positively when there is a perceived congruency between their own identity and the brand's identity (Fournier 1994; Reed 2004). Recent research, however, has shifted from demonstrating the importance of "fit" between consumers' identities and brand identities to evolving a deeper understanding of why consumers use brands to express their identity.

This shift in focus to understanding the motivational underpinnings of CBR has uncovered various contexts where CBR is used as a compensatory mechanism. For example, recent research focuses on how self-threat can influence consumers' choice of brands. In the IR context, it has been shown that when individuals experience a threat to self or a threat involving close relationships, it is expected that individuals cope by utilizing whatever external means are immediately available or accessible. Steele and colleagues (1993) suggest that when faced with a potential threat, people have "the option of leaving the threat unrationalized – that is, accepting the threat without countering it – and affirming some other aspect of self that reinforces one's overall self-adequacy" (Steele et al. 1993, 885).

One way to achieve higher self-esteem is to connect with reference groups or groups of individuals that the individual admires or aspires to be like. Mikulincer, Florian, and Hirschberger (2003) suggest that interpersonal relationships can protect individuals from threats and dangers. Park and Maner (2009) extend this argument and show that when individuals experience a threat to their physical appearance, some individuals connect to others as a way of coping. Greater favoritism towards the in-group can increase one's view of self (see Luhtanen and Crocker 1991 for a review). For instance, Tajfel and Turner (1986) suggest that in-group members exaggerate their superiority over out-group members in an effort to bolster self-esteem. Subsequent research has shown that engaging in group discrimination can promote feelings of self-worth (Lemyre and Smith 1985; Oakes and Turner 1980). Based on the preceding research findings, reaffirming their memberships in reference groups is one way by which individuals can restore their self-view that has been threatened.

Research in the CBR context has shown that brand names that are affiliated with a reference group can help bolster self-view following interpersonal rejection (Aaker 1999; Fournier 1998; Gao, Wheeler, and Shiv 2009; Loveland, Smeesters, and Mandel 2010; Rindfleisch, Borroughs, and Wong 2009; Swaminathan et al. 2009). Related literature in the context of brand communities reaffirms the idea that belonging to a brand community can increase self-esteem (Holt 2004; Muniz and O'Guinn 2001; Schouten and McAlexander 1995). Affiliating with reference group consistent brand names can exert significant value-expressive influence on consumer behavior (Bearden and Etzel 1982; Park and Lessig 1977). Specifically, in-group consistent brands can act as signaling mechanisms that convey the presence of ideal qualities to others (Swaminathan et al. 2009). Rindfleisch and colleagues (2009) also suggest that materialistic individuals are likely to seek attachment to material objects to compensate for faltering social connections or failing attachment to others. Gao, Wheeler, and Shiv (2009) showed that when a confidently held self-view (e.g., "I am an exciting person") is temporarily cast in doubt, individuals are motivated to choose products that bolster their original self-view (e.g., choosing brands with exciting brand personalities). Loveland, Smeesters, and Mandel (2010) argue that individuals with an active need for belongingness demonstrate a greater preference for nostalgic brands. Long and colleagues (in prep.) demonstrated that consumers evaluate preferred brands more positively when brand-relevant goals are activated, particularly for persons with a heightened need for belonging and friendship or as a compensatory mechanism for avoidant interpersonal attachment styles. Aggarwal and McGill (in prep.) demonstrated that consumer responses to anthropomorphized brands are highly goal-directed and driven by desire for successful social interaction, and that these responses vary with the type of relationship – partner or slave – that is expected from the brand.

Therefore, it appears that consumers engage in different types of brand relationships (e.g., partnerships, masters in a master–slave brand relationship, flings, and friends) with varying types of brands (e.g., sincere/exciting brands, nostalgic brands) to achieve various personal and social goals (e.g., greater social interaction, coping with relationship anxiety, belonging and social connectedness; and transitioning between various definitions of self). Previous research on consumer–brand relationship theory demonstrates that although brands as relationship partners can function in much the same way as humans do, differences between these relationship analogues do exist, which may limit the applicability of the relationship metaphor, but also provide opportunities for future research. We next highlight some potential areas for future research.

Future research

Despite the important role of IR theory, some differences between the two limit its applicability in the CBR context. As noted previously, a key difference is that the CBR context involves transfer of funds between the consumer and brands; such monetary exchange is more the exception than the norm in the IR context. Given this, an important area worthy of further investigation is how expectation of monetary exchange influences the extent and type of CBR. One may speculate that CBR development is limited to exchange-type relationships (as opposed to communal relationships) in conditions when monetary exchange norms are dominant, or when norms of monetary exchange are violated.

Another important area of further research is to expand our analysis from a focus on single consumer–brand relationships to multiple consumer–brand relationships. Indeed, unlike the IR context, consumers may engage in multiple relationships with brands; these relationships may vary in length as well as depth. In other words, there is greater potential for polygamous relationships between consumers and brands and perhaps "cheating" is a more acceptable practice in brand relationships than in interpersonal relationships. More research should be done across multiple consumer–brand relationships to uncover patterns in relationships that consumers engage in, rather than the current focus on single consumer–brand relationships. Further, much of our current understanding of CBR is based on cross-sectional studies. CBR has not gone beyond characterizing these relationships to describing (1) how one type of relationship can lead to another, e.g., a fling-like relationship to a commitment-type relationship, or (2) how a single consumer can move through these various relationship types over the duration of their relationship with a single brand. More research should be directed toward understanding the dynamic nature of consumer–brand relationships as they evolve over time. Such research, when conducted using longitudinal field studies, can provide important new insights into varying relationship development trajectories. Such understanding will prove crucial in developing frameworks that describe dynamic consumer behavior and their relationships with brands. Further, examining how consumers have varying relationships with brands could shed light on important questions surrounding brand strategy formulation (Keller and Lehmann 2006) as well as brand equity dilution (Keller and Sood 2003).

Much of the consumer–brand relationship literature has focused on the individual. The interpersonal relationship context has examined both partners within a dyad (e.g., Collins and Feeney 2000). Given the rich insights that dyadic analysis provides compared with an individual analysis, more research in the CBR context should focus on dyadic analysis, where possible. For instance, in the services industry context, this could be achieved by interviewing the consumer as well as the service provider.

More research is also needed to examine interactions between human personality and brand personality to see whether they are consistent or whether consumers use brand personality to compensate for what they lack in terms of human personality. Related to this, research could examine what attracts consumers and brands. In the interpersonal relationship context (Byrne 1971), a key question surrounds whether factors other than physical attractiveness contribute to interpersonal attraction. Factors such as similarity and complementarity of personalities and interests have been considered (e.g., Huston and Levinger 1978). Much of the consumer–brand relationship literature has focused on similarity of consumer to brand as a key driver of CBR (e.g., Belk 1988; Landon 1974; Sirgy 1982); much less research has focused on complementary roles that brands play in consumers' lives. Further, conditions that foster complementarity versus similarity between consumers' personalities and brand personalities could be an interesting area for further research.

One topic that needs greater research is how different segments of individuals vary in their CBR propensity. Chaplin and John (2005) examine this important question by investigating differences in self–brand connections between adults and children. Across three studies, their empirical research suggests that self–brand connections develop in number and sophistication between middle childhood and early adolescence. Melnyk, van Osselaer, and Bijmolt (2009) examine gender differences and find that female consumers tend to be more loyal than male consumers to individuals, such as individual service providers; this difference is reversed when the object of loyalty is a group of people. Monga and John (2007) examine cultural differences in reactions to brands and brand extensions. Despite these important contributions, more research should focus on understanding how different segments of potential consumers (e.g., males versus females, younger versus older consumers, consumers in independent versus interdependent cultures) vary in their propensity to develop relationships with brands as well as the types of consumer–brand relationships they are likely to engage in.

The whole area of relationship dissolution has received a great deal of attention in the IR literature, but has not had much attention paid to it in the CBR literature. How do consumers cope with dissolutions of CBR? How are their reactions similar or different to those of IR? Recent work by Johnson, Matear, and Thomson (2011) begins to examine this issue. According to the authors, some people identify so strongly with brands that they become relevant to their identity and self-concept. Thus, when people feel betrayed by brands, they experience shame and insecurity. More work could be directed toward developing a greater understanding of relationship dissolution similarities and differences between the realms of IR and CBR.

In addition to potential research opportunities in the CBR realm, some of the findings could also provide the basis for research in IR. For example, if CBR involves exchange of funds, then it is worthwhile to explore whether one's interpersonal relationships may be shaped by encounters with a business partner outside of the monetary exchange. Similarly, could the concepts of conspicuous brand consumption inform us about some unique kinds of interpersonal relationships which one might develop primarily to further one's status and prestige?

In sum, interpersonal relationship theory has proved to be a rich source of concepts, frameworks, and typologies that have been extensively applied in the CBR context. While IR and CBR share some similar motivations, some aspects of CBR are understudied compared with IR. This chapter summarizes the literature on the CBR topic, highlighting the similarities and differences between the two areas. It is hoped that the ideas outlined here will motivate future researchers to conduct further examination on CBR issues and develop a richer understanding of consumers' relationships with brands.

References

Aaker, J.L. (1997) "Dimensions of Brand Personality", *Journal of Marketing Research*, 34: 347–356.

—— (1999) "The Malleable Self: The Role of Self-Expression in Persuasion", *Journal of Marketing Research*, 36: 45–57.

Aaker, J.L., Fournier, S. and Brasel, S.A. (2004) "When Good Brands Do Bad", *Journal of Consumer Research*, 31: 1–16.

Aggarwal, P. and Law, S. (2005) "Role of Relationship Norms in Processing Brand Information", *Journal of Consumer Research*, 32: 453–464.

Aggarwal, P. and McGill, A. (in prep.) "Partners and Servants: Adopting traits of anthropomorphized brands", manuscript in preparation.

Ainsworth, M.D.S. (1989) "Attachments beyond Infancy", *American Psychologist*, 44: 709–716.

Bartholomew, K. and Horowitz, L.M. (1991) "Attachment Styles among Young Adults: A Test of a Four-Category Model", *Journal of Personality and Social Psychology*, 61: 226–244.

Bartz, J.A. and Lydon, J.E. (2004) "Close Relationships and the Working Self-Concept: Implicit and Explicit Effects of Priming Attachment on Agency and Communion", *Personality and Social Psychology Bulletin*, 30: 1389–1401.

Baumeister, R.F. and Leary, M.R. (1995) "The Need to Belong: Desire for Interpersonal Attachments as a Fundamental Human Motivation", *Psychological Bulletin*, 117: 497–529.

Bearden, W.O. and Etzel, M.J. (1982) "Reference Group Influence on Product and Brand Purchase Decisions", *Journal of Consumer Research*, 9: 183–194.

Belk, R.W. (1988) "Possessions and the Extended Self", *Journal of Consumer Research*, 15: 139–168.

Bowlby, J. (1969) *Attachment and Loss: Vol. 1. Attachment*, New York: Basic Books.

—— (1980) *Loss: Sadness and depression*, New York: Basic Books.

Brennan, K.A., Clark, C.L. and Shaver, P.R. (1998) "Self-Report Measurement of Adult Attachment: An Integrative Overview", in J.A. Simpson and W.S. Rholes (eds) *Attachment Theory and Close Relationships*, New York: Guilford Press.

Byrne, D. (1971) *The Attraction Paradigm*, Orlando, FL: Academic Press.

Chaplin, L.N. and John, D.R. (2005) "The Development of Self-Brand Connections in Children and Adolescents", *Journal of Consumer Research*, 32: 119–129.

Clark, M.S. and Mils, J. (1993) "The Difference between Communal and Exchange Relationships: What It is and is Not", *Personality and Social Psychology Bulletin*, 19: 684–691.

Collins, N.L. and Feeney, B.C. (2000) "A Safe Haven: An Attachment Theory Perspective on Support Seeking and Caregiving in Intimate Relationships", *Journal of Personality and Social Psychology*, 78: 1053–1073.

Collins, N.L. and Read, S.J. (1994) "Cognitive Representations of Adult Attachment: The Structure and Function of Working Models", in K. Bartholomew and D. Perlman (eds) *Advances in Personal Relationships, Vol. 5*, London: Jessica Kingsley.

Dommer, S.L., Swaminathan, V. and Gürhan-Canli, Z. (in prep.) "Who Forgives When Companies Err? Applying attachment theory to explain consumer responses to company transgressions", manuscript in preparation, The Joseph M. Katz Graduate School of Business, University of Pittsburgh.

Escalas, J.E. and Bettman, J.R. (2003) "You Are What They Eat: The Influence of Reference Groups on Consumers' Connections to Brands", *Journal of Consumer Psychology*, 13: 339–348.

—— (2005) "Self-Construal, Reference Groups, and Brand Meaning", *Journal of Consumer Research*, 32: 378–389.

Fournier, S. (1994) "A Consumer–Brand Relationship Framework for Strategic Brand Management", unpublished dissertation, The Graduate School, University of Florida.

—— (1998) "Consumers and their Brands: Developing Branding Theory in Consumer Research", *Journal of Consumer Research*, 24: 343–373.

Fournier, S. and Alvarez, C. (in prep.) "Brand Flings and the Transitional Self", manuscript in preparation, Boston University School of Management.

Gao, L., Wheeler, S.C. and Shiv, B. (2009) "The 'Shaken Self': Product Choices as a Means of Restoring Self-View Confidence", *Journal of Consumer Research*, 36: 29–38.

Griffin, D. and Bartholomew, K. (1994) "Models of the Self and Other: Fundamental Dimensions Underlying Measures of Adult Attachment", *Journal of Personality and Social Psychology*, 67: 430–445.

Hazan, C. and Shaver, P.R. (1987) "Romantic Love Conceptualized as an Attachment Process", *Journal of Personality and Social Psychology*, 52: 511–524.

Holt, D.B. (2004) *How Brands Become Icons: The principles of cultural branding*, Cambridge, MA: HBS Press.

Huston, T.L. and Levinger, G. (1978) "Interpersonal Attraction and Relationships", *Annual Review of Psychology*, 29: 115–156.

Johnson, A.R., Matear, M. and Thomson, M. (2011) "A Coal in the Heart: Self-Relevance as a Post-Exit Predictor of Consumer Anti-Brand Actions", *Journal of Consumer Research*, 38: 108–125.

Keller, K.L. and Lehmann, D.R. (2006) "Brands and Branding: Research Findings and Future Priorities", Marketing Science, 25 (6): 740–759.

Keller, K.L. and Sood, S. (2003) "Brand Equity Dilution", *MIT Sloan Management Review*, 45 (1): 12–15.

Kleine, R.E., III, Kleine, S.S. and Kernan, J.B. (1993) "Mundane Consumption and the Self: A Social-Identity Perspective", *Journal of Consumer Psychology*, 2: 209–235.

Kleine, S.S., Kleine, R.E., III and Allen, C.T. (1995) "How is a Possession 'Me' or 'Not Me'? Characterizing Types and an Antecedent of Material Possession Attachment", *Journal of Consumer Research*, 22: 327–343.

Landon, E.L., Jr (1974) "Self Concept, Ideal Self Concept, and Consumer Purchase Intentions", *Journal of Consumer Research*, 1: 44–51.

Lemyre, L. and Smith, P.M. (1985) "Intergroup Discrimination and Self-Esteem in the Minimal Group Paradigm", *Journal of Personality and Social Psychology*, 49: 660–670.

Levy, S.L. (1959) "Symbols For Sale", *Harvard Business Review*, 37: 117–124.

Long, C.R., Gable, P.A., Albee, C. and Boerstler, C. (in prep.) "Brands are Like Friends: Goals and interpersonal motives influence attitudes toward preferred brands", manuscript in preparation.

Loveland, K.E., Smeesters, D. and Mandel, N. (2010) "Still Preoccupied with 1995: The Need to Belong and Preference for Nostalgic Products", *Journal of Consumer Research*, 37: 393–408.

Luhtanen, R. and Crocker, J. (1991) "Self-esteem and intergroup comparisons: Toward a theory of collective self-esteem", in J. Suls and T.A. Wills (eds) *Social Comparison: Contemporary theory and research*, Hillsdale, NJ: Erlbaum.

McCall, G.J. (1970) *Social Relationships*, Chicago: Aldine.

McCracken, G. (1989) "Who is the Celebrity Endorser? Cultural Foundations of the Endorsement Process", *Journal of Consumer Research*, 16: 310–321.

Malhotra, N.K. (1988) "Self Concept and Product Choice: An Integrated Perspective", *Journal of Economic Psychology*, 9: 1–28.

Markus, H.R. and Kitayama, S. (1991) "Culture and the Self: Implications for Cognition, Emotion, and Motivation", *Psychological Review*, 98: 224–253.

Melnyk, V., van Osselaer, S.M.J. and Bijmolt, T.H.A. (2009) "Are Women More Loyal Customers than Men? Gender Differences in Loyalty to Firms and Individual Service Providers", *Journal of Marketing*, 73: 82–96.

Mikulincer, M. (1995) "Attachment Style and the Mental Representation of the Self", *Journal of Personality and Social Psychology*, 69: 1203–1215.

Mikulincer, M., Florian, V. and Hirschberger, G. (2003) "The Existential Function of Close Relationships: Introducing Death into the Science of Love", *Personality and Social Psychology Review*, 7: 20–40.

Monga, A.B. and John, D.R. (2007) "Cultural Differences in Brand Extension Evaluation: The Influence of Analytic versus Holistic Thinking", *Journal of Consumer Research*, 33: 529–536.

Muñiz, A.M., Jr and O'Guinn, T.C. (2001) "Brand Community", *Journal of Consumer Research*, 27: 412–432.

Murphy, B. and Bates, G.W. (1997) "Adult Attachment Style and Vulnerability to Depression", *Personality and Individual Differences*, 22: 635–644.

Norman, W.T. (1963) "Toward an Adequate Taxonomy of Personality Attributes: Replicated Factor Structure in Peer Nomination Personality Ratings", *Journal of Abnormal & Social Psychology*, 66: 574–583.

Oakes, P.J. and Turner, J.C. (1980) "Social Categorization and Intergroup Behavior: Does Minimal Intergroup Discrimination Make Social Identity More Positive?" *European Journal of Social Psychology*, 10: 295–301.

Park, C.W. and Lessig, V.P. (1977) "Students and Housewives: Differences in Susceptibility to Reference Group Influence", *Journal of Consumer Research*, 4: 102–110.

Park, C.W., MacInnis, D.J., Priester, J., Eisingerich, A.B. and Iacobucci, D. (2010) "Brand Attachment and Brand Attitude Strength: Conceptual and Empirical Differentiation of Two Critical Brand Equity Drivers", *Journal of Marketing*, 74: 1–17.

Park, J.K. and John, D.R. (2010) "Got to Get You into My Life: Do Brand Personalities Rub off on Consumers?" *Journal of Consumer Research*, 37: 655–669.

Park, L.E. and Maner, J.K. (2009) "Does Self-Threat Promote Social Connection? The Role of Self-Esteem and Contingencies of Self-Worth", *Journal of Personality and Social Psychology*, 96: 203–217.

Paulssen, M. and Fournier, S. (in prep.) "Attachment Security and the Strength of Commercial Relationships: A longitudinal study", manuscript in preparation, Boston University School of Management.

Pierce, T. and Lydon, J. (1998) "Priming Relational Schemas: Effects of Contextually Activated and Chronically Accessible Interpersonal Expectations on Responses to a Stressful Event", *Journal of Personality & Social Psychology*, 75: 1441–1448.

Price, L.L. and Arnould, E.J. (1999) "Commercial Friendships: Service Provider–Client Relationships in Context", *Journal of Marketing*, 63: 38–56.

Ratner, R.K. and Kahn, B.E. (2002) "The Impact of Private versus Public Consumption on Variety-Seeking Behavior", *Journal of Consumer Research*, 29: 246–257.

Reed, A., II (2004) "Activating the Self-Importance of Consumer Selves: Exploring Identity Salience Effects on Judgments", *Journal of Consumer Research*, 31: 286–295.

Rindfleisch, A., Borroughs, J.E. and Wong, N. (2009) "The Safety of Objects: Materialism, Existential Insecurity and Brand Connection", *Journal of Consumer Research*, 36: 1–16.

Schouten, J.W. and McAlexander, J.H. (1995) "Subcultures of Consumption: An Ethnography of the New Bikers", *Journal of Consumer Research*, 22: 43–61.

Shaver, P.R. and Brennan, K.A. (1992) "Attachment Styles and the 'Big Five' Personality Traits: Their Connections with Each Other and with Romantic Relationship Outcomes", *Personality and Social Psychology Bulletin*, 18: 536–545.

Sirgy, M.J. (1982) "Self-Concept in Consumer Behavior: A Critical Review", *Journal of Consumer Research*, 9: 287–300.

Snyder, M. (1974) "Self-Monitoring of Expressive Behavior", *Journal of Personality and Social Psychology*, 30: 526–537.

Steele, C.M., Spencer, S.J. and Lynch, M. (1993) "Self-Image Resilience and Dissonance: The Role of Affirmational Resources", *Journal of Personality and Social Psychology*, 64: 885–896.

Sternberg, R.J. (1986) "A Triangular Theory of Love", *Psychological Review*, 93: 58–83.

Swaminathan, V., Page, K.L. and Gürhan-Canli, Z. (2007) "'My' Brand or 'Our' Brand: The Effects of Brand Relationship Dimensions and Self-Construal on Brand Evaluations", *Journal of Consumer Research*, 34: 248–259.

Swaminathan, V., Stilley, K. and Ahluwalia, R. (2009) "When Brand Personality Matters: The Moderating Role of Attachment Styles", *Journal of Consumer Research*, 35: 985–1002.

Tajfel, H. and Turner, J. (1986) "The Social Identity Theory of Intergroup Conflict", in S. Worchel and W.G. Austin (eds) *Psychology of Intergroup Relations*, Chicago: Nelson-Hall.

Thomson, M. (2006) "Human Brands: Investigating Antecedents to Consumers' Strong Attachments to Celebrities", *Journal of Marketing*, 70: 104–119.

Thomson, M. and Johnson, A.R. (2006) "Marketplace and Personal Space: Investigating the Differential Effects of Attachment Style across Relationship Contexts", *Psychology & Marketing*, 23: 711–726.

Thomson, M., MacInnis, D.J. and Park, C.W. (2005) "The Ties That Bind: Measuring the Strength of Consumers' Emotional Attachments to Brands", *Journal of Consumer Psychology*, 15: 77–91.

Trinke, S.J. and Bartholomew, K. (1997) "Hierarchies of Attachment Relationships in Young Adulthood", *Journal of Social and Personal Relationships*, 14: 603–625.

Tupes, E.C. and Christal, R.E. (1958) "Stability of Personality Trait Rating Factors Obtained under Diverse Conditions", *USAF WADS Technical Report No. 58–61*, Lackland Air Force Base, TX: US Air Force.

Wish, M., Deutsch, M. and Kaplan, S.J. (1976) "Perceived Dimensions of Interpersonal Relations", *Journal of Personality and Social Psychology*, 33: 409–420.

2

EXPLORING RELATIONSHIP ANALOGUES IN THE BRAND SPACE

Felicia M. Miller, Susan Fournier, and Chris T. Allen

Most accept the premise that consumers desire brands and become devoted to them for reasons beyond functional performance. The idea that brands have symbolic value (Levy 1959; Solomon 1983), may contain deep meaning (Belk, Wallendorf, and Sherry 1989; Kleine, Kleine, and Allen 1995; McCracken 1986), foster community (Muñiz and O'Guinn 2001), or provide emotional value and self-enhancement versus functional benefits (Aaker 1991; Keller 2003) is well established in consumer research. Still, the nature of the bonds consumers form with brands remains enigmatic. It is common to find frustration expressed with extant theories and methods that promise an understanding of the quality of consumers' emotional attachments to brands (e.g. Brown 2005; Holt 2003; Zaltman 2003).

It is in this spirit that Fournier (1998) introduced the idea of the consumer–brand relationship, suggesting that brands can serve as viable partners in a range of different relationships, including Committed Partnerships, Flings, and Secret Affairs. As Aggarwal (2004) asserted, "The relationship metaphor offers a great opportunity to explore the complex but fascinating world of consumer–brand interactions" (p. 100). He borrowed directly from interpersonal relationship theory using Clark and Mills' (1979) Communal versus Exchange typology to demonstrate differences in consumers' brand evaluations and the processes underlying them. Recent studies continue to suggest value in thinking of consumer–brand interactions within the relational frame (MacInnis, Park, and Priester 2009). Still, empirical work such as this presents the tip of the iceberg. There exists a vast literature on human relationships that researchers could draw on more explicitly for understanding consumers' interactions with brands.

However, because we can apply the relationship metaphor to marketplace exchanges, should we? Put differently: do relationships analogous to those

existing between humans manifest in the brand space? As no
(2004, p. 88), the relationship metaphor has inherent limitati
cannot appropriately be conceived as "human-like." Arnould ¿
have been most strident in challenging the brand relationship n
tain that consumers have no interest in forming relationshi
(cf. Arnould and Price 2006; Twitchell 2004). Their point is tl
more important things to attend to than cultivating intimate relationships with
brands. When a brand assists with something important, as in spending "quality
time" at McDonald's with the kids, then that brand may be more highly valued,
but no adult wants to bring Ronald McDonald home for the weekend.

While the empirical examination of whether and how every interpersonal
relationship translates to the brand space would require a significant programmatic investigation, manageable steps can be made toward this goal. The present
research explores the consumer relevance of a subset of eight relationship types
identified by Fournier (1998) in her seminal brand relationship work. To accomplish our goals, we focus on the themes and defining elements that characterize
each of these relationships in the interpersonal realm. It seems reasonable that if a
given relationship is said to exist between a consumer and a brand, the defining
elements of the human analogue must be present in the brand space. Using the
lens of interpersonal relationships, we develop and assess parallel brand relationships and begin to address the question: do resonant analogues to interpersonal
relationships exist in the brand space?

Before turning to a description of our exploratory empirical work, we briefly
review the interpersonal and consumer literature on relationship types. We then
describe our methodology for examining our focal relationships and discuss the
process whereby we derived relational themes and refined our relationship
scenarios based on consumer feedback. We present results for the eight relationship types, providing insight into (1) the resonance of the relationship form
among consumers, (2) the extent to which consumers' relationship descriptions
play back interpersonal relational themes, and (3) the types of brands and product
categories elicited for each relationship. Our goal is to develop consumer-
relevant definitions and operationalizations of these core relationships for use in
consumer research. We close with a review of encouragements, caveats, and
future priorities for those looking to apply the relationship metaphor in the
branding domain.

Relationship types

The most basic conceptualization of brand relationship types is the dichotomy
explored by Aggarwal (2004) in his research on Exchange versus Communal
relationships. The Communal/Exchange paradigm was introduced in the interpersonal literature by Clark and Mills in 1979 and explored in many subsequent
papers over the past three decades (Clark and Mills 1993; Clark, Mills, and

owell 1986; Mills and Clark 1994). The Clark and Mills dichotomy has obvious marketplace applications. In the words of these originating researchers, "Exchange relationships are essential for the functioning of a modern economy" (Clark and Mills 1993, p. 690). Clark and Mills imply in their work that Exchange relationships are ubiquitous and Communal relationships are rare.

Dichotomies are theoretically elegant but yield conceptualizations at a high level of abstraction. Stated more concretely, if Exchange is appropriately conceived as the relationship type wherein one expects to give and receive functional benefits in equal measure, then within the Communal type there must be numerous variants wherein balanced reciprocity is not the norm. Indeed, Clark and Finkel (2005) indicate that Communal relationships include unique relationships such as friendships, romantic partnerships, and familial relationships, to name a few. The point is that one can go beyond Clark and Mills' dichotomy in proposing a relationship typology, and if one is interested in distinct characteristics in relationships, it makes perfect sense to do so (cf. Clarke, Allen, and Dickson 1985; Guerrero and Anderson 2000).

Beyond the Communal–Exchange dichotomy, there is no generally accepted typology of salient relationship types, and it is easy to become overwhelmed by the array of possibilities. There exist, however, studies of the dimensionality of the relationship space which can be useful for organizing typologies (Hinde 1979; Kayser, Schwinger, and Cohen 1984; Wish 1976; Wright 1985). Fournier (2009) explored the dimensionality of brand relationships and from dozens of dimensions (see page 12, Table 1.3), identified duration, power, emotionality, valence, and depth as among the most important. We use Fournier's dimensions as a guide in expanding our research focus beyond the Communal–Exchange dichotomy and select a subset of focal relationships for study that tap the diversity of the relationship space across these core dimensions. In addition to the Communal and Exchange relationship types popular in consumer research, we operationalize six others in this research: Abusive Relationships, Adversarial Relationships (Enmities), Committed Partnerships, Dependent Relationships, Master–Slave Relationships (Enslavements), and Secret Affairs. The negative affective space is represented by Adversarial and Abusive relationships. Power imbalance is captured in Dependencies and Master–Slave relations. Duration is a central defining element of Committed Relations; emotionality is a core facet of Secret Affairs. Our eight focal relations are diverse, provocative, and interesting, and serve as fertile candidates to explore the validity of relationship analogues in the brand space.

Methodology: development of brand relationship descriptions

Our research approach involves exposing consumers to a relationship scenario description and probing for familiarity and experiences with the focal relationship type. Scenario development was iterative and involved successive stages of data collection focused on the goal of "getting the relationship scenario right." Our research took place over a four-year period and involved up to four rounds of data collection to refine selected scenarios. In total, 1,639 subjects participated in our scenario-based research task.

We began the research with a relationship paragraph description designed to reflect the core defining features, characteristics, and facets of the focal relationship as revealed in the interpersonal relationships literature on that particular relationship type. Labels for the relationship were not provided. These initial paragraph descriptions were exposed to consumers in a subject lab using a between-subjects design wherein feedback was gathered on whether each description resonated with people's brand experiences and reflected a valid relationship in consumers' lives. Specifically, subjects were asked to read the paragraph description, identify up to five brands that fit the description, and select the one brand that best fit the description in their minds. Subjects were then asked to describe their relationship with the chosen brand and to explain why the selected brand was the best example of the probed relationship.

Subjects' open-ended responses were coded to create a "manipulation check" of sorts wherein we identified themes that were either consistent with ("got it") or inconsistent with ("did not get it") the relationship description. If a scenario had a high level (>50 percent) of "did not get it" responses, we made revisions to clarify, and in some cases simplify, the description to improve its focus on core themes. Another round of data was collected for relationships with high failure rates and the coding process was repeated. Six of the eight scenarios eventually evidenced strong resonance with consumers' stories. However, despite repeated rounds of refinement, the level of "did not get it" responses remained at or above 50 percent for the Committed and Communal relationship scenarios, indicating to us that these relationships did not translate directly from the interpersonal to the commercial space as theorized. We amplify these results below as we report on our culminating rounds of data collection for each focal relationship. A total of 750 respondents are included in these final research rounds. The final eight relationship descriptions used in this research are provided in Figure 2.1.

Results: within relationship types

Abusive relationship

For the Abusive relationship ninety-six subjects were asked to select a brand that:

> you *use or have used* which meet the following characteristics: the brand *just doesn't treat you right*; the brand *does not seem to value you as a customer*; no matter what you do to change or ignore the situation, the *wrongful treatment continues* just the same.

Abusive	Adversarial
A brand that you **use or have used** which meets the following characteristics: the brand **just doesn't treat you right**; the brand **does not seem to value you as a customer**; no matter what you do to change or ignore the situation, the **wrongful treatment continues** just the same.	A brand that you **adamantly refuse to buy, support, or use.** You think of this brand as an **opponent or rival**. This is a brand that you are **actively "against"** in some way.

Committed	Communal
A brand that you are **committed to in some significant and lasting way**. This is a brand that you **expect to be using for years to come**. Although your brand has competitors, **you stick only with "your brand."**	A brand that you **go out of your way to support**. This is a brand that you **really care about**. You have a strong desire **to help this brand succeed** in the marketplace.

Dependent	Exchange
A brand that you **"cannot live without."** This is a brand you feel is **truly irreplaceable**. It is **uncomfortable** for you to think about **being separated** from this brand for a long period, or **being prevented** from using it ever again.	A brand that you buy and use regularly and that meets the following characteristics: this brand provides a **straightforward benefit** for a **reasonable cost**; this brand simply **"does its job"** ... **nothing less, nothing more**.

Master–Slave	Secret Affair
A brand you **use on a regular basis**, but are somehow **"stuck with,"** **trapped into using**, or otherwise **forced to use**. This is a brand that you would say you use only because there is **no alternative** that is available to you and readily accessible. This is a brand you wish you didn't **"have to"** purchase or use. You would probably **not** select this particular brand if you had other options.	A brand whose **usage you downplay or keep hidden** from certain others for one reason or another. While you may use this brand regularly or often, this is a brand that you really **do not want others associating with you in any significant way**.

FIGURE 2.1 Relationship descriptions

The self-nomination process produced a diverse set of brands. Only thirteen brands were nominated by two or more of the ninety-six subjects; these brands accounted for 48 percent of the nominated brands. Within the brands that were nominated multiple times, we observe some patterns. Transportation providers were nominated most frequently including the MBTA-Massachusetts Bay Transportation Authority (ten), JetBlue (three), American Airlines (two), and US Airways (two). Two telecommunication brands were also nominated two or more times: Verizon (four) and Cingular (two). Table 2.1 provides the full list of brands nominated more than once for the Abusive relationship.

TABLE 2.1 Brands nominated more than once

Relationship type	Nominated brand	Number of nominations	Brands nominated twice
Abusive	MBTA	10	American Airlines
	Bank of America	6	Apple
	Dell	5	Best Buy
	Verizon	4	Cingular
	Comcast	3	Domino's Pizza
	Jet Blue	3	US Airways
	Toshiba	3	
Adversarial	Abercrombie & Fitch	6	Coca-Cola
	Dunkin Donuts	4	Colgate
	Pepsi	4	Crest
	Boston Red Sox	3	Gateway
	Dell	3	George W. Bush
	MBTA	3	Juicy Couture
	McDonald's	3	New York Yankees
	Wal-Mart	3	Olive Garden
			Pantene
Committed	Nike	9	Air Jordan
	Coca-Cola	7	General Motors
	Apple	5	Honda
	Colgate Toothpaste	5	Polo
	Crest Toothpaste	5	Revlon
	Dell Computers	4	Singapore Airlines
	Microsoft Windows	3	Skippy Peanut Butter
			Sony
			Victoria's Secret
Communal	Apple	7	Axe
	Coca-Cola	4	Budweiser
	Boston Red Sox	3	Dove
	Boston University	3	Google
	Burt's Bees	3	Microsoft
	Crest Toothpaste	3	Miller Beer
	Gap	3	New York Yankees
	Marquette University	3	Ralph Lauren
	Nike	3	Starbucks
	Sony	3	Verizon
Dependent	Apple	12	Google
	Microsoft	6	Nike
	Verizon	6	Victoria's Secret
	Blackberry	3	
	Coca-Cola	3	
	Dove	3	
	Starbucks	3	
	Tropicana	3	

Continued

TABLE 2.1 Cont'd

Relationship type	Nominated brand	Number of nominations	Brands nominated twice
Exchange	Colgate Toothpaste	8	Dell
	Crest Toothpaste	6	Domino's Pizza
	Dove	4	Kleenex
	Bic	3	Old Spice Deodorant
	Tide	3	Orbit Gum
			Paper Mate
			Poland Spring
Master–Slave	MBTA	10	Acuview
	Starbucks	10	Aquafresh
	Comcast	8	Breadwinners
	Boston University	6	Campus Convenience
	George W. Bush	6	Nike
	Microsoft	6	Shaw's
	Pepsi	4	
	Bic	3	
	BU Dining Hall	3	
	Cingular	3	
	Dell	3	
	N Star Electric	3	
	Verizon	3	
	Wal-Mart	3	
Secret Affair	Old Navy	5	Apple
	Marlboro	4	Budweiser
	Trojan	4	Dove
	Coach	3	Dunkin Donuts
	Payless	3	Durex
	Tampax	3	Marshalls
	Wal-Mart	3	Neutrogena
			Sensodyne
			Shaw's
			Starbucks
			Target

The Abusive description focused on on-going maltreatment within the context of a brand relationship. The open-ended manipulation check described earlier indicated that 76 percent of the subjects selected and described a brand relationship that was consistent with this general theme.

> They [AirTran] are always late with flights that you expected to leave at time you bought for. Do not care about customers' interests. One time my flight was delayed for over eight hours and they couldn't find a pilot.

Very irresponsible and they only compensated passengers with a $10 coupon for food! (#854)

Bank of America has always provided one with poor service over the phone and in banking centers. Their personnel are typically not helpful and I am always facing unwarranted charges and balances on my accounts. No matter how many complaints I make they don't change their service. (#778)

Verizon Wireless only seems interested in getting new customers and does not seem to care whether or not its current customers are satisfied. I'm frustrated with the brand and once I am outside my two-year contract I plan on switching services. (#845)

Responses from 24 percent of subjects included comments that were not consistent with the abusive relationship description. These exemplars focused on isolated incidences of poor product quality (70 percent) or service failure (13 percent) rather than the on-going maltreatment that typifies this relationship type. Table 2.2 provides a summary of all the coded responses.

I was ordering pizza [Dominos] at around 9 p.m. The guy who I was talking to on the phone wasn't nice nor did he sound happy. I had to repeat my order four times, but still, the wrong thing was delivered. (#679)

The company [Dell] provides a low quality product and only provides the customer with a warranty that will last for a couple of years after which point the product will most likely fail you or break. (#702)

Adversarial relationship

For the Adversarial relationship, 101 subjects were asked to select a brand that:

you *adamantly refuse to buy, support, or use.* You think of this brand as an *opponent or rival.* This is a brand that you are *actively "against"* in some way.

Again we see great diversity in nominated brands. Only seventeen brands were nominated more than once, accounting for 47 percent of the nominated brands. The brands that were nominated two or more times included a number of brands that compete against each other in leading brand/challenger scenarios or are intense rivals in some other sense: Crest (two) and Colgate (two) toothpaste, Coca-Cola (two) and Pepsi (four), New York Yankees (two)

TABLE 2.2 Resonance of relationship themes

Relationship type (sample size; rounds)	% Got it	Themes: Got it (% of responses[a])	% Did not get it	Themes: Did not get it (% of responses[a])
Abusive (96; 1)	76	Company does not value the customer (59) Powerless (26) Takes advantage of the customer (17) Doesn't listen to me; goose chase (14) Blames the customer (9) Entrapment (8) Grand scale or tipping point (3)	24	Just poor quality product (70) One isolated service failure (13) Master–Slave/entrapment only/no pattern of abuse (9)
Adversarial (101; 3)	76	Against my beliefs (60) Strongly hate the brand because of inferior product/service quality (23) Brand rivalry (16) Bad experience trigger-specific brand action creates adversary (5)	24	It is just not my favorite (57) Schema confusion – Master–Slave or Abusive (24) Continual usage (19)
Committed (103; 2)	41	Brand loyalty is part of a family tradition (33) Loyalty and commitment toward brand (24) My brand is my friend (24) The brand addresses my needs (21) My brand is better than your brand (19)	59	Description is solely quality or benefits-based/no evidence of emotional commitment (59) Shows a preference or liking but no real sense of commitment to brand (38) Schema confusion – Communal (2)
Communal (99; 2)	51	Brand supports me and my needs (32) Brand tries to make the world a better place (30) Brand is part of my family/tradition (26) Brand evangelist (20) It's all about love (16)	49	Brand provides me with product benefits (82) Schema confusion – Committed (16) No explanation/response (2)

Dependent (80; 1)	63	Brand is an integral part of my life (52) Nothing else suffices (30) Inseparability (26) Takes care of me (16) Always there for me (8) Object of obsession (6) Provides comfort (4)	37	Person likes quality of brand but isn't dependent upon it (53) No response/explanation (20) Person uses brand frequently but isn't dependent upon it (17) Schema confusion: miscellaneous (10)
Exchange (99; 3)	78	Does its job, solid functional benefits (56) Low/good prices (14) Simple/basic/no frills/purely functional (12) Reliable (9) Routine usage/habit (6) Indifference (3)	22	Strong affect/too much emotion (24) Miscellaneous (24) Evidence of strong relationship (19) Clear brand preference (14) Element of commitment (10) Investment of self-concept or values (10)
Master–Slave (96; 2)	60	No other options available (general)/monopoly (47) Authority dictates (26) Exclusive selling (10) Forced choice driven by convenience (9) Sunk cost investments prevent leaving (5) Forced choice driven by money constraint (3)	40	Miscellaneous (32) Love the product/failure on criteria: "wish you didn't have to purchase it" (30) Simply a bad product/service/lesser quality alternative (24) Schema confusion – Adversarial or Abusive (8) No other choice but happy with this alternative (5)
Secret Affair (92; 3)	66	Brand usage threatens desired social identity (66) Brand usage points out physical/biological problem (34)	34	Poor quality only (52) Dislike or embarrassment without any action (48)

and Boston Red Sox (three), and Dell (three) and Gateway (two) computers, for example. Brands nominated by two or more subjects are shown in Table 2.1.

The Adversarial description focused on the elements of opposition and distancing that characterize this relationship. The open-ended manipulation check indicated that 76 percent of the subjects selected and described a brand relationship that was consistent with these themes.

> I am a diehard Red Sox fan. Therefore, like most Sox fans, I hate the Yankees. That includes most of the players, management, ownership and especially the fans. (#460)

> Fox News is an example of what's wrong in the media, if not the world today. Besides being totally subjective, harmfully so, they report news that is often untrue. Many reporters and anchors reduce themselves to simply insulting people, ideas, or institutions they disagree with. As a news source, it's totally unreliable. (#480)

> I am very against the atmosphere, pricing, and quality of Starbucks. The prices are much higher than other coffee places and it has a very snobby atmosphere. (#470)

> I find this brand's [Abercrombie & Fitch] method of marketing to be overtly sexual. In recognizing that the target consumer for their products is probably pre-teens to teenagers, I find this method of marketing to be inappropriate and toxic to the youth of our country. (#411)

Explanations from the remaining 24 percent of subjects included comments that were not consistent with the adversarial relationship definition and theme. These included off-target exemplars of brands that were simply disliked or described as not being the subject's favorite (57 percent). In many cases, the elected brand was being used (19 percent), thus failing the avoidance behavior that is a hallmark of this relationship. Table 2.2 contains a summary of all the coded responses.

> I prefer Diet Coke to regular Coca-Cola because it tastes almost exactly the same and is much healthier for your body. (#343)

> I was a customer [Cingular] for three and a half years and continually had problems with things that customer service either took forever to fix because I had to argue with them or they didn't fix at all. (#268)

Committed relationship

For the Committed relationship, 103 subjects were asked to select a brand that:

you are *committed to in some significant and lasting way*. This is a brand that you *expect to be using for years to come*. Although your brand has competitors, *you stick only with "your brand."*

Diversity was again the norm in brand elicitation. A total of sixteen brands were nominated by two or more subjects, accounting for 46 percent of the nominated brands. There were no clear patterns within the most frequently nominated brands (see Table 2.1).

The Committed relationship description focused on the long-term, loyal nature of this relationship. Surprisingly, the open-ended manipulation check indicated that only 41 percent of the subjects selected and described a brand relationship that was consistent with this theme.

> I am from Detroit, so my life has revolved around American car companies. Also, my father does a lot of business with General Motors. Due to this I feel loyal to their products. (#860)

> I've grown up using Heinz and I will always think it is better than any other brand. If I have the opportunity to use Heinz (even if it means bringing my food home instead of eating it in the restaurant), I do. (#855)

> Nike has competitors such as Adidas and Reebok but if I had to choose between the same products from these three brands, I would choose the one with the Swoosh. (#904)

Responses from the majority of subjects (59 percent) were not consistent with the relationship description and its loyalty theme. Most common (59 percent) were descriptions that simply noted product attributes and benefits in support of a judgment of "a good brand." Respondents also frequently mentioned (38 percent) general brand preference without evidence of any brand commitment. Table 2.2 provides a summary of all the coded responses.

> I tried different types for a while and like Colgate best. It makes my mouth feel cleaner than the rest and doesn't hurt my gums when I brush, compared to others. (#801)

> It has a variety of products [St. Ives] for skin care. It is available at Target which is my favorite store. It is gentle on my sensitive skin. I also like the price. The commercials are always calming and reflect the nature of the products. (#807)

> Coca-Cola's taste and availability makes it a top-choice brand name for me. I enjoy the taste of Coca-Cola over Pepsi as well as many of its sister products (i.e. Sprite). Coke is reasonably priced which make me less likely to switch to a substitute product. (#902)

Communal relationship

For the Communal relationship, ninety-nine subjects were asked to select a brand that:

> you *go out of your way to support*. This is a brand that you *really care about*. You have a strong desire *to help this brand succeed* in the marketplace.

Twenty brands were nominated two or more times representing 48 percent of total nominated brands. A number of the brands nominated for the Communal relationship were also nominated for the Committed relationship (see Table 2.1); this overlap is examined further in the discussion section.

The Communal description focused on the supportive and caring nature of this altruistic relationship. The open-ended manipulation check indicated that only 51 percent of the subjects selected and described a brand relationship that was consistent with this theme.

> She [Nicole Richie] is a fashion icon of our time period that is constantly being criticized in the media for her lifestyle choices. I really respect her as a leader in fashion, and I always talk her up to everyone and back her up when people put her down. (#826)

> The reason why I circled this choice [Koko Sushi Bar and Lounge Restaurant] is because I'm constantly telling people that I know and do not know about how they should go to this restaurant. I even tell people who may live hours away from Green Bay to go there if they are ever in town. If the person is responsive, I often give them the name of the website as well. (#726)

> I have a vested interest in seeing Marquette University succeed and look good. I will be a Marquette Alum some day and I want it to have a good name and carry weight. (#725)

Responses from the remaining 49 percent of subjects were not consistent with the relationship theme of caring and support. Most often (82 percent), respondents described brand relationships for which they had a preference based solely on product attributes and benefits but with no mention of the care and concern that fuels the communal bond. In some cases (16 percent), subjects solely spoke of a loyalty trait more consistent with a Committed relationship than with the Communal form. Table 2.2 contains a summary of all the coded responses.

> The Yankees have a great reputation through their history of winning. (#720)

I have only ever used Crest toothpaste. It is the only one I have used since I was a child. My doctor also recommended it as the toothpaste for me to use. I have never had any problem with Crest and I guess because my parents have always used it, I continue to use it today. (#729)

I feel this company [Nuvidia] produces the best product [graphics cards]. Among its competitors, it takes care of their customers and has the strongest future company outlook. (#831)

Dependent relationship

For the Dependent relationship, eighty subjects were asked to select a brand that:

> you "*cannot live without.*" This is a brand you feel is *truly irreplaceable*. It is *uncomfortable* for you to think about *being separated* from this brand for a long period, or *being prevented* from using it ever again.

The selected brands for the Dependent relationship were the most diverse among all relationship types as only eleven were nominated by two or more subjects. These brands accounted for 54 percent of the selected brands and included five technology-related brands. The four most frequently nominated brands for the Dependent relationship were Apple (twelve), Microsoft (six), Verizon (six), and Blackberry (three). The Google brand was also nominated twice. The full list of brands that were nominated by two or more subjects is shown in Table 2.1.

The Dependent description focused on the obsessive attraction that characterizes this relationship bond. The open-ended manipulation check indicated that 63 percent of the subjects selected and described a brand relationship that was consistent with this theme.

> I am totally hooked on Facebook. I know it sounds dumb because it's not exactly a necessity, but I can't even begin to explain me and FB. It's like I totally get anxious if I can't check my FB account every hour even at night before I sleep. I know there are no new messages or wall postings, it's like I must check it and log on. I feel so much better when I finally log on. Friendster sucks and its only FB for me. I don't like it if I've gone one day without FB unless I am on a plane. (#1089)

> My Blackberry is my life. It has everything important to me there: passwords, schedules, texts, Facebook, BBM, bank info. In short, if I lose or cannot use my BB I will feel I have lost my identity. Whatever question or problem I have, BB has the answer. (#1143)

> I cannot live without it [Dove] because its products make my skin soft and it's the only deodorant that does not react badly (in a rash or dries out) with my skin. Having nice skin and smelling good are very important to me, as is having clean, shiny hair and I feel most comfortable with this brand. (#1113)

Responses from 37 percent of subjects included comments that were not consistent with the obsession core theme. Specifically, respondents expressed general liking based on quality (53 percent) and frequent or habitual use (17 percent) with no mention of the indispensability of the brand. Table 2.2 provides a summary of the coded responses.

> I've used it [Tropicana] since childhood and have made it for years a routine when waking up. (#1120)

> Lean Cuisine is a brand I very much enjoy and I eat a lot of their products because it's delicious and nutritious and convenient but I could switch brands fairly easily. (#1148).

> Because it [Victoria's Secret] is a brand that appeals to my femininity, something I can wear every day and feel sexy without outwardly showing it. (#1168)

Exchange relationship

For the Exchange relationship, ninety-nine subjects were asked to select a brand that:

> you buy and use regularly and that meets the following characteristics: this brand provides a *straightforward benefit* for a *reasonable cost*. This brand simply *"does its job"*. . . *nothing less, nothing more.*

Like the Dependent relationship, the brands nominated as exemplars of the Exchange relationship were very diverse. Only twelve brands were selected by two or more subjects and they represent 41 percent of the nominated brands. Table 2.1 provides all the brands nominated more than once for the Exchange relationship.

The Exchange description focused on routine use of a brand primarily for its precise balance of cost vs. reliable benefits. The open-ended manipulation check indicated that 78 percent of the subjects selected and described a brand relationship that was consistent with these themes.

> Crest toothpaste is a purely functional brand that I use twice a day strictly for cleaning my mouth. It is reasonably inexpensive and it does a good job protecting and cleaning my teeth and mouth. (#377)

These products [Great Value/Wal-Mart House Brand] are at a reasonable price and the product is the same as it would be if any other manufacturer had made it. It benefits me because it fills my need as well as is well priced. (#376)

Shaw's exemplifies this because you go into the store, expecting to find and buy food, and that's what you get. And that is the extent of my relationship to Shaw's – I go there when I need to, get what I need, and it's off my mind until next time. (#500)

Only 22 percent of subjects provided comments that were not consistent with the exchange relationship theme. These subjects expressed too much emotion (24 percent) or signaled strong brand preferences (14 percent). These subjects also failed to grasp the cost-benefit trade-off inherent to this relationship type. Table 2.2 contains a summary of all coded responses.

It remembers what I don't remember well, and gives me an opportunity to spend time by allowing me to play games. The brand [Nokia] is my best friend, telling me news from others. (#601)

Secret Platinum is probably the best deodorant I have ever used. I have tried about every brand but Secret has been the first to work effectively. It prevents sweating, goes on clear, doesn't stain my clothes, has a pleasant smell and relatively inexpensive. It is exactly what a deodorant should and must do. (#522)

Master–Slave relationship

For the Master–Slave relationship, ninety-six subjects were asked to select a brand that:

you *use on a regular basis*, but are somehow *"stuck with," trapped into using*, or otherwise *forced to use*. This is a brand that you would say you use only because there is *no alternative* that is available to you and readily accessible. This is a brand you wish you didn't *"have to"* purchase or use. You would probably *not* select this particular brand if you had other options.

The brands nominated for the Master–Slave relationship were the least diverse. A total of twenty brands were selected by two or more subjects. These brands represent 60 percent of the total nominated brands. These twenty brands have a ubiquitous presence in the marketplace and in many instances enjoy a virtual monopoly. The most frequently nominated brands were: Starbucks (ten), MBTA (Massachusetts Bay Transportation Authority) (ten), Comcast Cable (eight),

Microsoft (six), and George W. Bush (six). Table 2.1 provides a complete list of brands nominated two or more times.

The Master–Slave description focused on a lack of options resulting in perceived entrapment. The open-ended manipulation check indicated that 60 percent of the subjects selected and described a brand relationship that was consistent with this theme.

> My family cellular plan is on Verizon. I can't switch; I am forced to deal with this brand. They have poor customer service, the reception is just OK and the phone I have (the LG) is a piece of crap! All of those service features and products are bound within the dreaded family plan. (#218)

> I don't get a choice what textbooks [McGraw Hill] I buy. Regardless of how poorly written the textbook is, I still have to spend a lot of money to buy that particular textbook. There is no option. (#233)

> Living in Boston without a car I have to take public transportation everywhere I need to go. I don't choose to use the brand MBTA, but it is the only available option. Coming from Chicago, I have experienced better forms of transportation and if I had the chance to choose between the CTA and MBTA I would choose the CTA, but obviously in Boston I don't have that choice. (#289)

> I hate Comcast with a passion because it's such a freaking rip-off!! But there is nothing else I can really do about it because there are no other cable providers in the neighborhood where I live. It's expensive and keeps going out on me all the time and I never get installation or repair service on time. I hate it! The day RCN moves in I am switching. Screw you Comcast! (#308)

Forty percent of subjects included comments that were not consistent with the entrapment theme. Some reported strong positive feelings toward the brand, which is inconsistent with the desire for other alternatives (30 percent). Others simply expressed general dislike for the brand without actual entrapment (24 percent) and failed to register the captive nature of the Master–Slave relationship. There also existed some confusion between the Master–Slave template and more general Adversarial and Abusive relationship themes. Table 2.2 provides a summary of all coded responses.

> There aren't that many hair ties out there that are simple and cheap. Goody has a large variety and it comes in packs of twenty or more for a really good price. People stick with it because it is the one that is found most

conveniently in supermarkets and large mass merchandisers like Target. (#300)

I think Dell computer only fits for people who just "want" a computer. Their services are terrible. Once I had to wait for 20 minutes just to chat over the internet with a Dell rep. I found out that his knowledge about computers was worse than mine. (#185)

Secret Affair

For the Secret Affair relationship, ninety-two subjects were asked to select a brand:

> whose *usage you downplay or keep hidden* from certain others for one reason or another. While you may use this brand regularly or often, this is a brand that you really *do not want others associating with you in any significant way.*

A relatively large number of brands (eighteen) were nominated more than once for the Secret Affair relationship; however, these only accounted for 35 percent of the nominated brands. This relatively low percentage reflects the intensely personal nature of the Secret Affair. Many of the selected brands are associated with private and in some cases socially stigmatized behaviors such as smoking, alcohol, or premarital sex. The most frequently mentioned brands include Marlboro (four), Trojan (four), Tampax (three), and Budweiser (two). Table 2.1 provides the complete list of Secret Affair brands nominated more than once.

The Secret Affair description focused on the hidden and secluded nature of this relationship. The open-ended manipulation check indicated that 66 percent of the subjects selected and described a brand relationship that was consistent with this theme.

> Smoking is regarded as a terrible habit that is unhealthy and nasty. Instead of being criticized by others I choose to downplay my use of [Marlboro] cigarettes. Plus, I only smoke occasionally, so I can't be judged as a "smoker." (#3123)

> I enjoy looking at this website [PerezHilton.com], which is a celebrity gossip site, but I don't like to promote the fact that I read the garbage on the site and actually care what is going on in Hollywood gossip. The stars deserve more privacy and I don't need everyone knowing that I enjoy following the gossip. (#3101)

> I don't want people to know that I sweat a lot and need Clinical Strength Secret deodorant. I like to hide it. It works and I use it every day

but I just don't want everyone to know because it is embarrassing.
(#3154)

Responses from the remaining subjects (34 percent) included comments
that were not consistent with the hidden relationship theme. A large portion of
these subjects (52 percent) commented on the brand's poor quality with no
mention of the clandestine nature of the relationship. Others focused on the
embarrassment associated with using the brand but did not indicate any effort to
conceal the relationship (48 percent). Table 2.2 provides a summary of all the
coded responses.

Although Wal-Mart has some good, cheap products, most of the store is
garbage. Their workers are unfriendly and unhelpful from my experience.
(#3158)

Camel cigarettes are harmful to one's health and negatively affect other
people's perception of me. But I don't care. Cigarettes provide a mental
stress relief for me. I buy Camel (No. 9) cigarettes over other brands because
of the packaging. (#3121)

Results: across relationship types

By looking across relationship types, some additional insights into the interactions
between relationship types and brands emerge. Table 2.3 provides an analysis of
the top third of nominated brands in terms of mentions across all relationship
scenarios. The Apple brand was nominated a total of thirty times across scenarios:
the most of any brand. This was followed by the Massachusetts Bay Transportation
Authority (MBTA) (twenty-three mentions), Dell (nineteen mentions), Starbucks
(eighteen mentions), and Coke, Crest, and Microsoft (seventeen mentions each).
The distribution of cross type nomination drops off very rapidly, with the twenty-
second ranked brand, Old Navy, gathering only seven nominations among the
more than 750 respondents surveyed in the final round of this research. The
general observation here is that while some strong brands are more frequently
mentioned across scenarios, brand selection is largely idiosyncratic and dependent
on respondents' experiences with brands.

Still, some patterns in brand-by-relationship type can be noted. As Table 2.3
shows, select brands were disproportionately elicited for particular brand relationships. Apple was the most nominated brand exemplar for two relationship
types: Communal (seven) and Dependent (twelve). The second most nominated
brand overall, the MBTA, was nominated most often as an exemplar of the
Master–Slave (ten) and Abusive (ten) relationships. Starbucks, the third most
elicited brand overall, was nominated most often (ten times) for the Master–Slave
relationship. As indicated in Table 2.3, the most frequently nominated brand for

TABLE 2.3 Summary of nominated brands (top one-third of nominated brands)

	Abusive	Adversarial	Committed	Communal	Dependent	Exchange	Master–Slave	Secret Affair	Total
Apple	2	0	5	7[a]	12[a]	1	1	2	30
MBTA	10[a]	3	0	0	0	0	10[a]	0	23
Dell	5	3	4	1	1	2	3	0	19
Starbucks	0	0	1	2	3	0	10[a]	2	18
Coca-Cola	1	2	7	4	3	0	0	0	17
Crest	0	2	6	3	0	6	0	0	17
Microsoft	0	0	3	2	6	0	6	0	17
Nike	0	0	9[a]	3	2	0	2	0	16
Colgate	1	2	5	0	0	8[a]	0	0	16
Verizon	4	0	1	2	6	0	3	0	16
Boston University	1	0	1	4	0	0	6	1	13
Dove	0	0	1	2	3	4	0	2	12
Wal-Mart	1	3	0	0	0	1	3	3	11
Comcast	3	0	0	0	0	0	8	0	11
Pepsi	0	4	1	1	0	0	4	0	10
Bank of America	6	1	0	0	0	1	1	0	9
Dunkin Donuts	0	4	1	0	0	0	1	2	8
Boston Red Sox	0	3	0	3	0	0	1	1	8
Abercrombie & Fitch	1	6[a]	1	0	0	0	0	0	8
George W. Bush	0	2	0	0	0	0	6	0	8
Cingular	2	1	0	0	1	1	3	0	8
Old Navy	0	1	0	0	0	1	0	5[a]	7

Note: [a]Most frequently nominated brand for relationship type.

each relationship type falls within the top third of all nominated brands collected for this research.

A second set of insights emerge in considering relationship patterns within the most frequently mentioned brands. From this perspective, the relationship types represent a form of segmentation within the brand user base. As mentioned above, Apple is most often considered a Communal (seven) or Dependent (twelve) relationship partner, but Committed relationships (five) are also found. These insights are particularly interesting when relationships are viewed within a given category for competing sets of brands such that certain brands take on particular "relationship personalities." Looking at Coca-Cola and Pepsi, for example, we observe that the market leader Coca-Cola brand is most often (eleven out of seventeen nominations or 65 percent) selected as an exemplary partner in Communal and Committed relationships. This is in contrast with the Pepsi brand which has relatively low levels of nominations for these types and is seen much more as a partner in an Adversarial relationship (four of ten nominations or 40 percent) or as a Master–Slave (four of ten nominations or 40 percent) relationship. Through the lens of relationship-based segmentation, the Crest and Colgate brands appear quite similar. Both are seen most often as viable partners in Committed and Exchange relationships (twelve of seventeen nominations or 71 percent for Crest; thirteen of sixteen nominations or 81 percent for Colgate) with relatively low levels of negative relationship affiliation. Finally, Dependent and Abusive relationships most characterize Verizon (ten of sixteen nominations or 63 percent) while Cingular is defined mostly by Abusive and Master–Slave relationships (five of eight nominations or 63 percent). Figure 2.2 provides the complete relationship segmentation profiles for the above rival brands. Another general observation seems to hold: although a given brand is likely to manifest many different types of relationships across people in light of their personal experiences, for some popular brands there exists a narrow set of active brand relationship types that characterize consumer experiences.

Discussion

The purpose of this research was to begin empirically to address the question: do resonant analogues to interpersonal relationships exist in the brand space? We have made steps toward our goal by creating and attempting to validate relationship descriptions for eight popular brand relationship types. While some descriptions performed better than others, all eight provide a starting point for consumer researchers who wish to build on our efforts and explore these relationship forms.

Respondents' relationship stories were largely consistent with the grounded relationship themes derived from the literature, supporting parallel brand analogues for the Abusive, Adversarial, Dependent, Exchange, Master–Slave, and Secret Affair relationships. Although we obtain support for the validity of these

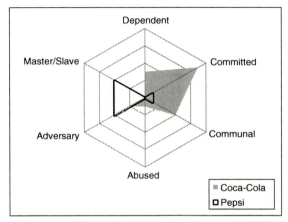

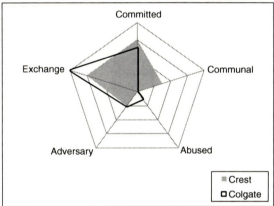

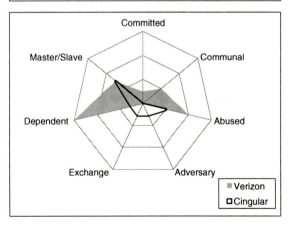

FIGURE 2.2 Relationship segments across competing brands

six relationships, relationship scenarios for the Communal and Committed relationships could not be calibrated, despite numerous attempts. This finding indicates that Communal and Committed relationships do not translate directly from the interpersonal to the commercial space as theorized in our field.

The Abusive, Adversarial, and Exchange descriptions have the most resonance with people's shared brand experiences. More than three-quarters of subjects were able to nominate and describe a brand relationship that reflected and resonated with the core themes defining these relationships in interpersonal research. It is also of note that two of our highest performing scenarios are negatively toned, suggesting value in this understudied domain of consumer behavior. Abusive, Adversarial, and Exchange relationships therefore translate well into consumer behavior, though some caveats regarding these high-performing scenarios seem to hold.

Exchange relationships stand as a primary relational paradigm in our literature and our research strongly supports the validity of this dominant relationship form. This said, subjects frequently described Exchange relationships that manifest strong preference and loyalty, which is inconsistent with the pure benefit-cost balance conception of this relationship. Exchange relationships, in other words, can sometimes look like Committed relationships and exhibit the emotions and behaviors that we expect Committed consumers to express. Our data question the belief that all Exchange relationships are purely functional and devoid of the deeper emotional connections that can instill habits over time.

Abusive and Adversarial relationships also resonated strongly but it is not clear from the data that these relationships manifest in the "strong forms" we anticipate when building from interpersonal research. Simple negative brand perceptions about quality and service were common themes among the subjects who "did not get" the Abusive and Adversarial relationship descriptions derived from the literature. These mild forms of brand dislike hardly qualify as enmities, adversarial opponents, or abusive engagements. There was also evidence of consumer confusion between Abusive and Adversarial relationship types, suggesting overlap in negatively toned commercial relationships and an avenue for future research.

The Secret Affair, Dependent, and Master–Slave descriptions were also promising, with significantly more than half of subjects identifying a brand relationship that was consistent with the themes in these descriptions. As with Abusive and Adversarial relationships, we conclude by observing that Dependent and Master–Slave relations are also extreme-form relationships: they have intense psychological consequences and barriers to freedom, and are thus relatively rare. The Secret Affair relationship was the most clear-cut of all relationships studied. There was no confusion between Secret Affairs and other relationships, and failed responses tended to focus mainly on negative attitudes associated with the brand. This understudied relationship has many implications for understanding consumers' experiences with brands.

By far, more questions about the validity of lived experience are raised for the Committed and Communal relationships than for the other six relationship types. For these two relationships, half or less of the subjects were able to describe a brand relationship experience that fits the theoretically inspired description. Interestingly, these two relationships also share a number of nominated brands: Apple, Coca-Cola, Crest, Microsoft Windows, Nike, and Sony. These six brands account for a full one-third of the brands that were nominated for either relationship by two or more subjects. Our data provide two possible explanations for these results. One explanation is that there exists inherent confusion and overlap between these two relationship types. The defining theme of the Committed relationship is loyalty while the focus for Communal is active support. These characteristics may not be sufficient to distinguish these relationship types from each other in the commercial realm: consumers in Communal relationships are likely loyal to brands, and at least some portion of brand loyal customers will act as evangelical brand supporters. And yet, consumer research treats these relationships as distinctive, common types. A second possible explanation for the failings of these descriptions may simply be that they are rare: subjects may be unable to identify brands that meet the lofty standards of commitment and support that emanate from the interpersonal literature. Our data and Clark and Mills' (1993) theorizing support this premise: while we focus as a field and discipline on Communal and Committed relationships, the majority of consumers' experiences are more likely characterized as mild forms of habit-based exchange.

Our research provides insight beyond the validation question and supports one overarching conclusion about the nature of people's brand relationships: the brands elicited as exemplary for a given relationship are very idiosyncratic. On average, less than half (48 percent) of all selected brands were nominated by more than one subject, with a modal selection within these brands of only two mentions per brand. Put differently, more than half of all nominated brands were unique selections made by just one subject. This finding is remarkable in light of our sample size of 750+ brand relationships in the final round of this research. The percentage of unique brands did vary by relationship: the Secret Affair relationship description generated the highest percentage of unique brands (65 percent) while the Master–Slave produced the lowest (39 percent), and Dependent the second lowest (46 percent). While there appears to be some cultural agreement as to which brands hold consumers captive in the marketplace, and which brands become addictive, brand relationships are for the most part uniquely colored through individual consumers' eyes.

This said, relationship patterns do emerge for some of the brands frequently elicited in our protocol, suggesting potential value in a relationship-based brand segmentation approach. A given brand can serve as an exemplary partner for multiple relationship types. Well-known brands like Apple, Starbucks, Coke, and Microsoft can be partners in a Committed relationship for one person and the subject of an Adversarial relationship for another person. This is consistent with the idiosyncratic nature of brand–consumer relationships discussed earlier, as even for a given brand there exists a diverse range of consumer experiences and, hence, relationship types.

In terms of method, the self-nomination process used in this research gives us additional confidence in the results as it ensures that the relationship of interest is embedded in the consumer's lived experience. This method of "stimulus" creation effectively produced a diverse set of brands including traditional consumer packaged goods, services, institutions, people, and places. Given the inherently personal nature of brand–consumer relationships uncovered here, we highly recommend that this type of self-nomination process be used to engage subjects in research dedicated to an increased understanding of the nature of people's interaction with brands. Our method calls into question the value in using imaginary brand scenarios to elicit a given relationship frame.

Future research

In terms of future research, there is a need for further delineation of relationship types beyond core themes. Can brand relationships be distinguished via characteristic profiles in terms of attitudes, emotionality, or behaviors, for example? Any useful typology must exhibit discriminant validity and these factors provide useful and relevant context for differentiating between relation types. In the interpersonal arena, emotionality has proved to be a useful discriminator and can be explored in the context of consumers' brand relationships (Guerrero and Anderson 2000). There is also a need for in-depth qualitative inquiry to further illuminate the lived experience of the different brand relationships. We analyze only for core themes in our open-ended descriptions of nominated brand relationships; our survey-based method is inherently limited in its ability to reveal relationship emotions, experiences, and ideals.

Beyond understanding the relationships and contributing to consumer behavior, there is an opportunity to consider brand relationships as a practical tool for better brand management. This study shows value in shifting focus to the relationship landscapes evoked for a given brand. Whether research designed specifically around a focal brand would reveal significant idiosyncratic variability, as with our self-nominating process, or whether segments of relationships would manifest for a given brand, is an important subject for future research. When provided with alternate relationship descriptions, which types do a brand's customers most frequently identify with? Can a brand's customers be segmented usefully not by attitudes and behaviors but by dominant relationship types? How do these segments relate to important branding concepts like loyalty, attachment, and evangelism?

References

Aaker, D.A. (1991) *Managing Brand Equity*, New York: The Free Press.

Aggarwal, P. (2004) "The Effects of Brand Relationship Norms on Consumer Attitudes and Behavior", *Journal of Consumer Research*, 31 (1): 87–101.

Arnould, E.J. and Price, L.L. (2006) "Market-Oriented Ethnography Revisited", *Journal of Advertising Research*, 46 (3): 251–62.

Belk, R.W., Wallendorf, M. and Sherry, J.F., Jr (1989) "The Sacred and the Profane in Consumer Behavior: Theodicy on the Odyssey", *Journal of Consumer Research*, 16 (1): 1–38.

Brown, S. (2005) "Fortune Favors the Brand", *Marketing Research*, 17 (2): 22–7.

Clark, M.S. and Finkel, E.J. (2005) "Willingness to Express Emotion: The Impact of Relationship Type, Communal Orientation, and their Interaction", *Personal Relationships*, 12 (2): 169–80.

Clark, M.S. and Mills, J. (1979) "Interpersonal Attraction in Exchange and Communal Relationships", *Journal of Personality and Social Psychology*, 37 (1): 12–24.

—— (1993) "The Difference between Communal and Exchange Relationships: What it is and is Not", *Personality and Social Psychology Bulletin*, 19 (6): 684–91.

Clark, M.S., Mills, J. and Powell, M.C. (1986) "Keeping Track of Needs in Communal and Exchange Relationships", *Journal of Personality and Social Psychology*, 51 (2): 333–38.

Clarke, D.D., Allen, C.M.B. and Dickson, S. (1985) "The Characteristic Affective Tone of Seven Classes of Interpersonal Relationship", *Journal of Social and Personal Relationships*, 2 (1): 117–20.

Fournier, S. (1998) "Consumers and their Brands: Developing Relationship Theory in Consumer Research", *Journal of Consumer Research*, 24 (4): 343–72.

—— (2009) "Lessons Learned about Consumers' Relationships with their Brands", in D.J. MacInnis, C.W. Park, and Joseph R. Priester (eds) *Handbook of Brand Relationships*, pp. 5–23. Armonk, NY: M.E. Sharpe.

Guerrero, L.K. and Anderson, P.A. (2000) "Emotions in Close Relationships", in C. Hendrick and S.S. Hendrick (eds) *Close Relationships: A Sourcebook*, pp. 171–216. Thousand Oaks: Sage.

Hinde, R.A. (1979) *Towards Understanding Relationships*, London: Academic Press.

Holt, D.B. (2003) "What Becomes an Icon Most?" *Harvard Business Review*, 81 (3): 43–9.

Kayser, E., Schwinger, T. and Cohen, R.L. (1984) "Laypersons' Conceptions of Social Relationships: A Test of Contract Theory", *Journal of Social and Personal Relationships*, 4 (1): 433–58.

Keller, K.L. (2003) "Brand Synthesis: The Multidimensionality of Brand Knowledge", *Journal of Consumer Research*, 29 (4): 595–600.

Kleine, S.S., Kleine, R.E. and Allen, C.T. (1995) "How is a Possession 'Me' or 'Not Me'? Characterizing Types and an Antecedent of Material Possession Attachment", *Journal of Consumer Research*, 22 (3): 327–43.

Levy, S.J. (1959) "Symbols for Sale", *Harvard Business Review*, 37: 117–25.

McCracken, G. (1986) "Culture and Consumption: A Theoretical Account of the Structure and Movement of the Cultural Meaning of Consumer Goods", *Journal of Consumer Research*, 14: 71–84.

MacInnis, D.J., Park, C.W. and Priester, J.R. (2009) *Handbook of Brand Relationships*, New York: M.E. Sharpe.

Mills, J. and Clark, M.S. (eds) (1994) *Communal and Exchange Relationships: controversies and research*, Hillsdale, NJ: Lawrence Erlbaum Associates.

Muñiz, A.M., Jr and O'Guinn, T.C. (2001) "Brand Community", *Journal of Consumer Research*, 27 (4): 412–32.

Solomon, M.R. (1983) "The Role of Products as Social Stimuli: A Symbolic Interactionism Perspective", *Journal of Consumer Research*, 10: 319–29.

Twitchell, J.B. (2004) "An English Teacher Looks at Branding", *Journal of Consumer Research*, 31 (2): 484–9.

Wish, M. (1976) "Comparisons among Multidimensional Structures of Interpersonal Relations", *Multivariate Behavioral Research*, 11 (3): 297.

Wright, P.H. (ed.) (1985) *The Acquaintance Description Form*, Beverly Hills: Sage Publications.

Zaltman, G. (2003) "The Hearing–Thinking Gap", *Across the Board*, 40 (6): 31–1.

3

MOTIVATIONS FOR THE BRAND AVOIDANCE RELATIONSHIP

Allyn White, Michael Breazeale, and
Cynthia Webster

Introduction

Effective marketing strategy requires understanding consumers' attitudinal and behavioral brand responses. Brands, by definition, can represent a collection of images, values, or even human qualities (e.g., Aaker 1997; Baker 2003; Keller 2003). The multi-dimensional nature of brands implies that any one brand may elicit a variety of positive or negative consumer responses, depending upon the qualities, brand users, events, or even memories a consumer associates with that brand (e.g., Banister and Hogg 2004; Braun-La Tour, La Tour, and Zinkhan 2007; Escalas and Bettman 2005; Meenaghan 2001a, 2001b; Roehm and Roehm 2007). While marketing literature is replete with studies on positive responses to brands (e.g., Coulter, Price, and Feick 2003; Fournier 1998), there is a dearth of research dedicated to the negative aspect of consumer brand responses, particularly in the form of brand avoidance. In addition, prior research has essentially limited the construct of "brand image" to formal names (e.g. Coca-Cola, Wal-Mart) related to specific products either produced or sold by a firm. Branding, considered in a broader context, however, can extend beyond marketer-specified meaning associations to the memories, images, and associations that an individual maintains with a basic consumption object (e.g., grapes instead of Dole brand fruits). Thus the notion of brand meaning should be explored from the consumer perspective in a wider realm of consumption processes, and not simply consumer responses to established brand names.

This lack of research is unfortunate, as understanding brand avoidance has implications for marketing researchers and practitioners alike. For instance, prior research has found that consumers reject brands to prevent bringing undesired meaning into their lives (e.g., Banister and Hogg 2004; Lee, Motion, and Conroy

2009; Muñiz and Hamer 2001; Thompson and Arsel 2004; Thompson, Rindfleisch, and Arsel 2006). Consequently, ultimate consumer brand choice may be driven simply by the rejection of another brand (Fournier 1998). Moreover, research on consumer decision making (e.g., Drolet, Luce, and Simonson 2009; Simonson 1989) suggests that the chosen brand may even be perceived as being of lower quality than the rejected brand, further underscoring the power of negative brand responses. From a marketing strategy perspective, practitioners need to gain an understanding of consumer brand avoidance in order to reshape effectively negative brand responses in the marketplace. Finally, a comprehensive theory of consumer brand behavior should integrate all types of consumer thoughts, feelings, and experiences related to a brand or product (Keller 2003). This notion charges marketing researchers with understanding not only positive, but *also* negative, brand responses, which are likely to be exhibited through brand avoidance behavior (e.g., Thompson *et al.* 2006).

As just mentioned, nearly all of the research on consumer brand behavior addresses positive responses to brands. In particular, research on attitudinal brand commitment (e.g., Coulter *et al.* 2003) and brand relationships (e.g., Fournier 1998) has investigated the origins of consumers' heightened, enduring positive responses to brands. Attitudinal brand commitment reflects an individual's emotional or psychological attachment to a brand within a product class (Chaudhuri and Holbrook 2001; Fournier 1998). An important finding from this stream of research is that consumers may be attitudinally committed to a brand regardless of their involvement with a product class (Coulter *et al.* 2003; Cushing and Douglas-Tate 1985). In addition, consumers can exhibit repeat purchase behavior – or behavioral brand commitment – without ever being attitudinally committed to a brand (Coulter *et al.* 2003). The other component of this intensely positive consumer brand response, brand relationship, underscores further the importance of the linkage that can exist between a consumer and a brand. Consumers may build relationships with a brand in order to add meaning to their lives (Fournier 1998). Indeed, many times consumers use brands as a means of constructing their self-concepts and expressing themselves to others (Escalas and Bettman 2005; Keller 1993). Taken together, these findings from prior research indicate that brands *themselves* – that is, apart from their respective products – play an integral role in consumer behavior. In summary, the overall importance of brands in consumers' lives merits equal research attention to the negative and positive impacts brands have on consumers. The current study addresses the currently under-researched, albeit extremely important, negative brand responses by exploring motivations for consumer brand avoidance. As previously noted, this research considers the branding phenomenon from a broad consumer perspective, exploring the brand meaning that consumers can attach to an object that is not related to brand user characteristics or perceived direct firm actions.

Review of literature on consumer rejection of brands

Recent years have witnessed a heightened interest in research on consumers' rejection of brands (e.g., Banister and Hogg 2004; Hogg, Banister, and Stephenson 2009; Iyer and Muncy 2009; Lee *et al.* 2009). For instance, research on symbolic consumption suggests that consumers maintain self-esteem by rejecting products and brands with which they associate negative meanings related to the undesired self (Banister and Hogg 2004; Hogg *et al.* 2009; Ogilvie 1987). Another study found that the perceived inauthenticity of a brand motivates consumers to avoid that brand (Thompson and Arsel 2004). Other research addresses consumer dislike of brands (Dalli, Romani, and Gistri 2006) and oppositional brand loyalty, which refers to playful opposition among users of competing brands (Muñiz and Hamer 2001).

Research on anti-consumption (i.e., deriving meaning from *not* consuming products or brands) is gaining popularity, as evidenced by a recent special journal issue dedicated to negative consumer behaviors in the marketing environment (*Journal of Business Research*, February 2009). In the only attempt to develop an instrument to measure anti-consumption, Iyer and Muncy (2009) limit avoidance motivations to two categories: intentions to preserve the global environment and desire to simplify consumer lifestyles. Other attempts at anti-consumption research are bounded by the context of specific holidays (e.g., Close and Zinkhan 2009) or political ideologies (e.g., Sandikci and Ekici 2009). Finally, Lee at al. (2009) present emerging motivations for consumer brand avoidance, which they describe as a consumer's conscious, active anti-consumption of a brand. The authors group these motivations under one of three general categories related to unmet expectations, undesired identity, and moral/ideological beliefs. A substantial contribution of Lee and colleagues' findings was the support for brand avoidance as a multi-faceted phenomenon, the motivations for which may vary across consumers. Their study represents the most comprehensive attempt to date that seeks to understand consumer avoidance, and thus provides a foundation for the current study.

The current research seeks to extend existing knowledge by executing a more in-depth exploration of the various motivations for consumer brand avoidance. This chapter focuses primarily on reasons for consumers' emotional or psychological "dis-attachment" to brands and the relationships with brands that add negative, as opposed to positive, meaning to consumers' lives. In other words, this study is one of few existing initial attempts to develop a comprehensive typology of negative brand responses. This research is novel in that the concept of branding is extended to capture idiosyncratic, individually derived meanings that consumers relate to products (e.g., meaning attached to the product as opposed to an established brand name) and established market brands.

Method

Sample

Interpretation was based on notes taken during and after phenomenological interviews with individuals who were aware of conscious avoidance of one or more brands. A combination of purposive, judgment, and snowballing sampling was used, geared at generating information-rich cases (Patton 1990). Overall, the sample selection process was guided by the goal of establishing an informant base characterized by variety and contrast (Lincoln and Guba 1985) to provide a varied perspective on the motivations of brand avoiders. The informant base comprised forty-one informants, which far exceeds the number suggested by McCracken (1988b, p. 17) as necessary for generating themes or cultural categories in this type of qualitative research. Unlike related research (e.g., Dalli *et al.* 2006), the informant base is varied in age, ethnic background, socioeconomic status, and household composition. The common themes that would emerge from such an eclectic set of depth interviews are deemed to be more representative of the lived experiences of brand avoiders than those resulting from a more homogeneous set of informants.

Data gathering

Interviews with key informants began with the researcher disclosing his or her name and affiliation, explaining the purpose of the interview, screening for brand avoidance behavior, and assuring confidentiality of informant identity. Informants were generally open and demonstrated remarkable willingness to disclose information about themselves and their brand avoidance behavior. To help further in building rapport as well as in gathering information, informants were asked general questions regarding such topics as their histories, family backgrounds, and current life situations. Although probing techniques were used, the interviews were kept as non-directive, non-evaluative (see, for example, McCracken 1988b), and loosely structured as possible, allowing informants the freedom to broach the topic and issues in their own ways and at their own paces. The informants had complete freedom when explaining the reasons and motivations for and attitudes toward their brand avoidance behaviors. As themes surfaced and as rapport with informants increased, it became possible to use more probing questions to test and explore these themes across informants.

Due to the highly personal nature of revealing underlying reasons for behavior, audio and video devices were not used during the interviews. Hand-written notes were taken instead and used to produce more complete field notes (including personal reflections) immediately afterward.

Analysis, interpretation, and validity checks

A considerable part of the analysis occurred simultaneously with data collection and helped determine the course of the study. In addition to coding the data for overgeneralizations, glosses, and claims of idiosyncrasy, an iterative process proposed by McCracken (1988b) of coding, categorizing, and abstracting the data was used in analysis. Data of obvious thematic similarity were identified throughout the interview notes, highlighted, and coded with key phrases. As new data were collected, they were analyzed in the context of the existing data and examined for points of similarity and contrast. The constant comparison of new data with old occurred both during and between interviews. As themes emerged, they were used to guide, but not restrict, the foci of future interviews. After each interview was interpreted ideographically, the interpretive context was broadened to more fundamental patterns that constitute the primary emergent themes. This back-and-forth process of relating a part of a text to the whole lends itself to an existential-phenomenological interpretation (Spiggle 1994; Thompson, Locander, and Pollio 1990).

The validation process was executed by conducting member checks and expert checks. As recommended by Lincoln and Guba (1985), member checks were carried out by providing selected conclusions to some of the informants for their responses. These informants were asked to assess whether the findings were consistent with their experiences. Expert checks were conducted by periodically submitting data and interim research findings to colleagues of differing backgrounds. An attempt was made to query a variety of individuals as heterogeneous as the sample under investigation. The colleagues were asked to ascertain the logic of the analytical categories and assess whether the conclusions were well established in the data. While both informants and colleagues generally agreed with the soundness of the interpretations, complete agreement was deemed less important than dialogue and a reexamination of the conclusions (Schouten 1991).

Findings

Coding analysis of the avoidance data revealed three overarching themes: Brand User–Self-concept Incongruity, Active Offender, and Passive Offender. Each theme was identified as the tie linking various subthemes. Briefly, respondents belonging to the first group, Brand User–Self-concept Incongruity, report avoiding the brand due to dissociative brand user characteristics. Active Offender individuals perceive a brands direct violation of societal norms or brand-created expectations. Finally, participants falling under the Passive Offender theme avoid the brand as a consequence of the brand's inclusion in a negative past experience. The emergent themes and subthemes are presented in further detail below.

Brand User–Self-concept Incongruity

As mentioned earlier, an important component of brand consumption is the construction and expression of consumer identities (Escalas and Bettman 2005; Keller 1993). Moreover, the theory of meaning transfer (McCracken 1988a) posits that brands often assume symbolic characteristics of their users. Consequently, brand choice – or rejection – is often the result of perceived correspondence between brand user imagery and a consumer's self-image (Escalas and Bettman 2003). Respondents in this category identify prevention of associations with other brand users as a primary motive for brand avoidance. Members of the first subtheme, Individual Self-concept, avoid brands or products whose users possess values that are incongruent with the respondents' own perceived value systems. In other words, the brand user images are not aligned with the consumers' actual or ideal self-concepts. These consumers refuse to consume products both privately and publicly. The second subtheme, Social Self-concept, is distinct from the first subtheme in that avoiders are less concerned about their own individual self-concepts (both actual and ideal) than they are about being publicly viewed as a typical consumer of a product. These respondents appear to base their avoidance behavior on how they want others to view them. Thus their motivations are founded upon their social self-concepts (again, both actual and ideal). Members classified under Social Self-concept are frequently not concerned about the actual characteristics of the avoidance object (for instance, some mention actually knowing the product is of acceptable quality), but are instead fearful of conspicuous association with the brand.

Individual Self-concept

As just mentioned, members of this subtheme avoid brands and products as a means of maintaining their own actual self-concepts, or realizing their ideal selves. Many respondents are driven by moral or ethical values, refusing to buy objects that add negative meaning to their lives. Johnston, a full-time college student, provides such an example:

> If there is anything Abercrombie and Fitch, I just throw it away or steer clear of it. They promote, support, and stand for immorality. When I found out about it, I threw all of my Abercrombie clothes away. I stand for Christian principles.

Eugenia also reports avoidance based on religious values:

> I used to be a big fan of Lance Armstrong and admired him, but then I heard that he didn't believe that it was God that helped him with cancer . . . that he did it all on his own. It was a big disappointment.

Other respondents avoid brands and products because they threaten the self-concept in terms of maintaining expectations for themselves. For example, LaToya believes in maintaining her wholesome female self-concept, even inconspicuously:

> I don't wear thong underwear. They're very uncomfortable, but they also make me feel like a piece of meat instead of a woman.

Not all members of the Individual Self-concept subtheme avoid for religious or moral reasons. Some respondents avoid brands and products based on their sense of individualism or other learned attitudinal characteristics. John sees himself as a non-conformist who is not a follower of the crowd:

> The North Face is just a name brand; other clothes are just as good and cheaper. A lot of my friends and my two brothers wear it. I guess you could just say I like to be different than the crowd.

Marianne does not believe in buying expensive brand name shoes based on her parents' beliefs:

> I can afford expensive brand name shoes, but growing up neither my mother nor father would buy them for my sister and me. They used to tell us that just because you have lots of money doesn't mean that you have to go around showing it off by wasting it on expensive shoes. My mother used to say it doesn't matter what kind of shoes you have because nobody is looking at your feet!

In summary, respondents from the Individual Self-concept subtheme avoid because they are devout in their beliefs about themselves. These individuals suggest a degree of self-confidence when discussing their motivations for avoidance, relying on themselves as good judges of character, as opposed to fearing the rejection of others. The latter is the case with the second subtheme in this category, Social Self-concept.

Social Self-concept

Respondents classified under this subtheme express the need to project a socially acceptable image to others. These consumers are essentially trying to maintain their status in the eyes of their peers. Many times, respondents report avoiding products so as not to risk their social standing in society. Janine, a college undergraduate, provides an example:

> I do not go to Marshall's [discount department store]. My mom used to make me go shopping there. That was the only store I didn't spend hours

shopping in. Everyone knew it was a knock off store and we talked about people who shopped there.

Liza also avoids based on fear of being what others consider "skanky":

Abercrombie and Fitch and Hollister were popular in high school, but when the trend died down socially unacceptable people started wearing them. It just made those brands tacky.

Cindy, a 27-year-old real estate professional, describes an association between a brand and a person whom she perceives as belonging to a lower social class:

I do not like to shop at Old Navy unless absolutely necessary. The clothes remind me of a girl I went to school with. I think of her every time I walk in the doors. She was always matching in those cheap, printed clothes. But I do actually love their pajama pants.

Cindy associates Old Navy with cheap tackiness, not because she dislikes their products, but because she identifies the brand as being worn by lower-class consumers. Her willingness to wear the brand in the privacy of her own home demonstrates a potentially important distinction between the public and the private self in understanding brand avoidance – the brand is good enough for her to wear but not good enough for her to be seen wearing.

Social status and the opinions of others play a dominant role in these respondents' avoidance motivations. The fear of conspicuous association with a dissociative group largely dictates the behaviors of these individuals in terms of the brands or products they refuse to purchase. It is this perceived public scrutiny that distinguishes Social Self-concept avoiders from Individual Self-concept avoiders. In summary, the Brand user–Self-concept Incongruence category reiterates the important influence of the perception of brand user on consumer brand behavior. Prior research (e.g., Banister and Hogg 2004; Hogg et al. 2009) has suggested that the self-concept, in the eyes of both the consumer (individual) and others (social), is a primary anchor upon which consumer decisions are made.

Active Offender

Many respondents avoid brands and products in response to negatively perceived direct firm actions and business practices. In line with related findings (e.g., Thompson and Arsel 2004; Thompson et al. 2006), these respondents oppose offending brands often for the sake of the culture with which they identify, or of society as a whole.

Countering Unfairness

Interestingly, the majority of respondents in this category report their brand avoidance as the only instance of assuming a strong position on societal issues. Additionally, most of them are vocal about their avoidance, undertaking a personal mission to punish the brand. Ariel is adamant about her avoidance of over-the-counter medicine, specifically Sudafed:

> Sudafed just treats symptoms and not the source. You can take a prescribed medication daily and eliminate an infection, or surgery is available. Sudafed is just an example of the entire pharmaceutical business and the way they prey on people. They target minor, yet chronic illnesses, give you pills with frequent dosage and collect the cash. They should be promoting long term health practices. Making money takes precedence over a healthy lifestyle in our society.

Emma also speaks out against America's large corporations, citing Starbucks as detrimental to the economics of society:

> Starbucks is a corporate machine. They're kind of like Wal-Mart, but not quite as bad. Of course they are trying to make money, but at the expense of Americans. The corporate monster is why the middle class is disappearing. There is such a gap between the rich and poor nowadays.

On a more personal note, Mei cites discriminatory practices as her motivation for avoiding Macy's department store:

> My daughter applied for a summer job online at Macy's when she was in college and got turned down because of her ethnicity. They gave a girl that did not even have a high school diploma the job instead. Macy's is where I got my favorite perfume, but now I just go to Stein Mart.

Broken Promises

Many avoiders do so based upon perceptions that certain brands have failed to uphold their promises to consumers and society. One distinguishing characteristic of this subtheme as compared with Countering Unfairness is that these respondents had previously established ideas about the *brand* promise. Whether expressed or implicit, these respondents had expectations regarding the desired behavior of the brand, which were ultimately unfulfilled. Individuals belonging to the Countering Unfairness subtheme, on the other hand, did not report their original expectations of the brand. Respondents report avoiding brands and products for a variety of broken promises. One segment of individuals in this subtheme has simply experienced product or service failures. Prior research is replete with studies on such failures (e.g., Maxham and Netemeyer 2003; Ringberg, Odekerken-Schröder, and Christensen 2007), and thus these respondents will not be elaborated upon. Other consumers classified under broken promises express feelings of resentment toward brands that have not lived up to perceived firm-created societal expectations. Jack, a business owner, is an example:

> Wal-Mart has misled the American public. When they started out they advertised the lowest prices and only American-made products. But they're not always the cheapest. Most of the products aren't even made in the USA. They said they would add jobs to the community, but many of their part-time employees are wards of the state. Target and Lowe's still have quality merchandise . . . better selection . . . full-time jobs. Not Wal-Mart . . .

Jack perceives Wal-Mart as contributing to the detriment of society by misleading consumers through marketing. The fact that he still shops at other "category killers" suggests that its abandoned promises to society are his true motivations for avoiding Wal-Mart.

Some offenders in this subtheme are faulted for not meeting what consumers perceive as implied promises. For example, Marcia refuses to shop at Old Navy because the firm has failed to maintain her expected brand image:

> Old Navy does not use the word "Christmas" in their commercials so they won't offend any non-Christians. I am very upset that such a family-oriented and recognized company would publicly stand for something so silly. If they would start recognizing Christmas I would forgive them though.

Passive Offender

A unique contribution of this study is the emergence of a theme whose likeness until this time has not been unveiled. For respondents in the Passive Offender theme, avoidance is based not on users of the brand or product, or direct offenses of the brand. These consumers harbor aversions to objects due to the brand's or product's incidental placement in the avoider's life story. Regarding the first two subthemes, Self-preservation and Tradition Lost, the brand represents the resurgence of negative feelings. Recent research suggests that brand encounters can inspire flashbulb memories (Roehm and Roehm 2007) that can ultimately exert significant influence on consumer brand choices (Braun-La Tour et al. 2007). In the words of one respondent, the brand happened to be "in the wrong place at the wrong time." Thus the brand serves as a conduit for negative feelings and emotions resulting from bad situations in the past. Respondents in this category avoid the brands in order to prevent the memories from resurfacing.

Self-preservation

Respondents in this subtheme avoid brands and products in efforts to prevent a loss of control over their emotional, psychological, or physical states. While some avoiders merely avoid products due to a mildly unpleasant association (e.g., one respondent avoids lemon-scented cleaning products because it reminds her of cleaning "dog mess" from her earlier job), other individuals report extreme aversion to brands or products in order to prevent psychological and/or emotional breakdown. Jennifer provides an example of such a respondent:

> I refuse to buy anything that is the color purple. For example, I love grapes, but if they do not have green ones then I just do not buy any. My parents divorced when I was seven years old. The walls in my room at that time were painted purple. I remember sitting in my room when my dad came in and told me that my mom was gone. I never have seen her again. Every time I see the color purple, I get a sick feeling and it reminds me of that day.

John, while engaging in an unhealthy behavior – smoking – avoids his father's type of cigarettes in order to prevent inheriting his parent's health complications:

> My father used to smoke cigarettes with brown filters and he was always coughing in the morning. I smoke regularly, and I know white-filtered cigarettes aren't healthy but something about not buying his cigarettes makes me think I'm making a better decision. I am fifty-two years old and I don't have the coughing problems my father had at my age. If he had smoked white filters I would probably smoke the brown ones!

These respondents' accounts underscore the importance of early or defining memories (Braun-La Tour *et al.* 2007) on consumer behavior. In addition, these memories can have long-lasting effects on both brand *and* product choice. Interestingly, these avoidance motivations may range from fear of mildly discomforting personal states to the other extreme of preventing complete loss of control over one's perceived well-being.

Tradition Lost

Respondents in this subtheme are related to those in Self-preservation due to the brand's placement in bad memories. However, to this group of consumers, the brand represents the termination of a routine from which respondents derived positive life meaning (e.g., Fournier 1998) until that point. James, a widower, provides an example:

> I do not buy red roses any more. They remind me of my wife. She passed away ten years ago. Red roses were the first gift I ever gave her. I gave

them to her every year on her anniversary until she passed. I do not mind talking about it. I just don't want anyone else to have that.

Marcia, a college professor, laments the loss of a closely held daily ritual:

When I was growing up in Louisiana, we were served coffee in bed every morning. My mother always bought the Louisiana specialty brands. Sharing that special coffee was something we did as a family. Even after we moved away from Louisiana, she always made sure we had those coffees. It was like a connection to home. Later, when my father died, she stopped buying them and started buying regular brands like Folgers. I hated it because that was our tradition and it was just gone.

Interestingly, this respondent demonstrates an important distinction between Tradition Lost and Self-preservation, evidenced by her willingness to consume Folgers coffee when necessary:

It's not true that I dislike Folgers. When someone serves me a cup of hot coffee – even my mother and even when I know it's Folgers – I enjoy it as long as I don't think about the associations I have with it. I would just never choose it for myself.

Both Self-preservation and Tradition Lost represent motivations desirous of preventing unpleasant prior associations with a brand or product. Other motivations exist, however, that are founded upon merely modeling an important other's behavior. These respondents avoid brands and products as a means of either paying homage to an admired individual, or maintaining a harmonious relationship with another person. Thus these consumers do not necessarily adopt the beliefs of the primary avoider, but mimic the avoidance behavior of that person.

Hero Worship

Respondents classified under this subtheme avoid products and brands due to their desire to be like another person. Family members and authority figures often serve as models for acceptable behavior; consequently, these respondents mimic avoiders as a means of maintaining a positive image in the eyes of role models. Jeanette, an undergraduate student, expresses such sentiments:

When I was about ten years old, my daddy told me that mayonnaise would make me fat. He's a health nut. We have a great relationship, and I look up to him very much. I want to be just like him. I do not want to get fat, and I certainly do not want my daddy to think less of me because I eat mayonnaise.

Mark, a college graduate, shares a similar story:

> Just about everybody in my family is Army – not Navy, not Marine, but Army – my grandfather, my dad, and my brother. I'm not, but I respect them for their service to this country. A few years ago my brother told me that Starbucks wouldn't send free coffee to the troops in Iraq, and that I shouldn't buy another damn thing from them. And I haven't ever since.

Pacification

Members of this last subtheme avoid in order to, in the words of one respondent, "keep the peace" with another person in their lives. For example, Frank feels that his wife's avoidance of Disney is exaggerated, but continues to model her behavior:

> I don't buy anything Disney. I had to turn a church down one time because they were asking for donations for a trip there. My wife hates them. I am just supporting her. I have seen the cartoons with the sexual things drawn in, but I don't think this is the Disney Corporation's fault.

Jan also avoids products in order to maintain her relationship with her boyfriend:

> My new boyfriend is from India, and they don't eat beef. So I don't either out of consideration for him. My last boyfriend left me because I wouldn't stay at home when he wanted to, and I lost him because I was stupid. I don't want to risk anything with my new boyfriend.

As mentioned earlier, a common theme underlying the Passive Offender category is the notion that consumers may avoid brands and products for reasons totally unrelated to perceived direct actions of the firm (i.e., Active Offender) or characteristics of typical users (i.e., Brand User–Self-concept Incongruence). This third category represents a unique contribution of the current research, as previous studies have not identified avoidance motivations founded upon the brand or product holding an incidental position in a bad prior memory (e.g., Self-preservation and Tradition Lost), or with the interest of another avoider as a goal (e.g., Hero Worship and Pacification).

Discussion

This study made a deep exploration into the motivations for consumer brand avoidance in order to understand more fully the negative aspect of consumer brand responses. As a result of in-depth interviews, several themes emerged, some of which are akin to findings from prior research (e.g. Banister and Hogg 2004; Lee *et al.* 2009; Thompson *et al.* 2006), and others that had not been previously unveiled, as in the case of the Passive Offender theme. Each category of avoidance motivations provides insight toward developing a comprehensive typology of consumer avoiders in the marketing environment.

Under the first theme of Brand User–Self-concept Incongruence, the sub-themes of Individual Self-concept and Social Self-concept relate to findings in symbolic research that describe consumer rejection of brands in order to avoid an undesired self-image (Banister and Hogg 2004; Lee at al. 2009; Ogilvie 1987). Interestingly, a consumer may avoid public associations with a brand, but still consume the brand in private. This notion captures the primary distinction between the two subthemes in this category: the social (public) versus the individual (private) self (Kleine, Kleine, and Kernan 1993; Ogilvie 1987). For example, the findings suggest that consumers belonging to the Social Self-concept subtheme may primarily be avoiding public associations with a brand, while those in the Individual Self-concept subtheme appear to refrain from both public and private consumption of the brand, exhibiting a more intrinsically motivated, intense negative response.

The second theme, Active Offender, also encompasses subthemes that align with consumer brand rejection motives found in prior research. Recent studies suggest that consumers reject brands as a means of waging war against brands due to some transgression committed by the firm (Lee et al. 2009; Thompson *et al.* 2006). First, under the subtheme of Countering Unfairness, Mei avoids Macy's in order to punish the retailer for its discriminatory practices. Second, in terms of Broken Promises, Jack avoids Wal-Mart because of his beliefs that the firm has not lived up to explicitly stated expectations. Both subthemes relate to moral or ideological avoidance (Lee *et al.* 2009; Thompson *et al.* 2006). In other words, these individuals avoid brands as a means of "doing the right thing" and preserving the good of society.

A unique contribution of this study was the unveiling of one previously undiscovered theme regarding consumer brand avoidance: Passive Offender. A common thread connecting each of the subthemes – Self-preservation, Tradition Lost, Hero Worship, and Pacification – is the essentially indirect negative relationship between the respondent and the object. Indeed, the brand itself is not the offender, but still receives the negative consequences of the avoidance behavior. Consequently, the revelation of the Passive Offender theme and related subthemes underscores the ability of a brand to transcend product-related charac-teristics (Aaker 1997) to take on not only an entirely unrelated meaning, but also a meaning that is *not* the result of the brand creator's actions. For example, John (in his avoidance of his father's brown-filtered cigarettes) and Marcia (in her avoidance of Folgers coffee) avoid consumption due to a product or brand's incidental placement in their respective life stories. These avoidance objects appear to serve as conduits for bad memories, as opposed to the negatively perceived brand users or active offenders described in other categories. Additionally, insights from these first two Passive Offender subthemes lend further support to prior findings regarding the significant influence of memories on consumer brand behavior (e.g. Braun-La Tour *et al.* 2007; Roehm and Roehm 2007). Finally, members of the two remaining subthemes, Hero Worship and Pacification, avoid products or brands with the goal of preserving a third party's interests (e.g., Frank's avoidance of Disney).

Conclusion

In conclusion, the overall contribution of the current research is an initial attempt toward developing a comprehensive typology of consumer brand avoidance. The emergent themes and subthemes provide substantially detailed insight into the emotional and psychological motivations for consumer brand avoidance. Moreover, the identification of the Passive Offender theme underscores the importance of viewing brand image in the broader context of consumers' idiosyncratically derived meaning that can become attached not only to an established brand name, but also to a basic consumption product.

Limitations and future research

As with similarly structured research, the current study was conducted in the "true spirit of discovery" (Fournier 1998, p. 368; Wells 1993), and thus lacks generalizability due to the exploratory objectives sought. Future research is needed in order to make inferences regarding motivations for consumer brand avoidance, and to further present implications for marketing researchers and practitioners alike. In particular, existing research would benefit from a more positivistic complement to what is primarily qualitative research. As such, this study has been conducted as a first step in the development of an instrument to measure consumer avoidance in the marketing environment. The second phase of this research will seek to develop and validate such an instrument, following established scale development guidelines in the literature.

References

Aaker, J.L. (1997) "Dimensions of Brand Personality", *Journal of Marketing Research*, 34 (3): 347–56.

Baker, W.E. (2003) "Does Brand Name Imprinting in Memory Increase Brand Information Retention?" *Psychology and Marketing*, 20 (12), 1119–35.

Banister, E.N. and Hogg, M.K. (2004) "Negative Symbolic Consumption and Consumers' Drive for Self-Esteem: The Case of the Fashion Industry", *European Journal of Marketing*, 28 (7): 850–68.

Braun-La Tour, K.A., La Tour, M.S. and Zinkhan, G.M. (2007) "Using Childhood Memories to Gain Insight into Brand Meaning", *Journal of Marketing*, 71: 45–60.

Chaudhuri, A. and Holbrook, M.B. (2001) "The Chain of Effects from Brand Trust and Brand Affect to Brand Performance: The Role of Brand Loyalty", *Journal of Marketing*, 65: 81–93.

Close, A.G. and Zinkhan, G.M. (2009) "Market-Resistance and Valentine's Day Events", *Journal of Business Research*, 62: 200–7.

Coulter, R.A., Price, L.L. and Feick, L. (2003) "Rethinking the Origins of Involvement and Brand Commitment: Insights from Post-Socialist Central Europe", *Journal of Consumer Research*, 30: 151–69.

Cushing, P. and Douglas-Tate, M. (1985) "The Effect of People/Product Relationship on Advertising Processing", in L.F. Alwitt and A.A. Mitchell (eds) *Psychological Processes, and Advertising Effects*, Hillsdale, NJ: Erlbaum.

Dalli, D., Romani, S. and Gistri, G. (2006) "Brand Dislike: Representing the Negative Side of Consumer Preferences", *Advances in Consumer Research*, 32: 87–95.

Drolet, A., Luce, M.F. and Simonson, I. (2009) "When Does Choice Reveal Preference? Moderators of Heuristic versus Goal-Based Choice", *Journal of Consumer Research*, 36: 137–47.

Escalas, J.E. and Bettman, J.R. (2003) "You Are What They Eat: The Influence of Reference Groups on Consumer Connections to Brands", *Journal of Consumer Psychology*, 13 (3): 339–48.

—— (2005) "Self-Construal, Reference Groups, and Brand Meaning (2005)", *Journal of Consumer Research*, 32: 378–89.

Fournier, S. (1998) "Consumers and their Brands: Developing Relationship Theory in Consumer Research", *Journal of Consumer Research*, 24: 343–73.

Hogg, M.K., Banister, E.N. and Stephenson, C.A. (2009) "Mapping Symbolic (Anti-) Consumption", *Journal of Business Research*, 62: 148–59.

Iyer, R. and Muncy, J.A. (2009) "Purpose and Object of Anti-Consumption", *Journal of Business Research*, 62: 160–8.

Keller, K.L. (1993) "Conceptualizing, Measuring, and Managing Customer-Based Brand Equity", *Journal of Marketing*, 57: 1–22.

—— (2003) "Brand Synthesis: The Multidimensionality of Brand Knowledge", *Journal of Consumer Research*, 29: 595–600.

Kleine, R.E., Kleine, S.S. and Kernan, J.B. (1993) "Mundane Consumption and the Self: A Social Identity Perspective", *Journal of Consumer Psychology*, 2 (3): 209–35.

Lee, M.S.W., Motion, J. and Conroy, D. (2009) "Anti-Consumption and Brand Avoidance", *Journal of Business Research*, 62: 169–80.

Lincoln, Y.S. and Guba, E.G. (1985) *Naturalistic Inquiry*, London: Sage.

McCracken, G. (1988a) *Culture and Consumption*, Bloomington: Indiana University Press.

—— (1988b) *The Long Interview*, Newbury Park, CA: Sage.

Maxham, J.G. III and Netemeyer, R.G. (2003) "Firms Reap What They Sow: The Effects of Shared Values and Perceived Organizational Justice on Customers' Evaluations of Complaint Handling", *Journal of Marketing*, 67 (1): 46–62.

Meenaghan, T. (2001a) "Sponsorship and Advertising: A Comparison of Consumer Perceptions", *Psychology and Marketing*, 18: 191–215.

—— (2001b) "Understanding Sponsorship Effects", *Psychology and Marketing*, 18: 95–122.

Muñiz, A.M., Jr and Hamer, L.O. (2001) "Us versus Them: Oppositional Brand Loyalty and the Cola Wars", *Advances in Consumer Research*, 28: 355–61.

Ogilvie, D.M. (1987) "The Undesired Self: A Neglected Variable in Personality Research", *Journal of Personality and Social Psychology*, 52 (2): 379–85.

Patton, M.Q. (1990) *Qualitative Evaluation and Research Methods*, 2nd edn, London: Sage.

Ringberg, T., Odekerken-Schröder, G. and Christensen, G.L. (2007) "A Cultural Models Approach to Service Recovery", *Journal of Marketing*, 71 (3): 194–214.

Roehm, H.A., Jr and Roehm, M.L. (2007) "Can Brand Encounters Inspire Flashbulb Memories?" *Psychology and Marketing*, 24: 25–40.

Sandikci, Ö. and Ekici, A. (2009) "Politically Motivated Brand Rejection", *Journal of Business Research*, 62: 208–17.

Schouten, J.W. (1991) "Selves in Transition: Symbolic Consumption in Personal Rites of Passage and Identity Reconstruction", *Journal of Consumer Research*, 17: 412–25.

Simonson, I. (1989) "Choice Based on Reasons: The Case of Attraction and Compromise Effects", *Journal of Consumer Research*, 16: 158–74.

Spiggle, S. (1994) "Analysis and Interpretation of Qualitative Data in Consumer Research", *Journal of Consumer Research*, 21: 491–503.

Thompson, C.J. and Arsel, Z. (2004) "The Starbucks Brandscape and Consumers' (Anticorporate) Experiences of Glocalization", *Journal of Consumer Research*, 31: 631–42.

Thompson, C.J., Locander, W.B. and Pollio, H.R. (1990) "The Lived Meaning of Free Choice: An Existential-Phenomenological Description of Everyday Consumer Experiences of Contemporary Married Women", *Journal of Consumer Research*, 17: 346–61.

Thompson, C.J., Rindfleisch, A. and Arsel, Z. (2006) "Emotional Branding and the Value of the Doppelgänger Brand Image", *Journal of Marketing*, 70: 50–64.

Wells, W. (1993) "Discovery-Oriented Consumer Research", *Journal of Consumer Research*, 19: 489–504.

4

BRAND FLINGS

When great brand relationships are not made to last

Claudio Alvarez and Susan Fournier

Although Fournier (1998) identified fifteen different types of consumer–brand relationships, disciplinary research has been limited to the exposition of but a few relationship forms. A strong bias toward committed, loyal brand relationships analogous to marital partnerships focuses our research attention, under the assumption that strong relationships are leverageable, resilient, and most importantly, made to last (Oliver 1999). This assumption is reinforced in research conducted using the Clark and Mills' (1979) relationship dichotomy, wherein communal relationships, which are guided by a lasting concern for the other, are contrasted with practical *quid pro quo* exchange relationships (Aggarwal 2004). Beyond the committed/communal/exchange paradigm, branding research focusing on specific relationship types is scant. Although marketing scholars have explored commercial friendships (Price and Arnould 1999), adversarial relations (Hill 1994), and addictions (Hirschman 1992), these studies do not draw primary inspiration from the relationship theories nor contribute centrally to this body of research.

The brand fling – a "short-term, time-bounded engagement of high emotional reward, but devoid of commitment and reciprocity demands" (Fournier 1998: 362) – is the relationship type most out of sync with the relationship strength–duration linkage assumption. Very little is known about this temporary relationship, in either the interpersonal or the brand relationship domain. This knowledge gap is particularly notable in light of the current cultural climate of instability and constant change (Bauman 2001), which renders less-enduring relationships more important and relevant. If the future is framed as nothing more than a discontinuous series of present moments, acting on impulse and seeking instant gratification become legitimized strategies to gain emotional rewards. In this environment, long-term commitments are no longer assets to be cultivated, but rather liabilities that restrict possibilities of what we might become.

This chapter advances knowledge of brand flings through the analysis of consumers' narratives of brand fling experiences. Related constructs and insights from the interpersonal relationships and consumer behavior literatures provide an initial lens through which to capture this phenomenon. Using a three-part survey methodology, we share evidence to support brand flings as a resonant consumer–brand relationship type. We also explore ways in which brand flings help consumers in the pursuit of their identity projects, and identify patterns in how these relationships evolve over time. Finally, we summarize similarities and differences between brand and interpersonal flings, contrast these with related consumer behaviors, and propose directions for research.

Flings in the interpersonal relationships domain

Interpersonal relationships research has used multiple terms to define emotionally laden, short-term relationships, including "hookups," "one-night stands," and "short-term mating." Despite important differences in the conceptualization of these constructs, they all share characterization as interactions (or brief series of interactions) between people who do not expect to form a lasting relationship and hence in which commitment does not play a role.

Research supports lack of trust in the relationship partner as a key element of short-term interpersonal relationships. Schmitt (2005) showed that both the dismissive attachment style (i.e., negative view of the relationship other and a positive view of the self) and the fearful style (i.e., negative view of self and other) (Bartholomew and Horowitz 1991) were consistently associated with higher levels of desire for and experience of short-term mating across fifty-six cultures. In a similar vein, hookups and one-night stands have been shown to help young adults who fear that intimacy leads to the loss of individuality (Paul, McManus, and Hayes 2000).

Lack of considered decision-making is also characteristic of short-term interpersonal relationships. People are generally less selective when choosing a short-term rather than a long-term partner (Stewart, Stinnett, and Rosenfeld 2000). Regan (1998) showed that the interpersonal qualities critical in long-term mate selection – someone relaxed in social situations, with a good sense of humor, easygoing, and friendly – mattered little in short-term relationship decisions, which were predominantly driven by the more surface-level criterion of physical attraction. Lehr and Geher (2006) demonstrate that reciprocity of shared feelings had a significant effect on liking for long-term partners but not short-term mates. The selection of a partner for a hookup is also generally more impulsive, providing additional support for this point (Paul and Hayes 2002).

Perhaps the most striking finding from the interpersonal literature is the deep and conflicted emotionality of short-term relationship experiences and, in particular, the stigma attached to these relationships, particularly when sexual intercourse is involved. Hookups and one-night stands are intrinsically enjoyable, inherently exciting, and allow a more playful and hedonistic approach to romantic relations than committed partnerships do (Garcia and Reiber 2008; Paul *et al.* 2000). After such engagements, however, college students typically feel "regretful or disappointed" (35 percent) in addition to feeling "good or happy" (27 percent) and "satisfied" (20 percent). Women experience regret more frequently than men, mention that they would not repeat the experience, and report that they felt like they were being "used" (Paul and Hayes 2002). Paul's (2006) focused analysis of college hookups supports the emotional complexity of this phenomenon. College hookups are generally conceived as fun and exciting experiences involving sexual gratification and confidence boosting. Alcohol consumption, the operation of "beer goggles," competitive games among friends, solidarity rules such as "no girl left behind" and other rituals (e.g., "hookup weekend") create a sanctioned atmosphere of licensed impulsivity supportive of these relationships. However, hookup experiences are difficult, particularly due to unarticulated expectations about what should or should not happen during the sexual encounter. Besides the negative stigma of "sluts" or "players" derived from excessive hookup behavior, or participation in the "walk of shame" ritual after a hookup, young adults in these relationships often feel pressured to behave in ways they are not comfortable with, sometimes to the point of sexual violation. This lack of clarity about roles further increases the probability of regret and disappointment, often overtaking the hedonistic enjoyment of the fling.

Brand flings

> Look in my shower here. Look! Seven bottles of shampoo and six conditioners and I use them all! In here [the closet]; this whole box is full of trial sizes that I pull from. Why? Because each one is different. It depends on my mood and what kind of a person I want to be.
>
> *Vicki (extracted from Fournier 1998: 357)*

Vicki is the consumer portrayed in Fournier (1998) whose relationships best exemplify brand flings. A 23-year-old woman about to finish her master's studies, Vicki's life projects involved experiencing different possible selves (Markus and Nurius 1986) and carving an initial definition of herself as an adult. Vicki's flings with not just hair care products but also clothing and other personal care brands enabled her to experiment with a variety of self-definitions at the same time, forging transitional versions of who she wanted to be in a given day.

Vicki's brand flings share the hedonic and time-bounded dimensions that characterize flings in the interpersonal domain and in this regard, evoke common conceptual ground with other constructs from the consumer behavior literature, notably impulsive purchases and variety seeking. In his seminal analysis of the buying impulse, Rook (1987) identified the same elements of excitement, hedonism, and self-control failure that characterize one-night stands and hookups (see also Baumeister 2002). Variety seeking and short-term interpersonal relations also share important motivational and experiential qualities. Variety seeking is a tendency to purchase a different product – oftentimes not as attractive as the preferred choice – just for the sake of change. The experience of buying a new and unfamiliar product is inherently pleasurable (McAlister and Pessemier 1982) and rooted in the search for sensorial stimulation (Sharma, Sivakumaran, and Marshall 2010). Sensory-emotional stimulation also serves as a core benefit of short-term relationships, hookups, and one-night stands.

Building from the literature, we propose a working definition: the brand fling is a hedonic, non-committed, time-bounded relationship driven by impulsivity and the need for experimentation and associated with post-termination feelings of shame and regret. Still, the application of insights from interpersonal relationships to brand flings remains as an empirical question, and the strong role of the physical in human flings presents obvious barriers to a direct translation of findings to the brand domain.

Research questions and methodology

The present study endeavors to advance our understanding of brand flings by looking for initial answers to the following research questions: (1) Does the idea of having flings with brands resonate with consumers' brand experiences? (2) What are the core characteristics of brand flings as described by consumers? (3) How do brand flings evolve over time? We provide a preliminary step toward possible phenomenological propositions and offer suggestions for future research developed from this base.

A series of three surveys informs our research questions. Because of the relevance of the college hookup as a critical variation of interpersonal flings, and due to the resonance of brand flings within the college student case reported by Fournier (1998), our samples are composed of US undergraduate students, balanced by gender.

Studies 1 and 2 sought understanding of the resonance of the brand fling construct. The first survey (N=195) probed consumer identification with the "brand fling" label; our analysis calculates the percentage of participants who said that they could recall and discuss a recent brand fling. In the second study (N=122), instead of using the "brand fling" label, we provided students with a brief scenario definition based on the above literature-based conceptualization of brand flings: "List up to five brands that you had a temporary but intense experience with. These are brands that you were 'obsessed with' at some point in your life, but your feelings faded and you moved on." The mechanism for assessing consumers' connection with the fling concept was also different in this study: instead of directly asking if people could recall a brand fling, we asked them to rate their brand fling exemplar on how transient ("not permanent," "no long-term commitment," "a phase") and emotional ("joy," "excitement," and "happiness") this relationship was. Factor analysis confirmed these two defining factors, which were then averaged to create an overall fling index. Respondents who rated their own best examples above the mid-point were considered to have elicited an appropriate brand fling exemplar, thus providing a percent estimate of the resonance and incidence of brand flings.

The third study (N=193) used a slightly modified scenario stimulus: "For a certain period of time you are really 'into' a particular brand. After a while these feelings fade away and you move on to other things." As with the other two studies, respondents were asked to nominate up to five brand relationships fitting the fling description/label, and to identify the brand relationship they felt was most representative of and true to the fling relationship type. The chosen brand fling was the subject of a respondent narrative (average word count =156) written to explain and illuminate the fling relationship type.

Our analysis summarizes brands and categories elicited as fling exemplars. We also conducted a content analysis of respondents' brand narratives and used as a framework for this analysis the three brand relationship tenets summarized by Fournier (2009), that is, that relationships vary in form and across multiple dimensions; are not an end in themselves but rather exist to bring meanings to consumers' daily lives; and have to be understood as temporal phenomena. We sought patterns in the data that allowed us to capture (1) specific dimensions or characteristics that stand out in consumers' narratives as defining elements of brand flings; (2) process insights about how flings start, develop, and end; (3) the different ways in which these characteristics are enacted in specific relationships, and the multiple forms that flings take; and (4) purposes or motives for engaging in flings. From our initial organizing framework, more specific categories were inducted and then quantified by two trained independent judges. Inter-rater agreement was 86 percent, with conflicts resolved through discussion.

Findings

Take-away #1: Brand flings are a resonant type of consumer–brand relationship

The concept of brand flings consistently resonated with the young adults in our three studies. In the first survey, 68 percent of respondents were able to recall a brand they had recently had a "fling" with. In the second survey, 89 percent of respondents provided appropriate examples of brand flings from their own experience. In Study 3, when participants were asked whether they could recall any brand from their recent past that fits the fling description, 72 percent answered affirmatively, and 65 percent were able to articulate an unambiguous and coherent narrative consistent with the conceptual description of flings. These results

TABLE 4.1 Fling brand exemplars by product category (ranked by total number of mentions across studies)

	Study 1 (133 qualified flings) %	Study 2 (108 qualified flings) %	Study 3 (126 qualified flings) %
Clothing and shoes	50	28	64
Food and beverages	17	12	10
Games and toys	–	35	3
Beauty and body care	19	6	5
Electronics	4	7	10
Accessories	6	–	5
Other	4	12	3

grant confidence in brand flings as a valid relationship construal that is very much present in a majority of young college students' lives.

We found strong patterns in the data regarding product and service categories in which brand flings take place (see Table 4.1). Across the three studies, the majority of brands mentioned as best exemplars of flings reside in the clothing/footwear category, with Abercrombie & Fitch, Nike, and American Eagle garnering significant mention. Games and toys were also notable in Study 2, garnering 35 percent of mentions. These results suggest that consumers may have brand flings in certain product domains more than in others, and that fling tendencies vary from brand to brand (see Table 4.2).

TABLE 4.2 Top ten most cited fling brands in each study

Study 1 (133 qualified flings)	Study 2 (108 qualified flings)	Study 3 (126 qualified flings)
Nike (14)	Beanie Babies (7)	Abercrombie & Fitch (19)
Starbucks (5)	Abercrombie & Fitch (6)	American Eagle (12)
Apple (5)	American Girl Dolls (5)	Hollister (7)
American Eagle (5)	Barbie (4)	Nike (5)
H&M (4)	Nintendo (4)	Guess (4)
Armani Exchange (3)	Sony (4)	Sony (4)
Brooks Brothers (2)	Limited Too (3)	Apple (3)
Express (2)	Nike (3)	Urban Outfitters (3)
Forever 21 (2)	Old Navy (3)	Aeropostale (2)
Gap (2)	POGS (3)	Blizzard (2)

Take-away #2: There exist five distinctive characteristics of brand flings

An analysis of consumers' fling narratives (Study 3) yielded five distinctive and qualifying characteristics of this understudied relationship type, some of which support ingoing assumptions and some of which challenge our conception of brand flings.

First and foremost, brand flings are highly emotional relational engagements. Specific feelings and emotions were explicitly mentioned by the majority (62 percent) of respondents. In general, brand flings are associated with very positive feelings. Many consumers (37 percent) expressed a general state of enjoyment, of feeling good:

> It felt like I was on top of the world while making its little pizzas.
>
> *Male, Lunchables*

> I was positively surprised by [how] much enjoyment I received.
>
> *Male, Apple iPod Touch*

When describing specific emotions, consumers used the word "love" (17 percent of mentions) to refer to an intense and almost instantaneous connection:

> Every time I would go into Macy's I would go straight into the wallet/ purse section and I would always fall in love with the Guess stuff.
>
> *Female*

> I went to Sephora and had an employee help me find my shade and try it out on me. I loved it right away.
>
> *Female, Bare Escentuals*

Brand flings also bring excitement to the lives of consumers (15 percent of mentions):

> I was extremely excited to purchase my new iPod.
>
> *Male*

These feelings are particularly evident in early relationship stages where consumers get to know the brand by purchasing and starting to use it:

> I felt extremely excited when I first purchased it, and then I felt super happy while playing it. I felt very happy when I was exploring the game; there were so many new things.
>
> *Male, Blizzard*

A small but insightful group of narratives (10 percent of mentions) portrayed a vivid picture of the emotional experience leading up to brand purchase. Respondents report a heightened sense of anticipation in which they found themselves craving the brand and consumed with a strong desire to buy or use it:

> I couldn't wait to get home to wear the new clothing I had to school.
>
> *Female, Hollister*

The second fling characteristic concerns the nature of people's interactions with fling brands. The high level of emotionality noted above leads consumers to engage intensively and somewhat obsessively with their fling brands, such that people (31 percent of respondents) invest a significant part of their available time, energy, and financial resources in the brand relationship. Brand flings involve a bit of effort to arrange for and accommodate the brand engagement. People in flings proactively search for the brand ("I loved Hollister clothes and was obsessed with seeing what they had in store every week"), carve out opportunities in the daily routine to be with it ("I would look forward to sales and go out of my way to use coupons there. I would always stop at Express when I went to the mall"), and invest psychological space so as to remain open and receptive to brand initiatives. This high level of engagement sometimes manifests in the usage realm:

> Once I got it I continuously used it for everything that I possibly could.
>
> *Male, Apple iPod*

In some circumstances, brand flings resulted in significant financial expenditures:

> If I were to estimate how much money I spent there it would be well over 3,000 dollars.
>
> *Female, Abercrombie & Fitch*

The brand fling is highly invested on many counts.

The third characteristic of brand fling relationships concerns the superficiality of the decision-making process surrounding the adoption of the brand. Consumers report that they were "carried away" by the fling and made buying decisions that were not necessarily thought through or rational when performance criteria were considered:

> After I bought my North Face I just wanted a warmer jacket and wish I had spent my money on something thicker to keep me warm.
>
> *Female*

> I used to play soccer and I used Puma Ferrari's, which is a flat-based kind of shoe. I did so because I liked the design of the shoe overall, even though the

fit was usually quite uncomfortable and the inside of the shoe used to heat up and cause blisters to form.

Male, Puma

Only four descriptions of how the relationship started (3 percent) included an explicit comparison with competitors' offers to determine "the best choice." On the contrary, superficial external cues such as the endorsement of notable social others were a more common precipitator of flings. Indeed, for a significant number of respondents (24 percent), the fact that "everyone else" was using the brand was the most important reason to buy it. The data suggest an underlying tension between more thoughtfully assessing one's needs against competitors' offers versus the hedonic triumph of the brand:

> At first if I had to buy something, I would only get it if it was from Nike. But that has changed now and I look into my needs. If I require any such related product, I look at the better product and its design rather than the brand.
>
> *Male*

The fourth defining characteristic of brand flings is identity signaling. Even though all symbolic brand engagements enable consumers to associate themselves with the coveted meanings that the brands convey, fling relationships stand out in the conspicuous nature of the consumer–brand image connection and its blatant role in self-presentation:

> Clearly they know you're shopping there. Shopping there means that I'm portraying a specific image of being cool.
>
> *Female, American Eagle*

Most of the fling brands mentioned by respondents (79 percent) are predominantly symbolic and publicly visible, not only in clothing (e.g., Abercrombie & Fitch, American Eagle, Guess) but also in electronics (e.g., Apple) and other categories (e.g., Starbucks). A significant number of respondents (27 percent) spontaneously described a very specific image of a brand user in their brief narratives of the relationship with the brand:

> It was cool to own and1 basketball shoes. It was cool because it was black culture, and it was cool to buy "black" products and wear baggy oversized clothes.
>
> *Male*

> I described myself as liking the "preppy" look of the brand, as I thought it fit into the zeitgeist of my school.
>
> *Male, Abercrombie & Fitch*

The fifth characteristic of brand flings is transience, which is certainly not a surprising theme given the inherently time-bounded nature of the engagement. However, two unexpected aspects of temporality need to be highlighted. First, although transience signals a formal "ending," the end of the fling brand relationship does not necessarily involve termination of engagement with the brand. Almost half of the respondents (46 percent) did not completely stop purchasing or using the brand though they claimed the fling was over. Hence, the high emotionality, intense engagement, and identity relevance that characterize the fling relationship may go away though the person still buys the brand. In short, the relationship lives on, but it is just not a fling anymore:

> My relationship with the brand isn't over, because I still wear the Uggs that I have. But . . . the allure is gone.
>
> *Female*

> It's not completely over, but now I just wouldn't go out of my way to shop there.
>
> *Female, Hollister*

The second unexpected quality of transience is that brand flings are typically not the one-time encounters that characterize hookups and one-night stands. Only 7 percent of the brand flings mentioned involved only one purchase of the brand. Transience in the brand fling domain was defined less in terms of temporality (58 percent of respondents did not explicitly state how long the relationship lasted) than as a generalized expectation that the relationship was "not made to last." Surprisingly, 26 percent of respondents stated that their flings continued over the course of several years. What makes something a brand fling is the realization that sooner or later the time will come to move on to other brands:

> Rain boots used to be unstylish so they made more stylish rain boots which are all the rage now, but it is only a matter of how long this will last. Rain boots will go out of style like scrunchies did.
>
> *Female*

> I got tired of wearing almost everything American Eagle and wanted a "new look." However, I feel the same will happen to the brand which I am currently favoring.
>
> *Female*

Take-away #3: Brand flings are phased, dynamic relationships with a characteristic pattern of growth and decline

Consumer–brand relationships are process phenomena: engagements that evolve over time in response to brand interactions and changes in life contexts.

The developmental pattern is particularly diagnostic in the case of brand flings because their defining characteristics (discussed in the previous section) vary in salience over the course of the relationship. Consumers' narratives indicate a sharp spike in emotionality at the early stage of the relationship when the person can feel "carried away" by the brand. This initial attraction then gives rise to a period of sustained energy and intense engagement with the brand, where consumers tend to become more invested with the identity signaled by it. An abrupt decline then follows, leaving consumers suddenly disengaged from the brand. Our analysis of people's brand fling narratives offers critical insights into how this relationship is initiated, develops, and ends.

In the dynamics of fling initiation, the most critical spark is the input of influential others. Many respondents (37 percent) got to know their fling brands through friends or close family members:

> I noticed American Eagle when my friends started to wear their products at school.
>
> *Female, American Eagle*

Consumers learned about the fling brand because "everyone" or "people around" them were using it (33 percent):

> I was in middle school and everyone who was someone was wearing Hollister.
>
> *Male*

> Everyone had an iPod and when I got to college, everyone had a MacBook.
>
> *Male*

Another mechanism for fling initiation is the magnetic attractiveness of product attributes and functionalities, especially in the context of technology brands. Many consumers (29 percent of those who mentioned non-clothing brands) described how they were fascinated by what the product had to offer:

> I loved the feeling of getting a new phone because I could explore the new features and learn how to use them.
>
> *Female, Nokia*

This fascination serves not only to attract consumers to the brand, but also to focus attention resources, generate excitement, and create stronger consumer–brand bonds:

> When a salesperson told me to just "try the tests" of what the EFX bracelets could do, it was mind-boggling and therefore exciting. It made me buy a

few and pass the word to other people about how effective the EFX bracelet was.

Male

The most striking finding from the middle development stage of flings is the extent to which the brand becomes integrated into people's lives. Most flings involve multiple brand purchases (79 percent), which, depending on the product category, may happen weekly or daily:

> I bought it multiple times; I have to say I bought A LOT of them.
>
> *Male, Ed Hardy*

Usage can be quite frequent too:

> I constantly used it and I enjoyed how it brought more music into my life.
>
> *Male, Apple iPod Touch*

Most notable in the final relationship stage is the drastic change in perspective associated with the end of flings. The end of a fling is often quite unexpected. Stories suggest that consumers suddenly "wake up" from an unreflective state to face the stark reality of the brand they are having a fling with:

> It's over. Pretty drastically, with my shirts going away for charity.
>
> *Female, Ed Hardy*

> I really liked Abercrombie & Fitch but all of the sudden, I started to hate it . . . I began to realize the products are overpriced and there are tons of brands that have prettier/cuter clothes.
>
> *Female*

> Yes it's over, I've moved on from the beachy look. I just look back on the brand and think about what a joke it all was.
>
> *Female, Abercrombie & Fitch*

This change in perspective brings to light some of the past actions of the brand that were not forthcoming for the consumer, or characteristics that escaped scrutiny in the context of the fling experience:

> Once I became interested in fashion, I finally realized that their clothes looked the same. Also they were so repetitive from season to season. Their prices also went up for what I thought was the same quality.
>
> *Female, American Eagle*

When the fling is "over," some respondents (25 percent) report strong negative attitudes toward the brand. For these consumers, the end of the fling constitutes a definitive breakup, replete with anticipated avoidance of future interchanges:

> Lunchables and I cannot be in the same room any more. It's quite the awkward situation.
>
> *Male*

> I would never wear their shirts any more if I was going out with friends.
>
> *Male, Quiksilver*

> At this point, I would probably never imagine myself buying, or wearing, any piece of American Eagle clothing.
>
> *Male*

Much more common than negative rejection, however, were cases (45 percent) of total mentions) where the brand was simply brought down from its pedestal to be perceived as "just another regular brand." Consumers' descriptions include many different articulations of a lack of differentiation and resonance for the brand:

> I just don't seek it out. I am indifferent about it now.
>
> *Male, Timberland*

> I'm apathetic about the brand now. I don't recommend it, but I don't hate it or talk poorly about it to others.
>
> *Female, Yankee Candle*

Interestingly, in a significant number of cases (25 percent) consumers left the fling while still feeling positively about the brand:

> I still like Nike and buy their things, but I'm more concerned about price and would be just as likely to purchase something from Adidas.
>
> *Male*

> I believe it is a great brand but just not suitable for the style I'm currently looking for.
>
> *Male, American Eagle*

Some of these consumers know the fling is over for them but still think the brand may be a good choice for others:

> It's over because I have too much of it and I would like to start wearing other brands. The brand is still fashionable and good for some people but it's repetitive for me.
>
> *Female, Marc Jacobs*

Take-away #4: Brand flings take multiple forms

Consumers find different ways to experience relationships with brands that are highly emotional, intensely engaging, relatively superficial, identity-relevant, and transient. Flings, in other words, come in different shapes and forms. Our survey suggests four variations of the fling relationship, each capturing different phenomenological experiences and emphasizing different personal and cultural factors that precipitate the relationship's initiation and fall.

Brand flings as a phase you go through in life

> Abercrombie & Fitch is the type of brand that everyone LOVES at some point in their life. There is a certain infatuation with the aroma, the good-looking people, the blasting music, and the scandalous clothes. But let's face it, if I were an Abercrombie & Fitch girl my whole life, I'd have zero friends! It's not what real life is like and I think when you grow up you also grow out of brands, it's natural.
>
> *Female*

The most prevalent type of brand fling evident in respondents' stories (43 percent of all qualified brand fling mentions) relates to brand relationships circumscribed in a particular developmental phase or period in life. Consumers in this situation feel like the brand represents who they are, but recognize that this brand–self connection is only temporary. The phase boundary was generally defined by age, such that people discussed "growing out of" the brand:

> I used to always shop at American Eagle Outfitters for all of my clothes, but I have since matured past this fashion.
>
> *Male*

> I just grew out of it. I no longer identify with the brand.
>
> *Female, Baby Phat*

For others, the boundary defining the phase is related not to age but to broader changes in life concerns and product needs:

> I decided money was more important than having clothes and sports equipment with a little check on it.
>
> *Female, Nike*

> It's over. I no longer enjoy wearing tight shirts at all.
>
> *Male, Abercrombie & Fitch*

The core idea embedded in flings as phases is the possibility of adopting specific styles or, more appropriately, specific versions of the self for a limited amount of time:

I was really into Quiksilver as a young teenager as it fit my needs of a "cool" young adult. As I got older, I moved on to higher end brands such as Ralph Lauren that had something different to say.

Male

Brand flings as social trends you jump into

When I was in middle school the hottest brand was Abercrombie & Fitch. It was pricey and carried status with it. It had such an attractive feel to it stemming from the store to the scented clothing. Throughout middle school and freshman year of high school I wore this brand extensively. But after a while, the high appeal slowly faded away. This brand went from the hottest brand to the brand everyone forgot about.

Female

A significant portion (17 percent) of brand fling narratives can be characterized as socio-cultural engagements with short-lived social fads and "hit brands." These brands quickly achieve popularity and status and become invested with an aura of inevitability that draws consumers to the brand:

The fact that everyone else was wearing the brand made everyone else want to wear it as well.

Female, Abercrombie & Fitch

Fads swamp individual tastes and preferences:

I was absorbed into the hype.

Male, Blizzard

I saw a lot of the girls walking around in these boots, and I didn't know what they were. I actually thought they were really ugly at first, but eventually that changed and I wanted a pair really badly.

Female, Ugg

Consumers did not describe themselves as being particularly oppressed by brand fads; they simply constituted another cultural norm to follow: "Crocodile logo, social convention" (Male, Lacoste). Brand flings-as-fads manifest the classic fling lifecycle and come to a quick and definitive end as cultural tastes change:

The Ed Hardy brand was hyped up for a summer, maybe two summers everywhere but California and then me and then everyone just got over it. Too sparkly and tacky to be permanent.

Female

Brand flings as the quick exhaustion of what the brand has to offer

I bought a Sony digital camera and at first was quite obsessed with learning about its new functions and taking more pictures than I really needed to. After a while, this new piece of exciting technology just became another digital camera.

Male

In our third type of fling, consumers engage with the fling brand in a fast cycle of excitement and boredom. Mentioned in 14 percent of brand fling stories, these flings are characterized by a period of intense relationship with the brand which seems to literally exhaust what the brand has to offer. Flings in this category simply burn out, a denouement that is variously driven by and sometimes due to a combination of (1) the voracity with which the consumer approaches the brand and (2) a lack of innovation or new branded offerings. Two consumers explain:

Used to love shopping there and would buy multiple items. However, the clothes have begun looking the same and not as exciting to buy.

Female, H&M

Eventually, I got sick of the same thing over and over again.

Female, Hollister

The onset of boredom that brings these fling relationships to an end often manifests in a relatively short period of time:

After less than a month, I got very bored of the product. I stopped playing.

Male, Blizzard

This form of brand fling was manifest in relationships with certain brands of food, wherein intense daily consumption of the same product leads the consumer to feel "sick of the taste" (Male, Barbara's cereal). As one consumer put it:

I just simply got tired of drinking it because I drank it so much.

Female, Gatorade

Forced flings

I was really excited to buy this shampoo/conditioner because it's a professional brand of hair care. I usually use the normal ones like L'Oreal, Pantene, Garnier. I wanted a fancier one that would make my hair unbelievably nice and silky. However, it was so bad for my hair that white stuff started appearing right after I shampooed. That killed my interest in the brand.

Female, Nexus hair care

In eliciting a brand relationship that qualified as a short-term fling, some respondents described brand relationships that would otherwise not have ended save for a bad experience with the brand (11 percent of mentions). These relationships can be thought of as "forced flings" in that respondents' loftier relationship plans were thwarted by unsatisfactory brand performance. Drawing an analogy with interpersonal relationships, brand flings in this category are the unintended consequences of a "bad date" with the brand; they are relationships that, for all intents and purposes, could have gone on to be something more special and somehow "bigger" than the circumscribed relationships that they become. Forced flings constitute a very particular type of brand fling because they are fundamentally based on the brand's failure to sustain an intended relationship with the consumer:

> I bought it just once. I thought it would feel a lot cooler than it actually did. I never bought anything after that.
>
> *Male, Gap*

> I thought the products would be terrific to use, but I was surprised at their quality. They seem to break so often. It was infuriating.
>
> *Male, Mac*

Take-away #5: Brand flings are purposeful relationships that support people in living their lives

One cannot capture the nature of brand flings without understanding what consumers are looking for in engaging in this type of relationship. Per the tenets of consumer–brand relationships, flings are not ends in themselves, but are instead sources of meanings that consumers appropriate in order to live their daily lives (Fournier 2009). The homogeneity of our undergraduate student sample allowed us to identify a limited number of purposes associated with brand flings, which collectively accounted for 36 percent of all responses. Specifically, brand flings served as important enablers of two life tasks related to the adolescence–adulthood transition: "fitting in" and expressing individuality, most notably by defining a sense of style(s).

One of the most critical concerns expressed by our sampled population is to become a part of the broader community, generally described in terms of "fitting in" or "blending in." Brand flings played an important role as a facilitator of this life task:

> I wanted to wear the brand because it would help me fit in with a crowd of friends who I thought would accept me if I wore the brand.
>
> *Female, Baby Phat*

> It feels like I'm part of the community of gamers whenever I play their brand.
>
> *Male, Blizzard*

This role of flings was at times coercive, such as in this example:

> Apple almost makes you feel you need to have an iPod. Everyone has them and you can't fit in unless you are walking down the street with those white earbud headphones connected to your ears.
>
> *Male*

But most often consumers put themselves in the driving seat of the fling relationship, and selected the brand most useful for their purpose:

> I really liked how popular the brand was and being associated with such a brand would evidently make me feel like I was part of the school and society.
>
> *Female, American Eagle*

> I felt exclusive and part of a club. It was cool to have Abercrombie clothes, so it was a good feeling to be considered part of it.
>
> *Female, Abercrombie & Fitch*

One consumer even showed appreciation for the brand's ability to communicate with family and friends:

> My older cousin always bought Coach bags. I wanted to be like her and also like every other popular girl in school and on TV so I always wanted these bags as well. I loved that they advertised the brand so largely on their bags because then everyone would be able to tell exactly what brand you were wearing and they associated you with the brand.
>
> *Female, Coach*

This need to "fit in" is counterbalanced by a similarly strong task of individuation. Young adults want to feel like they belong to a particular group or to the broader community, but at the same time they need to create identities of their own (Erikson 1956). Brand flings were powerful in their service of individuation needs.

One particularly salient aspect of individuation that was serviced by brand flings for our college-aged respondents involved the development of a sense of style. Being stylish generates recognition and positive feedback from friends and peers:

> I loved wearing the brand because I received many compliments.
>
> *Female, Marc Jacobs*

Having style also increases someone's attractiveness and makes them feel more desirable:

> You had this sort of sexy feeling when you wore their stuff because they had low rise fit jeans and pretty tight tops.
>
> *Female, Abercrombie & Fitch*

> Girls liked my clothes.
>
> *Male, Abercrombie & Fitch*

Flings with clothing brands provided ready-made solutions to the sense-of-style dilemma:

> It's cool for kids to wear their clothing because Urban Outfitters makes the creative decision for you, and all you have to do is carry enough change in your wallet to buy the product.
>
> *Female*

Flings also helped consumers learn how to combine different elements in a coherent yet non-conventional way:

> It helped me to develop a sense of style and the Abercrombie & Fitch girl was who I wanted to be.
>
> *Female*

In the extreme, a series of brand flings provided a testing environment wherein a true individual style could be defined:

> I grew up and gained a real fashion sense. I became conscious of trends and made decisions whether I should follow them or not. I also gained a lot more confidence and know how to put together outfits without relying on my friends.
>
> *Female, American Eagle*

Respondents' stories reveal a tension, however, between demarcating individuality and "fitting in." Even among the respondents who used flings to "follow the pack," there often surfaced an explicit concern about whether the person was using the same brand as everybody else. Indeed, the adolescence–adulthood transition is fundamentally characterized by the tension between integration and individuation (Erikson 1956). Our analysis suggests that this tension may be a core element in understanding consumers' cycles of engagement and disengagement with brand flings.

> I used to always buy American Eagle clothes and apparel a few years ago. However, when everyone started to catch on the American Eagle bandwagon, everywhere I walked, I saw people with the same clothes as

me . . . After a longer period, I ran into more and more people on the streets that had the same brand AND the same clothes as me. After that, I needed to move on to another brand, so I just stopped buying from there.

Male, American Eagle

More specifically, a core reason why consumers may engage in intense and temporary relationships with brands may be to continuously "blend in" and "stand out" in the context of their social environment: a cycle if you will of serial flings. One consumer articulated this tension very forcefully:

I began to become close with this brand, as it offered me clothing that couldn't be labeled, that couldn't depict my social class, that let me stand for myself and not make me stand for the brand. As I grew older, this brand struck the minds of other people, and they began to support this brand. By doing so, they let the world know about it, pushing it as a new trend, something to follow and support. The brand gladly took this direction, and left me in a group of people who didn't stand for what I stood for. I had to leave this group in order to hold my own individuality.

Female, Urban Outfitters

Summary thoughts and future research

The preceding analysis supports brand flings as a resonant consumer–brand relationship present in the lives of young adults. The phenomenological footprint of the brand fling is quite distinctive. Brand flings are highly emotional, intense identity-relevant relationships that are none the less superficial and transient. Brand flings manifest in different forms: as developmental phases in the lives of consumers, social trends, acts of brand exhaustion, or forced short-term engagements precipitated by the failures of a brand. Consumers appropriate the meanings of brand flings to serve multiple purposes, among which we highlight the needs to "fit in" and establish individuality. A distinct evolutionary pattern characterizes brand flings. They start with the pull of brand attraction and quickly become highly integrated focal objects of energy investment, only to end, sometimes quite abruptly, when emotions fizzle and perspectives change.

Our preliminary research suggests that impulsive and variety-seeking consumer behaviors can be usefully differentiated from brand flings. The excitement and hedonic elements of impulse buying are certainly a point of connection, but the self-control theme so central to impulsive behavior was remarkably absent in the consumers' narratives we analyzed. Further, the idea of searching for variety as a means of reducing boredom was not a defining motivation for brand flings, nor was the brand fling initiated in the context of a specific choice setting or with the decided focus on sensorial stimulation as a purposive goal. Most importantly, both impulsive and variety-seeking behaviors are restrictive, one-time buying occasions. Flings involve a longer time horizon and a series of meaningful interactions between consumer and brand.

Our analysis of consumers' relationship narratives also captures important differences between brand flings and their interpersonal analogues. The interpersonal fling is a complex phenomenon involving a social environment that reinforces licensed impulsivity and the negative consequence of shame. These factors were not salient in brand flings. Further, the short-term dimension fundamental to notions of the interpersonal hookup and one-night stand also commands a different perspective in the brand realm, one that is more appropriately labeled as transience and less directly tied to a brief time frame. Third, it is notable that the "absence of commitment" criterion that centrally defines human flings is not relevant in describing brand flings. Indeed, the investments of time, attention, and energy that characterize brand fling relationships, often for protracted periods of intense engagement, signal some sense of commitment to the brand on the part of the consumer, albeit a commitment that is short-lived. We cannot qualify flings as committed relationships in that they lack an enduring promise to stay together despite circumstances, but we cannot conclude that lack of commitment is part and parcel of brand flings. Lastly, while one-night stands and hookups can be motivated by fears of intimacy and lack of trust in relationship partners, we see no such relationship-aversion analogue driving brand flings. There exist important points of overlap between interpersonal and brand fling relationships, such as the driving role of attractiveness (of the person or the product), the centrality of fun and excitement, and the lack of considered decision making. Still, our analysis supports the general conclusion that conceptualizations borrowed wholesale from the interpersonal realm do not apply directly to brand flings.

Also of note, the importance of socially constructed and enacted identity themes in brand fling relations could hardly have been anticipated from the interpersonal literature. When superimposed on the dimension of transience, our findings help paint the picture of brand relationships forged to serve identities in flux. Just as the symbolic meanings of brands are in constant flux, as social trends come and go for example, consumers too go through phases, identifying themselves at one time with the California surfer culture, and then with urban professionals. Respondents' narratives stressed tensions and contradictions precipitated by the engagement and termination of brand flings: between "blending in" and expressing individuality, between the attempt to create a "cool" image that brings them closer to a particular brand and the frustration with the functional performance of the product that moves them apart from it. It may be argued that these identity contradictions are inherent in brand flings. They are what make flings so exciting . . . and so transient at their core.

The inevitability of the transience of brand flings is probably the most important finding in terms of implications for managers. As mentioned in opening our chapter, marketers may too easily have accepted the assumption that good brand relationships should last. The normative consequences of this assumption include branding programs that increase barriers to exit and disproportionate allocation of resources to consumers who stick around. Consumers engaged in flings thus escape managerial scrutiny, though leverage of the emotionality of this relationship could prove powerful. Judging by the intensity with which some flings are engaged – imagine a transient consumer spending $3,000 on one clothing brand, and at high speed! – fling relationships may be quite profitable as well.

Further research is in order if we are to deepen our understanding and address limitations of this study. The use of different methods such as ZMET (Zaltman and Coulter 1995) and expanded samples is critical in assessing the nature and manifestations of brand flings and probing the identity dynamics at play here. Other avenues for research include testing whether elements of the fling relationship can be added to everyday partnerships to make them more vivid and exciting, or whether marketing programs can engender programmatic cycles of flings.

References

Aggarwal, P. (2004) "The Effects of Brand Relationship Norms on Consumer Attitudes and Behavior", *Journal of Consumer Research*, 31(1): 87–101.

Bartholomew, K. and Horowitz, L.M. (1991) "Attachment Styles among Young Adults", *Journal of Personality and Social Psychology*, 61(2): 226–44.

Bauman, Z. (2001) "Consuming Life", *Journal of Consumer Culture*, 1 (1): 9–29.

Baumeister, R.F. (2002) "Yielding to Temptation: Self-Control Failure, Impulsive Purchasing, and Consumer Behavior", *Journal of Consumer Research*, 28 (4): 670–6.

Clark, M.S. and Mills, J. (1979) "Interpersonal Attraction in Exchange and Communal Relationships", *Journal of Personality and Social Psychology*, 37 (1): 12–24.

Erikson, E.H. (1956) "The Problem of Ego Identity", *Journal of the American Psychoanalytic Association*, 4: 56–121.

Fournier, S. (1998) "Consumers and their Brands: Developing Relationship Theory in Consumer Research", *Journal of Consumer Research*, 24 (4): 343–53.

—— (2009) "Lessons Learned about Consumers' Relationships with their Brands", in D.J. MacInnis, C.W. Park, and J.W. Priester (eds) *Handbook of Brand Relationships*, New York: M.E. Sharpe.

Garcia, J.R. and Reiber, C. (2008) "Hook-up Behavior: A Biopsychosocial Perspective", *Journal of Social, Evolutionary, and Cultural Psychology*, 2 (4): 192–208.

Hill, R.P. (1994) "Bill Collectors and Consumers: A Troublesome Exchange Relationship", *Journal of Public Policy & Marketing*, 13 (1): 20–35.

Hirschman, E.C. (1992) "The Consciousness of Addiction: Toward a General Theory of Compulsive Consumption", *Journal of Consumer Research*, 19 (2): 155–79.

Lehr, A.T. and Geher, G. (2006) "Differential Effects of Reciprocity and Attitude Similarity across Long- Versus Short-Term Mating Contexts", *The Journal of Social Psychology*, 146 (4): 423–39.

McAlister, L. and Pessemier, E. (1982) "Variety Seeking Behavior: An Interdisciplinary Review", *Journal of Consumer Research*, 9 (3): 311–22.

Markus, H. and Nurius, P. (1986) "Possible Selves", *American Psychologist*, 41 (9): 954–69.

Oliver, R.L. (1999) "Whence Consumer Loyalty?" *Journal of Marketing*, 63 (Special Issue): 33–44.

Paul, E.L. (2006) "Beer Goggles, Catching Feelings, and the Walk of Shame: The Myths and Realities of the Hookup Experience", in D.C. Kirkpatrick, S. Duck, and M.K. Foley (eds) *Relating Difficulty: The processes of constructing and managing difficult interaction*, Mahwah, NJ: Lawrence Erlbaum Associates.

Paul, E.L. and Hayes, K.A. (2002) "The Casualties of 'Casual' Sex: A Qualitative Exploration of the Phenomenology of College Students' Hookups", *Journal of Social and Personal Relationships*, 19 (5): 639–61.

Paul, E.L., McManus, B. and Hayes, A. (2000) "'Hookups': Characteristics and Correlates of College Students' Spontaneous and Anonymous Sexual Experiences", *Journal of Sex Research*, 37 (1): 76–88.

Price, L.L. and Arnould, E.J. (1999) "Commercial Friendships: Service Provider–Client Relationships in Context", *Journal of Marketing*, 63 (4): 38–56.

Regan, P.C. (1998) "What If You Can't Get What You Want? Willingness to Compromise Ideal Mate Selection Standards as a Function of Sex, Mate Value, and Relationship Context", *Personality and Social Psychology Bulletin*, 24 (12): 1294–303.

Rook, D.W. (1987) "The Buying Impulse", *Journal of Consumer Research*, 14 (2): 189–99.

Schmitt, D.P. (2005) "Is Short-Term Mating the Maladaptive Result of Insecure Attachment? A Test of Competing Evolutionary Perspectives", *Personality and Social Psychology Bulletin*, 20 (10): 1–23.

Sharma, P., Sivakumaran, B. and Marshall, R. (2010) "Impulse Buying and Variety Seeking: A Trait-Correlates Perspective", *Journal of Business Research*, 63 (3): 276–83.

Stewart, S., Stinnett, H. and Rosenfeld, L.B. (2000) "Sex Differences in Desired Characteristics of Short-Term and Long-Term Relationship Partners", *Journal of Social and Personal Relationships*, 17(6): 843–53.

Zaltman, G. and Coulter, R.H. (1995) "Seeing the Voice of the Customer: Metaphor-Based Advertising Research", *Journal of Advertising Research*, 35 (4): 35–51.

5

EXAMINING CHILDHOOD CONSUMPTION RELATIONSHIPS

Paul M. Connell and Hope Jensen Schau

The past is never dead, it is not even past.

William Faulkner, *Requiem for a Nun*

Popular culture abounds with references to childhood consumption referents in television shows, in books, and on the Internet. While there is a rich and continually evolving literature on children and consumption (cf., John 1999, 2008), the question of how consumption memories from childhood affect individuals into adulthood has only recently begun to be explored (Braun-LaTour and LaTour 2004; Braun-LaTour, LaTour, and Zinkhan 2007), and the question of how consumers draw on symbolic meanings (Holbrook and Hirschman 1982; Levy 1959) of childhood consumption referents as adults has been largely uncharted territory. This dearth of research persists despite the abundance of retro and nostalgic appeals in advertising (Brown, Kozinets, and Sherry 2003) and recent findings that exposure to brands in childhood has a profound effect on brand recognition in adulthood (Ellis, Holmes, and Wright 2010). Because preferences from childhood have the potential to extend into adulthood, and hold commonly held meanings in the popular culture, there are potential implications both for identity practices related to consumption (Epp and Price 2008; Schau and Gilly 2003) as well as intergenerational influences on consumption (Moore, Wilkie, and Lutz 2002). Finally, because children develop knowledge about advertising and its intent incrementally as they age and, particularly at young ages, tend to view advertising uncritically (Brucks, Armstrong, and Goldberg 1988; John 1999, 2008; Moore and Lutz 2000; Moses and Baldwin 2005; Ward, Reale, and Levinson 1972; Ward, Wackman, and Wartella 1977), there is the potential for brand-favorable biases that develop in childhood to extend into adulthood.

Fournier (1998) argues for the metaphor of a personal relationship between consumers and brands, and proposed a typology of fifteen different consumer–brand relationships. However, it was beyond the scope of her research to describe the nuances of each one of these fifteen relationships in detail; doing so could easily create a tome of epic proportions. One of the relationships described by Fournier (1998) is the childhood friendship. Childhood friendships represent those consumer–brand relationships that are rooted in childhood and follow an individual throughout the course of his or her lifetime. Fournier (1998) argues that people preserve these childhood friendships because they are emotionally rewarding, and asserts that they are infrequently engaged and provide feelings of comfort and security of the past self. Childhood friendships can be formed with products that are marketed specifically to children (e.g., Nestlé Quick for Vicki in Fournier's sample), or products that are not necessarily child-related, but remind one of childhood (e.g., Jean's use of Estée Lauder to evoke memories of her mother in Fournier's sample). We build on Fournier's construct by expanding childhood friendships to the constellation of consumption objects and activities that are remembered from childhood. We refer to these as Childhood Consumption Relationships (CCRs) to reflect this expanded positioning and also to avoid confusion with remembered friendships with other people during childhood.

How do CCRs originate, and what makes them so emotionally engaging? In the next section, we first provide a developmental explanation for how CCRs can be an important source of identity in childhood. After that, we follow with a theoretical foundation for how CCRs endure into adulthood, offer a typology of CCRs, and explore their implications for consumer creativity, intergenerational transfer, and public policy.

Origins of Childhood Consumption Relationships

Young children primarily use interests, possessions, and physical attributes in defining their selves rather than using psychological characteristics such as personality traits, as older children and adults tend to do (Damon and Hart 1988; Flavell, Miller, and Miller 2002; Harter 1988, 1999). Because consumption activities and possessions play such an integral part in identity in childhood, we believe that CCRs provide an important link to the past self. In addition, we believe that the way that children understand advertising also plays a role in the strength of the bond formed with CCRs. Developmental research demonstrates that children develop the ability to understand the purpose of advertising and cope with persuasive attempts as they age (John 1999, 2008; Moses and Baldwin 2005). Key milestones of development include recognizing advertisements as distinct from entertainment programming (Ward, Reale, and Levinson 1972), understanding the persuasive intent of advertising (Oates, Blades, and Gunter 2006; Ward, Wackman, and Wartella 1977), and effectively using cognitive defenses against advertising claims (Brucks, Armstrong, and Goldberg 1988). Children develop these abilities incrementally and at different paces, but by certain ages most children have consistently developed the knowledge structures for each of these milestones.

By about age seven, most children can recognize the distinction between advertising and entertainment programming (John 1999, 2008; Ward et al. 1972). However, advertising is still largely viewed uncritically until understanding of persuasive intent develops (Friestad and Wright 1994; John 1999, 2008; Oates et al. 2006; Ward et al. 1977). Development of persuasion knowledge appears to be related to the ability to take the perspective of others and infer their motives (Ward et al. 1977) and is consistently understood by about age eleven (John 1999, 2008; Ward et al. 1977). Even after developing persuasion knowledge, however, children have difficulty in effectively resisting persuasive attempts, and often have to be trained and prompted to defend themselves against advertising (Brucks et al. 1988; John 1999, 2008). By adolescence, children can effectively recognize bias and develop skepticism toward advertising claims (Bousch, Friestad, and Rose 1994; John 1999, 2008).

The goal of marketing communications directed toward children is to persuade them that consumption of what is being advertised will meet wants and needs, just as it is with any other target market. Industry experts recommend creating messages for children that are related to hedonic components of consumption experiences (e.g., Acuff and Reiher 1997). Together, positive affective associations toward advertising objects along with developmental cognitive constraints may make it difficult for young children to utilize persuasion coping behaviors effectively.

Because CCRs are formed during a distinct space in time where brands, consumption activities, and possessions form an integral part of identity and, simultaneously, marketing communications are viewed with lower degrees of skepticism while children respond to messages of fun and excitement, CCRs are likely to be highly affect-laden. Due to the developmental factors mentioned above, we believe that CCRs have unique properties that allow them to foster strong connections with consumers for years, even decades. In addition, we believe these strong connections can persist even in the absence of consumption, and potentially make CCRs highly resistant to negative information about them. In the next section, we offer a theoretical framework for how consumers related to their CCRs throughout their lifetimes.

Childhood Consumption Relationships and their impact on identity throughout the lifespan

At first glance, it may appear that nostalgia is the primary operating influence of CCRs, but nostalgia is usually described as involving a bittersweet longing for the past (Davis 1979; Holbrook 1993; Holbrook and Schindler 1994).

Indeed, nostalgia was originally considered a pathological homesickness (Davis 1979). While CCRs can indeed represent the preference and longing for bygone eras and consumption that are associated with nostalgia, we argue that it is not necessary for nostalgia to be present for an individual to relate to their CCRs. Instead, CCRs could be used to actively construct and maintain identity. Furthermore, we believe that CCRs are formed through the interaction between autobiographical memory and the self-concept.

Because CCRS are situated in the past, we argue that they are housed in the autobiographical memory store. Autobiographical memories are those memories that comprise one's life story, and are retrieved at varying levels of specificity (Conway and Pleydell-Pearce 2000). The most general autobiographical knowledge is related to lifetime periods, and includes relatively large spans of autobiographical time, such as "when I was a child" (Conway and Pleydell-Pearce 2000). McAdams (1985, 2004) refers to these periods as main chapters in the life narrative. General events include repeated scripts such as "watching cartoons" (Conway and Pleydell-Pearce 2000). The most granular memories, event-specific knowledge, are the most analogous to what Tulving (1983) described as episodic memory (Conway and Pleydell-Pearce 2000). Event-specific knowledge involves narratives situated in a particular place and time and with certain people (Conway and Pleydell-Pearce 2000), such as "the time I went to Disneyland with my grandparents."

Autobiographical memories are believed to be of fundamental significance to the self (Conway and Pleydell-Pearce 2000). Indeed, McAdams's life story theory of identity (1985, 2004) asserts that autobiographical stories are not an artifact of identity, but the primary means of construction and maintenance of identity (McAdams 1985, 2004; Singer and Blagov 2004). As a consequence of their importance to the self, autobiographical memories tend to be affect-laden (Conway 2005). We believe symbolic meaning is created through what Conway and Pleydell-Pearce (2000) describe as the self-memory system. The self and the autobiographical memory store interact with one another in a cyclical relationship. That is, the lens through which one sees the world is filtered through the self-concept; this affects perception, encoding of autobiographical memory, and later retrieval.

Goals of the self change over the lifespan (Conway and Holmes 2004; Erikson 1959). As this process unfolds over time, it leaves sets of highly accessible memories that were once highly goal relevant (Singer and Salovey 1993). Highly accessible autobiographical memories are those that had high self-relevance when originally encoded, and the most accessible are those that retain self-relevance at retrieval (Conway and Holmes 2004). For example, identity goals are particularly important in the teen years and early adulthood (Conway and Pleydell-Pearce 2000; Erikson 1959; Habermas and Bluck 2000). Memories formed during this stage of life when identity goals are paramount remain relevant throughout the life cycle and consequently remain highly accessible, second only to the most recent memories. This phenomenon is known as the reminiscence bump (Conway and Pleydell-Pearce 2000; Habermas and Bluck 2000). Habermas and Bluck (2000) assert that, at the same time that identity goals become highly salient, adolescents develop the social and cognitive abilities necessary for constructing a life narrative. Formation of identity for one's multiple selves, including the past self, is at its apex (Conway and Pleydell-Pearce 2000; Erikson 1959; Habermas and Bluck 2000). Because of the developmental constraints on forming identity during childhood mentioned in the previous section (Damon and Hart 1988; Flavell *et al.* 2002; Habermas and Bluck 2000; Harter 1988, 1999), adolescents have little fodder in which to construct an identity related to their past selves other than their CCRs. Indeed, because identity goals are at their height in adolescence, it is possible that CCRs could represent the most critical aspects of one's past self.

Conway and his colleagues ran several studies in which individuals were asked to write down the autobiographical memories they could remember and the age when their memory was encoded (Conway 2005; Conway and Holmes 2004; Conway and Pleydell-Pearce 2000). Coders then determined which psychosocial goals were associated with each memory. In individuals over 35, the most recent memories are the most accessible, with older memories becoming less accessible with the exception of the reminiscence bump, where there is a spike in accessibility.

In the context of CCRs, we are most interested in those memories that are encoded prior to adolescence. Children move through several psychosocial stages in this timeframe. Goals of trust, autonomy, and initiative all are highly salient at various stages prior to age six (Erikson 1959). However, because memories associated with these early-life goals are largely forgotten (Conway and Pleydell-Pearce 2000; Fivush 1997; Flavell *et al.* 2002; Hamond and Fivush 1991; Pillemer and White 1989), they are not likely to play a large role in the memories associated with CCRs. While young children have the ability to remember events and places, especially novel ones, they typically do not elaborate on them unless prompted to do so. Therefore, they tend not to and do not integrate them into a lifetime narrative; thus, most memories encoded at young ages are not retrievable in adulthood (Fivush 1997; Flavell *et al.* 2002; Hamond and Fivush 1991; Pillemer and White 1989). This phenomenon, known as childhood amnesia, is well established in the literature, but there are differing explanations as to why it occurs. Freud (1915) argued that the individual seeks to repress emotional trauma due to Oedipal conflict, whereas Fivush and colleagues (2003) and Nelson (2003) assert that language acquisition plays a key role in the development of autobiographical memory due to enhanced recall resulting from rehearsing and recounting experiences with others. Other researchers claim that development of autobiographical memory is more directly tied to cognitive development, and that young children simply lack the ability to encode and retain long-term episodic memories (Conway 2005). Due to these developmental constraints, we believe CCRs will be founded less on event-specific knowledge and will be more generalized in nature, corresponding more with the general lifetime period of childhood or general events such as eating breakfast (Conway and Pleydell-Pearce 2000).

So what exactly is the critical time period for formation of CCRs? According to Erikson (1959), the critical time period where industry goals (that is, being productive and enjoying it) are at their most salient is approximately between the age of six and the onset of adolescence. As previously mentioned, prior to the age of six, few memories are retained due to childhood amnesia (Conway and Pleydell-Pearce 2000). Therefore, while many children begin watching television and con-suming at a very young age, we argue that prior to the critical age of about six, so few memories are retained that they are not typically where CCRs take root. Similarly, after adolescence commences, when identity goals become important, children decrease consumption of childhood-related objects (Chaplin and John 2005) and begin to show skepticism toward advertising (Bousch et al. 1994), making it an unlikely time to form CCRs. Thus, we propose that CCRs are formed at the stage where industry goals are important, between the ages of six and adolescence. If these goals remain salient (or become salient), then we believe that the memories and CCRs associated with this stage in life will become an impor-tant component of individuals' identity projects, not only as a means of linking to the childhood self, but also as an active part of constructing adult identity.

While we believe that CCRs represent an important link to the past self as well as intersecting Erickson's (1959) industry and identity goals, we also recog-nize that not all CCRs are created equal. That is, some will be more resilient, some may go dormant for a time, and some might even become dissociative. In the next section, we offer a typology of different kinds of CCRs.

A proposed typology of Childhood Consumption Relationships

Based upon multiple research projects involving interviews (Connell and Schau 2007, 2009; Connell, Schau, and Price forthcoming; Schau 2000; Schau and Gilly 2003), netnographic inquiry (Connell and Schau 2007; Schau 2000; Schau and Gilly 2003), projective techniques (Brucks, Connell, and Freeman 2009), and experimental investigations (Connell, Brucks, and Nielsen 2009) with adults (concerning both their current childhood friendship consumption as well as retrospective accounts) as well as children, we have developed a typology of CCRs. This typology is by no means intended to be exhaustive, but rather offered as a starting point for spurring additional research in this substantive area.

Best friends forever (BFFs)

BFFs are the most enduring and beloved CCRs, and comprise most of the exam-ples that Fournier (1998) described. Examples include favorite childhood toys that are carefully maintained, movies or television shows from one's youth that are reconsumed throughout the lifetime (Russell and Levy 2011), or childhood vacation destinations that are visited time and time again. BFFs are those CCRs that were central to one's childhood identity, and remain highly accessible throughout the lifetime due to their centrality to the self-concept. Indeed, because consumption activities and objects form such an integral part of a child's sense of self (Damon and Hart 1988; Flavell *et al.* 2002; Harter 1988, 1999), BFFs are likely to be among the earliest of memories that people have about themselves. Thus, BFFs represent an important and powerful link to the past self.

Forbidden fruits

Most everyone remembers things they were not allowed to consume as a child, such as the movie whose content was not deemed appropriate for children. Unfortunately for parents, prohibiting consumption sometimes leads to an increase in its attractiveness to the child (e.g., Bushman and Stack 1996; Klein 1993; Pechmann and Shih 1999). Thus, when the parent no longer has control over the child, then the child readily consumes. Grandparents sometimes even become the conduit for consumption of forbidden fruits, especially those in the form of food (Lupton 1994). As the child ages and becomes autonomous from his or her parents, forbidden fruits might become guilty pleasures, such as the sugary breakfast cereals that were not allowed in childhood but are readily consumed during the college years. The growth of breakfast cereal cafés such as The Cereal Bowl and Cereality near college campuses demonstrates the power that forbidden fruits can hold.

Spoiled milk

Tastes change, and sometimes objects or practices that were readily and enthusiastically consumed in childhood become aversions in adulthood. Examples include the punch drink that is now just too sweet, the games that now seem dull, and the movies and television shows that are now unwatchable because they are just too silly and juvenile. Spoiled milk might even serve as a means of boosting current self-esteem, as individuals sometimes denigrate past selves as a means of boosting current self-esteem (Wilson and Ross 2001). While people might not wish to engage in consuming the spoiled milk per se, sometimes these CCRs have the potential to provide conduits for consumption that is unyoked to the original context. For example, adults who shudder at the thought of drinking Kool-Aid might become excited at seeing a t-shirt featuring the Kool-Aid Man. Spoiled milk can therefore retain its relevance by providing cultural meaning that can be communicated to peers. For instance, wearing a t-shirt featuring *Jabberjaw*, a cartoon that was popular in the 1970s but obscure today, conveys insider knowledge. The cartoon character is meaningless to those who aren't in the know, but could help to cement bonds among those in the same cohort.

Fine wines

While spoiled milk represents the CCRs that someone once adored but now abhors, fine wines are the converse. Examples include foods that were hated in childhood but come to be loved or films that were not understood in childhood but become favorites in adulthood. To illustrate this point, consider that Rozin and Schiller (1980) observed that children in the Zapotec culture in Mexico grew to love hot, spicy foods. Mothers gradually introduced their children to chili in their foods and over time, and children became accustomed to it and actually preferred spicy food as adults (Rozin and Schiller 1980; Zajonc and Markus 1982). Rozin and Schiller (1980) attributed their observations to the mere exposure effect, whereby repeated exposure leads to increased liking (Zajonc 1968; Zajonc and Markus 1982). While mere exposure might explain some fine wines, we believe there are other roots to these CCRs. Like spoiled milk, fine wines might develop as one's personal tastes change as they mature, which could be independent of repeated consumption of them. Consistent with Belk's (1988) notion that possessions can serve as a bridge to other people, fine wines could also evoke memories of loved ones and provide a pleasant, affect-laden link to these people. For example, several informants in our research indicated that their parent's favorite films have now become their own favorite films, and that these films evoke positive memories of their parents (Connell and Schau 2007, 2009). Thus, the consumption of fine wines might often be more about consuming memories than actual objects or practices.

Nefarious seeds

Nefarious seeds represent a sort of monstrous chimera of forbidden fruits and fine wines. While fine wines can be consumed by children, children eschew them until later in life. Nefarious seeds are forbidden for children to consume, but unlike forbidden fruits, the benefits that are derived from consumption are not salient to the typical child at the time they become familiar with them, but do become salient at a later time in life (Brucks et al. 2009). It is possible that nefarious seeds could be planted in a nonconscious manner from a variety of sources, including marketing activities, personal observation, and portrayals in the media (Dal Cin et al. 2007; Pechmann and Knight 2002; Pechmann and Shih 1999). For example, Brucks and her colleagues (2009) observed that ten-year-old children showed negative attitudes toward smoking, but demonstrated a sophisticated understanding of a number of perceived benefits related to smoking (e.g., social approval, self-esteem, mood management) that are typically not salient to children, but become highly salient during adolescence (Case 1985; Damon and

Hart 1988; Fischer 1980; Harter 1999; Harter 2003; Higgins 1991). These findings provide a potential explanation for why children, who commonly display highly negative attitudes toward smoking (Freeman, Brucks, and Wallendorf 2005), become highly susceptible to starting to smoke just a few years later (Illinois Department of Health 2011; Slovic 2000).

Long lost friends

Sometimes, CCRs are forgotten. Indeed, most of the consumption relationships that we formed in childhood likely fade into the mists of memory as they lose their resonance for us. However, in some cases long lost friends are linked to other associations. If these associations become activated, and the long lost friend is once again made salient, it has the potential to be reignited. Because long lost friends are all linked to childhood, we believe that having children of one's own will make a host of long lost friends salient as nodes in memory are activated, and these spread to other nodes (Collins and Loftus 1975). Activating one long lost friend could even unlock a panoply of other long lost friends if they have multiple associations with one another. For example, imagine a father is watching cartoons with his child. As the cartoons begin to show, he remembers the cartoons from his childhood, as images of *Scooby Doo* come to mind. Thinking of *Scooby Doo* makes him think of his childhood dog, Rex, who was an Irish Setter. Thinking of Rex makes him think of Alpo dog food, which is what Rex ate. He thinks, "Yeah, I should get an Irish Setter, and I would feed him Alpo." And so on . . .

Dearly departed

Sometimes CCRs are fondly remembered but are no longer available. Examples include books that are out of print, products that have failed, or television shows that are no longer being broadcast and are unavailable on video. Fournier (1998) touched on these, as informant Vicky fondly remembers Friendly's Ice Cream, which still exists but is not available where she currently lives. We believe that the dearly departed are the most nostalgic CCRs, because they are fondly remembered and missed (e.g., "they'll never make a show as funny as *The Little Rascals*"). In a sense, the individual experiences a type of grief over the dearly departed (Russell and Schau 2009). They represent a link to a time when things were better, even if it is as trivial as a television show.

Wishful longings

Sometimes people never had the opportunity to experience things in childhood and wished they had. Examples would include the child whose family could never afford to go to Disneyland or who lost her or his favorite doll in a fire.

Wishful longings are different than forbidden fruits in that their consumption was not merely prohibited. Rather, their consumption was impossible due to circumstances beyond the child's (and most likely the family's) control. Wishful longings are also likely to be highly nostalgic due to the yearning associated with them (Davis 1979). In the case of damaged objects, people might go to considerable expense to repair them. For example, the New York Doll Hospital repairs toys at an expense that far exceeds the cost of a new one. In the case of lost objects, a type of mourning could occur (Russell and Schau 2009), or the person might seek replicas that become surrogate, or indexical (Grayson and Shulman 2000) objects. As people age, they might seek to consume wishful longings themselves, or they might strive to make sure their own children are able to consume them (i.e., "I want to give my child what I didn't have"). In extreme cases, the individual might even construct a fantasy world around the wishful longing, where they imagined that consumption actually occurred. In these cases, the wishful longing becomes a type of imaginary friend, which we will discuss next.

Imaginary friends

A large body of research has converged on the finding that memory is malleable and vulnerable to suggestion (Braun 1999; Braun-LaTour, LaTour, Pickrell, and Loftus 2004; Loftus 2003). Thus, imaginary friends represent those CCRs that are believed to be remembered but were never actually consumed. For example, in one study, Braun-LaTour, and her colleagues (2004) exposed participants to two memory-evoking advertisements for Disneyland. One featured Mickey Mouse, a prominent fixture at Disneyland, and the other featured Bugs Bunny, a Warner Brothers character who has never appeared at Disneyland. Both advertisements call on the reader to remember their first visit to Disneyland, where they walked through the gates and shook Mickey Mouse's or Bugs Bunny's hand. Even though the Bugs Bunny condition was an impossible event, a significant number of participants in that condition reported remembering him at Disneyland. The experience felt so real that some participants strongly defended their memories in the study's debriefing, calling on the experimenters to contact their parents for verification. Thus, while imaginary friends never happened, they can be just as important to identity as other CCRs.

Summary

In this section, we have offered a typology of CCRs. These include CCRs that remain active throughout the lifespan or ebb and flow through it. While defining them, we have hinted at both positive and negative implications of these consumption relationships. In the section that follows, we will discuss in detail the implications of CCRs to consumer creativity, intergenerational transfer, and long-term biases.

Implications of Childhood Consumption Relationships

Consumer creativity

As previously mentioned, identity goals become important in adolescence and remain highly self-relevant across the lifespan (Conway and Pleydell-Pearce 2000). In the pursuit of fulfilling identity goals, individuals try to sort out who they are and how they fit into the world (Erikson 1959). This sense of self is constantly evolving. Therefore, the symbolic meaning of CCRs evolves along with the individual. We propose that when these persistent identity goals intersect with industry goals, then CCRs will comprise an important part of an individual's identity projects. Because industry goals represent being productive while having fun, and because many CCRs are pervasively advertised to children (thus resulting in commonly understood cultural meanings), we believe that they can become an important conduit for consumer creativity.

Conducting searches of personal webspace, we found abundant creative uses of CCRs (Connell and Schau 2007). In many of these, people playfully altered narratives that were originally associated with their CCRs. By virtue of the fact that these people posted websites or blogs, all of them were engaging in self-presentation. The Internet represents the ultimate in public presentation, but the individual can do so anonymously and has the freedom of choosing which self to present. Commercial referents can serve as cultural shorthand for public expression of the self (Schau and Gilly 2003). That is, since many CCRs have been ascribed symbolic meaning in popular culture, the author can be reasonably certain that audience members will understand what is being communicated. Jenkins (1992) refers to this type of narrative alteration as textual poaching. This behavior was not limited to written form; many bloggers also created graphic representations of altered story lines. Among them are images of the cereal mascot Booberry sitting in a bar cleverly called Boozeberry's with a martini and a cigar, and a doctored "Turnin' Trix" cereal box featuring images of Barbie prostitutes along with the Trix rabbit. Thus, the semiotics of CCRs becomes goal relevant to adults who commit to text or imagery their creative expression of the symbolic meaning of their CCRs. Consequently, textual poaching engages people in a creative process that enhances sense of self (Belk 1988; Csikszentmihalyi 1996).

However, it seems that consumers appear to ascribe to a belief that certain rules of engagement and reciprocity govern their CCRs. Specifically, while consumers freely alter advertiser narratives in order to playfully produce self-presentations, they often resist organizational efforts to change the narratives of their CCRs. For example, in the 1980s, Kellogg's changed the name of its product Sugar Smacks to Honey Smacks (at a time when many cereal brands were removing the word "sugar" from their names). The mascot for the product was changed from Dig 'Em the Frog, who had been in use for more than a decade, to a bear who was thought to better convey honey flavor. Consumer outcry, however, prompted the resurrection of Dig 'Em less than a year later. Similarly, UNICEF in Belgium had determined that its advertisements featuring images of children in war-torn countries were no longer resonating. It decided to create a shock campaign featuring the Smurfs, characters highly popular with the Belgian public since the 1950s. In the advertising spot, a Smurf village was bombed, killing all residents except for a baby Smurf who was left crying. Indeed, the account manager at the advertising agency that created the campaign stated, "We see so many images that we don't really react anymore. In 35 seconds we wanted to show adults how awful war is by reaching them within their memories of childhood." While the ads were only broadcast late at night when children would be unlikely to see them, the campaign created an outcry among Belgian consumers, forcing UNICEF to pull it. These cases demonstrate the pitfalls that companies can fall into if they fail to recognize the symbolic status of their brand emblems. Thus, while consumers give themselves license to take advantage of CCRs and alter narratives to convey meaning, they appear to expect marketers to maintain the myths that they hold dear. Otherwise, their fodder for self-expression changes meaning.

Intergenerational transfer

In the pursuit of fulfilling generativity goals, highly salient in middle adulthood, individuals become concerned with what they have produced in life (Erikson 1959). For many, bearing and raising children is a way to satisfy these goals. In close relationships, cognitive representations of the distinction between the self and the close other often become fuzzy (Aron, Aron, and Smollan 1992; Aron, Aron, Tudor, and Nelson 1991; Belk 1988). Thus, intergenerational transfer of consumption preferences and practices (Moore *et al.* 2002) could serve as a means of extending the identity portion of one's self (e.g., one's preferences, likes, and activities) into the genetic extension of one's self (i.e., family members). We believe that CCRs are especially prone to intergenerational transfer because of their importance to personal identity as well as because parents exert more control over their sons' and daughters' consumption during the child-rearing years.

If parents and children co-consume CCRs with similar engagement and commitment, then the relationship is synergistic and all parties involved benefit (Connell *et al.* forthcoming; Epp and Price 2008). However, what happens if the child refuses to adopt a parent's beloved CCR or if one child is included in a coalitional identity project with the parent but another child is excluded? For example, in interviews with family members, we observed child resistance to adopting a parent's consumption. In one case, the resulting conflict was so severe that the family resorted to group therapy to rectify the situation (Connell *et al.* forthcoming). We also observed several cases where family members were excluded from participating. In these cases, reactions from informants ranged from feelings of alienation and isolation, to jealousy, and even anger (Connell *et al.* forthcoming). Thus, such discordant elements of intergenerational transfer represent one potential "dark side" of CCRs. In the next section we will explore another potential negative influence of CCRs: long-term biases that originate in childhood and persist into adulthood.

Long-term biases

Previous research has demonstrated that cuing autobiographical memories can attenuate information processing and lead to more favorable evaluations of products (Baumgartner, Sujan, and Bettman 1992; Sujan, Bettman, and Baumgartner 1993). Because autobiographical memories are highly affect-laden (Baumgartner *et al.* 1992; Conway and Holmes 2004; Conway and Pleydell-Pearce 2000; Sujan *et al.* 1993), and because positive affect can lead to judgments toward products that are biased in an affect-congruent direction (Batra and Stayman 1990; Isen and Shalker 1982; Isen, Shalker, Clark, and Karp 1978; Mackie and Worth 1989; Schwarz and Clore 1983), there is significant potential for CCRs to harbor long-term biases toward them. In addition, these biases are likely to be highly resilient to negative information due to the consumer's attachment toward them (Ahluwalia, Burnkrant, and Unnava 2000). Because CCRs were formulated at a stage in life where children absorb marketing messages uncritically (Brucks *et al.* 1988; John 1999, 2008; Moore and Lutz 2002; Moses and Baldwin 2005; Oates *et al.* 2006; Ward *et al.* 1972, 1977), we believe they have special properties to make them especially prone to these effects.

While adults can correct for previous biases held in memory through a process called change in meaning (Friestad and Wright 1994), people must have both the ability and motivation to correct these biases (Wegener and Petty 1995). Research by Connell, Brucks, and Nielsen (2009) provides evidence that high levels of lingering positive affect toward early childhood advertising objects interfere with reconsideration of product beliefs in college-aged participants, even when they are prompted to correct their biases. This finding has important implications for marketers, consumer advocates, and policymakers alike. For example, if fond childhood memories are associated with less healthy food alternatives, adults who do not reconsider their childhood beliefs about these foods might be susceptible to misperceiving the nutritive value of these products for themselves and eventually for their own children many years later. Thus, in a sense, these BFFs can also fall into nefarious seed territory.

Conclusion

In this chapter, we have looked at childhood friendships, one of the many brand relationships described by Fournier (1998), in detail. We have expanded on her original definition and have introduced the term Childhood Consumption Relationships (CCRs). We have also provided theoretical insights into their origins and their impact on identity throughout the lifespan. We proposed our own typology of CCRs and discussed the implications of them in consumer creativity, intergenerational transfer, and potential long-term biases. We believe that much is yet to be learned about CCRs, and hope that further research will help to resolve unanswered questions about these fascinating consumption relationships.

References

Aaker, J.L. (1999) "The Malleable Self", *Journal of Marketing Research*, 36 (1): 45–57.
Acuff, D.S. and Reiher, R.H. (1997) *What Kids Buy and Why*, New York: The Free Press.
Ahluwalia, R., Burnkrant, R.E. and Unnava, H.R. (2000) "Consumer Response to Negative Publicity: The Moderating Role of Commitment", *Journal of Marketing Research*, 37 (2): 203–14.
Aron, A., Aron, E.N. and Smollan, D. (1992) "Inclusion of Other in the Self Scale and the Structure of Interpersonal Closeness", *Journal of Personality and Social Psychology*, 63 (4): 596–612.
Aron, A., Aron, E.N., Tudor, M. and Nelson, G. (1991) "Close Relationships as Including Other in the Self", *Journal of Personality and Social Psychology*, 60 (2): 241–53.
Batra, R. and Stayman, D.M. (1990) "The Role of Mood in Advertising Effectiveness", *Journal of Consumer Research*, 17 (2): 203–14.
Baumgartner, H., Sujan, M. and Bettman, J.R. (1992) "Autobiographical Memories, Affect, and Consumer Information Processing", *Journal of Consumer Psychology*, 1 (1): 53–82.
Belk, R.W. (1988) "Possessions and the Extended Self", *Journal of Consumer Research*, 15 (2): 139–67.
Bousch, D.M., Friestad, M. and Rose, G.M. (1994) "Adolescent Skepticism toward TV Advertising and Knowledge of Advertiser Tactics", *Journal of Consumer Research*, 21 (1): 165–75.
Braun, K.A. (1999) "Postexperience Advertising Effects on Consumer Memory", *Journal of Consumer Research*, 25 (4): 319–52.
Braun-LaTour, K.A. and LaTour, M.S. (2004) "Assessing the Long-term Impact of a Consistent Advertising Campaign on Consumer Memory", *Journal of Advertising*, 33 (2): 49–61.
Braun-LaTour, K., LaTour, M.S., Pickrell, J. and Loftus, E.F. (2004) "How and When Advertising Can Influence Memory for Consumer Experience", *Journal of Advertising*, 33 (4): 7–25.
Braun-LaTour, K., LaTour, M.S. and Zinkhan, G.M. (2007) "Using Childhood Memories to Gain Insight into Brand Meaning", *Journal of Marketing*, 71 (1): 45–60.
Brown, S., Kozinets, R.V. and Sherry, J.F. Jr. (2003) "Teaching Old Brands New Tricks: Retro Branding and the Revival of Brand Meaning", *Journal of Marketing*, 67: 19–33.
Brucks, M., Armstrong, G.M. and Goldberg, M.E. (1988) "Children's Use of Cognitive Defenses against Television Advertising: A Cognitive Response Approach", *Journal of Consumer Research*, 14 (4): 471–82.
Brucks, M., Connell, P.M. and Freeman, D. (2009) "Children's Ascribed Motivations for Smoking Elicited by Projective Questioning", in M.C. Campbell, J. Inman, and R. Pieters (eds) *Advances in Consumer Research, Vol. 37*, Duluth, MN: Association for Consumer Research.

Bushman, B.J. and Stack, A. (1996) "Forbidden Fruit Versus Tainted Fruit: Effects of Warning Labels on Attraction to Television Violence", *Journal of Experimental Psychology: Applied*, 2 (3): 207–26.

Case, R. (1985) *The Mind's Staircase: exploring the conceptual underpinnings of children's thought and knowledge*, Hillsdale, NJ: Erlbaum.

Chaplin, L.N. and John, D.R. (2005) "The Development of Self-Brand Connections in Children and Adolescents", *Journal of Consumer Research*, 32 (1): 119–29.

Collins, A.M. and Loftus, E.F. (1975) "A Spreading-Activation Theory of Semantic Processing", *Psychological Review*, 82 (6): 407–28.

Connell, P.M., Brucks, M. and Nielsen, J. (2009) "Long-term Effects of Advertising to Children on Judgment in Adulthood", in A. Chernev, S.P. Jain, and M. Herzenstein (eds) *Advances in Consumer Psychology, vol. 1*, Potsdam, NY: Society for Consumer Psychology.

Connell, P.M. and Schau, H.J. (2007) "Once Upon a Time: Childhood Relationships and their Role in the Self-Memory System", in S. Borghini, M.A. McGrath, and C.C. Otnes (eds) *European Advances in Consumer Research, volume 8*, Duluth, MN: Association for Consumer Research.

—— (2009) "The Pursuit of Identity Augmentation: Self-Expansion and Self-Extension as Distinct Strategies", in M.C. Campbell, J. Inman, and R. Pieters (eds) *Advances in Consumer Research, Vol. 37*, Duluth, MN: Association for Consumer Research.

Connell, P.M., Schau, H.J. and Price, L.L. (forthcoming) "Intergeneration Transfer of Consumption Practices within Families", in R. Ahluwalia, T.L. Chartrand, and R.K. Ratner (eds) *Advances in Consumer Research, Vol. 39*, Duluth, MN: Association for Consumer Research.

Conway, M.A. (2003) "Cognitive-Affective Mechanisms and Processes in Autobiographical Memory", *Memory*, 11 (2): 217–24.

—— (2005) "Memory and the Self", *Journal of Memory and Language*, 53: 594–628.

Conway, M.A. and Holmes, A. (2004) "Psychosocial Stages and the Accessibility of Autobiographical Memories across the Life Cycle", *Journal of Personality*, 72 (3): 461–78.

Conway, M.A. and Pleydell-Pearce, C.W. (2000) "The Construction of Autobiographical Memories in the Self-Memory System", *Psychological Review*, 107 (2): 261–88.

Csikszentmihalyi, M. (1996) *Creativity*, New York: Harper Perennial.

Dal Cin, S., Gibson, B., Zanna, M.P., Shumate, R. and Fong, G.T. (2007) "Smoking in Movies, Implicit Associations of Smoking with the Self, and Intentions to Smoke", *Psychological Science*, 18 (7): 559–63.

Damon, W. and Hart, D. (1988) *Self-Understanding in Childhood and Adolescence*, New York: Cambridge University Press.

Davis, F. (1979) *Yearning for Yesterday: A sociology of nostalgia*, New York: The Free Press.

Ellis, A.W., Holmes, S.J. and Wright, R.L. (2010) "Age of Acquisition and the Recognition of Brand Names: On the Importance of Being Early", *Journal of Consumer Psychology*, 20 (1): 43–52.

Epp, A.M. and Price, L.L. (2008) "Family Identity: A Framework of Identity Interplay in Consumption Practices", *Journal of Consumer Research*, 35: 50–70.

Erikson, E.H. (1959) *Identity and the Life Cycle*, New York: Norton.

Fischer, K.W. (1980) "A Theory of Cognitive Development: The Control and Construction of Hierarchies and Skills", *Psychological Review*, 87 (6): 477–531.

Fivush, R. (1997) "Event Memory in Early Childhood", in N. Cowan (ed.) *Development of Memory in Childhood*, Hove, UK: Psychology Press.

Fivush, R., Berlin, L.J., McDermott-Sales, J., Mennuti-Washburn, J. and Cassidy, J. (2003) "Functions of Parent–Child Reminiscing about Emotionally Negative Events", *Memory*, 11 (2): 179–92.

Fivush, R. and Reese, E. (1992) "The Social Construction of Autobiographical Memory", in M.A. Conway, D.C. Rubin, H. Spinner, and W.A. Wagener (eds) *Theoretical Perspectives on Autobiographical Memory*, Dordrecht: Kluwer Academic.

Flavell, J.H., Miller, P.H., and Miller, S.A. (2002) *Cognitive Development*, 4th edn, Upper Saddle River, NJ: Prentice Hall.

Fournier, S. (1998) "Consumers and their Brands: Developing Relationship Theory in Consumer Research", *Journal of Consumer Research*, 24 (4): 343–73.

Freeman, D., Brucks, M. and Wallendorf, M. (2005) "Young Children's Understandings of Cigarette Smoking", *Addiction*, 100 (10): 1537–45.

Freud, S. (1915) "Repression", in J. Strachey (ed.) *The Standard Edition of the Complete Psychological Works of Sigmund Freud (vol. 14)*, trans. J. Strachey, London: Hogarth Press.

Friestad, M. and Wright, P. (1994) "The Persuasion Knowledge Model: How People Cope with Persuasive Attempts", *Journal of Consumer Research*, 21 (1): 1–31.

Grayson, K. and Shulman, D. (2000) "Indexicality and the Verification Function of Irreplaceable Possessions: A Semiotic Analysis", *Journal of Consumer Research*, 27 (1): 17–30.

Habermas, T. and Bluck, S. (2000) "Getting a Life: The Emergence of the Life Story in Adolescence", *Psychological Bulletin*, 126 (5): 748–69.

Hamond, N.R. and Fivush, R. (1991) "Memories of Mickey Mouse: Young Children Recount their Trip to Disneyland", *Cognitive Development*, 6: 433–48.

Harter, S. (1988) "The Development of Self-Representations", in N. Eisenberg (ed.) *Handbook of Child Psychology, Vol. 3: Social, emotional, and personality development*, ser. ed., W. Damon, 5th edn, New York: Wiley.

—— (1999) *The Construction of the Self*, New York: Guilford Press.

—— (2003) "The Development of Self-Representations during Childhood and Adolescence", in M.R. Leary and J.P. Tanguy (eds) *Handbook of Self and Identity*, New York: Guilford Press.

Higgins, E.T. (1991) "Development of Self-Regulatory and Self-Evaluative Processes: Costs, Benefit, and Tradeoff", in M.R. Gunner and L.A. Sroufe (eds) *The Minnesota Symposia on Child Development, Vol. 23: Self processes and development*, Hillsdale, NJ: Erlbaum.

Holbrook, M.B. (1993) "Nostalgia and Consumption Preferences: Some Emerging Patterns of Consumer Tastes", *Journal of Consumer Research*, 20 (2): 245–56.

Holbrook, M.B. and Hirschman, E.C. (1982) "The Experiential Aspects of Consumption: Consumer Fantasies, Feelings, and Fun", *Journal of Consumer Research*, 9 (2): 132–40.

Holbrook, M.B. and Schindler, R.M. (1994) "Age, Sex, and Attitude toward the Past as Predictors of Consumers' Aesthetic Tastes for Cultural Products", *Journal of Marketing Research*, 31 (3): 412–22.

Illinois Department of Health (2011) "Healthbeat: Smoking", Online. Available at <http://www.idph.state.il.us/public/hb/hbsmoke.htm> (accessed January 11, 2011).

Isen, A.M. and Shalker, T.E. (1982) "The Effect of Feeling State on Evaluation of Positive, Neutral, and Negative Stimuli: When You 'Accentuate the Positive,' Do You 'Eliminate the Negative?'" *Social Psychology Quarterly*, 45 (1): 58–63.

Isen, A., Shalker, T.E., Clark, M. and Karp, L. (1978) "Affect, Accessibility of Material in Memory, and Behavior: A Cognitive Loop?" *Journal of Personality and Social Psychology*, 36 (1): 1–12.

Jenkins, H. (1992) *Textual Poachers: Television fans and participatory culture*, London: Routledge, Chapman, and Hall.

John, D.R. (1999) "Consumer Socialization of Children: A Retrospective Look at Twenty-Five Years of Research", *Journal of Consumer Research*, 26 (4): 183–213.

—— (2008) "Stages of Consumer Socialization: The Development of Consumer Knowledge, Skills, and Values from Childhood to Adolescence", in C.P. Haugtvedt, P. M. Herr, and F.R. Kardes (eds) *Handbook of Consumer Psychology*, New York: Psychology Press.

Kihlstrom, J.F., Beer, J.S. and Klein, S.B. (2003) "Self and Identity as Memory", in M.R. Leary and J. Price (eds) *Handbook of Self and Identity*, Tangney, NY: Guilford Press.

Klein, R. (1993) *Cigarettes are Sublime*, Durham, NC: Duke University Press.

Levy, S. (1959) "Symbols for Sale", *Harvard Business Review*, 37 (4): 117–24.

Libby, L.K., Eibach, R.P. and Gilovich, T. (2005) "Here's Looking at Me: The Effect of Memory Perspective on Assessments of Personal Change", *Journal of Personality and Social Psychology*, 88 (1): 50–62.

Loftus, E.F. (2003) "Make-Believe Memories", *American Psychologist*, 58: 867–73.

Lupton, D. (1994) "Food, Memory, and Meaning: The Symbolic and Social Nature of Food Events", *Sociological Review*, 42 (4): 664–85.

McAdams, D.P. (1985) *Power, Intimacy, and the Life Story: Personological inquiries into identity*, New York: Guilford Press.

—— (2004) "The Redemptive Self: Narrative Identity in America Today", in D.R. Beike, J.M. Lampinen, and D.A. Behrend (eds) *The Self and Memory*, New York: Psychology Press.

McAlister, A.R. and Cornwell, T.B. (2009) "Preschool Children's Persuasion Knowledge: The Contribution of Theory of Mind", *Journal of Public Policy & Marketing*, 28 (2): 175–85.

Mackie, D.M. and Worth, L.T. (1989) "Processing Deficits and the Mediation of Positive Affect in Persuasion", *Journal of Personality and Social Psychology*, 57 (1): 27–40.

Moore, E.S. and Lutz, R.J. (2000) "Children, Advertising, and Product Experiences: A Multimethod Inquiry", *Journal of Consumer Research*, 27 (2): 31–48.

Moore, E.S., Wilkie, W.L. and Lutz, R.J. (2002) "Passing the Torch: Intergenerational Influences as a Source of Brand Equity", *Journal of Marketing*, 66: 17–37.

Moses, L.J. and Baldwin, D.A. (2005) "What Can the Study of Cognitive Development Reveal about Children's Ability to Appreciate and Cope with Advertising?" *Journal of Public Policy & Marketing*, 24 (2): 186–201.

Nelson, K. (2003) "Self and Social Functions: Individual Autobiographical Memory and Collective Narrative", *Memory*, 11 (2): 125–36.

Oates, C., Blades, M. and Gunter, B. (2006) "Children and Television Advertising: When Do They Understand Persuasive Intent?" *Journal of Consumer Behaviour*, 1 (3): 238–45.

Pechmann, C. and Knight, S.J. (2002) "An Experimental Investigation of the Joint Effects of Advertising and Peers on Adolescents' Beliefs and Intentions about Cigarette Consumption", *Journal of Consumer Research*, 29 (1): 5–19.

Pechmann, C. and Shih, C. (1999) "Smoking Scenes in Movies and Antismoking Advertisements before Movies: Effects on Youth", *Journal of Marketing*, 63 (3): 1–13.

Pillemer, D.B. and White, S.H. (1989) "Childhood Events Recalled by Children and Adults", in H.W. Reese (ed.) *Advances in Child Development and Behavior*, Vol. 21, New York: Academic Press.

Rozin, P. and Schiller, D. (1980) "The Nature and Acquisition of Chili Pepper by Humans", *Motivation and Emotion*, 4: 77–101.

Russell, C.A. and Levy, S.J. (2011) "The Dynamics of Re-Consumption", working paper, American University, Washington, DC.

Russell, C.A. and Schau, H.J. (2009) "The Ties that Bind: Consumer Engagement and Transference with a Human Brand", in M.C. Campbell, J. Inman, and R. Pieters (eds) *Advances in Consumer Research*, Vol. 37, Duluth, MN: Association for Consumer Research.

Schau, H.J. (2000) "Consumer Imagination, Identity and Self-Expression in Computer Mediated Environments", unpublished doctoral dissertation, University of California at Irvine.

Schau, H.J. and Gilly, M.C. (2003) "We Are What We Post? Self-Presentation in Personal Web Space", *Journal of Consumer Research*, 30 (3): 385–404.

Schwarz, N. and Clore, G.L. (1983) "Mood, Misattribution, and Judgments of Well-Being: Informative and Directive Functions of Affective States", *Journal of Personality and Social Psychology*, 45: 513–23.

Singer, J.A. and Blagov, P. (2004) "The Integrative Function of Narrative Processing: Autobiographical Memory, Self-Defining Memories, and the Life Story of Identity", in D.R. Beike, J.M. Lampinen, and D.A. Behrend (eds) *The Self and Memory*, New York: Psychology Press.

Singer, J.A. and Salovey, P. (1993) *The Remembered Self*, New York: The Free Press.

Slovic, P. (2000) "What Does It Mean to Know a Cumulative Risk? Adolescents' Perceptions of Short-Term and Long-Term Consequences of Smoking", *Journal of Behavioral Decision Making*, 13 (2): 259–66.

Sujan, M., Bettman, J.R. and Baumgartner, H. (1993) "Influencing Consumer Judgments Using Autobiographical Memories: A Self-Referencing Perspective", *Journal of Marketing Research*, 30 (4): 422–36.

Tulving, E. (1983) *Elements of Episodic Memory*, Oxford: Clarendon Press.

Ward, S., Reale, G. and Levinson, D. (1972) "Children's Perceptions, Explanations, and Judgments of Television Advertising: A Further Explanation", in E.A. Rubinstein et al. (eds) *Television and Social Behavior, Vol. 4: Television in day-to-day life: patterns of use*, Washington, DC: US Department of Health, Education, and Welfare.

Ward, S., Wackman, D. and Wartella, E. (1977) *How Children Learn to Buy: The development of consumer information-processing skills*, Beverly Hills, CA: Sage.

Wegener, D.T. and Petty, R. (1995) "Flexible Correction Processes in Social Judgment: The Role of Naïve Theories in Corrections for Perceived Bias", *Journal of Personality and Social Psychology*, 68 (1): 36–51.

Wilson, A.E. and Ross, M. (2001) "From Chump to Champ: People's Appraisal of their Earlier and Current Selves", *Journal of Personality and Social Psychology*, 80: 572–84.

—— (2003) "The Identity Function of Autobiographical Memory: Time is on Our Side", *Memory*, 11 (2): 137–49.

Zajonc, R.B. (1968) "Attitudinal Effects of Mere Exposure", *Journal of Personality and Social Psychology*, 9 (1): 1–27.

Zajonc, R.B. and Markus, H. (1982) "Affective and Cognitive Factors in Preferences", *Journal of Consumer Research*, 9: 123–31.

6

MENTAL ACCOUNTING IN CONSUMER–BRAND RELATIONSHIPS

Pankaj Aggarwal and Maggie Wenjing Liu

Mental accounting is the set of operations that people perform to organize, evaluate, and keep track of their activities, especially those related to finances and expenses (Thaler, 1985, 1999). Prior research has shown the value of applying a mental accounting framework not just when people spend money on everyday products but also in the context of money spent on investments (Shafir and Thaler, 2006), financial products (Ranyard *et al.*, 2006), product disposal (Okada, 2001), immediate versus delayed consumption (Gourville and Soman, 1998), windfall spending (Arkes *et al.*, 1994), cross-cultural differences (Arkes *et al.*, 2010), and tracking time (Soman, 2001; Soster, Monga, and Bearden, 2010). In this chapter, we propose yet another important context in which a mental accounting framework is valuable: consumer–brand relationships, that is, to track, monitor, and assess interactions between consumers and brands. We propose that mental accounting framework applied in a consumer–brand relationship context allows us to gain deeper insights into consumer behavior, and offers specific strategic and tactical tools to marketers to improve the returns from their relationships with consumers.

Prior research has noted that brand relationships differ in what they stand for, what they mean to the consumer (Fournier, 1998), and the extent to which they attend to monetary versus non-monetary exchanges (Aggarwal, 2004). Prior research in mental accounting suggests that people adopt a mental accounting framework to track their expenses and benefits as well as to help manage their overall budget (Thaler, 1985). We suggest that people have a separate mental account for each of their brand relationships, and that the interactions between the consumer and the brand can be better understood by applying specific principles of the mental accounting framework. That is, the type of relationship that consumers have with a particular brand would lead to distinct ways in which they mentally account for their interactions, which in turn would result in predictable differences in their behavior. In this chapter, we propose a variety of contexts in which mental accounting principles can be applied to consumer–brand interactions. In particular, we suggest that if a mental accounting framework is adopted in a brand relationship context, then one could expect differences in, for example, the focal "currency" of exchange that is tracked, the length of time of the accounting period (for which the costs and benefits are tracked), the ease or difficulty with which the account may be closed, framing of the relationships, that is, narrow (sub-brands) versus broad (umbrella or corporate brands), as well as unique insights into different types of relationships including exchange versus communal relationships. We explore some of these ideas, and suggest ways in which employing this framework could help us better understand issues such as brand loyalty and brand extension, as well as provide useful research avenues for future investigation helpful for both academics and managers.

This chapter includes the following sections. First, we start with a brief literature review of mental accounting effects with particular relevance to brand relationships. Second, we note key findings from prior research in consumer–brand relationships highlighting the aspects that make them particularly appropriate for the application of mental accounting framework. Next, we propose a framework of mental accounting for consumer–brand relationships in a number of different contexts, and lay out specific testable propositions emanating directly out of an application of this framework. Finally, we discuss the theoretical and managerial implications of this framework and its important contribution to the field of consumer–brand relationships.

Mental accounting: a brief literature review

Thaler (1985, 1999) proposed that individuals follow a cognitive form of bookkeeping to track, record, organize, and interpret their consumption and expenses, and dubbed this cognitive structure as a mental accounting system. The main idea of mental accounting is that people act as though they maintain implicit accounts of their resources, especially financial resources (e.g., time, money, effort, etc.) and mentally book the costs and benefits as a result (Thaler, 1985). The accounting metaphor for payment and consumption provides a means of conceptualizing how consumers allocate their resources. The two main reasons that motivate people to use mental accounts is to constrain spending by budgeting specific limits to certain categories or accounts (Heath and Soll, 1996), and to keep track of transactions: to debit the expense and credit the benefits accruing from a specific consumption (Prelec and Loewenstein, 1998). One result of such transaction-specific mental accounts is that individuals are less likely to abandon products that they may have purchased but not consumed due to an imbalance between the debit and credit in that account (Thaler, 1985).

Prior research on mental accounting underscores that people constantly violate the economic principles of fungibility of money (Thaler, 1985). That is, people assign labels to sources and uses of funds, and are more likely to match the source of funds to its uses. Heath and Soll (1996) develop the notion of mental budget and suggest that these mental budgets act as a device to control against overspending. Thus, in addition to tracking expenses and benefits people also assign expenses to specific accounts and compare them against the budget allotted to that account. Put differently, people are less likely to put money from a pension account to a similar use as money from a checking account or money won in a lottery (Thaler and Shefrin, 1981). Researchers have also noted that people are flexible and self-serving in the allocation of specific expenses to certain accounts. For instance, if the expense is less prototypical of the account (Cheema and Soman, 2006), expenses and benefits are decoupled such as when buying on credit card (Prelec and Loewenstein, 1998). Similarly, costs and benefits are decoupled if the cost is seen as an investment rather than an expense (Kivetz, 1999).

For the purpose of this chapter, we will focus on four kinds of mental accounting effects that we believe are relatively more relevant to consumer–brand relationships, and are briefly reviewed below.

Loss aversion

Loss aversion is a basic principle of prospect theory (Kahneman and Tversky, 1979) and mental accounting (Thaler, 1985, 1999). The main thesis of this principle is that carriers of value are changes in wealth rather than the final state of welfare. Prospect theory suggests that the value function is (1) defined on deviations from the reference point; (2) generally concave for gains and convex for losses, and both gains and losses functions display diminishing sensitivity; (3) steeper for losses than for gains, indicating loss aversion. The S-shaped value function is steepest at the reference point. The reference point itself can be affected by individual expectations or framing of the outcome. People may use one or even multiple reference points when evaluating an outcome.

One important outcome of the shape of the value function is a model that predicts how people combine two or more financial outcomes in a single account. Thus, according to Thaler (1985) the principles of hedonic framing suggest that, in order to maximize utility from joint outcomes, people should:

1) segregate gains (because the gain function is concave);
2) integrate losses (because the loss function is convex);
3) integrate small losses with larger gains (to offset loss aversion); and
4) segregate small gains (silver linings) from larger losses.

Account labels, budgets, and balancing accounts

Another component of mental accounting is "labeling": resources and expenses are grouped into budgets. Each mental account has a label (such as entertainment account, education account, etc.), which is used to track and record costs and benefits related to that activity. Consumers utilize resources differently depending on the way they are labeled. Heath and Soll (1996) suggest that individuals create two types of labels that affect their consumption decisions: they label money for a certain class of products and they label products as relevant for a certain sum of money, that is, mental budget and expense tracking. Further, consumers label not only money but also time and other resources (Heath and Soll, 1996; Thaler, 1985).

Labeling not only facilitates trade-offs between alternative uses of funds, it also acts as an efficient device to control people's spending. Heath and Soll (1996) suggest that expenses are tracked against these budgets, and describe the mental accounting process of tracking expenditure in two stages – booking and posting. An expense must first be noticed and then assigned to a proper account. Failure to notice or book a benefit or a cost will not affect the balance of the mental accounts. Booking depends on attention and memory whereas posting depends on similarity judgments and categorization (Heath and Soll, 1996).

Since resources are generally non-fungible across accounts, individuals often justify their expenses through hedonic posting – posting items in a way that satisfies short-term interests and skirts the mental budgets. Since a more ambiguous expense could potentially be assigned to a different mental account, people are more likely to spend money on items that are less prototypical compared with those that are more prototypical if the budget for that mental account has been exhausted. Interestingly, many small expenses, such as money spent on coffee at work, may typically not be booked. Instead, this expense may be assigned to "petty cash" account which is not subjected to the principles of mental accounting that other accounts have to adhere to.

Currency

One way of framing outcome in mental accounting is to post the costs and benefits in specific currencies. It has been long noted in economics that people focus on the nominal face value of a given amount of money rather than its real value when making economic decisions. Fisher (1928) coined the term "money illusion" to describe this phenomenon. On the other hand, there are many other types of currencies used to post benefits and costs in mental accounts, such as time and effort. Okada and Hoch (2004) demonstrated systematic differences in the way that people spend time versus money. People are willing to spend more time for higher risk, higher return options ex ante. However, this pattern is reversed when they spend money and show the more standard behavior of increasing risk aversion.

The increasing popularity of loyalty programs and related marketing promotions has resulted in the abundance of new currencies (e.g., air miles, bonus points, store dollars) that consumers save, accumulate, budget, and spend much as they do with traditional paper money. Such new currencies have important implications in consumers' value perception. For instance, Dreze and Nunes (2004) found that consumers can be happier with prices presented in different currencies than with prices presented in a standard, single currency.

Decoupling and depreciation

It is a widely held view that consumers consider historic, non-recoverable transaction costs (e.g., time, money, and effort) when deciding on a future course of action, a phenomenon called the "sunk cost effect." Thaler (1985, 1999) argued that a consumer creates a mental account upon entering a transaction as a mechanism for tracking sunk costs. A consumer will close that account upon completing the transaction. By establishing a transaction-specific mental account, the consumer creates a psychological link between the costs and the benefits of a given transaction.

However, recent research suggests that the identification and consideration of such costs may not be straightforward. For example, it is significantly more difficult to identify and consider the cost of a purchased product when that cost is incurred by credit card or check than by cash (Prelec and Loewenstein, 1998; Soman, 2001). In transactions with greater ambiguity (e.g., what costs are paying for what benefits), psychological disassociation, or decoupling, of costs and benefits occurs. Such a disassociation between costs and benefits is labeled "transaction decoupling" (Soman and Gourville, 2001). There is also evidence that the decreased attention to sunk costs can be either cognitively driven (i.e., difficulty in allocating a single cost across multiple benefits) or motivationally driven (i.e., an underlying desire to avoid consumption).

Similarly, a temporal separation of costs from benefits will also make the mental account linkage weaker. When the cost occurs long before the benefit is consumed, a consumer might gradually adapt to a historic cost with the passage of time, thereby decreasing the sunk-cost impact. This process of gradual adaptation to costs is termed "payment depreciation" by Gourville and Soman (1998).

Consumer–brand relationships

The "brand-as-a-person" metaphor has proved to be an immensely valuable framework for both academics and practitioners interested in understanding consumer–brand interactions. Thus, important brand-related constructs such as brand loyalty (Mela, Gupta, and Lehmann, 1997), brand personality (Aaker, 1997; Plummer, 1985), brand image (Keller, 1993), as well as brand commitment (Chaudhuri and Holbrook, 2002) can all be traced back to social interactions in an interpersonal context. Fournier's (1998) seminal work on consumer–brand relationships more overtly exploited this idea of a brand-as-a-person and suggested that people form relationships with brands much like they form relationships with other people in a social domain. She further suggested that these relationships in a consumer–brand context often traverse a large spectrum, and described them using a rich conceptual vocabulary such as friendships, flings, arranged marriages, committed partnerships, secret affairs, courtships, and even enslavements (Fournier, 1998). Subsequently, there has been a great amount of interest in this area of investigation with researchers looking at relationship norms (Aggarwal, 2004), transgressions (Aaker, Fournier, and Brasel, 2004), loss aversion (Aggarwal and Zhang, 2006), self-construal (Swaminathan, Page, and Gurhan-Canli, 2007), anthropomorphism (Aggarwal and McGill, 2007), as well as semantic judgments via functional magnetic resonance imaging (fMRI) studies (Yoon *et al.*, 2006).

Clearly, the importance of branding for marketers cannot be disputed. It has been noted that brands are invaluable for organizations to ensure an ongoing stream of sales and revenue (Smith and Park, 1992) and a greater ability to charge a price premium (Starr and Rubinson, 1978) through increased loyalty from consumers, as well as through increased ability of manufacturers to successfully launch new products under the same brand name as extensions (Aaker and Keller, 1990). Branding also serves as a way to reduce consumers' search costs (Keller, 1993), and is a signal of quality (Zeithaml, 1988). Brands reduce consumers' risks by assuring standardization of products and by better matching expectations and deliveries. Consumers themselves use brands not just to reduce their time and effort in making decisions but also as a means to signal who they are or would like to be seen as (Belk, 1989). In fact, in this fast-changing world of technology and information, it is said that one of the biggest factors distinguishing successful organizations from others would be their ability to create and manage strong brands (McKinsey Company, 2002). Consequently, deeper insights into con-sumer–brand relationships would not be just theoretically interesting, but also provide immense value to managers who are constantly looking for ways to better manage the interface between their brands and consumers.

We propose that each consumer–brand relationship can be construed as a distinct mental account. Further, the principles of mental accounting are appli-cable in a consumer–brand relationship context. In addition, the specific applica-tion of these principles will depend on the particular relationship type. Some unique and insightful hypotheses that emanate out of this framework are testable, and proposed here to encourage future empirical studies in this area. Before we look at these hypotheses, it might be worthwhile to examine the appropriateness of applying a mental accounting framework to consumer–brand relationships.

Why is consumer–brand relationship like a mental account?

Prior research has noted that mental accounts are ways to assign expenses to specific categories (Thaler, 1985). Furthermore, the processes underlying mental accounting map very closely on to processes described in theories of categorization and schema (Henderson and Peterson, 1992). Brands are but one specific instance of categorization: brands are labels that manufacturers use to help consumers perceive the attributes, prices, and other marketing activities related to a particular product or service through a common lens; brands are "labels" that help categorize different aspects of the marketing activities under one name. Consequently, one can expect consumers' interactions with brands to follow the principles of mental accounting.

Consumer–brand relationships, like social relationships, involve multiple interactions over a period of time (Hinde, 1995). The exact type and frequency of these interactions would vary by the type of consumer–brand relationship. Some relationships are very active with interactions taking place on a daily basis (or even more often), such as between a consumer and her/his favorite brand of coffee, for example, Starbucks. Other relationships might be significantly more infrequent but potentially more emotionally intense such as between a woman and her DeBeers jewellery. In each relationship, people keep track of the benefits they receive and the costs they incur in order to assess the well-being of the relationship and the extent to which these relationships actually deliver what people expect them to deliver (e.g., Fong, 2006). The Investment Model of Relationships proposes that individuals are more likely to commit to relationships in which they invest heavily with resources such as time and money (Rusbult and Buunk, 1993), and that individuals remember and track costs and benefits in such relationships. Of course, the exact "currency" of exchange that people track in different relationships would be different, depending on the underlying nature of the relationship (Clark and Mills, 1993). The principles of mental accounting can help us understand what aspect of the interaction people pay attention to, how closely they keep track of their interactions (inputs vs. outcomes, costs vs. benefits), and how often they typically balance the account in different brand relationships.

Finally, like mental accounts, brands too can cut across categories, and can be conceived at a broad or a narrow level. Thus, one could have a mental account for a particular baseball game, or for sports, or for entertainment, and then track and assign specific expenses to these accounts depending on how they are labeled. Similarly, brands can be single product focused, such as Tetley tea, or straddle a wide variety of products and categories, such as Virgin (Drinks, Airline, Music, Mobile, Wines), or could even provide an umbrella under which any number of products can be sold, such as Wal-Mart. Further, brands could be thought of as Camry or Civic, or they could be construed as Toyota (with Camry and Civic under the same umbrella). This flexibility of what underlies a particular brand label maps quite closely to the flexibility that people have when assigning labels to their mental accounts.

For reasons just noted, we believe that consumer–brand relationships are indeed a very good context to apply the mental accounting framework to. In the next section, using the principles of mental accounting, we lay out a variety of specific testable predictions about consumer–brand interactions. Since this is a conceptual paper, we have not actually tested any of these proposed hypotheses. However, we do hope that other researchers will find some of these predictions worthwhile to test empirically in future investigations.

Proposed hypotheses: applying mental accounting principles to examine consumer–brand relationships

Some of the hypotheses based on the different principles and characteristics of mental accounting applied to consumer–brand relationships are noted below.

Currency of exchange

Relationships differ on many dimensions. One primary aspect on which various consumer–brand relationships may differ is the "currency" of exchange. Prior research on interpersonal relationships distinguishes between two types of relationships based on the underlying reason why people give benefits to others: exchange relationships and communal relationships (Clark and Mills, 1993). In exchange relationships, people interact with others to obtain something from them: individuals are concerned with what they receive and what they give. The relationship is based on the principle of quid pro quo, and people prefer to obtain comparable benefits in return for benefits given. In contrast, in communal relationships, people are motivated to take care of their partner's needs out of a genuine concern for their well-being. Individuals prefer to obtain benefits that signify a concern for their unique needs (Clark and Mills, 1993). Repayment of favor is desired relatively more in exchange relationships than in communal relationships (Fong, 2006).

Recent research has noted that consumer–brand interactions may be examined by using the communal versus exchange categorization (Aggarwal, 2004; Aggarwal and Law, 2005; Aggarwal and Zhang, 2006). Aggarwal (2004) finds that relative to consumers in an exchange relationship, those in a communal relationship evaluate the brand and its actions more positively when given a non-comparable benefit in return than when given a comparable benefit in return. As such, we expect that people will attend to, monitor, and report different aspects of the interaction in these two relationship types, and that the currency used to post benefits and costs would also vary. Accounts that are of an exchange nature may have a more transactional currency (such as money, or "value") to assess and track the (economic) value of continuing that relationship. Therefore, people in such a relationship are more likely to track interactions in monetary terms such as the price paid, cost of servicing, and fees, etc., and also more likely to convert all non-monetary transactions into monetary terms. On the other hand, relationships that are of a communal nature are more likely to use a currency that is relatively more personally relevant (such as effort, time, care, emotion, or even "self" identity) to assess and track the health of the relationship. Further, in such relationships, people are more likely to track their own emotions and feelings during and after different brand interactions, resulting in emotions taking on a much greater role in communal than in exchange relationships.

Activities in the accounts

Opening of account

Typically, mental accounts are opened as soon as people buy something. Prior research suggests relationships between consumers and brands can sometimes take the form of "flings" (see Fournier, 1998, for one such relationship between the consumer Vicki and her trial-size shampoo brands). Such relationships are charged with high emotion, and are based more on infatuation rather than on commitment. It can be hypothesized that the mental account for such a brand relationship might be opened even before the brand is purchased. In fact, just the initial infatuation may be sufficient to open the account; subsequent fantasizing about such brands may create a stream of benefits being accrued. Consequently, we propose that the purchase of the brand would not be a prerequisite for the relationship to start reaping benefits. On the other hand, mental accounts for most other relationship types may be opened only once the actual brand purchase has taken place.

Balancing accounts

As is the case for financial accounts, consumers practice hedonic posting to balance their brand accounts to justify their costs. Although consumers would generally like to see all relationship accounts being balanced, they may have a relatively greater tolerance for negative imbalance for accounts that are not evaluated on an everyday basis. Consumers may also have a greater tolerance for negative imbalance when the account balance is harder to calculate or when the account currency is harder to monitor (effort put in rather than money spent). Therefore, we suggest that exchange relationship accounts would be more likely to be balanced while communal relationship accounts would be more likely to be left unbalanced.

We also suggest that different types of relationship accounts can change consumers' methods of booking the costs and benefits in that account. For instance, in an exchange brand relationship (based on quid pro quo), consumers are more likely to aggregate the "net" value of brand interactions rather than tracking the gains separately from the losses (Aggarwal and Zhang, 2006). However, in a communal brand relationship (based on concern for others' needs), consumers are more likely to track the gains separately from the losses. Thus, we propose that when booking brand interactions, consumers are more likely to integrate costs and benefits in an exchange relationship but more likely to segregate them in a communal relationship.

Closing of accounts

One related issue is the duration of time for which mental accounts for some brand relationships are kept open. Certain accounts, such as childhood friendships, committed partnerships, and best friendships (Fournier, 1998), are likely to remain open even if there are long periods of inactivity in those accounts. Such relationships are less likely to be closed due to "entropy," since the emotions in such relationships are always likely to linger on beyond the actual transactions. On the other hand, brand relationships such as marriages of convenience, casual friendships, and even kinships are likely to be closed if there is little activity in these accounts for an extended period of time. Thus, people are more likely to cancel a store credit card if the store is no longer conveniently located than they are to cancel a frequent flyer membership to an airline like Virgin Atlantic, if they have fond memories of the one time they used the airline. One reason why relationships that have strong residual emotions may never be closed is because the consumers may secretly be hoping to get together with the brand again sometime in the future.

Similarly, mental accounting principles suggest that people like to keep track of the debits and credits in the account to assess whether the accounts are in balance or not. The frequency with which people assess the account's balance would also depend on the type of relationships. Some relationships are "short-term" where the balancing of the costs and benefits needs to be done fairly swiftly, since the relationship is likely to come to an end soon. Other relationships are "long-term" and are expected to last for years, obviating the need to balance the account early on. In fact, such accounts may go on almost indefinitely without there being a need to "check" the balance, as might be the case for relationships such as committed partnerships, and even secret affairs.

The relationship between educational institutions and their alumni is an interesting case in point, especially for those alumni who end up donating significant amounts to their alma mater. One could ask the question as to why some people donate so generously while others don't ever look back. Mental accounting principles can shed some light on this immensely important issue. People who do extremely well in life and attribute that success to their graduating school may "credit" a large value to their educational institution. The tuition that they paid in the past may come nowhere close to the contribution they assign to the school in their mental account. People find it very hard to live in an eternal debt of others. Further, the relationship seems so important (and probably nostalgic) yet inactive that people may yearn to rejuvenate it. By being a significant donor, they pay back the debt to the school; and by getting the school to acknowledge their contribution, the dormant and almost non-existent relationship with the school would be re-energized.

Account labels

One important feature of mental accounts is that each account has a label (such as entertainment account, education account, etc.) which is used to track and record costs and benefits related to that activity. We suggest that brand relationships too would have a "value" label associated with that relationship. Brand positioning is a key construct in marketing, which refers to how consumers perceive the brand in their mind space. Managers are constantly striving to create a distinct positioning for their brand, such that their brand is uniquely associated with something that is of crucial importance to the consumer. We suggest that one of the biggest factors driving the label that is given to a brand relationship account is the brand's positioning.

These brand relationships labels are important since they not only help track the costs and benefits, they may also guide people in their decisions when interacting with the brand. For example, when interacting with a brand that is seen as a "gift" brand (such as Hallmark cards) people may be less likely to evaluate the greeting card based on price than on the emotiveness of the message in it. Similarly, when eating out at a "value for money" buffet-style restaurant like Mandarin Chinese Cuisine people may find themselves holding back on tipping the waiter generously since the label attached to the account suggests attending to monetary factors. Conversely, the same person may find it significantly less painful to give a much larger tip in a "stylish and classy" restaurant like Sassafraz located in an upscale neighbourhood of Toronto, and known to be frequented by Hollywood stars.

Transaction utility vs. acquisition utility

One consequence of the type of label given to the account may be the difference in the relative importance of transaction utility from interactions with the brand versus its acquisition utility. Thaler (1985) gives the example of the beer on the beach and shows that people care about the value of the deal or the transaction utility that they derive from a particular exchange. We suggest that the degree to which people would care about deriving transaction utility would vary by the account label attached to that relationship. If the account label is one of "value for money," people may be disproportionately sensitive to it and insist on getting a good deal out of transaction with the brand. On the other hand, if the account label carries a lot of symbolic meaning (e.g., "long-term friends" account), then the relative weight of acquisition utility might be significantly larger relative to transaction utility.

Malleability of accounting principles

The term malleable mental accounting describes situations where consumers have flexibility in assigning ambiguous expenses to different mental budgets or create mental accounts to accommodate ambiguous expenses (Cheema and Soman, 2006; Read, Loewenstein, and Rabin, 1999). Given the opportunity and ambiguity in the situation, people may assign a particular expense to one or another account depending upon the final outcome they are motivated to achieve. Consumer–brand relationships, similarly, are likely to exhibit malleability of mental accounting principles.

Extra credits, fewer debits

Certain brand relationships, such as committed partnerships and courtships, are very dear to the consumer who may be motivated to see the relationship partner in a positive light. Consequently, we believe that consumers may intentionally overlook debiting the brand with "add-on" costs such as delivery charges, installation fees, and even sales taxes so that the account's debit side of the equation does not appear to be too negative. Conversely, in keeping with prior work (Rusbult and Buunk, 1993), the positive features of the brand may be overweighted, giving it "undue" credit for the benefits provided, thereby ensuring that the brand's account shows a surplus.

Pennies-a-day

Another example of malleability of accounting principles is to label costs incurred on certain brands as 'pennies-a-day' such that these expenses are never formally logged in (Gourville, 1998). This may be the case for relationships that are akin to secret affairs, as was noted by Fournier (1998), when Karen sneaks Tootsie Pops at work. By not accounting for these expenses, the consumer may be successful in keeping up the pretence that there is "nothing going on" between her and the brand!

Relabeling

It is also conceivable that brand relationship labels might create conditions for flexible mental accounting principles. Take, for example, consumers' relationships with a brand like the local zoo. If the relationship with the brand is one of committed partnership such that the consumer has purchased an annual membership, it is possible that the brand which was initially seen as an entertainment brand may be relabeled as "education" to reflect a more serious and deeper basis for the relationship, being based on education rather than the more frivolous fun aspect of the brand. Such a relabeling may be less likely for non-committed consumers, such as occasional visitors, who may not be motivated to give any deeper meaning to their relationship.

Non-topical accounting

Malleability may also be uncovered in contexts of negative brand interactions. For certain brands, consumers may be more likely and willing to overlook the brand's transgressions since they have a strong emotional bond and would not like that bond to be weakened. These consumers may be motivated to ignore the brand's topical indiscretions, and instead may bring to mind all the past positive experiences with the brand to counter its negative effect. On the other hand, for some other brand relationships, consumers may not be motivated to look beyond the immediate instance of the brand's transgression, thereby more closely following the mental accounting practice of treating these accounts as topical accounts. This unique prediction would shed some interesting light on the concept of brand equity and its temporal strength.

Narrow vs. broad brand accounts

Mental accounts for consumer–brand relationships can be narrow or broad, that is, the accounts could be brand-specific, category-specific, or even company-specific. The accounts could even be need-specific. The perceived breadth of a relationship can significantly affect a consumer's decisions. Thus, if consumers frame their account narrowly (e.g., with a sub-brand Corolla), it may become harder for the company (Toyota) to persuade its consumers to transfer the costs and benefits from that account to another account (such as the Camry or RAV4). On the other hand, if consumers frame the account broadly (e.g., at a larger family level), the costs and benefits from all the sub-brands might easily all go into the "Toyota" account. This would have significant implications for brand extensions and for life-time value assessment of consumers.

Temporal framing of brand accounts

The breadth of mental accounts for consumer–brand relationships can also be malleable temporally, that is, the brand accounts can be one-offs, short-term, long-term, or even multi-generational. Gourville (1998) proposes that temporal framing of an exchange can systematically affect the nature of the expenses that a consumer retrieves for the purpose of comparison. When consumers deal with a brand over the years, it is likely that they include interactions with both old and new generations of the product in one brand account. This way a temporally longer account is more likely to be balanced than two separate accounts of shorter duration. For instance, if a consumer feels that he or she overpaid when purchasing an iPhone 3G but got a good deal when purchasing the iPhone 4, it is easier for the consumers to balance his or her iPhone brand account by including both generations of products rather than having one account in the black and one in the red.

Temporal framing of brand accounts can also include booking both the new and old products in one account when making the upgrading decisions. Okada (2001) suggests that consumers consider the "mental book value" of the old product when getting the chance of upgrading to a new, high-quality product. Okada (2010) proposes that upgrade decisions differ from new purchase decisions because they are hindered by the psychological costs associated with the costs of the old product.

Sunk costs, decoupling, and depreciation

Similar to financial resources (time, money, and effort), investments in relationships can become "sunk costs" when the investments become historic and non-recoverable (Coleman, 2009; Little and Little, 2009). The sunk cost effect can happen in both interpersonal relationships (e.g., Coleman, 2009) and human–product relationships (Little and Little, 2009). The Investment Model (Rusbult, 1983) uses three factors as determinants of relationship commitment: satisfaction, quality of alternatives, and prior investment. The model distinguishes between extrinsic investment (e.g., shared friends or possessions in a relationship) and intrinsic investment (e.g., resources such as time, money, or effort put into a relationship) with intrinsic investments being seen as sunk costs (Coleman, 2009; Rusbult, 1983). Investment Model research indicates that sunk costs are one of the important factors that affect future commitment to the relationship (Coleman, 2009).

When the consumer–brand interactions have certain ambiguity as to what benefits are due to what costs, decoupling or disassociation between costs and benefits can happen in the brand accounts (Soman and Gourville, 2001). We suggest that decoupling and depreciation effects are more likely to occur in some types of brand relationships than in others. For instance, Aggarwal (2004) shows that consumers in an exchange brand relationship prefer to receive a benefit comparable to the one they give to the brand (e.g., monetary payment for answering questionnaires) while consumers in a communal brand relationship are more likely to evaluate the brand positively when receiving a non-comparable benefit (e.g., a free fitness class for answering a questionnaire). While consumers in an exchange relationship compare what they get back as reciprocal repayment from the brand with their own costs (Fong, 2006), those in a communal relationship are more likely to ignore prior (sunk) costs when assessing the benefits they receive from the brand. Therefore, we propose that decoupling and depreciation effects are more likely to occur in communal relationship accounts than in exchange relationship accounts.

Risky behaviors

Certain brand relationships are likely to promote risk aversive behavior from consumers while other relationships are more likely to promote risk seeking. For example, relationships such as committed partnerships and even arranged marriages (Fournier, 1998) may be characterized by lower levels of risk seeking. Consumers may perceive such relationships with brands to be exclusive, and any desire to seek out other options (i.e., trying other brands) may be seen as "cheating" in the existing relationship. For example, a consumer who is a committed Blackberry consumer may try to downplay the advantages of the latest model of the iPhone, lest she or he be tempted by it, or worse, be seen as betraying the brand. On the other hand, relationships such as friendships and flings have a certain level of excitement integral to them, and interactions with multiple partners may not be seen as cheating. In fact, in some sense, multiple partners are desirable in such relationships. Such a characterization of a relationship is more likely to promote risky behavior, such as variety seeking and trying out new flavors. As a corollary of this hypothesis, we suggest that committed partnerships and arranged marriages are more likely to be driven by a prevention goal while friendships and flings are more likely to be driven by a promotion goal.

Losses vs. gains

Endowment effect

Prior research has noted that people are generally loss averse (Kahneman and Tversky, 1979). Further, the rich stream of research on endowment effect suggests that loss aversion results in people asking for a significantly larger amount to give up an item they own than they are willing to pay for if they did not own it (Kahneman, Knetch, and Thaler, 1990). More recent work on consumer–brand relationships has shown that people show greater endowment effect in a communal than in an exchange relationship (Aggarwal and Zhang, 2006). We suggest that consumers' differential sensitivity to losses and gains will go beyond communal and exchange relationships. For example, we propose that relationships like kinships, casual friendships, and arranged marriages are likely to show lower levels of endowment effect compared with relationships like childhood friendships, committed partnerships, or courtships, driven primarily by the difference in the level of temporal and/or emotional investment.

Losses first or losses later

Another important finding from Prospect Theory (Kahneman and Tversky, 1979) is that losses loom larger than gains. In other words, the perceived pain of losing something is greater than the perceived joy of gaining an equivalent thing. An interesting twist to this result in the context of brand relationship relates to the sequencing of losses and gains. If losses loom larger than gains, then it is possible that for some relationships the pain of the loss would be greater if the loss-related interaction is experienced first, while for other relationships the pain would be greater if the gain-related interaction is experienced first in a sequence of brand interactions that involves loss and gain. That is, we suggest that perceived pain from a loss–gain sequence may be moderated by the type of relationship. Relationships that are past focused (such as childhood friendships, arranged marriages) may give greater weight to losses first; on the other hand, relationships that are future focused (such as courtships and flings) may give greater weight to losses later.

Dummy accounts

Finally, we think that there are some relationships in which consumers may not be quite happy with their brand partner and may be looking for a way out of the relationship. For example, in relationships that are seen as enslavements, consumers may feel that they do not have any other alternatives available. Such consumers may set up dummy accounts in order to track the competitor's brand – the brand that they would ideally like to have a relationship with. Such consumers may be actively seeking out information from competitive brands to switch their allegiance at the first opportunity they get. For instance, a consumer who bought an eBook reader such as Amazon Kindle may keep an eye on news about all the different features and prices of an iPad to assess the right time to get out of their current relationship.

Theoretical and managerial implications

In this chapter, we propose that the application of the principles of mental accounting to consumer–brand relationships is not just appropriate and interesting, but that it can also be used to generate a wide variety of hypotheses that would lead to some very insightful findings about consumer behavior. We have laid out a number of specific testable hypotheses that we believe would enrich our understanding of consumer–brand relationships as well as apply the mental accounting framework to a fairly novel context. By using these mental accounting principles we can go beyond the broad brushstrokes with which most prior marketing researchers have studied consumer–brand relationships. There are a number of insightful relationship-specific predictions made in this chapter that would help us better understand the multitude of facets on which consumer–brand relationship types differ from one another. The mental accounting framework helps us peel away some of those differences. Further, these principles are also very informative about the drivers and processes underlying consumer–brand interactions. We believe that this framework offers a vast array of possible avenues for consumer behavior researchers to explore in the future.

The application of this framework to better understand consumer–brand relationships has significant implications for marketing practitioners as well. By giving insights on the mechanism that motivates people to behave and feel the way they do when interacting with brands, this framework can help brand managers to fine tune their marketing strategies for maximum impact and to build stronger ongoing relationships with their consumers. Specific tactics on cost cutting, brand positioning, brand extensions, brand equity, as well as on how best to handle instances of perceived brand transgressions, all emanate directly out of seeing consumer–brand relationships through the mental accounting lens.

Although marketing researchers have generally stopped questioning the validity of applying the relationship metaphor to consumer–brand interactions, we think that extant research on brand relationships has only scratched the surface. The application of a mental accounting metaphor to consumer–brand relationships offers a great opportunity to explore the complex yet fascinating aspects of consumer–brand interactions. This framework can open a few more doors into the mesmerizing world in which consumers make friends and enemies, partners and buddies with brands, committing to them, courting them, having flings and secret affairs, and living under the same roof in arranged marriages. While this chapter has been written in the spirit of exploration, the true thrill of unearthing new knowledge about consumers awaits empirical validation of some of our proposed ideas.

References

Aaker, D.A. and Keller, K.L. (1990) "Consumer Evaluations of Brand Extensions", *Journal of Marketing*, 54 (1): 27–41.

Aaker, J.L. (1997) "Dimensions of Brand Personality", *Journal of Marketing Research*, 34: 347–56.

Aaker, J., Fournier, S. and Brasel, S.A. (2004) "When Good Brands Do Bad", *Journal of Consumer Research*, 31: 1–16.

Aggarwal, P. (2004) "The Effects of Brand Relationship Norms on Consumer Attitudes and Behavior", *Journal of Consumer Research*, 31: 87–100.

Aggarwal, P. and Law, S. (2005) "Role of Relationship Norms in Processing Brand Information", *Journal of Consumer Research*, 32: 453–65.

Aggarwal, P. and McGill, A.L. (2007) "Is that Car Smiling at Me: Schema Congruity as a Basis for Evaluating Anthropomorphized Products", *Journal of Consumer Research*, 34 (4): 468–79.

Aggarwal, P. and Zhang, M. (2006) "The Moderating Effect of Relationship Norm Salience on Consumers' Loss Aversion", *Journal of Consumer Research*, 33: 413–19.

Arkes, H.R., Hirshliefer, D., Jiang, D. and Lim, S.S. (2010) "A Cross-Cultural Study of Reference Point Adaptation: Evidence from China, Korea, and the US", *Organizational Behavior and Human Decision Processes*, 112: 99–111.

Arkes, H.R., Joyner, C.A., Pezzo, M.V., Nash, J.G., Siegel-Jacobs, K. and Stone, E. (1994) "The Psychology of Windfall Gains", *Organizational Behavior and Human Decision Processes*, 59: 331–47.

Belk, R. (1989) "Extended Self and Extending Paradigmatic Perspective", *Journal of Consumer Research*, 15 (1): 129–32.

Chaudhuri, A. and Holbrook, M.B. (2002) "Product-Class Effects on Brand Commitment and Brand Outcomes: The Role of Brand Trust and Brand Affect", *Journal of Brand Management*, 10 (2): 33–58.

Cheema, A. and Soman, D. (2006) "Malleable Mental Accounting: The Effect of Flexibility on the Justification of Attractive Spending and Consumption Decisions", *Journal of Consumer Psychology*, 16: 33–44.

Clark, M.S. and Mills, J. (1993) "The Difference between Communal and Exchange Relationships: What it is and is Not", *Personality and Social Psychology Bulletin*, 19: 684–91.

Coleman, M.D. (2009) "Sunk Cost and Commitment to Dates Arranged Online", *Current Psychology*, 28: 45–54.

Dreze, X. and Nunes, J.C. (2004) "Using Combined-Currency Prices to Lower Consumers' Perceived Cost", *Journal of Marketing Research*, 41(1): 59–73.

Fisher, I. (1928) *The Money Illusion*, New York: Adelphi.

Fong, P.S. (2006) "The Impact of Favor-Elicited Feelings on Reciprocity Behavior across Time", dissertation, Hong Kong University of Science and Technology.

Fournier, S. (1998) "Consumers and their Brands: Developing Relationship Theory in Consumer Research", *Journal of Consumer Research*, 24: 343–73.

Gourville, J.T. (1998) "Pennies-a-Day: The Effect of Temporal Reframing on Transaction Evaluation", *Journal of Consumer Research*, 24(4): 395– 409.

Gourville, J.T. and Soman, D. (1998) "Payment Depreciation: The Behavioral Effects of Temporally Separating Payments from Consumption", *Journal of Consumer Research*, 25 (2): 160–75.

Heath, C. and Soll, J.B. (1996) "Mental Budgeting and Consumer Decision", *Journal of Consumer Research*, 23 (1): 40–52.

Henderson, P.W. and Peterson, R.A. (1992) "Mental Accounting and Categorization", *Organizational Behavior and Human Decision Processes*, 51 (1): 92–117.

Hinde, R. (1995) "A Suggested Structure for a Science of Relationships", *Personal Relationships*, 2 (1): 1–15.

Kahneman, D., Knetch, J.L. and Thaler, R.H. (1990) "Experimental Tests of the Endowment Effect and the Coase Theorem", *Journal of Political Economy*, 98: 1325–48.

Kahneman, D. and Tversky, A. (1979) "Prospect Theory: Analysis of Decision under Risk", *Econometrica*, 47 (2): 263–91.

Keller, K.L. (1993) "Conceptualizing, Measuring, and Managing Customer-Based Brand Equity", *Journal of Marketing*, 57 (1): 1–22.

Kivetz, R. (1999) "Advances in Research on Mental Accounting and Reason-Based Choice", *Marketing Letters*, 10 (3): 249–66.

Little, D. and Little, A. (2009) "Looking for a Reason: Escalation in New Product Development", *Journal of Applied Management and Entrepreneurship*, 14: 82–101.

McKinsey Company (2002) "Building Strong Brands Better, Faster, Cheaper", Online. Available at <http://marketing.mckinsey.com> (accessed October 7, 2009).

Mela, C.F., Gupta, S. and Lehmann, D.R. (1997) "The Long-Term Impact of Promotion and Advertising on Consumer Brand Choice", *Journal of Marketing Research*, 34 (2): 248–61.

Okada, E.M. (2001) "Trade-Ins, Mental Accounting, and Product Replacement Decisions", *Journal of Consumer Research*, 27 (4): 433–47.

—— (2010) "Upgrades and New Purchases", *Journal of Consumer Research*, 37: 75–84.

Okada, E.M. and Hoch, S.J. (2004) "Spending Time versus Spending Money", *Journal of Consumer Research*, 31 (2): 313–24.

Plummer, J.T. (1985) "How Personality Makes a Difference", *Journal of Advertising Research*, 24 (6): 27–31.

Prelec, D. and Loewenstein, G. (1998) "The Red and the Black: Mental Accounting of Savings and Debt", *Marketing Science*, 17 (1): 4–29.

Ranyard, R., Hinkley, L., Williamson, J. and McHugh, S. (2006) "The Role of Mental Accounting in Consumer Credit Decision Processes", *Journal of Economic Psychology*, 27 (4): 571–88.

Read, D., Loewenstein, G. and Rabin, M. (1999) "Choice Bracketing", *Journal of Risk and Uncertainty*, 19: 171–97.

Rusbult, C.E. (1983) "A Longitudinal Test of the Investment Model: The Development (and Deterioration) of Satisfaction and Commitment in Heterosexual Involvements", *Journal of Personality and Social Psychology*, 45: 101–17.

Rusbult, C.E. and Buunk, B.P. (1993) "Commitment Processes in Close Relationships: An Interdependence Analysis", *Journal of Social and Personal Relationships*, 10: 175–204.

Shafir, E. and Thaler, R.H. (2006) "Invest Now, Drink Later, Spend Never: On the Mental Accounting of Delayed Consumption", *Journal of Economic Psychology*, 27: 694–712.

Smith, D.C. and Park, C.W. (1992) "The Effects of Brand Extensions on Market Share and Advertising Efficiency", *Journal of Marketing Research*, 29: 296–313.

Soman, D. (2001) "Effects of Payment Mechanism on Spending Behavior: The Role of Rehearsal and Immediacy of Payments", *Journal of Consumer Research*, 27 (4): 460–75.

Soman, D. and Gourville, J.T. (2001) "Transaction Decoupling: How Price Bundling Affects the Decision to Consume", *Journal of Marketing Research*, 38 (1): 30–45.

Soster, R.S., Monga, A. and Bearden, W.O. (2010) "Tracking Costs of Time and Money: How Accounting Periods Affect Mental Accounting", *Journal of Consumer Research*, 37 (4): 712–21.

Starr, M.K. and Rubinson, J.R. (1978) "A Loyalty Group Segmentation Model for Brand Purchasing Simulation", *Journal of Marketing Research*, 15: 378–83.

Swaminathan, V., Page, K.L. and Gurhan-Canli, Z. (2007) "'My' Brand or 'Our' Brand: The Effects of Brand Relationship Dimensions and Self-Construal on Brand Evaluations", *Journal of Consumer Research*, 34 (2): 248–59.

Thaler, R.H. (1985) "Mental Accounting and Consumer Choice", *Marketing Science*, 4: 199–204.

—— (1999) "Mental Accounting Matters", *Journal of Behavioral Decision Making*, 12 (3): 183–206.

Thaler, R.H. and Shefrin, H.M. (1981) "An Economic Theory of Self-Control", *Journal of Political Economy*, 89 (2): 392–406.

Yoon, C., Gutches, A.H., Feinberg, F. and Polk, T.A. (2006) "A Functional Magnetic Resonance Imaging Study of Neural Dissociations between Brand and Person Judgments", *Journal of Consumer Research*, 33 (1): 31–40.

Zeithaml, V. (1988) "Consumer Perceptions of Price, Quality, and Value: A Means–End Model and Synthesis of the Evidence", *Journal of Marketing*, 52: 2–22.

PART II

Understanding Consumer–Brand Relationship Bonds

Brand love and other strength indicators

7

LOVE ACTUALLY? MEASURING AND EXPLORING CONSUMERS' BRAND LOVE

Daniel Heinrich, Carmen-Maria Albrecht, and Hans H. Bauer

Nowadays marketers are highly interested in creating and maintaining relationships with their customers. While marketing research has a long tradition of exploring relationships in the business-to-business context (e.g., ties between manufacturer and supplier), attention has expanded to relationships between consumers and their brands (Fournier 1998) in recent decades. While management-oriented literature (e.g., the idea of lovemarks) has already revealed emotions as a core concept for establishing and upholding strong bonds between a consumer and a brand (Roberts 2005, 2006), academic research on this topic is still in its infancy. There are hardly any studies that have focused on consumer–brand love relationships (Ahuvia 1993; Albert, Merunka, and Valette-Florence 2008; Bauer, Heinrich, and Albrecht 2009; Carroll and Ahuvia 2006) in detail so far. Thus, the current study intends to contribute to filling this research gap by exploring the concept of brand love.

More precisely, the main objective of this study is to conceptualize and operationalize the construct of consumers' brand love by drawing on the concept of love from interpersonal psychology as well as on studies carried out in the consumer–object context. In order to emphasize the relevance of consumers' brand love to marketers, we link the construct to two marketing-related variables, namely price premium and the willingness to forgive.

Conceptualization and measurement of brand love

The concept of love

Love can refer both to a social relationship and to an emotional state. When people, for instance, speak of lovers, then the love relationship between two individuals is emphasized. When people speak of feelings of love, love is regarded as an emotion and is understood as a process or a momentary state that can also change over time and take on different forms (Lazarus 1991).

In social psychology, there are several theories (e.g., Freud 1922; Lee 1977; Maslow 1962; Reik 1944) that focus, amongst others, on the concept of love between individuals. One of the theories most often cited in literature that explicitly deals with love is Sternberg's (1986, 1987, 1988, 1997) triangular theory of love.

According to Sternberg, interpersonal love can be interpreted as a combination of three different components, namely intimacy, passion, and decision/commitment. Intimacy, the "warm" component, refers to "feelings of closeness, connectedness, and bondedness" (Sternberg 1986). Passion, the "hot" component, reflects "the drives that lead to romance, physical attraction, sexual consummation" (Sternberg 1988).

Decision/commitment, the "cold" component, represents the decision to love someone else in the short run and the commitment to maintain that love in the long run (Sternberg 1986). Using various combinations of these three components, Sternberg (1988) distinguishes between eight types of love: non-love, liking, infatuated love, empty love, romantic love, companionate love, fatuous love, and consummate love.

Nonlove is the state where all of the three components are absent and consummate love is the state where all components are present. Liking arises when there is only intimacy, infatuated love involves only passion, and empty love constitutes only decision/commitment. Romantic love is a combination of intimacy and passion, companionate love results from intimacy and decision/commitment, and fatuous love derives from passion and decision/commitment.

The concept of brand love

So far several studies (e.g., Ball and Tasaki 1992; Belk 1988, 2004; Richins 1997) have focused on emotional consumer–brand relationships, but only a few (e.g., Carroll and Ahuvia 2006) explicitly deal with brand love. Fournier (1998) has introduced the so-called "brand relationship quality model" into literature. Although she identifies, amongst others, consumer's love/passion for, intimacy with, and commitment to a brand as facets of brand relationship quality, she does not measure these facets. Ahuvia (1993, 2005) also addresses love in a consumer–object context by exploring different aspects of love, but without measuring consumers' brand love. Ji (2002), who focuses on children's brand love, does not measure it either. Whang et al. (2004) adopt Lee's love attitude scale for investigating the various bonds felt between individuals and their beloved objects, but also fail to measure non-interpersonal love.

Lacoeuilhe (2000) transfers the concept of "attachment between two people" to the marketing context and Thomson, MacInnis, and Park (2005) develop a scale for measuring "emotional attachment to brands." But as in social psychology, attachment and love are two different relationship concepts (Aronson, Wilson, and Akert 2006). Consequently, this scale cannot be used to investigate love in the context of brands. Saatchi & Saatchi CEO Kevin Roberts (2005, 2006) introduces his idea of "lovemarks" into management-oriented literature. But as no explicit definition can be found and causalities cannot be clearly identified, this concept has to be questioned from an academic point of view. Carroll and Ahuvia (2006) develop a scale for measuring brand love in general. Since their measuring items (e.g., "This is a wonderful brand"; "I love this brand"; "This brand is pure delight") only deal with love itself and do not reflect the three different aspects of Sternberg's complex idea of love, their scale has to be challenged. In their exploratory study, Albert, Merunka, and Valette-Florence (2008) identify eleven major dimensions of brand love. These are passion, duration of the relationship, self-congruity, dreams, memories, pleasure, attraction, uniqueness, beauty, trust, and declaration of affect. But they do not develop and provide a measurement scale for brand love either.

Since there is no adequate measurement model for brand love in marketing literature, the first objective of this study is to develop a scale for measuring consumers' love toward brands in a holistic, scientifically founded way based on Sternberg's social-psychological concept of love. We followed Shimp and Madden's (1988) reasoning for applying Sternberg's theory. Thus, the use of Sternberg's three-component model seems to be legitimate for our research purposes.

Developing a measurement model of brand love

In the current study brand love is analogously conceptualized to Sternberg's (1986) interpersonal triangular theory of love and can therefore be understood as a consumer's love relationship to a brand that can be characterized by the interplay of intimacy, passion, and commitment to that brand. By conceptualizing consumers' brand love analogously to Sternberg's (1986) interpersonal triangular theory of love, brand love has to be captured as a second-order construct with the factors intimacy, passion, and decision/commitment.

Intimacy is associated with "an awareness of the internal sphere, the most inward reality of the other person" (Perlman and Fehr 1987) and can be defined as "a recurrent preference or readiness for experiences of close, warm and communicative interpersonal exchange" (McAdams and Vaillant 1982). Emotional closeness without intimacy is therefore impossible by definition. Several studies (e.g., Chojnacki and Walsh 1990; Hendrick and Hendrick 1989; Lemieux and Hale 2000) have empirically validated Sternberg's concept of love in an interpersonal context. In line with these studies, Whitley (1993) highlights that intimacy can be seen as a facet "of a higher-order construct of love."

The idea that consumers can also establish strong connections and closeness to products and brands or even think of these objects and brands as parts of themselves and their personality is supported by many studies (e.g., Ahuvia 1993; Belk 1988, 1992, 2004; Price, Arnould, and Curasi 2000; Richins 1994a, 1994b; Schulz, Kleine, and Kernan 1989; Solomon 1986; Wallendorf and Arnould 1988). The results of these studies substantiate Sternberg's understanding of love. Hence:

H1: Brand love is reflected by brand intimacy.

Passion is used to describe "almost any strong emotional state" and can be defined as "a state of profound physiological arousal" (Baumeister and Bratslavsky 1999) or as "a state of intense longing for union with another" (Hatfield and Sprecher 1986). In the extant literature, passion has mostly been associated with interpersonal romantic love and has therefore been explored in this context (Aron and Westbay 1996; Brehm 1988; Fehr 1993; Fehr and Russell 1991; Hendrick and Hendrick 1986, 1989; Regan, Kocan, and Whitlock 1998). Davis and Todd (1982) focus on the differences between friendship and love relationships. They assume that these two types of relationships primarily differ in terms of passion. Consequently, passion turns out to be an essential component in establishing love relationships. Studies that build upon the triangular love theory in an interpersonal context are able to show empirically that passion constitutes a main facet of love (Hendrick and Hendrick 1989; Lemieux and Hale 2002; Overbeek *et al.* 2007; Whitley 1993).

Since the term passion is also used in the context of objects and brands (Belk, Ger, and Askegaard 2003; Duffy and Hooper 2003; Holbrook 1986; Matzler, Pichler, and Hemetsberger 2007), it is employed in the current study as well. Belk, Ger, and Askegaard (2003) consider passion as a strong emotion and as a motivating factor behind many consumption decisions. This assumption is supported by Yim, Tse, and Chan (2008) who highlight passion as a core element of people's affectionate bonds with brands. Hence:

H2: Brand love is reflected by brand passion.

Commitment can be interpreted as a person's intent to maintain a relationship (Rosenblatt 1977). Moreover, it is also associated with "feelings of attachments to a partner" (Rusbult and Buunk 1993). In Sternberg' triangular theory of love (Sternberg 1986, 1987, 1988, 1997), as well as in various concepts of interpersonal love, commitment constitutes a core component of love (e.g., Aron and Westbay 1996; Fehr 1988, 1993; Fehr and Russell 1991; Regan, Kocan, and Whitlock 1998).

Studies that have validated Sternberg's triangular theory of love in an interpersonal context have shown that commitment is another facet of love (Acker and Davis 1992; Aron and Westbay 1996; Lemieux and Hale 1999).

The construct of commitment can easily be transferred to the consumer–brand context since consumers can also display varying degrees of commitment to certain objects. Redden and Steiner (2000), for instance, even investigate consumers' fanatical commitment to brands. They describe these consumers as "brand worshipping consumers" or "obsessive consumers" of certain brands. Consumers who display strong commitment to brands are more likely to love these brands. Analogously to interpersonal relationships, commitment can consequently be considered as a facet of brand love. Hence:

H3: Brand love is reflected by brand commitment.

The consequences of brand love

Next, our study design is expanded in order to assess two more research objectives. First, we want to test the developed measurement scale of brand love for nomological validity. The second objective is to explore its predictive validity, showing that variations in brand love scores correspond to outcome measures of consumer behavior, such as willingness to pay a price premium and forgiveness. Therefore, we embed these two marketing-related variables and the brand love construct in a structural equation model.

Forgiveness

In interpersonal psychology, it is known that partners in close relationships are more willing to accommodate and to forgive mistakes made by their partners (Rusbult *et al.* 1991; Wieselquist *et al.* 1999). The emotional bond between the partners constitutes one factor that is responsible for even staying in a dissatisfying relationship since a separation would disrupt the partners' psychological homeostasis (Hazan and Shaver 1994).

Aaker, Fournier, and Brasel (2004) empirically show that the quality of a consumer–brand relationship has a significant effect on the consumers' willingness to forgive mistakes made by the brand. In the context of a consumer–brand love relationship, one can infer that a love relationship with a brand leads to a consumer's higher willingness to forgive mistakes made by the brand. Thus, the following hypothesis can be put forth:

H4: Brand love has a positive effect on forgiveness.

Price premium

Furthermore, according to Thomson, MacInnis, and Park (2005) consumers' willingness to pay a price premium is affected by their emotional attachment to the particular brand. This empirical finding is supported by brand equity literature, as it is widely recognized that to the extent an individual associates value with a brand he or she will be more willing to pay a higher price for it (Aaker 1996; Keller 2003; Vázquez, del Río, and Iglesias 2002; Yoo, Donthu, and Lee 2000). Hence, from the consumers' point of view their beloved brands are priceless, and therefore their willingness to pay a premium price will be higher. These considerations lead to the formulation of the following hypothesis:

H5: Brand love has a positive effect on willingness to pay a price premium.

Empirical study

Research design and sample

All proposed relationships were examined by means of an online questionnaire; no incentives were given. Test persons were first assigned to name a brand which they love or a brand to which they display the strongest feeling of love of all brands they can think of. After that, all questions for measuring the constructs were related to this brand.

During the five-week field study time, 519 consumers participated in the survey and 299 people completely filled out the questionnaire in an average time of seven minutes. The data sample consisted of 54.5 percent males and 45.5 percent females with an average age of 33.8 years (SD=12.8).

Analysis and results of the measurement models

Constructs are typically evaluated through a number of reliability and validity criteria, which can be divided into first and second generation parameters. Criteria of the first generation follow early methods derived from psychometrics (e.g., Churchill 1979). These are exploratory factor analysis (EFA), item-to-total correlations (ITTC), and Cronbach alpha (α). The most prominent method of second generation measures is confirmatory factor analysis (CFA), which was also applied in this case. Model parameters are estimated with the help of CFA using LISREL (Diamantopoulos and Siguaw 2000). The reliability and validity of the measurement models are assessed through global and local goodness of fit (e.g., Bagozzi and Baumgartner 1994; Hu and Bentler 1999). In the current study, all items were measured on seven-point Likert-scales ranging from "strongly disagree" (=1) to "strongly agree" (=7). A pre-test (n=44) served as a guarantee for the internal and external consistency of the measurement instruments.

To develop scales to measure brand intimacy, brand passion, and brand commitment, our approach followed the procedure proposed by Churchill (1979). At first fourteen items were generated by drawing on scales of the interpersonal or psychological context on the one hand and on the results of twelve qualitative in-depth interviews with consumers on the other hand. We had to delete some items due to ambiguous meaning and non-emotional context. The final measurement model of brand love contains a pool of nine items (see Table 7.1).

TABLE 7.1 Psychometric properties of the developed brand love scale

Factors	Items	Source	Factor loading	Indicator reliability	Factor reliability	α
Brand commitment	I am very focused on this brand.	on the basis of Yoo et al. (2000); Ahluwalia (2000)	0.899	0.71	0.89	0.888
	[. . .] would be my first choice.		0.921	0.75		
	I will not buy other brands if [. . .] is available at the store.		0.898	0.73		
Brand intimacy	Most of the time I feel very close to this brand.	on the basis of Aron et al. (1992); Miller and Lefcourt (1982)	0.944	0.86	0.90	0.936
	There is a close connection between me and this brand.		0.968	0.94		
	There is a certain intimacy between me and this brand.		0.913	0.73		
Brand passion	I am passionate about this brand.	on the basis of Thomson et al. (2005)	0.923	0.73	0.90	0.897
	[. . .] is a captivating brand.		0.934	0.79		
	I am enthusiastic about this brand.		0.884	0.75		
	Global Fit Indices: χ^2/df = 2.23; RMSEA = 0.061; SRMR = 0.022; NFI = 0.99; TLI = 0.99; CFI = 0.99					

Brand intimacy, brand passion, and brand commitment are three first-order factors that correspond to the higher order construct of brand love. All global and local fit indices are within the guidelines.

Moreover, it is also important to test for discriminant validity between the study constructs, which is analyzed with the help of the test recommended by Fornell and Larcker (1981). The test reveals that discriminant validity is given. Consequently, the estimated measurement model of brand love can be accepted. The constructs used as consequences of brand love are evaluated in the same manner as above.

Analysis and results of the structural equation model

To empirically test the proposed relationships stated in hypotheses H4 to H5, structural equation modelling (SEM) with LISREL using maximum likelihood

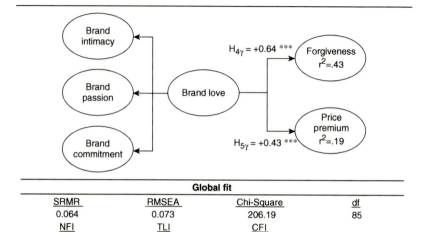

NOTE. γ = path coefficients; SRMR = Standardized Root Mean Square Residual;
RMSEA = Root Mean Squared Error of Approximation; CFI = Comparative Fit
Index; NFI = Normed Fit Index; TLI = Tucker-Lewis Index; df = degrees of
freedom; *** p ≤ 0.01

FIGURE 7.1 Conceptual model and results of the test of causal relationships

estimation was used. The calculated model (see Figure 7.1) shows an excellent fit with all global fit criteria met: χ^2=206.19, df=85, RMSEA=0.073, SRMR=0.064, NFI=0.97, TLI=0.98, and CFI=0.98. This allows the interpretation of the following results: brand love has a strong effect on price premium (γ=+0.64; H4) and on forgiveness (γ=+0.43; H5).

Exploring brand love styles

From interpersonal love theory we know that love can take different forms. Sternberg postulated eight different kinds of love existing in interpersonal relationships. Analogously, Shimp and Madden (1988) introduced eight kinds of consumer–object relations. However, empirical research discovering different brand love styles is still in its infancy. Only Whang *et al.* (2004) have started an approach to discover the structure of romantic consumer–brand relationships by applying Lee's love attitude styles on a sample of bikers who are in love with their machines. Thus, we address this research gap by analyzing our data as to differences in the way consumers love their brands.

Our developed measurement scale reveals the existence of brand intimacy, brand passion, and brand commitment as facets reflecting brand love. Depending on the presence or absence of these three components, different kinds of love derive. In this study, we use Sternberg's terminology for labeling the brand love styles. For interpretation, mean values of brand intimacy, brand passion, and brand commitment were computed for all datasets. Afterwards a median-split served as a cut-off criterion to identify whether the respective component of love is of high or low value. We assume that mean values > 4.5 indicate the presence and < 4.5 the absence of brand intimacy, brand passion, and brand commitment. A total of 299 datasets were analyzed in order to cluster homogeneous brand love categories. The results show that all kinds of love proposed by Sternberg could be identified within our data as follows.

A total of 115 consumers feel themselves in consummate love with their brands. Here the consumer feels an intimate relationship with the beloved brand, has a strong yearning to purchase or repurchase the brand, and is committed, at least in the short term, to support the particular brand (Shimp and Madden 1988). The second largest group is the cluster of fatuous love (n=50) which is characterized by a high level of passion and commitment but the absence of intimacy. This love style is fatuous in the sense that a commitment is made on the basis of passion without the stabilizing element of intimacy (Sternberg 1986). As everybody knows, love is sometimes blind! In this respect our findings are consistent because the brand love style of infatuated love can be identified. Infatuation is characterized by strong passion for a brand without any feelings of commitment or intimacy. This form of consumer–brand relationship basically applies to fad products (Shimp and Madden 1988) and is a result of passionate arousal. Furthermore, a group of 47 test persons showed neither high intimacy nor passion or commitment for the brand. Consequently, this group has to be labeled as nonlove. But nonlove does not mean disliking; it merely reflects that consumers do not have any love-like feeling for their brand. Nevertheless, the consumer–brand relationship can be solid and long lasting. Finally, we have to note that we also identified the love styles of empty love, companionate love, romantic love, and liking within our data. Table 7.2 shows these eight brand love styles classified in Sternberg's terminology.

Summary and discussion

The primary objective of this chapter was to develop a measurement scale reflecting consumers' love to brands. Based on the concept of love from interpersonal psychology literature as well as on studies focusing on consumer–object relations, we introduced a second-order brand love construct which is reflected by three first order factors, namely brand passion, brand intimacy, and brand commitment. In this way it is possible to capture all the facets of love analogously to Sternberg's triangular theory of love. The second aim of this study was to test hypotheses concerning the influence of brand love on marketing-related variables. The results offered evidence of predictive validity, showing that brand love has strong

TABLE 7.2 Eight brand love styles

Brand love style	#	Component		
		Brand intimacy	Brand passion	Brand commitment
Nonlove	47	–	–	–
Liking	2	O	–	–
Infatuated love	44	–	O	–
Empty love	20	–	–	O
Romantic love	18	O	O	–
Companionate love	3	O	–	O
Fatuous love	50	–	O	O
Consummate love	115	O	O	O

Note: O   love component present
        –   love component absent

positive effects on consumers' willingness to pay a price premium and that consumers turn a blind eye to the beloved brand when the brand makes a mistake. Thus, our findings underpin the relevance of brand love for marketers.

Although this research supports the increasing importance of consumer–brand love relationships, the study has some limitations that at the same time provide some avenues for future research. As a result of our research design, the present study has focused on a relatively small number of brands which possess affinity value and are clearly more powerful than the "average" brands whose influence struggles to get beyond awareness. So the question that arises is how love can be created in a consumer–brand context. Thus, antecedents of brand love have to be discovered. Future research should also explore how brand love is related to and different from well-established constructs like, for instance, brand attachment or brand trust. In addition, further consequences like positive word of mouth and brand loyalty should be verified. Furthermore, the product category and the consumption context can be regarded as moderators. Researchers are encouraged to address these questions.

References

Aaker, D.A. (1996) "Measuring Brand Equity across Products and Markets", *California Management Review*, 38 (3): 102–21.

Aaker, J., Fournier, S. and Brasel, A.S. (2004) "When Good Brands Do Bad", *Journal of Consumer Research*, 31 (1): 1–16.

Acker, M. and Davis, M.H. (1992) "Intimacy, Passion and Commitment in Adult Romantic Relationships: A Test of the Triangular Theory of Love", *Journal of Social and Personal Relationships*, 9 (1): 21–50.

Ahluwalia, R. (2000) "Examination of Psychological Processes Underlying Resistance to Persuasion", *Journal of Consumer Research*, 27 (2): 217–32.

Ahuvia, A.C. (1993) "I Love It! – Towards a Unifying Theory of Love across Diverse Love Objects", doctoral dissertation, Northwestern University.

—— (2005) "Beyond the Extended Self: Loved Objects and Consumers' Identity Narratives", *Journal of Consumer Research*, 32 (1): 171–84.

Albert, N., Merunka, D. and Valette-Florence, P. (2008) "When Consumers Love their Brands: Exploring the Concept and its Dimensions", *Journal of Business Research*, 61 (10): 1062–75.

Aron, A., Aron, E.N. and Smollan, D. (1992) "Inclusion of Other in the Self Scale and the Structure of Interpersonal Closeness", *Journal of Personality and Social Psychology*, 70 (3): 535–51.

Aron, A. and Westbay, L. (1996) "Dimensions of the Prototype of Love", *Journal of Personality and Social Psychology*, 70 (3): 535–51.

Aronson, E., Wilson, T.D. and Akert, R.D. (2006) *Social Psychology*, 6th edn, New York: Prentice Hall.

Bagozzi, R.P. and Baumgartner, H. (1994) "The Evaluation of Structural Equation Models and Hypothesis Testing", in R.P. Bagozzi (ed.) *Principle in Marketing Research*, Cambridge: Blackwell.

Ball, D.A. and Tasaki, L.H. (1992) "The Role and Measurement of Attachment in Consumer Behavior", *Journal of Consumer Psychology*, 1 (2): 155–72.

Bauer, H.H., Heinrich, D. and Albrecht, C.M. (2009) "All You Need is Love: Assessing Consumers' Brand Love", In M. Kamin and I.M. Martin (eds) *Proceedings of the American Marketing Association Summer Educators Conference*, Chicago: American Marketing Association 20: 252–3.

Baumeister, R.F. and Bratslavsky, E. (1999) "Passion, Intimacy, and Time: Passionate Love as a Function of Change in Intimacy", *Personality and Social Psychology Review*, 3 (1): 49–67.

Belk, R.W. (1988) "Possessions and the Extended Self", *Journal of Consumer Research*, 15 (2): 139–68.

—— (1992) "Attachment to Possessions", in I. Altman and S.M. Low (eds) *Place Attachment*, New York and London: Plenum Publishers.

—— (2004) "Men and their Machines", *Advances in Consumer Research*, 31 (1): 273–8.

Belk, R.W., Ger, G. and Askegaard, S. (2003) "The Fire of Desire: A Multisited Inquiry into Consumer Passion", *Journal of Consumer Research*, 30 (3): 326–51.

Brehm, S.S. (1988) "Passionate Love", in R.J. Sternberg and M.L. Barnes (eds) *The Psychology of Love*, New Haven and London: Yale University Press.

Carroll, B. and Ahuvia, A. (2006) "Some Antecedents and Outcomes of Brand Love", *Marketing Letters*, 17 (2): 79–89.

Chojnacki, J.T. and Walsh, W.B. (1990) "Reliability and Concurrent Validity of the Sternberg Triangular Love Scale", *Psychological Reports*, 67 (1): 219–24.

Churchill, G.A. Jr (1979) "A Paradigm for Developing Better Measures of Marketing Constructs", *Journal of Marketing Research*, 16 (1): 64–73.

Davis, K.E. and Todd, M.J. (1982) "Friendship and Love Relationships", *Advances in Descriptive Psychology*, 2: 79–122.

Diamantopoulus, A. and Siguaw, J. (2000) *Introducing LISREL*, 1st edn, London: Sage.

Duffy, N. and Hooper, J. (2003) *Passion Branding – Harnessing the Power of Emotion to Build Strong Brands*, 1st edn, Chichester: Wiley and Sons.

Fehr, B. (1988) "Prototype Analysis of the Concepts of Love and Commitment," *Journal of Personality and Social Psychology*, 55 (4): 557–79.

—— (1993) "How Do I Love Thee? Let me Consult my Prototype", in S. Duck (ed.) *Individuals in Relationships*, Newbury Park: Sage.

Fehr, B. and Russell, J.A. (1991) "The Concept of Love Viewed from a Prototype Perspective", *Journal of Personality and Social Psychology*, 60 (3): 425–38.

Fornell, C. and Larcker, D.F. (1981) "Evaluating Structural Equation Models with Unobservable Variables and Measurement Error", *Journal of Marketing Research*, 18 (1): 39–50.

Fournier, S. (1998) "Consumers and their Brands: Developing Relationship Theory in Consumer Research", *Journal of Consumer Research*, 24 (4): 343–73.

Freud, S. (1922) "Certain Neurotic Mechanisms in Jealousy, Paranoia, and Homosexuality", in *Collected Papers, vol. 2*, London: Hogarth.

Hatfield, E. and Sprecher, S. (1986) "Measuring Passionate Love in Intimate Relationships", *Journal of Adolescence*, 9 (4): 383–410.

Hazan, C. and Shaver, P. (1994) "Attachment as an Organizational Framework for Research on Close Relationships", *Psychological Inquiry*, 5 (1): 1–22.

Hendrick, C. and Hendrick, S.S. (1986) "A Theory and Method of Love", *Journal of Personality and Social Psychology*, 50 (2): 392–402.

—— (1989) "Research on Love: Does it Measure Up?" *Journal of Personality and Social Psychology*, 56 (5): 784–94.

Holbrook, M.B. (1986) "I'm Hip: An Autobiographical Account of Some Musical Consumption Experiences", *Advances in Consumer Research*, 13 (1): 614–18.

Hu, L.T. and Bentler, P.M. (1999) "Cutoff Criteria for Fit Indexes in Covariance Structure Analysis: Conventional Criteria versus New Alternatives", *Structural Equation Modeling*, 6 (1): 1–31.

Ji, M.F. (2002) "Children's Relationships with Brands: 'True Love' or 'One-Night' Stand?" *Psychology and Marketing*, 19 (4): 369–87.

Keller, K.L. (2003) *Strategic Brand Management: building, measuring, and managing brand equity*, 2nd edn, Upper Saddle River, NJ: Prentice-Hall.

Lacoeuilhe, J. (2000) "L'Attachement à la Marque: Proposition d'une Échelle de Mesure", *Recherches et Applications en Marketing*, 15 (4): 61–77.

Lazarus, R.S. (1991) *Emotion and Adaptation*, 1st edn, New York and Oxford: Oxford University Press.

Lee, J.A. (1977) "A Typology of Styles of Loving", *Personality and Social Psychology Bulletin*, 3 (2): 173–82.

Lemieux, R. and Hale, J.L. (1999) "Intimacy, Passion and Commitment in Young Romantic Relationships: Successfully Measuring the Triangular Theory of Love", *Psychological Reports*, 85: 497–503.

—— (2000) "Intimacy, Passion and Commitment among Married Individuals: Further Testing of the Triangular Theory of Love", *Psychological Reports,* 87: 941–7.

—— (2002) "Cross-Sectional Analysis of Intimacy, Passion, and Commitment: Testing the Assumptions of the Triangular Theory of Love", *Psychological Reports*, 90: 1009–14.

McAdams, D.P. and Vaillant, G.E. (1982) "Intimacy Motivation and Psychosocial Adjustment: A Longitudinal Study", *Journal of Personality Assessment*, 46 (6): 586–93.

Maslow, A.H. (1962) *Toward a Psychology of Being*, Princeton, NJ: Van Nostrand.

Matzler, K., Pichler, E.A. and Hemetsberger, A. (2007) "Who is Spreading the Word? The Positive Influence of Extraversion on Consumer Passion and Evangelism", in A.L. Dixon and K.A. Machleit (eds) *Proceedings of the American Marketing Association Winter Educators' Conference*, AMA online.

Miller, R.S. and Lefcourt, H.M. (1982) "The Assessment of Social Intimacy", *Journal of Personality Assessment*, 46 (5): 514–18.

Overbeek, G., Ha, T., Scholte, R., de Kemp, R. and Engels, R.C.M.E. (2007) "Brief Report: Intimacy, Passion, and Commitment in Romantic Relationships – Validation of a 'Triangular Love Scale' for Adolescents", *Journal of Adolescence*, 30 (3): 523–8.

Perlman, D. and Fehr, B. (1987) "The Development of Intimate Relationships", in D. Perlman and S. Duck (eds) *Intimate Relationships: development, dynamics and deterioration*, 1st edn, Newbury Park: Sage.

Price, L.L., Arnould, E. and Curasi, C.F. (2000) "Older Consumers' Disposition of Special Possessions", *Journal of Consumer Research*, 27 (2): 179–201.

Redden, J. and Steiner, C.J. (2000) "Fanatical Consumers: Towards a Framework for Research", *Journal of Consumer Marketing*, 17 (4): 322–57.

Regan, P.C., Kocan, E.R. and Whitlock, T. (1998) "Ain't Love Grand! A Prototype Analysis of the Concept of Romantic Love", *Journal of Social and Personal Relationships*, 15 (3): 411–20.

Reik, T. (1944) *A Psychologist Looks at Love*, 1st edn, New York: Farrar and Rinehart.

Richins, M.L. (1994a) "Special Possessions and the Expression of Material Values", *Journal of Consumer Research*, 21 (3): 522–31.

—— (1994b) "Valuing Things: The Public and Private Meanings of Possessions", *Journal of Consumer Research*, 21 (3): 504–21.

—— (1997) "Measuring Emotions in the Consumption Experience", *Journal of Consumer Research*, 24 (2): 127–46.

Roberts, K. (2005) *Lovemarks: the future beyond brands*, 1st edn, New York: Powerhouse Books.

—— (2006) *The Lovemarks Effect: winning in the consumer revolution*, 1st edn, New York: Powerhouse Books.

Rosenblatt, P.C. (1977) "Needed Research on Commitment in Marriage", in G. Levinger and H.L. Raush (eds) *Close Relationships: perspectives on the meaning of intimacy*, Amherst: University of Massachusetts Press.

Rusbult, C.E. and Buunk, B.P. (1993) "Commitment Processes in Close Relationships: An Interdependence Analysis", *Journal of Social and Personal Relationships*, 10 (2): 175–204.

Rusbult, C.E., Verette, J., Whitney, G.A., Slovik, L.F. and Lipkus, I. (1991) "Accommodation Processes in Close Relationships: Theory and Preliminary Empirical Evidence", *Journal of Personality and Social Psychology*, 60 (1): 53–80.

Schultz, S.E., Kleine, R.E. III and Kernan, J.B. (1989) "These are a Few of my Favorite Things: Toward an Explication of Attachment as a Consumer Behavior Construct", *Advances in Consumer Research*, 16 (1): 359–66.

Shimp, T.A. and Madden, T.J. (1988) "Consumer–Object Relations: A Conceptual Framework Based Analogously on Sternberg's Triangular Theory of Love", *Advances in Consumer Research*, 15 (1): 163–8.

Solomon, M.R. (1986) "Deep-Seated Materialism: The Case of Levi's 501 Jeans", *Advances in Consumer Research*, 13 (1): 619–22.

Sternberg, R.J. (1986) "A Triangular Theory of Love", *Psychological Review*, 93 (2): 119–35.

—— (1987) "Liking versus Loving: A Comparative Evaluation of Theories", *Psychological Bulletin*, 102 (3): 331–45.

—— (1988) "Triangulating Love", in R.J. Sternberg and M.L. Barnes (eds) *The Psychology of Love*, New Haven and London: Yale University Press.

—— (1997) "Construct Validation of a Triangular Love Scale", *European Journal of Social Psychology*, 27: 313–35.

Thomson, M., MacInnis, D.J. and Park, C.W. (2005) "The Ties that Bind: Measuring the Strength of Consumers' Emotional Attachments to Brands", *Journal of Consumer Psychology*, 15 (1): 77–91.

Vazquez, R., del Rio, B. and Iglesias, V. (2002) "Consumer-Based Brand Equity: Development and Validation of a Measurement Instrument", *Journal of Marketing Management*, 18 (1/2): 27–48.

Wallendorf, M. and Arnould, E.J. (1988) "My Favorite Things: A Cross-Cultural Inquiry into Object Attachment, Possessiveness, and Social Linkage", *Journal of Consumer Research*, 14 (4): 531–47.

Whang, Y., Allen, J., Sahoury, N. and Zhang, H. (2004) "Falling in Love with a Product: The Structure of a Romantic Consumer–Product Relationship", *Advances in Consumer Research*, 31 (1): 320–7.

Whitley, B.E., Jr (1993) "Reliability and Aspects of the Construct Validity of Sternberg's Triangular Love Scale", *Journal of Social and Personal Relationships,* 10 (3): 475–80.

Wieselquist, J., Rusbult, C.E., Foster, C.A. and Agnew, C.R. (1999) "Commitment, Pro-Relationship Behavior, and Trust in Close Relationships", *Journal of Personality and Social Psychology,* 77: 942–66.

Yim, C.K., Tse, D.K. and Chan, K.W. (2008) "Strengthening Customer Loyalty through Intimacy and Passion", *Journal of Marketing Research,* 45 (12): 741–56.

Yoo, B., Donthu, N. and Lee, S. (2000) "An Examination of Selected Marketing Mix Elements and Brand Equity", *Journal of Academy of Marketing Science,* 28 (2): 195–211.

8

BRAND LOVE

Investigating two alternative love relationships

Marc Fetscherin and Mary Conway Dato-on

Introduction

Researchers have examined the relationships between consumers and products and recently that between consumers and brands (Keller and Lehmann, 2006), using concepts such as brand satisfaction, brand loyalty, and brand love to distinguish among various types and intensities of relationships (Albert *et al.*, 2008). As consumers form relationships with brands, they often assign human characteristics (Levy, 1985) and personalities (Aaker, 1997) to them. Among the brand relationship constructs studied, the concept of brand love is one of the most recent and the least researched (Ahuvia, 2005a; Albert *et al.*, 2008; Fournier, 1998). Richins (1997) and others found that love is a typical consumer-related emotion and often has a strong connection to the individual's self-concept and identity (Ahuvia, 2005a, 2005b; Swaminathan *et al.*, 2007). Chaudhuri (1998) shows that emotions are linked to the perception of risk in products and purchase intention. Carroll and Ahuvia (2006: 87) define brand love as "the degree of passionate emotional attachment a satisfied consumer has for a particular" brand. Keh, Pang and Peng (2007: 84) define brand love as "the intimate, passionate, and committed relationship between consumers and a brand, characterized by its reciprocal, purposive, and dynamic properties." Building on this previous work, we define brand love as a multidimensional construct consisting of a satisfied consumer's experience with a brand, which leads not only to brand loyalty (a predecessor of brand love) but to a deeply emotional relationship. Ultimately, brand love is an emotional, affective fulfillment, while brand satisfaction refers to a more cognitive judgment. The objective of this study is to assess, on one hand, the relationship between brand love and existing branding concepts such as brand loyalty and, on the other hand, the suitable underlying love relationship theory in which brand love is nested. To achieve these objectives, we first review the current literature on consumer love toward products and brands, then develop hypotheses and examine this issue by conducting an explorative and confirmatory factor analysis. We conclude with a discussion of implications for marketing researchers and practitioners.

Literature review

Several recent studies offer empirical evidence for feelings of love toward products or brands (Ahuvia, 1993, 2005a, 2005b; Shimp and Madden, 1988). The marketing literature has applied the idea of love with two distinct approaches.

In the first approach, authors discuss consumer love towards a *product* (Ball and Tasaki, 1995; Rozanski *et al.*, 1999; Thomoson *et al.*, 2005; Wallendorf and Arnould, 1988). A number of studies assessed the emotional attachments of consumers to products (Ball and Tasaki, 1995; Rozanski *et al.*, 1999; Thomoson *et al.*, 2005; Wallendorf and Arnould, 1988), while others used terms like consumer–object or consumer–product relationships (Shimp and Madden, 1988; Whang *et al.*, 2004). Shimp and Madden's (1988) work on love in consumption and their corresponding model of consumer–object–love was inspired by the triangular theory of love of Sternberg (1986). Ahuvia (2005b) provided empirical support for this construct when she compared interpersonal love and love for an object. Whang *et al.* (2004) conducted "a study using the construct of love based on the interpersonal paradigm and measured this feeling with a shortened version of the love attitude scale initially" (Albert et al. 2008: 1064) proposed by Lee (1977). In sum, all these studies base their work on interpersonal relationship theories.

In the second approach, numerous studies have also examined consumer love for a *brand* or the consumer–brand relationship (Aggarwal, 2004; Fournier, 1998; Heinrich *et al.* 2009; Monga, 2002; Swaminathan *et al.*, 2007). These authors observed that consumers often consider brands as relationship partners (Keh *et al.*, 2007). Fournier (1998) found that consumers develop and maintain strong relationships with brands and proposed six major dimensions of brand relationships. The consumer's love or passion toward a brand measures the affective depths of such a relationship (Fournier, 1998; Keh *et al.*, 2007). One of the first works to thoroughly examine brand love was Ahuvia's study (1993). More recent studies by Whang *et al.* (2004) and Ahuvia (2005b) have further contributed to our understanding. In particular, Carroll and Ahuvia (2006) examined brand love, which elaborates the consumer's feelings toward a brand, including characteristics such as "passion for a brand, brand attachment, positive evaluation of the brand, positive emotions in response to the brand, and declarations of love toward the brand" (Albert *et al.* 2008: 1064).

As of today, and to the best of the authors' knowledge, only a few studies have empirically assessed brand love. Carroll and Ahuvia (2006) proposed a one-dimensional scale with ten measurement items. Keh, Pang and Peng (2007) developed a three-dimensional scale (intimacy, passion, and commitment) with eleven measurement items. Finally, Kamat and Parulekar (2007) proposed five dimensions (friendship, contentment, admiration, commitment, and yearning) with fifty-two items. However, all the brand love scales are based on the same relationship theory – Sternberg's (1986) triangular theory of interpersonal love. While we do not disagree, Albert *et al.* (2008) argue that the theory of interpersonal love relationships may be constraining. Furthermore, Yoon and Gutchess (2006) show that consumers process brand relationships in a different part of the brain than they do for interpersonal relationships. This suggests the need for caution in assuming the direct transferability of the theory of interpersonal love to explain the love relationship between consumers and brands.

Conceptualization of brand love and hypotheses

Parasocial love relationship

The first and perhaps most severe limitation in existing brand love literature is the assumption that love is a bi-directional relationship between a consumer and a brand, rather than a one-directional one. Existing studies are based on the triangular theory of interpersonal love (Sternberg 1986). However, as Whang *et al.* (2004: 320) noted, "although love is an outcome of bi-directional interaction between two partners, when the target of love is replaced with an object (e.g., product or brand), love becomes uni-directional." In other words, a brand cannot reciprocate the consumer's love except in the consumer's imagination. A consumer's love for a brand resembles more a parasocial relationship. Parasocial interaction (PSI), originally defined by Horton and Wohl (1956), is a perceived relationship of friendship or intimacy by an audience member with a remote media persona, leading to an illusion of a face-to-face relationship. PSI describes a one-sided interpersonal relationship where one party knows a great deal about the other, but the other does not reciprocate the knowledge. The one-sided relations between celebrities and audience or fans (Caughey, 1984) are the most common forms of such relationships studied so far in the literature. Although the parasocial relationship is similar in many ways to the interpersonal relationship, the former is uni-directional unlike interpersonal relationships. Brands, like celebrities, do not reciprocate knowledge of the lover and can only participate in a uni-directional or parasocial relationship. We define parasocial love as a perceived relationship of love by a consumer with a brand. Therefore, we would expect a positive relationship between parasocial love and brand love. Differently stated, consumers with a strong parasocial love for a brand will love the brand. We test the following hypothesis:

H1: The parasocial love construct significantly and positively influences overall brand love.

Interpersonal love relationship

The second shortcoming is that current brand love studies emanate from the theory of interpersonal love (Sternberg, 1986). Assuming brand love is grounded by the theory of interpersonal love relationships, rather than a parasocial love (see above), there are many other interpersonal love theories in addition to Sternberg's theory (1986). For example, Hendrick and Hendrick (1986) propose the Love Attitude Scale based on the original work of Lee (1977). Other love-related scales include Davis and Todd's (1985) Relationship Rating Form, Hatfield and Sprecher's (1986) Passionate Love Scale, and Shaver and Hazan's (1987) Attachment Styles. Masuda (2003) states in his meta-analyses of love scales that love encompasses two aspects, sexual attraction between romantic partners (erotic love) and non-sexual psychological closeness to partners (companionate love). The current brand love studies, based on Sternberg's (1986) triangular theory of interpersonal love, do not differentiate between erotic love (e-love) and companionate love (c-love). We argue that if a consumer's love toward a brand is based on interpersonal love theory, it is closer to companionate love (c-love) than to erotic love (e-love). We therefore test the following hypothesis (see Figure 8.1):

H2: The interpersonal love construct significantly and positively influences overall brand love.

Brand experience

The third limitation of existing brand love studies confirms the findings of Albert *et al.* (2008), who claim that no single interpersonal theory encompasses all emotions linked to love for a brand. One important aspect they found impacting brand love is the duration of the relationship with the brand and memories it evokes in the consumer. Both deal with a consumer's experience with the brand. Underscoring the importance of consumer experience with a brand, Fournier

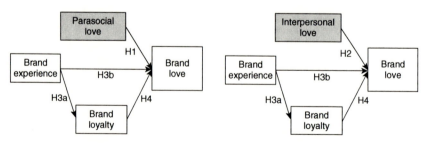

Model I : Parasocial love relationship   *Model II* : Interpersonal love relationship

FIGURE 8.1 Research models

and Yao (1997) stressed that a brand can generate nostalgic remembrances from childhood. Consumers with a longer experience with the brand might not only be more brand loyal, but also might have a positive feeling toward the brand and may exhibit brand love (see Figure 8.1). We therefore test the following two hypotheses:

H3a: A consumer's brand experience significantly and positively influences brand loyalty.

H3b: A consumer's brand experience significantly and positively influences overall brand love.

Brand loyalty

Busacca and Castaldo (2003) propose that the first stage of a consumer–brand relationship is brand satisfaction, which results from the consumer's positive experiences with the brand (see also Ha and Perks, 2005). As the relationship continues, satisfaction may become brand loyalty as numerous studies have found (Berry, 2000; Chaudhuri and Holbrook, 2001; Garbarino and Johnson, 1999; Lau and Lee, 2000). The relationship between brand satisfaction and brand loyalty has been discussed in the literature extensively and in general they are significantly positively related as numerous studies have shown over the past few decades (Bloemer and Lemmink, 1992; Kasper, 1988; Kraft *et al.*, 1973; LaBarbera and Mazursky, 1983). However, less is known about the relationship between brand loyalty and brand love. On one hand, Carroll and Ahuvia (2006) and Kamat and Parulekar (2007) argue that brand love precedes brand loyalty. On the other hand, Aaker's (1991) logic suggests brand satisfaction leads to brand loyalty and this leads then to brand love. In our model, we follow Aaker's (1991) logic and extend it by arguing that brand loyalty precedes brand love and we therefore test the following hypothesis (see Figure 8.1):

H4: Brand loyalty significantly and positively influences overall brand love.

Figure 8.1 illustrates the two models – one based on parasocial love relationship theory (left side) and the other based on the interpersonal love relationship theory (right side).

Dependent variables

We have chosen to take as the dependent variables items which assess how consumers "feel" about the brand, including items relating to composite affection for the brand. Respondents declare their love for the brand and contemplate life without the brand. We suggest that the more a consumer loves a brand, the more she or he acknowledges this love when asked. Similarly, a consumer who must live without the ability to express love (i.e., use the brand) would be miserable.

The expected acknowledgement and expression of separation anxiety from a brand accords with Fournier's (1998) work and reflects a deep relationship with a brand.

Method

Measurement items

Independent variables

(1) *Parasocial love*. The parasocial interaction scale was used in the current study employing the ten-item version of the original PSI scale, similar to previous studies (Conway and Rubin, 1991; Perse 1990). The scale was reworded to the context of brands. (2) *Interpersonal love*. We use the Love Attitude Scale (LAS) developed by Hendrick and Hendrick (1986) to measure interpersonal companionate love as applied to a brand. Similar to previous studies, we reworded original items in order to make them applicable to a brand rather than to a personal relationship. (3) *Brand experience*. Our research model includes three items suggested by Albert *et al.* (2008) to measure consumers' previous experience with the brand. Inspired by Fournier and Yao's work (1997), we added three additional items to measure the consumer's brand experience. (4) *Brand loyalty*. Gremler (1995) suggests that both the behavioral and attitudinal dimensions need to be incorporated in measuring of loyalty. We follow his advice and included both attitudinal and behavioral brand loyalty, using three items reworded from Quester and Lim (2003) to measure attitudinal aspects and two items to measure behavioral brand loyalty. For all the scales used, the respondents were asked to express their agreement or disagreement with certain statements along a five-point Likert scale.

Dependent variable

Overall brand love was measured by two items taken from Rubin's (1970) multi-item Romantic Love Scale and two items from Albert *et al.* (2008).

Product category

The brand love construct required looking at heavily branded products. As Albert *et al.* (2008: 1068) discovered, the product categories "strongly associated with the feeling of love include shoes, cars, lingerie, watches, perfumes and personal care, food items, music, cigarettes, and furniture." For our study, we selected cars as the product category. In presenting the car brands to survey participants, we used an unaided brand recall approach. Respondents were asked first to name three car brands that came to mind, which indicated that they had some level of brand awareness. We then asked which car brand was their favorite, and they used this brand to answer the survey.

Data collection

We collected data through a self-administered survey of undergraduate and graduate students. Students have often been used for marketing studies and scale testing, for example, the hedonic and utilitarian consumer attitude scale (Batra and Ahtolo, 1991), country image scale (Martin and Eroglu, 1993; Lala et al., 2009), multi-item measures of values (Herche, 1994), buying impulsiveness scale (Rook and Fisher, 1995), brand association scale (Low and Lamb, 2000), consumer based brand equity scale (Yoo and Donthu, 2001), revised country-of-origin image scale (Pereira et al., 2005), ad creativity scale (Smith and Schaefer, 1969), branded product meanings scale (Strizhakova et al., 2008). Students have also been used in consumer–brand relationship studies (Carlson et al., 2009; Hayes et al., 2006) and studies related to cars (Fetscherin and Toncar, 2009). Since student samples are commonly used (Tepper Tian et al., 2001; Voss et al., 2003), they are equally appropriate for the present study. While generalizing findings is always a concern, the fundamental nature of the feeling of love for a brand is more likely to generalize across diverse populations, making the use of student samples more legitimate in this case, than managerial-based scales where business experience is more important (Bello et al., 2009).

Analysis and results

Before conducting the survey, a pre-test with 20 respondents was performed in order to assess any potential issues with the survey and scale. We administered the initial survey to 196 students from the southern part of the United States; 180 usable surveys were drawn upon for the analysis. Through unaided brand recall, respondents mentioned three car brands and then were asked to mention their favorite one. Respondents then answered questions along a five-point Likert scale, ranging from 1 = strongly disagree to 5 = strongly agree. Using a five-point Likert scale for all items allowed consistent coding.

Reliability

The coefficient alpha and test-retest were used to assess the internal consistency, stability, and reliability of the proposed brand love construct (Churchill, 1979). The resulting Cronbach's alpha of .922 suggests a very well-defined item structure and internal consistency. The alpha values for the various dimensions are: interpersonal love (.905), parasocial love (.794), brand experience (.840), and brand loyalty (.850). As we only use one survey sample dataset, we conduct test-retest reliability by using the split-half coefficient estimates method, which is to split the scale items into two groups and then compare the groups as if they were two separate surveys. Two approaches can be used, the split-half reliability and the odd-even reliability. Reliability test results using the first approach yielded .728 and those using the second approach .927, both of which indicate good reliability. We also calculated the Guttman split-half reliability coefficient, an adaptation of the Spearman–Brown coefficient that does not require equal variances between the two split groups. Again, the reliability coefficients indicated a good internal consistency.

Validity

We also assessed content and construct validity. Content validity was assured by constructing the proposed items based on the current literature as well as by consulting and validating the proposed measurement scale with other marketing professors. Construct validity was assessed by convergence validity (internal consistency, see above) as well as the discriminant validity, by means of an explorative and confirmative factor analysis.

Explorative factor analysis (EFA)

We used the principal components extraction method with varimax rotation. The results reveal four factors with Eigen values greater than 1. Items with a factor load of less than 0.5 were excluded as well as those which had significant cross loadings (higher than 0.4) in order to prevent any multicollinearity. Of the twenty-six initial items, twenty-four were retained for the confirmatory factor analysis. Overall, our proposed model in Figure 8.1 is well specified. The proposed model seems to neatly reflect nomological validity since the factors that contribute to brand love are related to other constructs in the theoretical context of brand relationships.

Confirmatory factor analysis

We ran a confirmatory factor analysis (CFA) by means of a structure equation model (SEM) and obtained a satisfactory solution. Table 8.1 outlines the standardized regression weights for the relationship between the independent and dependent variables. Hypothesis 1, 2, 3a and 4 are all supported. Only hypothesis H3b is rejected. Moreover, our results show that the results based on the parasocial relationship theory are stronger compared to those based on the interpersonal relationship theory.

Moreover, the explained variance for brand love is 70 percent in the case of model I compared with 46 percent in model II. The Goodness-of-fit criteria are somewhat satisfactory with the Comparative Fit Index (CFI) of .816 (model I), .860 (model II); and Tucker-Lewis Index (TLI) of .770 (model I), .826 (model II). Unfortunately the Root Mean Square Error of

TABLE 8.1 Summary results

	Model I	Model II
H1: Parasocial love relationship $\rightarrow$ overall brand love (+)	.747***	
H2: Interpersonal love relationship $\rightarrow$ overall brand love (+)		.347***
H3a: Brand experience $\rightarrow$ brand loyalty (+)	.435***	.431***
H3b: Brand experience $\rightarrow$ overall brand love (+)	.061	.036
H4: Brand loyalty $\rightarrow$ overall brand love (+)	.347***	.600***

*** $p < .01$; ** $p < .05$; * $< .10$

Approximation (RMSEA) of .098 (model I) and .092 (model II) are higher than the .08 Hu and Bentler recommend (Hu and Bentler, 1998). These results suggest opportunities for future improvements of the model through adding variables or other measures items. However, the relative chi-square (Chi-square/df) is 2.733 (model I) and 2.525 (model II), well below the cutoff value of 3 (Schumacker, 1992; Schumacker and Lomax, 1996). Table 8.2 provides details of the summary fits.

A number of interesting observations can be drawn from our analysis. (1) As for our H1 and H2, our results show that both relationship theories explain brand love to some degree. However, the explanation power of brand love is higher when the model is based on the theory of parasocial relationship rather than interpersonal relationship theory. (2) We tested the idea that a consumer's experience with a brand positively affects brand loyalty (H3a) and brand love (H3b). Our analyses support our hypothesis that the experience with the brand does influence brand loyalty (H3a), but does not influence brand love directly (H3b). Future research should investigate this since much of the literature suggests strong connections between experience and product or brand evaluation (Fournier and Yao, 1997). (3) Another objective of this study was to understand more clearly

TABLE 8.2 Summary model fit

	Model I	Model II	Threshold
Overall Brand love	$R^2 = 70\%$	$R^2 = 46\%$	
Chi-square/df	2.733	2.525	≤ 3
Normal Fit Index (NFI)	.744	.792	$\geq .9$
Tucker-Lewis Index (TLI)	.770	.826	$\geq .9$
Comparative Fit Index (CFI)	.816	.860	$\geq .9$
Root Mean Square Error of Approximation (RMSEA)	.098	.092	$\leq .09$

the relationship between brand loyalty and brand love. The literature suggests two contradictory propositions: brand love precedes brand loyalty (Carroll and Ahuvia, 2006; Kamat and Parulekar, 2007) and brand loyalty precedes brand love (Aaker, 1991). We tested loyalty as a precursor to love, with our results supporting the notion that brand loyalty is a precursor of brand love (H4).

Conclusions and limitations

Both academics (Carroll and Ahuvia, 2006; Fournier, 1998) and practitioners (Roberts, 2004) highlight the importance of the feeling of love toward a brand. Although the literature on the emotional relationship between consumers and brands is increasing, only a few empirical studies on brand love have been conducted and all exhibit certain limitations. Our study provides an important contribution as we show that the construct of brand love is nested in the theory of parasocial love rather than interpersonal relationship love, which contradicts existing findings and provides a new perspective on this topic. We also show that brand loyalty precedes brand love. For marketing academics, this chapter provides a new perceptive on brand love. We encourage researchers to further investigate the suitable underlying theory for consumer–brand relationships and its operationalization. It would be interesting to further assess the similarities and differences exhibited by parasocial relationships between a person and a celebrity and the parasocial relationship metaphor used in the context of a relationship between a person and a brand, in line with the existing discussion of the interpersonal relationship between persons and the interpersonal relationship metaphor used in the context of a person and a brand.

There are some limitations. First, a second dataset is needed to test our findings. Moreover, surveying a larger, more diverse pool of respondents, including non-students and people from different countries, would allow us to generalize the current findings. Extending the research beyond the present US sample would allow investigation of the links between brand love and culture. Third, we should test the proposed model using other product categories as well as services. Fourth, we should extend the current model to incorporate other categories of variables influencing brand love in order to improve the model fit. Fifth, for the dependent variable, behavioral data should also be collected next to feeling expression. Finally, in asking respondents to choose their favorite brands for rating, there might be a bias of relationships, possibly constraining the sample to loved objects with little variance overall.

References

Aaker, D.A. (1991) *Managing Brand Equity*, New York: The Free Press.
Aaker, J. (1997) "Dimensions of Brand Personality", *Journal of Marketing Research*, 34 (3): 347–56.

Aggarwal, P. (2004) "The Effects of Brand Relationship Norms on Consumer Attitudes and Behavior", *Journal of Consumer Research*, 31: 87–101.

Ahuvia, A.C. (1993) "I Love It! Toward a Unifying Theory of Love across Diverse Love Objects", working paper, Northwestern University.

—— (2005a) "Beyond the Extended Self: Loved Objects and Consumers' Identity Narratives", *Journal of Consumer Research*, 32: 171–84.

—— (2005b) "The Love Prototype Revisited: A Qualitative Exploration of Contemporary Folk Psychology", working paper, University of Michigan – Dearborn.

Albert, N., Merunka, D. and Valette-Florence, P. (2008) "Loving a Brand across Cultures: A French/US Comparison", paper presented at Academy of Marketing Science Cultural Perspectives in Marketing Conference in New Orleans, LA, USA, 2008.

Ball, A.D. and Tasaki, L.H. (1995) "The Role and Measurement of Attachment in Consumer Behavior", *Journal of Consumer Psychology*, 1 (2): 155–72.

Batra, R. and Ahtolo, O. (1991) "Measuring the Hedonic and Utilitarian Sources of Consumer Attitudes", *Marketing Letters*, 2: 159–70.

Bello, D., Leung, K., Tung, R.L. and van Witteloostuijn, A. (2009) "Student Samples in International Business", *Journal of International Business Studies*, 40: 361–4.

Berry, L.L. (2000) "Cultivating Service Brand Equity", *Journal of Academy of Marketing Science*, 28 (1): 128–37.

Bloemer, J.M.M. and Lemmink, J.G.A.M. (1992) "The Importance of Customer Satisfaction in Explaining Brand and Dealer Loyalty", *Journal of Marketing Management*, 8: 351–64.

Busacca, B. and Castaldo, S. (2003) "Brand Knowledge, Brand Trust and Consumer Response: A Conceptual Framework", in 2nd workshop "Trust within and between organizations" special session "Trust in marketing". Amsterdam.

Carlson, B.D., Donavan, T. and Cumiskey, K. (2009) "Consumer–Brand Relationships in Sport: Brand Personality and Identification", *International Journal of Retail and Distribution Management*, 37(4): 370–84.

Carroll, B.A. and Ahuvia, A.C. (2006) "Some Antecedents and Outcomes of Brand Love", *Marketing Letters*, 17 (2): 79–89.

Caughey, J.L. (1984) *Imaginary Social Worlds: a cultural approach*, Lincoln, NE: University of Nebraska Press.

Chaudhuri, A. (1998) "Product Class Effects on Perceived Risk: The Role of Emotion", *International Journal of Research in Marketing*, 15 (2): 157–68.

Chaudhuri, A. and Holbrook, M.B. (2001) "The Chain of Effects from Brand Trust and Brand Affect to Brand Performance: The Role of Brand Loyalty", *Journal of Marketing*, 65 (2): 81–93.

Churchill, G.A., Jr (1979) "A Paradigm for Developing Better Measures of Marketing Constructs", *Journal of Marketing Research*, 16: 64–73.

Conway, J.C. and Rubin, A.M. (1991) "Psychological Predictors of Television Viewing Motivation", *Communication Research*, 18: 443–4.

Davis, K.E. and Todd, M.J. (1985) "Assessing Friendship: Prototypes, Paradigm Cases, and Relationship Assessment", in S.W. Duck and D. Perlman (eds) *Understanding Personal Relationships: an interdisciplinary approach*, Beverly Hills, CA: Sage.

Fetscherin, M. and Toncar, M. (2009) "Country of Origin Effect on the US Consumers' Brand Perception of Automobiles from China and India", *Multinational Business Review*, 17(2): 115–31.

Fournier, S. (1998) "Consumers and their Brands: Developing Relationship Theory in Consumer Research", *Journal of Consumer Research*, 24 (4): 343–72.

Fournier, S. and Yao, J.L. (1997) "Reviving Brand Loyalty: A Reconceptualization within the Framework of Consumer–Brand Relationships", *International Journal of Research in Marketing*, 14 (5): 451–72.

Garbarino, E. and Johnson, M.S. (1999) "The Different Roles of Satisfaction, Trust, and Commitment in Customer Relationships", *Journal of Marketing*, 63 (2): 70–87.

Gremler, D.D. (1995) "The Effect of Satisfaction, Switching Costs, and Interpersonal Bonds on Service Loyalty", unpublished doctoral dissertation, Arizona State University.

Ha, H. and Perks, H. (2005) "Effects of Consumer Perceptions of Brand Experience on the Web: Brand Familiarity, Satisfaction and Brand Trust", *Journal of Consumer Behaviour*, 4 (6): 438–52.

Hatfield, E. and Sprecher, S. (1986) "Measuring Passionate Love in Intimate Relationships", *Journal of Adolescence*, 9: 383–410.

Hayes, J.B., Alford, B., Silver, L. and York, R. (2006) "Looks Matter in Developing Consumer–Brand Relationships", *Journal of Product and Brand Management*, 15 (5): 306–15.

Heinrich, D., Bauer, H. and Mühl, J. (2009) "Measuring Brand Love: Applying Sternberg's Triangular Theory of Love in Consumer–Brand Relations", in Proceedings of the Australian and New Zealand Marketing Academy Conference, 2008. Available online at www.anzmac2008.org/_Proceedings/PDF/S05/Heinrich%20Bauer%20&%20Muh l%20S8%20PS%20P3.pdf> (accessed 15 November 2009).

Hendrick, C. and Hendrick, S.S. (1986) "A Theory and Method of Love", *Journal of Personality and Social Psychology*, 50 (2): 392–402.

Herche, J. (1994) *Measuring Social Values: a multi-item adaptation to the list of values (MILOV)*, Cambridge, MA: Marketing Science Institute.

Horton, D. and Wohl, R.R. (1956) "Mass Communication and Para-Social Interaction: Observation on Intimacy at a Distance", *Psychiatry*, 19 (3): 188–211.

Hu, L. and Bentler, P.M. (1998) "Fit Indices in Covariance Structure Modeling: Sensitivity to Underparameterized Model Misspecification", *Psychological Methods*, 3: 424–53.

Kamat, V. and Parulekar, A.A. (2007) "Brand Love – the Precursor to Loyalty", in J.R. Priester, D.J. MacInnis, and C.W. Park (eds) *New Frontiers in Branding: attitudes, attachments, and relationships*, Santa Monica, CA: Society for Consumer Psychology

Kasper, J.D.P. (1988) "On Problem Perception, Dissatisfaction and Brand Loyalty", *Journal of Economic Psychology*, 9: 387–97.

Keh, H.T., Pang, J. and Peng, S. (2007) "Understanding and Measuring Brand Love", in J.R. Priester, D.J. MacInnis, and C.W. Park (eds) *New Frontiers in Branding: attitudes, attachments, and relationships*, Santa Monica, CA: Society for Consumer Psychology.

Keller, K.L. and Lehmann, D.R. (2006) "Brands and Branding: Research Findings and Future Priorities", *Marketing Science*, 25 (6): 740–59.

Kraft, F.B., Granbois, D.H. and Summers, J.O. (1973) "Brand Evaluation and Brand Choice: A Longitudinal Study", *Journal of Marketing Research*, 10: 235–41.

LaBarbera, P.A. and Mazursky, D. (1983) "A Longitudinal Assessment of Consumer Satisfaction/Dissatisfaction", *Journal of Marketing Research*, 20: 393–404.

Lala, V., Allred, A. and Chakraborty, G. (2009) "A Multidimensional Scale for Measuring Country Image", *Journal of International Consumer Marketing*, 21 (1): 51–66.

Lau, G.T. and Lee, S.H. (2000) "Consumer's Trust in a Brand and the Link to Brand Loyalty", *Journal of Market Focused Management*, 4 (4): 341–70.

Lee, J.A. (1977) "A Typology of Styles of Loving", *Personality and Social Psychology Bulletin*, 3: 173–82.

Levy, S.J. (1985) "Dreams, Fairy Tales, Animals, and Cars", *Psychology and Marketing*, 2 (2): 67.

Low, G. and Lamb, C. (2000) "The Measurement and Dimensionality of Brand Associations", *Journal of Product and Brand Management*, 9 (6): 350–70.

Martin, I.M. and Eroglu, S.A. (1993) "Measuring a Multi-Dimensional Construct: Country Image", *Journal of Business Research*, 28 (3): 191–210.

Masuda, M. (2003) "Meta-Analyses of Love Scales: Do Various Love Scales Measure the Same Psychological Constructs?" *Japanese Psychological Research*, 45 (1): 25–37.

Monga, A.B. (2002) "Brands as a Relationship Partner: Gender Differences in Perspectives", in Susan M. Broniarczyk and Kent Nakamoto (eds) *Advances in Consumer Research, Vol. 29*, Valdosta, GA: Association of Consumer Research.

Pereira, A., Hsu, C. and Kundu, S.K. (2005) "Country-of-Origin Image: Measurement and Cross-National Testing", *Journal of Business Research*, 58 (1): 103–6.

Perse, E.M. (1990) "Media Involvement and Local News Effects", *Journal of Broadcasting and Electronic Media*, 34: 17–36.

Perse, E.M. and Rubin, R.B. (1989) "Attribution in Social and Parasocial Relationships", *Communication Research*, 16: 59–77.

Quester, P.G. and Lim, A.L. (2003) "Production Involvement/Brand Loyalty: Is There a Link?" *Journal of Product and Brand Management*, 12 (1): 22–38.

Richins, M.L. (1997) "Measuring Emotions in the Consumption Experience", *Journal of Consumer Research*, 24 (2): 127–46.

Roberts, K. (2004) *Lovemarks: the future beyond brands*, New York: Power House Books.

Rook, D.W. and Fisher, R.J. (1995) "Normative Influences on Impulsive Buying Behavior", *Journal of Consumer Research*, 22: 305–13.

Rozanski, H.D., Baum, A.G. and Wolfsen, B.T. (1999) "Brand Zealots: Realizing the Full Value of Emotional Brand Loyalty", *Strategy and Business*, 17: 51–62.

Rubin, Z. (1970) "Measurement of Romantic Love", *Journal of Personality and Social Psychology*, 16 (2): 265–73.

Schumacker, R.E. (1992) "Goodness of Fit Criteria in Structural Equation Models", paper presented at the Annual Meeting of the American Educational Research Association (San Francisco, CA, April 20–24, 1992).

Schumacker, R.E. and Lomax, R.G. (1996) *A Beginner's Guide to Structural Equation Modeling*, London: Lawrence Erlbaum Associates.

Shaver, P. and Hazan, C. (1987) "Being Lonely, Falling in Love: Perspectives from Attachment Theory", *Journal of Social Behavior and Personality*, 2: 105–24.

Shimp, T.A. and Madden, T.J. (1988) "Consumer–Object Relations: A Conceptual Framework Based Analogously on Sternberg's Triangular Theory of Love", in M.J. Houston (ed.) *Advances in Consumer Research, vol. 15*, Provo, UT: Association for Consumer Research.

Smith, J.M. and Schaefer, C.E. (1969) "Development of a Creativity Scale for the Adjective Check List", *Psychological Reports*, 25 (1): 87–92.

Sternberg, R.J. (1986) "A Triangular Theory of Love", *Psychological Review*, 93:119–35.

Strizhakova, Y., Coulter, R.A. and Price, L.L. (2008) "The Meanings of Branded Products: A Cross-National Scale Development and Meaning Assessment", *International Journal of Research in Marketing*, 25: 83–94.

Swaminathan, V., Page, K.L. and Gürhan Canli, Z. (2007) "'My' Brand or 'Your' Brand: The Effects of Brand Relationship Dimensions and Self-Construal on Brand Evaluations", *Journal of Consumer Research*, 34 (2): 248–59.

Tepper Tian, K., Bearden, W.O. and Hunter, G.L. (2001) "Consumers' Need for Uniqueness: Scale Development and Validation", *Journal of Consumer Research*, 20 (1): 50–66.

Thomson, M., MacInnis, D.J. and Park, C.W. (2005) "The Ties that Bind: Measuring the Strength of Consumers' Emotional Attachment to Brands", *Journal of Consumer Psychology*, 15: 77–91.

Voss, K.E., Spangenberg, E.R. and Grohmann, B. (2003) "Measuring the Hedonic and Utilitarian Dimensions of Consumer Attitude", *Journal of Marketing Research*, 40 (3): 310–19.

Wallendorf, M. and Arnould, E.J. (1988) "'My Favorite Things': A Cross-Cultural Inquiry into Object Attachment, Possessiveness, and Social Linkage", *Journal of Consumer Research*, 14: 531–47.

Whang, Y., Allen, J., Sahoury, N. and Zhang, H. (2004) "Falling in Love with a Product: The Structure of a Romantic Consumer–Product Relationship", in B.E. Kahn and

M.F. Luce (eds) *Advances in Consumer Research, vol. 31*, Provo, UT: Association for Consumer Research.

Yoo, B. and Donthu, N. (2001) "Developing and Validating a Multidimensional Consumer-Based Brand Equity Scale", *Journal of Business Research*, 52 (1): 1–14.

Yoon, C. and Gutchess, A.H. (2006) "A Functional Magnetic Resonance Imaging Study of Neural Dissociations between Brand and Person Judgments", *Journal of Consumer Research*, 33 (1): 31–40.

9

CONCEPTUALIZING AND MEASURING BRAND RELATIONSHIP QUALITY

Manfred Bruhn, Falko Eichen, Karsten Hadwich, and Sven Tuzovic

Introduction

Many consumer markets are now characterized by a high degree of market saturation and an increasing level of competition, in particular from retailer brands. Furthermore, consumers face an ever increasing level of product variety. For instance, about 30,000 new products in the fast moving consumer goods (FMCG) market have been launched in Germany in a single year representing about 600 products per week. The increasing number of consumer brands thus has led to a form of "brand inflation" in FMCG markets. In addition, the role of consumers in the marketplace has changed as well. Consumers are more price sensitive, they have higher expectations with regard to product quality and customer service, and they rely rather on word-of-mouth communication than on traditional advertising. In addition, it appears that consumers have become more critical with regard to the perception of brands. High levels of price competition have led to a decreasing level of brand awareness and increased switching intentions of brands. As a consequence, the role of customer loyalty has become an increasingly important topic for businesses in consumer markets.

However, most of these companies face the problem that they do not "know" their customers. Consumer markets are typically characterized by indirect distribution channels (e.g., wholesalers and/or retailers) as well as a large number of anonymous consumers. As a result, it is more difficult for them to initiate and maintain personal provider–customer relationships. Delgado-Ballester and Munuera-Aleman (2005: 189) conclude that in "consumer markets there are too many anonymous consumers making it unlikely that the company could develop personal relationships with each one." In the past, consumer goods companies have typically invested in building their brands with the purpose of creating a strong bond between the brand and the buyer. Alreck and Settle (1999: 130) argue that "the ultimate objective is to build a durable relationship between a specific brand and a particular customer group – to create a strong bond between brand and buyer!" However, the conditions in the marketplace have changed. Companies cannot rely on this form of "automatism" anymore, i.e., customer loyalty cannot be achieved solely as a result of strong brands. From a brand management perspective it is thus important to identify and understand the drivers of consumer–brand relationships. More recently researchers have noted that "consumers differ not only in how they perceive brands but also in how they relate to brands" (Aggarwal 2004: 87). According to this line of research, people build relationships with brands similar to social relationships among humans.

In this context, a number of scholars have started to investigate the area of relationship-oriented brand management, focusing on the relationships of consumers with brands and the resulting effects on brand loyalty and customer loyalty (Aggarwal 2004; Fournier 1994; Fournier and Yao 1997; Sheth and Parvatiyar 1995). Some authors (e.g., Fournier 1998; Veloutsou 2007) argue that an effective brand relationship management requires a comprehensive measurement of brand relationship quality (BRQ) which is defined as a "customer-based indicator of the strength and depth of a person–brand relationship" (Fournier 1994: 124). However, a review of the current literature on the measurement of BRQ reveals that important gaps still exist, both empirically and conceptually. For instance, existing approaches view BRQ mainly as a result of creating strong brand personalities, whereas the contribution of reciprocal relationship marketing activities on consumer–brand relationships has been neglected so far (Eichen 2010). Research studies, however, suggest that interpersonal interactions in the context of consumer brands can lead to increased brand attachment. For example, McAlexander et al. (2002: 43) note that "sustained interpersonal interactions can lead to relationships that transcend mere common interest in a brand and its applications." Patterson and O'Malley (2006) give a similar argument. According to the authors, managers need to monitor closely how customers themselves define their connections with brands. "If consumers . . . view these connections in terms of communal interaction with other consumers, then managers need to identify how best to facilitate that interaction" (Patterson and O'Malley 2006: 17). Consequently, a comprehensive analysis of consumer–brand relationships requires an interdisciplinary view instead of the common unilateral approach. Drawing on previous work on relationship marketing, branding, and consumer–company identification, Dimitriadis and Papista (2010) develop a conceptual framework to explain consumer–brand relationships. The authors argue that a cognitive overlap between a brand's image and the consumer's self-concept is a positive condition in order to develop relationship quality. Furthermore, they suggest several "in-role" and "extra-role" relational outcomes. However, Dimitriadis and Papista also conclude that the "development of measurement scales . . . is a research topic of high priority" (Dimitriadis and Papista 2010: 396).

In addition to some theoretical research deficits, several gaps can be identified with regard to empirical work. First, empirical studies have largely adopted a qualitative approach. For example, several scholars apply individual case studies to demonstrate the relevance of consumer–brand relationships (Coupland 2005; Fournier 1998; Fournier and Yao 1997; Ji 2002; Kates 2000; Lindberg-Repo and Brookes 2004; Morris and Martin 2000). Therefore, it is difficult to generalize the empirical results. Second, the majority of studies focus only on high-involvement products. Third, only few cross-industrial studies exist so far. The existing quantitative studies often focus on individual consumer goods industries in isolation (Hayes et al. 2000; Hess 1998; Kressmann et al. 2006; Swaminathan et al. 2007). Several authors suggest that cross-industrial studies are needed to advance the work on BRQ (Breivik and Thorbjørnsen 2008; Esch et al. 2006; Veloutsou 2007).

The objective of the present chapter is to contribute to the current discussion of consumer–brand relationships and to provide a better understanding of the antecedents of BRQ. Adopting an interdisciplinary view the authors develop a comprehensive third-order measurement model of BRQ. The model is then tested across eight different consumer markets in Germany including automobiles, cell phones, toothpaste, beer, tissues, tinned vegetables, car insurance, and wireless network operators. With a sample size of n=2,009 this study presents the largest cross-industry study in the German market so far. The large data set thus provides a strong context for the generalizability of the findings.

Brand relationship quality

Literature review

Even though there is a growing body of literature that deals with consumer–brand relationships, several authors note that research so far has been limited. Aggarwal (2004: 87) concludes that "even though there is growing interest of both researchers and practitioners in consumer–brand relationships work in this area has been fairly limited." Dimitriadis and Papista (2010) also note that little research has yet investigated the relationship of a consumer with a brand, the components of the strength of that relationship, and how it is expressed through consumer behavior. In this section we review the existing literature that has focused on consumer–brand relationship quality. In addition to literature in the field of brand management, we draw from research in the field of relationship marketing (Morgan and Hunt 1994; Palmatier et al. 2006) as well as previous work on the concept of relationship quality. Dimitriadis and Papista (2010) recently have argued that the "literature on brand management and relationship development has so far merged as two separate streams, despite the possibilities for complementarity between the two concepts" (Palmer 1996). Within the domain of relationship marketing, the concept of relationship quality has gained a central role as mediating variable between relationship marketing activities and their outcomes (Hadwich 2003; Roberts et al. 2003). As the construct relationship quality has been developed and empirically tested in the context of services and between businesses, some authors suggest that brand relationships are a logical extension of the idea of a brand personality (Blackstone 2000; Dimitriadis and Papista 2010). New research proposes that the construct of relationship quality is suitable as well to capture the nature of consumer–brand relationships (Aaker et al. 2004; Kressmann et al. 2006). Table 9.1 illustrates a list of dimensions of BRQ identified by various scholars.

Fournier (1998) identifies six dimensions: love and passion, self-connection, interdependence, commitment, intimacy, and partner quality. Subsequent studies have followed Fournier's original conceptualization (e.g., Aaker et al. 2004; Kressmann et al. 2006). However, new typologies have also emerged sharing some of the original dimensions (e.g., Hess and Story 2005; Veloutsou 2007). Some authors criticize the fact that a common definition and a measurement scale to capture BRQ are still missing (Dimitriadis and Papista 2010; Scarabis and Florack 2005).

Building the conceptual framework

Before building the framework it is necessary to develop a working definition for BRQ. According to Fournier, BRQ can be defined as a "customer-based indicator of the strength and depth of a person–brand relationship [which] reflects the intensity and viability of the enduring association between a consumer and a brand" (Fournier 1994: 124). Other authors only refer to dimensions to capture BRQ without actually defining the term BRQ (e.g., Thorbjørnsen et al. 2002; Veloutsou 2007). We suggest that a definition needs to capture three components: (1) the evaluation of brand relationships as the object; (2) an integrated perspective of ex-post evaluations as well as future evaluations; and (3) a relationship-oriented interpretation compared with individual transactions with the brand. We therefore define BRQ as follows:

> BRQ is the consumer-perceived ability of a brand to consistently develop the consumer–brand relationship according to the consumer's individual needs.

BRQ thus reflects the intensity and viability of the enduring association between a consumer and a brand (Fournier 1994). Theoretically, the expectations of the brand as a relationship partner determine the quality of the consumer–brand relationship from the consumer's point of view. Brand quality

TABLE 9.1 Dimensions of brand relationship quality

Source	Dimensions						Others
	Love/passion	Self-connection	Interdependence	Commitment	Intimacy	Partner quality	
Fournier (1994)	X	X	X	X	X	X	Brand attachment
Hayes, Capella, and Alford (2000)	X	X		X	X	X	Brand attractiveness
Thorbjørnsen et al. (2002)	X	X		X	X	X	
Park, Kim, and Kim (2002)	X	X		X	X	X	Nostalgia, brand trust
Aaker, Fournier, and Brasel (2004)	X	X		X	X	X	Brand satisfaction
Chang and Chieng (2006)	X	X		X		X	Brand attachment, functional connection
Kressmann et al. (2006)	X		X		X	X	
Smit, Bronner, and Tolboom (2007)	X	X	X	X	X	X	
Breivik and Thorbjørnsen (2008)	X	X	X	X	X	X	

as a relationship partner is derived from so-called animism theory (Gilmore 1919), which states that individuals tend to humanize inanimate objects, such as a passive brand. While brands represent lifeless objects, they are pushed into consumers' minds through continuous marketing activities (e.g., advertising), leading to an increased enlivenment among consumers (Fournier 1998). The perceived behavior of the brand then contributes to the development, maintenance, and even the termination of consumer–brand relationships. It further reflects in the cross-transactional judgment of brand quality as a relationship partner. The associations with brand quality as a relationship partner do not need to be the result of reciprocal interactive communication experiences; instead they can emerge from consumption experiences or in a one-sided interaction process, such as advertising (Fournier 1994).

Analogous to the expectations of a relationship partner in inter-human relationships, consumer expectations of the brand as a relationship partner vary with the nature of the relationship with the brand (Aggarwal 2004; Esch *et al.* 2006). While economically motivated consumer–brand relationships emphasize the fairness principle, socially motivated consumer–brand relationships are characterized by relationship feelings and altruism. In exchange-based or economically motivated consumer–brand relationships, brand satisfaction can be regarded as the primary target variable. For example, Esch *et al.* (2006: 100) note that the "primary positive outcome of an exchange relationship is satisfaction." Since the focus in exchange-based relationships is primarily on cost-benefit calculations, equity theory suggests that consumers expect performance and reward to be in balance (Mills and Clark 1982). As long as this occurs, the consumer is satisfied with the brand (Oliver and DeSarbo 1988). Various empirical studies confirm the relevancy of brand satisfaction for perceived BRQ (e.g., Aaker *et al.* 2004; Huber *et al.* 2008).

On the other hand, consumer–brand relationships that are primarily socially motivated (so-called community relationships) are determined less by a desire for fairness than by actual relationship feelings and altruism. This can be concluded from previous work by Esch *et al.* (2006) who suggest that "communal aspects of relationship involve feelings about other people; they transcend self-interest" (Esch *et al.* 2006: 100). The primary success factor of socially motivated relationships is seen in brand trust (Esch *et al.* 2006; Hess 1998), which is characterized by the consumer's confidence in the brand (cognitive trust) and the assessment of the brand as a reliable partner (affective trust) (Delgado-Ballester and Munuera-Aleman 2001). Brand trust is established as a central factor of BRQ in various studies (Park *et al.* 2002; Smit *et al.* 2007).

However, brand trust alone is not able to comprehensively capture consumer expectations in socially motivated consumer–brand relationships. Emotionally loaded community relationships distinguish themselves not only in the need for trust but also in the desire for emotional closeness (Berscheid 1994). The convergence of the relationship partners takes place on cognitive, emotional, and conative levels (Grau 2003). The significance of emotional closeness is derived from the psychological well-being related to close relationships: close relationships result in positive emotions like "feeling understood, validated, cared for, and closely connected with another person" (Reis and Shaver 1988: 386) and thereby contribute to the personality development and social integration of the relationship partners. Kressmann *et al.* (2003) and Scarabis (2006) confirm the relevance of emotional closeness as a factor for BRQ. Factor analysis of the samples in both studies resulted in four factors of love/passion, connection to identity, interdependence, and intimacy being grouped as one factor which Scarabis explicitly describes as affective brand closeness.

While quality of the brand as relationship partner (BRP) represents the first dimension of BRQ, our framework also includes quality of the brand as interaction platform (BIP) as second dimension. The relevance of interactions for BRQ is related to social penetration theory (Altman and Taylor 1973). In other words, the development of consumer–brand relationships requires repeated reciprocal interactions, in which mutual and continuous exchange takes place, fostering understanding and closeness between the relationship partners. Brand-related interaction platforms facilitate mutual influence and dialogue between the consumer and the brand. Consumer experiences, in regard to these brand interaction platforms, are the result of the additional consumer benefits provided by reciprocal interactions (Grönroos 1997). Due to the lifelessness of the brand, the reaction to consumer activities requires vocal brand representatives. Corresponding to the distinction between consumer–consumer interactions, employee–consumer interactions, and firm–consumer interactions in relationship marketing (Iacobucci and Hibbard 1999), consumers, employees, and communicative systems can be regarded as representatives, who jointly embody the spectrum of dialogic interaction partners for the foundation of BRQ.

Summing up, we measured BRQ on the basis of (a) the two formative dimensions BRP and BIP, and (b) two reflective items that captured BRQ as a uni-dimensional concept on a high level of abstraction ("There is a deep connection between me and this brand", "I have a good relationship with this brand"). Following Breivik and Thorbjørnsen (2008), who test reflective vs. formative BRQ model specifications, we decided to apply formative model specifications between the different measurement levels. Thus, BRQ is considered to be a consequence and not a driver of the quality dimensions. Figure 9.1 summarizes the conceptualization of BRQ as a multi-factor second-order construct.

Methodology

Sample and data collection

To test the theoretical model a cross-industry panel study was conducted. Data were drawn from the GfK Group's Global Online Panel consisting of 30,000

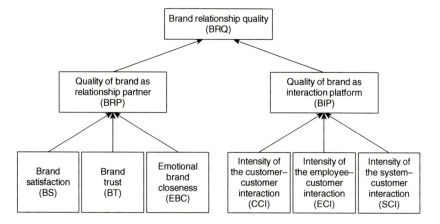

FIGURE 9.1 Conceptualization of BRQ and its antecedents

people for the German consumer market. An online survey was sent out to 2,241 panelists in May 2008. The survey entails a combination of random selection and quota sampling. Besides having a representative sample, the objective was to obtain a sufficient number of responses for each sector. For this study the goal was 250 responses per category. The selection of industries was determined by considering their variance (i.e., wide array of different consumer industries) as well as their relevance (i.e., adequate relevance to consumers and the national economy). Overall, eight different sectors were chosen: automobiles, cell phones, toothpaste, beer, tissues, tinned vegetables, car insurance, and wireless network providers. These categories represent a wide range in the consumer goods market as they differ with regard to the types of goods (e.g., FMCG vs. durables), the type of utility (functional vs. symbolic), and the degree of involvement (low vs. high). Table 9.2 summarizes the characteristics of the industry sample, whereas Table 9.3 provides an overview of all brands that are included per category (see Eichen 2010).

Of the 2,241 panelists, a total of 1,121 respondents completed the online questionnaire (response rate of 50 percent); 888 respondents evaluated two industries leading to a total data set of 2,009. The data set is equally distributed across all eight consumer goods sectors as well as within each consumer goods sector across all eighty-two brands. Overall, the goal of 250 responses per category was met. When looking at the brand level, the findings show that responses of stronger brands outnumber weaker brands across all eight categories. For instance, within the automobile sector 74 percent of all responses refer to the brands of Audi, BMW, Ford, Mercedes, Opel, and VW. Nokia is the market leader with 43 percent in the cell phone category. Within the beer category the brands Beck's, Bitburger, and Krombacher represent 57 percent of all responses.

TABLE 9.2 Characteristics of the industry sample

Industry	Goods type	Usage focus	Proportion of budget	Involvement	Frequency of purchase
Automobile	Consumer durable	Symbolic/ functional	High	High	Low
Cell phone	Consumer durable	Symbolic/ functional	Medium	High	Medium
Toothpaste	FMCG	Functional	Low	Medium	High
Beer	FMCG	Symbolic/ functional	Low	Medium	High
Tissues	FMCG	Functional	Low	Low	Medium
Tinned vegetables	FMCG	Functional	Low	Low	High
Car insurance	Contract goods	Functional	Medium	High	Low
Wireless network providers	Contract goods	Symbolic/ functional	Medium	Medium	Low

And in the market for cell phone subscriptions two brands, T-Mobile and Vodafone, combine almost 54 percent of all responses. With regard to gender, all sectors are almost equally distributed; however, the male proportion is slightly larger than the female one, varying between 50 and 59 percent. Only the beer sector shows a different composition with more than 70 percent of the respondents being male. The age distribution shows that the majority of respondents are between 21 and 60 years old.

Scale development and measures

Based on our conceptualization the construct BRQ comprises two second-order dimensions: quality of the brand as relationship partner (BRP) and quality of the brand as interaction platform (BIP). While scales from prior research were used as a source to measure BRP, the development of the items for BIP began with an initial item pool generated from fifteen in-depth interviews with consumers and experts (directors of marketing agencies). All measures are based on seven-point Likert scales. The anchors were "1 = strongly disagree" and "7 = strongly agree." We pretested the questionnaire using individual interviews with six marketing experts. This was followed by a quantitative pretest (n=188).

With regard to BRP, we drew on existing items to measure brand satisfaction and brand trust. Emotional brand closeness is not explicitly represented as a factor of BRQ in literature in any conceptualization approach. Thus, this relationship feature is implicitly measured through the factors brand intimacy, brand

TABLE 9.3 Overview of brands included per product category

Automobile	Cell phones	Toothpaste	Beer	Tissues	Tinned vegetables	Car insurance	Wireless network provider
Audi	Apple	Ajona	Beck's	Blümia	Bonduelle	Aachener und Münchner	Debitel
BMW	LG	Aronal	Bitburger	Kleenex	D'Aucy	Allianz	E-Plus
Citroen	Motorola	Blend-a-med	Hasseröder	Kokett	Gartenkrone	AXA	Mobilcom
Fiat	Nokia	Colgate	Jever	Öko Purex	Happy Harvest	Cosmos Direkt	O2
Ford	Sagem	Dentagard	König Pilsner	Regina	Jonker Fris	DEVK	Talkline
Mazda	Samsung	Elmex	Krombacher	Solo	Kingscrown	Gerling	T-Mobile
Mercedes	Sony Ericsson	Eurodont	Radeberger	Tempo	Noliko	Gothaer	Vodafone
Opel		Friscodent	Veltins	Zewa	Seidel	HDI Privat	
Peugeot		Odol-med3	Warsteiner		Sonnen-Bassermann	HUK-Coburg	
Renault		Perlweiss			Stollenwerk	LVM	
Skoda		Sensodyne				VHV	
Toyota		Signal				Victoria	
VW		Theramed				Würtembergische	
						Zürich	

interdependency, brand passion, and brand self-linkage, which represent cognitive, affective, and conative elements of closeness. Based on the qualitative in-depth interviews, we identified several existing items of these factors which closely capture emotional brand closeness. With regard to BIP, we developed new measurement scales based on the in-depth interviews that capture consumer–consumer (C2C) interaction, system–consumer (S2C) interaction, and employee–consumer (E2C) interaction. All constructs are reflective multi-item constructs. The scale items (after purification) are provided in Table 9.4.

Data analysis and results

We used Partial Least Squares (PLS) as the estimation approach to specify the model and estimate the parameters. PLS is a component-based structural equation modeling (SEM) technique developed by Wold (1974, 1985). The aim of the PLS methodology is to maximize the explained variance of dependent variables by disaggregating the overall causal model into partial equations that are solved simultaneously via regression analysis (Chin 1998; Herrman et al. 2010). PLS is similar to covariance-based techniques (e.g., LISREL which is a software package used for SEM) but offers more flexibility (Lee et al. 2008). We chose PLS because of the formative nature of the higher-order construct BRQ (Fornell and Bookstein 1982). Conventional covariance-based approaches such as LISREL tolerate formative indicators only in very restricted circumstances (Herrmann et al. 2010), whereas PLS can handle both reflective and formative types of measurement models (Fornell and Cha 1994; Henseler et al. 2009). Furthermore, PLS proves more robust for smaller sample sizes and when measures are not well established (Fornell and Bookstein 1982; Wold 1985). This is applicable to the industry-specific evaluations, avoiding the problem of under-identification which can occur when using covariance-based approaches such as LISREL (Bollen 1989).

As Table 9.4 reports, all constructs have acceptable levels of reliability with the composite reliability (CR) coefficients ranging from .92 to .96, exceeding the recommend threshold of .7 (Nunnally 1978). Cronbach's Alpha ranges from .87 to .94 exceeding the threshold as well. Furthermore, reliability of individual items has been assessed by analyzing the loadings of the items with their respective latent construct (see Table 9.4). All measurement items exceed the threshold of .5, loading significantly on the construct. Convergent validity has been assessed with the average variance extracted (AVE). The values range from .77 to .89, exceeding the benchmark of .5 (Fornell and Larcker 1981). In addition, we investigated discriminant validity using Fornell and Larcker's (1981) approach. The test reveals that discriminant validity is satisfactory with respect to all the variables (see Table 9.5).

Figure 9.2 shows the results of the PLS estimation. All parameter estimates, except for brand trust, are significant at p < .05. These findings indicate an adequate

TABLE 9.4 Measurement

Factor	Items	Loadings
Brand Satisfaction (BS) (α=.936; CR=.960; AVE=.888)	I am satisfied with this [brand].	.946
	The [brand] has come up to my expectations.	.952
	This brand is close to an ideal [brand].	.929
Brand Trust (BT) (α=.940; CR=.962; AVE=.893)	This [brand] is reliable.	.934
	This is an honest [brand].	.956
	I trust this [brand].	.946
Emotional Brand Closeness (EBC) (α=.904; CR=.932; AVE=.777)	I feel that I understand this [brand].	.879
	The [brand] and I are meant for each other.	.923
	This [brand] reveals a lot about my personality.	.941
	This [brand] plays a decisive role in my life.	.865
CCI (α=.870; CR=.920; AVE=.795)	I believe that this [brand] provides sufficient options to get in touch with other consumers/users of this [brand].	.824
	It is interesting to share experiences with other consumers/users of this [brand].	.937
	I use or would like to use the option to discuss with other consumers/users of this [brand].	.910
ECI (α=.874; CR=.922; AVE=.796)	I am of the view that this [brand] provides sufficient options to get in touch with employees of this [brand].	.859
	It is important to me being able to contact employees of this [brand].	.924
	I use or would like to use the option to discuss about [brand] with employees of this brand.	.893
SCI (α=.872; CR=.921; AVE=.795)	I think that this [brand] provides sufficient options to get in touch with the [brand] producer through interactive online applications.	.842
	It is important to me being able to get in touch with the [brand] producer through interactive online applications.	.934
	I use or would like to use the option to get in touch with the [brand] producer through interactive online applications.	.897

Note: α = Cronbach's Alpha; CR = Composite Reliability; AVE = Average Variance Extracted; CCI = consumer–consumer interaction; ECI = employee–consumer interaction; SCI = system–consumer interaction

TABLE 9.5 Discriminant validity

	Brand satisfaction	Brand trust	Emotional brand closeness	Intensity of consumer–consumer interactions	Intensity of employee–consumer interactions	Intensity of system–consumer interactions
Brand satisfaction	**.889**	.581	.206	.021	.013	.023
Brand trust		**.893**	.368	.084	.082	.095
Emotional brand closeness			**.774**	.300	.183	.189
Intensity of consumer–consumer interaction				**.793**	.523	.496
Intensity of employee–consumer interaction					**.797**	.697
Intensity of system–consumer interaction						**.795**

Notes: Bold numbers on the diagonal show the AVE. Numbers above the diagonal represent the squared correlations.

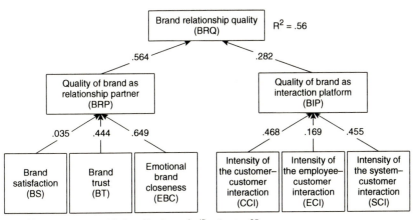

Note: All parameters, except for brand trust, are significant   p < .05

FIGURE 9.2 PLS estimations for the measurement model

model specification. As PLS does not provide statistics to measure overall model fit, we used the variance explained to assess nomological validity (Hulland 1999; Slotegraaf and Atuahene-Gima 2011). The formative and reflective measurement approaches share 56 percent of their variance, indicating predictive validity for the two formative quality dimensions.

To investigate the interrelationships between constructs across industries, Steenkamp and Baumgartner (1998) indicate that full or partial metric invariance must be given because the scale intervals of the latent constructs must be comparable across industries. Except for two constructs, full metric invariance was supported. By sequentially relaxing constraints on parameters, we conclude that partial metric invariance is supported for the two remaining constructs.

Discussion

On the level of the six relationship quality sub-dimensions we identify emotional brand closeness and brand trust as core drivers of BRQ, with the former (latter) accounting for up to 39.5 percent (27.1 percent) of the BRQ variance (see Table 9.6). These results are similar across all industries except the beer industry. Here, emotional brand closeness has the highest level with 73.6 percent, followed by consumer–consumer interactions that account for up to 26.4 percent of the BRQ variance. The findings also indicate that generally in the consumer goods market, brand satisfaction does not seem to be of any importance for BRQ. This suggests that consumer brand quality is solely influenced by communal aspects. An explanation is that brand satisfaction is considered as a basic requirement; therefore, it is of minor importance as a driver of BRQ. This assumption is confirmed by Jones and Sasser (1995).

Furthermore, our results suggest that the quality of the brand as relationship partner has a strong influence across all consumer markets. As Table 9.7 reports, BRP accounts on average for 67 percent of the BRQ variance. The strongest absolute effect is identified in the beer industry, whereas tinned vegetables show the lowest absolute effect (Table 9.7). Finally, there are some industries where the quality of the brand as interaction platform explains up to 47 percent of BRQ (e.g., car insurance).

Conclusion

In this study, we set out to contribute to the recent discussion on consumer–brand relationships and to develop a comprehensive measurement approach to capture brand relationship quality (BRQ). Our findings reveal important managerial implications and offer directions for future research. From a managerial perspective, this study supports the idea that emotional bonds with a brand are further dependent on the brand's ability to facilitate reciprocal interaction with other consumers, employees, and dialogic systems. Firms are thus encouraged to

TABLE 9.6 Influence of relationship quality sub-dimensions on BRQ

Ranking	Average (%)	Automobile (%)	Cell phones (%)	Toothpaste (%)	Beer (%)	Tissues (%)	Tinned vegetables (%)	Car insurance (%)	Wireless network providers (%)
1	EBC 39.5	EBC 37.5	EBC 37.6	EBC 57.1	EBC 73.6	EBC 48.1	EBC 36.8	BT 26.9	BT 31.3
2	BT 27.1	BT 21.6	BT 25.6	BT 29.2	CCI 26.4	BT 27.5	BT 25.2	EBC 25.7	EBC 22.7
3	CCI 14.3	BS 11.5	SCI 14.4	SCI 13.7	BS	SCI 12.3	CCI 19.0	ECI 20.1	CCI 17.7
4	SCI 13.9	SCI 10.8	CCI 13.1	BS	BT	CCI 12.1	SCI 19.0	SCI 17.6	SCI 17.6
5	ECI 5.2	CCI 10.1	ECI 9.3	CCI	SCI	BS	BS	CCI 9.7	BS 10.7
6	BS	ECI 8.5	BS	ECI	ECI	ECI	ECI	BS	ECI
	(n.s.)		(n.s.)	(n.s)	(n.s)	(n.s)	(n.s)	(n.s.)	(n.s)

Notes:
BS: Brand satisfaction
BT: Brand trust
EBC: Emotional brand closeness
n.s. Not significant at p < .05 level

CCI: Intensity of consumer–consumer interaction
ECI: Intensity of employee–consumer interaction
SCI: Intensity of system–consumer interaction

TABLE 9.7 Industry ranking regarding the influence of relationship quality dimensions on BRQ

Ranking	Quality of the brand as relationship partner		Quality of the brand as interaction platform	
	Industry	Influence (%)	Industry	Influence (%)
1	Automobile	.653 (71)	Car insurance	.399 (47)
2	Tissues	.619 (76)	Tinned vegetables	.389 (47)
3	Toothpaste	.599 (78)	Cell phones	.322 (37)
4	Network providers	.567 (64)	Network providers	.319 (36)
Average	Across industries	.564 (67)	Across industries	.282 (33)
5	Cell phones	.548 (63)	Automobile	.273 (29)
6	Beer	.544 (53)	Beer	.224 (29)
7	Car insurance	.447 (53)	Tissues	.194 (24)
8	Tinned vegetables	.436 (53)	Toothpaste	.165 (22)

establish an enhanced relationship orientation in their branding efforts. Our findings offer industry-specific guidelines for promoting the potential of interaction drivers to influence BRQ. However, the results further illustrate that brand relationship quality drivers are highly context-dependant. As a consequence, management and research of BRQ should be driven from an industry-specific perspective.

Our study also provides important contributions for research, from both a conceptual and also an empirical perspective. Conceptually, we have broadened the scope of brand relationship quality dimensions. The empirical findings support our proposed BRQ measurement model. In the past, the importance of the interactions for building and maintaining brand relationships has been neglected. Investigating the impact of interactions further (e.g., studies about how best to stimulate interactions among consumers from a brand relationship management perspective) remains a promising opportunity for future research. Furthermore, an indispensable advance would be achieved in this field by knowing how to identify successfully product-market-specific contextual factors, which could be used in formulating assumptions about their specific importance to different consumer goods markets. We hope that further research will continue to explore this area, expanding the analysis to other consumer markets as well.

References

Aaker, J., Fournier, S. and Brasel A.S. (2004) "When Good Brands Do Bad", *Journal of Consumer Research*, 31 (1): 1–16.

Aggarwal, P. (2004) "The Effects of Brand Relationship Norms on Consumer Attitudes and Behavior", *Journal of Consumer Research*, 31 (1): 87–101.

Alreck, P.L. and Settle, R.B. (1999) "Strategies for Building Consumer Brand Preference", *Journal of Product and Brand Management*, 8 (2): 130–43.

Altman, I. and Taylor, D.A. (1973) *Social Penetration: the development of interpersonal relationships*, New York: Plenum Publishers.

Berscheid, E. (1994) "Interpersonal Relationships", *Annual Review of Psychology*, 45 (1): 79–129.

Blackstone, M. (2000) "Observations: Building Brand Equity by Managing the Brand's Relationships", *Journal of Advertising Research*, 40 (6): 101–5.

Bollen, K.A. (1989) *Structural Equations with Latent Variables*, New York: John Wiley and Sons.

Breivik, E. and Thorbjørnsen, H. (2008) "Consumer Brand Relationships: An Investigation of Two Alternative Models", *Journal of the Academy of Marketing Science*, 36 (1): 443–72.

Chang, P.L. and Chieng, M.H. (2006) "Building Consumer–Brand Relationship: A Cross-Cultural Experiential View", *Psychology and Marketing*, 23 (11): 927–59.

Chin, W.W. (1998) "The Partial Least Squares Approach for Structural Equation Modeling", in G. Marcoulides (ed.) *Modern Methods for Business Research*, Mahwah, NJ: Lawrence Erlbaum Associates.

Coupland, J.C. (2005) "Invisible Brands: An Ethnography of Households and the Brands in their Kitchen Pantries," *Journal of Consumer Research*, 32 (1): 106–18.

Delgado-Ballester, E. and Munuera-Aleman, J.L. (2001) "Brand Trust in the Context of Consumer Loyalty", *European Journal of Marketing*, 35 (11/12): 1238–58.

—— (2005) "Does Brand Trust Matter to Brand Equity?" *Journal of Product and Brand Management*, 14 (3): 187–96.

Dimitriadis, S. and Papista, E. (2010) "Integrating Relationship Quality and Consumer–Brand Identification in Building Brand Relationships: Proposition of a Conceptual Model", *Marketing Review*, 10 (4): 385–401.

Eichen, F. (2010) *Messung und Steuerung der Markenbeziehungsqualität. Eine branchenübergreifende Studie im Konsumgütermarkt*, Wiesbaden: Gabler-Verlag.

Esch, F., Langner, T., Schmitt, B.H. and Geus, P. (2006) "Are Brands Forever? How Brand Knowledge and Relationships Affect Current and Future Purchases", *Journal of Product and Brand Management*, 15 (2/3): 98–105.

Esch, F., Rutenberg, J., Ströder, K. and Vallaster, C. (2005) "Verankerung der Markenidentität durch Behavioral Branding", in F.-R. Esch (ed.) *Moderne Markenführung. Grundlagen – Innovative Ansätze – Praktische Umsetzungen*, Wiesbaden: Gabler-Verlag.

Fornell, C. and Bookstein, F.L. (1982) "Two Structural Equation Models: LISREL and PLS Applied to Consumer Exit-Voice Theory", *Journal of Marketing Research*, 19 (4): 440–52.

Fornell, C. and Cha, J. (1994) "Partial Least Squares", in R. Bagozzi (ed.) *Advanced Methods of Marketing Research*, Cambridge, MA: Blackwell.

Fornell, C. and Larcker, D.F. (1981) "Evaluating Structural Equation Models with Unobservable Variables and Measurement Error", *Journal of Marketing Research*, 18 (1): 39–50.

Fournier, S. (1994) "A Consumer–Brand Relationship Framework for Strategic Brand Management", unpublished dissertation, University of Florida, Florida.

—— (1998) "Consumers and their Brands: Developing Relationship Theory in Consumer Research", *Journal of Consumer Research*, 24 (4): 343–73.

Fournier, S. and Yao, J.L. (1997) "Reviving Brand Loyalty: A Reconceptualization within the Framework of Consumer–Brand Relationships", *International Journal of Research in Marketing*, 14 (5): 451–72.

Gilmore, G.W. (1919) *Animism*, Boston: Marshall Jones.

Grau, I. (2003) "Emotionale Nähe", in I. Grauand and H.-W. Bierhoff (eds) *Sozialpsychologie der Partnerschaft*, Berlin: Springer.

Grönroos, C. (1997) "Value-Driven Relational Marketing: From Products to Resources and Competencies", *Journal of Marketing Management*, 13 (5): 407–19.

Hadwich, K. (2003) *Beziehungsqualität im Relationship Marketing*, Wiesbaden: Gabler-Verlag.

Hayes, B.J., Capella, L.M. and Alford, B.L. (2000) "The Brand Personality as a Basis for Consumer–Brand Evaluations", working paper, Mississippi State University.

Henseler, J., Ringle, C.M. and Sinkovics, R.R. (2009) "The Use of Partial Least Squares Path Modeling in International Marketing", *Advances in International Marketing*, 20: 277–319.

Herrmann, A., Henneberg, S.C. and Landwehr, J. (2010) "Squaring Customer Demands, Brand Strength, and Production Requirements: A Case Example of an Integrated Product and Branding Strategy", *Total Quality Management and Business Excellence*, 21 (10): 1017–31.

Hess, J. (1998) "A Multidimensional Conceptualization of Consumer–Brand Relationships: The Differential Impact of Relationship Dimensions on Evaluative Relationship Outcomes", unpublished dissertation, University of Colorado, Boulder.

Hess, J. and Story, J. (2005) "Trust-Based Commitment: Multidimensional Consumer–Brand Relationships", *Journal of Consumer Marketing*, 22 (6): 313–22.

Huber, F., Vollhardt, K. and Vogel, J. (2008) "Aufbau von Markenbeziehungen als Grundlage des Dienstleistungsmanagement", in M. Bruhn and B. Stauss (eds) *Forum Dienstleistungsmanagement: Dienstleistungsmarken*, Wiesbaden: Gabler-Verlag.

Hulland, J. (1999) "Use of Partial Least Squares (PLS) in Strategic Management Research: A Review of Four Recent Studies", *Strategic Management Journal*, 20 (2): 195–204.

Iacobucci, D. and Hibbard, J.D. (1999) "Toward an Encompassing Theory of Business Marketing Relationships (BMRs) and Interpersonal Commercial Relationships (ICRs): An Empirical Generalization", *Journal of Interactive Marketing*, 13 (3): 13–33.

Ji, M.F. (2002) "Children's Relationships with Brands: 'True Love' or 'One-Night' Stand?" *Psychology and Marketing*, 9 (4): 369–87.

Jones, T.O. and Sasser, W.E. Jr. (1995) "Why Satisfied Customers Defect", *Harvard Business Review*, 73 (6): 88–91.

Kates, S.M. (2000) "Out of the Closet and Out on the Street!: Gay Men and their Brand Relationships", *Psychology and Marketing*, 17 (6): 493–513.

Kressmann, F., Herrmann, A., Huber, F. and Magin, S. (2003) "Dimensionen der Markeneinstellung und ihre Wirkung auf die Kaufabsicht", *Die Betriebswirtschaft*, 63 (4): 401–18.

Kressmann, F., Sirgy, M.J., Herrmann, A., Huber, F., Huber, S. and Lee, D.J. (2006) "Direct and Indirect Effects of Self-Image Congruence on Brand Loyalty", *Journal of Business Research*, 59 (9): 955–64.

Lee J., Park, S.Y., Baek, I. and Lee, C.S. (2008) "The Impact of the Brand Management System on Brand Performance in B-B and B-C Environments", *Industrial Marketing Management*, 37 (7): 848–55.

Lindberg-Repo, K. and Brookes, R. (2004) "The Nature of the Brand Relationship Strength", Proceedings of the 12th International Colloquium on Relationship Marketing at Waikato Management School, Helsinki/New Zealand.

McAlexander, J.H., Schouten, J.W. and Koenig, H.F. (2002) "Building Brand Community", *Journal of Marketing*, 66 (1): 38–54.

Mills, J. and Clark, M.S. (1982) "Exchange and Communal Relationships", in L. Wheeler (ed.) *Review of Personality and Social Psychology*, Beverly Hills, CA: Sage.

Morgan, R.M. and Hunt, S.D. (1994) "The Commitment-Trust Theory of Relationship Marketing", *Journal of Marketing*, 58: 20–38.

Morris, R.J. and Martin, C.L. (2000) "Beanie Babies: A Case Study in the Engineering of a High-Involvement/Relationship-Prone Brand", *Journal of Product and Brand Management*, 9 (2): 78–96.

Nunally, J.C. (1978) *Psychometric Theory*, 2nd edn, New York: McGraw-Hill.

Oliver, R.L. and DeSarbo, W.S. (1988) "Response Determinants in Satisfaction Judgments", *Journal of Consumer Research*, 14 (4): 495–507.

Palmatier, R.W., Dant, R.P., Grewal, D. and Evans, K.R. (2006) "Factors Influencing the Effectiveness of Relationship Marketing: A Meta-Analysis," *Journal of Marketing*, 70 (10): 136–53.

Palmer, A.J. (1996) "Integrating Brand Development and Relationship Marketing", *Journal of Retailing and Consumer Services*, 3 (4): 251–7.

Park, J.W., Kim, K.H. and Kim, J. (2002) "Acceptance of Brand Extensions: Interactive Influences of Product Category Similarity, Typicality of Claimed Benefits, and Brand Relationship Quality", *Advances in Consumer Research*, 29 (1): 190–8.

Patterson, M. and O'Malley, L. (2006) "Brands, Consumers, and Relationships: A Review", *Irish Marketing Review*, 18 (1/2): 10–20.

Reis, H.T. and Shaver, P. (1988) "Intimacy as an Interpersonal Process", in S. Duck (ed.) *Handbook of Personal Relationships*, Chichester: John Wiley and Sons.

Roberts, K., Varki, S. and Brodie, R. (2003) "Measuring the Quality of Relationship in Consumer Services: An Empirical Study", *European Journal of Marketing*, 37 (1/2): 169–96.

Scarabis, M. (2006) "A Brand Like a Friend? Differenzielle Bindungsmuster durch Anthropomorphisierung", scientific presentation at the University of Münster, Münster.

Scarabis, M. and Florack, A. (2005) "Marken Werden Menschlich", *Planung and Analyse*, 32 (3): 64–8.

Sheth, J.N. and Parvatiyar, A. (1995) "Relationship Marketing in Consumer Markets: Antecedents and Consequences", *Journal of the Academy of Marketing Science*, 23 (4): 255–71.

Slotegraaf, R.J. and Atuahene-Gima, K. (2011) "Product Development Team Stability and New Product Advantage: The Role of Decision-Making Process", *Journal of Marketing*, 75 (1): 96–108.

Smit, E., Bronner, F. and Tolboom, M. (2007) "Brand Relationship Quality and its Value for Personal Contact", *Journal of Business Research*, 60 (6): 627–33.

Steenkamp, J.B. and Baumgartner, H. (1998) "Assessing Measurement Invariance in Cross-National Consumer Research", *Journal of Consumer Research*, 25 (1): 78–90.

Swaminathan, V., Page, K.L. and Gürhan-Canli, Z. (2007) "'My' Brand or 'Our' Brand: The Effects of Brand Relationship Dimensions and Self-Construal on Brand Evaluations", *Journal of Consumer Research*, 34 (2): 248–59.

Thorbjørnsen, H., Supphellen, M., Nysveen, H. and Pederson, P.E. (2002) "Building Brand Relationships Online: A Comparison of Two Interactive Applications", *Journal of Interactive Marketing*, 16 (3): 17–34.

Veloutsou, C. (2007) "Identifying the Dimensions of the Product-Brand and Consumer Relationship", *Journal of Marketing Management*, 23 (1/2): 7–26.

Wold, H.O. (1974) "Causal Flows with Latent Variables: Partings of the Ways in the Light of NIPALS Modeling", *European Economic Review*, 5 (1): 67–86.

—— (1985) "Partial Least Squares", in S. Kotz and N.L. Johnson (eds) *Encyclopedia of Statistical Sciences*, Vol. 6, New York: Wiley.

10

BRAND FORGIVENESS

How close brand relationships influence forgiveness

Leigh Anne Novak Donovan, Joseph R. Priester,
Deborah J. MacInnis, and C. Whan Park

Introduction

The early 1970s were a wonderful time for the upstart shoe company Nike. Nike had introduced a radical design (the waffle tread) that was clearly visible and widely perceived to be superior to the competition's designs. This radical innovation even came with a founding narrative that included one of America's most recognized running coaches using his wife's waffle iron to fashion the very first version. Nike had adopted a distinctive brand logo (the swoosh), and perhaps most importantly, Nike had recruited top international medium- and long-distance runners to wear Nike shoes in the Olympics and widely followed (by runners, at any rate) marathons and other long-distance races. With these steps, Nike had begun to make great inroads against the entrenched market share leader – Adidas. What could possibly go wrong?

In the spring of 1974, Nike introduced a new running shoe, the Nike LD-1000, based upon its famous waffle shoe, but with the additional innovation of a wider heel. The concept behind this change was that the wider heel would provide greater cushion support and stability. What looked good in design, however, did not translate to the actual shoe. The shoe was manufactured such that the heel was significantly wider than intended. This overly wide heel did deliver greater cushion and stability. However, it also reduced the amount that the foot could naturally move through each stride. The result: a shoe that was referred to internally at Nike as the knee breaker (Strasser and Becklund, 1991).

In retrospect, it is surprising that Nike was able to overcome this product failure. The most fervent Nike customers were undoubtedly the ones who purchased this faulty shoe. Given Nike's brief existence, and many readily available substitutes, why is it that customers returned to Nike, thereby fostering its growth to one day become the world's athletic shoe?

Our research is designed to help us to understand better what happens when customers of firms, such as Nike, experience product failures. Do certain factors reduce the negative impact of product failures on consumers' negative brand reactions? Our work specifically investigates behaviors following transgressions. We explore the role of brand relationship closeness and its subsequent impact on brand forgiveness as essential factors affecting the relationship between brand failure and negative brand outcomes, such as reduced purchase intentions, desires to avoid the brand, and desires to seek revenge against the brand. From this research, we hope better to understand customers' reactions following brand failures.

One can generalize beyond the Nike LD-1000 example, and even further to beyond brands: relationships, all too often, let us down. And brands, all too often, disappoint. However, we often maintain these relationships and continue to purchase these brands. What accounts for such behavior? Commitment to maintaining interpersonal relationships has been shown to increase forgiveness. Finkel *et al.* (2002) have found that relationship closeness is positively associated with behavioral intentions and forgiveness. In interpersonal relationships, forgiveness has been shown to have the ability to increase conciliatory behaviors in relationships (McCullough, Worthington, and Rachal 1997) and repair the relationship from the damage caused by the transgression (Fincham 2000). However, forgiveness in consumer–brand relationships has yet to be examined. What might cause some individuals to continue using, and others to abandon use of, a brand after a brand failure? We investigate the role of brand relationship closeness and forgiveness as key constructs in understanding the differences in behaviors following brand failures. Do close brand relationships lead to brand forgiveness? From the research on interpersonal relationships, we know that relationship commitment matters. Those with close, committed relationships are more likely to forgive than those with distant, uncommitted relationships (e.g. Finkel *et al.* 2002). As such, we explore whether brand relationship closeness similarly influences brand forgiveness. Thus, our research seeks to understand whether individuals engage in brand forgiveness, whether the forgiveness is indeed the result of relationship closeness, and whether such forgiveness fosters consumers' continued brand behavior.

We explore these questions in four studies, each using different methods, measures, and approaches. Study One manipulates a brand failure and examines the moderating role of brand relationship closeness on the relationship between brand failure and future purchase intentions. Study Two, which uses a real-world brand failure, examines whether brand relationship closeness (as assessed by two divergent measures) influences forgiveness. Study Three explores the role of forgiveness in a diverse set of post-transgression behaviors. Specifically, this study explores a richer set of consumer behaviors flowing from forgiveness.

We examine whether forgiveness impacts not just purchase intentions, but desires to avoid the brand, desires to seek revenge against the brand, and willingness to defend the brand. Study Four explores the mediating role of forgiveness in the influence of brand relationship closeness on purchase intentions and actual repurchase following a failure. In Study Four we use a different brand failure methodology, one which is common to research on interpersonal relationships – autobiographical recall. Specifically participants are asked to recall a specific brand transgression instance, and respond to questions concerning this autobiographic incident. Across all of these studies, our intent is to understand whether consumers' negative reactions to brand failure are impacted by brand relationship closeness through its impact on brand forgiveness.

Brand transgressions

Brand transgressions are costly. They can lead to attenuated purchase intentions (Smith and Bolton 1998; Tax, Brown, and Chandrashekaran 1998), increased brand avoidance (Grégoire, Tripp and Legoux 2009), reduced willingness to defend the brand (Park *et al.* 2009), and often public outrage (Ariely 2007; Grégoire, Tripp and Legoux 2009). That is, brand transgressions can undermine the customer value that is so difficult to build. In addition to costs to the firm, brand transgressions can be costly to the customers as well. They threaten the benefits offered by brands: customers may not be able to easily rely upon prior brand purchase as the basis of continued purchase, and may instead need to expend the mental and time cost of engaging anew in brand search. Given the costs of brand transgressions, it is clear that they are of theoretical and practical importance. Interestingly, consumers often react quite differently following transgressions: some consumers defect and try to find an alternative brand that will better meet their needs, whereas other consumers remain loyal to the brand. As Oliver (1999) stated, satisfaction is not enough to completely understand loyal behavior. We investigate whether understanding the role of brand relationship closeness and forgiveness following brand transgressions can better provide an understanding of and better predict consumer reactions and future behavior.

Relationship closeness

A useful perspective to understanding the nature of relationships is offered by research on interpersonal relationships. Specifically, within this field investigators have introduced the concept of relationship closeness (Clark and Lemay 2010). In the traditional context of interpersonal relationships, closeness is conceptualized as the extent to which an "other" individual is included in one's self concept. This perspective was advanced by Aron and Aron (1986) with the Self-Expansion Model. The proposed model suggests that we can incorporate others into our self-concepts. That is, we perceive close others to be part of ourselves. Integrating others into oneself enhances an individual's ability to accomplish goals, such that the other and the other's resources become part of the self (Aron, Aron, and Norman 2003; Aron, Norman, and Aron 1998; Aron *et al.* 2000). Recently, this relationship was hypothesized to extend also to consumer–brand relationships. Conceptually, the other person is replaced with the brand, and the construct captures the extent the brand is considered part of oneself (Reimann and Aron 2009). Such interpersonal, and brand, closeness is assessed with the Inclusion of the Other in the Self Scale (IOS). The IOS scale (Aron, Aron, and Smollan, 1992) consists of seven pairs of circle pairs. One circle represents the self and the other represents that other person (or brand). Each of the seven pairs represents a different depiction of closeness, overlapping to differing degrees from least overlapping (least inclusive) to most overlapping (most inclusive). Participants are asked to pick the pair of circles that best describes their relationship with the other (brand).

There is evidence that suggests a close relationship can help individuals overcome transgressions. In the interpersonal relationship literature in psychology, close relationships have been shown to positively influence the likelihood of forgiveness following transgressions (Fincham 2000; McCullough *et al.* 1997, 1998; Finkel *et al.* 2002; Hoyt *et al.* 2005). In the field of consumer behavior, researchers have found results consistent with the notion that brand relationships may be able to buffer brands from the negative effects of service failures. Tax, Brown, and Chandrashekaran (1998) demonstrated that positive prior service with a provider buffered the negative effects of deficient complaint handling. And Hess *et al.* (2003) demonstrated that the higher the number of past, quality, experiences with a provider, the lower the recovery expectations are, which results in more favorable evaluations following the failure. If the past positive prior service and greater number of past, quality experiences result in closer brand relationships, then both of these results can be understood within the framework of the present work.

We extend this construct of relationship closeness from interpersonal to brand relationships. Conceptually, brand relationship closeness can be thought of as the extent to which an individual considers a brand to be part of her- or himself (e.g., Escalas and Bettman 2003; Park *et al.* 2010; Reimann and Aron 2009). There are multiple ways with which to assess brand relationship closeness. As outlined above, one can assess the extent to which a brand is included with the self using Aron's IOS. Alternatively, one can assess the closeness of a relationship through more traditional measures. Notably, Escalas and Bettman (2003) have developed the brand self connection measure, in which participants respond to a set of questions designed to assess the extent to which a brand is considered to be connected to the self. Yet a third approach is offered by Park *et al.*'s brand attachment perspective. The research provides a conceptualization and methodology specifically for defining and exploring brand attachment. From this perspective, brand attachment can be understood as comprising (a) brand self connection (the extent to which a brand is perceived to be part of one's self) and (b) brand prominence (the extent to which one thinks about the brand without prompting).[1] This feeling of attachment to a brand influences a wide variety of behaviors towards the brand (Park *et al.*, 2010). In the current research, our interest is in the extent to which one feels close to a brand. In order to provide convergent support for our findings, we utilize all three approaches to brand relationship closeness across the four studies.

Forgiveness

One challenge of the present research has to do with the very definition of forgiveness. A review of the literature on forgiveness reveals a frequent tendency to conflate the definition of forgiveness with the behavior flowing from such forgiveness.[2] For example, a commonly used definition of forgiveness is provided by McCullough, Worthington, and Rachal (1997), who define interpersonal forgiveness as "the set of motivational changes whereby one becomes (a) decreasingly motivated to retaliate against an offending relationship partner, (b) decreasingly motivated to maintain estrangement (or avoidance) from the offender, and (c) increasingly motivated by conciliation and goodwill for the offender, despite the offender's hurtful actions." In other words, forgiveness, from such a definition, is measured by the behavioral intentions of decreased retaliation and estrangement, and increased goodwill. Such a definition is problematic for our research question, because at the most basic, we are interested in examining *if* and *when* brand forgiveness does lead to such behavioral and emotional resumption. Upon reflection, it seems possible that forgiveness and future behavior need not be related. For example, one can imagine instances in which an individual might forgive a brand, yet decide to adopt a different brand in the future. Or one might not forgive a brand, and yet continue to purchase this unforgiven brand due to factors such as habit or inertia. Additionally, past research has shown that forgiveness and reconciliation are two distinct constructs (e.g., Worthington 1998). Thus, forgiveness does not necessarily entail future behavioral intentions.

To disentangle forgiveness from subsequent behavioral intention, we use a simple, idiosyncratic approach to the definition and measurement of forgiveness. We define forgiveness as the neutralization of a transgression toward the offending brand or company. We conceptualize forgiveness as an emotional and/or cognitive decision which results in the neutralization of such a transgression. That is, what is necessary is the conscious decision to forgive. What this decision means to any one individual, however, may differ. What is invariant across any idiosyncratic personal beliefs of what forgiveness means, however, is that to forgive is to decide to forgive. As such, we measure forgiveness simply as (a) whether an individual has forgiven and/or (b) to what extent an individual has forgiven. This simple approach to forgiveness allows us to understand forgiveness, alone, and disentangles forgiveness from any possible future brand behavior. Specifically, by separating the decision to forgive from future behavior and behavioral intentions, we are able to empirically assess the extent to which forgiveness does foster future brand behavior.

Relationship to Forgiveness to Behavior Model

Our goal is to advance and explore the influence of brand relationship closeness on brand forgiveness, and the influence of brand forgiveness on brand behaviors following a brand transgression. We present four studies that examine this hypothesized model. Specifically, we propose and empirically test the Relationship to Forgiveness to Behavior Model. *A priori*, we expect that (a) those with close brand relationships will be more likely to forgive a brand following a transgression than those with distant relationships, (b) forgiveness will positively influence future behavioral intentions and actual post-failure behaviors, and (c) that forgiveness will mediate the influence of close brand relationships on future brand intentions. (see Figure 10.1)

Study One: iPod

We conducted Study One to address the question of whether brand relationship closeness moderates behavioral intentions following a brand success or failure. Of course, brand failure should lead to less positive brand behavioral intentions than brand success. In this study, we examine the extent to which brand relationship closeness affects the magnitude of these future behavioral intentions. Specifically, we examine whether brand relationship closeness moderates the relationship between brand failure and negative brand outcomes. Brand success/failure is manipulated using a hypothetical scenario. Brand relationship closeness and future purchase intentions are both measured.

Method

We explore the influence of brand relationship closeness using a scenario-based approach in which brand performance is manipulated to be either successful or unsuccessful. Individuals' brand relationship closeness was assessed through use of

FIGURE 10.1 Relationship to forgiveness to behavior model

brand self connection and brand attachment. Brand relationship closeness was measured at the beginning of the study. Participants then read a scenario in which the outcome was either a positive or negative. Following the scenario, participants provided their future behavioral intentions towards the brand.

Sixty-nine University of Southern California undergraduate students participated in a 2 (brand success vs. brand failure) x brand relationship closeness design study in partial fulfillment for course credit.[3] Each participant first completed a two-part booklet that (a) assessed their current relationship closeness with the iPod, (b) asked them to imagine a positive or negative experience with the iPod, and (c) assessed their repurchase intentions following the scenario. We chose the iPod as the focal product given college students' brand familiarity as well as the expected heterogeneity of brand relationship closeness for this brand.

Independent variables

Brand relationship closeness was assessed by 1) Park *et al.*'s (2010) brand attachment scale and 2) by brand self connection (the brand self component of the brand attachment scale). Specifically, two 11-point items assessed the brand self connection component of the scale: "To what extent do you feel that you are personally connected to the iPod?" and "To what extent is iPod a part of you and who you are?" Two additional items assessed the brand prominence component of the scale: "To what extent are your thoughts and feelings towards iPod often automatic, coming to mind seemingly on their own?" and "To what extent do your thoughts and feelings towards iPod come to you naturally and easily?" (0 = not at all; 10 = completely).[4]

Brand experience was manipulated by a scenario that described a successful or unsuccessful brand experience. All participants first read:

> I would like you to imagine that up to this point your iPod has delivered the performance that you expected when you purchased it. It has confirmed your expectations. Now, I would like you to imagine that you decided to compile a new playlist for your trip while you are on a one-week vacation. You compile this playlist from your existing music files. In order to compile this playlist you spend an hour and a half to complete the entire process. You are very excited to hear your new playlist on vacation.

In the successful outcome conditions, participants additionally read that:

> When you begin your Spring Break trip you first search for your new playlist. After finding your new playlist you listen to it on your trip and you are able to enjoy your iPod while on vacation.

In the unsuccessful outcome conditions, participants read that,

> However, when you arrive at your vacation destination your iPod screen is black and will not turn on. Your iPod will not play your new playlist or any of your songs on it. You contact Apple and they say that this has been a common problem and that if you send in your iPod they will fix it and mail it back to you. However, now you will not be able to listen to your iPod on your vacation.

Dependent variables

Two items indicated repurchase intentions: "In the future, do you think you would be willing to purchase an iPod again?" and "I would buy an iPod again next time." Both items were assessed by 11-point scales anchored with 0 (not at all) and 10 (completely). A composite future behavioral intention measure was created by averaging these two items.[5]

Results

A regression analysis examined the main effects of brand outcome (successful vs. unsuccessful), brand relationship closeness, and their interaction on repurchase intentions. Not surprisingly, we observed main effects of both brand outcome ($M_{success}$ = 8.78 and $M_{failure}$ = 6.74; $F(1, 67)$ = 16.9, $p < .0001$) and brand relationship closeness on future behavioral intentions, ($b_{brand\ attachment}$ = .73, $F(1, 67)$ = 25.04, $p < .0001$; $b_{brand\ self\ connection}$ = .44, $F(1, 67)$ = 17.73, $p < .0001$). People are more likely to intend to purchase following a brand success than a failure, and if they feel close versus distant. Of greater theoretical interest, there emerged the predicted significant interactions between brand relationship closeness and the brand outcome on repurchase intentions, $F(2, 66)$ = 10.72, p = .0017 for brand attachment; $F(2, 66)$ = 4.88, p = .03 for brand self connection . For ease of explication we decompose this interaction using the brand attachment measure – note, however, that the decomposition holds for brand self connection as well. Brand relationship closeness had no effect on repurchase intentions when the brand outcome was successful, ($F(1, 35)$ = 2.13, p = .15). In contrast, brand relationship closeness ($F(1, 32)$ = 15.07, p = .0005) did impact repurchase intentions following a brand transgression. In order to deconstruct this interaction, we created a tertiary split on brand relationship closeness, resulting in three brand relationship closeness categories: distant, moderate, and close. Those who reported close relationships had higher future behavioral intentions following the brand transgression (M_{close} = 9.06) than individuals reporting moderate ($M_{moderate}$ = 6.67) or distant brand relationships ($M_{distant}$ = 5.38). The difference between close and moderately close brand relationships was significant ($F(1, 46)$ = 5.16, p = .027), while the difference between moderate and distant brand relationships approached significance ($F(1, 45) = 3.34$, $p = .0745$). (see Figure 10.2)

An alternative examination of the interaction reveals that the brand outcome (successful or unsuccessful) was a significant predictor of future behavioral intentions for those with a distant brand relationship ($M_{distant} = 5.38$; $F(1, 21) = 8.84$, $p = .0075$) and those with a moderate brand relationship ($M_{moderate} = 6.67$; $F(1, 23) = 8.07$, $p = .0095$). However, the future behavioral intentions of those with a close brand relationship were not affected by the brand outcome manipulation ($M_{close} = 9.06$; $F(1, 22) = .01$, $p = .91$).[6]

Discussion

Study One provides support for the moderating effects of brand relationship closeness on the relationship between brand failures and resulting consumer brand purchase intentions. Participants who had a close brand relationship were unaffected by the brand failure, whereas those with moderate and distant brand relationships showed attenuated future behavioral intentions as a result of brand failure.

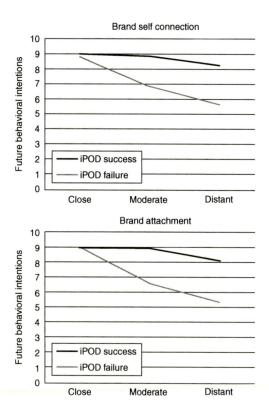

FIGURE 10.2 Future behavioral intentions by relationship closeness and outcome

While Study One provides initial evidence for the buffering effects of brand relationship closeness several questions remain. First, does brand relationship closeness influence forgiveness? Second, is brand relationship closeness influential for actual brand transgressions occurring in the real world? Third, are the results of Study One applicable to brand relationship closeness or are they due to the two approaches (brand attachment and brand self connection) used to operationalize brand relationship closeness? To examine these issues, we conducted Study Two. Specifically, we focus on an instance of a real-world brand transgression and we assessed brand relationship closeness by using brand attachment, brand self connection, and IOS. In addition, we measure the key concept – forgiveness.

Study Two: iPhone

We conducted Study Two following the release of the original Apple iPhone in April 2007. Recall that within several months of the phone's initial release Apple significantly reduced the brand's price. Such an immediate price reduction was viewed as a transgression by those who had already bought the brand. We examined how brand relationship closeness, as assessed by the IOS, brand self connection, and brand attachment influenced forgiveness.

Method

Two hundred twelve students enrolled in an introductory marketing course at the University of Southern California completed this study for partial fulfillment of course credit. All participants were given the brand failure information as follows:

> As you may know, Apple recently reduced the price of its iPhone from $599 to $399. We would like to ask you questions about your thoughts and feelings towards the iPhone.

Independent measures

Recall that there are at least three different approaches to measuring brand relationship closeness. The brand attachment (Park *et al.* 2010) and the brand self connection scales used in Study One, used traditional self-report measures to focus on brand self connection and brand prominence. A third approach, the Inclusion of Other in the Self (IOS) scale, advanced by Aron, Aron, and Smollan (1992), focuses on the extent to which the brand is perceived to be included in the self. To provide convergent validity that our results are not due to any idiosyncratic tendencies of the brand self connection and brand attachment scale, Study Two uses all three measures of brand relationship closeness.

Dependent measures

Participants stated how forgiving they felt following the brand transgression with a single item on an 11-point scale anchored with 0 (not at all) and 10 (extremely). Single-item measures of forgiveness are commonly used in psychology (e.g., Finkel, Burnette, and Scissors, 2007) and this measure is simple with high face validity. Additionally, this measure does not conflate forgiveness and the outcomes of forgiveness.

Results

To examine the key hypothesis, brand forgiveness was regressed on all three measures of brand relationship closeness in separate regression analyses. As predicted, there emerged main effects of brand attachment (b = .31, $F(1, 210)$ = 15.12, p = .0001), brand self connection (b = .26, $F(1, 210)$ = 11.48, p = .0008), and IOS (b = .40, $F(1, 210)$ = 10.43, p = .0014).

Recall that Study Two was conducted in order to examine whether brand relationship closeness influences forgiveness, and if such an effect would emerge in a real-world context. The results of Study Two are clear. Regardless of measure used, brand relationship closeness leads to forgiveness. Such a finding affords the opportunity to explore the consequences of brand forgiveness.

Study Three: Starbucks

Study Three is designed to examine the influence of forgiveness on repurchase intentions as well as a variety of other negative outcomes of brand failure – i.e., brand avoidance, revenge against the brand, and reduced willingness to defend the brand. Most importantly, Study Three is designed to determine whether forgiveness impacts how negatively consumers react to brand failure. The key question driving this study is whether brand forgiveness influences subsequent brand behavioral intentions. To elaborate, the possibility exists that people may forgive without continuing positive brand behavior, and that people may not forgive and continue positive brand behavior: forgiveness does not necessitate reconciliation (e.g., Worthington 1998).

In psychology, forgiveness is thought to engender the reduction of desire to avoid an offender and a reduction in desire to take revenge on an offender (McCullough, Worthington, and Rachal 1997). We use this perspective to formulate our approach. Specifically, does brand forgiveness have similar effects? To address such a question, we measured behavioral intentions traditionally associated with forgiveness in psychology literature, extended to a consumer–brand relationship context. Operationally, we assessed the extent to which individuals sought revenge on the brand, were willing to defend the brand, and planned to maintain the current level of brand behavior.

Method

One hundred seventy participants at the University of Southern California completed this study in partial fulfillment for course credit. All participants read a scenario in which the brand failed, and then reported their forgiveness, repurchase intentions, desires for revenge against the brand, willingness to defend the brand, and desire to avoid the brand in the future.

All participants were presented with the following brand failure scenario:

> I would like you to imagine that up to this point Starbucks has delivered the performance that you expected when you have purchased a beverage. Starbucks has confirmed your expectations. Now, I would like you to imagine that you have decided to go to Starbucks to order a hot beverage. You are looking forward to enjoying this hot beverage. You order your beverage, pick it up at the counter, and leave Starbucks. However, when you begin to drink your beverage, you realize that it is not the beverage you ordered. You were given the wrong drink and it is also cold. You are not able to enjoy your Starbucks beverage.

Repurchase intentions were measured with two items: "In the future, do you think you would be willing to purchase a Starbucks beverage again," on an 11-point scale anchored with 0 (not at all) and 10 (completely), and "In the future, do you think you would be willing to drink Starbucks," on an 11-point scale anchored with 0 (not at all) and 10 (very likely).[7] Desire to seek revenge was measured by "I want to take revenge on Starbucks," on an 11-point scale anchored with 0 (not at all) and 10 (completely). Willingness to defend the brand in the future was assessed with "In the future, do you think you would be willing to defend Starbucks to others who speak negatively of it," anchored with 0 (not at all) and 10 (very likely). Brand forgiveness was measured with a single item, "I have forgiven Starbucks," on an 11-point scale anchored with 0 (not at all) and 10 (completely).

Results

The key question driving this study is whether brand forgiveness influences subsequent brand behavioral intentions. The analyses reveal that forgiveness influences a wide variety of post-transgression intentions. The more consumers forgive a brand for brand failure, the more willing they are to repurchase the brand ($b = .65$, $F(1, 169) = 164.1$, $p < .0001$), consume the product in the future ($b = .47$, $F(1, 169) = 44.05$, $p < .0001$), and defend it against those who are disenchanted with it ($b = .53$, $F(1, 169) = 53.11$, $p < .0001$). The more consumers forgive a brand the less likely they are to seek revenge against the brand ($b = -.2$, $F(1, 169) = 9.53$, $p = .0024$).

Discussion

Study Three establishes that brand forgiveness matters. Whether and to what extent individuals forgive a brand fosters a variety of theoretically informative and predictive behaviors. Thus, we have established that brand relationship closeness influences future brand behavioral intentions (Study One), that brand relationship closeness influences brand forgiveness (Study Two), and that brand forgiveness influences repurchase intentions as well as a set of other brand behaviors (Study Three). These three studies lead to the most important question of this research: does forgiveness mediate the influence of brand relationship closeness on future behaviors? Study Four examines this issue.

Study Four: Autobiographical Recall of Brand Failure

Study Four examines brand failure, and determines whether the relationship between brand relationship closeness and future brand behavior is mediated by forgiveness. By examining the mediating role of forgiveness, we hope to demonstrate how close brand relationships positively impact future behavioral intentions following brand transgressions.

Study Four uses a different methodology to explore brand failure – autobiographical recall. Interpersonal relationship studies often ask participants to recall a specific past relationship failure (Enright and Coyle 1998; McCullough, Bono, and Root 2007). Doing so ensures that incidents are personally meaningful to respondents. This approach, in conjunction with the hypothetical scenario and real-world scenario, provides divergent methods to understanding forgiveness. The extent to which such multiple methods yield consistent results provides evidence for the robust nature of the model.

To utilize this autobiographical approach, all participants were asked to recall a time when a brand had failed them. They were then asked to describe the failure and provide assessments of their reactions towards the failure. Participants also indicated the extent to which they had forgiven the brand, and their behaviors and behavioral intentions following the failure. This method mirrors approaches used in interpersonal relationship research (e.g., Zechmeister and Romero 2002).

Method

One hundred twenty three undergraduate business students at the University of Southern California participated in exchange for partial course credit. All participants read:

> Please recall a specific incident when a brand failed you. For example, it didn't meet your expectations or it let you down. For example, perhaps

Starbucks gave you a supposedly hot coffee that was cold or your iPhone stopped working. Please tell us what happened in one to two sentences.

Brand relationship closeness was assessed with the brand attachment measure (Park et al. 2010) described in Studies One and Two.[8]

Participants indicated their reactions following the transgression. All items were measured on 11-point scales anchored by 0 (not at all) and 10 (completely), unless otherwise noted. Participants were asked to indicate the extent to which they had forgiven the brand following brand failure. Participants also indicated the perceived severity of the failure in order to examine whether brand relationship closeness influences perceived severity. To examine the consequences of brand forgiveness, participants were asked to indicate the extent to which they would be willing to purchase the brand again and whether they had purchased the brand since the failure (yes, no). Similar to Study Three, participants also indicated their desire to avoid the brand and their desire to take revenge on the brand. Forgiveness in interpersonal relationships is often measured with the TRIM inventory (transgression-related interpersonal motivations), which is an inventory composed of multiple items examining the desire for revenge and avoidance behavior (McCullough et al. 1998). Reductions in the desire to avoid and/or seek revenge on a transgressor are often used to explore forgiveness (McCullough, Bono, and Root 2007: McCullough, Fincham, and Tsang 2003; McCullough et al. 1998; McCullough, Worthington, and Rachal 1997). Thus, we formed a composite measure by averaging the two measures and we expected to find that forgiveness of a brand does predict a reduction in the desire of avoidance and revenge behaviors towards the brand.[9]

Participants, not surprisingly, reported a wide variety of brand failures. Examples of these include:

> My iPhone stopped working. I was walking in the rain and my phone fell out of my pocket. It was only in the rain for 3 seconds, but it completely stopped working and I had to get a new one.

> McDonalds messed up one of my orders at the drive-through window.

> My BenQ laptop stopped working. The computer became slower and slower but then one day when I opened it, nothing turned on. There was no response and this was only a year to a year and half after I bought it.

Results

Univariate analyses of the brand failures described by the participants are provided in Table 10.1.[10]

To rule out the alternative explanation that those with a close brand relationship simply report less severe failures and are thus more easily able to forgive, we

TABLE 10.1 Univariate analyses of the brand failures

Table of means			Brand relationship closeness	
	n=49		n=25	n=24
	Mean	Sig with brand relationship closeness	Distant	Close
Forgiveness	4.9	p = .004	3.9	5.9
Perceived severity	6.4	p = .41	6.4	6.25
Brand relationship closeness	3.8		1.89	5.85

Variables were measured on 0–10 scales

examined whether there was a main effect of brand relationship closeness on perceived severity of the failure. No effect was observed (b = .02, $F(1, 121)$ = .04, p = .85).[11] Additionally, in line with forgiveness in interpersonal relationships, we explored whether forgiveness influences the desires to avoid the brand and take revenge on the brand. As expected, there emerged a main effect of forgiveness on the desire to avoid and seek revenge on the brand (b = −.23, $F(1, 121)$ 4.39, p = .038).

In order to explore whether forgiveness mediates the influence of brand relationship closeness on future behavioral intentions, we conducted meditation analyses (Baron and Kenny 1986).[12] First, we regressed willingness to purchase the brand again upon brand relationship closeness. Replicating Study One, we find a main effect of brand relationship closeness on willingness to repurchase the product (b = .45, $F(1, 121)$ = 12.68, p = .0005). Second, we regressed forgiveness on brand relationship closeness. Replicating Study Two, we find a main effect of brand relationship closeness on brand forgiveness (b = .41, $F(1, 121)$ = 11.25, p = .0011). Third, we explore whether or not forgiveness has an influence upon future behavioral intentions. Replicating Study Three, a main effect of forgiveness on willingness to purchase the brand was observed (b = .77, $F(1, 121)$ = 147.17, p < .0001).

Of key importance and interest is the question of whether brand forgiveness mediates the influence of brand relationship closeness on future (and subsequent) brand related intentions. Evidence of such mediation is gleaned from the analysis in which brand behaviors are regressed simultaneously on both brand relationship closeness and brand forgiveness. And as hypothesized, the influence of forgiveness remains significant (b = .74, $F(1, 121)$ = 125.75, p < 0001), whereas the influence of brand relationship closeness is attenuated to non-significance (b = .15, $F(1, 121)$ = 2.51, p = .116).[13] (See Figure 10.3.)

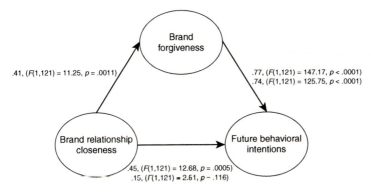

FIGURE 10.3 Mediation of brand relationship closeness and future behavioral intentions

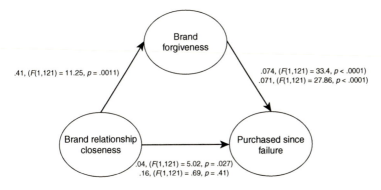

FIGURE 10.4 Mediation of brand relationship closeness and actual purchase following failure

Recall that participants were asked to report brand transgressions from the past. As such, it is possible to explore their post-brand failure actual purchase behavior. To do so, we analyzed whether the same brand had been purchased since the time of the failure. Regression analyses identical in nature to those described above revealed that the influence of brand relationship closeness on actual brand purchase is completely mediated by brand forgiveness (see Figure 10.4).

Discussion

Study Four replicates and extends Studies One, Two, and Three. More importantly, it highlights the mediating role played by brand forgiveness. Brand forgiveness underlies the influence of brand relationship closeness on both future brand behavioral intentions and on the report of past, post-brand failure behaviors.

General discussion

So, how was it that Nike was able to survive its horrific brand failure? The results of this research provide a plausible explanation. It is most likely that those who purchased the new shoe were those who felt closest to Nike (see Park *et al.* 2010). When these Nike customers experienced the brand failure (which to some of them, at least, may have resulted in injury!), the very reason that led them to purchase the shoes (their feelings of closeness with Nike) is the self-same reason that led them to be most likely to forgive Nike's failure. In a way, Nike owes its existence to its ability to make its customers feel as though Nike were part of themselves. Thus brand relationship closeness not only caused customers (a) to seek out and buy the new Nike shoes, but (b) to forgive Nike when those shoes injured, and (c) led those customers to buy Nike again.

It is worth noting that there have been mixed results regarding whether close brand relationships lead to increased negative reactions or decreased negative reactions. For example, there is evidence that consumers with strong brand relationships can react even more negatively following a brand failure. Grégoire, Tripp, and Legoux (2009) demonstrated the love-becomes-hate effect: following a double deviation (a failure followed by a failed recovery effort) consumers with a strong brand relationship hold a grudge the longest. This is especially interesting in relation to this research, because holding a grudge is the opposite of forgiveness (e.g., van Oyen Witvliet, Ludwig, and Vander Laan 2001). Additionally, individuals with high quality relationships have been shown to react even more negatively following service failures leading to an even greater decrease in repurchase intentions (Holloway, Wang, and Beatty 2009). In future research, we will explore when close brand relationships lead to more positive reactions versus more negative reactions and what role forgiveness plays in these opposing reactions.

In conclusion, at the most basic, this research advances the idea that brand forgiveness plays a key role, in effect, being the link between brand relationship closeness and future brand behaviors following a brand transgression. Understanding the role and importance of forgiveness has practical (e.g., Nike) and theoretical importance. And with this research, new questions arise. Perhaps of greatest interest is the question of how brand relationship closeness leads to brand forgiveness. Such future research will lead to greater insight into the psychological processes by which consumers maintain relationships with, and occasionally divorce themselves from, brands.

Notes

1 Park *et al.* (2010) developed a four-item measure that bears on brand relationship closeness. Brand relationship closeness may be revealed by the extent to which a consumer believes a brand is part of the self. Several studies have examined Brand Self-Connection (Escalas and Bettman 2003; Park *et al.* 2010). Park *et al.* (2010) examine brand relationship closeness as a component of a construct called brand attachment,

which indicates not only brand self-connection but also the extent to which the brand is prominent in consumers' minds. This measure is composed of two parts: a brand self-connection component and a brand prominence component. Brand self-connection captures the extent to which one feels the brand is a part of one's self and one's personal connection with the brand. Brand prominence measures the extent to which thoughts about the brand come naturally to mind and the extent to which individuals automatically think about the brand.

2 There also exists the tendency to conflate the definition of forgiveness with the psychological process believed to underlie forgiveness. This second conflation issue stands outside the current discussion, but is of importance to the authors.

3 Girard and Mullet (1997) demonstrated that older participants were more forgiving than young adults. Using relatively young undergraduate students as participants may thus provide a strong test of our hypothesis.

4 The alpha coefficient for the items assessing brand self connection was .84 and the items for brand prominence was .58. The overall alpha for the four items was .66. Note that though these alphas appear low, the alphas in subsequent studies are higher. Low alphas should make it more difficult (and thus a stronger test) to detect any proposed impact of brand relationship closeness.

5 The alpha for this measure is .98.

6 A conceptually similar analysis yields identical results. Specifically, we performed slope analyses. The slope for the positive condition was .19 ($t = 1.46$, $p = .15$) whereas the slope for the negative condition was 1.1 ($t = 4.42$, $p < .0001$).

7 The alpha for future behavioral intentions was .76.

8 The alpha for brand self connections was .88 and the alpha for brand prominence was .90 with an overall alpha of .81.

9 The alpha for this composite measure is .71.

10 Please note all analyses are performed with the continuous variable of BSC; split means are provided for ease of understanding.

11 Severity of the failure did negatively influence brand forgiveness ($F(1, 122) = 14.51$, $p = .0002$). We conducted the analyses reported below using severity of transgression as both a moderator and a covariate. Severity did not moderate any of the findings. And all of the reported effects remained significant when severity was used as a covariate. As such, severity is not examined further.

12 Note these analyses use brand attachment; however, analyses using brand self connection yield similar results, with the exception that mediation is partial rather than full.

13 The Sobel Test for mediation is significant, stat = 3.21, $p < .01$. See Figure 10.4.

References

Ariely, D. (2007) "HBR Case Study: The Customers' Revenge", *Harvard Business Review*, 85: 31–42.

Aron, A. and Aron, E.N. (1986) *Love as the Expansion of Self: understanding attraction and satisfaction*, New York: Hemisphere.

Aron, A., Aron, E.N. and Norman, C.C. (2003) "Self-Expansion Model of Motivation and Cognition in Close Relationships and Beyond", in M.B. Brewer and M. Hewstone (eds) *Self and Social Identity*, Oxford: Blackwell.

Aron, A., Aron, E.N. and Smollan, D. (1992) "Inclusion of Other in the Self Scale and the Structure of Interpersonal Closeness", *Journal of Personality and Social Psychology*, 63 (4): 596–612.

Aron, A., Norman, C.C. and Aron, E.N. (1998) "The Self-Expansion Model and Motivation", *Representative Research in Social Psychology*, 22: 1–13.

Aron, A., Norman, C.C., Aron, E.N., McKenna, C. and Heyman, R.E. (2000) "Couples' Shared Participation in Novel and Arousing Activities and Experienced Relationship Quality", *Journal of Personality and Social Psychology*, 60: 241–53.

Baron, R.M. and Kenny, D.A. (1986) "The Moderator–Mediator Variable Distinction in Social Psychological Research: Conceptual, Strategic, and Statistical Considerations", *Journal of Personality and Social Psychology*, 51 (6): 1173–82.

Clark, M.S. and Lemay, E.P., Jr (2010) "Close Relationships", in S.T. Fiske, D.T. Gilbert, and G. Lindzey (eds) *Handbook of Social Psychology*, Hoboken, NJ: Wiley.

Enright, R.D. and Coyle, C.T. (1998) "Researching the Process Model of Forgiveness within Psychological Interventions", in E.L. Worthington, Jr (ed.) *Dimensions of Forgiveness: psychological research and theological perspectives*, Radnor, PN: Templeton Foundation Press.

Escalas, J.E. and Bettman, J.R. (2003) "You Are What They Eat: The Influence of Reference Groups on Consumers' Connections to Brands", *Journal of Consumer Psychology*, 13 (3): 339–48.

Fincham, F.D. (2000) "The Kiss of the Porcupines: From Attributing Responsibility to Forgiving", *Personal Relationships*, 7 (1): 1–23.

Finkel, E.J, Burnette, J.L. and Scissors, L.E. (2007) "Vengefully Ever After: Destiny Beliefs, State Attachment Anxiety and Forgiveness", *Journal of Personality and Social Psychology*, 92 (5): 871–86.

Finkel, E.J., Rusbult, C.E., Kumashiro, M. and Hannon, P.A. (2002) "Dealing with Betrayal in Close Relationships: Does Commitment Promote Forgiveness?" *Journal of Personality and Social Psychology*, 82 (6): 956–74.

Girard, M. and Mullet, È. (1997) "Propensity to Forgive in Adolescents, Young Adults, Older Adults, and Elderly People", *Journal of Adult Development*, 4: 209–20.

Grégoire, Y., Tripp, T.M. and Legoux, R. (2009) "When Customer Love Turns into Lasting Hate: The Effects of Relationship Strength and Time on Customer Revenge and Avoidance", *Journal of Marketing*, 73: 18–32.

Hess, R.L., Jr, Ganesan, S. and Klein, N.M. (2003) "Service Failure and Recovery: The Impact of Relationship Factors on Customer Satisfaction", *Journal of the Academy of Marketing Science*, 31 (2): 127–45.

Holloway, B.B., Wang, S. and Beatty, S.E. (2009) "Betrayal? Relationship Quality Implications in Service Recovery", *Journal of Services Marketing*, 23 (6): 385–96.

Hoyt, W., Fincham, F.D., McCullough, M.E., Maio, G. and Davila, J. (2005) "Responses to Interpersonal Transgressions in Families: Forgiveness, Forgivability, and Relationship-Specific Effects", *Journal of Personality and Social Psychology*, 89 (3): 375–94.

McCullough, M.E., Bono, G. and Root, L.M. (2007) "Rumination, Emotion, and Forgiveness: Three Longitudinal Studies", *Journal of Personality and Social Psychology*, 92 (3): 490–505.

McCullough, M.E., Fincham, F.D. and Tsang, J.A. (2003) "Forgiveness, Forbearance, and Time: The Temporal Unfolding of Transgression-Related Interpersonal Motivations", *Journal of Personality and Social Psychology*, 84 (3): 540–57.

McCullough, M.E., Rachal, K.C., Sandage, S.J., Worthington, E.L., Jr, Brown, S.W. and Hight, T.L. (1998) "Interpersonal Forgiving in Close Relationships: II: Theoretical Elaboration and Measurement", *Journal of Personality and Social Psychology*, 75 (6): 1586–603.

McCullough, M.E., Worthington, E.L., Jr and Rachal, C. (1997) "Interpersonal Forgiving in Close Relationships", *Journal of Personality and Social Psychology*, 73 (2): 321–36.

Oliver, R.L. (1999) "Whence Consumer Loyalty?" *Journal of Marketing*, 63: 33–44.

Park, C.W., MacInnis, D.J., Priester, J., Eisingerich, A.B. and Iacobucci, D. (2010) "Brand Attachment and Brand Attitude Strength: Conceptual and Empirical Differentiation of Two Critical Brand Equity Drivers", *Journal of Marketing*, 74 (6): 1–17.

Park, C.W., Priester, J.R., MacInnis, D.J. and Wan, Z. (2009) "The Connection–
Prominence Attachment Model (CPAM): A Conceptual and Methodological
Exploration of Brand Attachment", in D.J. MacInnis, C.W. Park, and J.R. Priester
(eds) *Handbook of Brand Relationships*, Armonk, NY: M.E. Sharpe.

Reimann, M. and Aron, A. (2009) "Self-Expansion Motivation and Inclusion of Brands
in Self: Toward a Theory of Brand Relationships", in D.J. MacInnis, C.W. Park, and
J.R. Priester (eds) *Handbook of Brand Relationships*, Armonk, NY: M.E. Sharpe.

Smith, A.K. and Bolton, R.N. (1998) "An Experimental Investigation of Customer
Reactions to Service Failure and Recovery Encounters: Paradox or Peril?" *Journal of
Services Research*, 1: 65–81.

Strasser, J.B. and Becklund, L. (1991) *Swoosh: the unauthorized story of Nike and the men who
played there*, San Diego, CA: Harcourt Brace Jovanovich.

Tax, S., Brown, S.W. and Chandrashekaran, M. (1998) "Customer Evaluations of Service
Complaint Experiences: Implications for Relationship Marketing", *Journal of Marketing*,
62: 60–76.

van Oyen Witvliet, C., Ludwig, T.E. and Vander Laan, K.L. (2001) "Granting Forgiveness
or Harboring Grudges: Implications for Emotion, Physiology, and Health", *Psychological
Science*, 12: 117–23.

Worthington, E.L., Jr (1998) "The Psychology of Forgiveness: History, Conceptual Issues,
and Overview", in M.E. McCullough, K.I. Pargament, and C.E. Thoresen (eds)
Forgiveness: theory, research, and practice, New York: The Guilford Press.

Zechmeister, J.S. and Romero, C. (2002) "Victim and Offender Accounts of Interpersonal
Conflict: Autobiographical Narratives of Forgiveness and Unforgiveness", *Journal of
Personality and Social Psychology*, 82: 675–86.

11

RELATIONSHIPS ARE COMPLICATED

On construct validity when consumer–brand relationships are systems

Aaron Ahuvia

It may be a Hollywood cliché, but it is nonetheless true – *relationships are complicated*. Because of this complexity, relationships are generally not unidimensional constructs. What is more, relationships have many moving parts, and it is the way these parts fit together which often defines the relationship type. For example, if when a person arrives you feel happy and when they leave you feel sad, this relationship is typical of friendship. But if when a person arrives you feel sad and when he or she leaves you feel happy, that relationship is more typical of an enemy. Both relationships contain the same parts: someone comes, someone goes, you feel happy, or you feel sad. But these parts fit together differently in each case, and hence the relationships they typify are also quite different. I argue here that relationship types (e.g. friendship, love, enmity) are fairly complex systems whose parts typically include behaviors, emotions, thoughts, social norms, etc. Furthermore, the relationship type is defined not just by what its components are, but by the ways these components interact with each other. I suspect that for many readers, nothing said so far has been terribly controversial. Yet it has been my experience that if one tries to apply this thinking in one's research, it raises construct validity issues which have not been well explored the past literature. And these unresolved construct validity issues make it difficult to publish research in its most useful and insightful forms. My goal, then, is to begin addressing these issues in the hope that doing so will allow consumer–brand relationship researchers to publish the most theoretically appropriate models for their constructs.

In this chapter I will address a set of construct validity issues which are particularly prevalent in consumer–brand relationship research, although they are relevant in many other contexts as well. Figures 11.1 and 11.2 both contain hypothetical models of brand love which will be used as running examples

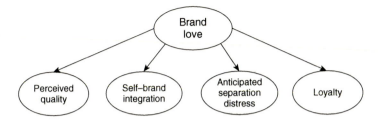

FIGURE 11.1 Hypothetical model of brand love as a second order multidimensional construct

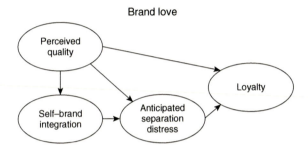

FIGURE 11.2 Hypothetical model of brand love as a system of constructs

throughout this chapter. These models are presented solely to facilitate this methodological discussion, and are *not* recommended as a substantive theory of brand love. Both figures 11.1 and 11.2 conceptualize brand love as a multidimensional construct consisting of the same components. Figure 11.1 depicts the more familiar approach to representing a multidimensional construct, in which the construct is a hierarchically organized. In figure 11.2, the multidimensional construct is conceptualized as what I will term a *system of constructs*. The approaches in figures 11.1 and 11.2 tell us different things and both can be useful. But should it be the case that meaningful predictive relationships of the type depicted in figure 11.2 exist between the lower order constructs within a larger multidimensional construct, then understanding these relationships is an essential part of understanding how the construct works. Investigating these relationships by modeling a single construct as an interconnected system of other constructs is a standard practice in CCT/interpretive/qualitative research. But some researchers with backgrounds in structural equations modeling would object to this practice. To be clear, the type of model depicted in figure 11.2 is entirely routine in SEM. But what is not routine is conceptualizing this type of predictive model as representing the interrelationships between subdimensions of a more abstract multidimensional construct. These critics of the approach advocated here might argue that figure 11.2 is a theory or model containing four distinct constructs, rather than a representation of a single multidimensional construct.

Unfortunately, what may seem at first to be a minor semantic difference has far-reaching implications for how consumer–brand relationships can be modeled and studied. This is because, for the most part, we study constructs. If one wishes to study a consumer–brand relationship such as brand love, using a hierarchical model such as figure 11.1 allows one to do so. But if one wishes to explore that consumer–brand relationship in more detail by investigating how the parts interact, the topic of your study may disappear before your eyes. For if the model depicted in figure 11.2 cannot be a construct, then it cannot be brand love. It must instead be a model about one or more of the labeled constructs (e.g. loyalty). And with that, the topic of the study has been turned in quite a different direction.

For researchers interested in consumer–brand relationships this leaves us with several options. First, one might abandon structural equations modeling and simply use CCT approaches, because the idea that a construct can be best described as a system of relationships between other constructs is well accepted in CCT research. But for obvious reasons, this is not the preferred course of action. Second, one could develop a model in the general style of figure 11.3.

Figure 11.3 is a hypothetical model containing both conventional paths between the first order constructs and the second order construct, as well as paths between some of the first order constructs themselves. In principle there is nothing wrong with the type of model depicted in figure 11.3, and models of this type have been published (Yi 1989). But in practice the paths linking the first order constructs in figure 11.3 are likely to be not significant or at most fairly weak, as the shared variance between these constructs has already been absorbed by the higher order (brand love) construct. This suggests that depicting multidimensional constructs in a manner similar to figure 11.2 will likely be necessary to study the interrelationships between the first order constructs that make them up. Therefore, the rest of this discussion will focus primarily on contrasting hierarchical multidimensional models such as depicted in figure 11.1 with system multidimensional models such as depicted in figure 11.2.

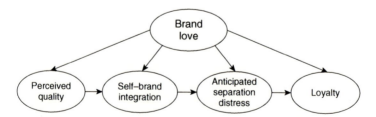

FIGURE 11.3 Hypothetical model of brand love as a second order reflective indicator construct with causal paths between first order constructs

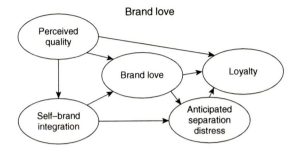

FIGURE 11.4 Hypothetical model of brand love as a directly measured construct within a system of constructs

As a third option, one might create direct measures of the consumer–brand relationship construct, which are distinct from the lower order constructs which make it up. Figure 11.4 depicts a hypothetical example of this type of model.

Figure 11.4 says something fundamentally different from figure 11.2 or 11.3. In figures 11.2 and 11.3 brand love consists of the four lower order constructs, whereas in figure 11.4 brand love exists separately from the other four constructs, although it interacts with them. There is nothing methodologically wrong with the type of model depicted in figure 11.4. But for relationships in general, and for consumer–brand relationships in particular, I would argue that it is a poor depiction of reality. A relationship is a system, analogous to a bicycle. If you take away the seat, the frame, the wheels, etc. you are not left with the pure essence of a bicycle, you're left with nothing at all. This can be seen clearly in a relationship like friendship. If you take away the high regard friends have for each other, the desire to spend time together, the enjoyment of each other's company, the normative commitments and expectations that come with being a friendship, etc., there is no friendship left over which is separate from these components.

This statement is a substantive claim about the nature of relationships, and is not always true with other categories of constructs. For example, unlike relationship constructs, satisfaction constructs (e.g. overall life satisfaction) are not constructed out of satisfaction with their sub-domains (marital satisfaction, job satisfaction, etc.). To continue with this example, overall life satisfaction exists as a separate psychological experience over and above our satisfaction with the various aspects of our lives such as our income or our health. In fact, the "top-down" influence of overall life satisfaction on individual life domains (e.g. "my life is good so I guess my job must be good") is generally stronger than the "bottom-up" influence of particular life domains on overall life satisfaction (e.g. "my job is good so therefore my life is good") (Lance, Alison and Michalos 1995). In the case of life satisfaction, if you removed from consideration each and every domain satisfaction – first eliminating from consideration job satisfaction, then marital satisfaction, then financial satisfaction, until every conceivable domain satisfaction had been removed – overall life satisfaction would still exist as a real experience and as a viable scientific construct. This is not the case, however, with relationships.

Why is it that life satisfaction and relationships differ in this way? Satisfaction is a judgment and corresponding experience that may be arrived at in many ways. It makes sense that our satisfaction with various aspects of our lives should influence our overall satisfaction, but it is not logically necessary that they do so. Put differently, overall life satisfaction is a phenomenologically separate experience from the various life domain satisfactions; it is not made up of them. In contrast, a relationship is not a specific experience or event. Rather, a relationship is a complex interconnected system of experiences, beliefs, social norms, etc., each of which can exist independently of any given relationship, but collectively constitute a relationship.

Perhaps this is why things like friendships are classified as "relationships." Social relationships are just one of many types of relationships, including mathematical relationships, causal relationships, etc. All these types of relationships occur *between* something and something else. The relationship itself has no independent substance over and above the things it connects together. *It is a mistake to create a theoretical model of a relationship which denies the fundamental nature of what it means for something to be a relationship.*

I used the friendship relationship rather than the love relationship in the previous example intentionally, because the word love has multiple meanings which could have blurred the issues. "Love" refers both to a type of relationship and to a collection of emotions which typify that relationship (Batra, Ahuvia and Bagozzi 2011). The most prototypical emotion in the love relationship is affection, although passion is also a prototypical aspect of romantic love (Fehr 1993). In consumer–brand *relationship* research, we are concerned firstly with love as a type of relationship, but also with the feelings of affection and passion which play a role in that relationship and are sometimes labeled as feelings of love. If a model of brand love is meant to describe the brand love relationship, it would be a substantive mistake to construct this model in the style of figure 11.4, because doing so would claim that the relationship existed independently of its constituent parts. But if a model of brand love is meant to describe the specific emotional experience of affection or passion for a brand, then a model in the style of figure 11.4 could be quite appropriate.

So far we have reviewed several options for modeling how the components (a.k.a. subdimensions or lower order constructs) of a relationship construct interact with each other. Models in the style of figure 11.1 assume that the parts of a higher order construct are only related to each other in the sense that they are all reflections of the same larger construct. This is sometimes, but not always, correct, as we will see below. Models in the style of figure 11.3 are unlikely to find statistically significant relationships between the lower order constructs, even when strong relationships may exist. Models in the style of figure 11.4

substantively misconstrue the nature of relationships by claiming that a relationship exists as an entity independent of the lower order constructs that make it up. This leaves models in the style of figure 11.2 which are designed to do precisely the type of analysis required, but meet with criticism from some researchers unaccustomed to seeing models of this type as representing predictive relationships between lower order constructs within a single more abstract construct. A primary thesis of this chapter is that using predictive models in the style of figure 11.2 will often be the best approach.

Multidimensional constructs as systems of subordinate constructs

All multidimensional constructs are, in a minimal sense, systems of subordinate constructs. In structural equations models this simple "system" is depicted as in figure 11.1, showing that each of the subordinate constructs (a.k.a. dimensions) are derived from the higher order construct brand love. Although figure 11.1 is a system of sorts, when I refer to a "system of constructs," I mean an interconnected system of relationships *between subordinate constructs* (e.g. figures 11.2 and 11.3).

It is the type of model exemplified in figures 11.2 and 11.3 that I have in mind when I described a construct as consisting of "a system" of other constructs. And it is the legitimacy of seeing a system of constructs such as figure 11.2 as a representation of a single larger complex construct that I wish to defend here. In my experience, models of this type have met with two major objections. The first holds that these models simply are *not* single constructs. The second objection consists of a series of related construct validity issues regarding the proper scope of these constructs and what construct they should be considered a model of. These objections are addressed in turn.

That's not a single construct

Researchers are accustomed to seeing higher order constructs which look like figure 11.1, so the idea that a single construct can consist of several other constructs is not problematic in and of itself. But when presented with constructs in the form of figure 11.2, some researchers have asserted that a system of constructs such as this cannot be considered a single construct. In fairness to this point of view, figure 11.1 is an abstract representation in which the lower order constructs (e.g. perceived quality) are more concrete subdimensions of the overall construct. Therefore, the claim that the four lower order constructs are all components of a single higher order construct can be supported (or not) both empirically and conceptually. In figure 11.2, however, it is possible to test the goodness of fit of the model, but this test does not really address the question of whether the constructs in the model should be seen as separate constructs or parts of a higher order construct. Therefore, for figure 11.2, the question of whether the model should be seen as four parts of a single construct or four different constructs must be decided on conceptual grounds.

To see why figure 11.2 can legitimately be described as depicting a single complex construct, let us begin with a review of Law, Wong and Mobley's (1998) taxonomy of multidimensional constructs. These authors create a trichotomy of multidimensional constructs based on different types of relationships between a construct's dimensions and the overall construct. This typology consists of latent model constructs, aggregate model constructs and profile model constructs. However, profile model constructs will not be presented here, as they are not relevant to the current discussion.

The distinction between latent model constructs and aggregate model constructs may bring to mind the distinction between reflective and formative indicators (Bagozzi 2011). However, formative and reflective indicators are both specific forms of measurement within structural equations models, and much of the debate about them is based on technical issues within this type of modeling, whereas latent model and aggregate model constructs refer to conceptual types of constructs which are not linked to any specific methodology. Although the current discussion uses SEM formatted models for purposes of illustration, the main issues addressed here are conceptual and philosophical in nature.

Figure 11.1 is an example of a *latent model construct*. These constructs posit the existence of a single underlying phenomenon, such as general intelligence (Spearman 1927), which manifests itself in a variety of ways (e.g. mathematical ability, linguistic ability, etc.). Each first order construct (mathematical ability, linguistic ability, etc.) is considered part of the higher order construct because the first order construct is either "caused"[1] by the higher order construct or is a manifestation of the higher order construct. In a latent model construct the relationship between higher order constructs and first order constructs is analogous to the relationship between first order constructs and the individual indicators of those constructs. For example, just as each mathematical problem on an IQ test is intended as a separate indicator of the same underlying construct (mathematical ability), each first order construct (mathematical ability, linguistic ability, etc.) is a separate indicator of the same higher order construct (general intelligence). As operationalized in SEM, in a latent model construct the higher order construct consists of the shared factor variance between the first order constructs.

Aggregate model constructs can best be explained through an example. The aggregate model construct Social Disruption (Holmes and Rahe 1976) is part of social readjustment theory which holds that various life events – like the birth of a child – can disrupt a person's established routines, relationships and ways of looking at the world. Following these disruptions, the person needs to engage in a process of social readjustment. The total, or *aggregate*, amount of readjustment a person must undergo depends on the total amount of disruption from all sources that person has recently encountered. To measure this aggregate level of disruption, Holmes and Rahe (1976) designed the Social Readjustment Rating Scale which measures how many of forty-three life-changing events a person has recently experienced, and assigns point values to each life-changing event. Hence, this rating scale measures needed social readjustment as an aggregate model construct with forty-three distinct dimensions, and each dimension measured by a single indicator. These forty-three first order constructs include events as diverse as moving to a new home or having a family member die, so the sources of each disruptive event may have nothing in common with one another. These forty-three dimensions are all considered part of the same higher order Social Disruption construct not because they have the same cause, but because they have the same effect, i.e. they create social disruption. Having the same effect is just one of several reasons first order constructs may be grouped together into a single aggregate model higher order construct. Nonetheless, the Social Disruption construct is a useful illustration of aggregate model constructs because it presents such a clear counterexample to the more familiar latent model constructs.

While in a latent model construct a person's score on the higher order construct is determined by the shared factor variance between the first order constructs, a person's score on an aggregate model construct is determined through an algebraic combination of the construct's indicators. In the social readjustment example, a person's overall score on the scale is determined by simply adding up the social disruption caused by each separate disruptive event. However, more complicated relationships between the dimensions of a construct and the overall construct are also possible, and would likely be needed to describe consumer–brand relationships (CBRs).

> Under the aggregate model, the multidimensional construct is formed as an algebraic composite of its dimensions. The multidimensional construct can be a linear or nonlinear function of its dimensions, and the dimensions may also have unit weights or differential weights while forming the overall construct.
>
> *(Law, Wong and Mobley 1998, p. 745)*

Relationships, whether they are interpersonal relationships or CBRs, are aggregate model constructs. For example, Davis, Todd and Perlman (1985) conceptualize friendship as an aggregate model construct consisting of nine first order constructs including enjoyment of the other and trust in the other. Comparing the aggregate model construct friendship with a latent model construct such as general intelligence can be instructive. The first order constructs mathematical ability and linguistic ability reflect both general intelligence and education (and other things as well). When measuring general intelligence through an IQ test, the goal is to sort out the effects of general intelligence on mathematical and linguistic performance from the effects of education, etc.

on performance. In this latent construct model, there is a single unified construct (general intelligence) giving rise to a certain amount of mathematical ability and linguistic ability; and only the variance in each of these first order constructs which is due to general intelligence is considered a part of general intelligence. In an aggregate model construct such as friendship, variance in the first order constructs (enjoyment, trust, etc.) also arises from multiple sources (the other's charm, honesty, etc.). But in an aggregate model construct, variance in the first order constructs arising from many different sources is nonetheless included in the higher order construct. For example, variance in enjoyment which is due to the other's charm (cause one), and variance in trust which is due to the other's honesty (cause two), are both included in the higher order construct friendship. As with all aggregate model constructs, the depth of a friendship can be measured by some aggregation of trust (from multiple sources) and enjoyment (from multiple sources), and other constructs as well.

As another example, Batra, Ahuvia and Bagozzi (2011) provide a description of the brand love prototype, which is the common mental model consumers have of love. In Batra, Ahuvia and Bagozzi (2011) this prototype is developed in a series of interpretive interviews and then assessed through two different structural equations models, both of which conceptualize brand love as a traditional latent model construct. But based on interpretive research reported as studies one and two of Batra, Ahuvia and Bagozzi (2011), brand love could be characterized as an aggregate model construct consisting of the following first order constructs:

1. *Great quality/qualities.* Loved brands are perceived to be excellent in virtually any way that a brand could excel, such as performance, trustworthiness, value for money, good-looking design, etc.
2. *Strongly-held values and existential meaning.* While loved brands were praised for providing a wide variety of benefits including very straightforward practical benefits, they were more likely to be loved when they also provided benefits which consumers felt connected to "deeper" issues such as self-actualization, close interpersonal relationships, existential meaning, or religious or cultural identities.
3. *Intrinsic rewards.* Consumers often adhered to the common distinction between performing an act "to get something" (extrinsic rewards) as opposed to doing it because "you love it" (intrinsic rewards). Loved brands provided intrinsic rewards when the process of using or interacting with the brand created happiness, pleasure, self-confidence, relaxation or some other psychological reward for the consumer.
4. *Self-identity.* Loved brands frequently played an important role in the consumer's construction and/or display of their identity (Ahuvia 2005).
5. *Positive affect.* Loved brands provided consumers with a wide variety of positive emotional experiences.

6. *Passionate desire and a sense of natural fit.* Consumers frequently experienced a sense of natural fit between themselves and their loved brands. Often the decision to purchase the loved brand was made rapidly and intuitively, an experience which was sometimes labeled *love at first sight.*

7. *Emotional bonding and anticipated heartbreak.* Consumers felt a strong sense of emotional attachment to loved brands. Consumers often expressed this emotional attachment by stating that they would be very upset were they to lose the loved item, a phenomenon known as "separation distress" in the attachment literature (Hazan and Zeifman 1999; Thomson *et al.* 2005; Park *et al.* 2010).

8. *Willingness to invest resources.* Consumers tend to invest high levels of time, energy and money in loved brands.

9. *Frequent thought and use.* Consumers frequently use and/or think about the brands they love.

10. *Length of use.* Consumers tend to have a relatively long history with loved brands and to anticipate that the relationship will endure long into the future.

Davis and Todd's (1985) friendship construct has nine dimensions, Batra, Ahuvia and Bagozzi's (2011) brand love construct had the ten original dimensions listed above which were rearranged into fourteen dimensions during the structural equations modeling, and Albert, Merunka and Valette-Florence's (2008) brand love construct has eleven dimensions. These examples reiterate a point made at the outset of this chapter: relationships are frequently complex multifaceted constructs. Scientists strive to create *parsimonious* theories. This means we prefer theories with the smallest possible number of parts and causal relationships between those parts. Yet to quote what is sometimes known as Einstein's razor, things should be made as simple as possible – *but not simpler.* In any complex multidimensional construct it is highly likely that some of the first order constructs will have theoretically important relationships with other first order constructs. There is nothing in the nature of aggregate model constructs to suggest that modeling these relationships is inappropriate. Quite to the contrary, a model of an aggregate construct which includes important relationships between the first order constructs is a more complete and more useful theory than one that does not.

As a practical matter, one advantage that latent model constructs have over aggregate model constructs is that established methodologies exist for measuring the intensity or extent of latent model constructs. For example, for both figures 11.1 and 11.2 the overall amount of love a consumer has for a brand is some combination of the four components of brand love depicted in each model. However, in figure 11.1 if one has measured the extent to which a consumer (a) perceives a brand to be of high quality, (b) has integrated the brand into his or her identity, (c) believes that losing the brand would be painful, and (d) is loyal to the brand, then combining this information into an overall measure of the extent to which that consumer loves that brand is fairly straightforward. However, if figure 11.2 is considered an aggregate model construct, we would know that a consumer's overall love for a brand is *some* function of the extent to which they experience each of the four components of brand love, but how exactly to specify that function remains an open question. In our example, to determine the extent of a person's love for a brand it may be tempting as a default simply to sum their scores on each of the four components. But there is no reason to believe this approach is optimal, unless of course the researchers have provided other conceptual or empirical arguments in support of that approach. Hence, one practical disadvantage of aggregate model constructs is that establishing how the components should be combined to create an overall measure of the construct is not a routine matter. Fortunately, measuring the overall extent or intensity of a construct is not required to answer many important research questions. Research seeking, for example, to understand the internal psychological dynamics of a CRB like brand love may not need to establish an overall brand love score for individuals. And treating CBRs as aggregate model constructs will allow researchers to produce predictive models (e.g. figure 11.2) which can investigate these issues effectively.

It may also be possible to use a two-step approach. In the first step a higher order construct is tested as a reflective model to determine which possible subdimensions should be included or excluded. Then in a separate step, a predictive model is developed and tested looking at influences of the subdimensions on each other. But exploring this option in detail is beyond the scope of this chapter.

Construct validity, or what's love got to do with it?

Scientific writing is, to a certain extent, rhetorical. While remaining honest, researchers aim to persuade reviewers and editors to publish their work. In this regard, latent model constructs currently have some rhetorical advantages over aggregate model constructs conceptualized as systems of interrelated constructs. Because in figure 11.1, brand love is a source of variance for each of the lower order constructs, factor analysis can be used to bring empirical evidence to bear on the question of whether any given lower order construct should, or should not, be considered part of brand love. This empirical evidence alone should not be determinative, but it can quite legitimately be effective when persuading the reader of the value of one's model. Researchers can establish construct validity (that the construct measures what they say it measures) in two steps. First, the lower order constructs are shown to be part of a single higher order construct. Then a name is assigned to that higher order construct based on what label best unites the lower order constructs. For example, using figure 11.1 it would be relatively easy to argue that of course this construct should be called brand love: what else would you call a construct containing all of those particular subdimensions?

In contrast, when constructs are conceived as aggregate model systems of lower level constructs, factor analysis cannot be used to help justify including or excluding lower order constructs from the model. Looking at figure 11.2, it is not obvious why those constructs should be considered parts of a single larger multidimensional construct. In addition to the legitimate scientific issues, at a rhetorical level figure 11.1 just *looks like* a single construct, whereas figure 11.2 does not (at least as SEM researchers are currently accustomed to seeing them). Therefore, if one tries to argue that, say, brand love is the best label for the system of constructs depicted in figure 11.2; a reviewer might legitimately ask why we should be looking for such a label in the first place? Why not leave them all as individual constructs? Or why not combine the individual constructs in figure 11.2 into two or more different multidimensional constructs?

To make matters worse, figure 11.1 has "brand love" visibly built into the diagram, whereas none of the constructs presented in figure 11.2 is called *brand love*. Where is the brand love in figure 11.2? Since brand love isn't a component of the diagram, why not see figure 11.2 as a theory of one of the named constructs in the model, such as brand loyalty?[2]

In response to these objections, it should be noted that many constructs do not include the name of the higher order construct in any of the subordinate constructs or their measures. For example, in Richins' well-established material-ism scale, none of its dimensions (i.e. success, centrality and happiness) is labeled "materialism," nor is the word "materialism" used on either the original scale (Richins and Dawson 1992) or the revised scale (Richins 2004). In the case of materialism it is not just possible, but advisable, to omit the word "materialism" from the measures because respondents are likely to react defensively to this term. I have reached the same conclusion, albeit for different reasons, about the word "love." Carroll and Ahuvia (2006) constructed a scale of brand love which included the item "I love this brand!" (responded to on a Likert agree/disagree scale). Researchers who have translated this scale into other languages have informed me that the use of the word "love" in this way is fairly idiomatic to English. For example, the word love is simply not used in this way in French (Albert, Merunka and Valette-Florence 2008) or in Greek. As a result, this scale item can sometimes cause measurement problems for non-English speaking populations. In retrospect, it is clear that this scale would be more useful had that item not been included. Nor would the meaning of this ten-item scale suddenly change from measuring brand love to measuring some other construct were this particular item to be dropped from the scale (a practice I recommend to cross-cultural researchers), even though doing so would remove the word "love" from the measure.

The situation where none of the lower order constructs bears the name of the larger multidimensional construct is particularly common when the multidimensional construct represents a system or a class of things. For example, the digestive system contains many parts including the stomach, large intestine and small intestine, but none of them is called the "digestive." Similarly, an automobile is a complex system of parts, none of which is called "car" or "automobile." This is also true for constructs which are classes/categories of things. The category New York City contains five boroughs, none of which is called New York. And the category New Yorker contains more than 8 million people, yet in all likelihood none of them is named New York. I suspect that it is not coincidental that all of these examples of systems or classes of things are aggregate model constructs.[3] Although examining this in detail is beyond the scope of this chapter.

At this point a critic might interject that these examples demonstrate that the type of model depicted in figure 11.2 *can* be considered brand love, but not that it *should* be considered brand love. More generally, if a multidimensional construct does not have its name included in the dimensions which make it up, or even the items which are used to measure it, on what basis can it be said to be that construct and not some other construct?

The short answer to this question is that one needs a clear definition of the term or construct in question. Then labeling a model such as figure 11.2 as a model *of* a particular construct is a matter of judging whether the model meets the definition of that construct. But this argument doesn't really resolve the issue; it just pushes the question back one level. Where does this construct definition come from and what distinguishes a valid definition from an invalid definition?

Answering these questions eventually brings us to an interesting and somewhat subtle point about the nature of much CBR research. To begin, we need to make a distinction between scientist-created constructs (e.g. object cathexis or advertising resonance) and ordinary language constructs (friendship, etc.). Whereas scientists have wide latitude in defining jargon such as "cathexis," scientific definitions of ordinary language constructs should *generally* refer to the same object or phenomenon as does the ordinary language term. For example, the word "fish" as used by a zoologist should generally refer to the same animal as when the word "fish" is used in everyday speech. I say generally, rather than always, because there may be important exceptions to this rule. As a case in point, in order to create a scientifically useful taxonomy of marine life, biologists do not consider dolphins to be fish, whereas a great many English speakers would consider a dolphin to be a fish. Occasional differences between ordinary language and scientific language of this kind arise because scientists construct more detailed and rigorous definitions for terms than are used by the general population. This is an important benefit of the scientific research process, and so long as the number of these exceptions remains reasonably small, it is still appropriate for scientists to use the ordinary language term. But, to continue our fishy example, should it become the case that a large number of animals scientists consider to be (or not to be) fish are different from what is described by the ordinary language use of that term, it would be advisable for scientists to create a new term to be used in place of "fish." In this way language can effectively perform its primary mission of facilitating communication.

Hence, for scientific constructs which begin life as ordinary language terms, data on how the term is used in everyday life are quite relevant when establishing what objects or phenomena the scientific term refers to.[4] To return to a CBR example, figure 11.3 should be considered a model of love, if an algebraic combination of its constituent constructs closely tracks ordinary language use of the term love. Put more plainly, if there are CBRs in the world which strongly have the attributes depicted in figure 11.3, these should also be CBRs in which consumers would normally talk about loving a brand or product.

When scientists attempt to introduce newly invented constructs, they need to justify that the added explanatory power provided by these constructs warrants the increased conceptual clutter introducing a new term will create. The central question these scientists need to answer is *why do we need this new construct?* And the main criterion for establishing a need for the new construct is showing that the new construct improves scientific understanding of some phenomenon within the domain of the discipline and is not redundant with existing terms.

In contrast, ordinary language constructs are not invented by scientists and hence scientists don't need to justify their creation. Encountering a new ordinary language construct is akin to a marine biologist's discovering a new kind of fish. The appropriate question is not *why do we need this fish?* Similarly, scientists should not adopt the stance which says "we will only study this new fish if doing so helps us understand the behavior of other fish we were already studying." Ordinary language constructs, like the newly discovered fish, are "out there" in the world whether scientists like it or not. Of course, not all fish or natural language constructs are equally important to the fields that study them. But the criteria for establishing that an ordinary language construct is worthy of study are different from the criteria used to justify the creation of a new scientist-defined construct. Specifically, ordinary language constructs are worthy of study to the extent that they are interesting and/or important to the mission of the field. In a nutshell, scientist-created constructs can be thought of primarily as independent variables whose existence is justified by their ability to explain something else, whereas ordinary language constructs can be thought of primarily as dependent variables, i.e. things to be explained.

This gives ordinary language constructs certain advantages over scientist-created constructs. The hurdles one needs to clear before introducing a new scientist-created construct should be considerably higher than the hurdles one needs to clear before introducing an ordinary language topic as a subject for study. Furthermore, ordinary language terms should trump scientist-created jargon. As a hypothetical example, imagine that for some time consumer researchers had studied "post-purchase negative affect and anxiety," and now a researcher wanted to study regret. The burden of proof should not be on the regret researcher to establish that regret is significantly different from "post-purchase negative affect and anxiety." Rather, if these two constructs turned out to be two names for the same thing, the field should adopt the term "regret" in place of "post-purchase negative affect and anxiety" in the interest of communicating clearly outside of the field.

This brings us to an interesting and somewhat atypical property of many constructs used in CBR research, such as friendship and love. These constructs fall somewhere in between typical ordinary language constructs and typical scientist-created constructs. When applied to interpersonal relationships, friendship and love are ordinary language constructs. But when applied to brands, they take a step in the direction of scientist-created constructs. In English, the term "love" is very commonly used in reference to products, brands and all sorts of things other than human beings. But the same cannot be said for friendship or most other types of CBRs. And as noted above, among non-English speaking populations the word love is also sometimes only used with reference to people. Given all this, should terms like friendship and love when applied to CBRs be granted the somewhat privileged status of ordinary language constructs?

The answer, I would argue, is partly an empirical issue. If it turns out to be the case that the underlying psychological mechanisms through which people form and manage their relationships with brands and with people are quite similar, then CBRs should be treated like ordinary language constructs. What it means to be friends or enemies is established through the primary use of these terms in interpersonal relationships. If a consumer uses highly similar psychological mechanisms to relate to a brand, then the friendship or enmity of that consumer towards that brand exists in some meaningful sense "out there" in the world, swimming merrily along its way like some previously undiscovered fish. But, if the underlying psychological mechanisms through which people form and manage their relationships with brands are quite different from the mechanisms they use with other people, then CBRs should be treated like any other scientist-created construct. The researcher wishing to argue that a consumer is an "enemy" of a certain brand would need to justify that the addition of this term adds enough explanatory power over existing terms like dissatisfaction to justify the additional linguistic clutter caused by yet one more piece of jargon.

In sum then, what constitutes a valid argument for construct validity depends on whether the construct in question is a natural language concept or a newly minted piece of scientific jargon. For a natural language term, the construct should refer to (i.e. point to) the same things as the natural language term, although scientific theories about how those things work need not match popular understanding. In contrast if a researcher is coining a new term, s/he must establish that the new construct has significant explanatory power and is not redundant with existing constructs. From this point, researchers can create definitions of the construct, which can in turn be used to establish which subdimensions should be included or excluded from a higher order construct.

Conclusion

In this chapter I have argued that relationships are frequently best conceived of as aggregate model constructs. Furthermore, research which specifies and demonstrates relationships *between* the lower order constructs within an aggregate model is not just legitimate but is preferable to research which ignores these relationships. Unfortunately, publishing this research presents a range of difficulties as reviewers and editors are relatively unaccustomed to aggregate model constructs. However, it is hoped that this chapter will present a platform on which to base further discussion of these issues and, with it, greater acceptance of the methods advocated here.

Notes

1 Bagozzi (2011) argues that because causation is generally defined as a relationship between two observable events, latent constructs do not, strictly speaking, cause anything. In the general intelligence example, then, it would be more accurate to say that certain in-principle observable aspects of a person's brain give rise to her or his tendency to perform well or poorly on mathematical tests. The construct *mathematical ability* is not the actual cause of anything; it is just an abstract representation of this tangible biological capacity. Bearing this in mind, I beg the indulgence of the reader if I speak somewhat figuratively through the metaphor of constructs as causes. I do so because I believe this metaphor can help elucidate my primary arguments.
2 And in fairness, figure 11.3 could legitimately be framed as a theory of loyalty or of brand love, just as many models of customer satisfaction could be framed as loyalty or satisfaction, depending on the perspective the researcher brings to the topic. Nonetheless, brand love and brand loyalty play different roles in figure 11.2. As depicted here, loyalty and the other constructs in figure 11.2 are parts of love, whereas the other constructs in the model are antecedents of loyalty, but not parts of loyalty.
3 It should be noted that there are counterexamples where a class of things such as eagles contains members which are also named eagles, e.g. bald eagles
4 This need for scientific and popular uses of the same term to share referents does not extend to other aspects of an object or phenomenon. For example, the person identified by political scientists as the president should be the same person the general population would identify by this term. But the theories created by political scientists to explain how one is elected president, or how presidents use their power once in office, etc., need not be the same as popular theories about these topics

References

Ahuvia, A. (2005) "Beyond the Extended Self: Loved Objects and Consumers' Identity Narratives", *Journal of Consumer Research*, 32 (1): 171–84.
Albert, N., Merunka, D. and Valette-Florence, P. (2008) "When Consumers Love their Brands: Exploring the Concept and its Dimensions", *Journal of Business Research*, 61 (10): 1062–75.

Bagozzi, R.P. (2011) "Measurement and Meaning in Information Systems and Organizational Research: Methodological and Philosophical Foundations", *MIS Quarterly*, 35 (2): 261–92.

Batra, R., Ahuvia, A.C. and Bagozzi, R.P. (2011) "The Brand Love Prototype: its nature and implications", manuscript under review.

Carroll, B.A. and Ahuvia, A.C. (2006) "Some Antecedents and Outcomes of Brand Love", *Marketing Letters*, 17 (2): 79–89.

Davis, K.E., Todd, M.J. and Perlman, D. (1985) "Assessing Friendships: Prototypes, Paradigm Cases, and Relationship Description", in S.W. Duck (ed.) *Understanding Personal Relationships*, Beverly Hills, CA: Sage.

Fehr, B. (1993) "'How Do I Love Thee . . .' Let me Consult my Prototype", in S. Duck (ed.) *Individuals In Relationships, vol. 1*, Newbury Park, CA: Sage.

Hazan, C. and Zeifman, D. (1999) "Pair Bonds as Attachments: Evaluating the Evidence", in J. Cassidy and P.R. Shaver (eds) *Handbook of Attachment: theory, research, and clinical applications*, New York: Guilford Press.

Holmes, T.H. and Rahe, R.H. (1976) "The Social Readjustment Rating Scale", *Journal of Psychosomatic Research*, 1: 213–18.

Jarvis, C.B., MacKenzie, S.B. and Podsakoff, P.M. (2003) "A Critical Review of Construct Indicators and Measurement Model Misspecification in Marketing and Consumer Research", *Journal of Consumer Research*, 30 (2): 199–218.

Lance, C.E., Mallard, A.G. and Michalos, A.C. (1995) "Tests of the Causal Directions of Global-Life Facet Satisfaction Relationships", *Social Indicators Research*, 34: 69–92.

Law, K.S., Wong, C.S. and Mobley, W.H. (1998) "Toward a Taxonomy of Multidimensional Constructs", *The Academy of Management Review*, 23 (4): 741.

MacKenzie, S.B. (2003) "The Dangers of Poor Construct Conceptualization", *Journal of the Academy of Marketing Science*, 31 (3): 323–6.

Park, C.W. and MacInnis, D.J. (2006) "What's In and What's Out: Questions on the Boundaries of the Attitude Construct", *Journal of Consumer Research*, 33 (1): 16–18.

Park, C.W., MacInnis, D.J., Priester, J., Eisingerich, A.B. and Iacobucci, D. (2010) "Brand Attachment and Brand Attitude Strength: Conceptual and Empirical Differentiation of Two Critical Brand Equity Drivers", *Journal of Marketing*, 74 (6): 1–17.

Richins, M.L. (2004) "The Material Values Scale: Measurement Properties and Development of a Short Form", *Journal of Consumer Research*, 31 (1): 209–19.

Richins, M.L. and Dawson, S. (1992) "A Consumer Values Orientation for Materialism and its Measurement: Scale Development and Validation", *Journal of Consumer Research*, 19 (3): 303–16.

Spearman, C. (1927) *The Abilities of Man*, Oxford: Macmillan.

Summers, J.O. (2001) "Guidelines for Conducting Research and Publishing in Marketing: From Conceptualization through the Review Process", *Journal of the Academy of Marketing Science*, 29 (4): 405–15.

Thomson, M., MacInnis, D.J. and Park, C.W. (2005) "The Ties that Bind: Measuring the Strength of Consumers' Emotional Attachments to Brands", *Journal of Consumer Psychology*, 15 (1): 77–91.

Yi, Y. (1989) "On the Evaluation of Main Effects in Multiplicative Regression Models", *Journal of the Market Research Society*, 31 (1): 133–8.

Youjae, Y. (1989) "An Investigation of the Structure of Expectancy-Value Attitude and its Implications", *International Journal of Research in Marketing*, 6 (2): 71–83.

PART III

How Goals and Identity Drive Consumers' Relationships with their Brands

12

THIS STORE JUST GETS ME! CUSTOMER CHEMISTRY AND ITS ROLE IN IDENTITY CONSTRUCTION

Michael Breazeale and Nicole Ponder

> . . . when I left there I couldn't stop thinking about it. It was like that place just got me!
>
> Stacy, 21-year-old informant, describing Anthropologie

Introduction

For more than two decades, consumer researchers have explored the role of possessions in the formation of consumers' identities. Belk (1988) established that consumers use possessions to both form and exhibit their identities to others. Fournier (1998) extended this work to demonstrate that consumers can form relationships with the brands they use and that these relationships often reinforce their own identities. In related research, Ahuvia (2005) found that consumers' narratives could shed light on their relationships with brands and the identities they help to construct. Scholars no longer question whether consumers' relationships with brands provide information about those consumers and the way they perceive themselves. A concept that has received little attention, however, is whether consumers can form similar relationships with retailers. Furthermore, can these relationships contribute to the consumer's sense of self?

The concept of customer chemistry is proposed to describe the consumer process of developing a positive, environmentally derived attachment to a retailer (Breazeale 2010). Empirical evidence suggests that consumers form emotional attachments to retailers based largely on the consumer's feelings of self-image congruity with the retailer's perceived personality as conveyed by the visual servicescape. For example, a consumer who thinks of himself as casually sophisticated and fashionable might be inclined to bond with a retailer such as Hollister whose upscale beach shack interiors tap into his sense of identity. Also playing a role in the formation of the customer chemistry attachment is the emotional significance that the consumer attributes to the retailer based on associations with important events or people in the consumer's life (Breazeale 2010). So a consumer who remembers shopping as a child with her beloved grandmother at Macy's on special occasions might feel an emotional attachment to Macy's because of the retailer's proximity to those fond memories.

The purpose of this chapter is to explore the possibility that the customer chemistry relationship serves as a consumer heuristic that allows consumers not only to shape their own identities but also to signal that identity to others. Ten consumers who participate in depth interviews describe just such a relationship with a favorite retailer and shed light on this relationship's significant implications for the consumer *and* the retailer.

Conceptual foundation

Research is replete with evidence of the self-image as a determining factor of a consumer's behavior (Barnes 1998; Bjerke and Polegato 2006; Park, Jaworski, and MacInnis 1986; Sirgy 1982, 1985). Balance theory (Heider 1946), cognitive dissonance theory (Festinger 1957), parallel-constraint satisfaction (Shultz and Lepper 1996), and many other consumer behavior theories all consider self-image to be the driving force for much consumption. Accordingly, self-image congruity with brands has been shown to play a significant role in brand preferences and purchase intentions (Belk, Bahn, and Mayer 1982; Ericksen 1996; Zinkhan and Hong 1991).

Only recently, however, have researchers begun to explore the idea that the self-image itself may be partially formed through consumption and that the objects and brands that consumers love may be of particular importance. Aron *et al.* (1991) suggested that interpersonal love involves a fusion of identities with one's sense of self growing to include the loved other. Numerous studies have built upon this concept to describe the importance of love of special possessions (Csikszentmihalyi and Rochberg-Halton 1981), of fashion (Thompson and Haytko 1997), and of collections (Ahuvia 2005) among other things.

The basis for much of the aforementioned research is Belk's (1988) "Possessions and the Extended Self." Belk codifies the belief that consumption plays a role in consumers' definition of their sense of self and supports the idea that consumers utilize *possessions* to extend, expand, and strengthen sense of self. Two components of the self are discussed. Core self relates to "the body, internal processes, ideas, and experiences," while extended self relates to "persons, places, and things to which one feels attached" (p. 141).

Two more recent developments in consumer research serve to further extend Belk (1988). First, conceptualization of self as narrative (Escalas and Bettman 2000; Fournier 1998; Giddens 1991; Thompson 1996, 1997) suggests that not only do consumers see themselves as a list of attributes but that those attributes relate in memory to pivotal episodes in one's life – episodes which are strung together to form a story. The resulting story allows consumers to understand who they are and connects past, present, and imagined future identities into a cohesive whole. Also explained by the narrative are one's affiliations with some people and rejection of affiliation with others, based upon the roles they play in the narrative. Ahuvia (2005) suggests that this view is consistent with metaphors that describe identity as a performance in which consumers employ consumed goods to enact personalized versions of cultural scripts (Murray 2002).

The second relevant development since Belk (1988) involves a focus on the complexities of developing and maintaining a sense of self. Discovery of one's personal preferences, making choices, and representing one's self to others have become major concerns for both consumers and researchers (Gergen 1991; Giddens 1991). Two primary theories have evolved to address these concerns – fragmented self and empty self. Postmodernist researchers have described fragmented multiple selves which consumers feel no driving need to reconcile (Firat and Venkatesh 1995). Other researchers have countered the suggestion that consumers do not feel the need to search for a unified self with studies indicating an intense need to define an authentic self (Gould and Lerman 1998; Murray 2002; Thompson and Hirschman 1995). In stark contrast to the postmodernist ideas is Cushman's (1990) suggestion that consumers' identities are actually nothing more than black holes that can never be filled despite lifelong attempts to fill them with consumed objects. In Cushman's view, consumers with an empty sense of self engage in ongoing episodes of lifestyle consumption in a fruitless effort to find their true identity, an identity that can never be found, due in part to a lack of social and cultural support for that project.

A recent study addresses both of these identity issues in a way that is contrary to Cushman's dark view. The concept of belief harmonization suggests that humans possess certain sacrosanct beliefs, among which is the belief that they are moral, loveable beings for whom fate has planned a benevolent future (Dunning 2007). Based on that belief, the research suggests that consumers' beliefs, needs, and preferences actually form a dynamic network which strives to reduce any tension among its elements. For instance, if a consumer wants to buy an expensive luxury item but thinks of himself as a frugal person, the desire for the luxury item may cause the value placed on frugality to become less salient and the belief that he is worth the splurge to become more salient. Therefore, identity is fluid and adaptive to the situation or life stage in which the consumer finds him or herself.

Missing from all of these studies is the concept that consumer love of place can also play a significant role in developing consumers' sense of self. Tourism research has examined consumer reactions to place in the context of travel destinations (Dinnie 2008; Gilmore 2002; Hankinson 2004), while marketing researchers have discussed the concept of place love only in the context of "third places" and then only in regard to the social bonds that lonely consumers form there (Rosenbaum *et al.* 2007). Consumer behavior researchers have not yet explored the possibility that consumers' love of the consumption space may drive consumption which informs identity and which in turn reinforces love of the space. The current chapter addresses this deficiency in the context of consumers' love of a retailer as it attempts to answer the question, "What is the role of customer chemistry in identity construction and signaling for consumers?"

Method

Study design and data collection

Qualitative research in the form of depth interviews was used in this study. A depth interview approach allows the researcher to uncover the subjective meanings of consumers' lived experiences and to explore the way that those experiences inform the consumers' sense of self (Fournier 1998). All of the interviews were conducted by the primary researcher in order to allow a holistic perspective (Fournier 1998).

Ten informants were purposively selected with the goal of achieving greater insight regarding the role of loved retailers in consumers' identity construction. The use of a non-random sample is justified in exploratory stages of research such as this (Erlandson *et al.* 1993). Informants from various life stages and occupations were included in the sample. Table 12.1 provides information on the ten informants. Each of the participants provided valuable insight into the phenomenon of interest, but three interviews were especially illuminating and will be described here in greater detail.

The interviews were semi-structured and focused on the informant's relationship with their loved retailer. Each interview progressed quickly from a discussion of the informant's relationship with the retailer to more detailed life history information with several informants divulging personal information. The fact that the discussions of a favorite place to shop led so easily into discussions of personal matters only serves to reinforce the researchers' belief that the relationship with a loved retailer plays a role in identifying one's self-concept.

Informants were told that the interviewer was interested in better understanding what it is about the store that makes it their favorite. They were told that this understanding could lead to better relationships between all retailers and their customers. Interviews lasted from five to nine hours each and were conducted in a place of the informant's choosing to allow for a sense of comfort and relaxation. Conversations and interviewer observations were documented in shorthand and transcribed immediately following each meeting.

Data collected from the informants determined the direction that each interview took. The transcripts of the interviews yielded a first-person description of the informant's own thoughts and feelings about the retailer and the role it plays

TABLE 12.1 Informant descriptions

Informant name	Gender	Age	Occupation	Family status	Customer chemistry with:
Bill	M	79	Retired attorney/CPA	Married father of 2	Barnes and Noble
Cole	M	30	Mortgage processor	Partnered	The Gap
Darla	F	27	Insurance coding clerk	Single	Bass Pro Shops
Jane	F	45	Real estate agent	Married mother of 2	Best Buy
Kris	F	29	Bank loan officer	Single	Old Navy
Kurt	M	46	College professor	Married father of 3	Best Buy
Laura	F	19	High school student	Single	Plato's Closet
Lu	F	60	Personal assistant	Married mother of 2	Lowe's
Marc	M	45	Business owner	Married	Z Gallerie
Stacy	F	21	College student	Single	Anthropologie

in their life. These descriptions provide a thorough understanding of the customer chemistry process as perceived by the participant informant. Details of each case were compared as they relate to the theoretical foundations of customer chemistry and to the role of the retailer in the informant's identity construction. To further stimulate discussion and to enhance the validity of the findings, an additional interview technique was employed. The shopping with consumers (SWC) protocol suggested by Lowrey, Otnes, and McGrath (2005) involved taking the informants on a field trip to the retailer that is the object of their affection. Informants were asked to consider the shopping trip to be as typical as possible and to regard the interviewer as someone with whom they wish to share the experience. To better simulate an actual shopping experience, each informant was provided $100 to spend on anything they wanted in the store.

During the shopping visit, the interviewer made efforts to document the informant's behavior while minimizing the effects of observation on the informant. Verbal prompts designed to assess the informant's state of mind were provided during the shopping trip. These prompts varied based on the type of retailer and were tailored to each situation. General probes explored favorite areas, the amount of merchandise from the retailer that the participant already owns, and how often the participant shops with others in the store. Other prompts encouraged the participant to discuss her or himself in the context of her or his everyday life outside of the shopping experience to allow comparison of in-store demeanor with that already exhibited outside of the shopping experience.

Because the goal of the SWC protocol is to duplicate the actual shopping experience as closely as possible, prompts were delivered as unobtrusively as possible. Immediately following the shopping trip, the primary researcher transcribed his notes which recreated the behavior, the dialogue, and the mood of the time spent in the store.

By combining the informants' own descriptions of their relationship with the retailer with the researcher's observations of the shopping experience, the researchers were able to achieve a better understanding of the actual emotional processes at work while the informant was actually exhibiting the effects of customer chemistry. This understanding should provide a useful opportunity to describe the dynamic between the informant and the retailer, shedding further light on the role of customer chemistry in identity construction. The findings should then allow a better understanding of retail consumer behavior in general and customer chemistry specifically.

Data analysis

In the tradition of grounded theory (Strauss and Corbin 1988), analysis was conducted on each of the interview/SWC transcripts, beginning with a reading of the transcripts and description of recurrent themes for the individual informants. Through the informants' own perspectives, identity construction issues were explored. Careful attention was paid to the particular events and feelings that related to the way that the informant perceives him/herself and wishes to be perceived by others. The researchers then examined patterns that exist among the ten informants' stories, an attempt to provide structure to an overall understanding of customer chemistry and identity construction. A framework of sensitizing concepts guided this interpretation. These concepts are presented in Table 12.2.

The analysis employed the constant comparison technique (Lincoln and Guba 1985), which involves reading and rereading of the text until common patterns are discerned. Of particular interest was the range of possible relationships, the various meanings placed on consumption episodes by the informants, and the outcomes of the relationships as perceived by the informants.

Case studies

Three of the ten interviews and shopping trips are described below. Each of these cases represents an informant who has expressed love for a particular retailer and reports a high level of customer chemistry. Their narratives provide rich descriptions of the role that this retailer plays in their lives. Important episodes in the consumer–retailer experience are highlighted in an attempt to weave together

TABLE 12.2 Themes that guided this research

A priori theme		Suggested γ:
Transformation of self into a desired form		Wong and Ahuvia (1998)
Loved objects are connected to the self in that they express the self by making visible to others one's internal dispositions, preferences, and impulses, and in that they transform the self into a desired form.		Greenwald (1988)
Version of self that is most salient		
Humans, utilizing limited cognitive capacities, base self-worth on observing and imitating others. The self comprises four components – the diffuse self, the public self, the private self, and the collective or social self. The diffuse self, present at birth, bases self-worth on achieving hedonic satisfaction. The public self is driven by social recognition and bases self-worth on the approval of others. The private self seeks individual achievement and places value on that achievement based on a personal standard. The collective self strives to attain the goals of a reference group – goals which are internalized by the individual as her/his own.		
Trilateral nature (person–thing–person) of consumption relationships		Belk (1988)
Relationships with objects are never two-way (person–thing), but instead three-way (person–thing–person). Due in part to the social nature of consumption, people always experience a somewhat competitive nature in consumption because there may be other people who want to consume the same object.		
Life stage and its impact on customer chemistry		Mick and Fournier (1998)
No single stage of life can contain the ongoing struggle that all consumers face as they resolve identity conflicts only to find that resolution challenged by new events in one's life. Each stage of life involves a synthesis of identities that represents an evolving sense of who one is at any given time		
Empty-self conceptualization of identity construction		Cushman (1990)
Consumers can never be satiated and spend their lives in a constant state of non-fulfillment. Ahuvia (2005) alternatively suggests that consumers personalize the objects they consume, bringing them into a "web of meaning" (p. 182) that impacts them internally (through synthesis into a life narrative) and externally (through sharing their experiences with a larger community).		
"Purity of pleasure" vs. "focal practices"		Borgmann (2000)
Advancing technology has created a consumptionscape in which the benefits consumers derive from consumed objects are far removed from the skill and work that was necessary to create those objects. Borgmann (2000) suggests a "purity of pleasure" (p. 421) for these objects because the hard work of creating them has been removed from the consumer. In contrast, "focal practices" (p. 421) require more effort on the part of the consumer, but the consumer does not mind because the experience of consuming these objects is exactly what the consumer most wants to be doing.		

a coherent story. Each case is followed by a brief description of a theme as perceived by the researcher.

Cole and Gap

At thirty, Cole's appearance does not match the impression the interviewer had before meeting him. He appears several years younger and his small frame, long blonde hair, and trendy, expensive-looking clothes do not match his career as a mortgage company accountant. Growing up gay in a small town, he escaped the monotony by studying the clothes in celebrity and fashion magazines. Dreaming about the styles he would one day be able to afford got him through difficult days of feeling that he was the only gay person in the world. The confident young man that he is today has evolved as he moved to a bigger city, settled into a job that is rewarding if not very exciting, and entered a long-term relationship that brings him much happiness and security.

Cole's appreciation of fashion is still quite strong, and even among his new circle of fashion-conscious friends, he is considered a style guru. He and his partner travel extensively and he has the opportunity to shop at exclusive stores all over the world, but he chooses clothing that supports his personal sense of style, one that might best be described as sophisticated all-American. The interviewer is not surprised by the store Cole describes as his favorite. Gap, a San Francisco-based company, is the largest specialty apparel retailer in the United States (www.gapinc.com), and parent company for retail brands Old Navy and Banana Republic. Purveyor of "cool, confident, casual . . . American style," the retailer has successfully created iconic status, being careful to maintain the distinctions among its unique brands. Its primary brand, Gap, is the one that Cole admires and his personal style seems quite consistent with the retailer's intended identity.

Asked why this retailer is his favorite, Cole responds pensively,

> Well, they really represent everything I like about fashion. They have clean lines and traditional styling in their stores and in their clothes. When I go in there, I feel like I'm stepping into my own closet. Everything is really neat and in its place and they tend to place everything by color. That's the same thing I do in my closet.

The interviewer notes that Gap is known for fairly traditional clothing and that its sister store, Banana Republic, is often considered by many to be more upscale and is usually more expensive. ["What is it about the Gap's style that draws you to it more than Banana Republic that has a similar style?"]

> I have a lot of friends who only buy Banana Republic clothes, but I don't really think they're worth the money. You go in there and the clothes aren't that different from Gap but the whole atmosphere seems sort

of affected, kind of put on. It's like they're trying to be something they're not.

["Have you always felt this way about Gap?"] Gosh, as long as I can remember anyway. I know that when I was first old enough to go shopping for my own clothes, I would drive myself out of town to the nearest mall – I wasn't really supposed to leave town by myself, but I had to if I wanted good clothes. As soon as I found Gap, I knew I had found my store. They had all of the clothes that I saw people wearing in magazines but I could afford them. Sometimes I would sneak away and just kind of hang out in there even if I didn't have any money to spend. It was my escape.

["Do you tell people that you love Gap, or do you keep it your little wardrobe secret?"] Oh, I tell everybody. It just makes sense to go there for the basics. They carry all the basics you need for a solid wardrobe, and if I have the basics, I can make them look expensive. ["What do you think it says about you to others that Gap is your favorite store?"] I think it tells them that I appreciate classic men's fashion, maybe that I know how to put myself together. I mean you can just feel it when you walk in the store. It's neat and organized and you just feel calm when you're in there. Maybe that's how I make people feel!

As Cole enters the store, the young man who has been fairly sedate until this point becomes more animated. He makes his way toward the back of the store where the clearance section sits. As he walks in that direction, though, he touches an article of clothing on nearly every rack that he passes.

I always come to this section first. [He seems rather excited.] I wear a small and they must not sell a lot of smalls, so I can always find really great deals. Look at these pants! [He holds up a pair of khaki pants.] These normally cost $35 but look at this price – they're only $6 now! [As he continues to shop the clearance rack, the interviewer notices that he has picked up and is holding four pairs of similar looking khakis. "Are you buying each of those?"] Yeah, they're all different shades and I need these. You have to be sure to wear the right color of khaki with the right shirts and sweaters. If they don't match, you just look sloppy. [The interviewer can't see the difference in any of the pants that Cole is holding but makes a note to himself to check his khakis when he gets home.]

Before he finishes shopping, Cole has spent nearly two hours carefully perusing the menswear on every rack and shelf in the store. The only things he has elected to purchase are those first items that he found on the clearance racks. The interviewer asks if he didn't find anything else he wanted.

Oh, I found lots of things I want, but it would be silly to buy them now when I know they'll probably have my size on the clearance rack in a few weeks. I go ahead and pick out what I want and then wait until it goes on clearance. That's how I always shop for clothes. I never pay full price for anything unless I know the store doesn't put stuff on clearance, and almost all of them do.

Cole continues to beam as he exits the store, seeming invigorated by the experience of spending time in his favorite store. He clutches his purchases close to his chest and turns to inform the interviewer that he will probably head to a couple more Gap locations nearby before going home. He does and yet, of all the interview participants, Cole is the only one who does not spend more than the hundred dollars that was provided by the interviewer.

Cole's theme

Cole spent his early life feeling alone and out of place in a small town. His method of coping with the loneliness was to dream of the life he would one day have. He used fashion and celebrity magazines to show him what that life could be. During his formative years, Cole developed a sense of what it meant to be fashionable and to be accepted. As a young man, he moved away from the home where he felt so alone and built a life for himself, a life that more closely matched his dreams. A large part of that life was dedicated to the clothes that symbolized success and acceptance to him. Whether through shopping for clothes for himself or through sharing fashion advice with his circle of friends, Cole defines himself in large part by his sense of fashion. The store that allows him to display his personal style is Gap.

Cole could go to any number of stores to find the clothes that he likes. He always goes to Gap first, though. He loves it because the store's servicescape reminds him of his own closet and the clothes they have represent the style that he feels defines him. His earliest experiences with the store as a young consumer allowed him to feel a sense of belonging that he lacked in his life. His trips to Gap showed him what life could be like for him one day and helped him to express his personal style. Then, rather than leaving the store behind, he held on to Gap as a reminder that he has achieved the life he wanted so badly as a teenager. He now goes to the store, not to dream about what life will be, but instead to prove to himself and others that he has made it.

Darla and Bass Pro Shop

Darla is a single, twenty-seven-year-old insurance coding clerk. She has always filled her spare time with friends and family and has only recently left her parents' home and moved several states away from them. Settling into the new life she is creating for herself, she has quickly made a small group of new friends who enjoy her quick wit and ready smile. Darla has always been a little overweight even though she was very athletic growing up. In high school and college she hiked, camped, fished, and participated in team sports, but her weight was always an issue. As she has grown older and her lifestyle has become more sedentary, weight has become an even bigger issue for her, causing her to leave behind many of the physical activities that she once cherished. Employing a coping mechanism to deal with the isolation she feels because of her weight, Darla strives to be the go-to person whenever any of her friends has a question on virtually any topic. While some may perceive her as a know-it-all, her ability to answer obscure trivia questions and provide the appropriate responses in almost any situation makes her a valuable resource to many of her friends.

On the day of the interview, Darla seems comfortable talking about several topics, even though she comes across as somewhat frenetic. The conversation quickly turns to Bass Pro Shop and the place that the retailer holds in her life. She grew up near Springfield, Missouri, also the hometown of this retailer that calls itself "The Granddaddy of All Outdoor Stores" (www.basspro.com). Bass Pro Shop, as described by the company's website, is a destination retailer that strives to create "a truly unforgettable shopping experience" that is "as close to the Great Outdoors as you can get indoors." The store delivers on its promise by providing an indoor space that mimics the outdoors in many ways. From indoor waterfalls and giant aquariums to wildlife mounts and life-sized mountaineering displays, Bass Pro plays like a theme-park for the outdoors enthusiast. The massive interior sports polished concrete floors, giant fireplaces, and log-style columns in a setting that feels like a giant's hunting lodge. The individual departments feel cozy while the overall store is designed to provide an atmosphere "where shoppers may shop and dream in comfort." A huge indoor boat gallery sits next to a shooting range and mounted wildlife appears to have wandered into the store just as intrigued by what is inside as the customers. Rich earth tones ensure that the customer feels grounded even though the intent is to make the imagination soar. The sounds of waterfalls and wildlife create a sense of being a part of the natural environment that is artificially recreated indoors. Customers do not have to imagine how their purchases would make them feel in the outdoors because the interactive environment allows them to experience it in-store.

But what is it about Bass Pro Shops that Darla loves?

> Well, it's part of my hometown so I guess there's a pride issue there, but I think I would love it anyway. It's just the best store I've ever been in. I go in there and I get completely lost. In fact, when I lived in Springfield, if I was having a bad day, I would leave work and go right to Bass Pro to wander around and get centered. ["Why do you think Bass has that effect on you?"] Well, first of all, nobody who really likes it would ever call it just "Bass." It's Bass Pro. And I go in there because it feels comfortable, like it's my store. That store is everything I am and everything I want to be! It's outdoorsy and fun and it's really cool. When I go in there, I think about all

of the fun times I've had camping with my friends or fishing with my dad. It's almost like I'm back in those memories because it really feels like the outdoors in there. Then I think about all of the stuff I could do with the things they sell and I get excited about the fun times that I could have.

As she enters the massive wooden doors that lead into the nature wonderland that is Bass Pro, Darla points to the massive fireplace that has giant tree trunks burning in it, a crackling fire that would be out of place anywhere but here or in some of the largest castles in Europe. Her childlike enthusiasm for this store seems matched by that of many other patrons who are milling about the wide-open space. ["Do you ever chat with any of the other people you see in here?"]

If I have a question, I'll ask someone for help, but I kind of think of this as my time. When I'm in here, it's my time. I like to wander around and be by myself. It's therapeutic. Every now and then if I see someone who looks like they may need help with a fishing lure or something, I may offer some advice.

Darla treks through each section of the store rather methodically, making sure that she does not skip any area that might hold some unseen treasure. She tries on jackets and caps, occasionally asking the interviewer how things look on her. She handles camping gear and goes through tackle boxes to see which has the appropriate number of compartments for her apparently huge collection of fishing lures. Her demeanor, which had come across as somewhat hurried and imposing outside the store, seems to have become calmer and even her speech is slower. She truly seems relaxed. ["Why do you think this store has such a calming effect on you?"]

I guess it's because I feel at home here. Even though I'm not in Springfield anymore, it takes me right back there. It feels like I could walk out those doors and be home again. Like I said, it makes me think about all the good times I've had with my friends, and I guess it makes me think that I could have some of those times again. ["You seem nostalgic for those times. Do you still do this kind of stuff with friends?"] Not really. My life has gone in a different direction and the friends I have now aren't into the same kinds of fun. I mean, I love the friends I have now – it's just different. But when I'm in here, it's like I'm camping and fishing with my old friends all over again.

By the time she leaves the store, Darla has purchased a new rain-proof jacket, a sports water bottle, and a new tackle box that she plans to use in reorganizing her lures. The calmness that came over her as she shopped still remains, although her step is noticeably quicker. As she drives away, the interviewer notices her looking back at the store several times in her rearview mirror.

Darla's theme

The image of Darla looking at Bass Pro Shop in her mirror as she pulls away is symbolic in many ways of the relationship she has with the retailer. For her, Bass Pro is a reminder of good times she had and of a lifestyle that no longer fits her. When she goes there, she is back in an environment that brought her joy and contentment. She continues to define herself as the outdoorsy, athletic girl even though the friends that she has made in her new home would probably not perceive her in that way. Yet as long as she has a Bass Pro Shop to wander, she can envision herself as that girl.

The corporate website for Bass Pro Shop suggests that the store is designed to be a place where consumers can shop and dream in comfort. Their intention is probably for those dreams to be of future outdoor adventures that shoppers can enjoy with their purchases. In Darla's case, however, those dreams are no less real and no less meaningful just because they are dreams of times past. The retailer allows her, as many old friends do, to be the person she was when they first met, and through her relationship with the store, Darla is able to present that persona to people she has met even after it has ceased to be representative of her.

Kurt and Best Buy

Kurt is a forty-six-year-old college professor in the southwestern United States. A husband and father of three young children, he is also a prolific researcher and a favorite among his students partly because of his frequent inclusion of his own irreverent real-life experiences in his classroom instruction. And his life provides him with plenty of material to keep those students entertained.

In his self-described "misspent youth," Kurt spent a great deal of time as the center of attention. Whether on the hockey ice or in the classroom, he stood out. His outgoing and sometimes outrageous personality ensured that people noticed him. He particularly prides himself on the fact that he was very popular with the ladies and even with the men who frequented the gay dance club where he worked as a regular DJ during the 1980s. Even though he is not gay, the attention paid him by the male club patrons still makes him beam more than twenty years later. As Kurt describes it, he was a celebrity within the club culture of his hometown area.

Indeed that time in his life, before he met his wife and began his current career, provides him with many of his fondest memories. He talks often about his adventures as a club DJ and his huge collection of music, proud not only of his prowess but also of the focus with which he put together his sets. Many of his current friends know that Kurt is the person they can ask even the most obscure music question and get the right answer. He is quick to point out that his knowledge is not limited to the music that he played but also covers the equipment that he used to play it. Still quite the techie, Kurt indulges himself whenever possible with the latest music-oriented gadget, although family responsibilities usually come first now.

When the conversation turns to the reason for the meeting, Kurt seems equally confident talking about his favorite retailer. Even though he is no stranger to the tools that retailers use to woo their customers, Kurt claims to be drawn in completely whenever he enters a Best Buy and he tells anyone who asks that Best Buy is his favorite store.

> Oh, I love that place. Everybody knows that when I do get the chance to go shopping, I'm going to Best Buy first. They know what they're doing there. As soon as you walk in, you get overwhelmed by all the great merchandise they carry, but it's laid out in such a way that you're not overwhelmed by the space itself. It's smart that they make sure that every special interest a customer could have is in its own separate store-within-a-store. Whether you're in there to shop for CDs or for laptops, you get the feeling that they specialize in that.

But what is it that first attracted Kurt to Best Buy?

> I used to go into any music store that I found just to see if they carried anything that I needed to add to my collection. As traditional music stores got harder to find, I started looking at places like Circuit City and Best Buy. I think Best Buy was just the best non-traditional music store I found. And when I went in there, I noticed that they carried pretty much everything I was interested in and I could take my family in there, too, and they wouldn't be bored. Even the kids could shop for video games while I looked at the stuff that interested me. [Kurt would later sheepishly admit that the video games interested him as well.] And I love the feel of the store. It's kind of techno like some of the clubs where I played, even though it's really bright in there and no club I ever worked in would ever be lit that bright.

Entering the store Kurt seems not to notice the greeter who welcomes him, walking briskly to the display area that holds the mp3 players and looking like a man with a mission.

> I need a new mp3 to hold my music. I keep filling them up. I'm getting ready to chaperone a group of students to Ireland and I want to be sure I have enough music to keep me occupied the whole trip, plus I like the idea of having one that just has music for this trip! [As he browses, Kurt

explains that the brand of the music player doesn't matter to him because he's "not caught up in labels." He eventually chooses a brand that is unfamiliar to the interviewer.] This one is just as good as an iPod. If Best Buy carries it, then I know it's good and they'll stand behind it.

Then as quickly as he had walked to the music players, he turns and walks to the video game section of the store. His children have multiple gaming systems and he makes sure to select something for each of them. ["I notice that you seem pretty self-contained while you shop. You haven't asked for any help and didn't speak to the greeter as we walked in." The interviewer is curious about the total lack of interaction Kurt has with the store's personnel or even any of the other patrons who mill about the sections where he is looking. His in-store demeanor had been quite different than the outgoing persona he had exhibited previously.]

I hate to shop. I like to get in and get out. I know what I want and I come in and get it and then leave. [The interviewer is afraid that he has just wasted several hours and a hundred dollars. "But you said this is your favorite store."] Oh, it is. I love this place. You wouldn't find me spending this much time in most stores. I guess I get wrapped up in myself when I'm here. I know I may not get to come back for a while, [this location, the nearest to his home, was nearly an hour and a half away] so I'm pretty focused on what I'm getting. I've been thinking about it for days. And it's like a vacation, getting to come in here without the family. I can look at the stuff I want to and take my time.

Before he pays for his purchases and leaves the store, Kurt browses the small "Dance Music" section of CDs. He doesn't select any to purchase, but he seems deep in thought as he browses and then moves on. ["You're not buying any?"]

I guess not. I don't need them anymore. I just like to know what's hot. I don't even recognize a lot of it anymore. [He shrugs and pays for his purchases.]

On the drive home, Kurt makes several phone calls as he coordinates the trip he has planned for his students. He jokes and laughs loudly with his colleagues. The extroverted academic has returned as the focused club DJ recedes into his past.

Kurt's theme

Consistent with his Baby Boomer status, Kurt has enjoyed multiple careers and lived a variety of divergent life experiences. He remembers most of them fondly and cherishes a select few. One of the memories that makes him especially proud is that of his life as a club DJ. That time in his life allowed him to feel like a celebrity. His days were spent exploring the now nearly extinct record stores and his nights were spent as the center of attention in dance clubs and bars. The party didn't start until he entered the club and began to spin. Anyone who has ever experienced such a life understands that the warmth of the spotlight is hard to duplicate. Now, even though he is well-respected by his colleagues and students alike, he shares the spotlight with other researchers and other favored professors. The only time he is truly the center of attention is when he delivers his classroom lectures.

Best Buy takes Kurt back to those heady times. When he steps into Best Buy, he is on a mission to reclaim his identity as the music expert who knows how to whip a crowd into a frenzy. In the brightly lit substitute for a techno club that Best Buy provides, Kurt is an expert again. He is surrounded by the current equivalent of the music equipment and vinyl records that occupied so much of his time. The persona that he has developed as a college professor slips away and the serious young man who spun records for a living returns. He is concerned only with finding the best equipment with which to play his favorite music mixes through its earphones – a rather isolating alternative to booming club speakers. It is not until his family responsibilities become salient and the decreasing selection of tangible music for purchase reminds him that he is no longer that person that he transforms back into the outgoing college professor who quietly yearns to again be the center of attention. Best Buy serves as a palpable reminder of the times that he cherished and a veritable time tunnel that carries him back to them.

Summary of case studies

The three cases described in this chapter all tell of a unique but not uncommon individual experiencing customer chemistry with a retailer. Like the other seven interviewees not reported here, each informant provides different reasons for the love they feel, yet each is actually describing the way that their retailer helps them create a sense of self and convey that to others. Kurt uses Best Buy to transport him back in time to a lifestyle that no longer fits him. For Cole, Gap is a touchstone that centers him, reminding him that he has attained so many of the things that mattered to him as a teenager. Similarly, Darla loves Bass Pro Shop for the memories that it stirs within her.

What the informants have in common is love for a particular retailer. Several of the ten respondents love the retailers because the relationships allow them to move closer to an ideal self that each of them wishes to be. Through their relationships with these stores, they see their own personalities mirrored, and in that reflection they also see what they hope to one day become. While they each report that their retailer's personality is similar to their own actual personality, each also suggests that perhaps the retailer represents an ideal version of themselves, the person they *want* to be.

For the three participants described here, their favorite retailers allow them a glimpse into the past. Darla and Kurt have cherished memories that their relationships allow them to relive even though their current situations differ from those that bring them joy. In Bass Pro Shop, Darla is the younger, more physically fit girl who camps and fishes with her friends and family. In Best Buy, Kurt is the club DJ who brought the party with him. For Cole, however, his retailer is a reminder of times that weren't as positive. As a young gay man yearning to escape small-town boredom and homophobia, Gap appeared to be a way out. Now when he goes into the store, he is reminded of how far he has come. The personalities that Darla and Kurt perceive in their favorite retailers represent the ideal selves that they feel they once represented but have left behind. This is unlike Cole's perception of the personality of Gap that represents the ideal self that he once strived to achieve and now embodies.

The primary difference among the cases lies in the role of the retailer in signaling the identity of each informant. Cole uses his relationship with Gap to signal to others that he has achieved the things that he holds important while still choosing to spend frugally, another value learned early in life. For both Kurt and Darla, their selection of their favorite retailer signals identities that they once had and perhaps wish they could again have.

Discussion

This chapter compiles the stories of consumers who report customer chemistry with a loved retailer. The willingness of the informants to speak with total candor about their lives and the roles that the retailer plays in them created a unique opportunity to delve in-depth into the customer chemistry relationship and to explore the role it plays in constructing their identities. These case studies confirm Belk's (1988) previous research which proposes that identity issues are central to consumption and that consumed objects contribute to the formation of identity. Additionally, the narratives contained herein offer evidence of the ability of a place to invoke the same kind of identity construction associations as loved possessions have been proved to do (Ahuvia 2005).

Ahuvia (2005) describes the role of loved possessions in the resolution of identity conflicts that consumers experience on an ongoing basis as they form their life narratives. One of the primary contributions of that research is the suggestion that consumers often synthesize conflicting identities through consumption of loved objects. The current research extends both studies to show that, for the consumers who share their stories here, consumption of a loved place serves that same function, allowing each of them to create an identity that is informed by the relationship with the retailer. Therein lies the primary contribution of this research.

Loved possessions and favorite brands play a vital role in consumers' lives. To date, no research has explored the role of the loved place in consumers' identity construction. These case studies offer proof that a loved retailer can indeed serve as a place that allows consumers to create, extend, and express their identities. The loved place can be a testing ground for desired identity, a proving ground for newfound identity, a reminder of identities left behind as they are for Kurt and Darla, or a touchstone signaling adherence to core values as it is for Cole.

Implications and future research

Future research should continue to explore the role of loved places not only in the retail setting but in other consumption contexts such as service provision and online consumption. As more consumers shift their consumption habits to the virtual world, there is much to be learned about their relationships with favorite websites, blogs, and community forums.

A common thread among many of the informants was their belief that the employees of their loved retailer were somehow more qualified, kinder, and smarter than the employees of other stores. The transfer of meaning (McCracken 1986) that this suggests could have implications not only for the employees of loved retailers but also for private label brands (PLBs) or for other retailer-sponsored endeavors such as concerts, sporting events, or even television programs. Researchers should examine the possibility that the customer chemistry relationship provides benefits to all whom it touches.

The primary implication of this research for retailers lies in the importance that consumers attach to their relationships with them. Retailers must understand and appreciate their own potential to play a role in the construction of their customers' identities. If they elect to take this responsibility seriously, the potential exists for them to build stronger, more resilient relationships with customers who love them for doing so.

Limitations

All studies have limitations, but the very things that might be considered limitations in many empirical studies are the factors that make this type of research meaningful. While a purposively selected sample does not allow for broad generalization, it does provide a diverse base for exploratory phenomenological research. A small sample size of ten does not allow the researcher to test hypotheses for statistical significance but does provide for the kind of thick description that is necessary for discovery-oriented research. Finally, a heavy reliance on self-reported consumer histories does not ensure the reliability of those stories but does allow the researcher unique access to the very thought processes that make this research worthwhile.

Conclusion

This research extends existing research in a way that allows for theory-building. The findings establish the importance of relationships with place and position them squarely in the domain of consumer research, also suggesting multiple avenues for future research. The researcher wishes to thank all of the informants for their willingness to share so much of themselves and for the valuable information they have provided. This information will allow future researchers to develop new streams of research, future retailers to develop more meaningful relationships with their customers, and future consumers to more fully develop identities that, although unique to themselves, are informed by those described herein.

References

Ahuvia, A.C. (2005) "Beyond the Extended Self: Loved Objects and Consumers' Identity Narratives", *Journal of Consumer Research*, 32 (1): 171–84.

Aron, A., Aron, E.N, Tudor, M. and Nelson, G. (1991) "Close Relationships as Including the Other Self", *Journal of Personality and Social Psychology*, 60 (2): 241–53.

Barnes, J.G. (1998) "Closeness, Strength, and Satisfaction: Examining the Nature of Relationships between Providers of Financial Services and their Retail Customers", *Psychology and Marketing*, 14 (8): 765–90.

Bass Pro Online: <basspro.com/webapp/wcs/stores/servlet/CFPage?storeId=10151&cat alogId=10001&langId=-1&appID=64&option=3&page=12> (accessed January 16, 2011).

Belk, R.W. (1988) "Possessions and the Extended Self", *Journal of Consumer Research*, 15 (2): 139–68.

Belk, R.W., Bahn, K.D. and Mayer, R.N. (1982) "Developmental Recognition of Consumption Symbolism", *Journal of Consumer Research*, 9 (1): 4–17.

Best Buy Online: <Bestbuyinc.com/about/history.htm> (accessed February 24, 2010).

Bjerke, R. and Polegato, R. (2006) "How Well Do Advertising Images of Health and Beauty Travel across Cultures? A Self-Concept Perspective", *Psychology and Marketing*, 23 (10): 865–84.

Borgmann, A. (2000) "The Moral Complexion of Consumption", *Journal of Consumer Research*, 26 (4): 418–22.

Breazeale, M. (2010) "Three Essays on Customer Chemistry", unpublished dissertation, Mississippi State University, Mississippi.

Csikszentmihalyi, M. and Rochberg-Halton, E. (1981) *The Meaning of Things: domestic symbols and the self*, Cambridge: Cambridge University Press.

Cushman, P. (1990) "Why the Self is Empty: Toward a Historically Situated Psychology", *American Psychologist*, 45 (5): 599–611.

Dinnie, K. (2008) *National Branding: concepts, issues, practice*, Elsevier: Oxford.

Dunning, D. (2007) "Self-Image Motives and Consumer Behavior: How Sacrosanct Self-Beliefs Sway Preferences in the Marketplace", *Journal of Consumer Psychology*, 17 (4): 237–49.

Ericksen, M.K. (1996) "Using Self-Congruity and Ideal Congruity to Predict Purchase Intention: A European Perspective", *Journal of Euro-Marketing*, 6: 41–56.

Erlandson, D.A., Harris, E.L., Skipper, B.L. and Allen, S.D. (1993) *Doing Naturalistic Inquiry: a guide to methods*, Newbury Park, CA: Sage.

Escalas, J.E. and Bettman, J.R. (2000) "Using Narratives and Autobiographical Memories to Discern Motives", in S. Ratneshwar, D.G. Mick, and C. Huffman (eds) *The*

Why of Consumption: perspective in consumer goals, motives, and desires, New York: Routledge.

Festinger, L. (1957) *A Theory of Cognitive Dissonance*, Stanford, CA: Stanford University Press.

Firat, F.A. and Venkatesh, A. (1995) "Liberatory Postmodernism and the Reenchantment of Consumption", *Journal of Consumer Research*, 22 (3): 239–67.

Fournier, S. (1998) "Consumers and their Brands: Developing Relationship Theory in Consumer Research", *Journal of Consumer Research*, 24 (3): 343–73.

GAP Online: <gapinc.com/public/OurBrands/brands_gap.shtml> (accessed January 17, 2011).

Gergen, K.J. (1991) *The Saturated Self: dilemmas of identity in contemporary life*, New York: Basic Books.

Giddens, A. (1991) *Modernity and Self-Identity*, Stanford, CA: University Press.

Gilmore, F. (2002) "A Country – Can It Be Repositioned? Spain – The Success Story of Country Branding", *Brand Management*, 9 (4/5): 281–93.

Gould, S.J. and Lerman, D.B. (1998) "'Postmodern' versus 'Long-Standing' Cultural Narratives in Consumer Behavior: An Empirical Study of NetGirl Online", *European Journal of Marketing*, 32 (7/8): 644–54.

Greenwald, A.G. (1988) "A Social Cognitive Account of the Self's Development", in D.K. Lapsley and F.C. Power (eds) *Self, Ego, and Identity: integrative approaches*, New York: Springer-Verlag.

Hankinson, G. (2004) "Relational Network Brands: Towards a Conceptual Model of Place Brands", *Journal of Vacation Marketing*, 10 (2): 109–21.

Heider, F. (1946) "Attitudes and Cognitive Organization", *Journal of Psychology*, 21: 107–12.

Lincoln, Y.S. and Guba, E.G. (1985) *Naturalistic Inquiry*, Beverly Hills, CA: Sage.

Lowrey, T.M., Otnes, C.C. and McGrath, M.A. (2005) "Shopping with Consumers: Reflections and Innovations", *Qualitative Market Research: An International Journal*, 8 (2): 176–88.

McCracken, G. (1986) "Culture and Consumption: A Theoretical Account of the Structure and Movement of the Cultural Meaning of Consumer Goods", *Journal of Consumer Research*, 13 (1): 71–84.

Mick, D. and Fournier, S. (1998) "Paradoxes of Technology: Consumer Cognizance, Emotions, and Coping Strategies", *Journal of Consumer Research*, 25 (2): 123–43.

Murray, J.B. (2002) "The Politics of Consumption: A Re-Inquiry on Thompson and Haytko's (1997) 'Speaking of Fashion'", *Journal of Consumer Research*, 29 (3): 427–40.

Park, C.W., Jaworski, B.J. and MacInnis, D.J. (1986) "Strategic Brand Concept: Image Management", *Journal of Marketing*, 50 (4): 135–45.

Rosenbaum, M.S., Ward, J., Walker, B.A. and Ostrom, A.L. (2007) "A Cup of Coffee with a Dash of Love", *Journal of Service Research*, 10 (1): 43–59.

Shultz, T.R. and Lepper, M.R. (1996) "Cognitive Dissonance Reduction as Constraint Satisfaction", *Psychological Review*, 103: 219–40.

Sirgy, M.J. (1982) "Self-Concept in Consumer Behavior: A Critical Review", *Journal of Consumer Research*, 9 (3): 287–300.

Sirgy, J.M. (1985) "Using Self-Congruity and Ideal Congruity to Predict Purchase Intention", *Journal of Business Research*, 13 (3): 195–206.

Strauss, A. and Corbin, J. (1988) *Basics of Qualitative Research: techniques and procedures for developing grounded theory*, Newbury Park, CA: Sage.

Thompson, C.J. (1996) "Caring Consumers: Gendered Consumption Meanings and the Juggling Lifestyle", *Journal of Consumer Research*, 22 (4): 388–407.

—— (1997) "Interpreting Consumers: A Hermeneutical Framework for Deriving Marketing Insights from the Texts of Consumers' Consumption Stories", *Journal of Marketing Research*, 34 (4): 438–55.

Thompson, C.J. and Haytko, D. (1997) "Speaking of Fashion: Consumers' Uses of Fashion Discourses and the Appropriation of Countervailing Cultural Meanings", *Journal of Consumer Research*, 24 (1): 15–42.

Thompson, C.J. and Hirschman, E.C. (1995) "Understanding the Socialized Body: A Poststructuralist Analysis of Consumers' Self-Conceptions, Body Images and Self-Care Practices", *Journal of Consumer Research* (22), 2: 139–53.

Wong, N. and Ahuvia, A. (1998) "Personal Taste and Family Face: Luxury Consumption in Confucian and Western Societies", *Psychology and Marketing*, 15 (5): 423–41.

Zinkhan, G.M. and Hong, J.W. (1991) "Self-Concept and Advertising Effectiveness: A Conceptual Model of Congruency, Conspicuousness, and Response Mode", *Advances in Consumer Research*, 18 (1): 348–54.

13

THE TRANSFER AND LIMITATIONS OF THE RELATIONSHIP METAPHOR IN IDENTITY-RELEVANT CONSUMPTION SITUATIONS

Hazel H. Huang

Introduction

In 1998, Susan Fournier published her seminal paper "Consumers and Their Brands: Developing Relationship Theory in Consumer Research" in *Journal of Consumer Research*. Her study has encouraged many researchers to investigate the new, exciting concept of brand relationship. Studies using interpersonal relationship theory (Hinde 1979) indicate that through the interaction between consumers and brands, consumers are able to use brands in various ways, both functional and emotional. Undoubtedly, at the product level, brands serve basic functional attributes to allow consumers to perform required activities. For example, we need a pen to write. In addition to functional attributes, brands are embedded with meanings that help consumers enrich their desired life narratives (Elliott and Wattanasuwan 1998). We need a pen to write, but some of us may need a Mont Blanc pen to write. These emotional meanings reflect consumers' self-identities and become prevalent in their lives. Life narratives are thus composed of brand experience in which interaction between brands and individuals demonstrates the concept of brand relationship akin to interpersonal relationship. This concept has been supported by many studies in the past fourteen years (Commuri 2009; Esch *et al.* 2006; Ji 2002; Story and Hess 2006; Sung and Choi 2010, to name a few).

While we may celebrate the breakthrough in devising the brand relationship concept, we are inclined to overlook the critiques, as documented in the literature. Such critiques challenge the theoretical foundation of the brand relationship concept by rejecting a legitimate application of interpersonal relationship theory (Bengtsson 2003; Iacobucci and Ostrom 1996; O'Malley and Tynan 1999, 2000; Patterson and O'Malley 2006). It has been argued that a brand partner is not an active relationship partner, as is required to shape the relationship. Communication from brands is seen as a standard, and thus, cannot generally be sufficiently personal to be meaningful for a simulated interpersonal relationship. These critiques may have neglected the fact that brand relationship is a metaphor; as a metaphor, a brand relationship does not require a perfect transfer from the interpersonal relationship concept. Nevertheless, these critiques have raised some important conceptual issues for us to consider.

Traditionally, we have simplified the definition of brand relationship to the relationship of brand as an interpersonal relationship partner without explicitly considering the metaphoric transfer from interpersonal relationship to brand relationship. What properties (i.e., generic space) do these two concepts share? How do these two concepts differ? How do we combine the generic space and dissimilarities to create a new meaning (i.e., blend space) for the metaphor – brand relationship? This chapter will use the three concepts – generic space, dissimilarities, and blend space – which compose Fauconnier and Turner's (1998) conceptual integration networks model, to evaluate the brand relationship metaphor transfer. The chapter begins with a discussion of critiques of brand relationships followed by an introduction of the conceptual integration networks model. This model will then be applied to evaluate the brand relationship metaphor. Finally, future directions for research are proposed.

Critiques of the brand relationship metaphor

Critiques of the brand relationship concept have centered on the issue of transferring the relationship metaphor (Bengtsson 2003; O'Malley and Tynan 1999, 2000; Patterson and O'Malley 2006). The arguments are on the grounds that (1) interdependence, vital to an interpersonal relationship, is missing from a brand relationship, and (2) the nature of interaction between interpersonal relationships and brand relationships is different. Therefore, it is difficult for the values produced from brand relationships to simulate those from interpersonal relationships. These critiques may explain why consumers have scored low on Fournier's (1994) brand relationship quality scale with regard to favorite brands, below 2.5 on a 5-point scale (Huang 2009) and below 4 on a 10-point scale (Park, Kim, and Kim 2002).

According to interpersonal relationship theory (Kelley and Thibaut 1978; Rusbult, Arriaga, and Agnew 2003), interdependence between partners must be evident for an interpersonal relationship to exist. As a result, partners must collectively affect, define, and redefine the relationship (Hinde 1979: 14–15). On this basis, brand relationship explicitly considers a two-way communication between person and brand (Fournier 1994: 21). Hence, the central assumption on which the brand relationship is established is the consumer's ability to personify a brand, which then becomes an active partner with the consumer. However, "the personification of brands does not necessarily imply that the brand can become an active partner with the consumers. A brand is an inanimate object and cannot think or feel; thus it is likely to respond to consumers in a highly standardized manner" (Bengtsson 2003: 154). In fact, research has shown that brands as relationship partners are passive, if indeed a relationship exists (Coupland 2005). While it is obvious that brands need consumers to survive, their survival may not be "personal" enough to the consumers in the business competitive sense. Thus, a lack of interdependence between partners in a brand relationship suggests that the analogy of reciprocity, which is anchored in the benefits the relationship can bring to the partners involved (Giddens 1991: 89–90), is hard to find. Hence, a passive brand relationship partner does not have the key property of interdependence, which maintains an interpersonal relationship.

Moreover, imitation of interpersonal interaction between the consumer and the brand is limited (O'Malley and Tynan 1999). For an interpersonal relationship, the interaction is only between the relationship partners; therefore, it is simple and straightforward. Thus, the interaction is usually single-dimensioned. On the other hand, the interaction in a brand relationship is multiple-dimensioned. In other words, while interpersonal relationship partners depend solely on the interaction with their relationship partners to define their relationships, consumers tend to have more dynamic sources that define their relationships with brands. These sources are derived from what the brands represent (O'Malley and Tynan 1999; Patterson and O'Malley 2006), including brand usage (Fournier 1998; Swaminathan, Page, and Gürhan-Canli 2007), the possession of the brand (Belk 1988), the interaction with service or sales personnel (Price and Arnould 1999) and the organization (the brand company, technology, and system) (Iacobucci and Ostrom 1996), and sometimes other brand users (Belk and Tumbat 2005; McAlexander, Schouten, and Koenig 2002; Muñiz and O'Guinn 2001). These multi-dimensional interactions involve real interpersonal interactions (e.g., interaction with service personnel) as well as simulated ones, which complicates the process of transferring the metaphors.

In addition, a relationship partner frequently has a clear idea of the role of the other party in her or his life, thereby generating expectations for the relationship. For example, a boss in a boss-and-subordinate relationship expects the subordinate to perform her/his job well while the subordinate expects the boss to give sufficient support to carry out her/his job. Although it can be argued that the roles in immature relationships can be ambiguous (e.g., the two parties at the initial stage in an intimate relationship), most roles are either fixed (such as father-and-son) or have a clear expectation of how to perform within a relationship (such as colleagues). With brand relationships, not all consumers are able to identify the role of brands clearly. To them, brands are brands (Bengtsson 2003). This leads to a difficult evaluation of the brand relationship quality, even with their favorite brands (Huang 2009; Park et al. 2002).

As mentioned before, these critiques forget the fact that metaphors are used as figurative language; each metaphor is "literally impossible but imaginatively suggestive" (Stern 1988: 85). Although a metaphor is literally impossible, it is connotatively true to some extent (Hunt and Menon 1995). Hence, appropriate use of metaphors can liberate our imagination (Van den Bulte 1994) by bringing together two separate concepts and by using meaning to indicate implications of one concept in order to understand another concept (Black 1979). However, there may be a danger when using metaphors in an unduly creative (and careless) fashion (Davies and Chun 2003) because we are still obliged to recognize meaning from literal language (Ortony 1975). Borrowing these meanings from literal language to project to different concepts may disguise reality and thus mislead or hinder the development of research (Pinder and Bourgeois 1982). The next section will discuss the assessment of a metaphor transfer upon which an evaluation of the brand relationship metaphor transfer will be carried out.

Assessing metaphoric transfer

Before assessing the relationship metaphor to describe brand relationships, we first look at what constitutes the criteria for evaluating metaphoric transfers. A metaphor can be successfully transferred only when the borrowed concepts and values remain valid during the process of metaphoric transfer (Hunt and Menon 1995), which involves the source domain and the target domain. The source domain refers to the borrowed concepts, in this case metaphorical expressions that we use to understand the target domain. A set of systematic correspondences between the source and the target domain reveals explicitly the manifestations of the target domain; these systematic correspondences are known as mappings from the source domain on to the target domain (Lakoff and Johnson 1980). These mappings are referred to as pre-existing similarities, which are composed of human experience and perceived structural similarity (Kövecses 2002: 69–74).

The pre-existing similarities are in the "generic space" in Fauconnier and Turner's (1998) conceptual integration networks model. To put it simply, the generic space signifies what the source and target domain have in common. While commonality is the key to understanding a metaphoric expression and is used mainly to assess metaphoric transfer (Cornelissen 2003; Hunt and Menon 1995), Pinder and Bourgeois (1982) argue that dissimilarities are equally important in shaping precisely the metaphoric concepts. That is, a precise use of metaphor needs to specify important properties that the source and the target domain do *not* share. It is not enough to demonstrate the similarities, that is, the shared properties, because "[t]o speak only of similarities leaves open the possibility of implied identity, which should be ruled out if no identity is intended" (Pinder and Bourgeois 1982: 642). Based on the invariance principle, a coherence of the mapping knowledge from source domain to target domain is required, while an incoherence of the mapping should be clearly explained (Kövecses 2002: 103). To fuse dissimilarities into similarities requires a process called "blend space,"

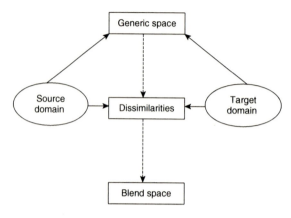

FIGURE 13.1 Metaphoric transfer mapping process

which involves a selective projection to create a new structure for the metaphoric meanings of the target domain (Fauconnier and Turner 1998). Therefore, the assessment of a metaphor starts from the generic space and then moves on to focus on the dissimilarities and blend space with regard to the abstract structure of the source and target domain (Figure 13.1).

Transferring the brand relationship metaphor

Fauconnier and Turner's (1998) conceptual integration networks model will be used to evaluate the metaphor – brand relationship – transfer by using generic space, dissimilarities, and blend space (see Table 13.1). The metaphoric transfer will focus on the conceptual level; that is, the abstract structure of both interpersonal relationship (the source domain) and brand relationship (the target domain). The abstract structure here refers to the ontological entities of relationships: the values of relationships and types of relationships.

The values of a relationship

The values of an interpersonal relationship are derived from functional and social benefits (Smith and Mackie 2007: 398). In terms of the functional aspect, interacting with people can be interesting and useful, for example, self-arranged study groups are applied to facilitate learning efficiencies during the process and improve learning outcomes as a result. Meanwhile, in terms of the social aspect, interacting with people can provide us with a window to better understand ourselves by seeking other people's reactions. With others, we can share enjoyable moments in life. Their companionship can help us overcome difficult times by providing social support. In short, companionship helps us understand the world that surrounds us, interpret realities, and, finally, master our lives.

TABLE 13.1 Metaphoric transfer – brand relationship

Abstract structure	The source domain: **interpersonal relationship**	The target domain: **brand relationship**	Transferability of metaphoric meanings
Values of the relationship partner	Values derived from interaction with human beings	Values derived from interaction with brands through: (1) brand usage – object (2) company – marketing communication (direct: emails; indirect: generic advertisements) (3) personnel (e.g., sales or service personnel) (4) other brand users	Generic space: The meanings of the interaction reside in the partner's life narratives. Dissimilarities: (1) Active (interpersonal relationship) versus passive (brand relationship) relationship partners (2) Single (i.e., the relationship partner in an interpersonal relationship) versus dynamic sources (i.e., brand usage and mass marketing communication in a brand relationship) Blend space: Shift the focus on interdependence to dependence
Types of relationships	Types determined by the role in the relationship: (1) Kinship (parent–child dyad, siblings, etc.) (2) Marriage – husband-and-wife (3) Informal relationships (e.g., acquaintances, friendship and romantic relationship) (4) Professional relationship (e.g. boss–subordinate, colleagues, clients, business partners, competitors)	Types determined by consumers' emotions: (1) Friendships • Casual friends/ buddies • Best friendships • Compartmentalized friendships (2) Marriages/partnerships • Arranged marriages • Marriage of convenience • Committed partnerships (3) Romantic relationships • Courtships • Rebounds/ avoidance-driven relationships • Secret affairs • Flings • Dependencies (4) Nostalgia relations • Kinships • Childhood relationships (5) Reluctant relations • Enmities • Enslavement	Generic space: Different emotions are generated by different relationships Dissimilarities: (1) The determinants of the relationship types are different: social role (interpersonal relationships) versus emotional factors (brand relationships) (2) Emotions driven by interpersonal relationships are stronger than are those driven by brand relationships (see Table 13.2). Blend space: Emotions from interpersonal relationships are adjusted to the brand context (see Table 13.2)

The functional benefits of a relationship belong to the generic space shared by interpersonal relationships and brand relationships. The functional aspect provided by brands is the primary building block necessary for a brand relationship to develop (Fournier 2009). A consumer would not use a brand that does not function properly. Without wanting to use the brand, the consumer is unlikely to use it to create his or her life stories. For example, people need clothes to keep themselves warm and maintain their roles in different social interactions. They do not simply need any clothes, but different types of clothes for different occasions, such as going out with friends or attending an important business meeting. The meanings that different brands represent may help people associate themselves with the desired others and therefore identify their group membership. For example, the meanings associated with Gap jeans and Chanel business suits are located in completely different spheres. Hence, the most basic and intimate interaction between consumers and brands lies in their daily brand usage through which they are able to engage their life themes and fulfill their self-identity goals (Little 1983; McAdams 1996). This functional aspect transcends to a social benefit that helps consumers "master" their lives.

Similarly, the social benefit of an interpersonal relationship relates to life themes and self-identity goals. The social as well as functional benefits from interpersonal relationships and brand relationships are categorized to generic space. This self-identity related social benefit could be observed from three aspects. Liking, as a fundamental element in an intimate interpersonal relationship (Blumstein and Kollock 1988), is the first aspect. Similarity plays an important role in determining liking (Rodin 1978). To some extent, an individual is a reflection of those to whom he or she is close – a "looking glass self" (Cooley 1964). The construction of self is a continuous process so that during the course of the interaction with the relationship partner, the self will become more like the partner (Zajonc et al. 1987). This "birds of a feather flocking together" effect has also been observed between consumers and brands (Levy 1959; Sirgy 1982), by using the consumer–brand congruence model (Belch and Landon 1977; Sirgy et al. 1991).

The second instance involves the behavioral confirmation mechanism through which relationships seem to affect self-identity (Darley and Fazio 1980). Behavioral confirmation refers to the process which an individual adopts to confirm the expectations of others. For an interpersonal relationship, the behavioral confirmation effect is presented through an interaction with a relationship partner, and this effect is able to shape an individual's behavior and subsequently self-identity (Berk and Andersen 2000). Although the brand is not able to "confirm" the behavior of the brand owner, the brand owner is able to obtain such confirmation from their social intercourse. An extreme example of this is obtaining confirmation through brand community, where owners of the same brand get together to interact with the brand as well as other brand owners (McAlexander et al. 2002; Muñiz and O'Guinn 2001). Through brand-related interaction, brand owners maintain, modify, or eliminate their behavior and attitudes in order to conform to social norms and receive social acceptance. This process is similar to the behavioral confirmation mechanism of interpersonal relationships.

Third, another way in which relationships affect the self is by incorporating the relationship partner's resources (social and material), ideas (perspectives), as well as identities (Aron, Aron, and Norman 2001), because in a close relationship, the other is included in the self (Aron *et al.* 1991). In other words, the self and her or his close relationship partners share the elements of the knowledge structures (Aron *et al.* 1991; Smith, Coats, and Walling 1999). It is recognized that the brand is unable to "share" the knowledge structure of its owner, but the owner is able to share the knowledge structure of the brand. Consumers interact with their brands when they use them and when they receive formal information from the company (e.g., newsletters or advertising campaigns) or engage in informal conversation with other social agents (e.g., colleagues, friends, or family). For example, if a brand company emphasizes ethical and environmental issues (e.g., the Body Shop), the brand user may incorporate these ideas into her or his knowledge structure. Therefore, the meanings bestowed on the relationship partners (either human partners or brand partners) are used as a basis for constructing their counterparts' self-identities through events embedded in their life narratives. In sum, the fact that "relationships shape one's conceptions of the self in general" (Aron 2003: 443) is evident in both interpersonal and brand relationships. These concepts, which reflect the functional and social benefits of interpersonal and brand relationship that are transferrable (i.e., generic space), exist in the meanings of a relationship partner, and enrich our lives.

However, there are dissimilarities between interpersonal and brand relationships. An interpersonal relationship is based on "the elementary phenomena of interaction [reflecting] interpersonal patterns of events" (Kelley *et al.* 1983: 22), from physical movement, such as eye contact, to exchange of feelings, such as anger in a lovers' quarrel. Interaction can be seen as a sequence of causally interconnected events between two people (Kelley *et al.* 1983) and thus is featured with (1) the individual actions, (2) coordination of actions, and (3) sequential patterns (Kelley *et al.* 1983). The actions and reactions are part of the coordination of actions. These actions indicate that two parties in an interpersonal relationship behave, both verbally and nonverbally, in ways that are meaningful to each other through a causal, sequential pattern.

On the other hand, as discussed in the section on the critiques of brand relationship, the nature of the interaction between interpersonal relationships and brand relationships is different, thereby leading to a lack of interdependence in a brand relationship. Therefore, the concept of interdependence of an interpersonal relationship is a concept that the brand relationship metaphor should not, and cannot, borrow. However, to fuse this dissimilarity into the brand relationship metaphor, dependence on brands may be more relevant than interdependence in articulating a brand relationship. Therefore, in addition to the generic space, which interpersonal and brand relationships share, the blend space in a brand relationship transfers interdependent relationship to dependent one.

Types of relationships

The second ontological entity is the type of relationship. There are different interpersonal relationships, depending on the relationship dyads: (1) the family domain involves parent–child and siblings dyads; (2) the marriage domain involves wife and husband; (3) the close relationship domain involves friendships and romantic relationships; and finally (4) the work environment domain involves boss–subordinate relationships, colleague relationships, relationships with clients or business partners, and relationships with competitors. Some of the relationship dyads, for instance the parent–child dyad, are predetermined as the roles are fixed when an individual is born. The type of relationship does not exist by choice. Therefore, the discussion of these types of relationships usually involves the development of attachment and the shift in the balance of role dominance.

Other relationship types are determined by legal (such as marriage), occupational (such as professional relationships in a work environment), or emotional relations (such as friendship). Although these relationships exist by choice, people may not be completely free to choose, since each relationship comes with some strings attached. For example, in a professional relationship, if a boss does not like her subordinate, she may be unable to freely fire the subordinate because of legal reasons. Similarly, if a subordinate does not like his boss, he may not be able to terminate the relationship at his own behest, considering the income he would lose when quitting the job. Economic reasons as well as emotional ones account for the difficulty in breaking off a relationship. Having said this, if the relationship partners are not satisfied with the quality of their relationship, dissatisfaction may eventually (but not necessarily) lead to dissolution of the relationship.

By using the interpersonal relationship concepts and by evaluating the emotions in a brand relationship, Fournier (1998) has identified fifteen types of brand relationships, namely casual friends (or buddies), best friendships, compart-mentalized friendships, arranged marriages, marriage of convenience, committed partnerships, courtships, rebound (or avoidance-driven) relationships, secret affairs, flings, dependencies, kinships, childhood relationships, enmities, and enslavement. Interpersonal and brand relationships seem to share the properties of different relationship types. However, dissimilarity lies in the determinants of the relationship types. Concerning an interpersonal relationship, the types depend on the role of the relationship partner in a relationship, as discussed previously. On the other hand, brand relationship types depend on the interpersonal-relationship-simulated emotions originating from the relationships. Therefore, the blend space relies on the emotions instead of roles.

Although the relationship types are transferred from interpersonal to brands on the basis of emotions, further dissimilarities between emotions with interpersonal relationship partners and those with brand relationship partners arise. First, each interpersonal relationship type has its own unique feature. For example, when assessing the relationship quality between boss and subordinate, key assessors include the supervisor's role competency, role clarity, leadership style, and strategic vision (Chell and Tracey 2005). Although trust as an element in emotional bonding appears to be a crucial feature of effective employment relationships, love is rarely discussed. Notwithstanding, love is an important emotional element of kinship, friendship, and romantic relationships. Therefore, emotions should be addressed in blend space if we are to use interpersonal relationship types to discuss brand relationship types successfully. This is particularly important for assessing brand relationship quality since Fournier's (1994) brand relationship quality scale does not seem to tackle this issue; hence, it may be difficult to distinguish the true relationship quality (Huang 2009; Park *et al.* 2002).

A further dissimilarity concerns the fact that different interpersonal relationship types evoke different emotions, even though the word we use to describe that emotion is the same. For example, different types of love are identified for different types of interpersonal relationships (Lee 1977). According to Rubin (1973), the love that exists in a friendship is called liking, which is known as companion love. Companion love is characterized by affection as well as tenderness, and it is established on a foundation of trust, respect, honesty, care, and commitment (Brehm 1992). Companion love is different from passionate love (Hatfield and Rapson 1993), which involves physiological arousal, sexual attraction, extremes of emotion, and instability (Fehr 2001).

While there are many different types of love in interpersonal relationships, brand love is more straightforward and less directly related to relationship types (Ahuvia 2005). Brand love involves "passion for the brand, attachment to the brand, positive evaluation of the brand, positive emotions in response to the brand, and declarations of love for the brand" (Carroll and Ahuvia 2006: 81). However, it does not necessarily include the "tenderness" of a companion love or "sexual attraction" of a passionate love. Moreover, the affection or passion towards brands rarely demonstrates self-sacrifice, as is the case in an interpersonal relationship context (Albert, Merunka, and Valette-Florence 2009). The intensity of the emotional dimensions is generally weaker in brand relationships compared with interpersonal relationships. Therefore, the blend space focuses on such properties as yearning, commitment, and liking (Shimp and Madden 1988; Sternberg 1986), leaving out the properties related to physical (e.g., sexual attraction) and altruistic (e.g., self-sacrifice) behavioral tendency. Table 13.2 summarizes the emotions (including love, trust, commitment, connectedness, and attachment) that have been identified and transferred from interpersonal relationships to brand relationships.

TABLE 13.2 Theory application

Theoretical constructs for assessing relationship quality	*The source domain: interpersonal relationship*	*The target domain: brand relationship*	*Theory transfer*
Investment model	Rusbult's (1980) investment model includes commitment and satisfaction to examine the relationship quality. Commitment is a function of (1) the relationship outcome value, (2) the outcome value of the best available alternative, and (3) functional (extrinsic) and emotional (intrinsic) investment size. Satisfaction is a function of (1) relationship reward value and (2) relationship cost value.	Sung and Campbell (2009) applied Rusbult's investment model to evaluate consumer brand relationships. Sung and Choi (2010) found that a high level of commitment was dependent on investment size when satisfaction was low, and that regardless the level of satisfaction, the influence of alternative attractiveness on commitment remained consistently negative.	Similar to interpersonal relationships, consumers remain in an unsatisfactory relationship because of the investment size. Departure from interpersonal relationships implies that consumers will not remain in a relationship if there is a better alternative. This may be because consumers are less involved in moral obligations to continue the brand relationships compared with interpersonal relationships when there is a better alternative (Johnson and Rusbult 1989).
Interpersonal relationship model		Fournier (1994) used various components of interpersonal relationship and devised a relationship quality scale for brand relationships.	Breivik and Thorbjørnsen (2008) found that the investment model was better at distinguishing various degrees of intensity of a brand relationship. This may be because the nature of brand relationships is less involving, compared with interpersonal relationships.
Love	Hatfield (1988) distinguished passionate love from companion love. Sternberg (1986) identified three elements of love: liking, yearning, and commitment.	Carroll and Ahuvia (2006) identified five elements for brand love: (1) brand passion (Belk, Ger, and Askergaard 2003), (2) brand attachment (Thomson, MacInnis, and Park 2005), (3) positive evaluation of the brand, (4) positive emotions in response to brand, and (5) declarations of love for the brand.	Love for brands focuses on self-joy in using the brands, without physical attraction or altruistic behavior that may take place in love for people.

Trust	Rempel, Holmes, and Zanna (1985) identified three dimensions for trust: predictability, dependability, and faith.	Morgan and Hunt's (1994) trust construct focused on confidence in a relationship partner's reliability and integrity. Elliott and Yannopoulou (2007) highlighted that functional trust (i.e., reliability and integrity) would transcend to emotional trust (i.e., faith) when emotional investment in brands increased.	Trust in a person and trust in a brand have been defined and researched in a similar manner.
Commitment	Kiesler (1971) defined commitment as the binding of oneself to a course of action (p. 26). Binding occurs for three reasons: personal, structural, and moral (Johnson, Caughlin, and Huston 1999).	Traylor (1981) defined brand commitment as the binding of oneself to a certain brand within a product category. Satisfaction (Bloemer and Kasper 1995) and trust (Morgan and Hunt 1994) are the antecedents to commitment.	Only personal commitment in interpersonal relationships can be transferred to brand relationships. Commitment in interpersonal relationship does not necessarily imply satisfaction or trust because of the structural or moral reasons for staying in a relationship (Fehr 2001).
Connectedness	Aron et al. (1991) argued that a close relationship includes other in the self (see Aron 2003 for a comprehensive review).	Brands have been argued to reflect the extended self, as brand users use brand meanings to identify themselves (Belk 1988; Escalas 2004; Escalas and Bettman 2003; Thompson and Haytko 1997).	Connectedness in an interpersonal relationship and that in a brand relationship have been conceptualized and researched in a similar manner.
Attachment	Bowlby identified three features for attachment: proximity maintenance (staying near), safe haven (turning to for comfort), and secure base (using as a base from which to engage in nonattachment behavior) (Hazan and Shaver 1994).	Thomson et al. (2005) identified three elements in brand attachment: affection, connection, and passion.	Thomson et al. (2005) used Hazan and Shaver's (1994) and Hazan and Zeifman's (1999) attachment behavior to validate their brand attachment scale, but they also found that strong emotional attachment to brands was rare. This rarity may result from the fact that brand relationship is seen as a commercial relationship. Further research is needed to clarify this.

Directions for future research

A different property between interpersonal and brand relationship concerns single versus multiple channels of interactions (see Table 13.1). One task for future researchers is to conceptualize a brand relationship according to different levels of firm and interpersonal involvement, in addition to brand involvement. For example, the relationship with aspirational brands is based mainly on the brands' advertisements. Individuals do not own these brands, but appreciate (or worship!) them at a distance, because they may not be able to afford them. What values of interpersonal-like relationship might one derive from such brand interaction?

Moreover, the interaction with service or sales personnel or other users merits consideration. Although an abundance of literature has discussed the relationship between consumers and service providers (Iacobucci and Ostrom 1996; Price and Arnould 1999) and the relationships among brand users (i.e., brand community, cf. Belk and Tumbat 2005; Cova and Pace 2006; McAlexander et al. 2002; Muñiz and O'Guinn 2001; O'Guinn and Muñiz 2009; Schau, Muñiz, and Arnould 2009), the way in which consumers transfer the real interpersonal relationship to brand relationship requires further investigation. Are there any carry-over effects? If so, how strong are they? When the true interpersonal relationship ceases (for example, the service personnel leave the company or the brand user leaves the community), does the brand relationship continue? Would it change for better or for worse?

Most importantly, the research on different levels of true interpersonal involvement in a brand relationship would provide us with more insights into how the brand relationship metaphor can be transferred appropriately in various situations. Would the borrowed interpersonal relationship properties remain the same across different levels of interpersonal involvement? Many interesting questions are worth answering once we peel back the layers of brand relationship interaction.

The second direction for future research is to investigate how brand relationship changes its type as it evolves. The types of interpersonal relationships are determined by the roles that the relationship partners assume in the relationship. Hence, the type will remain unchanged until the roles change. On the other hand, types of brand relationships are based on the values derived from consumers' perception of brands. The relationship type may migrate to a different type when values change. Is there a best relationship type for consumer and brand? If relationship type and quality are arranged on a continuum (can it be a continuum?), what might that look like?

Conclusion

A lack of clarity in the brand relationship metaphor transfer "has allowed for various interpretations, and provided researchers [with] the luxury of being able to choose whichever relationship best fits their research agendas at any given time" (O'Malley and Tynan 1999: 592). The development of a new concept from various perspectives has facilitated the richness of our understanding of brand relationships and moved this area of research forward in the past fourteen years. However, we have arrived at a point that requires more specific definition of a brand relationship, and a split in the types of brand relationships to cultivate future research in different fields, such as the field of interpersonal relationship studies.

This chapter has examined metaphoric transfer from interpersonal relationship to brand relationship. Metaphors are used as a figure of speech, as it is *not* expected that brand relationships are the same as interpersonal relationships. If consumers are able to attribute the values and emotions of interpersonal relationships to a brand relationship, then a brand relationship exists even without using the relationship metaphor (Fournier 1998). However, for research to be scientific, it has to identify systematically the shared and non-shared properties between these two relationships. Fauconnier and Turner's (1998) conceptual integration networks model is used for this purpose. By using the model, we have observed that although some of the values and emotions are transferrable, they need to be modified to better suit the brand relationship context, for example, to change interdependence between relationship partners to dependence on brand partners. Through the metaphor transfer process, some directions for future research have been identified to enrich the yet to be completed metaphoric transfer. I hope that this chapter provides some insights into doing so and serves as a starting point for further work in the area.

References

Ahuvia, A.C. (2005) "Beyond the Extended Self: Love Objects and Consumers' Identity Narratives", *Journal of Consumer Research*, 32 (June): 171–84.

Albert, N., Merunka, D. and Valette-Florence, P. (2009) "The Feeling of Love toward a Brand: Concept and Measurement", *Advances in Consumer Research*, 36: 300–7.

Aron, A. (2003) "Self and Close Relationships", in M.R. Leary and J.P. Tangney (eds) *Handbook of Self and Identity*, New York: Guilford Press: 442–61.

Aron, A., Aron, E.N. and Norman, C. (2001) "Self-Expansion Model of Motivation and Cognition in Close Relationships and Beyond", in G.J.O. Fletcher and M.S. Clark (eds) *Blackwell Handbook of Social Psychology, vol. II: Interpersonal processes*, Malden, MA: Blackwell: 478–501.

Aron, A., Aron, E.N., Tudor, M. and Nelson, G. (1991) "Close Relationships as Including Other in the Self", *Journal of Personality and Social Psychology*, 60 (2): 241–53.

Belch, G.E. and Landon, E.L., Jr (1977) "Discriminant Validity of a Product-Anchored Self-Concept Measure", *Journal of Marketing Research*, 14 (May): 252–6.

Belk, R.W. (1988) "Possessions and the Extended Self", *Journal of Consumer Research*, 15 (September): 139–68.

Belk, R.W., Ger, G. and Askergaard, S. (2003) "The Fire of Desire: A Multisited Inquiry into Consumer Passion", *Journal of Consumer Research*, 30 (December): 326–51.

Belk, R.W. and Tumbat, G. (2005) "The Cult of Macintosh", *Consumption, Markets and Culture*, 8 (3): 205–17.

Bengtsson, A. (2003) "Towards a Critique of Brand Relationships", in P.A. Keller and D.W. Rook, *Advances in Consumer Research, vol. 30*, Valdosta, GA: Association for Consumer Research: 154–58.

Berk, M.S. and Andersen, S.M. (2000) "The Impact of Past Relationships on Interpersonal Behavior: Behavioral Confirmation in the Social-Cognitive Process of Transference", *Journal of Personality and Social Psychology*, 79 (4): 546–62.

Black, M. (1979) "More about Metaphor", in Andrew Ortony (ed.) *Metaphor and Thought*, Cambridge, UK: Cambridge University Press: 19–43.

Bloemer, J.M.M. and Kasper, H.D.P. (1995) "The Complex Relationship between Consumer Satisfaction and Brand Loyalty", *Journal of Economic Psychology*, 16 (2): 311–29.

Blumstein, P. and Kollock, P. (1988) "Personal Relationships", *Annual Review of Sociology*, 14: 467–90.

Brehm, S.S. (1992) *Intimate Relationships*, New York: Random House.

Breivik, E. and Thorbjørnsen, H. (2008) "Consumer Brand Relationships: An Investigation of Two Alternative Models", *Journal of the Academy of Marketing Science*, 36 (4): 443–72.

Carroll, B.A. and Ahuvia, A.C. (2006) "Some Antecedents and Outcomes of Brand Love", *Marketing Letters*, 17 (April): 79–89.

Chell, E. and Tracey, P. (2005) "Relationship Building in Small Firms: The Development of a Model", *Human Relations*, 58 (5): 577–616.

Commuri, S. (2009) "The Impact of Counterfeiting on Genuine-Item Consumers' Brand Relationships", *Journal of Marketing*, 73 (May): 86–98.

Cooley, C.H. (1964) *Human Nature and the Social Order*, New York: Schocken Books.

Cornelissen, J.P. (2003) "Metaphor as a Method in the Domain of Marketing", *Psychology and Marketing*, 20 (3): 209–25.

Coupland, J.C. (2005) "Invisible Brands: An Ethnography of Households and the Brands in their Kitchen Pantries", *Journal of Consumer Research*, 32 (June): 106–18.

Cova, B. and Pace, S. (2006) "Brand Community of Convenience Products: New Forms of Customer Empowerment – The Case 'My Nutella the Community'", *European Journal of Marketing*, 40 (9/10): 1087–105.

Darley, J.M. and Fazio, R.H. (1980) "Expectancy Confirmation Processes Arising in the Social Interaction Sequence", *American Psychologist*, 35 (10): 867–81.

Davies, G. and Chun, R. (2003) "The Use of Metaphor in the Exploration of the Brand Concept", *Journal of Marketing Management*, 19 (1/2): 45–71.

Elliott, R. and Wattanasuwan, K. (1998) "Brands as Symbolic Resources for the Construction of Identity", *International Journal of Advertising*, 17 (2): 131–44.

Elliott, R. and Yannopoulou, N. (2007) "The Nature of Trust in Brands: A Psychosocial Model", *European Journal of Marketing*, 441 (9/10): 988–98.

Escalas, J.E. (2004) "Narrative Processing: Building Consumer Connections to Brands", *Journal of Consumer Psychology*, 14 (1/2): 168–80.

Escalas, J.E. and Bettman, J.R. (2003) "You Are What They Eat: The Influence of Reference Groups on Consumers' Connections to Brands", *Journal of Consumer Psychology*, 13 (3): 339–48.

Esch, F., Langner, T., Schmitt, B.H. and Geus, P. (2006) "Are Brands Forever? How Brand Knowledge and Relationships Affect Current and Future Purchases", *Journal of Product and Brand Management*, 15 (2): 98–105.

Fauconnier, G. and Turner, M. (1998) "Conceptual Integration Networks", *Cognitive Science*, 22 (2): 133–87.

Fehr, B. (2001) "The Status of Theory and Research on Love and Commitment", in G.J.O. Fletcher and M.S. Clark (eds) *Blackwell Handbook of Social Psychology: interpersonal processes*, Malden, MA: Blackwell: 331–56.

Fournier, S. (1994) "A Consumer–Brand Relationship Framework for Strategic Brand Management", unpublished doctoral thesis, University of Florida, Gainesville, Florida.

—— (1998) "Consumers and Their Brands: Developing Relationship Theory in Consumer Research", *Journal of Consumer Research*, 24 (March): 343–73.

—— (2009) "Lessons Learned about Consumers' Relationships with their Brands", in D.J. MacInnis, C.W. Park, and J.R. Priester (eds) *Handbook of Brand Relationships*, New York: M.E. Sharpe: 5–23.

Giddens, A. (1991) *Modernity and Self-Identity: self and society in the late modern age*, Stanford, CA: Stanford University Press.

Hatfield, E. (1988) "Passionate and Companionate Love", in R.J. Sternberg and M.L. Barnes (eds) *The Psychology of Love*, New Haven, CT: Yale University Press: 191–217.

Hatfield, E. and Rapson, R.L. (1993) *Love, Sex, and Intimacy: their psychology, biology, and history*, New York: HarperCollins.

Hazan, C. and Shaver, P.R. (1994) "Attachment as an Organizational Framework for Research on Close Relationships", *Psychological Inquiry*, 5 (1): 1–22.

Hazan, C. and Zeifman, D. (1999) "Pair Bonds as Attachments", in J. Cassidy and P.R. Shaver (eds) *Handbook of Attachment: theory, research, and clinical applications*, New York: Guilford Press: 336–54.

Hinde, R.A. (1979) *Towards Understanding Relationships*, London: Academic Press.

Huang, H.H. (2009) "Self-Identity and Consumption: A Study of Consumer Personality, Brand Personality, and Brand Relationship", unpublished doctoral thesis, Warwick Business School, University of Warwick, Coventry, UK.

Hunt, S.D. and Menon, A. (1995) "Metaphors and Competitive Advantage: Evaluating the Use of Metaphors in Theories of Competitive Strategy", *Journal of Business Research*, 33 (2): 81–90.

Iacobucci, D. and Ostrom, A. (1996) "Commercial and Interpersonal Relationships: Using the Structure of Interpersonal Relationships to Understand Individual-to-Individual, Individual-to-Firm, and Firm-to-Firm Relationships in Commerce", *International Journal of Research in Marketing*, 13 (1): 53–72.

Ji, M.F. (2002) "Children's Relationships with Brands: 'True Love' or 'One-Night Stand'?" *Psychology and Marketing*, 19 (4): 369–87.

Johnson, D.J. and Rusbult, C.E. (1989) "Resisting Temptation: Development of Alternative Partners as a Means of Maintaining Commitment in Close Relationships", *Journal of Personality and Social Psychology*, 57 (6): 967–80.

Johnson, M.P., Caughlin, J.P. and Huston, T.L. (1999) "The Tripartite Nature of Marital Commitment: Personal, Moral, and Structural Reasons to Stay Married", *Journal of Marriage and the Family*, 61 (February):160–77.

Kelley, H.H. and Thibaut, J.W. (1978) *Interpersonal Relations: a theory of interdependence*, New York: Wiley.

Kelley, H.H., Berscheid, E., Christensen, A., Harvey, J.H., Huston, T.L., Levinger, G., McClintock, E., Peplau, L.A. and Peterson, D.R. (1983) "Analyzing Close Relationships", in H.H. Kelley, E. Berscheid, A. Christensen, J.H. Harvey, T.L. Huston, G. Levinger, E. McClintock, L.A. Peplau, and D.R. Peterson (eds) *Close Relationships*, New York: W. H. Freeman: 20–67.

Kiesler, C.A. (1971) *The Psychology of Commitment*, New York: Academic Press.

Kövecses, Z. (2002) *Metaphor: a practical introduction*, Oxford: Oxford University Press.

Lakoff, G. and Johnson, M. (1980) "The Metaphorical Structure of the Human Conceptual System", *Cognitive Science*, 4 (2): 195–208.

Lee, J.A. (1977) "A Typology of Styles of Loving", *Personality and Social Psychology Bulletin*, 3 (2): 173–82.

Levy, S.J. (1959) "Symbols for Sale", *Harvard Business Review*, 37 (July/August): 117–24.

Little, B.R. (1983) "Personal Projects: A Rationale and Method for Investigation", *Environment and Behavior*, 15 (3): 273–309.

McAdams, D.P. (1996) "Personality, Modernity, and the Storied Self: A Contemporary Framework for Studying Persons", *Psychological Inquiry*, 7 (4): 295–321.

McAlexander, J.H., Schouten, J.W. and Koenig, H.F. (2002) "Building Brand Community", *Journal of Marketing*, 66 (January): 38–54.

Morgan, R.M. and Hunt, S.D. (1994) "The Commitment-Trust Theory of Relationship Marketing", *Journal of Marketing*, 58 (July): 20–38.

Muñiz, A.M., Jr and O'Guinn, T.C. (2001) "Brand Community", *Journal of Consumer Research*, 27 (March): 412–32.

O'Guinn, T.C. and Muñiz, A.M., Jr (2009) "Collective Brand Relationships", in D.J. MacInnis, C.W. Park, and J.R. Priester (eds) *Handbook of Brand Relationships*, New York: M.E. Sharpe: 173–94.

O'Malley, L. and Tynan, C. (1999) "The Utility of the Relationship Metaphor in Consumer Markets: A Critical Evaluation", *Journal of Marketing Management*, 15 (7): 587–602.

—— (2000) "Relationship Marketing in Consumer Markets: Rhetoric or Reality?" *European Journal of Marketing*, 34 (7): 797–815.

Ortony, A. (1975) "Why Metaphors are Necessary and Not Just Nice", *Educational Theory*, 25 (1): 45–53.

Park, J., Kim, K. and Kim, J.K. (2002) "Acceptance of Brand Extensions: Interactive Influences of Product Category Similarity, Typicality of Claimed Benefits, and Brand Relationship Quality", in S.M. Broniarczyk and K. Nakamoto (eds) *Advances in Consumer Research, vol. 29*, Valdosta, GA: Association for Consumer Research: 190–98.

Patterson, M. and O'Malley, L. (2006) "Brands, Consumers and Relationships: A Review", *Irish Marketing Review*, 18 (1/2): 10–20.

Pinder, C.C. and Bourgeois, V.W. (1982) "Controlling Tropes in Administrative Science", *Administrative Science Quarterly*, 27 (4): 641–52.

Price, L.L. and Arnould, E.J. (1999) "Commercial Friendships: Service Provider–Client Relationships in Context", *Journal of Marketing*, 63 (October): 38–56.

Rempel, J.K., Holmes, J.G. and Zanna, M.P. (1985) "Trust in Close Relationships", *Journal of Personality and Social Psychology*, 49 (1): 95–112.

Rodin, M.J. (1978) "Liking and Disliking: Sketch of an Alternative View", *Personality and Social Psychology Bulletin*, 4 (3): 473–8.

Rubin, Z. (1973) *Liking and Loving*, New York: Holt, Rinehart and Winston.

Rusbult, C.E. (1980) "Commitment and Satisfaction in Romantic Associations: A Test of the Investment Model", *Journal of Experimental Social Psychology*, 16 (2): 172–86.

Rusbult, C.E., Arriaga, X.B. and Agnew, C.R. (2003) "Interdependence in Close Relationships", in G.J.O. Fletcher and M.S. Clark (eds) *Blackwell Handbook of Social Psychology: interpersonal processes*, Malden, MA: Blackwell: 38–56.

Schau, H.J., Muñiz, A.M., Jr and Arnould, E.J. (2009) "How Brand Community Practices Create Value", *Journal of Marketing*, 73 (September): 30–51.

Shimp, T.A. and Madden, T. (1988) "Consumer–Object Relations: A Conceptual Framework Based Analogously on Sternberg's Triangular Theory of Love", in M.J. Houston (ed.) *Advances in Consumer Research*, Provo, UT: Association for Consumer Research: 163–68.

Sirgy, M.J. (1982) "Self-Concept in Consumer Behavior: A Critical Review", *Journal of Consumer Research*, 9 (December): 287–300.

Sirgy, M.J., Johar, J.S., Samli, A.C. and Claiborne, C.B. (1991) "Self-Congruity versus Functional Congruity: Predictors of Consumer Behavior", *Journal of the Academy of Marketing Science*, 19 (4): 363–75.

Smith, E.R., Coats, S. and Walling, D. (1999) "Overlapping Mental Representations of Self, In-Group, and Partner: Further Response Time Evidence and a Connectionist Model", *Personality and Social Psychology Bulletin*, 25 (7): 873–82.

Smith, E.R. and Mackie, D.M. (2007) *Social Psychology*, New York: Psychology Press.

Stern, B.B. (1988) "Medieval Allegory: Roots of Advertising Strategy for the Mass Market", *Journal of Marketing*, 52 (July): 84–94.

Sternberg, R.J. (1986) "A Triangular Theory of Love", *Psychological Review*, 93 (2):119–35.

Story, J. and Hess, J. (2006) "Segmenting Customer–Brand Relations: Beyond the Personal Relationship Metaphor", *Journal of Consumer Marketing*, 23 (7): 406–13.

Sung, Y. and Campbell, W.K. (2009) "Brand Commitment in Consumer–Brand Relationships: An Investment Model Approach", *Journal of Brand Management*, 17 (2): 97–113.

Sung, Y. and Choi, S.M. (2010) "'I Won't Leave You Although You Disappoint Me': The Interplay Between Satisfaction, Investment, and Alternatives in Determining Consumer–Brand Relationship Commitment", *Psychology and Marketing*, 27 (11): 1050–74.

Swaminathan, V., Page, K.L. and Gürhan-Canlı, Z. (2007) "'My' Brand or 'Our' Brand: The Effects of Brand Relationship Dimensions and Self-Construal on Brand Evaluations", *Journal of Consumer Research*, 34 (August): 248–59.

Thompson, C.J. and Haytko, D.L. (1997) "Speaking of Fashion: Consumers' Uses of Fashion Discourses and the Appropriation of Countervailing Cultural Meanings", *Journal of Consumer Research*, 24 (June): 15–42.

Thomson, M., MacInnis, D. and Park, C.W. (2005) "The Ties that Bind: Measuring the Strength of Consumers' Emotional Attachments to Brands", *Journal of Consumer Psychology*, 15 (1): 77–91.

Traylor, M.B. (1981) "Product Involvement and Brand Commitment", *Journal of Advertising Research*, 21 (December): 51–6.

Van den Bulte, C. (1994) "Metaphor at Work", in G. Laurent, G.L. Lilien, and B. Pras (eds) *Research Traditions in Marketing*, Boston: Kluwer Academic: 405–25.

Zajonc, R.B., Adelmann, P.K., Murphy, S.T. and Nidedenthal, A.M. (1987) "Convergence in the Physical Appearance of Spouses", *Motivation and Emotion*, 11 (4): 335–46.

14

TEENAGERS' PURPOSIVE BRAND RELATIONSHIPS

From social filters to shoulders to lean on

Samil A. Aledin

Introduction

Research area

Brands have become important elements of youth and popular culture in our society, which educates and fosters more brand-dependent consumers than any other constructing cultures and societies that are heavily influenced by brands and the importance of symbolic consumption. The aim of this study is to enhance understanding of what brands mean at the peak of their influence, and the focus is on their relationships with teenagers aged between thirteen and fifteen. Brand consumption is known to have an important role especially in early adolescence when children start to form their identities.

Given the results of brand studies suggesting that a substantial number of consumers stay loyal to their childhood brands, marketers are understandably keen to influence their future consumers as early as possible. The link between a consumer and a brand and its consequences are well documented in the literature concerning adults (e.g., Escalas 2004; Fournier 1998; Muñiz and O'Guinn 2000; Solomon 1983). However, evidence of the connection between children or adolescents and brands is more limited (e.g., Chaplin and John 2005; Ji 2002; Robinson and Kates 2005).

Purpose of the study

The aim of this study is to give an account of teenagers' brand relationships in daily life. Since meanings facilitate understanding of relationships the psychological and socio-cultural aspects of brand relationships are explored through the respective brand meanings and motives. In doing so, teenagers will be consider from the thematic perspectives of self-construction and self-expression, self-esteem, and the aspect of fitting in and sticking out in daily social interaction. As results of the analyses, six new consumer–brand relationship types are presented. These types are characteristic, but not limited, to teenagers' lives with brands.

Conceptual foundation

Self, identity and social identity

The self could be defined as the sense of who and what we are. It is an organizing concept through which we can understand people's everyday activities (Kleine *et al.* 1993: 209). In the literature self and identity are commonly used as synonyms as they both answer to the question "Who am I?"

Weigert *et al.* (1986) make a distinction between the self and identity suggesting that an individual has one self that becomes situationally defined through a variety of identities (Weigert *et al.* 1986: 57–8). The self-concept used in this study is grounded in this idea of the self as the sum of diverse situational identities (see Kleine *et al.* 1993).

The central concept of social identity refers to the particular aspects of the self-concept that derive from an individual's knowledge of and feelings about the group memberships he or she shares with others (Smith and Mackie 2000: 205). Social identity is "the systematic establishment and signification, between individuals, between collectivities, and between individuals and collectivities, of relationships of similarity and difference" (Jenkins 1996: 4). Adolescents in particular are eager to identify themselves with groups, which may be based on some subcultures, post-subcultures or hobbies (Helenius 1996: 5).

Brand and product meanings

Consumers buy brands for the value and benefits they provide. According to Richins (1994) the value of possessions is rooted in their meanings. In order to understand the value, she divides meanings into private and public meanings (Richins 1994: 504). Public meanings are subjective meanings that outside observers (non-owners) assign to an object. The private meanings of a brand are the sum of the subjective meanings for which the brand stands for a particular individual. This sum of meanings may also include elements of brand's public meanings, but in that case the owner's personal history with the brand also plays an important role (Richins 1994: 505–6).

The hermeneutically oriented theory of meaning is generated from the narrative structuring of identity and the role of stories in constructing self-identities (e.g., Gergen and Gergen 1986; Polkinghorne 1988). Thompson (1997) bases his understanding and interpretation of consumers' consumption stories on the model (see also Thompson *et al.* 1994) that is based on the metaphor of the person's life history as a text. This hermeneutic model not only conceptualizes consumption meaning as a type of narrative, but also argues that consumers are "self-narrators". The reciprocal movement in the model occurs when a specific consumer narrative is derived from a consumption experience and then is incorporated into the interpreting of a consumer's broader life narrative (Thompson 1997: 440–1).

Finally, McCracken's approach (1986) to the "stage" of brand and product meanings is grounded in notions of structural anthropology: the cultural meanings of consumer goods are constantly in transit, and they move continually between their several locations in the social world. Meanings are found in three different locations: the culturally constituted world, the consumer good and the individual consumer (McCracken 1986: 71–2).

Connections between consumers and brands

Fournier (1998) offered a comprehensive relationship view of consumer–brand interactions – one that starts with basic relationship principles and builds on an integrative framework to explain and explore the frame and dynamics of those interactions in everyday life (see Fournier 1998: 344). Within Fournier's theoretical framework, the brand is treated as an active contributing member of a relationship dyad that connects the consumer and the brand (see Aaker and Fournier 1995: 392). Additionally, Fournier used her typology of brand relationship qualities (BRQs) to categorize the relationship forms of her interviewees. BRQs included, for example, "arranged marriages", "casual friends", "childhood friendships" and "enslavements" (Fournier 1998: 362; see also Fournier 1995: 661; Olsen 1999).

An alternative way to consider the link between brands and consumers is meaningful self–brand connections. Meaningful self–brand connections are created by linking the brand to the self, and to be more specific by taking brands as meaningful and important components of a person's self-narrative. People tend to construct stories or narratives to give their lives coherence and create their identities (Escalas 2004: 67). People use brands to create and represent their self-images and communicate to others who and what they are or wish to be. Self–brand connections are preferred to specific brand associations, because the brand meaning is most often dependent on the entire constellation or the set of brand associations (Escalas and Bettman 2003: 340).

Personal and social roles of brands

Brand meanings, consumer–brand relationships and self–brand connections are prerequisites for the various ways to use brands. Brands are consumed for both their social and private meanings (Solomon 1983: 324). Thus, the consumer often relies upon the social information inherent in products to formulate self-image and to maximize the quality of role performance (see Solomon 1983: 319–20).

Belk (1988) argued that people tend to extend the core self and reflect their various identities by their possessions. He stated that the construct of extended self offered more insightful alternative to examine self-related consumer research than formulations positing the relationship between self-concept and brand image-driven consumer brand choice (Belk 1988: 140, 160).

Rather than being solely symbolic resources for the construction of personal identities, communal brands are the foundation of group identification and experiences of social solidarity (Thompson 2004: 98; see also Wattanasuwan 2005: 182). Miles *et al.* (1998) concluded that the consumption of brands with embedded meanings is a tool by which teenagers can manage the constant balancing between fitting into a group and standing out from the crowd. A teen-ager wants both to be a special and interesting individual and fit in with his peers and gain acceptance (Miles *et al.* 1998: 88–93; see also Bourdieu 1984). Escalas and Bettman (2003) showed that consumers actively construct themselves by using brand association that arise through reference group usage and the result-ing self–brand connections. A brand used by a reference group is a source of brand associations, which become linked to consumers' mental representation of self as consumers actively construct their current selves (Escalas and Bettman 2003: 341). Auty and Elliot (2001) studied teenagers and discovered that this movement of meaningful properties of brands from group to the self did not explain adolescent brand behaviour as much as the human need for social approval did. It was more important for the teenagers to be liked by others than to be like others (Auty and Elliot 2001: 240).

Methodology

Research approach

This study can be characterized as qualitative with emic- and etic-focused interpretations. The analysis is driven by abductive reasoning, since the researcher's thinking process moves between the empirical findings and prior theories.

The research process (Figure 14.1) started with the sensitizing concepts, self, identity and social identity, based on the pre-understanding and research interests of the author. They guided the first phase of the data collection in which eighty-eight Finnish and eighty-two British teenagers (male and female) were asked to write an essay entitled "Brands in my Life". A thematic analysis was executed in order to see what aspects of brands teenagers con-sidered relevant.

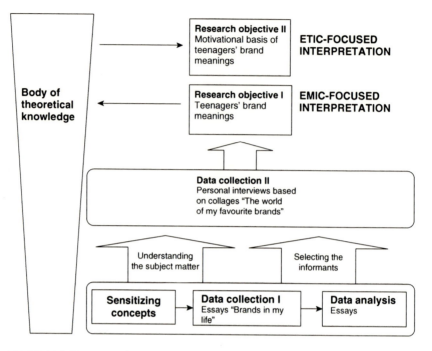

FIGURE 14.1 The research process

The informants for personal interviews were selected based on the essays. The main selection criterion was the importance of brand consumption (e.g., brands in self-expression and with reference to diverse in- and out-groups). The primary data were collected at personal interviews and the data analysis was executed through an interplay between empirical findings and the body of theoretical knowledge.

Informants

Twelve teenagers were chosen for personal interviews in both Helsinki and London. In order to ensure the above average potential for consumption the Finnish participants were recruited from the wealthier areas of Helsinki and British participants from private schools. The British teenagers were included in the empirical data in order to gain a deeper and more diverse understanding of the research topic. Focusing solely on Finnish teenagers and the commercial environment in Helsinki would have given a narrower and more localized perspective. The chosen adolescents were between thirteen and fifteen years of age. At this stage, a heightened awareness of other people's perspectives, along with a need to shape one's own identity and to conform to group expectations, results in a stronger focus on the social aspects of being a consumer, making choices, and consuming brands (John 1999: 187).

Data collection

The personal interview data were collected during a single session lasting from one hour and a half to two hours. In the beginning of the interviews the respondents were asked to make a collage (on A2 paper) of their favourite brands: "Create a world of your favourite brands". The magazines used for the collages included fashion and lifestyle magazines, youth magazines, sports magazines and other hobby-related publications. The collages of the informants were used as an aid and stimulus in the interviews, when they were asked to discuss the meanings linked with these selected brands. If they did not find pictorial material related to some of their favourite brands, the interviewees were instructed to draw pictures or write about them using crayons.

The interviews were conducted in line with the notions of intensive interviewing in which the structure ranges from a loosely guided exploration of topics to semi-structured, focused questions. Thus, the interviewees were likely to expect the interviewer to take a very active role and to express great interest.

Data analysis

The data were analysed from the transcribed personal interviews in the form of emic-focused and etic-focused interpretation (see Thompson 1996). The emic-focused interpretation included an intratextual and an intertextual analysis (see Thompson 1997).

The intratextual analysis consisted of analysing the four separate sets of empirical data (Finnish/British/Girls/Boys). One set of empirical knowledge (e.g., the meanings of brands to Finnish girls), rather than the individual interviews, was taken as one text to be analysed. After the analyses of these four texts separately the intertextual analysis followed. In the intertextual analysis the findings in these four bodies of empirical knowledge were compared and the construction of a holistic and synthesized categorization of brand meanings began. In this concluding categorization, which comprised self- and group-driven brand meanings as the most abstract categories, the aspects of teenagers' brand relationships in their daily lives were identified, including common characteristics, and special gender-driven and cultural features.

The etic-focused interpretation represents a deductive approach to identifying the motives behind the meanings teenagers attribute to brands, in line with the respective body of theoretical knowledge. This body of knowledge developed and evolved as a result of interplay between the empirical findings and the theoretical knowledge during the stages of data collection and analysis.

Results

Teenagers' brand relationships – six new types

Brands offer a way to a world of meanings in which an individual consumer can adopt ready-made solutions from the socio-cultural environment or engage in their development in order to achieve self-related goals. On the other hand, selves and identities of individuals steer participation and activeness in the creation process in which consumers give new meanings to brands through their consumption.

The reactions and comments of other teenagers about one's brands reflect the brand image back to him or her, and increase his or her self-knowledge. Embedded in their self-construction and self-expression is the image of teenagers as trapeze artists balancing between standing out in the crowd as a unique individual and fitting in by seeking group memberships as an adolescent, a member of a new generation, a friend in a group or a skateboarder, for example.

The findings of this study elucidate teenagers' lives with their brands through the respective brand meanings and the motives behind them. So far, the relationship types have been grounded in adults (Fournier 1998) and children (Ji 2002; Robinson and Kates 2005). Grounded in the findings, six new consumer–brand relationship types, particularly characteristic of teenagers, are presented. The relationship types are defined through the diverse roles brands have in relationships with consumers (see Ji 2002).

Social filter

This metaphor describes a relationship where a brand acts as a means of fitting in. A teenager can cover his or her individual characteristics by using international fashion brands (mainly girls) or commonly used athletic brands (mainly boys), such as H&M, Only (in Finland), Topshop (in GB), Puma and Nike, and be at social ease without the fear of being labelled in any way.

Although brands are symbolic sources for the construction and expression of the self, Thompson (2004) also stresses the importance of communal brands as foundations of group identification and experiences of social solidarity (Thompson 2004: 98). The findings of this study were consistent with Thompson's notions. The informants' accounts were not endless manifestations of individuality and uniqueness: they also concerned brands that were "used by everyone", "for everyone", "casual" and "normal". The status of being a "standard and normal teenager" was achieved through wearing clothing brands that were widely accepted and worn either by peers or by the masses in the social environment. As one Finnish teenage girl said, using normal and not too striking brands made her feel safe and secure in her daily social interactions. Shoes carrying sports brands such as Adidas, Nike and Puma were usually the casual options that helped the boys to melt into the crowd. Similarly, the girls used common brands such as

Topshop, Office (shoes) and Only (jeans) in order to comply with the pressure to fit in.

> Interviewer (I): "Okay, Nike, Adidas and Puma, they are comfortable and casual. Can you name me some other features that are common to them or typical to them?"
>
> Boy 14 years, London: "Probably because, you know, a lot of teenagers, normally people of my age, wear those sorts of shoes, you know, when you're older, it's ok to wear like smarter shoes but in this age you don't really want to wear those smarter shoes. Fit in with the crowd more, casual shoes, Nike, Adidas and Puma, mostly people in this age wear instead of Lacoste or Dolce & Gabbana or stuff like that."
>
> I: "What kind of person are you in other people's opinion?"
>
> Girl 14 years, Helsinki: "Probably quite normal, because a lot of people wear Only jeans. So, if they were to classify me based on them, I'd be quite a normal person. 'A standard person' . . ."
>
> I: "What is a standard person?"
>
> Girl 14 years, Helsinki: "A person who doesn't wear radical clothes or use radical brands, but prefers clothing brands that are like normal . . . Or I mean brands that in a way others know about and approve of."

These findings were consistent with Auty and Elliot's (2001) suggestion that teenagers' need to be liked and approved takes precedence over the need to be like others in the case of fitting in. The fact that it was "safely nice" not to stand out from one's peers was clear evidence of the need for social acceptance, as was the reference to the "increased sense of togetherness" that using the same brands evoked. Thus, these teenagers' accounts also suggested a need to be like their peers. This is in line with Auty and Elliot's notions: they acknowledged that often the simplest way to be liked and approved was to be like the people a person chose to be liked by (see Auty and Elliot 2001: 240).

Match maker

This metaphor describes a relationship where a brand enables a friendship between two teenagers who would not otherwise become friends owing to different interests. An iPod and Sony Playstation are examples of brands that lower the obstacles to becoming acquainted with other teenagers.

Whereas clothing brands connected groups of friends and made them feel part of a face-to-face in-group, iPod and Playstation seemed to take the matter of bonding even further. Given the interactive nature of these branded products, they were also likely to make people socialize and communicate, and at best function as an admission ticket to a group. According to one of the British boys, a teenager not particularly interested in music or video games might buy an iPod or a Playstation just to enter into social interaction with his peers and try to make new friends. Talking about songs on iPods and sharing them, and the contents and special features of video games gave a natural access to groups and new friendships.

> Boy 14 years, London: "Maybe somebody would get an iPod even though they don't like music. Or like a Playstation, someone would buy one to start talking to a person about what happens, 'cos they've overheard, they want to get into the conversation, be someone's friend or something."

The notions of connecting and friendships were also touched on by one girl when she talked about exchanging songs among iPod users. In addition, she suggested that it was not only the brands she and her friends used that connected them, but also the brands they desired. Thus, some of these desired brands were topics of social interaction, and united the girls in this "day-dreamy" manner.

> Girl 14 years, London: "I think a lot of people like the iPod thing. Everyone has an iPod therefore they can talk about it. I think that kind of binds a lot of different friendships because people could borrow it and use it and that keeps people friends together as well."
>
> I: "Are there any other brands (other than iPod) that people talk about a lot in your class?"
>
> Girl 14 years, London: "I think sometimes it's not stuff they have, it's stuff they want to have they can talk about as well. So it's sometimes the top designers like Chloe and Dolce & Gabbana, these are just the kind of things that hold people together as well, it is not all about what they have."

Mature friend

This metaphor describes a relationship where a brand makes its user feel superior to his or her peers through maturity. The expression of maturity is used to make an impression on others. A typical brand for the expression of (cool) maturity is Lacoste, since a sporty adult is commonly linked to its user image. In addition, Gucci (sunglasses) is considered as a maturing brand.

Brands in these visible and publicly perceivable product categories were relevant in the context of self-extension by means of material possessions. Whereas in the case of symbolic self-completion it seemed that teenagers exploited brands that made them feel more satisfied, for example with their athletic identity, using "maturing" brands to express maturity was related to self-extension. These products enabled them to show a trait they would not otherwise display.

One of the boys extended his self by wearing Lacoste clothes that he associated with people aged eighteen and above. He was fourteen, and the Lacoste brand made him and his friends feel and look more mature. His account implied that it was cool to look older, not least in order to attract admiration from others.

> Boy 14 years, London: "Well if I bought it . . . It may be for older as well . . . If something that, I mean, probably is for sort of eighteen-year-olds, I'm fourteen, so it is for older people, but if you wear it, it does sort of make you look older or more mature, so it's like a maturing product."

In addition, one of the girls had chosen an "adult-like, but not too much adult-like" model of Gucci sunglasses in order to appear more mature among her peers. Her expression of maturity was based on the typical users of such eyewear, adults. Although she clearly wanted to appear more mature, however, by choosing a "not too much adult-like" model she was not abandoning the idea of being a teenager.

> Girl 13 years, Helsinki: "Yes it is, since the sunglasses are really good for me."
>
> I: "What makes them good?"
>
> B: "I don't know . . . They're somehow adult-like, but on the other hand not too adult-like, so they're not really adult-like, what adults tend to wear. They are like something in between . . . And then they protect you from that sun . . ."

Reputation wrecker

This metaphor describes a relationship where the self-image of a person is threatened by the commonly linked negative brand meanings. An asocial and obnoxious group can adopt a brand and as a consequence the original users of the brand may abandon it in order to avoid association with this group. Burberry and Miss Sixty were dropped after asocial post-subcultural groups had "adopted" these brands. In addition, clothing private labels of retail chains were likely to result in avoidance for the sake of not damaging one's reputation.

Out-groups also played an important role in the definition and expression of the informants' identities in that they are defined in terms of what a person is and what he or she is not. Escalas and Bettman (2005) suggest that when out-group members start to use a brand associated with an in-group, its members may form an association with the brand that the in-group members would not want transferred to them. In a case like this a brand may become meaningful through the process of avoiding out-group symbolism in constructing one's possible self (Escalas and Bettman 2005: 379). Thus, brand association employed by members of an out-group may influence the construction and expression of the self in this inverted manner. In this study, "Polluted brands" were abandoned as constructive and expressive tools of the self.

A post-subcultural group of "chavs" seemed to have ruined the reputation of Burberry and in part sports-related brands (e.g., Adidas) in the United Kingdom. Both the male and female informants acknowledged these brands to be "chavish", but since Adidas, together with Nike, also represented casual and hobby-related brands for the boys, they did not rule them out as strongly as the girls did. Similarly, some of the Finnish girls would avoid wearing Miss Sixty jeans because the brand image had been stained by "piss-Lizzys", a Finnish post-subcultural group of teenage girls that was commonly associated with cocky as well as arrogant attitudes and behaviour. Some of the informants said that they had distanced themselves from the brand in order to avoid being associated with "piss-Lizzys". That was not how they wanted to construct and express themselves.

> Girl 14 years, London: "But yeah, like a lot of chavs wear like Adidas, like trackies and things and most people wouldn't wear those things in case like they got assumed they were a chav."
>
> I: "Okay. Can you name some other chavish brands?"
>
> Girl 14 years, London: "Well, now, like Burberry is like a huge chav brand and like it used to be cool but now it's really not because chavs started wearing it and it's more, also another thing which is really chavish is like fake designer things like fake Burberry, or fake anything, really, is like seen as less classy."
>
> I: "Can you tell me about the brands that are not for you?"
>
> Girl 14 years, London: "Things like Adidas and a lot of sports brands . . ."
>
> I: "Why is that?"
>
> Girl 14 years, London: "Because I think it's the association with townies and chavs as well because I don't really like that, because I wouldn't want to have an association."
>
> Girl 14 years, Helsinki: ". . . then Pepe Jeans also has really good jeans, for example, I'm wearing a pair now. They're really expensive, but of really good quality. I mean Miss Sixty used to be a close brand for me, but then it turned into a piss-Lizzy brand . . ."

Furthermore, one of the British girls alluded to more prominent out-group brands such as Tesco and Marks & Spencer's. She claimed that Tesco clothes would be worn by young children who were incapable of buying their own things, and Marks & Spencer's clothes were worn by old people and not by normal teenagers. In addition, a concrete Finnish equivalent of these "abnormal Tesco teenagers" was the group of boys that I labelled "brand-sissies" on the basis of the accounts. They were also stigmatized for wearing private label clothing purchased in department stores.

> Girl 14 years, London: "Tesco is a supermarket. It's for either really young people when their mums buy their clothes and it's just not right, a supermarket selling clothes. It's wrong. It's just not a place where anyone would go. If you ask like, anyone my age, like, one person out of 20 million people would say yes."

> Boy 14 years, Helsinki: "Then I guess there's a group that are dictated by their mothers, if I can say so. They like wear what their mum says in the morning . . ."

> I: "What brands do they use?"

> B: "They might wear Stockmann's own labels like 'Cap Horn' and 'Bodyguard', and then what else they have . . ."

A shoulder to lean on

This metaphor describes a relationship where a brand, usually an exclusive luxury brand such as Louis Vuitton, gives a teenager comfort in the context of feeling sad and blue. In a relationship like this, a brand makes its user feel special and "worthy". The essential notion behind comfort and raised self-esteem can be "despite all the afflictions at least I have a luxury bag".

Teenagers' brand meanings were not solely related to the self-concept, and also included meanings that affected the other side of self-knowledge, self-esteem. Self-esteem concerns how individuals feel about themselves, in other words their positive or negative self-evaluations (Smith and Mackie 2000: 116–17).

According to the accounts of the girls in particular, brands provided protection to the self by affecting feelings and self-confidence. In one case a designer-brand leather bag gave comfort and increased self-esteem when the girl was feeling down and blue, because although things in her life were not as they should be, she "at least had a Louis Vuitton leather bag". Designer jeans from Miss Sixty would also increase her self-confidence in contexts in which she did not need comforting, so she would just feel more secure on the basis of the status and prestige of the brand. Here the designer jeans would enhance her self-esteem for reasons related to social distinction or identification.

I: "Why is this brand important to you?"

Girl 13 years, Helsinki: "It would just be something special. Maybe something primarily for me, it could like raise my self-esteem. If I wasn't doing so well I could think 'Well, at least I have a Louis Vuitton leather bag.'"

I: "Why does Miss Sixty suit you?"

Girl 13 years, Helsinki: "It doesn't necessarily suit me, but I just buy them. I don't know . . . I just want to own them. Sometimes it feels like clothes are like ornaments that you collect and just have to have. And sometimes you just wear them. When you wear Miss Sixty you get more self-confidence . . ."

Mood sensor

Brand meanings seemed to regulate the mood of the female informants. In this metaphor a brand expresses the mood of a user. This is characteristic to brands with a wide range of colours. It was indicated that, for example, United Colors of Benetton and Esprit were used for the purposes of mood expression. The colour of the piece of clothing was likely to change as teenagers' moods did.

One of the girls implied that she exploited the wide variety of colours of the Benetton clothing brand to express her mood. In this case the mood had an influence on her choice of brand (and the particular colour), not the other way round.

I: "Tell me what kind of person would Benetton be?"

Girl 14 years, Helsinki: "It has a frame of mind that . . . It might be sad someday, glad some other day, sometimes depressed and again sometimes hyperactive. So, its nature and opinions would change quite often . . ."

I: "Which of these brands do you think are like you?"

Girl 14 years, Helsinki: "Maybe Benetton and Puma. Puma because I like to do sports. And then Benetton is nice, because my mood changes quite often . . ."

Discussion and implications

As addressed earlier, the research on consumer–brand relationships has either involved children or adults, leaving a gap regarding teenagers. This study fills this gap and increases the understanding of teenagers' lives with brands. This exciting stage of life between a child and an adult involves developmental characteristics that have an effect on the nature of teenagers' relationships. The six new types of brand relationships complement the theory of consumer–brand relationships basically in a similar manner as Ji's (2002) children's brand relationships do.

Teenagers' lives with brands can be understood by elucidating the roles of brands in diverse contexts of everyday life. This is the leading notion behind the presented six consumer–brand relationship types. *Social filter, match maker, mature friend, reputation wrecker, a shoulder to lean on* and *mood sensor* all generate consumer insight into teenagers' relationships with brands beyond the more general consumer–brand relationship types of Fournier (1998). They imply what kinds of brands teenagers use as well as how and why they use them. Teenagers use their brands in a purposive manner; they help master their daily social interaction, seek connectedness and acceptance as well as deal with their self-esteem.

Marketing practitioners are commonly guided by "brand management perspective" (e.g., Keller, Aaker, Kapferer) while they plan and implement marketing actions in line with respective strategies. Although they "always are consumer-oriented", they still tend to approach consumers predominantly guided by identities and images of their brands, and try to find ways to persuade diverse consumer segments to buy their branded product or service more than before. This study brings forth the consumer side of the equation and discusses what consumers actually do with their brands. It offers insight into how consumers interact with their brands in their daily lives, "in good and in bad" from the managerial perspective. Maybe marketing practitioners should not only develop their brands with functional, emotional and self-expressive benefits in mind, but also consider the category of social benefits. Self-expressive benefits offer a too narrow view of the social aspect.

Thus, with regard to marketing practitioners, this study reflects the psychosocial roles brands play in teenagers' lives. An understanding of these roles can be used in brand building and communication strategies. The understanding of a brand being a social filter, match maker, a shoulder to lean on or a mood sensor may give an edge to help reposition the brand against the competition. In addition, in order to attract early adolescents a brand or its sub-brand can be positioned to play the role of a mature friend. The need to impress their peers with maturity was one of the things teenagers seemed to desire at this stage of their personal development.

However, marketing practitioners should also be aware of the damaging power consumers may wield over their brand. This study implied that less positive brand meanings, created particularly at the cultural level, can turn a brand into a reputation wrecker. A reputation wrecker in a company's brand portfolio demands immediate counter and revival strategies. Burberry struggled with the damaging effect of the chavs more and for longer than they would have wanted to, for example.

Conclusions and trustworthiness

Brands are relationship partners teenagers love to hate and hate to love; they help them to express and construct their identities, and give them confidence in the exciting and insecure search for a balance between fitting in and standing out. Today's teenagers on their journey to adulthood, engulfed in a consumer culture, exploit the meaningful qualities of the brands that help them to manage the psycho-social challenges of everyday life. The passage from childhood to adulthood is eased, to some extent, through the fostering of socially rewarding brand relationships, and avoiding or terminating involvement with brands that are "non grata" (Aledin 2009: 140).

The six presented consumer–brand relationship types evolved from the findings of the author's dissertation. A number of techniques were employed to increase the trustworthiness of the study. During the writing process cross-disciplinary scholars and the reviewers shared their views with the author. With regard to the data collection and analysis diverse forms of triangulation were executed. Each informant wrote an essay "Brands in my Life" at high school, made a collage "The World of my Favourite Brands" and participated in personal interviews that were grounded in the collages. "Various copies" of one type of source were used as twenty-four informants participated in the research interviews. Finally, multiple theories and perspectives were used to interpret and explain the data.

In a qualitative study transferability replaces generalizability. A thick description of the study was provided to enable the reader to make the transfer or to reach a conclusion about whether transfer can be considered a possibility. The presented consumer–brand relationship types are a result of a subjective interpretive process of analysis. The metaphors presented here are to be understood primarily in the context of this study. However, similar findings on many aspects of teenagers' brand relationships, despite the varying sizes of the commercial environments and the stages of consumer culture of Helsinki and London, would suggest that the interpretations and results could apply to city teenagers in other industrialized countries and developed societies.

References

Aaker, D. (2010) "Marketing Challenges in the Next Decade", *Journal of Brand Management*, 17 (5): 315–16.

Aaker, J. and Fournier, S. (1995) "A Brand as a Character, a Partner and a Person: Three Perspectives on the Question of Brand Personality", *Advances in Consumer Research*, 22: 391–5.

Aledin, S.A. (2009) "Teenagers' Brand Relationships in Daily Life: A Qualitative Study of Brand Meanings and their Motivational Ground among Teenagers in Helsinki and London Metropolitan Areas", doctoral thesis, Turku School of Economics.

Auty, S. and Elliot, R. (2001) "Being Like or Being Liked: Identity vs. Approval in a Social Context", *Advances in Consumer Research*, 28: 235–41.

Belk, R.W. (1988) "Possessions and the Extended Self", *Journal of Consumer Research*, 15: 139–68.

Bourdieu, P. (1984) *Distinction: a social critique of the judgement of task,* Cambridge, MA: Harvard University Press.

Chaplin, L.N. and John, D.R. (2005) "The Development of Self–Brand Connections in Children and in Adolescents", *Journal of Consumer Research*, 32: 119–29.

Escalas, J.E. (2004) "Narrative Processing: Building Consumer Connections to Brands", *Journal of Consumer Psychology*, 14: 168–80.

Escalas, J.E. and Bettman, J.R. (2003) "You Are What They Eat: The Influence of Reference Groups on Consumers' Connections to Brands", *Journal of Consumer Psychology*, 13: 339–48.

—— (2005) "Self-Construal, Reference Groups, and Brand Meaning", *Journal of Consumer Research*, 32: 378–89.

Fournier, S. (1995) "Toward the Development of Relationship Theory at the Level of Product and Brand", *Advances in Consumer Research*, 22: 661–2.

—— (1998) "Consumers and their Brands: Developing Relationship Theory in Consumer Research", *Journal of Consumer Research*, 24: 343–72.

Gergen, K.J. and Gergen, M.M. (1986) "Narrative Form and Construction of Psychological Science", in T.R. Sarbin (ed.) *Narrative Psychology: the storied nature of human conduct*, New York: Praeger.

Helenius, P. (1996) *Nuorten Kulutus ja Identiteetti 90-Luvun Suomessa*, Helsinki: Ykköspaino Oy.

Jenkins, R. (1996) *Social Identity*, London: Routledge.

Ji, M.F. (2002) "Children's Relationships with Brands: 'True Love' or 'One Night Stand'?" *Psychology and Marketing*, 19: 369–87.

John, D.R. (1999) "Consumer Socialization of Children: A Retrospective Look at Twenty-Five Years of Research", *Journal of Consumer Research*, 26: 183–213.

Kapferer, J.N. (2005) "The Post-Global Brand", *Journal of Brand Management*, 12 (5): 319–24.

Keller, K.L. (2001) "Brand Research Imperatives", *Journal of Brand Management*, 9 (1): 4–6.

Kleine, R.E. III, Kleine Schultz, S. and Kernan, J.B. (1993) "Mundane Consumption and the Self: A Social-Identity Perspective", *Journal of Consumer Psychology*, 2: 209–35.

McCracken, G. (1986) "Culture and Consumption: A Theoretical Account of the Structure and Movement of the Cultural Meaning of Consumer Goods", *Journal of Consumer Research*, 13: 71–84.

Miles, S., Dallas, C. and Burr, V. (1998) "Fitting In and Sticking Out: Consumption, Consumer Meanings and the Construction of Young People's Identities", *Journal of Youth Studies*, 1: 81–96.

Muñiz, A.M. Jr and O'Guinn, T.C. (2000) "Brand Community", *Journal of Consumer Research*, 27: 412–32.

Olsen, B. (1999) "Exploring Women's Brand Relationships and Enduring Themes at Mid-Life", *Advances in Consumer Research*, 26: 615–20.

Polkinghorne, D.E. (1988) *Narrative Knowing and the Human Sciences*, Albany, NY: SUNY Press.

Richins, M.L. (1994) "Valuing Things: The Public and Private Meanings of Possessions", *Journal of Consumer Research*, 21: 504–21.

Robinson, P. and Kates, S.M. (2005) "Children and their Brand Relationships", *Advances in Consumer Research*, 32: 578–9.

Smith, E.R. and Mackie, D.M. (2000) *Social Psychology*, 2nd edn, Philadelphia, PA: Psychology Press.

Solomon, M.R. (1983) "The Role of Products as Social Stimuli: A Symbolic Interactionism Perspective", *Journal of Consumer Research*, 10: 319–29.

Thompson, C.J. (1996) "Caring Consumers: Gendered Consumption Meanings and the Juggling Lifestyle", *Journal of Consumer Research*, 22: 388–407.

—— (1997) "Interpreting Consumers: A Hermeneutical Framework for Deriving Marketing Insights from Texts of Consumers' Consumption Stories", *Journal of Marketing Research*, 34: 438–55.

—— (2004) "Beyond Brand Image: Analyzing the Culture of Brands", special session summary, *Advances in Consumer Research*, 31: 98–9.

Thompson, C.J., Pollio, H.R. and Locander, W.B. (1994) "The Spoken and the Unspoken: A Hermeneutic Approach to Understanding the Cultural Viewpoints that Underlie Consumers' Expressed Meanings", *Journal of Consumer Research*, 21 (3): 432–52.

Wattanasuwan, K. (2005) "The Self and the Symbolic Consumption", *Journal of American Academy of Business*, 6: 179–84.

Weigert, A.J., Teitge, J.S. and Teitge, D.W. (1986) *Society and Identity: toward a sociological psychology*, Cambridge: Cambridge University Press.

15

BRANDS CAN BE LIKE FRIENDS

Goals and interpersonal motives influence attitudes toward preferred brands

Christopher R. Long, Philip A. Gable, Courtney Boerstler, and Christina Albee

Recently, one of the authors of this chapter was in a movie theater with his six-year-old daughter watching Pixar's *Toy Story 3D*. As the film approached its conclusion, he noticed that he was trying unsuccessfully to suppress the urge to cry. At this moment, he lowered his 3D glasses and listened: the sound of sniffling adults emanated from several directions.

Someone who had only a dispassionate understanding of Sheriff Woody and Buzz Lightyear might find this situation odd: why were grown-ups crying in response to fictional events befalling an animated toy cowboy and his animated plastic space ranger sidekick? What characteristics of people lead us to relate intensely to non-human entities, like fictional characters or brands?

From the authors' perspective, one likely culprit for these relational tendencies is humans' essentially social nature. Humans have evolved as social creatures, and much of our cognitive and emotional processing is oriented toward facilitating social connection. Lacking horns, claws, fangs, shells, or scales, humans have always needed other humans to facilitate each other's survival, and our patterns of behavior typically reflect a drive toward acceptance, support, and closeness. To be sure, much of what researchers have learned about human social psychology is grounded upon the assumption that social belongingness is a primary and necessary motivator for human behavior (e.g., Baumeister and Leary, 1995).

Of course, most of our species' social psychological functions evolved in eras pre-dating animated space rangers, not to mention social media, broadcast media, or even status updates via hieroglyphics. In today's world, we can receive tweets from an insurance-peddling Geico gecko, Mr. Clean can be our friend on Facebook, our cars can park themselves, and microwaves, smoke alarms, and blood pressure monitors can speak to us. Our engagements with brands and products are increasingly life-like, and it is not difficult to imagine that such engagements implicate social psychological tendencies typically associated with interpersonal interaction.

The purpose of the present chapter is to consider two of these tendencies – namely, the need to belong and attachment – and how these tendencies interact with our goals to influence consumer–brand relationships. Along the way, we will consider research-based evidence for our ideas, and we will conclude by offering applications of our ideas for practicing marketing professionals.

Belongingness and attachment: two interpersonal relationship-relevant individual differences

A fundamental dimension underlying human social relationships is our species' need to belong. The desire for social affiliation and inclusion shapes our interpersonal behavior and decision-making, as we attempt to cultivate acceptance and avoid the harsh emotional penalties that come with rejection (Leary, 2010). For reasons having to do with survival and reproduction (and not always in that order), feeling liked, invited, and included yields rewards both emotional and biological. For example, when people feel accepted, we experience an increase in positive emotions, such as happiness and contentment, whereas when we feel a lack of acceptance, we are at increased risk for negative emotions, as well as physical and psychological illness (e.g., Baumeister and Leary, 1995). To some extent, our self-esteem rises and falls as an index of how well we are doing socially (Baumeister, Dori, and Hastings, 1998).

For some of us, the relative intensity of our need to belong is particularly high, and this sensitivity to social acceptance has an impact on our interpersonal relationships. Specifically, people who are relatively preoccupied with belongingness behave in ways that show a longing to connect with others. They pay close attention to others' social cues (Pickett, Gardner, and Knowles, 2004), they tend to downplay the possibility that others might be discriminating against them (Carvallo and Pelham, 2006), and they are at increased risk for feeling homesick (Watt and Badger, 2009). Of course, in the search for social acceptance, almost everyone occasionally conforms to trends or tries to present themselves as attractive and interesting (e.g., Leary and Cox, 2008). For all of us, as belongingness needs become more acute, we become increasingly motivated to seek social connection. However, for many of us, this motivation is easily and habitually activated.

A similarly motivating set of personality traits involves humans' drive for interpersonal attachment, which refers to a particular variety of belongingness. Whereas belongingness motives implicate a general need for social acceptance and inclusion, attachment motives involve goals associated with close connections with significant others. Typical adults manifest their own distinctive attachment style, or set of expectations for how they and their partners will feel and act in the context of close relationships (Brennan, Clark and Shaver, 1998;

Hazan and Shaver, 1987). Although individuals may exhibit different attachment styles across different relationships, relationship researchers tend to believe that attachment tendencies are rooted in early childhood experiences, which inform individuals' expectations for how others will respond in the context of close relationships. As a result, people develop characteristic attachment styles that influence most of their close relationships. These styles are often described in terms of two more or less independent dimensions: attachment anxiety and attachment avoidance. Attachment anxiety refers to insecurity with respect to whether or not partners will be available, committed, and supportive, whereas attachment avoidance refers to difficulties allowing oneself to depend upon or grow close to partners. Individuals whose relationships are characterized by relatively low levels of both attachment anxiety and avoidance are described as having secure attachment styles.

Interpersonal attachment is one of the most widely studied topics in relationship psychology; therefore, researchers have developed detailed profiles of people whose romantic relationships are characterized by attachment anxiety or avoidance (e.g., Shaver and Mikulincer, 2007). In brief, attachment anxiety is associated with hypervigilance toward one's current and past partners (Davis, Shaver, and Vernon, 2003; Hazan and Shaver, 1987), self-reported ease of falling in love (Hazan and Shaver, 1987), and stress, depression, and anxiety, in general (e.g., Hankin, Kassel, and Abela, 2005; Mikulincer and Florian, 2001). Attachment avoidance is associated with relatively low acceptance of one's partner (Hazan and Shaver, 1987), reduced seeking of caregiving from one's partner (Collins and Feeney, 2000), and the belief that romantic love rarely lasts for long (Hazan and Shaver, 1987). In contrast, attachment security comprises positive alternatives to the anxious and avoidant tendencies mentioned above, including an increase in self-reported positive emotion in one's romantic relationships (Simpson, Collins, Tran, and Haydon, 2007).

Belongingness and attachment are brand relevant

Brands are often represented as having human characteristics, whether these representations are generated independently by consumers or as a part of brand presentation strategy. In either case, the perception of brands as human (Levy, 1985) or having personalities (Aaker, 1997) is a key assumption among researchers who emphasize brands' roles as relationship partners (Aaker, Fournier, and Brasel, 2004; Fournier, 1998). Researchers who share this perspective, several of whom have contributed chapters to the present volume, emphasize the varied implications of the processes whereby "people form relationships with brands in much the same way in which they form relationships with each other in a social context" (Aggarwal, 2004: 87). In many cases, consumer–brand relationships are born from humans' tendency to anthropomorphize brands (Fournier, 1998).

Brand anthropomorphization by consumers is widely encouraged by marketers. Brands are instilled with personalities and distinct images, and sometimes, marketers design an anthropomorphized depiction of the brand, as with the M&M's characters or the Pillsbury Doughboy. In marketing research, the study of brand anthropomorphization is quickly developing into an area of emphasis, and researchers are developing new approaches to elaborate this concept. For example, Aggarwal and McGill (2007) propose schema congruity as a theoretical foundation for investigating the effectiveness and consequences of product anthropomorphism. Specifically, they have found that the ability of consumers to anthropomorphize a product and their evaluation of the product is dependent on the perceived fit between the features of the product and an activated human schema; the better the fit, the more consumers liked the product. More recently, these researchers have shown that consumers are particularly likely to adopt the traits of anthropomorphized brands when the brands are liked and when they are portrayed as partners with the consumers (Aggarwal and McGill, 2010). Work such as this offers an initial framework both to understand the product anthropomorphism phenomenon and to identify conditions leading to favorable evaluations.

It is important to note that people's tendencies to relate to brands, and to other non-human entities, in social ways are dependent upon interpersonal needs and motives. Epley, Akalis, Waytz, and Cacioppo (2008a) examined two typically social motivational factors that impact the tendency to anthropomorphize non-human entities: the need for belongingness and the need for control. In one study, belongingness needs influenced individuals' tendency to anthropomorphize non-human entities, which, in this case, were their pets. The results indicated that chronically lonely people may create agents of social support by anthropomorphizing their pets. In another study, those authors explored effects of the need for control on anthropomorphization. They found that when the need for control is high, anthropomorphism increases – for example, with respect to unpredictable non-human entities – and when the need for control is low, anthropomorphism decreases.

Epley, Waytz, Akalis, and Cacioppo (2008b) have extended these findings to further account for loneliness as a factor influencing people's tendencies (1) to anthropomorphize non-human agents such as non-human animals and products and (2) to believe in commonly anthropomorphized supernatural agents (such as God). Across three studies, these authors demonstrated that chronically lonely people, as well as those induced to feel lonely, tend to anthropomorphize non-human entities in their environment (i.e., animals, products, and supernatural agents). Loneliness not only leads people to seek companionship from non-human entities, but it also alters the way in which those entities are conceptualized. Epley, Adam, and Cacioppo (2007) and Epley *et al.*'s (2008a, 2008b) research has been applied to brand anthropomorphization by Puzakova, Kwak, and Rocereto (2009), who suggest that congruence between self-concept and brand image may facilitate brand anthropomorphism and who argue that the needs for belongingness and control moderate the relationship between self-concept/brand congruence and anthropomorphized brands.

Brand-relevant effects of belongingness motivation are not limited to anthropomorphism; for example, the need to belong has recently been shown to impact consumption behavior. Specifically, consumers for whom the need to belong is an active goal show increased interest in consuming a variety of nostalgic products, perhaps because these products facilitate feelings of connection to warm social contexts from the consumers' pasts (Loveland et al., 2010). Likewise, consumers who have recently experienced (or who anticipate) social exclusion are particularly likely to spend and consume in ways that may lead to social affiliation (Mead et al., 2011).

As they have done with belongingness motives, researchers have begun to study interpersonal attachment motives' effects on brand relationships. Swaminathan et al. (2009) examine ways in which attachment style moderates the effects of brand personality on brand perceptions. They showed how activating particular interpersonal attachment styles can impact which consumers are most likely to be influenced by particular aspects of brand personality. For example, individuals primed to be temporarily high in attachment avoidance and anxiety prefer brands that seem exciting, whereas individuals primed to be temporarily low in avoidance but high in anxiety prefer brands that seem sincere.

With respect to the present chapter, findings like Epley et al.'s (2007, 2008a, 2008b), Loveland et al.'s (2010), and Swaminathan et al.'s (2009) underscore the brand relevance of interpersonal motives toward belonging and attachment.

Goal regulation in interpersonal and brand relationships

As we have noted above, the field of social psychology rests upon the idea that we are social animals who are strongly influenced by the presence of others (e.g., Asch, 1955; Zajonc, 1965). However, research specifically examining how interpersonal relationships affect goals and goal-directed behavior has increased in popularity within the past decade (Fitzsimons and Finkel, 2010). A review of this literature suggests that interpersonal relationships have strong and predictable effects on particular aspects of goal initiation and pursuit.

The social environment provides the background against which goals are initiated. For example, the needs for belonging and attachment are robust initiators of a wide range of social goal-relevant behaviors. Within the context of specific interpersonal relationships, the mere presence of a significant other can facilitate pursuit of relationship-relevant goals. Laboratory studies have shown that when close others (e.g., one's mother) are associated with a particular achievement goal (e.g., academic achievement), activating thoughts of the significant other results in better achievement of subsequent goal-relevant tasks (Fitzsimons and Bargh, 2003). However, just as social relationships are complex, so are the ones between goal initiation and interpersonal relationships: significant others facilitate goal performance when individuals have close relationships with these people and believe that they care about goal performance (e.g., the status of one's academic achievement; Shah, 2003).

Studies of goal contagion indicate that noticing others pursuing a goal makes people more likely to pursue the same goal, even if they have no prior relationship with the observed actor (Aarts, Gollwitzer, and Hassin, 2004). However, esteemed others may inspire people to see themselves as capable of similar future achievements (Lockwood and Kunda, 1997), though such outcomes seem to depend upon several factors. For example, if people feel like their relationship partner is controlling, then they may find goals modeled by the partner aversive and behave in ways opposite to those of the controlling other (Chartrand, Dalton, and Fitzsimons, 2007).

The role of relationship quality in goal influence is further illustrated by several aspects of interpersonal interactions in goal achievement. Interpersonal interactions that require one to expend more effort because they are high-maintenance can lead to poorer performance on a subsequent task (Finkel *et al.*, 2006). In contrast, after efficient interactions, individuals perform better at tasks and exert more persistent effort when compared with individuals who have engaged in inefficient interactions. Also, interactions that may be particularly difficult for some individuals (e.g., prejudice-conscious White participants interacting with a Black partner) can have detrimental effects on performance in subsequent cognitively difficult tasks (Richeson and Trawalter, 2005). In contrast, interpersonal relationships that are less difficult can facilitate goal achievement. Individuals whose close relationship partner is supportive and encouraging of the individual's goals are more likely to achieve these goals (Brunstein, Dangelmayer, and Schultheiss, 1996).

In the same way, turning to brand relationships, it is likely that certain types of brand relationships facilitate goal achievement. However, just as interpersonal relationships are complex, the relationships between brands and individuals are complicated (Fournier, 1998). Although much has been learned about the nature of consumer–brand relationships in general, there is little research linking consumer–brand relationship to goals. In a call for a more person-centered approach to the study of consumer goals, Baumgartner (2002: 288) expresses the view that

> consumer researchers have not paid much attention to the purposive element of consumer behavior. It would appear that viewing consumers as goal-striving individuals and investigating consumer behavior in terms of midlevel motivational concepts that are accessible to conscious awareness and strike a balance between meaningfulness and manageability

(Little, 1989) should contribute to a greater understanding of a very fundamental question about the behavior of consumers – what purposes they are trying to accomplish by purchasing, consuming, and disposing of things.

Indeed, there seems to be a need for more research investigating the role of goals in brand relationships.

Bridging the gap: from the interpersonal to the consumer–brand relationship

As indicated above, it is clear that people use brands and other people to help them meet goals. However, the authors of this chapter argue that there is more than a passing similarity between the ways in which people incorporate brands and other people into their goal pursuits. In fact, we suspect that in many situations, the psychological functions of brands are interchangeable with the psychological functions of other people.

To identify the viability of this claim, our research group has begun revisiting important findings in interpersonal relationship psychology from the following perspective: what happens when we insert brands into the roles that, in the original psychological research, were played by relationship partners? For example, because of the functional dynamic that underlies many consumer–brand relationships, it is worth considering the ways in which this functionality mirrors that of many interpersonal relationships. That is, to what extent does the question of "How do I feel about my favorite brand of deodorant when it helps me do well on a job interview?" mirror "How do I feel about my relationship partner when she or he helps me do well on a job interview?" For reasons that will become clear below, our work suggests that processes typically thought of as "interpersonal" can influence your evaluations of your deodorant in the same ways that they influence your evaluations of your partner.

Using goals to draw people closer to people

An innovative set of studies by Gráinne Fitzsimons and James Shah (2008) demonstrates a simple method for changing how people think about acquaintances they perceive as helpful. Specifically, merely reminding people of particular goals yields powerful positive effects on people's thoughts about acquaintances whom they believe to be helpful with those goals.

For example, in one of Fitzsimons and Shah's (2008) studies, university students were initially asked, as part of an unrelated experiment, to list acquaintances who helped them reach any of a series of particular goals (e.g., acquaintances who help me have a fun social life, achieve academically, stay in shape, etc.). Then, a month later, these same students were tasked with creating a list of their acquaintances. Just before creating this list, some students received subtle reminders of the goal of academic achievement while they were unscrambling a series of sentences, several of which included achievement-related words (e.g., *achieve* and *accomplish*). The other students' sentences contained no achievement-relevant words. As a result, when listing their acquaintances, the achievement-primed students were quicker to include acquaintances whom they had weeks earlier noted as helping them with academic achievement than were students who had unscrambled irrelevant sentences.

Perhaps more tellingly, when the students rated how close they felt to acquaintances on their lists, the achievement reminder led them to rate themselves as closer to achievement-helpful acquaintances than did students who did not receive the reminder. (The reminder had no effect for closeness to goal–irrelevant acquaintances or for acquaintances who were successful themselves – but not helpful – with meeting the goal.) As Fitzsimons and Shah point out, results like these highlight how evaluations of our acquaintances depend upon our moment-to-moment goals.

Those same researchers notes that there is good reason for their findings: shifts in the evaluation of acquaintances as a function of our active goals turn out to be quite adaptive. In another study, Fitzsimons and Shah (2008) saw successful outcomes for the students who, following a subtle reminder of the goal of academic achievement, increased their closeness ratings for achievement-helpful acquaintances: these students studied more and earned better grades on their next exams.

In short, Fitzsimons and Shah (2008, 2009) have shown that people categorize their interpersonal relationships based on goal instrumentality. In a utilitarian way, people amplify their feelings of closeness to specific relationship partners who seem likely to facilitate active goal pursuit.

Using goals to draw people closer to brands

The above findings inspired our research group to consider the extent to which goal-dependent evaluations take place in people's brand relationships. Due to successful brands' inherently functional nature, this connection between brands and acquaintances seems worth exploring. Brands, like acquaintances, help people meet particular goals, whether those goals are to have a fun social life (e.g., by checking Facebook or drinking Budweiser), to achieve academically (e.g., by using Microsoft Office or Wikipedia), or to stay in shape (e.g., by eating Lean Cuisine or running with Nike+ on our Apple devices). Increasingly, brands, like acquaintances, often show up just at the right times to be useful: they contact people via text, tweet, email, or location-based messaging, they network with people online, and they place themselves in online and offline locations where people search for relevant information and products. As people's goals shift, it only makes sense that their attention to and evaluations of brands, like acquaintances, might shift accordingly.

However, while it is easy to establish that brands, like acquaintances, are functional, it is less simple to establish the extent to which brands are social. One way to learn more about brands' social nature would be to explore the relationship dynamics of situations in which brands and acquaintances are interchangeable with respect to outcomes. For example, in a series of studies, we sought to show that activation of brand-relevant goals boosts feelings of closeness toward goal-helpful brands. In these studies, which we describe below, we hypothesized that we would replicate Fitzsimons and Shah's (2008) findings of goal-dependent shifts in evaluations, except that the objects of these evaluations would be brands instead of acquaintances.

Another way to learn about brands' sociality might be to show how brand-relevant evaluations and biases can be influenced by interpersonally oriented processes, like belongingness and attachment. For instance, we attempt to show that goal-dependent shifts in brand evaluations are influenced by people's idiosyncratic levels of belongingness needs or attachment motivation. Across the studies described below, this was exactly our hypothesis: specifically, as might be expected in evaluations of acquaintances, brand closeness will shift as a function of goal activation, and increased brand closeness should be associated with relatively high levels of belongingness needs and relatively low levels of attachment avoidance.

Study 1

The research participants in all four of the studies we describe were university students in the United States, some from a large state university (Studies 1 and 2) and others from a small private university (Studies 3 and 4). Across the studies, each participant completed the research tasks while alone in a one-person cubicle.

The purpose of Study 1 was to establish the existence of a relationship between an interpersonally oriented personality trait, one's relative level of belongingness motivation, and one's evaluation of a goal-helpful brand. Here, participants completed several tasks, including a measure of their need to belong, a task asking them to list goal-helpful brands, and an evaluation of a series of athletic shoe brands. Between each of these tasks, participants completed unrelated activities included to disguise the purpose of the present study.

For the belongingness measure, participants completed Leary, Kelly, Cottrell, and Schreindorfer's (2007) Need to Belong (NTB) scale, a ten-item scale assessing the degree to which individuals desire social acceptance and experience difficulty when they are without social contacts. Items include "I want other people to accept me" and "I do not like being alone." Higher scores indicated responses consistent with higher levels of NTB.

On the brand listing measure, participants responded to a series of items prompting them to write the name of a brand that increases the likelihood that they will succeed at a particular goal. For example, they were asked to provide the name of a brand of shoes that most helps them achieve the goal to be healthy or fit, and they were asked to provide the name of a brand of shampoo that most helps them achieve the goal of cleaning their hair. For each goal, we also asked them to provide the name of a brand from the helpful brand's product class that does not help them achieve the goal (e.g., a shoe brand that does not help them achieve the goal of being healthy or fit).

The athletic shoe evaluation task presented participants with the names of six different popular brands (i.e., Adidas, Asics, Converse, New Balance, Nike, and Reebok), drawn from pilot testing. For each brand, participants indicated the extent to which they liked the brand, used the brand often, perceived the brand as good value, intended to purchase the brand in the future, and felt close to the brand, which, because of its explicitly social dimension, is the measure in which we were most interested. For each item, higher numbers indicated responses consistent with a more positive evaluation.

Of the 101 participants who completed the measures, 88 listed a helpful shoe brand that was one of the six they later evaluated. Of these, the most popular responses included Nike and Asics. Likewise, 27 listed unhelpful shoe brands that were among the six brands later evaluated. Of these, the most frequent unhelpful brands were Converse and Nike. Based on these 88 and 27 participants, respectively, the results of Study 1 were as expected: There was a positive association between NTB and feeling close to one's goal-helpful brand of shoes. Moreover, there was a negative association between NTB and liking one's unhelpful brand of shoes. In short, as belongingness needs increased, feeling close to one's helpful brand increased and dislike for one's unhelpful brand increased.

Study 2

Having established a link between belongingness motives and feeling close to helpful brands, our next objective was to assess whether brand evaluations shifted as a function of goal activation, as Fitzsimons and Shah (2008) had shown with acquaintances. To this end, Study 2 adapted Fitzsimons and Shah's goal activation methodology. As in Study 1, participants completed a series of questionnaires, among which was a version of the brand listing task, in which they listed brands that help them achieve certain goals. Again, the product category and goal in which we were interested was the brand of shoes that helped them achieve the goal of being healthy or fit.

After unrelated filler activities, participants completed what we called a "Cognitive Task." This task involved unscrambling twelve sentences and was a version of a technique widely used by researchers for subtly activating specific goals (e.g., Chartrand et al., 2010; Geers et al., 2005; Srull and Wyer, 1979). In the present study, the sentence scrambling task was designed to subtly activate either the goal of being healthy or health-irrelevant concepts. Half of the participants were randomly assigned to receive scrambled sentences in which health-related words were included (e.g., "active" or "well"), and the other half received sentences with no health-related words. For instance, a sentence unscrambling item intended to activate a health goal was "ACTIVE THE WAS PUPPY," whereas the equivalent goal-irrelevant item was "SNIFFING THE WAS PUPPY." Once they had unscrambled the sentences, all participants completed the brand evaluation task used in Study 1, evaluating the same series of shoe brands.

Of the thirty-one participants who completed all the tasks, twenty-nine listed a helpful shoe brand that was among the six they later evaluated. Of these twenty-nine, the most popular responses included Nike and Adidas. With respect to the primary analyses, the results of Study 2 were as anticipated: an active health goal, as manipulated via the sentence unscrambling task, enhanced participants' evaluation of their helpful shoe brand. Specifically, those exposed to health-related words perceived their helpful brand as better value than did the neutral goal group. The effect for brand closeness was in the same direction but was not significant. (It is important to point out that all of our studies were fighting a ceiling effect, as we attempted to enhance people's ratings of brands that they already used and viewed in a positive light.) Nevertheless, with respect to perceived brand value, evaluation was more positive among those for whom a relevant goal was activated.

Study 3

To provide stronger evidence for goal-dependent shifts in brand evaluations, Study 3 incorporated a subtler, non-conscious method of goal activation (i.e., subliminal priming). In addition, to verify that the evaluation effects would occur with a non-fitness goal, Study 3 focused on evaluations of websites that help participants connect with friends. Moreover, to increase methodological rigor, Study 3 eliminated the conceptual ambiguity associated with activating nothing in particular (i.e., goal-irrelevance). Now the two versions of the goal activation task involved activating a social goal or, in place of the goal-irrelevant prime, a health goal, respectively. Finally, to increase the delay between the brand listing and goal activation tasks, this study comprised a multi-session design: at the first session, participants completed a version of the brand listing task, which included an item asking for a website that helped with the goal of social connection. After a week-long delay, the second session entailed only the subliminal goal activation task followed by the brand evaluations.

The subliminal goal activation task was adapted from a similar task developed by Arndt, Greenberg, Pyszczynski, and Solomon (1997) and was presented as a computer-based "Word-Relation Task." The task presented participants two emotionally neutral words, like "LETTUCE" and "CALCULATOR," and the participants responded by pressing a certain key if they thought the words seemed related, or a different key if they thought the words seemed unrelated. What the participants didn't know was that for 27 milliseconds between the first and second word of each pair, they were being exposed subliminally to a word. For fifteen trials, half the participants were exposed to the word "SOCIAL," which should activate concepts relevant to social connection, and the other half saw the word "HEALTH," which should active concepts irrelevant to social connection. In general, when masked by the neutral words that preceded and followed the primes, 27 milliseconds is enough display time for non-conscious perception of these words but is insufficient for conscious recognition of what they saw. Therefore, this task served as a proxy for non-conscious goal activation.

Following the subliminal goal activation task, participants completed a brand evaluation task. Although the evaluation dimensions were the same as those used in Studies 1 and 2 (i.e., liking, frequency of use, value, purchase intent, and closeness), each participant in Study 3 received a list of brands customized to include the website brand that she or he had nominated as helping her or him connect with friends. Participants' goal-helpful websites were surrounded by filler brands, including beverage brands (e.g., Starbucks and Coca-Cola) and other website brands.

Of the forty participants who completed the study, a majority listed Facebook as the website brand that helped them connect with friends. With respect to the major analysis, the results of Study 3 were as predicted: an active social goal, as manipulated via the subliminal task, enhanced participants' evaluation of their helpful website. Specifically, those exposed to the word "SOCIAL" felt closer to the website that helped them connect socially than did participants exposed to "HEALTH." This finding suggests that even non-conscious activation of relevant goals can modify people's brand evaluations.

Study 4

Designed to build upon Study 2 and Study 3's demonstrations of goal-dependent shifts in brand evaluation, Study 4 used a more complex design to replicate these findings and to examine the role of attachment style in goal-dependent shifts in brand evaluation. We hypothesized that attachment avoidance, which inhibits closeness in interpersonal relationships, might do the same in brand relationships, even for goal-helpful brands. Also, we wondered whether any inhibitory effects of attachment avoidance on brand closeness might disappear when goals relevant to the helpful brands are activated.

To explore these possibilities, we modified Study 3 in two ways. First, during the initial session and just after the brand listing task, participants completed Brennan, Clark, and Shaver's (1998) Experiences in Close Relationships (ECR) scale. This 36-item scale assesses how people typically feel in emotionally close relationships (i.e., not specific to a particular relationship partner). The ECR comprises two subscales on which higher scores indicate responses consistent with higher levels of attachment anxiety and attachment avoidance, respectively. Items include "I worry a lot about my relationships" from the anxiety subscale and "I get uncomfortable when a romantic partner wants to be very close" from the avoidance subscale.

The second difference from Study 3 was that the subliminal goal activation task was replaced with a sentence unscrambling goal activation task. A week after the first session, participants returned for the second session and were presented with twelve sentence unscrambling items. Half the participants were randomly assigned to unscramble sentences in which social-related words were included (e.g., "relate" or "affiliate"), and the other half received sentences with health-related words. For instance, a sentence unscrambling item intended to active a social goal was "I WISHES MY COMMUNICATED," whereas a health-goal item was "THE WHOLESOME LOOKED FOOD." Once they had unscrambled the sentences, all participants completed the brand evaluation task used in Study 3, in which each participant evaluated the social website that she or he had provided in the first session as well as filler brands.

Of the fifty-one participants who completed the study, a majority listed Facebook as the website brand that helped them connect with friends, as in Study 3. With respect to the primary analyses, an active social goal again enhanced participants' evaluation of their helpful website. Specifically, participants who unscrambled sentences with social words felt closer to the website that helped them connect socially than did those exposed to health-related words. Likewise, participants who unscrambled sentences with social words indicated that they more frequently used the website that helped them connect socially than did those exposed to health-related words.

With respect to attachment, we found a significant relationship between attachment avoidance and closeness to the social website brand. Specifically, as is typically the case with respect to interpersonal closeness, mean-centered attachment avoidance negatively predicted brand closeness. This effect did not go away when we added the goal activation condition to the model. Rather, attachment avoidance remained a significant negative predictor of brand closeness, while in this particular model the effect of goal activation condition was only marginally significant. (There was no interaction between attachment avoidance and goal activation condition.) The same pattern held when using attachment avoidance and goal activation to predict the frequency with which participants reported using the social website brand. In short, attachment avoidance was negatively related to reported brand closeness or frequency of use, whether or not the effects of goal activation were taken into account.

Applications and implications

Across these four studies, we have shown how evaluations of goal-helpful brands become more positive when relevant goals are brought to mind. What is more, these results highlight connections between interpersonal relationships and brand relationships: goal-activated shifts in closeness seem to occur in both interpersonal relationships and brand relationships. Likewise, belongingness needs and interpersonal attachment motives are predictive of brand closeness, as they are predictive of interpersonal closeness.

Of course, the above findings are limited in several respects. They rely upon university student participants and these participants' self-reported brand evaluations, and they focus on particular goals and product classes. However, given the consistency of the findings with one another and with previous research on interpersonal and brand relationships as described above, they are worth noting. They provide opportunity to consider some specific, actionable applications and broader, thought-provoking implications.

For instance, these findings suggest that brand managers could use associations between brands and goal-helpfulness in order to boost brand evaluations. If reminders of brand-relevant goals enhance consumers' brand closeness, then identification of the specific goals to which a brand's users are applying the brand's products could lead to increased loyalty among users. Although this may sound obvious, it is clear that brands from similar product classes may be associated with very different goals.

For example, many people use Facebook to maintain relationships with friends and family, while using LinkedIn to promote their professional interests and using Twitter to converse and be entertained. Similarly, one night someone may drink Budweiser to have fun with friends at a party or sporting event, whereas the same person the next night might drink a regional brewery's microbrew with the same friends as part of a relaxing dinner at home. Furthermore, different segments of a brand's users might associate the brand with different goals. For one group, the consumption of Doritos might be a component of a warm after-school environment for entertaining their children's friends, but for another group, Doritos might represent a rewarding self-indulgence after a hard morning on the job.

Once brand-relevant goals have been identified, brand managers should consider reinforcing this association by emphasizing connections between these goals and the brand. As indicated by the studies by Fitzsimons and Shah (2008) and our own research group, subtle activation of relevant goals should be enough to enhance subsequent brand evaluations among consumers who already believe a brand to be helpful with those goals. It stands to reason, although it is left to future research to confirm, that more positive evaluations by this group of consumers would stimulate their brand loyalty and possibly reinforce purchase behavior. On the other hand, to the extent that goal-dependent shifts in brand evaluations are short-lived, it might make sense to provide subtle but noticeable reminders of these goals at and around locations where consumers purchase the brand. In-store and online product presentation could incorporate goal-relevant language (e.g., words like "friends" or "sharing" for brands helpful with social goals) or images (e.g., appropriating the look and feel of online social networks for brands helpful with social goals).

To approach consumers who do not yet view a particular brand as goal helpful, building connections between brands and goals would be an obvious priority for brand managers. New or less established brands in a product class would be particularly well positioned to benefit from helping consumers learn how those brands could help them meet specific goals. If managers have identified brand-relevant (or even potentially brand-relevant) goals for consumers who currently use their brands, then these goals should be useful targets for building associations between the brands and goal helpfulness. Product placements in goal fulfillment contexts, goal-relevant event sponsorships, online microsites associated with particular goal-relevant online keyword searches, goal-relevant applications for mobile phones, and goal-relevant brand mascot or spokesperson strategies are only a few ways in which brand–goal associations could be enhanced. As with interpersonal relationships (e.g., Rusbult, 1980), the belief that one's brand provides clear rewards should predict a brand relationship that is quite satisfactory.

However, it is important to remember that when relationships become less useful for an individual, the status of those relationships may be in jeopardy. Indeed, this is what Fitzsimons and Fishbach (2010) found: when individuals perceive themselves as successfully progressing toward a particular goal, preference for the goal-instrumental other decreases. This falling out with the goal-instrumental other occurs when individuals believe there is at least partial attainment of the goal and occurs to the degree that individuals seek to re-focus on additional goals. Moreover, this utilitarian orientation leads individuals to move away from the former goal-facilitating friend and toward new others who are perceived to facilitate goals that may not be progressing as well. To the extent that these processes occur in brand relationships, it is possible that when an individual feels that she or he has attained a brand-relevant goal, the brand would decrease in importance to that consumer. This could indicate that managers should emphasize their brand's ability to facilitate ongoing goals (e.g., social affiliation or health) as opposed to more acute goals (e.g., having a memorable high school prom or removing a wart).

Similarly, brands positioned to meet narrow goals will face different challenges than brands positioned to meet broader goals. For example, as noted above, LinkedIn is a social media site that is positioned specifically as facilitating enhancement of one's professional social network, whereas Twitter is a social media site positioned as meeting the more general goals of entertainment and conversation. LinkedIn will therefore not be of interest to the many consumers who hold these more general goals, and, unless it works to change its positioning, it must strive to maintain a dominant position among the smaller segment of consumers who hold a narrower goal. In contrast, Twitter must contend with an array of strong competitors from across platforms and industries that can plausibly claim to help consumers meet more general goals associated with entertainment and conversation. In short, the scope of the goals with which a brand becomes associated will help determine – and will in turn be influenced by – the scope and identity of the brand's competition and consumers.

While each of the applications of the research findings presented in this chapter should prove useful, they are not entirely unintuitive. What most engages the authors of this chapter – and what could eventually yield radical implications for brand managers – are the larger implications associated with our findings about the nature of consumer–brand relationships. That is, the association between consumers' belongingness motives and attachment styles and their evaluations of brand value and closeness raise fascinating and challenging questions. To what extent are consumer–brand relationships influenced by consumers' interpersonal relationship-relevant individual differences? Under what circumstances might individual differences related to belongingness and attachment shape consumers' feelings of brand closeness and commitment? If these interpersonal motives do influence brand evaluations and behaviors, in what specific ways is the "consumer–brand relationship" metaphor more than just a figure of speech?

Definitive answers to these questions will not arrive immediately, although researchers have illuminated many intriguing aspects of consumer–brand relationships (e.g., see the other chapters in this volume and MacInnis, Park, and Priester, 2009). Nevertheless, in the near future, technological developments (e.g., in online behavioral profiling and location-based messaging) should increase the possibilities for brand managers to make strategic decisions related to differences in consumers' levels of belongingness and attachment. It may soon make sense, for instance, to segment messaging to address individuals' or groups' typical attachment motives (e.g., perhaps by emphasizing brand warmth to attachment-anxious consumers and emphasizing brand competence to attachment-avoidant consumers). Already, representative national surveys have shown how different attachment styles characterize large divisions of the US population. Around 25 percent of American adults tend toward attachment avoidance, and another 11 percent tend toward attachment anxiety (Mickelson, Kessler, and Shaver, 1997). These tendencies co-vary in interesting ways with ethnicity, age, and relationship status, population segments that many brand managers already take into consideration. As brand managers focus on meeting different groups of consumers' general goals, we encourage them to think about how their brands can be positioned to fulfill these many consumers' enduring attachment and belongingness concerns. This kind of thinking may well yield successful results for managers and researchers for years to come.

References

Aaker, J. (1997) "Dimensions of Brand Personality", *Journal of Marketing Research*, 34 (3): 347–56.

Aaker, J., Fournier, S. and Brasel, S.A. (2004) "When Good Brands Do Bad", *Journal of Consumer Research*, 31 (1): 1–16.

Aarts, H., Gollwitzer, P.M. and Hassin, R. (2004) "Goal Contagion: Perceiving is for Pursuing", *Journal of Personality and Social Psychology*, 87: 23–37.

Aggarwal, P. (2004) "The Effects of Brand Relationship Norms on Consumer Attitudes and Behavior", *Journal of Consumer Research*, 31 (1): 87–101.

Aggarwal, P. and McGill, A.L. (2007) "Is that Car Smiling at Me? Schema Congruity as a Basis for Evaluating Anthropomorphized Products", *Journal of Consumer Research*, 34 (4): 468–79.

—— (2010) "Partners and Servants: Adopting Traits of Anthromorphized Brands", in D.W. Dahl, G.V. Johar, and S.M.J. van Osselaer (eds) *Advances in Consumer Research*, *vol. 38*, Duluth, MN: Association for Consumer Research.

Arndt, J., Greenberg, J., Pyszczynski, T. and Solomon, S. (1997) "Subliminal Exposure to Death-Related Stimuli Increases Defense of the Cultural Worldview", *Psychological Science*, 8: 379–85.

Asch, S.E. (1955) "Opinions and Social Pressure", *Scientific American*, 193 (5): 31–5.

Baumeister, R.F., Dori, G.A. and Hastings, S. (1998) "Belongingness and Temporal Bracketing in Personal Accounts of Changes in Self-Esteem", *Journal of Research in Personality*, 32 (2): 222–35.

Baumeister, R.F. and Leary, M.R. (1995) "The Need to Belong: Desire for Interpersonal Attachments as a Fundamental Human Motivation", *Psychological Bulletin*, 117 (3): 497–529.

Baumgartner, H. (2002) "Toward a Personology of the Consumer", *Journal of Consumer Research*, 29: 286–92.

Brennan, K.A., Clark, C.L. and Shaver, P.R. (1998) "Self Report Measurement of Adult Attachment: An Integrative Overview", in J.A. Simpson and W.S. Rholes (eds) *Attachment Theory and Close Relationships*, New York: Guilford Press.

Brunstein, J.C., Dangelmayer, G. and Schultheiss, O.C. (1996) "Personal Goals and Social Support in Close Relationships: Effects on Relationship Mood and Marital Satisfaction", *Journal of Personality and Social Psychology*, 71: 1006–19.

Carvallo, M. and Pelham, B.W. (2006) "When Fiends Become Friends: The Need to Belong and Perceptions of Personal and Group Discrimination", *Journal of Personality and Social Psychology*, 90 (1): 94–108.

Chartrand, T.L., Cheng, C.M., Dalton, A.N. and Tesser, A. (2010) "Nonconscious Goal Pursuit: Isolated Incidents or Adaptive Self-Regulatory Tool?" *Social Cognition*, 28 (5): 569–88.

Chartrand, T.L., Dalton, A. and Fitzsimons, G.J. (2007) "Relationship Reactance: When Priming Significant Others Triggers Opposing Goals", *Journal of Experimental Social Psychology*, 43: 719–26.

Collins, N.L. and Feeney, B.C. (2000) "A Safe Haven: An Attachment Theory Perspective on Support Seeking and Caregiving in Intimate Relationships", *Journal of Personality and Social Psychology*, 78 (6): 1053–73.

Davis, D., Shaver, P.R. and Vernon, M.L. (2003) "Physical, Emotional, and Behavioral Reactions to Breaking Up: The Roles of Gender, Age, Emotional Involvement, and Attachment Style", *Personality and Social Psychology Bulletin*, 29 (7): 871–84.

Epley, N., Adam, W. and Cacioppo, J.T. (2007) "On Seeing Human: A Three-Factor Theory of Anthropomorphism", *Psychological Review*, 114 (4): 864–86.

Epley, N., Akalis, S., Waytz, A. and Cacioppo, J.T. (2008a) "Creating Social Connection through Inferential Reproduction: Loneliness and Perceived Agency in Gadgets, Gods and Greyhounds", *Psychological Science*, 19 (2):114–20.

Epley, N., Waytz, A., Akalis, S. and Cacioppo, J.T. (2008b) "When We Need a Human: Motivational Determinants of Anthropomorphism", *Social Cognition*, 26 (2): 143–55.

Finkel, E.J., Campbell, W.K., Brunell, A.B., Dalton, A.N., Chartrand, T.L. and Scarbeck, S.J. (2006) "High-Maintenance Interaction: Inefficient Social Coordination Impairs Self-Regulation", *Journal of Personality and Social Psychology*, 91: 456–75.

Fitzsimons, G.M. and Bargh, J.A. (2003) "Thinking of You: Nonconscious Pursuit of Interpersonal Goals Associated with Relationship Partners", *Journal of Personality and Social Psychology*, 84: 148–64.

Fitzsimons, G.M. and Finkel, E.J. (2010) "Interpersonal Influences on Self-Regulation", *Current Directions in Psychological Science*, 19: 101–5.

Fitzsimons, G.M. and Fishbach, A. (2010) "Shifting Closeness: Interpersonal Effects of Personal Goal Progress", *Journal of Personality and Social Psychology*, 98: 535–49.

Fitzsimons, G.M. and Shah, J.Y. (2008) "How Goal Instrumentality Shapes Relationship Evaluations", *Journal of Personality and Social Psychology*, 95 (2): 319–37.

—— (2009) "Confusing One Instrumental Other for Another: Goal Effects on Social Categorization", *Psychological Science*, 20: 1468–72.

Fournier, S. (1998) "Consumers and their Brands: Developing Relationship Theory in Consumer Research", *Journal of Consumer Research*, 24 (4): 343–73.

Geers, A.L., Weiland, P.E., Kosbab, K., Landry, S.J. and Helfer, S.G. (2005) "Goal Activation, Expectations, and the Placebo Effect", *Journal of Personality and Social Psychology*, 89 (2): 143–59.

Hankin, B.L., Kassel, J.D. and Abela, J.R.Z. (2005) "Adult Attachment Dimensions and Specificity of Emotional Distress Symptoms: Prospective Investigations of Cognitive Risk and Interpersonal Stress Generation as Mediating Mechanisms", *Personality and Social Psychology Bulletin*, 31 (1): 136–51.

Hazan, C. and Shaver, P. (1987) "Romantic Love Conceptualized as an Attachment Process", *Journal of Personality and Social Psychology*, 52: 511–24.

Leary, M.R. (2010) "Affiliation, Acceptance, and Belonging: The Pursuit of Interpersonal Connection", in S.T. Fiske, D.T. Gilbert, and G. Lindzey (eds) *Handbook of Social Psychology*, 2nd edn, Hoboken, NJ: John Wiley & Sons.

Leary, M.R. and Cox, C.B. (2008) "Belongingness Motivation: A Mainspring of Social Action", in J.Y. Shah, Y. James, and W.L. Gardner (eds) *Handbook of Motivation Science*, New York: Guilford Press.

Leary, M.R., Kelly, K.M., Cottrell, C.A. and Schreindorfer, L.S. (2007) "Individual Differences in the Need to Belong: Mapping the Nomological Network", unpublished manuscript, Duke University.

Levy, S.J. (1985) "Dreams, Fairy Tales, Animals, and Cars", *Psychology and Marketing*, 2 (2): 67–81.

Little, B.R. (1989) "Personal Projects Analysis: Trivial Pursuits, Magnificent Obsessions, and the Search for Coherence", ing D.M. Buss, and N. Cantor (eds) *Personality Psychology: recent trends and emerging directions*, New York: Springer.

Lockwood, P. and Kunda, Z. (1997) "Superstars and Me: Predicting the Impact of Role Models on the Self", *Journal of Personality and Social Psychology*, 73: 93–103.

Loveland, K.E., Smeesters, D. and Mandel, N. (2010) "Still Preoccupied with 1995: The Need to Belong and Preference for Nostalgic Products", *Journal of Consumer Research*, 37 (3): 393–408.

MacInnis, D.J., Park, C.W. and Priester, J.R. (2009) *Handbook of Brand Relationships*, Armonk, NY: M.E. Sharpe.

Mead, N.L., Baumeister, R.F., Stillman, T.F., Rawn, C.D. and Vohs, K.D. (2011) "Social Exclusion Causes People to Spend and Consume Strategically in the Service of Affiliation", *Journal of Consumer Research*, 37 (5): 902–19.

Mickelson, K.D., Kessler, R.C. and Shaver, P.R. (1997) "Adult Attachment in a Nationally Representative Sample", *Journal of Personality and Social Psychology*, 73: 1092–106.

Mikulincer, M. and Florian, V. (2001) "Attachment Style and Affect Regulation – Implications for Coping with Stress and Mental Health", in G. Fletcher and M. Clark (eds) *Blackwell Handbook of Social Psychology: interpersonal processes*, Oxford: Blackwell Publishers.

Pickett, C.L., Gardner, W.L. and Knowles, M. (2004) "Getting a Cue: The Need to Belong and Enhanced Sensitivity to Social Cues", *Personality and Social Psychology Bulletin*, 30 (9): 1095–107.

Puzakova, M., Kwak, H. and Rocereto, J.F. (2009) "Pushing the Envelope of Brand and Personality: Antecedents and Moderators of Anthropomorphized Brands", *Advances in Consumer Research*, 36: 413–20.

Richeson, J.A. and Trawalter, S. (2005) "Why Do Interracial Interactions Impair Executive Function? A Resource Depletion Account", *Journal of Personality and Social Psychology*, 88: 934–47.

Rusbult, C.E. (1980) "Commitment and Satisfaction in Romantic Associations: A Test of the Investment Model", *Journal of Experimental Social Psychology*, 16: 172–86.

Shah, J.Y. (2003) "Automatic for the People: How Representations of Significant Others Implicitly Affect Goal Pursuit", *Journal of Personality and Social Psychology*, 84: 661–81.

Shaver, P.R. and Mikulincer, M. (2007) "Attachment Theory and Research: Core Concepts, Basic Principles, Conceptual Bridges", in A.W. Kruglanski and E.T. Higgins (eds) *Social Psychology: handbook of basic principles*, 2nd edn, New York: Guilford Press.

Simpson, J.A., Collins, W.A., Tran, S. and Haydon, K.C. (2007) "Attachment and the Experience and Expression of Emotions in Romantic Relationships: A Developmental Perspective", *Journal of Personality and Social Psychology*, 92 (2): 355–67.

Srull, T.K. and Wyer, R.S. (1979) "The Role of Category Accessibility in the Interpretation of Information about Persons: Some Determinants and Implications", *Journal of Personality and Social Psychology*, 37 (10): 1660–72.

Swaminathan, V., Stilley, K.M. and Ahluwalia, R. (2009) "When Brand Personality Matters: The Moderating Role of Attachment Styles", *Journal of Consumer Research*, 35 (6): 985–1002.

Watt, S.E. and Badger, A.J. (2009) "Effects of Social Belonging on Homesickness: An Application of the Belongingness Hypothesis", *Personality and Social Psychology Bulletin*, 35 (4): 516–30.

Zajonc, R.B. (1965) "Social Facilitation", *Science*, 149: 269–74.

PART IV

Managerial Applications of Consumer–Brand Relationship Ideas

16

FIRING YOUR BEST CUSTOMERS

How smart firms destroy relationships using CRM

Jill Avery and Susan Fournier

A customer is fired

When Norma answered the telephone and the person on the other end said he was calling from Filene's Basement, her heart soared. Finally, someone from corporate headquarters was calling to apologize for the abominable treatment she had received yesterday in a Filene's Basement retail store. Norma immediately began recounting the story of how the store manager, someone Norma had known for twenty years, had yelled at her and had made her cry in front of other customers after she asked him to extend a sale price so that she could buy some flatware at a discounted price. She conveyed the manager's response: "He screamed 'NO! When are you gonna realize you are nothing special to us?'"

Norma thought about the hundreds of thousands of dollars she had spent at Filene's Basement, a retail chain selling designer labels at discounted prices, since the early 1970s, the hundreds of friends she had introduced to the store, and the many special favors and gifts she had given to various Filene's Basement employees who had become her personal friends over the span of her thirty years as a loyal customer. She thought back to the special invitations she enjoyed as a member of the Filene's Basement Insiders Club, a group created to reward the firm's best customers with special offers and invitations to intimate events. She also remembered the many times employees had bent the rules for her, in deference to her status as one of "The Regulars," a group of women well-known because of their frequent shopping activity and first-in-line position for all of the store's sales events and new store openings. She knew she was worthy of such acknowledgement. This is what had made the store manager's reaction to her simple request so puzzling and so upsetting.

As she paused to catch her breath, the voice at the other end of the telephone asked for her address. Norma remembers the moment: "I honestly thought they were going to send me flowers! And then this gruff voice says, 'You are never to call Filene's Basement again, you are never to set foot in any of our stores again.' I was so flabbergasted. I honestly don't think they knew how much I spent. I honestly don't think they knew I was such a good customer."

The customer is no longer king

How, in a business climate in which building relationships with customers has dominated both managerial thought and marketing budgets (Shah *et al.* 2006), could Filene's Basement have fired a loyal customer, one who was formally and informally recognized as a best customer? In today's world, Filene's Basement is not alone: firing your customer, once unheard of in a world where "the customer is king," is becoming a more common occurrence (Mittal, Sarkees, and Murshed 2008), albeit one that still makes the national news when it happens.

We begin this chapter by tracing the recent history of the "fire your customers" paradigm, and its radical divergence from the tenets of customer-centricity that inspired the rise of relationship marketing. Then, we analyze the relationship trajectory of a fired customer to illuminate that a bad customer is often the result not of inherent consumer shortcomings, but of a poorly managed customer relationship at the hands of the firm. Our findings indicate that firing customers is often, ironically, a case of blaming the victim: managers remain largely unaware of their own roles in creating the unprofitable customers they seek to shed. Our case study shows how a firm's CRM programs can paradoxically transform good customers into bad customers, whose value stemming from their frequent purchasing is eroded by their increasing cost-to-serve. We conclude with practical advice on how managers can improve the overall quality of the customer relationships in their portfolios, and turn troubled relationships around.

Customer-centricity is dead: long live customer-centricity

Sam Walton, the founder of Wal-Mart, famously claimed that "the secret of successful retailing is giving your customers what they want" (Walton and Huey 1993). He advocated that customers were the lifeblood of a company and that success lay in attracting them and then delighting them so as to retain them over their purchasing lifetimes. "There is only one boss. The customer. And he can fire everybody in the company from the chairman on down, simply by spending his money somewhere else" (Walton and Huey 1993). For decades, companies embraced his customer-centric approach, following Levitt's (1960) advice that managers should work to fulfill customers' needs rather than focus on selling products. Companies lived in fear that their customers would leave them by switching to their competitors; the thought of firms firing their own customers was ludicrous.

However, more recently, companies have begun firing their customers. The first wave of firings occurred in the 1990s when stock keeping unit (SKU) rationalization became a popular cost-cutting strategy. Following a proliferation of new product launches which filled grocery shelves to their bursting point, managers began to realize that carrying so many different brands and SKUs was costly for companies that were struggling to trim the fat from their supply chains. Large consumer product companies like Procter & Gamble and Unilever were first to slim down, eliminating flavors, scents, sizes, forms, and sometimes even entire brands and product lines. Competing brands owned by the same parent company were merged; smaller brands were sold or discontinued altogether. Consumers of these brands and product variants were left hanging, summarily fired en masse from their favorite brands.

The 1990s also ushered in the age of relationship marketing. Don Peppers and Martha Rogers' classic book *The One to One Future* (1993) advocated shifting managerial focus from managing products and brands to managing customers. The authors recognized that all customers were not worth the same amount and, therefore, that there was value in understanding customers as individuals and customizing for them products and marketing programs that reflected their personalized value. Since then, we have lived through two decades of investment in CRM systems; sales of sophisticated CRM software designed to collect and analyze the purchase histories of individual consumers reached $9 billion in 2008 (Mertz 2009). Companies across industries have embraced the notion of quantifying the current and future value each customer contributes to the firm and then assigning them to a tier in a hierarchically arranged customer profitability pyramid (Zeithaml, Rust, and Lemon 2001). Customers in different tiers receive differential treatment commensurate with their expected profitability. The most profitable customers occupy the top Platinum tier, followed by Gold, Silver, and Bronze level customers. The least profitable customers are classified as Lead, representing their tendency to weigh down corporate profits.

Following a study conducted by Bain and Company that indicated that, on average, 30 percent of a company's customers are unprofitable, customers in the lowest Lead tier were branded "below-zero" customers and increasingly wound up as targets for firing by firms looking to boost their profits (Peppers and Rogers 2004). Initially, firms were subtle about firing their Lead customers. Companies tried to shed their unprofitable customers by raising prices, fees, or premiums to flush out the bottom tier. Banks instituted minimum balance requirements and charged Lead-tier customers fees to use live teller services rather than self-service ATM machines. Insurance companies raised the premiums of some existing customers to encourage them to switch to their competitors. eBay raised the fees it charged sellers who were not selling enough volume (Glagowski 2006). Best Buy dropped its worst customers from its promotional mailing lists, refusing to notify them of upcoming sales and special events (McWilliams 2004). Then, companies tried to persuade lower-tier customers to leave: American Express offered customers $300 to cancel their credit cards (Pilon 2009), while Citibank offered a $500 incentive to leave. Finally, companies became aggressive about firing unprofitable customers: Allstate Insurance dropped homeowners in coastal regions from its homeowners' insurance customer portfolio (Conlon 2010), ING Direct closed the bank accounts of customers with low credit scores (Taylor 2005), and AT&T and T-Mobile cut off service to customers who were ringing up excessive roaming charges on "unlimited" cell phone plans (Price 2008). Sprint-Nextel cut loose a thousand customers who were demanding too much customer support (MSN Money 2007).

Taking responsibility for bad relationships

CRM systems have been successful at matching companies' marketing efforts to the perceived profit potential of individual customers. CRM metrics indicate which customers can support the higher marketing costs that come from specialized attention, product customization, and promotional discounts. Companies with sophisticated CRM systems utilize software that automatically calculates the worth of a customer and directs customer-facing employees to the appropriate level of service. Traffic light colors, flashing green for Platinum and Gold customers, yellow for Silver and Bronze customers, and red for Lead customers, appear on the employees' screens, guiding their choices in how much to offer each customer in terms of discounts, free goods, service levels, or access. For example, hotels use traffic light colors to indicate whether a guest checking in should be offered a free room upgrade and airlines use them to indicate whether a passenger deserves to move up in the standby list.

One of the gross simplifications implicated in these practices is the belief that customers can be treated like economic assets that have a measurable and predictable value to the firm, often determined by a customer lifetime value calculation that calculates the cost to acquire the customer and then estimates the expected annual profit generated by the customer and the length of the customer's expected relationship with the company. What is missing is the realization that the value of a customer is not an inherent, stable, and predictable characteristic of the customer, but rather a dynamic outcome of a negotiated relationship between a customer and the company. Both the customer and the company are responsible for determining the value of the consumer–brand relationship and the actions of both of them create, build, nurture, and negotiate the terms of their agreement (Fournier and Avery 2011). Therefore, there is rarely such a thing as a bad customer, just a poorly negotiated customer relationship.

Relationship marketing is not only about motivating good customers and firing the bad. Relational success is also about navigating through relationships when they get messy, and turning troubled relationships around. Once a customer has been classified into the Lead tier, is she doomed to trigger a red light for the rest of her tenure, or be fired? Or can companies look for ways to renegotiate their relationship with her to increase her profitability so that she can climb back into the higher tiers of the profitability pyramid? Current practice suggests that firms are too quick to close the door on troubled relationships. They shirk from analyzing their own role in creating the problem and blame the customer when the relationship goes bad. Below, we trace the evolution of a customer to highlight ways in which firms can become actively involved in renegotiating relationships.

Customer alchemy: the evolution of a best customer

In an effort to understand how consumer–brand relationships fall apart, we conducted a series of depth interviews with a consumer we will call Norma, who was forbidden to patronize the Filene's Basement retail stores after a long history as a customer. We reverse-engineer Norma's relationship with Filene's Basement to uncover the critical incidents and behaviors of each party that shaped their relationship trajectory. We trace Norma's rollercoaster path from a new customer, to a Gold customer, to a Platinum customer, and watch as Platinum painfully turns to Lead.

We begin this story at its end. Why was Norma fired? According to the letter she received, Norma was fired for her "excessive returns history" and "frequent registered complaints." The company's decision to fire Norma focused on her high cost-to-serve: her numerous returns cost the company money to process and her frequent complaints took up valuable employee time. Filene's Basement relied on economic data to define and diagnose the relationship, and these numbers indicated a Lead-level customer. The firm threatened Norma with legal action if she entered any of Filene's Basement retail stores, severing their relationship with her.

Norma looked at the numbers too, but she focused on revenues rather than profits: "A six-digit customer," by Norma's analysis. She also recognized the value that she brought to the company that was not captured by her purchasing record. "I was loyal. I was there shopping. I was buying. I was telling others to shop there. I was getting others to come. People from all over – I would bring them." Besides supporting her own accessorized lifestyle, Norma acted as others' personal shoppers, and introduced countless friends to the store.

But why did Norma underestimate her service costs? How could Norma's and Filene's Basement's conceptions of the relationship be so very misaligned? To understand Norma's returns behavior, we have to rewind to the beginning of her relationship to understand the relationship rules and norms that were established when she first became a customer.

A new customer: relationship rules are established

When Norma began shopping at Filene's Basement in the 1970s, the seventy-year-old retail chain had already established a unique shopping culture, into which this new customer was acculturated. Filene's Basement was the United States' original outlet store, offering discounted prices on overstock designer goods from Boston's and New York's finest department stores and boutiques. Filene's Basement was known for its fantastic bargains, sometimes offering 50–75 percent off designer prices, and for its fleeting inventory, most of which was made up of one-of-a-kind items that disappeared as soon as they hit the sales floor.

The Boston store, the original location and the chain's flagship store, was known for its frenetic sales, when people lined up for hours just to be let in the doors. By 1990, 15,000–20,000 customers lined the aisles of Filene's Basement's Boston store each day, rummaging through racks, tables, and counters of discounted merchandise ("Filene's Basement" 2011). Merchandise went quickly: in 1992, brides participating in Filene's Basement's bridal sale cleared racks of wedding dresses within 37 seconds of the store's opening (Foxman and Dobscha 1997). Norma explained what it was like: "It was crazy. I would leave Monday mornings free because there were sales. Huge line-ups. We were held back with a rope. A security guard was always present. When the bell rang, it was everyone for herself. The doors were held open for us and we would feast on the bargains. The bargains were phenomenal." Shopping was a contact sport at Filene's Basement and customers were ruthless in their quest to grab the most desirable merchandise. "The women would go absolutely crazy. One day, this woman hit me. I was in line for a markdown. I got there first. She said, 'You can't have it.' I called security and they said, 'We didn't see anything.' You were taking your life in your own hands when you shopped there. It was brutal. Another time a woman was trampled. Customers just walked by. I ran to the manager and told him. I thought he would care. But he said, 'There are people who look after that.' I was surprised." As Norma's recollections report, employees often looked the other way when customers misbehaved.

As Filene's Basement opened new stores in the Boston suburbs and expanded to other cities, the company began to split designer shipments so that each store received only a few items to sell. This made shopping more difficult and sent consumers running to different stores to find what they needed to make a set. Norma explained, "It's crazy, you have no idea. You don't know what you have. It's always discombobulated . . . we would go from store to store. I'd buy pants in one store, a matching jacket in another. I'd get one wine glass in Boston, then run to Framingham to see if I could make a matching set. Every purchase is a gamble; everything is hunt and peck."

The first fitting rooms were installed in 1991; prior to that time, customers stripped down in the aisles to try on the merchandise. Norma and her friends wore leotards so that they could easily try on clothing or grabbed their approximate size and then tried the merchandise on at home, returning unwanted items to the store to receive merchandise credit. Norma explained, "Returns are a big part of the experience. There are no fitting rooms. You can't inspect anything. Merchandise gets bounced around. It's crazy. You cannot think in the Basement. You charge it all up – then try it on at home." Returns were costly in both time and money, as customers had to pay for parking and then stand in long lines waiting for customer service to process them. A bartering system evolved among customers. "We'd call each other later and filter discards amongst ourselves. There was a big coat sale. This beautiful white coat was $29.99. My mother saw a woman with it and said to her, 'My daughter would love that coat. Can I have your name and number so that I can call you and see if you want to keep it? If you decide that you don't want it, you can call me.'"

When questioned by us about her excessive returns, Norma laughed. Those were not only justifiable in her mind, but appropriate to the shopping culture that Filene's Basement had cultivated. "That's ridiculous. Everyone returns stuff. That's just what you do." Filene's Basement's 4P marketing decisions – product strategy, pricing strategy, place strategy, and promotion strategy – were largely to blame for Norma's behavior. Filene's Basement's chaotic store design, one-off and incomplete product assortments, limited-time sales, and automatic discounted pricing contributed to creating a shopper culture in which customers were frantic to buy in the moment, leading many to regret their purchases and return unwanted items later. With this perspective, Norma appears largely innocent of blame for her chronic returns, and becomes a more sympathetic character – a shopper doing the best she can within a broken system that encourages bad behavior.

There are many examples of company behaviors that unwittingly encourage "bad customer behavior." In the telecommunications sector, programs offering customers incentives to change providers spark chains of switching behavior to take advantage of the free cash. In retail, frequent sales train customers to wait if they want to buy at discount prices. Promotional deals for data-hungry smart phones encourage users to liberally surf and download, creating system overloads.

A golden customer is recognized

Norma did not fixate on a revenue/cost equation to define her brand relationship. She looked to the relational signals the firm was sending her, and the signals she provided in return. Early on in her relationship, the staff acknowledged Norma as one of "The Regulars" and most employees addressed her by name. The Regulars were a group of women who shopped frequently, purchased in great quantities, and were first in line for every sale. The Regulars met for brunch each Sunday before embarking on their weekly shopping ritual, shopping together and helping each other with their purchases. When a new store location opened, the Regulars were the first ones to arrive and soon became a store's most prodigious shoppers.

The Regulars were granted special privileges that other customers did not enjoy. Norma recounted the many times employees had bent rules for her, granting pre-sale prices and sale extensions, or peeks at just-in merchandise that had yet to reach the floor. "The fur buyer called me about a silver fox. They held things for me even though they weren't really supposed to." In the days when there were no dressing rooms, Norma and her friends were invited into the staff's private offices to try on the clothing. "Mr. X, the store manager, used to say 'sure' to whatever I asked. They did it for some customers. But not for everyone."

Importantly, these practices created a history of interactions in the life of Norma's relationship that served as clues to the type of relationship the store wished to establish with her. Norma understood the official rules of the standard Filene's Basement customer relationship; she was savvy enough to understand the protocols regarding sale prices, sale notification, and product returns, but she was trained over time to understand that these rules did not apply to her. New rules and norms for behavior were forged during interactions, as employees pointed the way to a deeper, more special relationship. The company was an enabler for Norma's rule breaking.

No matter how she looked at it, Norma was singled out as a best customer. She was invited, through the firm's own CRM efforts, to engage in a deep, close, and highly personalized relationship. For more than thirty years, Filene's Basement differentiated Norma from the masses. Norma was special, appreciated, even loved. The appreciation was mutual. Norma told us about her interactions with Filene's Basement employees over the years, people who she regarded not as service representatives, but as close, personal friends. When she walked into a Filene's Basement, she felt like she was coming home. "We were like family," she explained. "I brought presents when they got married or had babies. They showed me their family pictures. There was a lot of camaraderie."

Transforming Gold into Platinum

Over the years, Norma's relationship with Filene's Basement deepened. With pride, Norma recalled the special invitations she enjoyed as a member of the Filene's Basement Insiders Club, a group that rewarded the company's best customers with special offers and events. It was here that she mingled with store managers and executives from the corporate headquarters who always seemed so pleased to hear her ideas for improving the store.

Norma happily performed the extra-role behaviors characteristic of the deepest relationships, recognizing the special favors she was receiving from employees. "It's a two-way street. When they do good, you want to go back and give them a favor in return. Like, if they call me before sales, I give them a gift for their baby." She brought the staff Italian pastries after Christmas, "so when everyone returned stuff, they would not feel so bad. At least they knew some customers appreciated them." She took a stock girl diagnosed with cancer out to dinner. "It was not a big deal. Just a nice thing. She was walking home from work one day and was hit by a car and killed. I called Mr. Z (the CEO). 'You better do something,' I said. So they had a memorial service for her. I did a little bit of pushing to make sure they knew it was important." She also pushed to help employees get promoted, writing letters to senior management to express her thoughts about their merit. When a Filene's Basement executive passed away, she attended his funeral and made sure other customers accompanied her. She recognized the special treatment accorded her by Filene's Basement and reciprocated with her own special gifts.

Norma also reciprocated by working hard to maintain her good-customer status. She went outside her role as a customer to serve as a collaborative teammate. She offered floor employees product information for new lines, suggested merchandising tips to move inventory faster, and caught labeling mistakes on the floor. "They were selling Barovier glass. I printed a bunch of information about the brand and the product so that the salesgirls would know what they were selling. I helped them." The employees were grateful for her assistance and often sought her advice on new merchandise. "I showed them how the tags they used ruined the leather gloves and the silk scarves. Now they put scarves in brass rings instead of tagging them." Norma envisioned herself not just as a customer, but as a partner to Filene's Basement and actively looked for ways to improve the firm's performance.

When Filene's Basement declared bankruptcy in 2009, Norma was shocked to hear the news. Her first response was sympathy for the employees. Then she realized what the bankruptcy might mean for her and grieved for the loss of her partner and community. "I first heard about the bankruptcy when I was chatting with M, the giftware buyer. She said, 'I want you to be the first to know.' When she told me, I came to tears. I started to cry. She started to cry. 'What's going to happen to your job, your pension?' I said. Why did I come to tears? Because I wouldn't have that store to shop in anymore. The community would be broken up."

Platinum turns to Lead

Things started to go downhill as Norma's expectations escalated in response to continued special treatment. Validated through the firm's reinforcement of her behaviors, Norma came to expect personalized recognition and attention from all employees all of the time. An evolving relationship norm developed in her mind: "I will be honored with benefits and information not available to other customers; normal rules and policies do not apply to me." However, not all employees were on board with her definition of their relationship. "I came in for the

Ferragamo sale and the size 7½ shoes were not out on the floor. I asked the girl to go get them and she refused and told me to come back later. I said, 'I am here now. Go down to the stock room and get my size 7½ Ferragamos.' The shoes were just sitting there in the stockroom." As the company grew larger, new employees were not familiar with Norma and failed to give her the specialized attention she thought she deserved.

The more the company acknowledged Norma's status via CRM outreach, the more she came to expect. And, as the effort needed to serve Norma increased, her direct profit contribution declined. She recounted a story about how she was able to get her way through leveraging her relationships with various employees. "They were having a sale – Waterford lamps were 25 percent off. I bought two. Six months later, the sale was over, but there was one lamp still there. The tag said $375. But it read $210 when the tag was scanned. There was a 25 percent store-wide sale going on, so I told the cashier that I should get 25 percent off of the $210 price. She said, 'No, I can only give you $375 minus 25 percent.' So I bought it and later asked the store manager about reducing the price for me, and he said, 'Oh no, I can't give it to you for the lower price.' But then B (a salesclerk) gave it to me for $210 minus 25 percent and said, 'Don't tell the manager.' I kissed her." As ownership of the company transferred from Federated Department Stores to various retail holding companies over the years, profit margins tightened, corporate strategy evolved, and managers were under pressure to perform, making it more difficult for them to accommodate Norma's special requests.

Just as the company's CRM had helped build Norma into a Platinum-level customer, it also slowly transformed her into a high-maintenance Lead customer whose value was eroded by her high cost-to-serve. The first clue came when she was not invited to join the Insiders Club for the Newton store, after being a member at the Boston store: "I always felt a little excluded in Newton. They had an Insiders Club and no one ever told me. It was five minutes from my house. I felt very bad when I found out. We had spent so much money. I felt I should have been invited." Norma was confused and hurt that her strong relationship with the company was not recognized, but rebounded when a new manager at the store later invited her to join the club when he heard she was upset.

These events served as critical incidents in the life of Norma's relationship with Filene's Basement. While all behaviors in a consumer–brand relationship constitute signals and hence hold the potential to change one partner's understanding of the relationship, research has shown that certain behaviors are more diagnostic of the type of relationship being executed and its rules. Signals that possess a higher probability of precipitating revisions to the relationship include actions taken by partners in response to situations when the immediate interests of one partner are at odds with the collective interests of the relationship (Wieselquist et al. 1999). Filene's Basement employees' resolution of these two incidents reinforced Norma's belief that she was a Platinum customer, entitled to respect, special treatment, and her own set of rules. When the relationship was put to the test, Norma's needs won out over the company's.

Then, suddenly, overworked employees started rejecting her merchandising help, telling her to go directly to headquarters executives with her ideas. "I bought a necklace in an ugly box. The necklace cost $1,499. I drove to a jewelry store in Boston to get a nice box so that I could give it as a gift. I showed Mr. X (the store manager) and asked him, 'Why don't you put the necklaces in nice boxes like this?' He said, 'Talk to Mr. Y (the CFO). Don't talk to me.' I also told him that I didn't like the newspaper ad coming out the same day as the sale because then you couldn't plan in advance. I got the same response: 'Talk to Mr. Y. Don't talk to me.'" Norma was puzzled by his response. He had always been open to her suggestions in the past. "He took it as a complaint I guess. I was just making a suggestion . . . trying to make it a better store, a better place to shop. I just wanted a better store for us all to shop in. I thought I was doing them a favor. I thought I was being helpful." What Norma failed to realize was that Filene's Basement's new holding company was centralizing decision-making at corporate headquarters, stripping managers and floor employees of their decision-making power and leaving them discouraged and disillusioned.

Leveraging her relationships formed through the Insiders Club, Norma decided to go to the corporate headquarters to air her ideas. "I had to speak to the top. I arrived unannounced on a Friday. There was no one there. Then I went in another time. Mr. Z (the CEO) would not see me. About two weeks later, I called him again. His secretary practically hung up on me. When I finally reached the CFO, he said, 'You have all these complaints. Maybe you don't need to shop here.'"

Following her visit to headquarters, Norma received a telephone call and a letter informing her that she was no longer welcome to shop at Filene's Basement owing to her excessive levels of returns and complaints. She was devastated. How could a company fire its "best customer"?

A relationship in ruins

Norma's story indicates that company actions taken in the name of CRM contributed to the creation and subsequent demise of a certain type of relationship unique to the commercial world: *the best customer*. The best customer is cultivated and recognized by company employees as special and receives increasing rewards. But a "trap" of sorts presents itself in managing best customers. These company behaviors start a downward spiral which paradoxically turns a Platinum-level customer into a Lead-level customer as the expectations of best customers escalate over time. CRM programs which continuously recognize and reward customers transform best customers from highly profitable, loyal customers into high-maintenance customers whose value stemming from their frequent purchasing is eroded by their increasing cost-to-serve.

How could a firm and its so-called "best customer" become so misaligned? Norma continues to struggle to understand what happened. She pins the blame on the store's inability to track her purchase history. "I honestly don't think they knew how much I spent. I honestly don't think they knew I was such a good customer." Unlike Filene's Basement, she recognizes the intangible value her brand evangelism brought to the firm. Were excessive returns the culprit? Norma's reasoning rejects this idea as well: returns were part of the Filene's Basement shopping experience and everyone returned goods to the store. How about the chronic dissatisfaction and complaining that were mentioned in the letter that Filene's Basement sent? In her mind, Norma was not complaining: she was trying to collaboratively help build a better store and increase Filene's Basement's profitability. She struggles to understand how the stores' employees did not appreciate that distinction.

In the final analysis, Norma's lack of profitability was mutually determined, and Filene's Basement failed in its relationship oversight role. Management failed to see how its own actions fed a downward spiral in the relationship. They neglected to play by the rules of the evolved relationship that they themselves helped to create. Trapped in an untenable situation, Filene's Basement failed to renegotiate their relationship with Norma. They fired her instead of working to turn things around.

Can bad customer relationships be saved?

Ironically, firing customers is often a case of blaming the victim: many managers remain unaware of their own roles in creating unprofitable customers. Managers who execute CRM programs without a deep understanding of the meaning of relationships and a process understanding of their dynamic evolution embark on a dangerous path. Before firing a customer, managers should take a hard look at their own CRM practices to see whether they bear or share responsibility for creating the problem. Is the firm punishing customers for problems that managers themselves enabled? Has the blind and optimistic application of CRM programs ignored relationship realities?

Below, we outline a series of practices that managers must consider in analyzing how actions taken in the name of CRM may be creating problems in the customer portfolio.

Attraction and acquisition stage

Relationship problems can occur at many stages of a relationship, but most can be traced back to the relationship's earliest days. The time during which a company works to attract and acquire a new customer is rife with opportunities to invite bad customers into the customer portfolio. Managers need to take a hard look at their customer acquisition practices to determine whether they are targeting the wrong customers with their marketing outreach. Smart companies know that CRM begins *before* someone becomes a customer. Getting to know prospects before signing them on as customers helps companies like Progressive Insurance and HubSpot maximize the value of their customer portfolios. Progressive Insurance uses its comparison quotes system to weed out unprofitable drivers before they enroll as customers. Progressive provides prospective customers with their own price quote and a comparison price quote from three of their competitors. Progressive prices its own quotes below the competition for customers that it wants, but raises them above those of its competitors for customers whose profiles indicate that they may be unprofitable, thereby driving bad customers towards its competitors (Frei 2004). HubSpot, a company that sells software products that help companies execute inbound marketing programs, takes time upfront to analyze the potential of prospective customers before investing in a relationship with them. Rather than firing customers in whom the firm has invested significant financial and human resources, HubSpot weeds out 50 percent of the people who come looking for its product, firing prospects rather than customers, based on its knowledge of which types of customers will most benefit from the company's product and therefore remain as customers the longest (Steenburgh, Avery, and Dahod 2010).

Managers should also look at the marketing communications that are used to attract customers to the firm. Some messages attract the wrong kinds of customers. For example, price-based advertising will attract price-sensitive customers who are likely to switch to competitive brands when a better price deal can be had. Other messages transform good prospects into bad customers. Programs like Tweeter's automatic price protection guarantee taught customers to value the electronic retailer's low prices, rather than its enhanced service and support.

Relationship exploration and templating stage

The first few interactions between a company and a new customer are critically important for setting the stage for their relationship. It is during this phase that relationship rules and norms are formed that will guide the customer's behavior and create expectations for relating with the company. It is also during this time period that the customer is oriented into the culture that defines the company's relationships with its customers at large. Managers must examine what explicit rules are specified during these early interactions and what implicit rules organically emerge as the customer interacts with employees and with other customers. Dissecting bad customer behaviors and tracing them back to their origins offers the opportunity for managers to discern whether any employee actions contribute to the creation of rules or norms that engender unprofitable relationships. For example, Best Buy realized that its return policies were creating opportunities for customers to misbehave; customers were purchasing products at full price, returning them to a store, and then returning to repurchase these same products at lower, used-product prices. By rewiring its returns process and sending returned goods to faraway stores, Best Buy was able to nip this bad behavior in the bud (McWilliams 2004).

The rules that emerge during the early interactions begin to suggest the type of relationship at play. Consumer–brand relationships come in many shapes and forms and each type of relationship is governed by a unique set of rules. Thus, managers need to think about what kind of relationships they would like to have with their customers and then work backwards to determine what kind of rules need to be established to seed those relationship types that can be profitable for the firm.

Critical incidents and relational renegotiation

Opportunities for renegotiating relationships arise during each interaction between the company and its customer. Interactions serve to either buttress the existing relationship when both parties play by the existing rules, or adjust its path towards the operative goals of either party when one party deviates from the rules. Customers often test their relationships with companies by behaving in ways that break the rules. For example, a frequent patron of a restaurant may ask the hostess to seat him/her ahead of other patrons who are waiting for a table, or a frequent customer of a grocery store may ask to purchase more than the allowed minimum of a sale item. It is during these times when the company must assess the state of the current relationship and whether there is a strategic desire on the part of the company to deviate from the existing relational path. Importantly, in the moment, managers must look forward into the future to ascertain how its response will affect the ongoing profitability of the customer.

Companies should also keep a keen eye out for opportunities to intervene to change the trajectory of relationships that are veering astray. HubSpot watches to see whether customers are receiving value from the use of the product by closely monitoring their online activity. Customers are given a Customer Happiness Index score based on the frequency and depth of their usage, and those with scores that drop below a certain level are targeted for relational intervention. A customer service representative contacts the customer, offering assistance, additional training, or resources to get the relationship back on track.

Another critical intervention comes at the point of the decision to fire a customer. Before firing a customer, managers must look inward and carefully analyze how their own actions are contributing to the relationship state. Table 16.1 contains a checklist of questions managers can ask to illuminate their role as a relational partner. It is through this understanding that relationships can be properly assessed, renegotiated as needed, and set along a profitable path for both the customer and the company.

Today, Norma still grieves for her relationship with Filene's Basement. "I will never go in, never ever. No . . . definitely not. Well, maybe. It breaks my heart.

TABLE 16.1 Illuminating the company's role as a relational partner

Attraction and acquisition stage	• Did we do something to attract the wrong kind of customers? Do we need to adjust our market segmentation and targeting strategies? • Are we promising too much in our customer acquisition marketing communications? Do we need to adjust our promotion strategies? • Are we taking any customer we can get or are we discriminating about who we hire as a customer? • Are we analyzing our prospects before they become customers and weeding out those that are likely to become unprofitable?
Relationship exploration stage	• How are we orienting our customers to our relationship? • What explicit rules are we communicating to new customers? • What implicit rules are organically developing? • What are customers learning about how to relate to us from our customer culture? • What expectations are we building in new customers? • How might our explicit rules contribute to the creation of bad customer behaviors?
Relationship definition stage	• What type of relationship do our emerging rules suggest? What are the rules of that type of relationship? • Does our interpretation of the relationship match the customer's? Do we share a common vision for who we are together?
Critical incidents	• What important relational tests occurred and did we pass or fail them? How might we have unknowingly escalated a relationship that was unprofitable to the firm? • How did we test the relationship to make sure it was healthy?
Ongoing renegotiation	• How did our ongoing interactions cement or change the relationship? • Where did things go wrong and how might we have contributed to them? • Did we actively and explicitly work to renegotiate terms that were detrimental to the firm? • Did we try to fix our relationship when it went off track?

Is there anything they could do to bring me back? Yeah! Just let me in. I want to go back. I really miss the store. I have fantasies. My little heart starts to palpitate." Norma is open to relationship renegotiation, but Filene's Basement still isn't listening.

References

Conlon, G. (2010) "When is it OK to Fire your Customers?" *Think Customers: The 1 to 1 Blog,* January 8, 2010.

"Filene's Basement: Our Story". Online. Available at *www.filenesbasement.com* (accessed January 31, 2011).

Fournier, S. and Avery, J. (2011) "Putting the 'R' Back into CRM", *MIT Sloan Management Review*, 52 (3): 63–72.

Foxman, E. and Dobscha, S. (1997) "The Filene's Basement Bridal Sale: A Content Analysis of Store-Authored and Media-Authored Communications about a Retail Event", *Conference of the Academy of Marketing Science*, June 1997, 321–6.

Frei, F.X. (2004) "Innovation at Progressive: Pay-as-You-Go Insurance", Harvard Business School Teaching Case, 9-602-175.

Glagowski, E. (2006) "eBay Fires Customers", *Think Customers: The 1 to 1 Blog* (accessed August 29, 2006).

Levitt, T. (1960) "Marketing Myopia", *Harvard Business Review*, 38 (7/8): 138–49.

McWilliams, G. (2004) "Minding the Store: Analyzing Customers, Best Buy Decides not All are Welcome: Retailer Aims to Outsmart Dogged Bargain-Hunters and Coddle Big Spenders", *Wall Street Journal*, November 8, 2004: A.1.

Mertz, S.A. (2009) "Dataquest Insight: CRM Software Market Share Analysis, Worldwide, 2008", *Gartner Inc.* available at www.gartner.com/DisplayDocument?id=1059116 (accessed July 6, 2009).

Mittal, V., Sarkees, M. and Murshed, F. (2008) "The Right Way to Manage Unprofitable Customers", *Harvard Business Review*, 86 (4): 95–102.

MSN Money (2007) "Sprint to 1000 Customers: You're Fired", *MSN Money*, available at http://articles.moneycentral.msn.com/Investing/Extra/SprintDumpingCustomers. aspx (accessed July 9, 2007).

Peppers, D. and Rogers, M. (1993) *The One to One Future*, New York: Currency Doubleday.

—— (2004) *Managing Customer Relationships: a strategic framework*, New York: John Wiley and Sons.

Pilon, M. (2009) "Amex Encourages Cardholders to Leave", *Wall Street Journal*, February 25, 2009.

Price, C. (2008) "Sprint Follow Industry to Terminate Customers over Roaming, Data", *PhoneNews.co*, available at www.phonenews.com/sprint-follows-industry-to-terminate-customers-over-roaming-data-3468/ (accessed May 19, 2008).

Shah, D., Rust, R.T., Parasuraman, A., Staelin, R. and Day, G.S. (2006) "The Path to Customer Centricity", *Journal of Service Research*, 9 (2): 113–24.

Steenburgh, T., Avery, J. and Dahod, N. (2010) "Hubspot: Inbound Marketing and Web 2.0", Harvard Business School Teaching Case, 9-509-049.

Taylor, W.C. (2005) "Rebels with a Cause, and a Business Plan", *New York Times*, January 2, 2005.

Walton, S. and Huey, J. (1993) *Sam Walton: made in America*, New York: Random House.

Wieselquist, J., Rusbult, C.E., Foster, C.A. and Agnew, C.R. (1999) "Commitment, Pro-Relationship Behavior and Trust in Close Relationships", *Journal of Personality and Social Psychology*, 77 (5): 942–66.

Zeithaml, V.A., Rust, R.T. and Lemon, K.N. (2001) "The Customer Pyramid: Creating and Serving Profitable Customers", *California Management Review*, 43 (4): 118–42.

17

ON THE COMPLEXITY OF MANAGING BRAND RELATIONSHIPS IN A SOCIAL MEDIA WORLD

Thomas W. Leigh and Scott A. Thompson

> The marketer in peer-to-peer environments is an interloper, more talked about than talking. At best, its role is to provoke conversations among consumers, and at worst, it becomes the enemy, attacked with invective or parody
>
> (Deighton and Kornfield 2009)

Introduction

Traditionally, the marketer has enacted a brand curator role, literally seeking to control brand management processes with respect to designing, promoting, and preserving the brand to target customers and users over its life cycle. Accordingly, the brand marketer's role has been examined from a perspective of creating and managing consumer brand meaning, or its cognitive brand architecture (Aaker 1997; Keller 1993). Recently, this role has been expanded to include managing brands metaphorically in terms of their brand personalities (Aaker 1997) and consumer–brand relationships (Fournier 1998). In these recent conceptual views, the marketer is the brand authority who designs and manages the brand's meaning, value proposition, and marketing campaign. The marketer is assumed to author the brand's narrative and manage its authenticity and trajectory over time. However, these perspectives are now recognized as limiting in a world of large-scale social media, fan networks, brand communities, and oppositional groups that use brands as foils in their cause-related agendas (Fournier and Lee 2009; Schau, Muñiz, and Arnould 2009).

An appreciation of the opportunities and perils created by these environments involves the recognition that traditional marketing, often referred to as outbound, "appointment," or "interrupt" marketing, has lost effectiveness and efficiency. Some of this productivity loss is due to active consumer efforts to enhance their

TV experiences, better control their time, and eliminate ad intrusions. Consumers joined no call lists, used caller ID, and skipped ads using VCR tools.

However, Web 2.0 media, including search (Google), smartphones (Apple), social media (Facebook), blogs (Twitter), peer-to-peer sites (YouTube), online consumer communities (slickdeals.com), online and offline brand communities (Nutella, Harley-Davidson), and advocacy groups (Fatwallet.com, Greenpeace), have enabled the consumer to be online ubiquitously. Hence, the challenge is for marketers to reframe their role to fit socially mediated markets: to better understand the role players, value creation practices, and social identity dynamics for a social media world designed to enable people to participate in peer-to-peer conversations, social networks, and interest-based communities, rather than commerce.

Web 2.0 media empower consumers to be more active in managing their consumer experiences and social exchanges. Marketers, in a sense, are Web 2.0 party crashers who found that their efforts to join were considered intrusive and inauthentic (Fournier and Avery 2011). Hence, marketers need to learn how to behave more appropriately in a world where consumers more actively manage their experiences using internet searches and content, online promotions, and shared online opinions and complaints. Simply viewed, this would mean that the marketer needs to learn how to work in two-way networks where the consumer is likely to have access to countervailing information to that provided by the marketer.

However, the marketer's dilemma is more complex than simply adopting and practicing inbound marketing practices. Web 2.0 media embed consumers and marketers in social networks, webs, and communities that collectively create value in ways that are complex and evolutionary. Brand and social identities are constructed among the members of a social network, collective, or community as they manage their everyday lives. Consumers may influence the brand's identity by merely recommending it to a set of peers online. Hence, conversations are multi-way, not simply two-way.

Social network members may also seek social status by openly displaying online their consumption practices, product category expertise, and enthusiasm or undying love for a brand. In enthusiast social networks, true believers are distinguished from "fan-boys" and "poseurs." Similarly, brand communities often define themselves as in-groups and out-groups that battle over the merits of specific brands (Apple vs. RIM). Finally, advocacy groups may seek to promote their own agendas by using as a social tool a brand that has cultural resonance: anti-obesity groups promote healthy eating, while lobbying against McDonald's; political activists such as Greenpeace attack the BP brand; and media commentators, comedians, and even self-promoting brand terrorists may employ brands in their "acts."

In light of these new realities, recent commentators have suggested that the marketer is no longer able to control the brand narrative, has been stripped of the power to persuade, and may need to cede control of the brand to consumers, collectives, or the broader culture (Deighton and Kornfield 2009). In fact, Schau *et al.* (2009) assert that consumer–marketer co-creation is the key to value creation in brand communities. Thus, it is not a far stretch to agree with these academics that "a revolution in marketing thought and practice" (Schau *et al.* 2009, p. 30) is needed as marketing "grapples with the question of how to work with social media" (Deighton and Kornfield 2009, p. 5).

Our contention is that defining the marketer's role is not as simple as merely ceding the brand narrative to the social web or collective. The marketer clearly has a stake in both the brand and the social milieu that surrounds it. As Fournier and Lee (2009) note, there are many roles that the marketer might adopt in a social collective. And brand consumers and stakeholders may or may not have the best interests of the brand at heart. Hence, the marketer's decision as to whether or not to employ traditional marketing practices or participate in brand-relevant social networks, collectives, and communities requires an analysis of: how consumers individually gather and employ information in making brand-related choices; how consumers employ social media information in their consumption decisions; the role of social media in consumers' management of their social relationships and social identity projects; and the nature of the value creation practices that govern consumers' social web actions and participation in brand-related groups and communities.

Our purpose is twofold. First, we present a conceptual typology to guide our thinking about the nature of the consumer's role and involvement with brands across (1) three brand-consumer contexts: consumers as brand message receivers, peer-to-peer conversational networks, and casual social networks; and (2) three brand–consumer collective contexts: enthusiast social networks, brand communities, and select brand clubs. This framework incorporates the distinctions among (1) traditional brand consumption, with its emphasis on outbound marketing to consumers, versus conversational brands, with the emphasis on Web 2.0 inbound search and community (Fournier and Lee 2009); (2) mere information collection versus meaningful interpretation, and mere accessibility versus the power to establish social identities, in marketplace dialogues (Deighton and Kornfeld 2009); and (3) consumer or brand collectives that may seek to co-create value by sharing practices with marketers versus those that may seek to build their own personal or group agendas by opposing the brand or its consumer loyalists (Schau *et al.* 2009). We illustrate the typology by anecdotal references to a set of brands, collectives, and advocacy groups.

Second, given the insights from this brand-consumer typology, we will revisit the issue of defining the brand marketer's role and practices. We will discuss a typology of marketer practices that seeks to identify and describe marketer-relevant characteristics and practices to fit each of the brand-consumer contexts, including appropriate marketer roles and practices for traditional authority brands; conversational brands emphasizing opinion leaders; casual social networks emphasizing multi-way dialogues; enthusiast social networks emphasizing product category loyalty and status; brand communities emphasizing social collective values and practices; and select brand clubs emphasizing collective capital and institutional membership. We note the need for theoretical interpretations of experientially emerging marketer practices, as well as some controversy over the relative roles of consumers and marketers.

Conceptual framework

To specify our brand-consumer typology, we identified seven consumer-relevant characteristics as a basis for distinguishing how the consumers learn about the brands, relate to brands, and the degree to which the consumer is involved in social media and groups for either personal or brand-related issues. We drew on a variety of sources to identify these core characteristics (Deighton and Kornfield 2009; Kozinets *et al.* 2010; McAlexander, Schouten, and Koenig 2002; Muñiz and O'Guinn 2001; Schau *et al.* 2009; Thompson and Sinha 2008). We also drew on our own personal experiences as consumers, social network participants, and brand community members. Our brand-consumer typology is presented in two exhibits: (1) the brand-consumer contexts that emphasize individual consumers operating with the marketer or in simple conversational or casual social networks (see Table 17.1); and (2) the brand-consumer collective contexts, including enthusiast social networks, brand communities, and select brand clubs (see Table 17.2). We will first conceptually describe the seven consumer-relevant characteristics we selected to define the typology. We will then discuss each of the six brand-consumer contexts in terms of these seven attributes and illustrate each anecdotally.

The first consumer-relevant characteristic is the *consumer unit of analysis*, or whether or not the consumer is operating as an individual, a participant in a two-way or multi-way dialogue, or a member of a collective, community, or club. Consumers may be primarily involved with brands as *individuals*, either relying on the brand marketer for information about the brand or integrating marketer-provided information with direct personal experiences to inform brand value, choices, and loyalty. Consumers may also participate in *peer-to-peer personal exchanges* about the brand, sending or receiving word-of-mouth (WOM) information from friends or opinion leaders about a brand in a variety of media formats. Consumers may participate in *casual social networks* such as Facebook that enable the posting of personal information and opinions to many friends simultaneously. Consumers may also participate in *product category enthusiast collectives* that enable social exchanges among serious product or brand users. Finally, they may participate in commitment-based *brand communities* or institutionalized *select social clubs*.

A second consumer-relevant characteristic is the *consumer role in brand-related communications*. In the three brand-consumer contexts, this roughly corresponds to

TABLE 17.1 Brand-consumer contexts

Consumer Relevant Characteristics	Consumer As Brand Message Receiver	Peer-to-Peer Conversational Networks	Casual Social Networks
1. Consumer Unit of Analysis	Individuals as Consumers	Consumers in Peer-to-Peer Webs	Consumers in Social Networks
2. Consumer Role in Brand Related Practices Communications	Outbound Message Receiver or Target WOM Recommender	Outbound Message Receiver or Target WOM Buzz Recommender	In-Bound Information or Entertainment Seeker/User Outbound WOM Provider
3. Consumer's Self-Identification with Brand	Brand Loyalty or Consumer–Brand Relationship	Brand Loyalty or Consumer–Brand Relationship	Brand is Self-Identity and Socially Relevant
4. Consumer Social Interaction & Commitments	Passive Badge Value In Everyday Life (One–way communication)	Active Self-Identifier in Inter-Personal Conversations (Two-way Conversations)	Active Party in casual social web dialogue or Entertainment (Use Experiences; Self-Identity or Expertise)(Multi-way exchanges)
5. Consumer Benefits Motivating Behavior	Functional Value; Brand Image Value	Functional Value; Brand User Status & Expertise	Brand Use Status and Self Image on Web
6. Consumer Capital Resources Accumulated through Brand and Social Participation	• Economic Capital (Personal Use) • Human Capital (Product/Brand Expertise)	• Economic Capital • Brand–Consumer Relationship Capital • Interpersonal Badge & Social Capital	• Human Capital (User Expertise and Experiences) • Social Status and Friend-Web Capital • Economic Capital (Personal Use)
7. Consumer Role in Brand-Related Value Creation Practices	Passive and Limited: Receiver of Brand Information & Brand User	• Passive Receiver of Brand Information; Active Recommender or Critic of Brands to Peers	• Active Searchers for Product or Brand; Active Users of Social Networks for Non-Brand Activities; Active Promoter of Self to Friends

TABLE 17.2 Brand–consumer collective contexts

Consumer Relevant Characteristics	Enthusiast Social Networks	Brand Communities	Select Brand Clubs
1. Primary Consumer Unit of Analysis	• Product Category Enthusiast Networks	• Consumers in Brand Collectives or Communities	Consumers as Formal Members & Leaders in Brand Institution
2. Consumer Role in Brand Related Communications	• In-Bound Searcher or Outbound Promoter of Product Category or Preferred Brand	• Passionate Brand Believer, User, and Proselytizer/Protector	Brand Consumption and Preservation is Rationale for Club Membership and Work
3. Consumer's Self-Identification with the Brand	• Active Player in Status Hierarchy for Product Category (May Trump Brand Identity Issues)	• BC is Identity Relevant in an In-Group vs. Out-Group Sense	Select Club is Identity Relevant & Demands Member Investments
4. Consumer Social Interaction & Commitments	• User Experience as Deep, Revealing in Identity-Based Social Dialogues (Multi-Way Exchanges)	• Brand provides Social Meaning for In-group Roles and Experiences (Individual-in-Group)	Select Club is Brand Authenticity & Formal Network Event Manager
5. Consumer Benefits Motivating Brand + Social Behavior	• Product or Brand Use is Instrumental to Social Network Role & Status (Expert, Poseur)	• Brand Community is Instrumental to the Member for Intellectual & Social Commitment	Select Club is Consumption and Leadership Experience Provider

6. Consumer Capital Resources Accumulated through Brand & Social Participation	• Human Capital (Expertise) • Social Status in Web • Economic Capital (Expertise Buyer/Seller)	• Human Capital (Expertise) • Symbolic Status & Recognition • Cultural Capital • Economic Capital Social Capital; Support; Help	• Concentrated Collective Capital (Human; Social; Cultural; Economic) • Institutional Role & Status as Brand Curator & Marketer • Partner with Marketers in Co-creating Brand Meaning
7. Consumer Role in Brand-Related Value Creation Practices	• Competitive and Active Player in Fan Nets • Active WOM Recommender • Technology Beta Tester Role in NPD • New Product Adviser to Firms • Expertise Builders & Displayers • Altruistic Social Contributors • Severe Critic of Poseurs	• Active Player in BC Practices • BC Outbound Marketing Impression Manager • Status Competition: In-Group and Out-Group Roles • Brand Preservation & Authenticity Role • Shared Sense of Responsibility for Preservng the BC	• Active Club Member and Leader • Defining Shared Tasks & Practices • Protect Brand & Brand Heritage in Use • Formalize Club as Brand Marketer • Define Authentic or Acceptable Club Brand Practices

the recent distinction between outbound and inbound, or Web 2.0, marketing. In the former, the consumer is considered to be the passive receiver of brand-related messages, or possibly a WOM recommender. In the latter, the consumer is considered to be an active information seeker on brands that are personally relevant and valuable. In addition, this casual networker may be an active seeker of entertaining content or activities who may be attracted to a brand through Web 2.0 social networks and may actively share worthwhile content in their friendship network.

In the three brand-consumer collective contexts, the consumer is actively interested in receiving or searching for product or brand content from a variety of sources. In enthusiast social networks, this information is likely to be specifically focused on product category attributes, benefits, and performance. Enthusiasts are also likely to serve as active promoters of the product category (both preferred and non-preferred brands) to non-users. In brand communities and select clubs, the information sought is likely to be selectively focused on the communal brand. Information about other brands in the product category may be discounted, ignored, or disparaged. As true believers, community members are likely to proselytize on behalf of their brand community or select club.

The third consumer-relevant characteristic is the *consumer's self-identification with the brand*, or the relative degree to which the brand meaning is relevant to the consumer's self-identity. This aspect may include the individual consumer simply acquiring the brand for the personal meaning it has for the owner; having the consumer form a personal relationship with the brand (Fournier 1998); having the brand be self-identity and socially relevant in social networks; involving the consumer in an elite fan product category group and its status hierarchy; involving the consumer as an in-group member in a BC; or involving the consumer in a select brand club involving formal commitments to the brand and the club.

The fourth characteristic is *consumer social interactions and commitments*, or the nature and extent of the consumer's participation and involvement with the brand in individual or social contexts. In brand-consumer contexts, this could range from passive, one-way communications to others in everyday life (e.g. badge value); to active, two-way interpersonal conversations; to active participation in casual, multi-way social network dialogue or entertainment activities. The brand could be embedded in these one-way to multi-way communications in many ways, from mere access to information to complex interpretations about the brand, or its role in establishing self-identity or reputation in social dialogues (Deighton and Kornfield 2009). In brand-consumer collective contexts, this ranges from being an active player in a product category status hierarchy to being an active member in the brand community in-group or select club. Thus, in collectives, the social network may be more or less exclusive, as well as more demanding in the expectations and/or practices placed on members.

The fifth characteristic is the *consumer benefits that motivate their brand and social behavior*. Consumer benefits may range from the strictly functional value-in-use and brand image benefits to the individual consumer; to the consumer's status as a product or brand expert in interpersonal dialogues or network exchanges; to the fact that the product or brand use, experience, and knowledge may be fundamentally instrumental to the consumer's role and respect among the social collectives, communities, and clubs in which s/he participates.

The sixth characteristic is the *consumer capital resources collected* through individual involvement with the brand, social networks, and/or brand-consumer collectives. Four fundamental capital types have been identified in the sociological theory of practices in consumer and brand community contexts (Holt 1995; Schau *et al.* 2009). *Economic capital* involves the conversion of resources such as labor, expertise, property rights, or creative ideas into products and services that are, in turn, convertible into money (Bourdieu 1984, 1985). For example, a consumer who buys a branded classic car exchanges money for the objectified attributes embodied in the car's functionality-in-use and/or its social value due to its brand image. *Human capital* is the skills or expertise embodied in people that have been acquired through their personal efforts in formal education or experiences (Ratchford 2001). People who are certified as possessing human capital are recognized and compensated for their relative effectiveness and efficiency in value creation.

Social capital is the actual or potential resources that are linked to the possession of a durable network of acquaintance and recognition (Bourdieu 1984, 1985). The value of an individual's human capital can be leveraged through social capital, or the degree to which the individual knows who to contact and how to operate in a social network (Bourdieu and Wacquant 1992). An individual's social participation may involve dyadic exchanges (Sirsi *et al.*, 1996), complex social webs linked by friendship and reciprocity (Iacobucci and Hopkins 1992), or collective social identity (Schouten and McAlexander 1995).

Cultural capital encompasses a variety of forms (Bourdieu 1984, 1985). It is objectified in the cultural characteristics or qualities that socially define a product or brand's value and rarity. It is also embodied in the practical knowledge, skills, and dispositions that define individual or group mastery and commitment to a collective's habitus, or social definition of what is culturally acceptable (versus vulgar). Identical product or brand experiences may be differentially interpreted by insiders (those in the know) and outsiders (those not in the know) (Holt 1998).

The final characteristic is the *consumer's role in brand-related value creation practices*. The role of value creation practices by both individual consumers in social contexts, such as a baseball game (Holt 1995), and brand communities such as an H-D Posse ride (McAlexander, Schouten, and Koenig 2002) has been recognized. In fact, Schau *et al.* (2009) identify a set of value creating practices that BCs offer their members. We first examine the consumer's role in value creating practices in brand-consumer contexts. For example, we note that the consumer's role may encompass being a passive message receiver and user; being passive as a message receiver, but active as an opinion leader; being an active searcher, user, and promoter of product, brand, or self-identity markers. Then, we examine value creation distinctions among enthusiast social networks, brand communities, and select brand clubs as consumers seek to fulfill entertainment, camaraderie, expertise, social status, and altruistic goals. Finally, we note that the value creating activities of BCs and select clubs generate significant costs that must be negotiated if the collective is to preserve its vitality.

Consumers as brand message receivers

In traditional brand marketing, the consumer unit of analysis is the individual brand decision-maker, acting on their own or for their family unit. The consumer's role is considered to be a receiver of outbound marketing messages. The consumer is generally presumed to follow some variant of a psychological hierarchical effects model of communications in which marketer messages sequentially drive brand awareness, knowledge, interest, intention, and purchase. This communications process is now referred to as outbound, or interrupt, marketing because it involves the placement of one-way marketer messages in media environments selected to reach desirable target market customers as they read, drive, listen, or entertain themselves. In particular for TV media, consumers were offered entertainment content by "appointment," in that they needed to be available at a given time in order to watch desired content. Ads are embedded in TV shows as the price of admission. Many consumers considered the ads intrusive and, when alternate technologies appeared, expressed their dissatisfaction by changing their viewing habits or skipping the ads.

In these mass media environments, marketers were considered to be the brand's authors and their goals involved designing a branded product that would be recognizable and memorable, offered differentiated functional or image value, and could be promoted aggressively to achieve extensive retail distribution, stimulate store visits, and control the consumer's in-store buying experience. While purchase and product use was often the end of the marketing cycle, considerable emphasis was placed on building and leveraging cognitive and affective brand loyalty (Keller 2003), brand personalities that link to customer identities (Aaker 1997), consumer–brand relationships (Fournier 1998), and customer loyalty (Kumar and Reinartz 2002) in the belief that these brand connections would transcend transactions over time and provide the brand a unique and sustainable market position. The consumer's role in brand-related practices was presumed to be limited to being a passive receiver of brand content and, as part of the brand or customer loyalty models, a valued walking badge or face-to-face WOM recommender.

The debate over the role of the marketer in a social media world is partially focused on how alternative social media have altered the consumer's role in this marketer model. However, several social media issues have arisen as a consequence of marketers' attempts to employ this traditional marketing paradigm in social media. The first is that many marketers merely attempted to translate their outbound marketing model to social media, trying to reach new consumers or desiring to cut their marketing costs to their current customer base (Fournier and Avery 2011). Hence, similar to the debate that ensued concerning whether firms were sincere or manipulative in applying CRM strategies, processes, and technologies (Fournier, Dobscha, and Mick 1998), there is rising debate about appropriate and sincere practices by marketers in the social media world.

The second issue is that marketers often fail to provide the brand value they promise to their customers. In the traditional marketing model, customer dissatisfaction and complaints tended to be handled individually by customers. Indeed, sophisticated marketers worried about getting customers to voice their complaints so they could be resolved in a timely fashion to maintain customer loyalty and avoid negative WOM. Only rarely were brand breakdowns (e.g. Tylenol) sufficiently newsworthy for mass media attention. With the social media model, marketers have found that a single dissatisfied customer can virally spread negative WOM. David Carroll's YouTube song about his experiences with United Airlines as he tried to get his broken guitar replaced resonated with consumers.

The third issue is that popular brands may become cultural icons that are employed as celebrity tools by advocacy groups, subcultures, or entertainers to advance their own agendas or burnish their images. Coca-Cola is a foil in the fight on obesity. And Starbucks and Dove had been widely parodied for their brand successes relative to their pollution, climate, and poverty externalities. Hence, the fact that consumers can now harness the power of social media for their own purposes creates an open source media world that may have significant consequences for brands and the firms that own them (Fournier and Avery 2011). Individual brand consumers, as well as a variety of external stakeholders, or groups with non-brand-relevant identities and agendas, may surprise the brand marketer with counter-strategy meanings and influence brand trajectories.

Peer-to-peer conversational networks

In peer-to-peer conversational networks, the unit of analysis is individual consumers operating in peer-to-peer relationships. As Kozinets *et al.* (2010) note, these peer relationships may involve organic, or unprompted, face-to-face conversations among consumers as a natural consequence of their consumption experiences and friendship. However, they may also involve marketer-prompted campaigns to influence opinion leaders for the product category to recommend a particular brand. Kozinets *et al.* (2010) call this the linear marketer influence model. In each of these approaches, the consumer is treated by the marketer as a passive receiver of brand-related content or, if credible as an opinion leader, an active WOM brand recommender. A key to this model is that consumers would be more likely to listen to the advice of a credible opinion leader than to the recommendations of a salesperson.

Individual consumers who recommend a brand to a peer are presumed in this model to do so out of brand loyalty or some form of consumer–brand relationship. Brands are eligible to be a focal topic in two-way interpersonal conversations because the brand has passed muster in their shared consumption projects. Hence, the consumer can serve as an expert recommender because s/he has found the brand to be self-relevant in either a functional problem-solving or self-identity sense and, therefore, is willing to risk suggesting it to a friend. There is an extensive literature on opinion leaders and how marketers might best manage their role in new product diffusion and brand choice processes (Feick and Price 1987; King and Summers 1976). However, it is important to note that consumers in a social media or open source environment (Pitt *et al.* 2006) are increasingly able to cross-check information presented by their friends and/or opinion leaders for its relevance, accuracy, and credibility.

It is also important to note that consumer WOM has always involved personalized messages created by the consumer on the product's behalf. Hence, everyday conversational processes of dialogue, story-telling, and self-impression management are likely involved. However, in social media WOM contexts, consumers may be more active, creative, idiosyncratic, or even resistant in regard to marketer-initiated content and persuasion (Kozinets et. al. 2010). In a fashion similar to the attempt to transfer traditional outbound marketing to social media, some marketers have been attracted to the obvious opportunity to adapt WOM marketing to social networks in order to stimulate consumer "buzz" to a wider audience. Others have tried to influence social media opinion leaders and celebrities to mention the marketer's products or promotions in their blogs, forums, or white papers. Kozinets et. al. (2010) examined one such marketing campaign involving the "seeding" of a new cell phone to product category bloggers. They reported that 84 percent of the bloggers mentioned the product in their blogs. However, they also noted some complex distinctions that appear to be related to the self-identity projects of the bloggers themselves. Apparently, this reflects an increased role of any blogger-generated content about the brand beyond the immediate friendship exchanges to self-identity implications in the larger social network. Thus, WOM in networked contexts differs in significant ways from the linear opinion leader model (Kozinets *et al.* 2010). First, the opinion leader is personally exposed in the social media world to many consumers or followers. Hence, the opinion leader openly presents his or her personal character to the public and, thus, is likely to be more concerned about self-identity and consistency across messages and consumers.

Second, the WOM occurs within the context of the blog forum or website. Thus, the nature and expectations concerning the blog as media may affect the audience's interpretations. Finally, some individual consumers may, like media celebrities or critics, become quite active in producing personal scripts or productions that involve brand-related WOM content in order to build an audience. In fact, Kozinets *et al.* (2010) investigated WOM communicator strategies and found that consumer motivations extended beyond mere reciprocal exchange and altruism to include interpersonal concerns about self-presentation, communal involvement, and their own character narratives.

Casual social networks

The unit of analysis in casual social networks is the individual consumer in the social network. In general, social networks concentrate capital resources for use by their members in conducting their life projects. However, in more casual social networks, capital is concentrated in individual agents. The volume of capital concentrated in a network member depends on "the size of the network of connections he can effectively mobilize and in the volume of capital (economic, human, or cultural) possessed in his own right by each of those to whom he is connected" (Bourdieu 1984, p. 249). No group-level solidarity or commitment is necessarily applied. However, as task interdependency increases, social networks are driven to formalize, perhaps in the form of a clique (Iacobucci and Hopkins 1992), a situated community of practice (Wenger, McDermott, and Snyder 2002), or a select club (Bourdieu 1984).

The rise of massive casual social networks on Facebook, Second Life, and LinkedIn has drawn a great deal of attention by marketers. In these social environments, the interactions are not about brands or products. Instead, brands and products are merely social tools or topics of conversations. A Facebook member may ask friends which type of cell phone they recommend. For example, Nick wrote to Robert:

> Read this http://www.facebook.com/l/c858c/www.popularmechanics. com/technology/gadgets/news/4G-wireless-network-guide if you are going to use a phone on a "4G", of which Verizon kicks the pants off everyone, go Droid. The apps are far and beyond Apple. I love Apple, they are innovative, but they have become Microsoft, only in it for the quarterly report to wall and broad.

Or a Second Life player may create a pair of virtual Nike shoes to wear. A LinkedIn member may post a picture of themselves wearing a new Hickey Freeman suit.

In each case, the product or brand serves a supporting role. Thus, marketers who attempt to insert themselves into these interactions risk being regarded as interlopers (Deighton and Kornfield 2009). This problem is illustrated by the numerous, sometimes disastrous, efforts firms have made to insert themselves into Second Life. Despite the support of the developers, brand managers have often found themselves unwelcome. Players have crashed helicopters into Nissan's virtual building. Other companies have had their virtual marketing properties attacked with virtual nuclear weapons. An in-game group calling itself the Second

Life Liberation Army (SLLA) even formed to conduct further attacks. As a result, marketing managers were often disappointed with the result of their efforts. As Erik Hauser, the creative director of Wells Fargo's digital agency, stated, "Going into Second Life now is the equivalent of running a field marketing program in Iraq" (see http://members.forbes.com/forbes/2007/0702/048.html).

However, marketers' forays into casual social networks don't have to end in nuclear revolution. Some firms have managed to interject themselves into these environments without engendering negative responses. For example, Skittles has a Facebook page with more than 16 million FB members. From this site, the brand has launched a variety of well-received campaigns to engage FB consumers. For example, 44,000 FB users participated in Skittles' Valentine's Day campaign (www.digitalbuzzblog.com/skittles-facebook-mob-of-love/; http://www.ignitesocialmedia.com/social-media-examples/skittles-facebook-fan-page-example/).

Enthusiast social networks

Enthusiast social networks are organized informally around a product category instead of a single brand, although consumers may still be a "fan" of a particular brand. Their product interest is more intense than that of the casual social network. They typically involve intense strong commitments to a product category and may involve inclusionary product category loyalty or use standards, or even active efforts, to exclude individuals who exhibit limited value to the collective. Product category enthusiasts share a social identification with fellow users and/or admirers of a product category, whether it be computers, golf clubs, or sports cars. These enthusiasts actively search for product-relevant information using both traditional marketing sources (enthusiast magazines) and the more inbound Web 2.0 product-related sources. More importantly, they are active players in the expertise-fueled status hierarchy that forms around product category use and network participation. The user's direct and personal experience in product use and expertise is revealed in social media dialogues and interpersonal communications and is instrumental to their social network status and role. Enthusiasts also take on product membership identities and personalities that define their community self-identity and their relative status (i.e. product "newbie," "expert," or "poseur"). As detailed below, examples of enthusiast social networks include the personal computer community (i.e. "computer geeks") and the watch community (i.e. the self-described "watch idiot savants" or "WISs").

Brand ownership and loyalty to a brand matters less in enthusiast groups than they do in brand communities. While members have personal brand preferences and may own only certain brands, they still feel a bond with others who share their passion for the product category, even if they own different brands. As a result, owners of competing brands share information about brands they own as well as ones they don't. In a sense, the product category is superordinate, brand ownership and/or loyalty is subordinate. Hence, while the presence of a status hierarchy distinguishes an enthusiast from a casual social network, an enthusiast network allows and encourages dialogue among owners of a variety of approved brands as a natural aspect of network value and exchange. Enthusiasts welcome new members, either admirers or new buyers in the focal product category, and encourage their active participation and commitment. The out-group consists of the people who do not appreciate the product category as a whole or who ridicule the product category or its consumers. In the case of WISs, this may lead to poking fun at people who refuse to appreciate the "value" of an expensive watch or use cell phones to tell time. And special derision is reserved for those who buy or promote fakes because they represent a direct threat to the group's beloved products and their sense of status as owners.

One consequence of the superordinate status of the product category is that the strong brand based in-group and out-group rivalry that exists between competing brand communities is lessened or absent in enthusiast social networks. This lack of hostility among brand owner subgroups allows consumers to altruistically share product information about many brands, to demonstrate their expertise, to comment and/or resolve questions or problems being experienced by both regular and novice members, to recommend products and/or brands that fit another member's requirements, and even to serve as a beta tester for new product concepts offered by marketers who are considered legitimate by enthusiast members. Hence, an ethic of altruism in regard to sharing information with non-members about the focal product, the passion and feelings of ownership and membership, and the self-identity and self-efficacy benefits of consumer community participation guide consumer practices in enthusiast groups.

At the same time, it must be recognized that the presence of a status hierarchy largely based on expertise and credibility as a product category loyalist can engender competitiveness among individual enthusiast groups as they vie for recognition and status. Human capital is the currency through which members acquire social network status. So, members who want to be recognized must demonstrate the currency and relevance of their expertise. The downside is that individuals who are active in the social network and do not demonstrate knowledge or currency may be severely criticized or ignored. Indeed, individuals who do not show the proper appreciation, or own "fakes," may be labeled "poseurs" – individuals who claim membership but do not really belong and, hence, are ostracized.

Case 1: Computer geeks

People who are interested in computers are notorious for their high level of involvement. Indeed, forums and message boards in which "computer geeks" socialize as well as trade information and advice have been a prominent part of the internet since its inception. Popular activities include exchanging information and advice on overclocking computer components – the risky practice of running them at faster speeds than were intended. Overclocking can destroy the central processor or other components. However, overclocking can also lead to perform- ance gains for little or no additional cost. Thus, the ability to achieve the highest possible speed while avoiding disaster is respected and admired. Members con- tinually exchange information on their experiences, as well as advice on how to successfully optimize the latest computer products. Two websites with extensive forums on computer product categories and overclocking are http://hardforum. com/ and www.techpowerup.com/forums/.

Case 2: Watch idiot savants

Watch enthusiasts refer to themselves as WISs (watch idiot savants). WISs enjoy discussing the joys and intricacies of watches, especially mechanical watches. They have long "wrist check" threads in which they post pictures of the watches they have on their wrists that day: http://forums.watchuseek.com/f109/longest- wrist-check-thread-ever-38748-post214130.html; http://forums.watchuseek.com/ f381/iwc-chronoswiss-515244-post3770808.html?highlight=chronoswiss.

WISs include people who enjoy everything from "affordable" and "Chinese watches" to those who love "high end" watches that cost $10,000 to more than $100,000. They share advice on buying, selling, and servicing watches as well as rumors and pictures of upcoming products. Spring is a particularly lively time for WISs since the European Basel trade show, where new models are announced, occurs at this time. Members traveling to the show gather information and post pictures for fellow members. Then, they mark the wait to new product release on various WIS forums and post "siting" threads when one of them spots a model actually up for sale. WISs are also noteworthy for the internal trading that occurs within the group. To fund new purchases or to buy a prized "Grail" watch, mem- bers frequently sell part of their collections to fellow members. Many members buy and sell watches regularly for the sheer joy of the chase (referred to as "catch and release"). It is not uncommon for a post in the For Sale forum to state that they are making the watch available to fellow WISs before putting it on eBay (they prefer to place it in a good home). Finally, sellers cite their status as members on the watch forum as evidence of their trustworthiness when selling or trading watches. This is not a trivial issue as the frequent buying and selling that occurs involves wire transfers of $1,000 to $10,000 or more to fellow members whom the buyer has never personally met. A sample of such forums includes: http://forums.watchuseek.com/forum.php; For sale between individuals (NO DEALERS): http://forums.watchuseek.com/f29/; Want to Trade (WTT): http:// forums.watchuseek.com/f31/. The following is an example of a thread illustrating the social interactions on a WIS network: http://forums.watchuseek.com/f381/ iwc-chronoswiss-515244-post3770808.html?highlight=chronoswiss.

Brand communities

In brand communities, the unit of analysis is individual consumers as members of a brand community, defined as "a specialized, non-geographically-bound community, based on a structured set of social relationships among admirers of a brand" (Muñiz and O'Guinn 2001, p. 412). These consumers possess a shared social identification based on their interest in a particular brand which gives rise to *consciousness of kind*, or a connective bond to fellow brand users and/or admirers (McAlexander, Schouten, and Koenig 2002). The brand community is self-identity relevant in both an in-group and out-group sense. This bond in turn leads to *shared community practices*, including rituals, practices, and traditions concerning the brand, its heritage, and consumption practices. These include shared stories about the brand's attributes or history; a shared sense of belonging, *communitas*, and phatic communion (Celsi, Rose, and Leigh 2003); and a shared sense of joy, flow, and nostalgia about brand or brand community experiences. Finally, brand collectives share a *sense of moral responsibility* that drives instrumental and social behavior among the members to share brand-related information, to help others in the community, to protect the brand's authenticity, and to proselytize the brand and the community to both members and non-members.

Several unresolved issues concerning brand communities are relevant to our brand-consumer collective framework. In the first place, brand communities may be either geographically or virtually based. Some brand communities develop around a physical location, or third place, that is closely identified with the brand community and may become a recognized meeting space or even sacred ground. British car community members gather for regular meetings at a local pub, hold tech sessions at a local garage, and display their cars at annual car shows held at a specific venue. Brand communities may also be virtually based and are increasingly multi-media and geographical in their social interaction processes.

Second, the sense of social identification within a brand community, as well as its idiosyncratic consumption and community practices, leads to in-group and out-group biases and status competition that may be expressed in various forms, including negative word of mouth towards rival brands, unwillingness to notice or consider information about competing brands, reduced likelihood of adoption, or even direct, outright disparagement of out-group brand owners, admirers, or members of "competing" communities. Thus, as consumers become more committed to their brand community, they are less likely to be in the market for other brands in the product category regardless of the source of the information, be it marketer, consumer recommender, or independent analyst. This is referred to as "oppositional loyalty" (Muñiz and Hamer 2001) and it would tend to insulate members of a brand community from adopting a competing brand. On the other hand, brand community members are presumed to be brand loyal to the community brand. Hence, they may be active seekers of new information about their focal brand. This would, seemingly, make marketing efforts to a brand community that is consistent with the community's values and practices more effective and efficient. Hence, this message receptivity may result in marketing savings and competitive advantage.

The benefits, and challenges, associated with brand communities can be readily seen at brandfests and conventions dedicated to particular brands. An excellent example is BlizzCon. Demand for the tickets is so high, Blizzard resorts to a lottery system to award them.

Case 3: BlizzCon

Blizzard is a leading developer of computer games, including the largest massive multiplayer online game, "World of Warcraft," with more than 12 million monthly subscribers and 62 percent share. Large and enthusiastic communities have grown up around its games. In response, Blizzard stages an annual fan convention called "BlizzCon." The 2010 conference attracted 27,000 attendees and was available as a live pay per view event on DirectTV. Many attendees dress up as their World of Warcraft characters, appearing as heavily armed trolls or well-armored elves. BlizzCon allows Blizzard to reinforce the bonds between these players who spend long hours together in game, but often only see one another face to face at the convention. Blizzard also uses the conference as an opportunity to announce new games and generate excitement and WOM about its products. Basically, BlizzCon provides a venue where WoW fans can socialize with fellow players and bask in their shared identities.

Of course, not everyone is a fan of World of Warcraft. The game has a number of well-established competitors with their own communities such as Everquest 2. Reading accounts of BlizzCon posted by Everquest 2 players provides a study of out-group bias. For example, players of Everquest 2 ridicule WoW players, portraying them as young and immature. WoW players reciprocate this out-group bias and portray Everquest 2 members as elitists, snobs, and people who just can't appreciate the best product on the market (http://en.wikipedia.org/wiki/BlizzCon).

A third issue is multiple brand community membership, either across or within product categories (Thompson and Sinha 2008). Brand communities in their most general, non-geographical, and informal form do not require a sense of place and may be joined merely by buying or admiring the brand. Hence, consumers may show overlapping patterns of brand community membership across product categories that may share similar consumer core benefits (i.e. BMW car owners may be Ritz Carlton vacationers owing to their interest in exceptional performance). Consumers may be members of two car brand communities, even ones that are rivals. For example, a BMW owner may also own a British or American collector car and actively participate in each brand's community. As Thompson and Sinha (2008) note, these issues have not been sorted out and are complicated by the fact that even minimal membership participation can influence social identification effects. Admittedly, rivalry among brand communities may be friendly or tongue in cheek. However, serious rivalries may also occur to the degree that they initiate psychological or even physical actions. Thus, the issue of degree of participation and its effect on information bias, brand loyalty, new product adoption, or social disagreements requires attention.

A fourth issue involves the role of economic markets in brand communities. Economic markets and exchange have always been part of community (Mauss [1923] 1990). However, there is controversy concerning the role and extent of consumer versus marketer agency in brand communities. On one hand, Muñiz and O'Guinn (2001) suggest that brand community members are more informed and influential than they would be as individuals and, therefore, will likely play a stronger role as consumers.

Alternatively, Kozinets (2002) conceptualizes community as re-gatherings that band consumers together to assert their brand agency and ownership, and may even criticize marketers and incite activism against them as they seek to manage the brand for its meaning and profits. In our framework, brand communities aggregate capital resources for the benefit of their members, including human (or expertise), social (support, help, friendship), and symbolic or cultural capital in the form of expert status, authenticated brands and artifacts, or the community's values and practices. Hence, we would presume that the community could adopt a stance against commercialization as one of its core values. The brand community itself could also define the conditions under which it would provide exchange mechanisms for either altruistically or economically trading these resources among in-group members. This mechanism might involve defining the practices governing conversions of member and /or collective capital into economic forms.

A final issue involves the consumer and brand community's roles in specific brand-related value creation activities and their link to the collective capital of the community. Schau et al. (2009) identified four value creation practices for members that were served by the brand communities in general. These are (1) social networking practices that enable and sustain the social bonds that provide the glue that binds BC members to the collective (e.g. welcoming, empathizing, and governing); (2) social impression practices focused on reinforcing in-group identity and proselytizing to relevant external parties (evangelizing and justifying); (3) community engagement practices that concern the status hierarchy and members' standing within it (badging, milestoning, and documenting); and (4) brand use practices that concern appropriate care, respect, and preservation of the focal brand object (grooming, customizing, commoditizing). These practices govern the operations of the brand community and how it provides consumption experiences and individual social distinctions in human, social, and cultural capital among members. The capability of the brand community to collect and share these value creating practices and capital may be a key determinant of a brand community's role, relative to the marketer or other brand stakeholders, in influencing the brand's meaning heritage and trajectory.

Select brand clubs

For select brand clubs, the unit of analysis is the select club, or formal institution that organizes the value creating practices and formal leadership structure that defines and legitimizes the shared values, capital resources, and consumption practices of the BC. The nexus of the select brand club's influence is that it collectively concentrates the BC's economic, human, social, and cultural capital and employs them to provide its members with a degree of influence concerning the brand. Select clubs offer a degree of formalization, permanency, and leadership to the BC, an aspect that resonates with the BC's project of altruistically preserving the brand's heritage and the brand community's vitality. In this sense, the BC aspects of consciousness of kind, rituals and traditions, and moral responsibility (Muñiz and O'Guinn 2001) may be delegated by the BC to select club leaders in order to enhance the BC's functions of consumer agency, economic and social exchange, and brand stewardship. Hence, select brand clubs may largely define the symbolic capital for the BC, with particular emphasis on preserving brand authenticity; defining the rules of the BC which determine distinctive social status (i.e. self-work and mastery); and, establishing the BC's terms of exchange that govern the relative value of the various forms of capital (Leigh, Peters, and Shelton 2006).

Bourdieu's notion of practice (1992) provides a lens for interpreting how select brand clubs operate. The fundamental notion is that shared projects and problems in a social field generate interest in shared practices directed at shared instrumental goals (Brown and Duguid 2001). Select brand clubs are "deliberately originated in order to concentrate social capital and to derive full benefit from the multiplier effect" (Bourdieu 1985, p. 249). In select brand clubs, consumer practices would stress how to play the social status game in order to earn material and symbolic profits (Bourdieu 1984). Thus, a select brand club may deliberately employ its social network connectedness, shared commitments, and solidarity in order to concentrate cultural capital and profits in its network for the benefit of its members.

Once established, a select brand club within a BC is likely to try to employ its capital resources to ensure its vitality. Hence, select clubs are likely to be motivated to participate in governing the nature of the brand playground, in particular with respect to the BC's definition of what constitutes rare and distinctive tastes and practices (Bourdieu 1984). This ability to define tastes enables the select club to bestow status on its members. Furthermore, the vitality of the select club would be enhanced to the degree that it is able to concentrate the ownership of authentic branded products, expertise, and consumption practices in its formal network. Through this process, the select club endows itself with the authority to influence the economic market for authentic products, to certify authentic restorations and disparage modifications, to recognize the mastery credentials of its members or service providers, and to vie with the marketer for control over the brand's heritage.

Personal efforts and social investments by club leaders distinguish select clubs from enthusiast networks and BCs. Formalizing the practices of a collective requires "an unceasing effort at sociability" (Bourdieu 1985, p. 250) to define the group's identity, as well as delimit its boundaries. Becoming a leader in a select brand club requires legitimate participation in the club's collective events (meetings, shows, or rallies) and recognized practices (cultural ceremonies, workshops, and competitions). An individual builds social capital in the collective by sincerely participating in its sanctioned activities and exchanges. The virtue of "being known," that is "being known by more people than they know" (Bourdieu 1985, p. 250), supposedly justifies the efforts invested in sociability in terms of symbolic, cultural, and economic profits. However, a select club's efforts to formalize and administer the BC's structure and practices create a "fundamental paradox of connectedness that can be exhausting" (Wheatley and Kellner-Rogers 1998, p. 13) to those who serve as leaders. Hence, while leadership powers are valued for their symbolic capital and status, the personal costs to earn them may be onerous.

Given that the select club's existence depends on whether its capital is deployed in terms consistent with the group habitus, it seems reasonable that leaders will retain their roles only to the degree that they act in consonance with the interests of the group. Attributions of incompetence, neglect, misappropriation, or misuse of collective social capital would quickly compromise a leader's position. This has implications for the role of the marketer. We argued that marketers have always been a part of BCs owing to the role that commerce may legitimately play in enabling members to realize their brand-related consumption and identity projects. The select club is interesting in that it may formally define the roles of brand marketers and decide who is legitimate and who is not. Hence, it is likely that successful marketers must adhere to the select club's fundamental values and practices, as both a member and a commerce provider. A second marketer-related aspect is that the select club itself is a marketer of its brand and its communal values to its members, non-members, and society. Hence, the select club *as an organization* is likely to actively seek a role as co-producer of brand-relevant content, or co-creator of value creating practices.

Marketer practices

Our perspective is that the role of the marketer in the Web 2.0 world is contingent on the nature of the form of social system that provides the context for the brands and its trajectory. Hence, we offer a set of indicated marketer practices that might fit the realities identified in our brand-consumer typology analysis. We also isolate a few controversial issues resulting from the fact that social media marketing understanding is emerging largely through the practical case-based experiences offered by marketers.

Brand-consumer contexts

In brand-consumer contexts, the marketer's role has been that of brand authority, value creator, and active persuasive agent in a one-way communications process directed at desirable consumers (see Table 17.3). Marketers employed outbound marketing messages to promote their brand's benefits and stimulate WOM among consumers. Marketers were respected to the degree that they provided legitimate value and satisfaction to consumers with their products and their media efforts. Some brands and commercials even achieved cultural icon status. And brand failures or promotional gaffes were relatively low-risk events because they were typically between the consumer and the marketer, the opinion leader, or the media.

However, the advent of the internet and social media changed this model. Traditional marketers found themselves with new tools for reaching and relating to consumers with potentially greater effectiveness and reduced costs. Marketers found that new outbound marketing approaches could be used to generate WOM buzz among large networks of consumers and opinion leaders. And, most importantly, marketers found that a whole new set of inbound marketing approaches could or must be used as consumers were empowered to actively perform their consumer roles of searching, learning, buying, and using social media applications. They found that social media contexts are also highly entertaining to consumers and that success in these media demanded relevant, timely, and entertaining content if marketing was to be persuasive. On the other hand, they found that both consumers and other social media users could be very demanding or even dismissive of marketers as interlopers in a friendship-based world. As Fournier and Avery (2011) note, marketers flocked to social media platforms only to find that they risked control of their messages, brand images, and corporate reputations.

There are many views on how marketers should operate in the new social media. We will discuss three here. One is that the traditional brand marketer faces a challenging and unpredictable marketing context purely and simply because social networks are ubiquitous, and hence uncontrollable by marketers in the old-fashioned sense. For example, Leslie Gaines-Ross (2010) argues that "corporations now face landscapes rife with new threats to their reputations" (p. 70). Moreover, these threats can come from anywhere: a single disaffected customer, such as David Carroll attacking United Airlines for breaking his guitar may reach millions of YouTubers, a single satirical tweeter who led an attack on BP (Leroy Stick @BPGlobalPR), or an activist group or church, such as that which attacked Caterpillar.

TABLE 17.3 Marketer practices in brand-consumer contexts

Marketer Relevant Characteristics & Practices	Traditional Authority Brand Marketing	Conversational Brand Marketing	Casual Social Network Marketing
Communication Frame Facing the Marketer	Organic Consumer WOM (One-Way)	Opinion Leader WOM with Active Marketer Targeting Trusted Buzz Leaders (One-Way)	Locse Friendship Based Social Network (Multi-Way)
Market – Consumer Influence Model	Consumer ⟶ Consumer Marketer	Consumer Opinion Leader ⟶ Many Potential Consumers Marketer	Many Consumers ⟶ Many Consumers Marketer
Marketer's Core Communications Role	Marketer as Brand Authority & Value Creator	Marketer as Brand Authority & WOM Buzz Creator	Marketer as Social Network Friend & Listener

Continued

TABLE 17.3 Con'd

Marketer Relevant Characteristics & Practices	Traditional Authority Brand Marketing	Conversational Brand Marketing	Casual Social Network Marketing
Marketer Campaign Issues & Practices	• Out-Bound Marketing – Stimulate Awareness – Trigger Hierarchy of Effects – Trigger Retail/Web Visits & Purchase – Remove Barriers to Buying (Finance) – Measure Sales, Satisfaction, Complaints – Use Internet as Content & Efficiency Driver	Out-Bound Marketing to Stimulate WOM Buzz – Trigger Buzz Conversations & Engage Opinion Setters – Ads that Are Controversial & Topical – Product Placements in Entertainment Venues – Celebrity and Comedy Shows – Personal Media (YouTube) – Monitor and Counter Bad Buzz (United)	– In-Bound Marketing Based on Consumer Curiosity or Interest – Provide Relevant, Timely & Entertaining Content – Join Social Networks as Friends – Post Banner Ads to Attract WEB Visitors – Provide Content that is Personal, Relevant, Timely, Entertaining (Blogs, Webcasts, Videos, White Papers)
Marketer Control & Risk Levels	• Marketer is In-Group • Assumes Marketer is Intelligent Brand Curator • Few Risks to Brand in Targeted Media	• Marketer is In-Group • Assumes Opinion Leaders are Brand Supporters • Risks that Brand Enters Social Conversations Outside Selected Media	– WOM Can Be Idiosyncratic, Creative, or Dismissive in Brand Meanings – Risk When Brand-Related Communication is Co-Produced or Co-Created – Marketer may be in Out-Group

Case example: Caterpillar's "Death Bulldozers"

Caterpillar (CAT) was attacked by Palestinian activists because its D9 bulldozers are used by the Israel Defense Forces (IDF). While the IDF buys equipment from many companies, activists chose CAT as their poster child, branding its products as "Death Bulldozers." In response to shareholder activists, CAT's board stated: "Caterpillar shares the world's concern over unrest in the Middle East and we certainly have compassion for all those affected by the political strife. However, Caterpillar machines and engines are at work in virtually every country of the world each day. We have neither the legal right nor the means to police individual use of that equipment. We believe any comments on political conflict in the region are best left to our governmental leaders . . ." Earlier in July 2010, the largest Presbyterian denomination in the USA called on CAT to "carefully review its involvement in obstacles to a just and lasting peace in Israel-Palestine, and to take affirmative steps to end its complicity in the violation of human rights."

This example highlights the risks facing marketers. While it may be argued that United Airlines should have had a more effective customer complaint process in place, it had yet to realize the power of social media. BP met only the minimums of the law with its disaster plan, so maybe it deserved to have its reputation tarnished. However, there is little that CAT could have done to anticipate that its brand rather than that of another firm would be singled out by these activist groups. Maybe, as Gaines-Ross (2010) asserts, the best marketers can do is to detect such problems early and diffuse them using aggressive PR strategies: avoid excessive shows of force; act quickly; tell your side's story; find sympathetic third-party advocates; and fully utilize social media to your advantage. To be able to do this, a firm must cross-functionally commit to brand risk management as a core corporate strategy in dealing with social media. BP did not have an integrated media and PR program in place. Hence, it was blindsided when its "green and yellow starburst" and media messages were so rapidly attacked, hijacked, and parodied. BP's "Blogs from the Gulf," such as one that described the disaster as "a mesmerizing ballet at sea," its failure to effectively deal with the official BP Twitter account and its satirical and fake content, its lack of third-party ambassadors, and even its unwillingness to have Twitter remove rogue posts point to its lack of anticipatory risk management assessments.

A second point of view is that marketers can choose among three social media strategies: (1) cede control to consumers and become a citizen of the web; (2) try to fit in unobtrusively on the web by adapting inbound marketer practices; or (3) figure out how to leverage the web to involve consumers in the brand's playground (Fournier and Avery 2011). As discussed below, ceding control to *true consumer collectives* may be sensible as they have a stake in the brand. However, ceding control of the brand in the casual social web contexts ignores the fact that the brand marketer has significant economic capital at stake when consumers and non-consumers are freely allowed co-producer privileges with respect to the brand.

Attracting desirable and interested target consumers to the brand is consistent with the appropriate use of inbound marketer practices, in particular the notion of offering active consumers the brand-relevant content and entertaining messages they seek. However, extending the brand to new market segments or marketing new product innovations may require the employment of more sophisticated outbound mass media campaigns that have direct links to embedded marketing in social media networks or entertainment venues, or more sophisticated and believable opinion leader campaigns through marketing efforts via bloggers, social website postings, or content sharing. These marketer practices are not well understood, despite the efforts of consulting firms to encode Best Practices for social media marketing (www.toprankblog.com/2009/02/best-worst-practices-social-media-marketing/).

Companies, such as Newell Rubbermaid, that have actively invested in social media marketing recognize that the social media world is complex and rapidly evolving in ways that are difficult to anticipate. Hence, while they may not have ceded control of their brand or their desire to manage it as an asset, they do recognize that brand management in social media contexts requires adaptive and emergent strategy and learning. For example, Newell Rubbermaid recognized several years ago the need to be active in social media. It hired an experienced marketer/PR executive to build a social media role and platform for the firm. The firm's use of social media, as well as the nature of the social media organization and team, has continually evolved as the firm solves emergent social media problems. At Newell, the first step was to find a sponsor in the firm. Graco provided the opportunity with its need for social media practices for the appropriate use of blogs for its Graco Baby Strollers. It has also had major successes with Sharpie pens. Examples of the emergent marketer practices include treating the blog as the cement for the relationship; strict transparency because customers will let you know otherwise; organizing meetings with consumer bloggers; diversifying the set of Newell bloggers to include brand managers and customer service personnel; providing recognition to regular consumer bloggers; transparency in using the blog as a social media site for YouTube videos and a Christian Science article during a Graco stroller recall; personalizing the bloggers by name and @Newell address; establishing ambassador roles for regular customer bloggers; and showing customers on the blog with their Sharpie pen art.

A third point of view is that marketers are going to continue investing in WOM and, hence, need to develop new marketer-initiated practices to stimulate consumer WOM and opinion leader content in social media (Kozinets et al. 2010). We agree that marketers have too much at risk with significant brands not to attempt to work within social media to influence the brand narrative. However, WOM and inbound marketing practices in general (blogs, webcasts, marketer-inspired videos, consumer-developed content) need to be examined for their legitimacy and authenticity. The seeding practice examined by Kozinets et al. (2010) is instructive. In the first place, the acceptance rate of the willing bloggers was high, product-relevant messages were very common, and the commentary was very positive. Hence, it is reasonable to assume that the marketer had done some homework on the seeding campaign and its upside/downside risks. Thus, the marketer appears to have been very interested in brand development and control. It would be useful to examine how this firm and others think through the WOMM decision process. Second, it points to the inherent complexity of working with a diverse set of bloggers. Bloggers present personalized and self-identity-based points of view. They are often celebrity brands in and of themselves with their reputations to manage. And they recognize, as probably do their audiences, that a seeding campaign is the marketer inserting itself into social media seeking its own self-interest. Hence, blogger strategies such as seeding need to be carefully considered from the perspectives of message credibility, transparency, co-branding risk, and boomerang possibilities. Finally, the sheer complexity and diversity of the blogger discourse processes that Kozinets *et al.* (2010) noted, should both encourage and give pause to marketers. While most of the bloggers willingly convert the marketer's offering into a narrative that fits the norms and expectations of their audience, the diversity of the bloggers' meaning conversion processes should give pause to marketers concerning how to balance the marketers' need for consistency with the bloggers' interests.

Brand-consumer collective contexts

Our consumer typology distinguished three types of brand-consumer collectives. A marketer practices framework to fit these enthusiast social networks, brand communities, and select brand clubs, respectively, is presented in Table 17.4.

Enthusiast social networks

Enthusiast social networks stress product category over brands with members acting as fans of the product category as a whole, as well as one or more brands. Hence, there is little hostility to marketers of non-preferred brands as they are providing valuable information about related products within the product category. The marketer role is thus a co-producer of user-desired content and value regardless of brand.

The lack of hostility toward opposing brands makes enthusiast social networks a promising environment for marketers. These communities are composed of individuals who are active, passionate consumers in the product category. While they own brands and may have brand preferences, their sense of identity revolves primarily around the product category. Thus, they do not show an automatic out-group bias against particular brands or companies. Within the confines of these communities, the marketer can interact with consumers who own competing brands without the hostility and outright rejection that characterizes rival brand communities.

TABLE 17.4 Marketer practices in brand-consumer collectives

Marketer Relevant Characteristics & Practices	Enthusiast Social Network Marketing	Brand Community Marketing	Select Brand Club Marketing
Communications Frame Facing the Marketer	• Consumption Group that Stresses a Product Category Consumption Activity That Yields Fan-Based Loyalty and Passion	Brand Community that Espouses an Emotional Commitment to A Brand and Builds A Social Group to Support it	Formal Brand Related Membership Club That Operates As a Brand Marketer and Status Provider
Market-Consumer Influence Model	Brand A Owner ⟷ Brand B Owner / Marketer	In-Group Consumers ⟷ Out-Group Consumers / Marketing	Marketer ⟷ Select Club Leaders / Club Members
Marketer's Core Communication Role	Marketer as Co-Producer of User Desired Content and Value	Marketer as Co-Member & Co-Participant in Brand-Space for In-Group	Marketer as Brand Co-Creator with Formal Club Hierarchy

Marketing Campaign Issues & Practices			
	• In-Bound Marketing • New Media Approaches • Blog-Based, "Seeding" Campaigns • Identify Close-Knit Social Groups and Seek to Co-Produce Content & Advice • Identify Consumer Promotion Sites and Co-Promote Deals Offerings to Site Users • Review User Complaints' Teach How to Use Product Properly or Improve Product	• Be Transparent In-Group Member at a Distance • Identify Community Value Creating Practices and Seek to Enable These Efforts • Social Networking • BC Impression Creation • BC Event Opportunities • BC Status & Reputation • Promote BC Consumption Experiences • Enable External Badging & Recognition • Support Preservation Efforts	• Respect Select Club's Role in Defining & Legitimizing Brand Consumption Practices • Share or Cede Control Over to Brand's Meaning Trajectory to Select Club • Support Select Club's Efforts to Formalize its Marketing Activities that Support the Brand's Heritage • Enable Select Clubs to Efficiently Develop & Manage Brand-Related Events and Symbols • Help Ensure the Select Club's Vitality as an Organization • Involve Select Club in Co-Creating New Products & Marketing Problems • Enable Select Club Leaders to Receive Recognition & Status

Marketers seeking new users or market share gains should focus on enthusiast social networks. These groups are made up of active and often heavy consumer spenders within the product category including collectors and traders. Furthermore, members are more open to new products and product innovations regardless of brand, with many owning multiple brands simultaneously and sequentially. As a result, they will not reject the marketer's offerings out of hand simply based on brand loyalty. Indeed, they are open to switching brands and thus are readily "attainable" as new customers for an innovative product or a new brand. Moreover, their high level of involvement and enthusiasm makes many of them market mavens and gives rise to extensive word of mouth among the enthusiast group itself, as well as to its more peripheral admirers. This makes these networks fertile ground for successful seeding and viral marketing campaigns. However, the non-brand specific nature of the enthusiast social networks also means that members are receptive to a broad range of messages from a variety of sources, including new entrants. Hence, established product category leaders must keep on top of the enthusiast social networks as their loyalties are changeable. By the same token, enthusiast social networks are particularly valuable to new entrants. Firms seeking to leapfrog established competitors will find enthusiast social networks to be open to and even welcoming of new products, innovations, and brands.

Brand communities

Unlike enthusiast social network members, brand community members possess social identities and emotional commitments to both a brand and the brand community. This leads to a range of benefits for marketers in loyalty marketing programs and being an in-group member of the brand community. Furthermore, brand community members are more likely to adopt products and spread positive WOM about their preferred brand. At the same time, they are less likely to adopt products from competing brands and more prone to spread negative WOM about them. Therefore, marketing actions aimed at creating and growing a brand community can pay off handsomely. This is why most studies on brand community emphasize the positive effects to the marketer to the degree that they can influence the extent and quality of the value creation processes (see Table 17.4) for the brand community (Schau et.al. 2009). These authors advocate co-creation practices with brand communities and argue that the marketer can advance its agenda by working as a partner on community event development, new product development, or extend the community's array of consumer practices. Subject to the marketer's assessment of the value of these investments versus their unidentified costs, we agree.

However, the existence of brand communities can also severely limit the marketer's opportunities. Once built, brand communities can actually offer fewer opportunities than enthusiast social networks. On the one hand, marketing efforts aimed at the firm's own brand community amount to "preaching to the choir." BC consumers are already prone to purchase the brand's product and engage in positive WOM about it. Thus, marketing actions are likely to show incremental results. Furthermore, marketing actions aimed at members of rival brand communities are not very promising. These consumers are not likely to switch brands and are prone to use any information to simply further their efforts to cast their own brand in a positive light, but at the marketer's expense. Therefore, to achieve growth and keep the BC vital, marketers need to be creative in their focus on encouraging non-brand community members to join and participate in the firm's brand community. Marketer's efforts in this regard may be more or less successful depending on the degree of commitment that brand community membership implies. In the simplest BC contexts (Muñiz and O'Guinn 2001), where BC membership is essentially proffered based on brand ownership, these marketer efforts may show relatively high yield. However, as the BC requires investments in the more community-oriented practices, consumers may show more resistance and resources dedicated to enhancing WOM or purchase behavior may produce only modest returns.

Select brand clubs

The communications frame facing the marketer in select brand clubs is that of a formal brand-related membership club that operates in its own right as a brand marketer and service provider (see Table 17.4). The marketer–consumer influence model that is relevant involves a two-way dialogue between the brand marketer and the select club leadership; a two-way dialogue between the club's leaders and members; and one-way communications from the marketer and individual club members. Because of the degree of rotation in select clubs among membership and leader roles, as well as member participation in the club as consumers of particular brand-related events, the select club maintains many of the characteristics of a brand community from a marketing perspective. However, it is the institutional aspects of select brand clubs that set them apart from a marketing point of view. In particular, the marketer needs to respect the select club's role in defining brand consumption practices; to arrive at a shared agreement concerning the degree to which it will share or cede control over the brand's trajectory; and how it can best work to ensure that the club is able to formalize its own marketing role in the BC, manage its brand-related service offerings efficiently, and ensure the longer-term vitality of the select club. At the same time it must recognize the risk that a well-run select club may pose when marketer self-interest initiatives indicate that brand and brand community changes are required.

The presence of a select club at the heart of a BC has derivative implications for the social negotiation of brand meaning. On the surface, select clubs may appear to be focused on altruistically preserving their authentic branded products and their shared experiences. However, at a deeper level, they may seek to act institutionally in the role of brand curator. This is far from the notion that brand communities are imagined and atomistic relationships among consumers with a common interest (Muñiz and O'Guinn 2001). Thus, the notion of co-creation of consumption practices suggested by Schau *et al.* (2009) may involve more than ceding control implicitly to a brand community. Rather, it would likely involve co-creation in a more strategic sense in which the brand marketer and the select club are jointly and formally interested in negotiating and managing the brand's heritage and trajectory. Furthermore, it suggests that the balance of power between the select brand club and the brand marketer is largely determined by the respective capital resources each brings to bear on the brand. In a sense, the brand's trajectory may reflect the symmetry or asymmetry in the power between the marketer and the select club.

However, it is very likely that the select club and the marketer will diverge in their desired brand trajectories as marketplace changes occur. Marketers seek new markets and new customers, and may need to redesign their products or brands for business purposes. However, much like fan cultures (Hill 2002), BCs and select clubs may tend to be textual conservatives because they have invested emotionally in the brand, their consumption experiences, the community network, and the select club itself. They may emphasize the authenticity of their brand-related values relative to the larger society and, hence, may become locked into their own "rigidly maintained sets of values, authenticities, textual hierarchies, and continuities" (Hill 2002, p. 38). The brand marketer thus may be presented with the tension of choosing between the select brand club niche market and the opportunities in a larger market. Yielding to the select club or its BC in this case may compromise the brand's economic viability or ultimately spell an end to the brand narrative. Thus, the marketer may have to take the initiative to lead brand-changing initiatives and socially negotiate with the select club.

Select clubs, because they are attempting to formalize the amorphous aspects that define a BC, yet maintain the camaraderie that defines its essence, possess value chain management issues of their own. On the one hand, the select club must provide a range of consumption, personal development, and self-identity experiences so its members can emotionally connect with brand. Developing and participating in these activities is a time-consuming social aspect of being an active, authentic member. Often, select club leaders find that the task of building a club activity plan and executing it also requires considerable expertise. An additional issue is lack of continuity as club leaders come and go. Hence, the notion of co-creation of consumption practices by the marketer and BCs (Schau *et al.* 2009), as well as the notions of community scripts (Fournier and Lee 2009), may be particularly relevant to select clubs as they seek to please their members and keep the select club vital. Further, marketers may be in a strong position to work with select club leaders on their value chain planning and management issues.

They may add value for the select club leaders by helping them formalize club's planning process; by providing managerial tools, websites, or materials; by helping them institutionalize their value creation processes so that members realize their expected social and identity projects and status; and by helping the select club achieve continuity and collective mastery in the leadership process itself. In offering this support, it is essential that the firm stresses creating conditions and processes that enable the select club to add value with reduced effort, rather than turning the club into a formal aspect of the firm's marketing plan (Fournier and Lee 2009).

References

Aaker, J.L. (1997) "Dimensions of Brand Personality", *Journal of Marketing Research*, 34: 347–56.

Bourdieu, P. (1984) *Distinction: a social critique of the judgment of taste*, trans. Richard Nice, Cambridge, MA: Harvard University.

—— (1985) "The Forms of Capital", in J.G. Richardson (ed.) *Handbook of Theory and Research for the Sociology of Education*, Westport, CT: Greenwood Press.

—— (1992) *Outline of a Theory of Practice*, Cambridge, UK: Cambridge University Press.

Bourdieu, P. and Wacquant, L.J.D. (1992) *An Invitation to Reflexive Sociology*, Chicago, IL: The University of Chicago Press.

Brown, J.S. and Duguid, P. (2001) "Knowledge and Organizations: A Social-Practice Perspective", *Organization Science*, 12 (2): 198–213.

Celsi, R., Rose, R. and Leigh, T. (1993) "An Exploration of High-Risk Leisure Consumption through Skydiving", *Journal of Consumer Research*, 20: 1–23.

Deighton, J. and Kornfeld, L. (2009) "Interactivity's Unanticipated Consequences for Marketers and Marketing", *Journal of Interactive Marketing*, 23, 1: 4–10.

Feick, L.F. and Price, L.L. (1987) "The Market Maven: A Diffuser of Marketplace Information", *Journal of Marketing*, 51: 83–97.

Fournier, S. (1998) "Consumers and Their Brands: Developing Relationship Theory in Consumer Research", *Journal of Consumer Research*, 24 (4): 343–53.

Fournier, S. and Avery, J. (2011) "The Uninvited Brand", *Business Horizons*, 54 (3): 193–207.

Fournier, S., Dobscha, S. and Mick, D.G. (1998) "Preventing the Premature Death of Relationship Marketing", *Harvard Business Review*, January–February: 43–51.

Fournier, S. and Lee, L. (2009) "Getting Brand Communities Right", *Harvard Business Review*, April: 105–11.

Gaines-Ross, L. (2010) "Reputational Warfare", *Harvard Business Review*, December: 70–6.

Hill, M. (2002) *Fan Cultures*, London and New York: Routledge.

Holt, D.B. (1995) "How Consumers Consume: A Typology of Consumption", *Journal of Consumer Research*, 22: 1–16.

—— (1998) "Does Cultural Capital Structure American Consumption", *Journal of Consumer Research*, 25: 1–25.

Iacobucci, D. and Hopkins, N. (1992) "Modeling Dyadic Interactions and Networks in Marketing", *Journal of Marketing Research*, 29: 5–17.

Keller, K.L. (1993) "Conceptualizing, Measuring, and Managing Customer-Based Brand Equity", *Journal of Marketing*, 57: 1–22.

King, C.W. and Summers, J.O. (1976) "Overlap of Opinion Leadership across Product Categories", *Journal of Marketing Research*, 7: 43–50.

Kozinets, R.V. (2002) "Can Consumers Escape the Market? Emancipatory Illuminations from Burning Man", *Journal of Consumer Research*, 29: 20–38.

Kozinets, R.V., de Valck, K., Wojnicki, A.C. and Wilner, S.J.S. (2010) "Networked Narratives: Understanding Word of Mouth Marketing in Online Communities", *Journal of Marketing*, 74 (2) (March): 71–89.

Kumar, V. and Reinartz, W. (2002) "The Mismanagement of Customer Loyalty", *Harvard Business Review*, July: 4–12.

Leigh, T.W., Peters, C. and Shelton, J. (2006) "The Consumer Quest for Authenticity: Multiplicity of Meanings within the MG Subculture of Consumption", *Journal of the Academy of Marketing Science*, 31 (4): 1–13.

McAlexander, J., Schouten, J. and Koenig, H. (2002) "Building Brand Community", *Journal of Marketing*, 66 (1): 38–55.

Mauss, M. ([1923] 1990) *The Gift: forms and function of exchange in archaic societies*, New York: Routledge.

Muñiz, A.M. and Hamer, L. (2001) "Us versus Them: Oppositional Loyalty in the Cola Wars", *Advances in Consumer Research*, (28): 355–61.

Muñiz, A.M. and O'Guinn, T. (2001) "Brand Community", *Journal of Consumer Research*, 27: 412–32.

Pitt, L.F., Watson, R.T., Berthon, P., Wynn, D. and Zinkhan, G. (2006) "Corporate Brands from an Open Source Perspective", *Journal of the Academy of Marketing Science*, 34 (2): 115–27.

Ratchford, B.T. (2001) "The Economics of Consumer Knowledge", *Journal of Consumer Research*, 27: 397–411.

Schau, H.P., Muñiz, A. and Arnould, E. (2009) "How Community Brand Practices Create Value", *Journal of Marketing*, 73: 30–51.

Schouten, J. and McAlexander, J. (1995) "Subcultures of Consumption: An Ethnography of the New Bikers", *Journal of Consumer Research*, 22: 43–61.

Sirsi, A.K., Ward, J.C. and Reingen, P.H. (1996) "Microcultural Analysis of Variation in Sharing of Causal Reasoning about Behavior", *Journal of Consumer Research*, 22: 345–72.

Thompson, S.A. and Sinha, R.K. (2008) "Brand Community and New Product Development: The Influence and Limits of Oppositional Loyalty", *Journal of Marketing*, 72: 65–80.

Wenger, E., McDerrmott, R. and Snyder, W.M. (2002) *Cultivating Communities of Practice*, Boston, MA: Harvard Business School.

Wheatley, M.J. and Kellner-Rogers, M. (1998) "The Paradox and Promise of Community", in F. Hesselbein, M. Goldsmith, R. Beckhard, and R. Schubert (eds) *The Community of the Future*, San Francisco, CA: Jossey-Bass.

18

CORPORATE IDENTITY AND ITS REFLECTIVE EFFECT IN DEVELOPING BRAND RELATIONSHIPS

Jean Yannis Suvatjis and Leslie de Chernatony

Introduction

In this challenging information age, the effective management of business "relationships" is a mandatory task. Building "relationships" necessitates creating a succession of new sources of brand value, and revitalizing internal and external contacts, so organizations can present contemporary and relevant behaviors to stakeholders.

Building corporate relations is a key goal of any organization and is attracting research interest amongst academics. Several academics and practitioners developed various theories regarding brand management, brand equity, brand associations, brand relations, corporate reputation, brand and company associations, stakeholders, corporate identity and image, all based entirely or partially on social relationship theory. All of them aimed to delineate the approach and to synthesize the core elements and relationship mix needed to build strong relations for the benefit of the entire organization and the interacting stakeholders. Recently, corporate identity studies have attracted major attention from academics and practitioners owing to their contribution to an organization's performance.

The corporate identity concept is multidimensional by its context and nature, since it encompasses a number of components, and each one of them constitutes a variable serving a specific role in the process of creating, managing and preserving corporate identity. On the other hand, all these components must be properly aligned to create and maintain an organization's relationships internally and externally. More specifically, branding, reputation, corporate personality, corporate image, stakeholder theory, advertising, culture, visual symbolism and communication are only a few areas of study along the spectrum of corporate identity. Our study addresses the issue of corporate identity modeling and its "relationship" development process within the internal and external environment through the newly designed six-station corporate identity model.

The philosophical framework on which the six-station corporate identity model was based focused entirely on devising the appropriate links and relationships to create a strong corporate identity. The study introduces a corporate identity construct which also demonstrates and illustrates the "relational bridges" for achieving "successful consumer interface."

The six-station corporate identity model aims to create a strong corporate identity, strengthen brands, help in the formulation of corporate strategy, encourage more transparent communication, engender a unique corporate personality and strengthen reputations, all based on the creation and management of corporate "relationships."

The model was grounded in a review of the literature. Qualitative research was conducted to assess the model's relational pragmatism, usefulness and managerial applicability. The model provides a conceptual framework for analysis of the identity development process. It emphasizes the continuous and synergistic efforts needed for "relationship" management.

The relationship concept

Social, organizational, brand and corporate relationships are only a few types of relationships which dominate the research agenda of academics and practitioners. What actually is a "relationship" and what does it come from? "A relationship is what the relationship means; understanding a given relationship requires a mastery of the meanings the relationship provides to the person who engages it" (Fournier, 1998: 345). The development of a relationship must be based on the alignment of intentions, beliefs, principles and motives of the involved parties.

Hinde (1979) noted that in order for a relationship to exist, the characteristic of interdependence among parties must be dominant, where parties must communally affect, define and redefine the relationship.

Any kind of a relationship can be characterized as a dynamic praxis since its status can change in any given time depending of the behavior of the partners, and the events that influence the equilibrium of the relationship. "Thus, relationships are constituted of a series of repeated exchanges between two parties known to each other; they evolve in response to the interactions and to fluctuations in the contextual environment" (Fournier, 1998: 346).

Relationships affect and are affected by the contexts in which they are embedded. Psychological, socio-cultural and relational meanings are identified in the relationship-forming process. Psychological meaning usually refers to identity activity in which the relationship is grounded. People always want to deal with a company with strong status, corporate personality and image (Fournier, 1998: 346).

Relationships are purposive, involving at their core the provisions of meanings to the people who are involved in them. Relationships are multiplex phenomena: they range across several dimensions and take many forms, providing a range of possible benefits for their participants.

Yet, relationships are process phenomena: they evolve and change over a series of interactions and in response to fluctuations in the contextual environment (Hinde, 1995).

Social relationship theory indicates that relationships communicate norms of behavior that guide people's evaluations of the relationship partner (Aggarwal, 2004). Using the same syllogism, business relationships are created as an outcome of the evaluation of people's experience with an organization.

When organizations focus on their business activities and consumers are satisfied with the outcome of the primary experience with the organization, they may think of the organization as a living partner or as an associate.

There is evidence suggesting why consumers might interact with brands in ways that closely reflect their social interactions. First, consumers most of the time do not distinguish between brands and manufacturers of brands. According to them, the company is the brand and the brand is the company (King, 1991).

Relationships are frequently distinguished by the nature of the benefits they deliver to the participants (Weiss, 1974; Wright, 1995). Relationships appear in different schemes, analogous to the purpose which they intend to fulfill and the domain in which they operate and belong. The diversity of relationships evolves around people, organizations, tangible objects, services or group of people and group of companies. Relationship schemes such as consumers and brands, organizations and consumers, monopolize the business world and have become a favorite research subject.

The peculiar nature, the formation process, the structure and the idiosyncrasy of the "social relationship" phenomenon, studied extensively from the point of view of psychology and social relationship theory, shed light on the investigation into business and corporate relationships. Yet, metaphors and similes are incorporated in the analysis of the relationship in order to facilitate the understanding of any voluntarily or involuntarily formed relationships.

More specifically, Nida and Smalley (1959) suggested that there is an apparent need to anthropomorphize objects so that one can facilitate interactions with a non-material world.

In essence for any brand to serve as a legitimate relationship partner, it must surpass the personification and behave as an active, contributing member of the dyadic relationship. Animism also is used in the anthropomorphization of the brand, with conveyance of the human qualities of emotion, thought and volition. Athropomorphized identity characters serve as examples (Fournier, 1998: 346).

Animism is not only recognized in the domain of products (Gilmore, 1919; McGill, 1998; Moon, 2000), it applies to organizations as well. Consumers sometimes think of companies as having a soul. Once organizations are associated with values that originate from human qualities, people interact with them in ways that parallel social relationships, and their interactions are guided by the norms that govern these relationships (Aggarwal, 2004).

Metaphorical anthropomorphization of the organization emphasizes the conveyance not only of human qualities but of all tangible and intangible attributes intended to be shared in the relationship. For example, insurance companies serve as "guardian angels," to secure consumers' wellbeing in good or bad times, thus forming a corporate relationship. This example may apply to the context of a company's management of corporate identity and image process. Business relationships are created to satisfy specific needs, to advance organizational harmony, to ensure mutual shared benefits and to deal with organizations with particular styles of business behavior.

Conversely, there is no parallelism in applying the reciprocity criterion to a lifeless brand – object (company). A brand may enjoy selected animistic properties, but it is not a vital entity. In fact the brand has no objective existence at all – it is simply a collection of perceptions held in the mind of the consumer (Fournier, 1998: 345) as well as their hearts. Through its people, a company can think, feel, execute, hurt or satisfy needs. Accepting the behavioral significance of marketing actions, one accepts the legitimacy of the brand as contributing relationship partner (Fournier, 1998: 345).

Furthermore, an organization's relationships with consumers can be a strategic asset and a source of competitive advantage. Although corporate relationships are part of the marketing spectrum, is not clear how, when and what types of corporate relationships influence people's responses to accept a company and to form a favorable corporate image. It is important to identify how information transmitted to consumers creates an environment of favorable association with the organization (Dacin and Brown, 1997). Marketing needs to identify "the value of corporate identity and image" and the value of being seen as a "builder" of corporate relationships.

Finally, corporate relationships can be formed from perceptions, inferences and beliefs about the organization; a consumer's knowledge of their prior behavior with respect to the company; information about the company's prior actions; moods and emotions experienced by the person with respect to the company; and overall and specific evaluations of the company and its perceived attributes (Dacin and Brown, 1997).

The corporate identity concept

Corporate identity is a very important business concept because it demonstrates corporate ethos, aims and values and presents a sense of individuality that can help to differentiate an organization from its competitors (Hatch and Schultz, 1997). According to Zinkhan et al. (2001: 154), corporate identity represents "the ways a company chooses to identity itself to all the publics." As Baker and Balmer

(1997) noted more simply, albeit far more generally, corporate identity is what an organization is. Corporate identity can be viewed as a vehicle by which a company's character is conveyed to different audiences (Erikson, 1960). It reflects the sense of "essential character," since each company has its own personality, uniqueness and individuality (Bernstein, 1984).

Effective corporate identity management can build understanding and commitment among an organization's various stakeholders. It helps attract and retain customers and employees, achieve strategic alliances, gain support from financial stakeholders and generate a sense of direction and purpose (Hatch and Schultz, 1997). Senior managers attach considerable importance to corporate identity modeling and regard it as a strategic marketing issue (Balmer, 1994).

There are various models that incorporate advanced knowledge about forming and managing corporate identity, but their varied approaches and perspectives have led to questions about each model's capabilities and limitations. In the beginning the lack of consensus in defining a standardized corporate identity construct has led to confusion in determining the corporate identity context (Melewar and Jenkins, 2002) and managing it. The need for an in-depth analysis to decode the essence of corporate identity construct and its derivates (Cornelissen and Elving, 2003) led academics and practitioners to deeply scrutinize the concept. Recent findings and studies regarding the dimensions of corporate identity transmitted the first signs of convergence among researchers (Otubanjo and Melewar, 2007).

Based on the last developments a strong need was perceived for a new corporate identity model. All of this motivated an intense research program that is briefly described below.

The first review of the corporate identity literature involved exploring traditional and new areas of general management, marketing management, brand management, advertising, communication, corporate symbolism and corporate visual identity systems, organizational behavior, interpersonal relationship psychology, digital technology, corporate image and reputation studies. Indeed, the expression of corporate identity is a dynamic process, evolving as the organizational context changes (Gioia, 1998) and requiring effective management through the use of an appropriate model.

A second thorough literature review explored the area of business and corporate identity modeling to assess the limitations of existing models and to consider the need for a new one. Ten criteria emerged that were deemed important for a robust model, namely, visual clarity, ease of interpretation, logical sequence, adjustment and adaptability, production of synergies, employee operationalization, ease of memorizing, effectiveness, modularity and proactivity. These criteria were applied to introduce a clear, workable, useful and valid visual model, which encompassed all dimensions that could possibly comprise the corporate identity construct according to the literature review.

The idea of constructing the model was, first of all, to create a model that would include all acceptable, meaningful and salient aspects of corporate identity. Secondly, the model had to incorporate only those components/variables that were directly related to and accepted in the corporate identity context used by researchers. Addressing and interpreting each component/variable, both individually and in terms of their interrelationships, can facilitate understanding for everyone, especially for organizations willing to investigate, evaluate and adapt the model and that might implement it as a strategic attempt to formulate and manage their corporate identity. Thirdly, in developing a corporate identity model, all endogenous and exogenous forces had to be considered that impact on corporate identity and its incorporated variables to reveal practical managerial applications.

The six-station corporate identity model: its dyadic role

The present study will introduce the framework and the relationships produced by the mechanics of the six-station corporate identity model which can create a favorable identity. The proposed corporate identity construct will attempt to answer basic questions of whether, how and in what ways companies create on-going relationships with consumers.

The model will attempt to develop a grounded and fully articulated relationship framework for the study of company–consumer interaction within the context of corporate identity. The six-station corporate identity model describes basic relationship principles and develops an integrated framework, explaining and exploring the formation of interactions and associations.

The intent of this model, beyond its primary objective to build a strong corporate identity, is to develop a solid conceptual foundation from which corporate identity relationships can be cultivated and to further illustrate the dynamism of the relationships produced. Indeed, corporate identity can serve as a relationship bridge to create a partnering association which will make the consumer the most "loyal" friend or associate of the organization.

Primarily, the six-station corporate identity model attempts to build and manage a strong corporate identity by identifying how consumers evaluate the organization and its actions, depending upon whether an organization's actions match consumers' perception, the norms of their relationship and their acceptance.

The model suggests that when an organization attempts to form a particular relationship within the context of its business activities, the company is assessed in the same way as other members within society – according to the norms of social behavior.

It seems that, when consumers form relationships with brands, brands too are evaluated as though they were members of a culture and need to conform to its norms. If the actions of the brand are in violation of the norm of a relationship, then the brand is evaluated negatively, but if the actions are in conformity with the norms of a relationship, then the evaluation is positive.

The model takes into account and reveals relationships based on economic factors, social factors such as exchange and communal relationships (Clark and Mills, 1993), and also relationships based on associations related to an organization's corporate ability and corporate social responsibility (Dacin and Brown, 1997).

According to Clark and Mills (1993), in exchange relationships the stimulus for giving a benefit to the partner is to get something back in return. In the business world relationships between organizations and consumers who interact for business purposes can be characterized most of the time as typical exchange relationships. In communal relationships, organizations and people offer benefits to others to demonstrate a concern for wellbeing.

These relationships have distinct norms: Organizations or people in exchange relationships expect to receive monetary reward for providing any kind of service, wish to receive analogous benefits in return, and expect prompt compensation for benefits offered to a partner. Organizations or citizens in a communal relationship do not expect monetary reward for assisting partners, prefer to receive non-comparable benefits in return, and do not expect prompt compensation for benefits offered.

Communal and exchange relations are part of the corporate identity concept because corporate identity relies heavily on the exchange of messages (cues) sent and received at the point of interface between the organization and its external audiences. The six-station corporate identity model radiates communal and exchange relationships, firstly because it is addressed solely to audiences of different type; secondly because these two relationship types are directed to different audiences with a different purpose; and thirdly because these distinct relationships are salient in the corporate interaction process where consumers interpret these norms to formulate their behavior and their evaluations of the organization.

The model's synergies and relationships also reveal and develop the organization's corporate ability and corporate social responsibility role which empower the relationship-building process. Corporate ability refers to an organization's expertise in producing and delivering its outputs, and corporate social responsibility reflects the organization's status and activities with respect to its perceived societal obligations (Dacin and Brown, 1997).

The model demonstrates what consumers should holistically know about an organization that can influence their evaluations about the organization, its behavior, products or services. The model attempts to reveal that different types of corporate relations can have important influences on company and product evaluation.

The typology of the six-station corporate identity model

Corporate identity serves as the reflected microcosm of the organization's macrocosm, structured by a chain of related elements that converge to consolidate a corporate identity as the organization's characteristically representative image, for both external and internal consumption. For example, one can conceive of IBM's total corporate identity as "Big Blue," this being a logo, an image, an attitude, a style of communication and a corporate history, all of which exemplify a business model, a way of working and a corporate view of life.

The skeleton of the six-station model is set out below; it is presented as the new corporate identity mix.

1. Top management, mission/vision/values, leadership – Head Station
2. Brands/products and services, corporate strategy, marketing – Strategy Station
3. Visual dentity, corporate visual identity systems, sdvertising – Creativity Station
4. External, internal communication, digital communication (internet) – Communication Station
5. Stakeholders, organization's staff, company's group dynamism – Human Power Station
6. Reputation, corporate image, corporate personality – Critical Triplet Station.

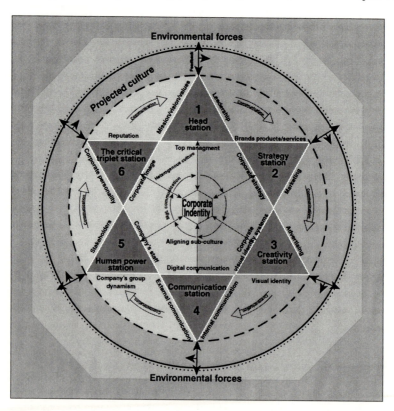

FIGURE 18.1 The six-station corporate identity model

The six-station corporate identity model is a comprehensive model that provides a clearer definition of the corporate identity formation process, and reveals all possible relationships produced. All major mechanisms that influence an organization and act in synergy with others create either a dynamic relay of favorable outcomes or gaps that must be bridged in the process of corporate management.

The literature review has provided the theoretical basis that has assisted in conceptualizing a model appropriate for business professionals and managers. Managers must take into account that corporate identity is the presentation of the firm, but they must also consider this notion more broadly, for although corporate identity is indeed the presentation of the company, it also involves a continuous effort to manage all its dynamics, maintain its distinctiveness and manage effectively all relationships being produced. For this reason, a conceptual definition of corporate identity will be presented, along with a practical operational approach to the formulation and analysis of identity and its subsequent corporate relationships.

The conceptual definition calls for the strategic orchestration and total management of the multiple dynamics which affect a company's mechanisms and which contribute to a favorable image in the consumer's mind. The operational approach aims to include and measure all shifting parameters that alter the status of the identity. Therefore, corporate identity is defined as the organization's icon, the mental image, that manifests a company's culture, conveys its self-image and earned reputation, transmits its corporate personality, reflects its unique characteristics and protects it from imitators.

The six-station model's architecture: relationship builder

The six-station model introduces the major components that contribute to the initial process of corporate identity formation and to its management after formation. Its significance lies in providing an analytic framework for the identity formation process. This formation process is facilitated through the synergistic effect, the voluntarily and involuntarily formed relationships and the successful management of them.

Nevertheless, the model considers and draws special attention to both esoteric and exoteric relationships which arise within the model due to fermentation of social, business, individual and group interactions, facilitating the channeling of the appropriate behavior needed to advance and accelerate the formation and management of corporate identity.

Metaphorically, the entire model represents a "corporate neural network," composed of different "neuron stations," each one connected circularly, but allowing interaction along and within the area enclosed by all stations. Owing to the openness of this system, interaction can occur from any direction. Each of the station triangles depicts major components analyzed firstly as separate entities, and secondly in relation to each other. The components must be able to advance their properties and associations to prepare a path and a relay of succession to the next station triangle of parameters.

The model contains two stages or sides, the right and the left side. This is indicated by the different shading of the areas on the right and left in the central circle.

The model's mechanisms

The model assumes that the image formation process starts immediately after an organization transmits even its slightest messages to the outer environment, and the formation process continues and is dependent on the density of messages sent and accumulated by the internal and external environments.

As a result of the model's typology and clockwise motion, the messages produced by the entire organization are multiplied when information is processed, thus producing outcomes. These communication cues initiate the first stage of the "corporate invitation" to extend bilateral relationships.

When information is managed and transferred from one station to another, messages are produced that go through an interaction process, receiving and providing feedback from each station. Feedback is then manipulated and directed to the entire organization, abandoning the area of the nucleus culture, which is the area in which most negotiations and dealings take place.

In the corporate identity management process, every station maintains a role and seeks incorporation and interaction with the next station to ensure smooth management of the concept of corporate identity. In the event of the need for some identity change, modification or improvement, interaction is necessary not only between adjoining stations, but with all stations, regardless of order or sequence.

In both circumstances, every point on the outer circle of the projected culture generates and reveals a degree of minimum or maximum image interface, depending on the level of information involved, sent, interpreted and digested by the market and by the external and internal stakeholders at any particular time.

If events and messages are isolated and unrelated to other activities and if no affiliation exists between the related corporate components, the degree of image interface is assumed to be low, not significant with weak impact forming relationships externally. If messages and information are functions of various parameters and decisions are aligned with groups' interest, the degree of image interface is assumed to be high and significant, thus possibly creating new relationships.

The location of station number 1 conveys certain messages that are analogous to the content and purpose of its parameters, thus creating certain synergies esoterically and externally. It releases data, promotes activities and seeks connections and affiliation with the next station. At this point, image interface is assumed to be low, owing to the release of limited information.

In the second corporate station (2), it is assumed that image interface is significantly higher, due to the fact that messages produced by the company increase, since they incorporate messages originating from both stations 1 and 2 and seeking relationships with wider audiences mainly externally. Station 2 now becomes the site of new sets of parameters that produce new messages. These incorporate the pre-existing and still active messages from station 1, since the market and all major stakeholders continue to consider and respond in order to incorporate them into the newly obtained messages from the second corporate station.

This model assumes that the more one progresses through the defined corporate identity stations, the higher the degree of image interface obtained and the more there are potential relationships to form. The highest level of interfacing occurs in the last station (6), with its critical parameters of corporate personality, corporate image and corporate reputation. It is assumed that most images can be found in this part of the model, since all the different publics have formed an idea of the company based on all previous parameters, and more particularly have formed an image of the company based on the concepts of corporate personality and reputation. If resemblance of impressions occurs between organization and potential external constituencies, multiplication of relationships exists.

The "relationship bridges" of the right side of the model

The management relational bridge – Head Station

The model can be broken down in terms of stages/sides or spheres to illustrate the internal relations of adjacent components (see Figure 18.1). The right side of the model is composed of corporate stations 1, 2 and 3.

It includes station 1 as the Head Station in which, under the leadership of senior management, with the company's vision, mission and values, the objectives are set for the company's operation. The effect of the leadership of top executives on the firm itself is considered a major factor, since an implemented leadership model affecting not only people but also the market is critical in the formation of a company's corporate identity.

Top executives are assigned the most important role in this station in that they "kindle" the system through their effective leadership. Management's definition of a clear company vision, mission and objectives, managed by capable executives and managers through a facilitative management style, will assist the transition from the first station to the second station (strategy).

Beyond the aim of beginning to form a strong corporate identity, management attempts to create "relational bridges." Primarily these relationships will be built based on a company's vision, mission, values and leadership style, and secondarily they will be built to facilitate diffusion of the image of the existing organization aura and corporate sentiment to external audiences. The role of top executives is critical, since their contribution, attitudes, values and policies and the degree of leadership they exercise will have an enormous effect on the firm's continuing existence in the market, future longevity, relationship development and corporate association mental formation.

This station will initiate communal relationships (Clark and Mills, 1993) in two different directions. Firstly, the formation of in-company communal relationships between top management and personnel will assist the organization to collectively embrace the company's vision, mission and values and objectives established by the top management, thus achieving a strong internal corporate consensus. Secondly, formation of out-company communal relationships with external audiences will occur, the homogeneous "corporate climate" will be diffused to consumers who will be acquainted with the strategic and social intent of the organization.

Also, relationships connected to corporate social responsibility are in the initial stage of formation with external groups. Usually, organizations try to introduce their social responsible identity and social contribution through their expressed vision, mission and values statements as first indicators of the organization's future behavior and philanthropic intent vis-à-vis its societal obligations.

The strategic relational bridge – Strategy Station

This station's major component is the formulation of a corporate strategy. It involves the selection of certain branding strategies related to products and services, always in conjunction with, and under the direction of, the marketing department. Marketing has the potential to make an important contribution to the multidisciplinary concept of corporate identity, since it is expanding into new areas which have direct and indirect links to corporate identity, such as social marketing, marketing of services and corporate branding (Hatch and Schultz, 1997). Moingeon and Ramanantsoa (1997) noted that the methods of diagnosing identities should be of special interest to marketing executives responsible for managing corporate identity, image and corporate communication.

Yet, today's executives must be globally literate, seeing the world's challenges, enacting global-centric leadership and mobilizing multicultural teams (Rasmussen, 2000).

Strategy is set by the general consensus achieved among top executives and managers, and by other tactical moves designed for each of the firm's different strategic units under its marketing umbrella. All strategic activities of such a nature are marketing-oriented; the related functions deal mainly with the study of the market, consumer tastes and demands, product development and other prerequisites that precede final decisions on corporate branding.

In this station the organization also attempts to build relationships based on their amicable strategies, branding relationships and marketing's socially acceptable character through the strategic relational bridge.

In this station exchange relationships will be under development, since all corporate marketing strategies are aimed toward market development and target specific segments which appear receptive to a company's product and services.

Actually, the aim is dual exchange relationships. Firstly, the company will extend an exchange relationship invitation to consumers, expecting a monetary reward for providing any kind of product or services. Secondly, consumers will seek to receive analogous benefits in return if they concede to relationships based on the value and utility of the products and services being purchased.

These relationships will form as outcomes of consumer association with the organization, and will be activated by the contribution and the "relational bridge" of this station. An organization's integrated brand strategy and marketing's dynamic involvement will reveal the organization's corporate ability to produce and deliver its outputs, thus persuading consumers of the service efficiency, quality and usefulness guaranteed them.

The strategy station and its mechanisms must align cooperation among team members in the station, and only then extend these synergies to station 3, the so-called "Creativity" Station.

The semiotic relational bridge – Creativity Station

This station incorporates the necessary corporate creativity functions, their evolution and interrelation with corporate advertising. The Creativity Station is informed by feedback from the two previous stations regarding the firm's strategic intent and decision making. The creative process explores and creates a "visual essence" not only to label and symbolize the company and its products, but also to visualize its objectives, vision, mission, values, and tangible and intangible products. It is also concerned with the already formulated corporate strategies, human attitudes and behaviors, physical premises, corporate objects and tools. The process culminates in selecting a total and distinct visual representation of the whole organization.

This station employs the concept of the traditional theory of visual identity presentation. It is recommended that adaptation of visual symbolism be considered on a gradual basis and be executed in two phases.

Firstly, visual artifacts and symbols must be selected to represent the company and its products, after careful examination and research into traditional symbolism, so that they are indicative of the company's nature, products, beliefs, attitudes, management philosophy and employees, as well as its social and business behavior.

Completion of this stage will call for an evaluation of the effectiveness and efficiency of the selected "visual" representations and their effects on the entire organization.

After positive feedback has been received regarding the effectiveness of the selected artifacts, logos, colors, shapes and slogans, the second phase will be introduced. This will require the adaptation of unique integrated systems of total visual representation, known as corporate visual identity systems.

It would be more useful, appropriate and effective to take into account the evolution of the corporate visual identity system concept, not only as a tool in developing company representation, but as an alternative to the more ambitious and unique visual identity representations utilized in local or international markets. Finally, in this station, the visual representation of the company has been considered as part of the firm's organizational culture with all its related artifacts – logo, trademark, slogan, and color – as establishing the company's total emblematic apparatus. Upon completion of all processes in the three stations of the model's right side, it will be seen that all the first and most critical strategic decisions and activities fall within the firm's control. All parameters appearing in these three stations contain elements that are designed, directed, executed, modified and initiated under the care, supervision and direct control of top management and are affected by its technocratic nature and idiosyncrasy.

The role of the marketing department is very important, since it can be a dual one. It can maintain its technocratic nature, while also playing a more flexible role, focusing on integrated marketing approaches, without neglecting "relationship marketing," the pulse of the market and the desires, tastes and preferences of consumers.

This station facilitates the process of building relationships, based on the power of symbolism through the semiotic relational bridge.

The formulation of communal relationships is pursued by the organization with the use of its corporate symbolism. In essence the selected corporate visual symbols can act as communication channels to convey the organization's nature, products, beliefs, attitudes and management philosophy to its employees internally, as well as its social and business behavior to consumers externally.

Consumers always react positively to artifacts, symbols, colors and slogans that transmit reliability, security, dependability, safety and trustworthiness. Also, there is an evident connection between refined and friendly corporate symbols and an organization's corporate behavior towards socially responsible activities and programs.

Friendly and socially acceptable corporate symbols set the foundations for communal relationships between the organization and consumers. These communal relationships are the outcome of the organizational culture, strategic intent, corporate behavior and corporate identity, airing a corporate invitation to consumers to accept the organization's philosophy and to initiate a partnering relationship.

The "relationship bridges" of the left side of the model

The communication relational bridge – Communication Station

The left side of the model comprises corporate stations 4, 5 and 6. The fourth station is called the Communication Station, since it operates as a two-way channel performing communication duties for the company's internal and external environment. It transmits and receives information. The firm conducts its normal communication with its various internal and external stakeholders, receives feedback and conducts the communication activities necessary for its operation. All of the firm's formulated messages, types of business communication and related communications activities are transmitted in any direction to the market, with the aid of traditional print, as well as electronic and digital means of marketing communication.

Since communication is multidirectional, its properties, functions, role, messages, processes and policies must be fully utilized and absorbed to a great extent by the next station. The concept of communication concerns the entire organization, especially the stakeholders and company staff, who are significantly affected by the flow of communication and by the pattern employed. They are affected both formally and informally, since management and organizational communication play a contributing role in the organization. Managing communication effectively will contribute positively to the corporate identity formation process.

An additional aim of this station is to intensively utilize transparent communication to enhance the dyadic (two-way channel) communicative process between organization and consumers, thus establishing a communication relation bridge with external audiences willing to be involved in a partnering relationship.

More specifically this station attempts to structure communal relationships through transmitting communication cues. In essence, the organization attempts to create direct communal relationships through the use of an integrated communication process with consumers, to increase the consumers' knowledge about the company's corporate ability to fulfill its tangible and intangible promises, along with the ability of its products and services to respond to customers' needs and tastes.

The organization aims to convert the majority of these communal relationships to exchange relationships, thus benefiting the company with an increased customer base and satisfying consumers in return.

The anthropocentric relational bridge – Human Station

This is the "human corporate power station," the most important component of the corporate ecology. It deals entirely with the human factor and all its corporate synergies and mechanisms, producing conscious or unconscious attributes in the formation of corporate identity. Internal and external stakeholder roles, attitudes, values, ethics, actions and interests act as transmitters of information to the outside world. Within the group of internal and external stakeholders, staff constitutes a critical determinant. In this model, a company's staff includes all people working in the company, especially those at the lower employment level (production line and factory employees). The company's personnel might have dual status, with both internal and external stakeholder property status, or might be either an internal or external stakeholder.

It is believed that junior employees can greatly affect the firm's corporate identity, simply because they usually outnumber the rest of the firm's employees, and consequently have more direct and immediate contact with consumers. They communicate daily with their own constituencies, either as consumers or as firm employees; they do not hesitate to discuss the prevailing environment within their organization, comment on it favorably or unfavorably, and make concerted efforts to convey the message with respect to their own benefits (compensation, working conditions, etc.). However, further research may be needed to support this assumption before it can be regarded as a valid parameter in the formation of corporate identity.

Human behavior always tends to initiate conflicts, since group dynamics can produce multiple conflicts within organizations. As an unavoidable phenomenon, conflict within and among groups can create a major obstacle in the process of forming corporate identity. This station is also crucial for the formation of corporate identity, since consensus within these groups advances corporate identity. The fewer conflicts in this station, the fewer disturbances are caused in the entire model, contributing to a more stable and solid process for the formulation of corporate identity.

The extra role of this station is to create a "double-way relational bridge." In the beginning the organization attempts to use the aura of organization culture to build relationships with internal and external audiences. All relationship efforts are focused on the human factor.

More specifically, the "double-way relational bridge" is centered on the development of communal and exchange relationships with a company's internal and external stakeholders' involvement.

Internally, communal relationships will be created from the shared emotions, beliefs, impressions and perceptions among the employees of the company. Strong communal relationships are created upon the establishment of "mutual corporate love and respect" between employees and the organization.

The internal communal relations between interorganizational partners are transferred intentionally and unintentionally through their constituencies (personnel) to the public. If external audiences accept these communal relationships and maintain their apparatus, then these relationships might transform to exchange relationships for the benefit of the partnering scheme.

The nurturing of the initial communal relationships will indirectly trigger consumers' associations about a company's corporate ability. These positive associations on behalf of the consumers will create "trust" towards the company, will reduce perceived risk, and will increase confidence in the company-consumer relationship. Thus it will solidify communal relationships and set the foundations for converting them to future exchange relationships.

The bonding relational bridge – Critical Triplet Station

The introduction of the last station completes the circuit of the corporate identity process model, in which all stations contribute equally to the formation of a coherent corporate entity. Also, the previous five stations initiated the development of communal and exchange relationships along with relationships based on associations regarding a company's corporate ability and social corporate responsibility role. In this station, the organization and the consumer should have formed a strong relationship based on those formed in the previous five stations.

The establishment of a company's corporate personality, reputation and image is ultimately left to the consumers' judgment. The components of this station constitute the company's critical "reaching out" to the consumers. This is probably the most crucial station in the entire model, as it defines consumer perceptions of the company and fulfills the goal of "relationship marketing."

The criteria that determine the success of this model are the strategic and operational goals initially set by management: to synchronize efforts, connect synergies, adapt existing strategies, implement new strategies and tactics, eliminate corporate parasitism, communicate effectively, exercise ethical business practice, and so on. The resulting analysis is always focused on facilitating the creation of a strong corporate personality, leading to a strong corporate reputation and positive image. The final corporate station comes last in the cycle, so its effect may not be instantaneous, as consumers require time to form perceptions and opinions of the company's image, reputation and personality. Yet it is the first station to be negatively affected when consumers convey signs of dissatisfaction and discontent with the company. If "corporate perishability" occurs as a result of the firm's heterogeneous sub-cultures, a misalignment of human behavior and lack of clear communication will weaken the relay of the system. The resulting blockage of the circular flow of synergies will be due to the broken flow of the successive synergies that must be maintained as a full-time, continuous corporate practice.

Assessing the "building relations": qualitative research findings and discussion

Qualitative research was used to investigate, firstly, the model's applicability and, secondly, the contribution of the relationship formation process to the concept of corporate identity.

Purposeful sampling was employed in the qualitative research (Sabiote-Fernandez and Roman, 2005). In-depth, semi-structured interviews were conducted with twenty-eight corporate identity consultants and business managers. This sample was selected from highly reputable companies in manufacturing, commerce, industry and services, and the interviewees were CEOs, general managers, corporate identity managers, marketing managers, advertising managers and human resources managers. The respondents provided a foundation for the initial stage of the research, giving through their responses a good indication of issues relating to corporate identity.

The model was presented so that they could comment on its managerial applicability and on the corporate relationship process development. Interviews were recorded and transcribed and content analysis was performed by two researchers (Krippendorf, 1980). Emergent coding was used to evaluate responses, and categories were established following preliminary examination of the data. Some broad descriptive codes were redefined further, and more indicative sub-codes were developed as the researchers became better acquainted with the data. Inter-researcher differences were resolved through discussion (Miles and Huberman, 1994). Inter-coder reliability was calculated at 89 percent.

Content analysis revealed that the model was regarded as useful and having managerial applicability. Finally, the model was perceived as being representative of corporate identity and as clearly depicting it as a concept. Respondents felt the model presented the many components of corporate identity in an interlinked, holistic manner.

Findings on consumer relations

The findings directly and indirectly revealed a series of interesting issues. One interesting theme which emerged is the role of corporate relationships in the creation and management of corporate identity. Initially, the six-station corporate identity model described and promoted the importance of the development of corporate relationships with its audiences through internal and external mechanisms. Respondents also highlighted the "relationship" aspect either directly or indirectly.

Corporate identity concept and its relationship effect

The themes that emerged from the respondents' interpretation and definitions of the corporate identity concept revealed a variety of statements containing important aspects, variables and parameters concerning the context of corporate identity. The most important themes that were revealed, and which composed the core body of the corporate identity definition, included the following.

Corporate reputation and its relationship effect

The purpose for seeking to identify the contribution of corporate reputation to corporate identity is firstly to analyze respondents' views and secondly to explore its relationship to other elements of corporate identity.

Corporate reputation was perceived as a central element for defining corporate identity. Consultants recognized that reputation can be formed over time and it is a product of aggregate experiences maintained by the stakeholders. A general manager of a consulting firm observed that "Corporate reputation is derived generally through a company's perceived corporate image formed in the mind of the stakeholders over time, including all its actions and activities and specifically through consumer concrete interactions and relationships with the company." This statement reflects the perception that the objective of corporate identity management is to acquire a favorable corporate image among stakeholders which, over time, results in the acquisition of a favorable reputation, leading to the stakeholders' propensity to deal more actively with the organization (Baker and Balmer, 1997). A communications manager highlighted the importance of the company's reputation, but in combination with the important contribution of symbolism. He stated that corporate identity is defined "as the symbols, beliefs and values combined with the corporate reputation formed among all stakeholder groups of a company that had an experience with that company or somehow a relationship with it." The nature of this definition involves the concept of corporate reputation as a focal point, supported by the significant contribution of visual symbolism and adopted corporate beliefs.

It was also expressed that corporate image stimulated the creation of corporate reputation and that corporate images formed in the market create the notion of corporate reputation. A communications manager explained the interrelation and the synonymous nature of these two concepts in the following way: "corporate reputation is a dimension of the perceived corporate image formed in the mind of the stakeholders. It must be considered an important factor." This reflects two schools of thought: one which perceives corporate reputation as synonymous with corporate image, and another that regards corporate reputation as different from but interrelated with corporate image (Gotsi and Wilson, 2001). The remarks obtained from a creative director of a consulting company expressed his own interpretation that "corporate reputation is the reflection of the many corporate images of a firm in the market; after images are encountered, experienced and interpreted by the different publics, corporate reputation is formed, thus a firm can become distinguishable and unique." This is another opinion, which reveals the interrelation and the origin of corporate reputation in the concept of corporate image. This view is in line with Mason's (1993) stance that corporate reputation is only one dimension of corporate image. Also Fombrun (1996: 72) argues that a company's corporate reputation is influenced by the multifarious images held by different constituencies and audiences. According to this view, corporate reputation is an amalgam of the multiple images of a company held by all.

Also, a marketing manager stated that "corporate reputation is built over time since it is composed of aggregates of image and experience of the firm, is greatly associated with employee behavior, corporate communication and corporate symbolism." The above statement can be related to Herbig and Milewicz's (1995: 24) findings that reputation involves a historical dimension as it represents "the estimation of the consistency over time of an attitude of an entity . . . based on its willingness and ability to perform an activity repeatedly in a similar fashion."

A human resources development manager also noted that "a firm's willingness and ability to perform well along with good image sustainability constitutes a solid corporate reputation. It's mainly the outcome of the company's holistic business behavior in the market. It is built over a specific period of time and reflects the corporate standing of the company." This statement is also verified by Fombrun and Van Riel (1997: 10) who emphasize the historical nature of reputation since they suggest that reputation is a "subjective, collective assessment of an organization's trustworthiness and reliability" based on past performance.

Company's idiosyncrasy to build relationships

Few consultants defined the concept of corporate identity in a holistic matter. Their definition appeared to be general, but it involved the corporate relationship concept. For example, a marketing consultant stated that "corporate identity is the company's specific outlook that reveals its certain characteristics that make the company identifiable and customer friendly to the market in general," while a public relations manager in the same consulting firm stated that "the company's presentation, total appearance and relationship approach in the market environment constitute the company's corporate identity." Statements such as these are in line with the view that corporate identity refers to attributes which make an organization distinct (Abratt, 1989; Balmer, 1995, 1998; Gray and Balmer, 1998; Van Riel and Balmer, 1997). Moreover, a communications manager defined corporate identity as "the DNA of a corporate organization, determining its visual and behavioral forms of expression and interaction within the environment in which the corporation operates." This definition offered the expanded nature of the subject, its multidisciplinary character, and designated its importance using the power of metaphor. Finally the CEO of an established consulting firm stated that "corporate identity consists of all those elements that differentiate one corporation from another and contribute to the awareness (cognition) and preference (emotion) of the corporation." Actually this executive referred to all elements that are relevant to the concept of corporate identity in a general and concise way. The above perception is in accordance with Larcon and Reitter (1979) who argue that identity is a set of interdependent characteristics of the organization that give specificity, stability and coherence, and which make it identifiable.

Corporate culture as a conduit to create customer interaction

Corporate culture has been referred to by many consultants as one of the main aspects for defining corporate identity. A CEO from a well-known corporate identity-consulting firm stated that "the symbols, concepts, codes and relationships that unify the corporate culture and distinguish it in the corporate world compose the heart of the corporate identity concept." This response defines the concept of corporate identity by focusing directly on the corporate culture along with the importance of corporate symbolism, concepts and codes that assist in the revelation of the culture. A general manager of another consulting firm observed through his definition that "corporate culture is all the beliefs, norms, actions and interactions that exist within the company that are directly and indirectly communicated to all its audiences, and define the corporate identity of the firm." Generally these respondents expressed the importance of corporate culture and placed it at the heart of the corporate identity concept. This is also noted by Baker and Balmer (1997) who state that while culture is an integral element of corporate identity formation, it is arguably the most important element of the corporate identity mix.

Corporate identity consultants claimed that their unique company culture constitutes the major identifiable attribute of their firm. Indicatively, a public relations consultant stated that "our homogeneously unique culture is communicated through our well trained employees and through the direct communicational strategy. Fortunately, in being a traditional company our projected culture is our most reliable communication message." Indeed culture is a major corporate identity attribute for those who understand its importance. On the same note a creative consultant commented that "our business culture supported by our business ethos, good product and services and use of clear communicational channels to our stakeholders compose the most compelling core elements our identity." Corporate identity and corporate communication consultancy may be seen as providing a mirror and a window, reflecting and revealing the organization's culture and personality (Balmer and Dinnie, 1999).

Corporate visual symbolism and its effects on customer interaction

Visual symbolism remains for many consultants the most prominent aspect of corporate identity. Visual symbolism, however, along with a mixture of other factors, was designated by corporate identity consultants as contributing to the uniqueness of corporate identity. Indicatively, a creative consultant referred to the contributing factors of corporate identity "as the factor of standardized corporate symbolism, logo, slogan and other artifacts as predominant factors." This is in accordance with Olins (1995) who states that the symbols of the company should present the central idea of the organization with impact, brevity and immediacy. Also Melewar and Saunders (2000) state that corporate visual identity systems can widen the communication mix through symbol, logo and slogan.

The same consultant also stated that "visual symbolism which reflects a degree of friendliness towards the consumer contributes incredibly to favorable consumer evaluation and association with the company."

This same consultant also added that "a company's visual presentation, culture, business activity strategy, brands, and unique products and services complement some of the most important factors." A public relations manager shared an almost identical view since he advocated that "the most important factors that contribute to corporate identity are unique and homogeneous appearance, appropriate business behavior, unique entrepreneurial activity and powerful corporate brands."

Corporate symbolism was regarded as a major component of corporate identity and was mentioned in combination with other factors. For example, a sales manager stated that "mainly, corporate identity is a mixture of appropriate symbolism, always in accordance with its values, business activities, the corporate manner, structure and behavior of the company towards the consumers." Partly, this supports Bernstein's (1984) perception that symbolism can become a type of shorthand for the identity of the company and its values. An analogous definition was offered by a marketing manager who insisted that "corporate identity is all visual, standardized, universal, concrete, abstract, behavioral and non-behavioral elements that a company adopts consciously and unconsciously in its process to present itself in the market, approaching strategically its audiences through mutually beneficial relationships." Such a definition reveals not only major core elements of corporate identity, but also concepts that act directly and indirectly in its formation and management. Markwick and Fill (1997) also observe that corporate identity is the organization's presentation of itself to its various stakeholders and the means by which it distinguishes itself from all other organizations. Another marketing manager observed that his company's recognizable corporate identity characteristics are "its powerful corporate symbolism, a very approachable and friendly way of customer service, its manageable market strategy, our brand names, and the quality of our products." Similarly but under a different scope, Baker and Balmer (1997) highlighted the importance of visual identity that contributes to strategy formulation as well as revealing symbolism as being a significant element of the corporate identity mix.

Image and relationships

Proponents of the corporate image concept maintained that corporate identity is an image-derived and related subject. A CEO of a manufacturing organization noted that "all those elements which help build a distinctive and identifiable image of a company within the market can contribute to the identity concept. So, corporate identity can be defined as the final perception and relationship-based experiences the different publics have concerning a company or an organization." This view matches partly that of Bersnstein (1984) and Topalian

(1984), who believe that images are formed in conjunction with the characteristics of an organization, being the net result of the interaction of all the experiences, beliefs, feeling, knowledge and impressions that each stakeholder has about the organization.

Also, a general manager in his attempt to define corporate identity highlighted the image factor as the most essential. Specifically, he stated that "corporate identity is the combination of image, corporate values, vision, general impressions, development relationships and behavioral norms of an organization." In a similar fashion, Bernstein (1984) points out that image is a construction of a public impression created to appeal to an audience.

Contributing factors of corporate identity

The purpose of this question was to collect comments associated with factors that were considered important by the respondents and that also contributed to the development and management of corporate identity.

Communication to facilitate consumer association and interaction

Business consultants commented on the importance of communication in developing corporate identity. A CEO stated colorfully that "a well-defined mission, vision and values, along with a company's overall strategic intent, uniquely communicated with all means of communication, digital and non, create a favorable message to consumers in order for them to explore possible association with the company, contributing fundamentally to the initial development of corporate identity." This statement reinforces the idea that the explicit role of top management in the formulation of corporate identity requires strong links to the company's vision (Abratt, 1989; Dowling, 1993). There is evidence for a positive effect of direct, as well as two-way, communication on relationship strength and outcomes (Lindberg-Repo and Gronroos, 2004; Verhoef, 2003).

Communicating tangible and intangible company values along with measurable salient attributes is the most appropriate way of projecting the characteristics of corporate identity. A financial manager noted that appropriate communication to the market clearly projects identity characteristics. He stated, "Our everyday communicational dialogue with the consumer includes reminders of our core values, promotion of our business ethos, showing our reliability, cultivating relationships/interpersonal bonds, promoting quality, reliable service and dependability, stimulating consumer willingness to associate with our company." This statement reveals that an important way to build relationships with consumers is to interact and to establish a communicational dialogue of any kind (Berthon, Hulbert and Pitt, 1999) and also that communication is an antecedent of trust (Morgan and Hunt, 1994).

A creative director of a consulting firm observed that "we constantly construct and air messages to our customer. These advertising signals are properly aligned with our vision and values and corporate activities to fit consumer expectations, thus contributing positively to the corporate identity context."

Business executives considered a company's communication strategy as a prevalent factor contributing to the development of corporate identity. It is remarkable how managers and executives insist on the central role of communication in diffusing a company's values, visionary planning, mission, strategy and societal obligations in the business world. A marketing manager noted, "Our multidimensional corporate communication based on the company's corporate culture facilitated the development and management of corporate identity, making communication one of the major factors in building consumer relationships and strong corporate identities." Therefore, companies should strive to begin an on-going dialogue with their consumers, address them directly and treat them individually (Gronroos, 2000; Winer, 2001). Similarly, a sales manager highlighted that "customer relationships should only be built with proper communication and continuous interaction." This is in line with the observation that there is evidence that direct, as well as two-way, communication has a positive effect on relationship strength and outcomes (Gronroos and Lindberg-Repo, 2004; Verhoef, 2003). Also, Muñiz and O'Guinn (2001) found indications of a positive long-term impact in relationship building efforts.

A multifactor synthesis

In many cases consultants and business managers were hesitant to address only one or a few factors that they considered significant for the development of corporate identity. A marketing-oriented consultant pointed out that "corporate visual identity, corporate philosophy, mission vision and values statements, corporate communication, reputation, marketing, strategy, branding portfolio, strong corporate ethics, efficient personnel and strong administration and developing consumer relationships" are some of the factors that contribute to corporate identity. The involvement of the above factors supports statements expressed by Van Riel and Balmer (1997) that corporate identity can be a powerful means of integrating the many disciplines and activities that are essential to organizational success.

A public relations consultant also stated that "Visual identity, corporate culture, clear corporate vision, consistent external communication, reputation management, corporate strategy, advertising and social responsibility of the firm could be some major contributing factors, but it is not limited to only those."

The importance of corporate culture for corporate identity

The purpose of addressing this question was to obtain responses about and discuss the importance of corporate culture in the development and management of corporate identity.

Culture's contribution to building relationships

Corporate identity consultants were convinced of the importance of corporate culture in the context of corporate identity. With their background and their familiarity with the corporate identity issue, they replied with assurance and conciseness about this importance. A communications consultant replied that "corporate culture is critical, important and very crucial for the identity context, because it conveys not only beliefs, values, ethics, behavioral patterns and executive actions, but the entire heart of a company's essence. A friendly corporate culture accelerates the relationship formation process with consumers simply because they consider the company part of their own environment." Hatch and Schultz (2001) also note that culture is the organization's values, behaviors and attributes, that is, the way employees all through the ranks feel about the company. A public relations consultant noted in more detail that "corporate culture is crucial in building corporate identity. Also, it is among the most critical factors for maintaining corporate identity in cooperation with the human factor, since culture formation originates with the employees primarily and is secondarily related to stakeholders' actions, associations and type of relationships."

Business executives believed that corporate culture and a company's employee role are directly related in the context of identity. Regardless of their designated sensitivity towards corporate culture, they took a step forward in designating "employee roles" as a related factor of corporate culture. A human resources development manager stated that "culture is very important, since it reveals employee roles, relationships, involvement and impact on the entire organization for the present, future and sustainability in the market." The same perception was conveyed by a CEO who stated that "our corporate culture formulates the basis upon which the corporate identity is structured and developed via its employee and stakeholder contribution and participation, characterized by the type of relationships developed within and outside the company." Actually, corporate culture is based on the staff's intention about perceptual homogeneity internally, and conveyance of this to external stakeholders. The view that the behavior of personnel has a direct effect on an organization's corporate identity and image is expressed by Kennedy (1977). Furthermore, that the personnel should identify with an organization's ideals and goals and that this contributes to the formation of company culture is noted by Van Riel and Balmer (1997).

Corporate personality, corporate identity and consumer relationships

The purpose of raising the issue of corporate personality was, firstly, to identify how corporate personality was perceived by the respondents in relation to the identity context, and secondly, what its contribution is to this context, and, thirdly, to collect responses regarding evaluation ratings. Based on the received feedback the following themes emerged regarding the contribution and importance of corporate personality to the identity context.

Corporate personality as a derivative of cultural and corporate relationships

A manager of a consulting company stated that "corporate personality is a corporate component formed and derived from the prevailing blended cultural and relationship environment that exists within the company." This is in line with Balmer (1995) who argues that corporate personality refers to the mix of cultures within the organization.

He further explains that "corporate personality is formed from aggregate elements originating in the culture of every organization. Since corporate culture is unique for every company, its corporate personality must be aligned with the uniqueness of its culture."

Corporate personality was considered as a concept associated with corporate values. The interrelation of these two concepts focused on the values that affect corporate personality and the impact of these on the concept. Loose corporate values result in weak corporate personality; strong values will contribute to a strong and unique personality. A communications consultant expressed in detail the contribution of corporate personality: "Values and beliefs contribute to the formation of corporate personality. These begin with and depend on the value structure, the prevailing company culture or the types of culture, the company's projected characteristics, its actions, decisions, its executive behavior and personnel behavior. The cohesiveness of these elements can contribute to the formation of corporate relationships that will lead to corporate personality, and consequently, it will contribute to the corporate identity context. It is one of the important factors of identity." This agrees with Abratt and Shee (1989) who state that corporate personality reflects the characteristics that serve as the totality of the behavioral and intellectual characteristics of the organization.

Many business executives supported passionately the contribution of corporate culture in the formation and management of corporate identity. They stated with vigor the necessity of serious involvement in the identity concept. A marketing manager declared that "corporate personality is a new term but it has always existed, hidden, within the concept of corporate identity. Its significance was overlooked. Corporate personality is always formed within the limits of the corporation, developing and refining the many corporate images into socially accepted realities for enhancing the entity of the firm's actions and symbolism." This statement is in accordance with Van Herdeen (1995), who notes that personality is projected through visual identification cues, and through behavioral cues such as the level of customer satisfaction.

Conclusion

The six-station corporate identity model constitutes a feasible approach to creating and managing corporate identity and generating value and trust in the company.

Conveying corporate identity is like developing an exchange relationship with all stakeholders. The model shows how organizations should transmit all their attributes, values and characteristics. It is also clear what the company expects the stakeholders to appreciate in return. Thus, management should pursue a long-term commitment to excellence in order to preserve positive relationships through the management of corporate identity.

Management should observe and monitor the individual employee's contribution to the management of corporate identity. Enthusiastic and positive employee behavior in the market results in conveying the organization's goals and values proudly. Such behavior indicates employee satisfaction and is a signal that employees act instinctively in ways that benefit the organization.

The six-station model calls for the initiation and adaptation of an empowerment program among all internal stakeholders and employees. Empowerment promotes and communicates satisfied and pleasant behaviors, excellent customer service, quicker response to needs and problems, productive employee-generated ideas and warm, interactive employees.

Yet, an aim of the six-station model is to communicate a series of consistent and favorable corporate attributes to stakeholders, as well as to collect multiple data through the organization's multi-stage interactions with its stakeholders.

This model offers practitioners an overall, flexible but well-defined approach to corporate identity management that is suited not only to the rapidly changing environments in which a company operates, but also to the behavioral context in which stakeholders form relationships, initiate responses and establish behavioral patterns that affect the firm's corporate identity.

The management of corporate identity differs from one corporation to the other, as the application of any corporate model is a sensitive managerial practice. Managers must be able to relate to the model so they feel comfortable dealing with it and to be sure that it suits their corporate environment and business case. Managers who fail to select an appropriate corporate identity model to deal with their own business reality are doomed to be unsuccessful in managing corporate identity issues effectively.

The elaboration of variables to produce manageable data is a key goal in applying the model successfully. Every variable is structured to present and maintain its own complexity, framework, idiosyncrasy and contribution to the corporate identity model.

Management should balance and properly manage all variables involved in the formation and management of corporate identity by identifying the best way of measuring those variables and by defining their contribution to the context of corporate identity. It is up to management to define an evaluation system based on a continual monitoring of the variables related to corporate identity, and to define the impact of each one separately and all of them as a whole.

The six-station corporate identity model offers this capability of examining each variable separately in order to examine its impact on corporate identity.

Finally, in this chapter the six-station corporate identity model was introduced along with explanations and justifications. The metaphor of a neural network was used to characterize the model in order to stress both its multi-synthesis and its multidirectional synergistic property. The structure of the model was analyzed, while special emphasis was given to all its components. The chronology or time sequence of the events depicted within the model facilitated an understanding of its processes and stages. All stations and their elements were explained, their presence and interaction supported and justified. The circular motion of events, their synergies and points of intersection and the interactions among variables were elucidated.

A logical approach was employed in constructing the model, which was tested for validity and managerial applicability. The model depicts corporate identity management as a circular process that designates the sequential synergies and effects produced within each station. It links the sequential events produced at each station, thus connecting all the stations together.

The stations are strategically located so that each one depicts the production of specific benefits that can be transmitted to the next station. This process produces synergies that will contribute to the overall process of establishing corporate identity.

Findings from the qualitative research have shown that this model is managerially acceptable and manageable within the corporate identity context. The model provides a conceptual framework for analyzing the identity development process, and is not intended as a mechanical model of what is in reality a continuous, synergistic and non-linear process. Developments in later stages do not always depend exclusively on causes arising from the previous stage.

It is believed that by postulating a corporate identity model that meets key criteria for robustness, and by providing some indication of its managerial applicability, researchers will be stimulated to consider how refinements can be made to corporate identity models by initiating and implementing closer dialogue between researchers and practitioners.

References

Abratt, R. (1989) "A New Approach to the Corporate Image Management Process", *Journal of Marketing Management*, 5 (1): 63–76.

Abratt, R. and Shee, P.S. (1989) "A New Approach to the Corporate Image Management Process", *Journal of Marketing Management*, 5 (1): 63–76.

Aggarwal, P. (2004) "The Effects of Brand Relationship Norms on Consumer Attitudes and Behavior", *Journal of Consumer Research*, 31: 87–100.

Baker, M.J. and Balmer, J.M.T. (1997) "Visual Identity: Trappings or Substance", *European Journal of Marketing*, 31 (5/6): 366–79.

Balmer, J.M.T. (1994) "The BBC's Corporate Identity: Myth, Paradox and Reality", *Journal of General Management*, 19 (3): 33–47.

—— (1995) "Corporate Identity, the Power and the Paradox", *Design Management Journal*, 6 (1): 39–44.

—— (1996) "The Nature of Corporate Identity: An Explanatory Study Undertaken within BBC Scotland", unpublished Ph.D. thesis, University of Strathclyde, Glasgow, UK.

—— (1998) "Corporate Identity and the Advent of Corporate Marketing", *Journal of Marketing Management*, 14 (8): 963–96.

—— (2001) "Corporate Identity, Corporate Branding and Corporate Marketing: Seeing through the Fog", *European Journal of Marketing*, 35 (3/4): 248–91.

Balmer, J.M.T. and Dinnie, K. (1999) "Corporate Identity and Corporate Communications: The Antidote to Merger Madness", *Corporate Communications: An International Journal*, 4 (4): 182–92.

Bernstein, D. (1984) *Company Image and Reality: a critique of corporate communication*, London: Cassel.

Berthon, P., Hulbert, J.M. and Pitt, L.F. (1999) "Brand Management Prognostications", *Sloan Management Review*, 40 (2): 53–65.

Clark, M.S. and Mills, J. (1993) "The Difference between Communal and Exchange Relationships: What it is and is Not", *Personality and Social Psychology Bulletin*, 19 (December): 684–91.

Cornelissen, J. and Elving, W.J.L. (2003) "Managing Corporate Identity: An Integrative Framework of Dimensions and Determinants", *Corporate Communications: An International Journal*, 8 (2): 114–20.

Dacin, P.A. and Brown, T.J. (1997) "The Company and the Product: Corporate Associations and Consumer Product", *Journal of Marketing*, 61 (1): 68–84.

Dowling, G.R. (1986) "Managing your Corporate Images", *Industrial Marketing Management*, 15 (2): 109–15.

—— (1993) "Developing your Image into a Corporate Asset", *Long Range Planning*, 26 (22): 101–9.

Erikson, E.H. (1960) "The Problem of Ego Identity", in M.M. Stein, A.J. Vidich, and D.M. White (eds) *Identity and Anxiety*, Glencoe, IL: The Free Press.

Fombrun, C.J. (1996) *Reputation: realizing value from the corporate image*, Boston: Harvard Business School Press.

Fombrun, C. J. and Van Riel, C. (1997) "The Reputational Landscape", *Corporate Reputation Review*, 1 (1): 5–13.

Fournier, S. (1998) "Consumers and their Brands: Developing Relationship Theory in Consumer Research", *Journal of Consumer Research*, 24 (March): 343–73.

Gilmore, G.W. (1919) *Animism*, Boston: Marshall Jones.

Gioia, D.A. (1998) "From Individual to Organizational Identity", in D.A. Whetten and P. Godfrey (eds), *Identity in Organizations: building theory through conversations*, Thousand Oaks, CA: Sage.

Gotsi, M. and Wilson, M.A. (2001) "Corporate Reputation: Seeking a Definition", *Corporate Communication: An International Journal*, 6 (1): 24–30.

Gray, E.R. and Balmer, J.M.T. (1998) "Managing Corporate Image and Corporate Reputation", *Long Range Planning*, 31(5): 695–702.

Gronroos, C. (2000) "Creating a Relationship Dialogue: Communication, Interaction and Value", *Marketing Review*, 1 (1): 5–14.

Hatch, M.J. and Schultz, M. (1997) "Relations between Organizational Culture, Identity and Image", *European Journal of Marketing*, 31 (5/6): 356–65.

—— (2001) "Are the Strategic Stars Aligned for your Corporate Brand?" *Harvard Business Review*, 79 (2): 128–36.

Herbig, P. and Milewicz, J. (1995) "To Be or Not to Be . . . Credible that is: A Model of Reputation and Credibility among Competing Firms", *Marketing Intelligence and Planning*, 13 (6): 24–33.

Hinde, R.A. (1976) "On Describing Relationships", *Journal of Child Psychology and Psychiatry and Allied Disciplines*, 17 (January): 1–19.

—— (1979) *Towards Understanding Relationships*, London: Academic Press.

—— (1995) "A Suggested Structure for a Science of Relationships", *Personal Relationships*, 2 (March): 1–15.

Kennedy, S.H. (1977) "Nurturing Corporate Images", *European Journal of Marketing*, 11 (3): 120–4.

King, S. (1991) "Brand Building in the 1990s", *Journal of Marketing Management*, 7: 1–22.

Krippendorff, K. (1980) *Content Analysis: an introduction to its methodology*, Newbury Park: Sage.

Larcon, J.P. and Reitter, R. (1979) *Structures de pouvoir et identité de l'entreprise*, Paris: Editions Nathan.

Lindberg-Repo, K. and Gronroos, C. (2004) "Conceptualizing Communications Strategy from Relational Perspective", *Industrial Marketing Management*, 33: 229–39.

McGill, A.L. (1998) "Relative Use of Necessity and Sufficiency Information in Causal Judgement about Natural Categories", *Journal of Personality and Social Psychology*, 75 (July): 70–81.

Markwick, N. and Fill, C. (1997) "Towards a Framework for Managing Corporate Identity", *European Journal of Marketing*, 31 (5/6): 396–410.

Mason, C.J. (1993) "What Image Do You Project", *Management Review*, 82 (11): 10–16.

Melewar, T.C. and Jenkins, E. (2002) "Defining the Corporate Identity Construct", *Corporate Reputation Review*, 5 (1): 76–90.

Melewar, T.C. and Saunders, J. (2000) "Global Corporate Visual Identity Systems: Using an Extended Marketing Mix", *European Journal of Marketing*, 34 (5/6): 538–51.

Miles, M.B. and Huberman, A.M. (1994) *Qualitative Data Analysis: an expanded sourcebook*, London: Sage.

Moingeon, B. and Ramanantsoa, B. (1997) "Understanding Corporate Identity: The French School of Thought", *European Journal of Marketing*, 3 (5/6): 383–95.

Moon, Y. (2000) "Intimate Exchanges: Using Computers to Elicit Self-Disclosure from Computers", *Journal of Consumer Research*, 26 (March): 412–32.

Morgan, R.M. and Hunt, S.D. (1994) "The Commitment-Trust Theory of Relationship Marketing", *Journal of Marketing*, 58 (3): 20–38.

Muñiz, A.M., Jr. and O'Guinn, T.C. (2001) "Brand Community", *Journal of Consumer Research*, 27 (4): 412–32.

Nida, E.A. and Smalley, W. (1959) *Introducing Animism*, New York: Friendship.

Olins, W. (1995) *The New Guide to Identity*, Aldershot: Gower.

Otubanjo, O.B. and Melewar, T.C. (2007) "Understanding the Meaning of Corporate Identity: A Conceptual and Semiological Approach", *Corporate Communications: An International Journal*, 12 (4): 414–32.

Rasmusson, E. (2000) "Becoming a Multicultural Manager", *Sales and Marketing Management*, 152 (6): 140.

Sabiote-Fernandez, E. and Roman, S. (2005) "Organizational Citizenship Behaviour", *International Journal of Market Research*, 47 (3): 163–83.

Topalian, A. (1984) "Corporate Identity: Beyond the Visual Overstatements", *International Journal of Advertising*, 25 (3): 55–62.

Van Heerden, C.H. (1995) "Factors that Determine the Corporate Image of South African Banking Institutions", *International Journal of Bank Marketing*, 13 (3): 12–18.

Van Riel, C.B.M and Balmer, J.M.T. (1997) "Corporate Identity: The Concept, its Measurement and Management", *European Journal of Marketing*, 31 (5/6): 340–56.

Verhoef, P.S. (2003) "Understanding the Effect of Customer Relationship Management Efforts on Customer Retention and Customer Share Development", *Journal of Marketing*, 67 (10): 30–45.

Weiss, R.S. (1974) "The Provisions of Social Relationships", in Zick Rubin (ed.) *Doing unto Others: joining, molding, conforming, helping, loving*, Englewood Cliffs, NJ: Prentice Hall.

Winer, R.S. (2001) "A Framework for Customer Relationship Management", *California Management Review*, 43 (4): 89–105.

Wright, G. (1995) "The Delineation and Measurement of Some Key Variables in the Study of Friendship", *Representative Research in Social Psychology*, 5: 93–6.

Zinkhan, G.M., Jaiskankur, A.J. and Hayes, L. (2001) "Corporate Image: A Conceptual Framework for Strategic Planning", in G. Marshall and S. Grove (eds) *Enhancing Knowledge Development in Marketing, vol. 12*, Chicago: American Marketing Association.

9

BRAND HUMANITY

Transforming the business of building brands

Stephen Springfield and Padmini Sharma

Introduction

How does a brand evoke true love? Most marketers ponder this question deeply and frequently during their careers and we are no exception. Certainly, there are many iconic brands in our culture – Apple, Nike, Harley-Davidson, Disney, Oprah, to name a few – that evoke admiration and envy. This is especially true when one works with brands in categories that are relatively low-involvement, like chips. While we have the privilege at Frito-Lay of working on big and popular brands such as Lay's®, Cheetos®, Doritos® and Tostitos®, we are also acutely aware of the fact that popularity does not equate to brand love. This was the reason why we found ourselves repeatedly drawn to brands that do inspire adoration, love and fanaticism. We approached these brands with a sense of awe and a desire to understand the principles driving their success in both the marketplace and the hearts and minds of their consumers.

This was an important endeavor at Frito-Lay, a company that has traditionally focused on building strong businesses more than strong brands. Obviously, the ideal goal is to build both and, in fact, strong brands are also successful businesses. Perhaps the right way to characterize the internal culture of our company is to say that we are so adept at managing the day-to-day business, we are challenged to maintain the necessary balance between the short term and the long term. For instance, we rely heavily on tangible levers such as pricing and trade incentives rather than on intangible levers such as brand equity. Our company has also traditionally relied on its distribution and sales muscles to set itself apart from competition; however, these are becoming less and less effective in our category today. As Marty Neumeier points out in his book *ZAG*, competition today does not emanate from other companies, but from the clutter in consumers' minds. Somehow, Frito-Lay had yet to come to terms with this new reality of competition, in which the only asset that can provide true competitive insulation is a differentiated brand.

Faced with this realization, we looked inward at how we approached the business of building differentiated brands in our company. After all, we own some of the biggest snack brands in the world, so we must be doing something right. And indeed we are. Our product quality is unmatched, thanks to an ace R&D team. Our distribution system is unparalleled. And for a large company, we are surprisingly nimble and responsive to competitive threats. But all things considered, we are still adjusting to the new business reality of competing for a share of the consumer's mind, rather than competing for retail shelf-space.

In all fairness, we did focus some of our efforts on building brands. The problem was that the process was stuck in a time warp. We used models (the standard brand pyramid) that once were good tools, but were no longer relevant in the era of competitive clutter and a battle for the consumer's share of mind. These models were not actionable or prescriptive. They did not help bring the brand to life in a magnetic way. Last but not least, they did not lead to advantaged positions in the marketplace. If there was one overwhelming indictment of these tools, it was that they were product-oriented, rather than brand-based. They lacked the ability to shape brand distinction, which is ultimately the driver of choice in a cluttered category. Without distinction, there is no choice, and without choice, no preference, and without preference, no loyalty.

What you will read in this chapter is our approach to building differentiated, competitively insulated brands with the ability to evoke love and loyalty among their consumers. We call this approach "Brand Humanity" because it is a viewpoint on building brands based on three very human principles:

1.   Authenticity
2.   Relationship
3.   Story.

To put these principles into practice, we created a model which has three core building blocks:

1.   Understanding the *Brand Lover's* self-identity and conflict;
2.   Defining the *Brand's Distinction* within its competitive context;
3.   Articulating the *Brand's Social Ideal* or its ideological reason for being.

We believe that strong brands activate these three building blocks authentically and consistently. Ultimately, this creates a brand narrative or story that confers meaning to a brand well beyond the sum of its tangible attributes. It is this meaning that provides sustained growth for the brand by making its competition completely irrelevant.

Let us start by dissecting the three principles of Brand Humanity.

Authenticity

Our journey started by discussing what makes brands iconic. In all likelihood, they did not originate from either brand pyramids or Madison Avenue. Brands like Apple, Virgin, Wal-Mart and Disney, to name a few, share one common characteristic – they all have notably passionate founders with strong convictions about how they could make the world better through their brands. Apple's anthem is about Thinking Different. Sam Walton, the founder of Wal-Mart, believed that everyone should have affordable access to things that make their lives better. Richard Branson refused to conform to the norms of air travel and believed that flying should be fun and pleasurable. Disney keeps the magic of childhood alive for all of us.

In fact, these brands seem to exist for the sole reason of expressing their founders' points of view. Do any of us believe that Walt Disney's true motive was anything other than wanting to keep the magic of childhood alive? Or that Steve Jobs wasn't a different thinker himself, who wanted to shake up the world of computing and technology? Consumers find these brands different and magnetic because they stay true to their founding intent through every action they take. By doing so, they become enduring symbols of belief in a crowded consumer culture.

This is all good and true for founder brands. But how is this relevant to brands like ours, which are embedded within a largely impersonal corporate entity? In fact, the challenge with our brands is that the only ideology that consumers ascribe to them is the profit motive, which is neither flattering nor worthy of sustained loyalty. An obvious solution is to *adopt* a point of view, but that can feel dishonest and manipulative. On the other hand, if the point of view is a natural extension of the brand's DNA, it is completely authentic. Many brands have done this well. Las Vegas, with its "What happens in Vegas, stays in Vegas" campaign, has adopted the viewpoint that carefree adult behavior deserves a place of its own. This feels authentic to the brand. Similarly, Dove's "Real Beauty" campaign espouses the view that beauty comes from within. This too feels authentic to it, while it might feel inauthentic for MAC Cosmetics, which is all about glamor, to hold that ideological position.

So, how does one determine whether an adopted ideology is authentic or inauthentic? There's a highly reliable method for it, called the "man (or woman) on the street" interviews. Stop a person on the street and ask if it makes sense for Cheetos to espouse a lighthearted and playful approach to life. Or if Axe deodorant could authentically fund literacy for girls in developing countries. This method is extremely reliable because the meaning of established brands resides in the collective consciousness of consumer culture. They intuitively understand which points of view are consistent with the brand's DNA and which ones feel "off."

Once you have an ideology for your brand, it's not enough to just say what it is. The brand must live it. Every action should demonstrate it. And it needs to stay the course, regardless of short-term pressures.

Relationship

Authenticity matters if a brand wants to evoke a committed, monogamous relationship with its consumers. In fact, Brand Humanity in practice needs no special skills and techniques other than the intent to build sincere and meaningful relationships between brands and consumers. While we did build a model to make some of these principles more "tangible," it's worth stressing that no model or template can replace or compensate for the guiding intent of the brand. In fact, in our training sessions, we often ask the question, "Thinking about human relationships, can you imagine building a relationship using a model or checklist, rather than operating from an authentic place of caring?" We assert that the same is true of consumer–brand relationships. Intentions matter and actions speak louder than any communication campaign.

Referring back to iconic brands like Harley, it is easy to see how these brands have become great not through the theatrics of empathy, but through actions that reveal how committed they are to their founding or guiding intent. This creates a legion of consumers who don't just "buy" the product, but *buy into* the brand. Also, the people who manage these brands typically fit their own consumer profile, so it's easy for them to stay true to their ideology and consistently make decisions that put the consumer first, even at the expense of the company. Paradoxically, this doesn't hurt them financially in the long run because they earn undying love and loyalty through their actions.

Frito-Lay's challenge, ironically, comes from its tremendous success in the marketplace. While we are privileged to work on billion-dollar brands that are category leaders, their size and ubiquity have the unintended consequence of making them seem broadly appealing and impersonal. When brands lack humanity, they can't inspire relationships. In the movie, *Castaway*, Tom Hanks couldn't see his volleyball as a companion and friend until he created the character of "Wilson." This is why brand characters are so effective. They humanize the brand, making it easier for consumers to form relationships with them.

But what about big brands that don't necessarily have brand characters? We were inspired by Susan Fournier's (1998) work on consumer–brand relationships, in which she demonstrated that brands can become viable relationship objects when they reinforce a person's critical self-image (more on this later). Even more insightful was her demonstration that this does not happen just with brands in high-involvement categories like automotives, technology and fashion. Even brands in low-involvement categories can inspire relationships with consumers if they demonstrate that they truly understand their consumers at a deep level.

Story

Last but not least, we decided that we needed a metaphor for thinking about brands that would make it easier to practice the principles of authenticity and relationships, while being intuitive and inspirational. Story is the perfect metaphor for brands. This is not a new thought by any means; however, it's pretty provocative in a corporate culture that views brands primarily as weapons in competitive warfare rather than as entities that can foster relationships with consumers. We are a sales-driven culture which believes that the battle takes place in the grocery store during the moment of purchase. We needed to show that the battle may well be taking place in the snack aisle, but the real war is being waged in consumers' minds. This is why story as a metaphor for brand has immense power, because stories are mechanisms of meaning and memory. The "story" we tell ourselves about a brand, rather than any fact about it, is the ultimate arbiter of choice, preference and loyalty. So, as marketers, our primary job is to make sure that our brands are conveying the right stories.

It is worth clarifying here that "story" is not meant to suggest fiction and fantasy. It is not license to exaggerate or deceive. The stories that we find most magnetic are those that contain universal truths about what it means to be human. Similarly, the best brand stories are those that are true to their internal ideology and offer their consumers a similar insight into their own selves.

Take Disney for example. The story of Disney is the story of Peter Pan. It's about never growing up and keeping the magic of childhood alive. Everything that Disney does is in service of expressing and living this story. Disney is loved by those who embrace a similar aspect about themselves – the desire to retain the innocence of childhood, no matter their age. To take another example – Harley's story is about rebeling against the establishment. Harley's business strategy serves no other purpose than to bring this story to life. By doing so, they have cultivated a fanatic following with people who share the same belief system.

In summary, Brand Humanity operates on the principle that authentic brand stories will result in strong consumer–brand relationships, which are ultimately the only way to succeed in today's consumer culture.

Now let's turn our attention to the Brand Humanity model.

Introduction to the model

The intent of this model is to help translate the principles of Brand Humanity into a tangible thinking tool. As mentioned earlier, the model has three building blocks that in totality constitute the brand story.

- *Brand Lover's* self-identity and conflict.
- *Brand's Distinction* within its competitive context.
- *Brand's Social Ideal* or its ideological reason for being.

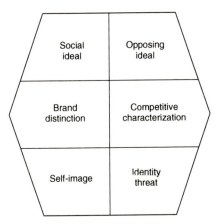

FIGURE 19.1 Conflicts that form the brand's story

It is important to note that each of these constructs is listed as a "conflict" (IS vs. IS NOT) so that we understand not only what the brand is, but also what it's NOT. This is critical in defining boundaries and guardrails for the actions of the brand.

Brand Lovers

Strong brands are very clear about who they are for. They don't try to be everything for everyone. This was our first mandate in building this model – understanding who the brand story is for. We call them "Brand Lovers" for the simple reason that they have an intense love and devotion for the brand that separates them from others who simply use or appreciate the brand.

From Susan Fournier's work on consumer–brand relationships, we understood that this kind of devotion occurs when a brand reinforces a consumer's vital self-concept. In other words, brand lovers strongly identify with the brand and use it to signal core aspects of their self-image to others. But more importantly, they also use the brand to signal that they are NOT a certain type of person. To illustrate, a Harley brand lover uses the brand to signal the rebellious part of his identity. Equally important to him is to portray that he's *against* conformity. Similarly, an Apple brand lover is motivated to signal that she's cool and creative just as much as she wants to signal that she's NOT a tech geek.

Our deepest attachments are to people and things that reinforce what we need to believe about ourselves. Our most critical identity traits are ones that we believe make us uniquely valuable, and yet, deep down fear that they may not be true. As such, our vital self-concept is fragile and constantly needs reinforcing. As Nietzsche once said, "Even he who despises himself nevertheless esteems himself as a self-despiser."

Hence, when people use brands to reinforce their identities, the resulting relationship is strong for precisely that reason and highly resistant to competitive threats. A case in point – Apple's fans are extremely forgiving when the brand stumbles because it is a vital part of who they are and how they'd like to be seen. They won't switch to a non-Apple product because that would be akin to rejecting a core part of their self-identity. This is wonderfully portrayed in Apple's television ads, with two antithetical personalities that serve as the ideal self-image (socially confident, cool, witty, young) and the identity threat (geeky and socially inept).

The concept of Brand Lovers and Brand Love makes complete sense in the case of high-involvement categories when brands have badge value and are obvious social signals. But the snack category in which we operate is pretty low-involvement. We wondered if we could even find brand lovers for our brands, let alone confirm that they used our brands to reinforce their self-image. In all honesty, it sounded far-fetched even to us. But thanks to an implicit association method based on the proprietary ABA/POE model (Reid and Gonzalez-Vallejo, 2009), we were able to validate that our brands do indeed have brand lovers who associate their self-image with our snack brands. We will discuss this later through a Cheetos case study.

It is important to point out that the brand lover may not necessarily be the communication target. The latter is a group with whom the brand needs to grow in order to meet business goals, while the brand lovers may not be a big enough group to achieve financial goals. However, they are the oracles and stewards of the brand story, so everything that a brand does must pass muster in their eyes. To bring this point home, while the Harley brand lover is the "rebel," the business target is most likely a forty-year-old accountant with a high disposable income, going through a mid-life crisis, who finds the rebel image highly aspirational.

Next we'll see how the main function of a brand is to build a distinction in service of reinforcing and signaling the brand lover's vital self-identity.

Brand Distinction

Brand distinction starts with understanding those elements of your brand that make it what it is. These include both tangible and intangible attributes. However, in our model we take neither type of attribute at face value and go a step further to understand the holistic experience they deliver *in support of the Brand Lover's vital self-concept*. For instance, some of Harley's key attributes might hypothesized to be Black, Loud, Leather, Intimidating, etc. We sum them all up into one expression, "Disturbing the Peace," which becomes Harley's brand distinction, appealing to the rebellious brand lover. (Disclaimer: This is our hypothesis for illustrative purposes; Harley may articulate its brand distinction differently.)

Harley's distinction has such a strong point of view embedded in it that it becomes the only possible choice for someone who considers him/herself a rebel, because in light of Harley's distinction, other motorcycle brands seem more socially approved and conforming. Similarly, one might add up Apple's core attributes of Simple, White, Minimal, Cool, Intuitive to a distinction of "Instrument of Human Expression," which appeals to its brand lover's self-concept of being creative. It makes other brands seem irrelevant, because they appear too technical and machine-like, in contrast to Apple.

A "good" brand distinction is one that does the following:

1. supports the brand lover's desired self-concept, and
2. characterizes the competition in such a way as to make it irrelevant.

The resulting brand distinction should make the brand an "ONLY." This is a concept espoused by Marty Neumeier in his book *ZAG*. He says that a strong brand should be able to state that it is the ONLY one in its competitive category with that particular distinction, which is why understanding the competitive frame of reference is extremely important.

It is worth pointing out that we think of the Brand Distinction as being tightly linked to the concept of Brand Stretch. Because the Distinction is a statement separate from (but supported by) combinations of attributes, it can be applied to multiple categories. For instance, as long as Apple's distinction is "Instrument of Human Expression," it can move from computers to MP3 players to cell phones. The key requirement for a successful stretch is for the brand to be able to stay true to its distinction in any competitive category that it stretches to.

Brand's Social Ideal

It should come as no surprise that we explicitly capture the brand's ideology in our model. Also, following the pattern of duality in the model (self-concept vs. identity threat and distinction vs. competitive characterization), we capture the opposing ideal as well. The reason for this is quite simple: opposing ideals held by an out-group make the social ideals held by one's in-group even more salient and motivating. For instance, Harley's rebellion would not be nearly as energizing without the opposing ideal that we should all "adhere to social norms."

In some sense, the social ideal becomes the moral of the brand story. It is the reason for the brand's existence beyond the obvious purpose of making money. One of the ways in which we've asked marketers at Frito-Lay to bring this construct to life is by imagining that the brand they're working on is a non-profit organization with the mandate of creating social change. What would the brand do? It's important to note that social ideals do not have to be altruistic. They have to stay true to the core of the brand. For instance, Harley's social ideal might be "go your own way," which is not altruistic in the same sense as saving the rainforests or finding a cure for cancer, but is highly motivating to the brand lover.

Ideals are important because they become the guiding principle for everything the brand does. Most of the time, firms assume that if brands take on a strong point of view, they may end up alienating part of the audience. However, we believe that it's riskier not to take a clear stand, because that means that the brand isn't particularly relevant to anyone. Such brands become vanilla – liked by all, loved by none. Paradoxically, brands with strong views end up attracting more and alienating less, because they take on timeless human dilemmas that are felt by everyone at some level or the other. Harley might speak directly to the rebel, but the idea of going one's own way without being stifled by society's norms has broad appeal. Ideals give a brand strong conviction. And sticking to one's ideals is what makes a brand feel authentic and, over time, results in a brand story that builds strong relationships with consumers.

Of all the constructs in the model, this is perhaps the most challenging and rewarding for the brands that we work with. To associate snack brands with social ideals is ambitious in and of itself, but to persuade the organization that ideals-led branding is a pathway to sustained growth is another matter altogether. Fortunately, we have established proof of concept through several of our brands. We will now discuss one of them, Cheetos, to bring to life the Brand Humanity approach and demonstrate the success we've had with it.

Cheetos case study

Cheetos had always been marketed as a family-brand during its sixty-year history, enjoying strong marketplace success and growth. But when the company decided to take a proactive approach in the fight against childhood obesity by shifting its advertising to those over twelve years of age, the Cheetos brand found itself in a challenging position. How does a billion-dollar brand walk away from a strategy that had worked exceptionally well for it in the past?

The first thing we did was dig into who exactly was eating Cheetos snacks. Surprisingly, we discovered that almost half of Cheetos' consumers were adults. We decided to take a closer look at them. Through projective research techniques, we found that the reason that adults love Cheetos is because it lets them feel like a kid again. In fact, the emotional experience of eating Cheetos is more powerful for adults because they have more constraints, in the form of responsibilities and obligations that get in the way of their letting loose once in a while. Cheetos helps these adults feel playful and a tad naughty because it's so quirky with its bright orange color, irregular shapes and cheesy messiness.

We characterized the Cheetos brand lover as the "Rejuvenile," based on a book by Christopher Noxon of the same title. Essentially, Rejuveniles are Gen Xers, who reject the idea that physically growing older requires the adoption of grown-up behavior and norms. They face a strong internal conflict – being responsible vs. being kidlike. A few other brands in alternate categories have successfully positioned themselves around a similar insight. The popularity of the animated series *South Park* is one such example. It has an animation and voiceover style that's juvenile, yet requires an adult perspective on political and social issues to truly understand the content. With "Rejuveniles" as our brand lovers, we defined the vital self-concept as "playful," with the identity threat as being "mature," based on perceived conformity to an adult-like mindset.

Next, we delved into Cheetos' brand distinction. We started with the attributes mentioned previously – bright orange, irregularly shaped, cheesy, etc. We also discovered that brand lovers loved to lick the powdery cheesy residue off their fingers when they ate Cheetos – it made them feel like they were breaking the rules of snacking. Taking all these attributes and behavioral insights together, we expressed Cheetos' brand distinction as "Breaks Social Norms," with the competition juxtaposed as being "Conventional." With a distinction such as "Breaks Social Norms," you can see how prescriptive it is about the types of communication and innovation that the brand would do. If it feels too safe or something that a cracker would do, it's probably not a good fit for Cheetos.

Articulating Cheetos' social ideal was quite simple because we had such a rich understanding of our brand lover. We knew that Rejuveniles refuse to take themselves or the world around them too seriously. The brand itself had a strong history of promoting this view through its decidedly juvenile mascot, Chester Cheetah. We felt that if Cheetos were to become a non-profit organization with one clear mandate, it would be to tell the world to "lighten up" in the face of the opposing ideal of "social propriety."

Now that we understood the foundational story of the brand, we translated it into a consumer-facing campaign targeted at adults for the first time in the brand's history. The resulting marketplace success was further enhanced by the renewed cultural momentum and energy for the brand.

Outcome and impact

One of the most beneficial outcomes of the Brand Humanity process at Frito-Lay is an acknowledgment that the rules of branding and consumer engagement have changed. This has also led to the recognition that what made us successful in the past is no longer sufficient to get us to the future. In this section, we highlight some key outcomes of this process.

Brand vs. business building

As a company, we are focused on building the business (short-term view) vs. investing in the brand (long-term focus). While both are important, the Brand

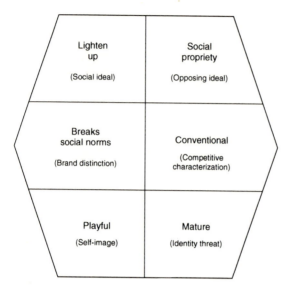

FIGURE 19.2 Cheeto's Brand Humanity framework

Humanity process helps marketers build the business *by* building the brand. Though we still face pressures to demonstrate quick wins, we are slowly but surely persuading the organization that investment in building strong, authentic relationships with consumers is the pathway to sustained growth.

Common vocabulary

This framework and approach has created a common vocabulary internally as well as externally, with our agency partners. It has fostered a collaborative approach to brand building that's a good blend of art and science. The debates and discussions are richer because we are focused on getting the concepts right and demonstrating the insights leading to those ideas.

Empathy

The Brand Humanity framework necessitates a deep empathetic understanding of the consumer because it deals with concepts such as vital self-concept and identity-threat.

This understanding has shifted the way we go about understanding our consumers. We've broadened our lens from understanding their snacking behavior to understanding them as people with dreams, hopes, aspirations, fears and challenges. This empathic research approach is leading to better insights and more authentic marketing efforts.

Limitations and challenges

As with any story, there are always some bumps in the road before the happy ending. Brand Humanity is no exception. We faced (and continue to face) some challenges. However, we are also finding that addressing them is leading to better thinking and greater adoption. The following are the key tension points in the adoption of Brand Humanity.

The framework conundrum

An ongoing area of debate is regarding the primary objective of this tool. Currently, it serves many purposes – it's a thinking tool to debate and discuss the building blocks of a brand story; it's a framework to build consensus and alignment among multiple teams (both internal and external); and it's also an evaluative tool used by senior management to ensure that brands have distinct roles within the overall portfolio. Sometimes, these multiple objectives do not work as harmoniously as we'd like them to. This is probably a fundamental issue with all such frameworks; however, we do need to establish a clear objective if we are to see ongoing adoption and success with this approach.

Casting the right people in the right roles

We have come to the realization that the process of Brand Humanity is neither intuitive nor easy for some. There seems to be a divide between those who find this approach liberating and those who find it too soft and intangible. Currently, everyone in our department is required to undergo the training and have some level of familiarity and skill in working with these concepts. Even those who are analytic wizards and are uncomfortable with anything that does not have a number attached to it are not exempt. This stems from a desire to democratize Brand Humanity, especially in a culture where job rotations occur frequently. However, it may not be the best implementation and adoption strategy.

Measurement

A big question is how do we make ourselves accountable for creating strong consumer–brand relationships when we don't know for certain how to measure the payoffs? Without the right type of accountability, Brand Humanity can seem too conceptual or worse, simply a checkpoint to get through in the annual planning process.

What the future holds

Despite seeing greater adoption and success with Brand Humanity in our company, we need to make sure that we address the limitations outlined above.

To that end, we are keen to collaborate with academics especially to solve the measurement question and quantify the payoffs of Brand Humanity. We have strong early indications with some of our brands that this is a powerful approach to building iconic brands.

Acknowledgment

Brand Humanity would've remained a glimmer in our eyes but for the unstinting and passionate support of our Chief Marketing Officer, Ann Mukherjee. She saw the potential in this that even we didn't and became the catalyst for its adoption at Frito-Lay. She continues to inspire us to take Brand Humanity to greater heights.

References

Dick, A. and Basu, K. (1994) "Customer Loyalty: Toward an Integrated Conceptual Framework", *Journal of the Academy of Marketing Science*, 22: 99–113.
Escalas, J. and Bettman, J. (2005) "Self-Construal, Reference Groups, and Brand Meaning", *Journal of Consumer Research, Inc.*, 32: 378–89.
Fournier, S. (1998) "Consumers and Their Brands: Developing Relationship Theory in Consumer Research", *Journal of Consumer Research*, 24: 343–73.
Freling, T. and Forbes, L. (2005) "An Examination of Brand Personality through Methodological Triangulation", *The Journal of Brand Management*, 13(2): 148–62.
Holt, D. (2004) *How Brands Become Icons*, Boston, MA: Harvard Business School Publishing.
Neumeier, M. (2007) *ZAG, The Number-One Strategy of High-Performance Brands*, Berkley, CA: Peachpit Press.
Park, C., MacInnis, D., Priester, J. and Wan, H. (2005) "Emotional Attachment, Brand Evangelism, and Brand Equity", Marshall School of Business, University of Southern California.
Reid, A. and Halgren, S. (2011) "In Defense of Marketing, The Peacock's Plume and Dancing Birds of Paradise", White Paper Series / Winter 2011, Portsmouth, NY, Sentient Decision Science.
"Rejuvenile by Christopher Noxon-Book-EBook-Random House." Random House – Bringing You the Best in Fiction, Nonfiction, and Children's Books. Web. 07 Oct. 2011. <http: www.randomhouse.com/book/122975/rejuvenile-by-christopher-noxon/>.
Schmid, K., Hewstone, M., Tausch, N., Cairns, E. and Hughes, J. (2009) "Antecedents and Consequences of Social Identity Complexity: Intergroup Contact, Distinctiveness Threat, and Outgroup Attitudes", *Personality and Social Psychology Bulletin*.
White, K. and Argo, J. (2009) "Social Identity Threat and Consumer Preferences", *Journal of Consumer Psychology*, 19: 313–25.

MUSINGS AND MEDITATIONS

Where do we go from here?

Michael Breazeale and Susan Fournier

The chapters in this book serve not only to reveal leading-edge research on the nature and process of consumer–brand relationships, but also suggest many important avenues of research for scholars and practitioners who seek to advance knowledge in this domain. Our purpose in these concluding remarks is not to restate or repackage that which our contributors have already discussed. Rather, we hope to build on these collective insights to suggest eight conundrums, opportunities, and must-haves that are implicated as critical paths for advancing brand relationship scholarship along needed lines.

Maximizing the psychology connection

Brand relationship theory has progressed largely through the leverage and adaptation of interpersonal relationship theories developed in the social, clinical, counseling, developmental, and cognitive psychology realms. Still, the human relationships discipline is deep and well established and there exist many concepts and frameworks that have yet to be considered for their consumer–brand implications. For example, works-in-progress consider Bowlby's (1969) attachment theory and the effects of secure, avoidant, and anxious styles of relating in the commercial realm (Paulssen and Fournier 2011). McAlexander (2011) takes on the complicated task of explaining how close and socially embedded relationship ties are effectively severed, providing much needed attention to the dissolution of relationship bonds (see also Coulter and Ligas 2000). Many personality factors are known to influence interpersonal relationship behaviors, and these too offer avenues for consumer research: for example, the need to belong (Baumeister and Leary 1995), interpersonal orientation (Swap and Rubin 1983), intimacy and affiliation motives (McAdams and Constantian 1983), and relationship proneness

(Cheek and Buss 1981). Matthews (1986) offers the promising notion of friendship styles, wherein an individual is accumulative, discerning, or independent in their friendship patterns across time.

The vast field of possible relationship types provides another rich area for brand relationship research. While early-stage works in the field of personal relationships were centered primarily on close relationships (Kelley *et al.* 1983), dedicated research streams now focus on specific relationship forms including courtships, boyfriends/girlfriends, divorced couples, friendships (with distinctions among casual, best, close, same-sex, and childhood friends), secret affairs, abusive relations, kin, peer groups, work relations, communal relations, task-related relations, love/hate relations, and dysfunctional relationships, to name but a few. In marketing there exists a strong bias toward committed, loyal brand relationships analogous to marital partnerships, under the assumption that strong relationships are leverageable, resilient and made to last. Aggarwal (2004) broadens our perspective to Clark and Mills' (1979) relationship dichotomy, wherein communal relationships, which are guided by a lasting concern for the other, are contrasted with practical *quid pro quo* exchange relationships. Beyond the committed/communal/exchange paradigm, branding research focusing on specific relationship types is scant. Several chapters in this volume (Chapters 2, 3, 4, and 5) are dedicated to the phenomenology of particular relationship forms. Marketing scholars have also variously explored commercial friendships (Price and Arnould 1999), adversarial relations (Hill 1994), and addictions (Hirschman 1992), though these studies do not draw primary inspiration from the relationship theories or contribute centrally to this body of research.

In terms of process mechanisms, Rusbult's (1980) investment theory provides a rich avenue for explaining and measuring brand loyalties, as indicated in the recent work of Sung and Campbell (2009). Account making (Burnett, McGhee, and Clarke 1987), relationship narratives (Gergen and Gergen 1987), idealization (Murray, Holmes, and Griffin 1996), attribution style (Bradbury and Fincham 1990), and accommodation (Rusbult *et al.* 1991) provide interesting perspectives on the cognitive processes involved in developing relationships. Also of note is work on relationship-serving biases that support relationship functioning including selective memory, biased partner perceptions, and biased perceptions of non-partners (Clark *et al.* 1994). Recent consumer research also suggests promise in theories of implicit attitudes (Graiko *et al.* 2011) and deprivation (Long and Yoon 2011) for explaining and measuring consumers' affective brand bonds.

For understandable reasons, marketing is fixated on close relationships generally and the notions of love, commitment, and relationship strength specifically, and a significant proportion of published brand relationships research circles around these well-trodden grounds. A brief scan of recent issues of the journal *Personal Relationships* suggests many exciting topics capable of broadening the scope of brand relationship research: gratitude as a relationship booster, relationship sacrifice, maintaining spatially strained relationship ties, relationship prototypes and personal templates, authenticity in relationships, intrusive snooping behavior within close relationships, linguistic patterns in relationship interactions, partner complementarity, relationships and mental health, and the experience of being loyal but ignored. There is much to be leveraged in the annals of personal relationship research.

From the dyadic to the social

Despite the traction of Consumer Culture Theory (CCT) among consumer behavior scholars and the realities of a socially embedded, web-enabled world, consumer–brand relationship theory remains for the most part just that: a dyadic exercise focused on the relationship of an individual consumer with a brand. Much has been written about the need to expand brand relationship research to more forcefully include the socio-cultural. As O'Guinn and Muñiz (2009, p. 173) eloquently state: "A brand relationship is more than the thoughts and feelings of individual consumers about a brand. There are meaningful collective brand relationships. Further all 'individual' relationships pass through collectives. Brand relationships are made through social forces." Beyond the extension of individual brand relationships to collective brand community relationships (Schouten and McAlexander 1995; Muñiz and O'Guinn 2001), little relationship scholarship is conducted at the social level of analysis. Brand relationships remain, for all intents and purposes, dominated by psychologists and an individualistic sensibility; there is little discussion of sociology, society, collective action, the role of institutions (e.g., retailers, equity markets, governments, fashion gatekeepers, and media) or the collectivity in general in our theories of relationships with brands. Brand relationship research remains a matter of "individual consumers and their minds" (O'Guinn and Muñiz 2009, p. 173).

There exists much potential in motivating the field toward a cultural and sociological interpretation of brand relationships. Co-creation remains the lynchpin of the new marketing paradigm (Vargo and Lusch 2004) and this process critically influences brand relationships. While advances have been made in understanding how individual consumers make meanings for the brands they love (Escalas and Bettman 2005; Fournier 1998), the processes whereby societies and cultures constitute brands and thereby govern brand relationships are less understood. Relationship-inspired research concerning select meaning makers and meaning production systems such as celebrities (Parmentier and Fischer 2010; White 2011), branded entertainment (Allen, Fournier, and Miller 2008), adolescent peer groups (Wooten 2006), status-granting systems (Ordabayeva and Chandon 2011), and cultural mythologies (Thompson and Arsel 2004) can provide needed insight. Research concerning specific instantiations of co-creation such as consumer-generated ads (Campbell et al. 2011), brand parodies (Michel, Sabri, and Lagroue 2011), and product design (Moreau 2011) can also inform how consumers relate to their brands. The various social processes that facilitate, contribute to, and govern brand relationships also offer promising avenues for research, as for example with gossip and rumors (Muñiz, O'Guinn, and Fine 2005), politics (Luedicke, Thompson, and Giesler 2010), and cultural disruption (Holt 2004). As Leigh and Thomson (Chapter 17, this volume) point out, researchers also need to reconceptualize marketing's role when interfacing with consumers in the various collective contexts that embed their brands (e.g., brand communities, formalized brand clubs, enthusiast discussion groups, casual social networks such as Facebook, and opinion-led peer-to-peer communications networks such as blogs).

Drawing inspiration from the study of business-to-business relationships

As we enter into a second phase of inspired relationship research, it behooves us to step back in order to more fully appreciate our scholarly relationship roots not just in the social sciences, but in the marketing discipline itself. Relationship applications in marketing started in business-to-business environments wherein dyadic, reciprocating partnerships are legitimately engaged (Dwyer, Schurr, and Oh 1987). Though the relationship tradition has remained a staple in B-to-B scholarship, this sub-discipline has, for all intents and purposes, not been tapped for brand relationship inspiration. Relationships and the contracts that implicitly and explicitly define them have been studied extensively in the business-to-business context (Heide 1994; Williamson 1975) and yet brand relationship processes have yet to be conceived in contracting terms. Contracting theory (Rousseau and Parks 1992) introduces a wide array of promising constructs that can usefully extend brand relationship research, including psychological and implied contracts, relationship rules and norms, relationship promises, relationship schemas and prototypes, contract breach, contract drift, and supra-contracting. Heide and John's (1992) insightful typology of contract norms (norms of flexibility, solidarity, and information exchange) within exchange relationships can also be readily extended to the brand context.

Also of note is Heide and Wathne's (2006) probe of the phenomenology of friend versus businesspeople relationship role archetypes, which has direct application to company and service relationships in the business-to-consumer realm. Narayandas and Rangan's (2004) conceptualization of extra-contractual relationship behaviors as the foundation for increased commitment in business relationships can similarly inform our study of the process dynamics underlying consumers' loyalties to their brands. So too can we draw insight from the dependency structures that define supplier–buyer relationships and drive relationship performance (Lusch and Brown 1996) and explore the operation of dependency in consumers' brand relationships. We cannot do justice in this limited context to the rich stores of relationship knowledge developed in the business marketing context, but we can encourage researchers to ground themselves in these foundational works.

Spotlight on the brand as relationship partner

Research on consumer–brand relationships is decidedly lopsided, with significant attention to the consumer side of the relationship equation and scant research dedicated to the role of the brand. Within this research stream, brand personality serves as the dominant inquiry frame. For example, Aaker, Fournier, and Brasel (2004) provide insight into how sincere versus exciting brand personalities affect the strength of consumers' relationship bonds, particularly under conditions of partner-induced stress. Specific traits of trustworthiness, credibility, and benevolence have also played a central role as these qualities have been shown to govern the loyalty connection. Advances in brand relationship theory can be obtained by broadening beyond the trust-satisfaction-loyalty framework to consider other possible partner qualities and effects. Which brand partners foster and sustain engagement, for example? Which partners enable the storytelling and myth-making that facilitates cultural relationship foundations?

While effective and relevant, however, the human personality framework is limiting nonetheless. If we are to understand the role of brands as relationship partners, we need to move beyond the big five personality traits to consider partner qualities with marketing inspiration and implication. Alex (2011), for example, focuses on hubris to explain the misinformed actions of brands within escalating crisis environments. A practitioner paper presented at the Second International Colloquium on Consumer–Brand Relationships revealed how the Canadian coffee shop Tim Horton's makes its big brand feel small (Hollis 2011). Research by Paharia et al. (2011) on underdog brands pursues a similar relational dynamic in highlighting the forever struggling underdog brand. Fournier and Avery (2011b) also call out brand size as a detriment in the consumer-controlled internet age. The big/small dichotomy has great potential to help us understand brand relationship dynamics on marketing terms, and is especially interesting in its stark contrast to accepted business goals of increased share at all costs. The notion of relationship role archetypes (e.g., friends versus businesspeople, Heide and Wathne 2006) provides a promising alternative to trait-based frameworks when conceptualizing the partner brand. As we push to develop substantively driven brand relationship theory, we must adopt a sharp focus on and sensitivity to the marketing context in which this theory will be applied.

Anthropomorphism, the tendency to attribute human characteristics, emotions, intentions, and behaviors to nonhuman objects, also provides a powerful theoretical window on the fundamental processes governing people's relationships with brands (Fournier 1998). Anthropomorphism has captured renewed attention among psychologists interested in why and when people anthropomorphize nonhuman entities (Epley et al. 2008). In consumer research, Aggarwal and

McGill (2007) explore how anthropomorphism affects brand liking through the process of schema congruity; Kim and McGill (2011) explore the effects of anthropomorphizing objects on risk perceptions and behaviors. Whether brands that are anthropomorphized through brand characters (e.g., the M&M guys or Keebler Elves) or product characteristics (e.g., computer design features that heighten human attributions) make better relationship partners because they are seen as more relatable, approachable, or empathetic, and whether these human-like traits translate into stronger brand relationships has yet to be explored. Research is also needed to consider processes beyond the cognitive realm that may govern the effects of anthropomorphizing, such as the need for belonging or social connection. Brown (2011) offers a provocative suggestion for further expanding this work by considering the relationships that anthropomorphized brand characters have with each other, as, for example, in online social worlds.

Relationships engage, but what does that mean?

Moving in the direction of a more thorough understanding of consumer–brand relationships requires an understanding of the "alpha point" of the relationship. Where does it begin? What is the spark that ignites the passion that fuels relationships, both positive and negative? One possible answer is that the relationship begins when the consumer is engaged by the brand. The dictionary definition of the word engagement references a "promise, obligation, or other condition that bonds" (Collins 2011). We feel it is appropriate that the bonding moment for consumer–brand relationships is engagement. But how can the *construct* of engagement be operationalized for brand relationship research?

Numerous disciplines claim investment in the engagement construct. Advertisers look at viewer engagement to measure the impact of advertising; educators study student engagement as an indicator of learning outcomes; public policy researchers and environmental planners consider investor engagement, stakeholder engagement, public engagement, and corporate engagement to gauge the impact of policy; psychologists measure task engagement as an important indicator of testing outcomes; and management researchers have long studied worker or employee engagement as a predictor of workplace involvement and performance. But these disciplines do not share a common definition of engagement, and marketing researchers have effectively borrowed whatever definition best suits their needs in a given research situation. A recent special issue of the *Journal of Business Research* (2010) devoted to engagement proves interest in the topic as well as the fact that there is little common ground among marketing researchers as to what engagement implies.

Efforts to conceptualize consumer engagement can be noted. Mollen and Wilson (2010) incorporate definitions from the education and management literature to describe a tripartite engagement construct, composed of cognitive, personal, and emotional dimensions. Kahn's (1990) work suggests that a fourth dimension might be included to incorporate behavioral engagement. Even more recent research considers a fifth – social engagement – to describe consumers' "interactions at an interpersonal or social level that serve to unite, express, or clarify membership in a cultural group" (Lawrence, Fournier, and Brunel 2011). A common supposition that accompanies each of these definitions is that not all dimensions must be present for engagement to occur for any given consumer. If that is the case, then isn't there an underlying engagement construct that essentially produces these outcomes? Regardless of the discipline that produces the definition that underlies a particular research project or the ultimate dimensionality of the construct, a clear understanding of the meaning of engagement seems necessary if consumer–brand relationship research is to progress.

A walk on the dark side

The realm of consumer–brand relationship research would appear to be a very happy place to anyone who has read the majority of that research. We describe love-like relationships and favorite brands and the kinds of bonds that form between consumers and the brands that hold special memories for them. Researchers have been less likely to shine the bright light of intellectual curiosity into the darkness with regard to brand relationships – to explore the negative consequences of brand relationships or to examine the reasons that consumers avoid certain brands or to consider brand relationships that might result in injurious consumption. Clearly, some consumption that consumers regularly undertake can leave them feeling conflicted, ambivalent, or even stressed.

Among the research that could be considered relevant to the dark side of consumer–brand relationships is the stream that explores brand avoidance. Other than Chapter 3 of this volume, several published articles explore aspects of the negative brand relationships that, on one end of the spectrum, cause consumers to avoid a brand (Lee, Motion, and Conroy 2009) or, on the more extreme end of the same spectrum, cause them to actively seek revenge against a brand (Gregoire, Tripp, and Legoux 2009). An entire issue of the *Journal of Business Research* (February 2009) devoted to brand avoidance confirms the topic's relevance to both researchers and practitioners, but still the concept remains under-researched.

Another important dark-side aspect of relationships is that which explores the addictive relationships many consumers form with brands. A recent edited volume by Mick *et al.* (2011) explores several problematic consumer behaviors including unhealthy eating, alcohol and tobacco abuse, pornography, gambling, and credit card mismanagement. Cotte and Latour (2009) suggest that consumers exhibit stronger addictions to online gambling than casino gambling. Given that more than $10 billion is spent each year by online gamblers (Cotte and Latour 2009), this is an issue of interest not only to relationship researchers but to the social policy domain as well. Hirschman (1992) describes compulsive consumption, raising the question as to "How many consumer–brand relationships are actually the result of addictive or compulsive behaviors?" Compulsive binge eating is one such behavior that has received some attention (Faber, Christenson, De Zwann, and Mitchell 1995), and more recently the de-marketing of tobacco is an addiction issue that has been studied (Inness, Barling, Rogers, and Turner 2008). Consumer–brand relationships form with nonaddictive products as well, but might there be an addictive or compulsive component to what we consider normal or healthy consumption relationships, and might this be masked by what the marketer sees as a "strong brand relationship"? Several authors represented in this book are currently studying the effects of favorite brand deprivation on consumers (Long, Breazeale, Fournier, and Yoon 2011), attempting to determine the role that compulsive behaviors play in the relationship, but there is much more that could be studied.

Another issue that is quite relevant, given the current worldwide economic climate, involves the marketing of financial products and institutions. Pre-crisis research delved into topics such as strategies for building affective commitment to retail banks (Menon and O'Connor 2007), while more recent research explores attempts to restore consumer confidence in the post-crisis era (Gounaris and Prout 2009). If consumers develop relationships with their banks, credit unions, real estate agents, and investment bankers, could the loyalty and trust that typically accompanies these types of relationships have played a role in the financial crisis as consumers turned a blind eye to the misbehavior of some professionals in these industries? More critically, how do we understand the experience and meaning of what is now known as one of the most abusive brand relationships precipitated at the hands of marketing? Research is required that explores consumer–brand relationships in the context of brands which may not hold as paramount the best interests of the consumer.

Relationships with brands in the healthcare industry represent a relatively new stream of research as healthcare providers have begun to realize the importance of relationship-building activities with patients/customers. Improving patient outcomes through relationship-building (Hausman 2004), the difficulty of building relationships in the healthcare industry when many services are being outsourced (Foxx, Bunn, and McCay 2009), and the necessity of capitalizing on relationships by healthcare professionals (Seltman 2005) are topics that have only recently begun to be studied. Capella et al. (2009) ask whether marketing efforts directed at building relationships actually raise the cost of healthcare, thus disincentivizing these efforts. Similarly, Amaldoss and He (2009) question the strategic impact of consumer advertising that encourages relationships with over-the-counter medications. These studies demonstrate the importance of consumer relationships in the healthcare and pharmaceutical industries, but they only scratch the surface of the potential incongruities that occur when brand relationships are sought and formed with both personal and product brands within the healthcare solutions industry.

Dissolution provides yet another context for examining the less-than-rosy side of relationship life. McAlexander (1991) examines the emotional and economic impact of dissolution of brand relationships in the context of divorce. But what happens when a consumer and a brand essentially divorce from each other? The dissolution of once happy consumer–brand relationships is an area that has only recently been considered. As in the process of customer de-selection described in this book (Chapter 16), the end of a relationship can be traumatic for all parties involved. Pressey and Matthews (2003) explore relationship dissolution and create a typology of dissolution styles, yet there is a paucity of research delving deeper into the ongoing effects of this phenomenon for either the marketer or the consumer. With the ubiquitous nature of the internet, the apparent willingness of consumers to share their experiences via blogs, complaint websites, and other forums, and the ever-present enticement from attractive "brand relationship alternatives," the dissolution of a given brand relationship is no longer an isolated or rare event. Indeed, break-ups can garner the kind of attention once reserved for celebrity coupling and uncoupling. Based on the public nature of many consumer–brand break-ups, it is vital that research examines and describes the process that accompanies both mutual dissolutions as well as the more one-sided break-up.

A question of method more than content perhaps, the recent attention paid to neuromarketing techniques which study consumer brainwaves in attempts to uncover the magic "buying button" brings up the issue of the ethicality of exploiting unconscious consumer processes. While this stream of research has been thus far exploratory in nature, a strategic focus of the findings raises "ethical questions involving consumers' consent and understanding to what may be viewed as an invasion of their privacy rights" (Wilson, Gaines, and Hill 2008, p. 389). If this research yields the relationship buttons that must be pushed in order for consumers to form strong bonds with their brands, then will that consumer "love potion" be used against unwitting consumers, an apparent violation of the unspoken pact that many consumer researchers hold with their informants?

Many opportunities exist to understand the dark side of the consumer–brand relationship domain. These suggestions scratch the surface of a fertile area that deserves investigation in order to achieve a full picture of the phenomenon and fully realize the impact of consumers' relationships with brands.

CRM may be a four-letter word

Those who study relationships through the lens of the customer relationship management (CRM) paradigm tend to diverge from consumer–brand relationship researchers on one important point. CRM research, with its reliance on the economics view of consumers as rational beings seeking to maximize utility at all costs, seems to leave the consumer out of the relationship, or at minimum, to trivialize the input of the consumer in the relationships that are formed and maintained (Fournier and Avery 2011a). The very premise of CRM implies that customers and their attitudes toward the company must be "managed" such that they deliver value to the firm. If we look to personal relationships, the fallacy inherent in that premise becomes clear. In healthy friendships, romantic partnerings, and even casual acquaintanceships, the relationship is not *managed* by either of the partners. The participants are in the relationship because both of them *want* to be. To suggest that marketers can impose relationships on their most attractive customers "is akin to the notion of Neanderthal man clubbing and dragging home the Neanderthal woman who seems most likely to provide him with healthy children – it is outdated and impractical" (Breazeale 2010, p. 54).

It is perfectly understandable that marketers interested in monetizing the benefits of consumer–brand relationships would attempt to administer the relationship themselves. But if the research in this volume teaches anything, it is that the consumer is the primary determinant of the existence and continuation of a consumer–brand relationship. Indeed, the claimed focus of many practitioners has shifted in recent years toward a more customer-centric perspective as companies have realized that the customer is – at a minimum – an equal partner in the relationship. Despite well-conceived intentions, we can nevertheless question the degree to which practitioners' behaviors deliver against this customer-first goal. As Chapter 19 in this volume attests, buying into a relationship perspective is one thing; getting an organization behind it with supportive structures and operations is quite a different – and difficult – task to pull off.

It is time for CRM researchers and practitioners to follow the lead of CBR researchers, abandoning their economics-informed view of consumers and instead acknowledging the importance of the relationship as well as the essential input of the consumer partner. Future operationalizations could, for example, segment customers based not on lifetime value or costs to serve, but rather on the different roles that consumer–brand relationships play in consumers' lives (Fournier and Avery 2011a). In accounting for the importance of these relationships, researchers would achieve a more holistic view. In turn, this renewed focus would allow them to more effectively describe and capitalize upon the dyadic dynamic between the consumer and the marketer, allowing them to more effectively monetize relationship benefits.

Maybe CRM is not a four-letter word, but it may be the wrong *three* letters. Perhaps customer relationship nurturance (CRN) would better describe the actual process that takes place between consumers and the marketers who have found that cultivating bi-directional relationships with their consumers is the best way to reap ongoing economic rewards.

The "so-what" of consumers' relationships with their brands

There is no escaping the fact that the notion of brand relationships is fundamentally practical, though substantive contributions have yet to drive consumer–brand relationships research. Perhaps as a consequence of method or, on a deeper level, a subconscious attempt by relationship researchers to avoid exploitation of the very informants who inform our research, brand relationship researchers have been reticent in drawing conclusions that will produce quantifiable, monetized outcomes for practitioners. To truly have an impact, brand relationship theory and research must prove actionable for firms and other stakeholders. We must address the matter of finding the "so what" in consumers' brand relationships and demonstrate empirically whether and how building relationships matters to societies and firms.

Answers to the "so what" question will require different skill sets and research paradigms than the tools applied in brand relationship research to date. The modeling tradition in marketing, particularly as concerns the growing area of marketing finance, has much to contribute in advancing brand relationships along needed lines. Over the past decade, academics and practitioners have expressed increased interest in connecting marketing initiatives to financial performance so as to bridge the so-called marketing–finance divide (Srinivasan and Hanssens 2009). This is not an easy task. A defining characteristic of brand assets (e.g., brand relationships and brand equity) is that they are inherently slow-moving and not immediately visible such that changes in a well-managed brand's equity take time to manifest on a firm's bottom-line. For these same reasons, long-term brand equity value is less likely to be captured by backward-looking accounting measures such as profit and return on assets. Given these realities, the gold standard metric for assessing branding's impact on the firm is shareholder value, which is determined by levels of stock returns and the volatility or risk associated with those returns.

Within this framework, brand relationships can prove valuable if they serve to generate abnormal returns or, perhaps more significantly, operate as strategic tools for managing the risk exposure of the firm. Strong brand relationships, for example, can encourage broader stock ownership among individual investors, insulate a company from market downturns, grant protection from equity dilution in the case of product failures, and reduce variability in cash flows through loyalties and relationships with the trade. Strong brand relationships can reduce psychological ego risks and the financial risks of making wrong decisions. Empirical research that leverages the concepts and models of finance can consider whether and how brand relationships generate shareholder value and exacerbate or control firm risk.

The "so what" of brand relationships also demands attention to a second key stakeholder: society. Though much research has been conducted under the materialism umbrella, we have yet to offer unequivocal evidence as to whether the quality and quantity of brand relationships affects individual well-being and the health of societies overall. Drawing from interpersonal relationships research, a paradox exists in how brand relationships influence health and well-being (Rook 1994). Do brand relationships contribute an important source of meaning that improves or deteriorates life satisfaction and happiness? Do brand relationships play a role in alleviating or exacerbating stress? Do individuals with strong brand relationships exhibit less or more loneliness and despair? Are brand relationships a source of comfort and affiliation, or a source of conflict and disappointment? Interpersonal relationships research documents the rewards and benefits of social relationships as well as their hazards and costs. Which of these realities weighs more significantly on health and well-being in the brand relationship realm? Daily existence is more connected to consumer behaviors than ever before, raising many unresolved issues around well-being and quality of life.

Toward a science of brand relationships

Since Fournier (1998) opened the door to consumer–brand relationship research, academics and practitioners alike have explored this fascinating domain, most often employing qualitative techniques and scale development exercises that provide a necessary foundation for a stream of research that describes a phenomenon that is in many ways unique to each individual who experiences it. An important step in the evolution of brand relationship scholarship requires the development of generalizable relationship systems from our in-depth studies of individual and collective relationship instantiations. Idiosyncratic experiences can form the basis of generalizable relationship systems. Individuals and communities may clearly manifest relational principles that with dedication and focus can be shown to be generalizable: we just need to apply ourselves specifically to these scientific goals. Progressing from descriptive research to more explanatory, prescriptive research requires a deeper and more systematic understanding of the trajectory of consumer–brand relationships and the processes that unfold as relationships evolve.

In order to achieve a macro perspective that regards consumer–brand relationships in a sociocultural context which recognizes their impact on society as a whole, cross-disciplinary research that combines research paradigms will be necessary. Metaphors relating brand relationships to personal relationships described by psychological theories have provided an essential basis for our research, but they will not be sufficient to advance our understanding of a cultural phenomenon that is much larger in scope than is implied by existing research. The disciplines of experimentation and modeling will also prove critical in this exercise, particularly as they consider longitudinal processes in real-world contexts. While modeling and experimental research are not completely neglected in the brand relationship research domain, they are clearly not the norm. Aggarwal (2004) provides a notable exception with research based on Clark and Mills' (1979) communal-exchange theory and then a series of experiments designed to test the operation of these basic processes in the consumer realm. Aaker, Fournier, and Brasel (2004) report on a longitudinal field experiment in which different brand partner personalities encourage relationships which are then strained by a brand transgression. Breazeale (2010) utilizes structural equation modeling to describe the process that consumers follow when forming relationships with beloved retailers. Loughran-Dommer and Swaminathan (2010) use experiments to confirm that when individuals experience anxiety in their interpersonal relationships, they use brands that assert their in-group identities to cope with this self-threat. Long and Yoon (2011) employ experiments to explore consumers' anxiety levels in the face of being separated from their beloved brands. These and other similarly inspired studies represent the type of research that will advance consumer–brand relationship research from a descriptive foundation to a prescriptive stream that provides substantive and actionable results.

Where do the metaphors end?

Most chapters in this book explore the consumer–brand relationship in the context of the interpersonal relationship metaphor. Some (Chapter 1) qualify the applicability of that metaphor, and others (Chapter 8) suggest instead that a para-social metaphor may be more appropriate. The parasocial framework has certain appeal in its suggestion of a one-sided relationship. This non-reciprocating relationship fits with the realities of a mass-marketing mediated environment as well as dominant CRM practices which maintain that the brand holds the power to manage customer relationships. Still, the realities of a co-created branding world enabled through conversational social media directly challenge this assumption and renew trust in the leverage of the interpersonal relationship metaphor for brand research. The list of applications is extensive: the majority of brand relationship research involves the identification of relevant constructs in the personal relationships realm and their adaptation to the context of brands.

We have been accumulating evidence for more than a decade using this research strategy, and the powerful personal relationship frameworks that have served as impetus and inspiration for the nascent brand relationships field have without a doubt been productive in getting the discipline off the ground. Still, the interpersonal relationships frame serves as metaphor, not reality, and questions of the limitations of this metaphor have not yet been critically engaged. Regardless of one's stance, most researchers in this domain would agree that there are inadequacies in any metaphorical application to the study of consumer–brand relationships. As Zaltman (2003) notes, metaphor is a powerful explanatory device for the progression of science, but it obscures as much as it reveals. As a field, it is time we systematically consider where the notions of brand relationships and personal relationships intersect and where they diverge. There exists a need to describe how and where, for lack of a better term, mutation occurs.

True advances in brand relationship theory will not derive from merely borrowing concepts and insights from interpersonal theories and demonstrating their applications in the consumer–brand realm. This metaphoric argument has been repeatedly proposed and reinforced. True progress requires that we do more than prove the manifestation of known relationship principles within a different and broadened scope of application. We need our own relationship concepts, frameworks, and operationalizations if impact on theory and practice is to be obtained. Future research efforts require a focus on the uniqueness inherent in consumer–brand relationships and sensitivity to the marketing contexts in which they are engaged.

References

Aaker, J., Fournier, S. and Brasel, A. (2004) "When Good Brands Do Bad", *Journal of Consumer Research*, 31 (June): 1–25.

Aggarwal, P. (2004) "The Effects of Brand Relationship Norms on Consumer Attitudes and Behavior", *Journal of Consumer Research*, 31: 87–100.

Aggarwal, P. and McGill, A. (2010) "Partners and Servants: Adopting Traits of Anthropomorphized Brands", presentation at the Association for Consumer Research Conference, Jacksonville, FL, October 7–10.

Alex, K. (2011) "The Hubristic Brand: Transgressing Brand Values in Consumer–Brand Relationships", presentation at the Second International Colloquium on Consumer–Brand Relationships, Winter Park, FL, Rollins College, March 17–19.

Allen, C., Fournier, S. and Miller, F. (2008) "Brands and their Meaning Makers", in C. Haugtvedt, P. Herr, and F. Kardes (eds.) *Handbook of Consumer Psychology*, Mahwah, NJ: Lawrence Erlbaum Associates.

Amaldoss, W. and He, C. (2009) "Direct-to-Consumer Advertising of Prescription Drugs: A Strategic Analysis", *Marketing Science*, 28 (3): 472–87.

Baumeister, R. and Leary, M. (1995) "The Need to Belong: Desire for Interpersonal Attachments as a Fundamental Human Motivation", *Psychological Bulletin*, 117 (3): 497–529.

Bowlby, J. (1969) *Attachment and Loss, vol. 1: Attachment*, New York: Basic Books.

Bradbury, T. and Fincham, F. (1990) "Attributions in Marriage: Review and Critique", *Psychological Bulletin*, 107 (1): 3–33.

Breazeale, M. (2010) "I Love that Store! Toward a Theory of Customer Chemistry", in "Three Essays on Customer Chemistry", dissertation, Mississippi State University, 53–106.

Brown, S. (2011) "If Consumers Can Have Relationships with Brands, Why Can't Brand Characters Relate to Each Other?" presentation at the Second International Colloquium on Consumer–Brand Relationships, Winter Park, FL, Rollins College, March 17–19.

Burnett, R., McGee, P. and Clarke, D. (1987) *Accounting for Relationships: explanation, representation, and knowledge*, London: Methuen.

Campbell, C., Pitt, L.F., Parent, M. and Berthon, P.R. (2011) "Understanding Consumer Conversations around Ads in a Web 2.0 World", Journal of Advertising, 40 (1): 87–102.

Capella, M., Taylor, C.R., Campbell, R.C. and Longwell, L.S. (2009) "Do Pharmaceutical Marketing Activities Raise Prices? Evidence from Five Major Therapeutic Classes", *Journal of Public Policy and Marketing*, 28 (2): 146–61.

Cheek, J. and Buss, A. (1981) "Shyness and Sociability", *Journal of Personality and Social Psychology*, 41 (2): 330–9.

Clark, M., Helgeson, V., Mickelson, K. and Pataki, S. (1994) "Some Cognitive Structures and Processes Relevant to Relationship Functioning", in R.S. Wyer and T.K. Srull (eds) *Handbook of Social Cognition, vol. 2: Applications*, Hillsdale, NJ: Lawrence Erlbaum Associates.

Clark, M.S. and Mills, J. (1979) "Interpersonal Attraction in Exchange and Communal Relationships", *Journal of Personality and Social Psychology*, 37 (1): 12–24.

Collins (2011) "Engagement", in *Collins English Dictionary – Complete & Unabridged, 10th Edition*. Available at http://dictionary.reference.com/browse/engagement (accessed June 22, 2011).

Cotte, J. and LaTour, K.A. (2009) "Blackjack in the Kitchen: Understanding Online Versus Casino Gambling", *Journal of Consumer Research*, 35 (5): 742–58.

Coulter, R. and Ligas, M. (2000) "The Long Good-Bye: The Dissolution of Customer-Service Provider Relationships", *Psychology & Marketing*, 17 (8): 669–95.

Dwyer, F.R., Schurr, P. and Oh, S. (1987) "Developing Buyer–Seller Relationships", *Journal of Marketing*, 51 (April): 11–27.

Epley, N., Akalis, S., Waytz, A. and Cacioppo, J. (2008) "Creating Social Connection through Inferential Reproduction: Loneliness and Perceived Agency in Gadgets, Gods, and Greyhounds", *Psychological Science*, 19 (2): 114–20.

Escalas, J. and Bettman, J. (2005) "Self Construal, Reference Groups and Brand Meaning", *Journal of Consumer Research*, 32 (December): 378–89.

Faber, R.J., Christenson, G.A., De Zwaan, M. and Mitchell, J. (1995) "Two Forms of Compulsive Consumption: Comorbidity of Compulsive Buying and Binge Eating", *Journal of Consumer Research*, 22 (3): 296–304.

Fournier, S. (1998) "Consumers and their Brands: Developing Relationship Theory in Consumer Research", *Journal of Consumer Research*, 24 (March): 343–73.

Fournier, S. and Avery, J. (2011a) "Putting the Relationship Back in CRM," *Sloan Management Review*, April: 63–72.

—— (2011b) "The Uninvited Brand", *Business Horizons* (special issue on Web 2.0, Consumer-Generated Content, and Social Media), 54: 193–207.

Foxx, W.K., Bunn, M.D. and McCay, V. (2009) "Outsourcing Services in the Healthcare Sector", *Journal of Medical Marketing*, 9 (1): 41–55.

Gergen, K. and Gergen, M. (1987) "Narratives of Relationship", in R. Burnett, P. McGee, and D. Clarke (eds) *Accounting for Relationships: explanation, representation, and knowledge*, London: Methuen.

Gounaris, K.M. and Prout, M.F. (2009) "Repairing Relationships and Restoring Trust: Behavioral Finance and the Economic Crisis", *Journal of Financial Service Professionals*, 63 (4): 75–84.

Graiko, S., Reid, A., Sharma, P. and Springfield, S. (2011) "Understanding Brand Lovers at Frito-Lay", presentation at the Second International Colloquium on Consumer–Brand Relationships, Winter Park, FL, Rollins College, March 17–19.

Grégoire, Y., Tripp, T.M. and Legoux, R. (2009) "When Customer Love Turns into Lasting Hate: The Effects of Relationship Strength and Time on Customer Revenge and Avoidance", *Journal of Marketing*, 73 (6): 18–32.

Hausman, A. (2004) "Modeling the Patient–Physician Service Encounter: Improving Patient Outcomes", *Journal of the Academy of Marketing Science*, 32 (4): 403–17.

Heide, J. (1994) "Interorganizational Governance in Marketing Channels", *Journal of Marketing*, 58 (January): 71–85.

Heide, J. and John, G. (1992) "Do Norms Matter in Marketing Relationships?" *Journal of Marketing*, 56 (April): 32–44.

Heide, J. and Wathne, K. (2006) "Friends, Businesspeople, and Relationship Roles: A Conceptual Framework and a Research Agenda", *Journal of Marketing*, 70 (July): 90–103.

Hill, R.P. (1994) "Bill Collectors and Consumers: A Troublesome Exchange Relationship", *Journal of Public Policy & Marketing*, 13 (1): 20–35.

Hirschman, E.C. (1992) "The Consciousness of Addiction: Toward a General Theory of Compulsive Consumption", *Journal of Consumer Research*, 19 (2): 155–79.

Hollis, G. (2011) "Brand Love: A Case Study of Tim Horton's", presentation at the Second International Colloquium on Consumer–Brand Relationships, Winter Park, FL, Rollins College, March 17–19.

Holt, Douglas (2004) *How Brands Become Icons*, Boston: Harvard Business School Publishing.

Inness, M., Barling, J., Rogers, K. and Turner, N. (2008) "De-marketing Tobacco through Price Changes and Consumer Attempts to Quit Smoking", *Journal of Business Ethics*, 77 (4): 405–16.

Kahn, W.A. (1990) "Psychological Conditions of Personal Engagement and Disengagement at Work", *Academy of Management Journal*, 33 (4): 692–724.

Kelley, H., Berscheid, E., Christensen, A., Harvey, J., Huston, T., Levinger, G., McClintock, E., Peplau, L. and Peterson, D. (1983) *Close Relationships*, New York: W.H. Freeman.

Kim, S. and McGill, A.L. (2011) "Gaming with Mr. Slot or Gaming the Slot Machine? Power, Anthropomorphism, and Risk Perception", *Journal of Consumer Research*, 38 (1): 1–15.

Lawrence, B., Fournier, S. and Brunel, F. (2011) "Consuming the Consumer-Generated Ad", working paper.

Lee, M.S.W., Motion, J. and Conroy, D. (2009) "Anti-consumption and Brand Avoidance", *Journal of Business Research*, 62 (2): 169–80.

Long, C. and Yoon, S. (2011) "I Miss My Brand: Brand Deprivation and Consumers' Interpersonal Relationship-Relevant Traits", presentation at the Second International Colloquium on Consumer–Brand Relationships, Winter Park, FL, Rollins College, March 17–19.

Long, C.R., Breazeale, M., Fournier, S. and Yoon, S. (2011) "I Miss My Brand! A Longitudinal Study of Brand Deprivation", working paper.

Loughran-Dommer, S. and Swaminathan, V. (2010) "Relationship Anxiety, In-Group Identity, and Brand Relationships", presentation at the Second International Colloquium on Consumer–Brand Relationships, Winter Park, FL, Rollins College, March 17–19.

Luedicke, M., Thompson, C. and Giesler, M. (2010) "Consumer Identity Work as Moral Protagonism: How Myth and Ideology Animate a Brand-Mediated Moral Conflict," *Journal of Consumer Research*, 36 (April): 1016–32.

Lusch, R. and Brown, J. (1996) "Interdependency, Contracting and Relational Behavior in Marketing Channels", *Journal of Marketing*, 60 (October): 19–38.

McAdams, D.P. and Constantian, C. (1983) "Intimacy and Affiliation Motives in Daily Living", *Journal of Personality and Social Psychology*, 45 (4): 851–61.

McAlexander, J. (2011) "Where Are We Going with this . . . Relationship?" , Keynote address at the Second International Colloquium on Consumer–Brand Relationships, Winter Park, FL, Rollins College, March 17–19.

McAlexander, J.H. (1991) "Divorce, the Disposition of the Relationship, and Everything", *Advances in Consumer Research*, 18 (1): 43–8.

Matthews, S. (1986) *Friendships through the Life Course: oral biographies in old age*, Beverly Hills, CA: Sage.

Menon, K. and O'Connor, A. (2007) "Building Customers' Affective Commitment towards Retail Banks: The Role of CRM in Each 'Moment of Truth'", *Journal of Financial Services Marketing*, 12 (2) 157–68.

Michel, G., Sabri, O. and Lagroue, P. (2011) "Using Brand Parodies to Build Brand Equity: Are Parodies Harmful to the Brand Relationship?" presentation at the Second International Colloquium on Consumer–Brand Relationships, Winter Park, FL, Rollins College, March 17–19.

Mick, D.G., Pettigrew, S., Pechmann, C. and Ozanne, J. (2011) *Transformative Consumer Research for Personal and Collective Well-Bring*, London: Psychology Press.

Mollen, A. and Wilson, H. (2010) "Engagement, Telepresence, and Interactivity in Online Consumer Experience: Reconciling Scholastic and Managerial Perspectives", *Journal of Business Research*, 63 (9/10): 919–25.

Moreau, P. (2011) "Inviting the Amateurs into the Studio: Understanding How Consumer Engagement in Product Design Creates Value", *Journal of Product Innovation Management*, 28 (3): 409–10.

Muñiz, A. Jr. and O'Guinn, T. (2001) "Brand Community", *Journal of Consumer Research*, 27 (March): 412–32.

Muñiz, A.M., Jr., O'Guinn, T.C. and Fine, G.A. (2005) "Rumor in Brand Community", in D.A. Hantula (ed.) *Advances in Social and Organizational Psychology: A Tribute to Ralph Rosnow*, Hillsdale, NJ: Lawrence Erlbaum Associates.

Murray, S., Holmes, J. and Griffin, D. (1996) "The Benefits of Positive Illusions: Idealization and the Construction of Satisfaction in Close Relationships", *Journal of Personality and Social Psychology*, 70 (1): 79–98.

Narayandas, D. and Rangan, V.K. (2004) "Building and Sustaining Buyer–Seller Relationships in Mature Industrial Markets", *Journal of Marketing*, 68 (July): 63–77.

Ordabayeva, N. and Chandon, P. (2011) "Getting Ahead of the Joneses: When Equality Increases Conspicuous Consumption among Bottom-Tier Consumers", *Journal of Consumer Research*, 38 (June): 27–41.

O'Guinn, T. and Muñiz, A. Jr. (2009) "Collective Brand Relationships", in D. MacInnis, C.W. Park, and J. Priester (eds) *Handbook of Brand Relationships*, Armonk, NY: M.E. Sharpe.

Paharia, N., Keinan, A., Avery, J. and Schor, J.B. (2011) "The Underdog Effect: The Marketing of Disadvantage and Determination through Brand Biography", *Journal of Consumer Research*, 37 (February): 775–90.

Parmentier, M. and Fischer, E. (2010) "Wannabes: Toward an Understanding of Relationship Formation between Consumption Communities and Aspiring Celebrities", presentation at the First International Colloquium on Consumer–Brand Relationships, Winter Park, FL, Rollins College, April 22–24.

Paulssen, M. and Fournier, S. (2011) "Attachment Security and the Strength of Commercial Relationships", working paper, Boston University.

Pressey, A.D. and Mathews, B.P. (2003) "Jumped, Pushed, or Forgotten? Approaches to Dissolution", *Journal of Marketing Management*, 19 (1/2): 131–55.

Price, L.L. and Arnould, E.J. (1999) "Commercial Friendships: Service Provider–Client Relationships in Context", *Journal of Marketing*, 63 (4): 38–56.

Rook, K. (1994) "Investigating the Positive and Negative Sides of Personal Relationships: Through a Lens Darkly?" in B.H. Spitzberg and W.R. Cupach (eds) *The Dark Side of Close Relationships*, Mahwah, NJ: Lawrence Erlbaum Associates.

Rousseau, D. and Parks, J.M. (1992) "The Contracts of Individuals and Organizations", *Research in Organizational Behavior*, 15: 1–43.

Rusbult, C. (1980) "Commitment and Satisfaction in Romantic Associations: A Test of the Investment Model", *Journal of Experimental Social Psychology*, 16 (2): 172–86.

Rusbult, C., Verette, J., Whitney, G., Slovik, L. and Lipkus, I. (1991) "Accommodation Processes in Close Relationships: Theory and Preliminary Evidence", *Journal of Personality and Social Psychology*, 60 (1): 53–78.

Schouten, J. and McAlexander, J. (1995) "Subcultures of Consumption: An Ethnography of the New Bikers", *Journal of Consumer Research*, 22 (June): 43–61.

Seltman, K. (2005), "Feels Good and it Works", *Marketing Health Services*, 25 (2): 3–3.

Srinivasan, S. and Hanssens, D.M. (2009) "Marketing and Firm Value: Metrics, Methods, Findings, and Future Directions", *Journal of Marketing Research*, 46 (3): 293–312.

Sung, Y. and Campbell, W.K. (2009) "Brand Commitment in Consumer–Brand Relationships: An Investment Model Approach", *Journal of Brand Management*, 17 (2): 97–113.

Swap, W. and Rubin, J. (1983) "Measurement of Interpersonal Orientation", *Journal of Personality and Social Psychology*, 44 (1): 208–19.

Thompson, C. and Arsel, Z. (2004) "The Starbucks Brandscape and Consumers' Anticorporate Experiences of Glocalization", *Journal of Consumer Research*, 31 (December): 631–42.

Thomson, M., MacInnis, D.J. and Park, C.W. (2005) "The Ties that Bind: Measuring the Strength of Consumers' Emotional Attachments to Brands", *Journal of Consumer Psychology*, 15 (1): 77–91.

Vargo, S. and Lusch, R. (2004) "Evolving to a New Dominant Logic for Marketing", *Journal of Marketing*, 68 (January): 1–17.

White, A. (2011) "Building Celebrity Brands: Understanding Consumer Responses to Endorser Failures", presentation at the Second International Colloquium on Consumer–Brand Relationships, Winter Park, FL, Rollins College, March 17–19.

Williamson, O. (1975) *Markets and Hierarchies: analysis and antitrust implications*, New York: The Free Press.

Wilson, R.M., Gaines, J. and Hill, R.P. (2008) "Neuromarketing and Consumer Free Will", *Journal of Consumer Affairs*, 42 (3): 389–410.

Wooten, David B. (2006) "From Labeling Possessions to Possessing Labels: Ridicule and Socialization among Adolescents", *Journal of Consumer Research*, 33 (September): 188–98.

Zaltman, G. (2003) *How Customers Think: Essential Insights into the Mind of the Market*, Boston: Harvard Business School Press.

NAMES INDEX

BRANDS INDEX

GENERAL INDEX

Lightning Source UK Ltd.
Milton Keynes UK
UKOW04f0351270315

248634UK00001B/7/P